Serfdom, Society, and the
Arts in Imperial Russia

RICHARD STITES

Serfdom, Society, and the Arts in Imperial Russia

THE PLEASURE AND THE POWER

Yale University Press
New Haven &
London

Published with assistance from the Annie Burr Lewis Fund.

Published with assistance from the Mary Cady Tew Memorial Fund.

Library of Congress Control Number: 2001012345
ISBN 978-0-300-13757-6 (pbk. : alk. paper)

Set in Sabon type by Keystone Typesetting, Inc.
Printed in the United States of America by Sheridan Books.

A catalogue record for this book is available from the Library of Congress and the
British Library.

The paper in this book meets the guidelines for permanence and durability of the
Committee on Production Guidelines for Book Longevity of the Council on
Library Resources.

10 9 8 7 6 5 4 3 2 1

In memory of Reginald Zelnik (1936–2004),
beloved friend, colleague, human being

Contents

Acknowledgments

I have benefited a great deal from the generosity of donors over the years spent on this book. I thank the Fulbright Program for an award in 1995; the National Endowment for the Humanities for its fellowship in 1997–8 and for the Summer Institute on Art and Artifact in Russian History in St. Petersburg, organized by George Munro and Alison Hilton in 1992; the Social Science Research Council for financing, Jane Burbank for organizing, and the University of Iowa, Portland State University, and the Kennan Institute for hosting, three seminal conferences on Imperial Russia; IREX (the International Research and Exchanges Board) for an Academy of Science Fellowship in Moscow and St. Petersburg in 1997–98, one of a long chain of IREX awards supporting my work; the Georgetown University Graduate School, School of Foreign Service, Provost's Office, and Center for Eurasian, Russian, and East European Studies for innumerable research grants.

The Public Library of the Performing Arts at Lincoln Center in New York offered up its rich resources. In Washington, I thank the staffs of the Georgetown University Library, the Library of Congress Music and Performing Arts Division, and the Hillwood Museum—particularly Kristen Regina, Karen Kettering, and Anne Odom. The bright young Georgetown freshman Katherine Magalif helped me check sources during the final stages of the book and David Hagen made the pictures.

The bulk of the research was carried out in Moscow, St. Petersburg, a few provincial towns in Russia, and Helsinki. It would be superfluous to list all the archivists and librarians in the Russian cities, but I heartily thank them for their patience and industry. Special recognition however is in order: in Moscow, to Vitold Petyushenko, Research Director of the Tretyakov Gallery; Olga Butkova and Kirill Razlogov for my backstage tour of the Maly Theater; Anya Salnykova for the endless stream of books; and the guide to the Ostrovsky House-Museum. In St. Petersburg, I am indebted to Elena Barkhatova of the print and photography collection of the Russian National Library; Neli and Vasily Kuznetsov of the recordings collection at the Rimsky-Korsakov Conservatory for many hours of listening to and copying obscure music; Pavel Lyssakov and Andrei Tolshin for a backstage tour of the Alexandrinsky Theater; Yuliya Shkitina for an inside tour of the Academy of Arts; and Liya Yangulova for copying much-needed books. At the Russian Museum, Evgeniya Petrova, Irina Karaski, Raya Dashkina, Elena Stolbova, Kira Mikhailova, and Ekaterina Shilova showed me how to unlock the treasures stored in the attic of that great museum and to view a Russia-in-pictures rarely seen on museum walls.

In Smolensk, thanks go to the archivists, librarians, local studies people, and faculty assembled for an international conference by Catherine Evtuhov, Boris Gasparov, and Andrew Wachtel; in Novospasskoe, Smolensk Oblast, to the guide at the Glinka manor house museum; and in Kursk to Alexander Reprintsev and especially Tatyana Alentieva for revealing to me more of the wonders of provincial Russian life in Tula, Orël, Kursk, the Korennaya Monastery, Voronezh, and other sites connected with this book.

The Slavonic Library in Helsinki, Finland, has been my scholarly base each summer and several winters over the last twenty-five years. Its nearly complete collection of nineteenth-century journals on open shelves a few feet from the readers' desks, its enormous collections, its machine-like efficiency, and its superbly accommodating staff make it the best library in the world outside Russia for prerevolutionary Russian studies and much else. I salute Irina Lukka, Maire Aho, Jarmo Suonsyrjä, Saara Talasniemi, Eila Tervakko, and Leena-Riitta Peltola for their incomparable services. I have gained much also from the Finnish National Gallery and the White Hall from their periodic shows of Russian art; and from the city's art, music, and theater libraries, with a special thanks to Liisa Byckling for theatrical expertise. At Helsinki University's Renvall Institute of History and Area Studies, my second home for many years, I thank Julia Azbel, Elena Hellberg-Hirn, Tuomas Lehtonen, Arto Luukkanen, Timo Vihavainen, Mikko Ylikangas, and Pirkko Hautamäki. Most of all I cherish the friendship and support of Natalia Baschmakoff of Joensuu University.

Just as rehearsals are mandatory in theater, try-out talks can help shape and refine ideas for a book. I was lucky enough to present some of them in North America at Brown, Harvard, Johns Hopkins, Toronto, Brock, Grand Valley, and Miami of Ohio universities, the University of Southern California, and the Hillwood Museum; and in Europe at the Renvall Institute, the Baltic and East European Graduate School in Södertorn (Sweden), the European University of St. Petersburg, Joensuu University in Finland, Cambridge University, and the State University of Kursk.

Good friends have supplied me with information, contacts, manuscripts, and CDs to feed my interests: Steven Marks, David Schimmelpenninck van der Oye, Tanya Stites, Hubertus Jahn, Abraham Ascher, Jeffrey Burds, David Moon, Fred Skinner, Paul Heineman, Andrew Wachtel, Lindsey Hughes, David Ransel, Douglas Smith, and Stuart Campbell. Scholars too numerous to mention have shared their unpublished dissertations and other materials listed in the bibliography. Priscilla Roosevelt, Boris Gasparov, Alison Hilton, and Murray Frame by their wisdom, learning, and close reading of my book, have added immensely to its value, as has Gavin Lewis for Yale University Press. Personal thank-yous can really get out of hand in a preface. I wish I could say a few words about my cat Blackie, but my publishers won't allow it. So I thank with all my heart my daughter Sasha; my sons Tod, Tom, and Andrei and his wife Holly Stevens; and, in addition to those mentioned above, Harley Balzer, Donald Duffy, Abbott Gleason, Ray Hanna, Brendan Humphreys, Daniel Orlovsky, Tom Quinn, Claus Westmeier, and the late Reginald Zelnik; the crowd at the Sea Horse in Helsinki and Martin's Tavern and Café Milano in Georgetown; the old gang from the Kibbutz on Maneesikatu; and, most of all, the incomparable Peter Dunkley, David Goldfrank, Amy Leonard, and Howard Spendelow.

Note: for clarity and economy, I have used the now-out-of-use term "actress." For variety I translate *dvoryanstvo* as both "gentry" and "nobility" and use the less-than-ideal "Gentry Club" for *Dvoryanskoe Sobranie*. In the text, Russian words are transliterated in a reader-friendly mode, but in a more scholarly way for the notes. The dates are all Old Style, thus two weeks behind the Western calendar in the nineteenth century.

Introduction: What's in a Title?

In this book a historian takes a look at the arts; or better, a historian looks at the broad canvas on which society — its structures, practices, mentalities — interacted with the arts. Historians do different things from musicologists, art historians, and theater scholars; or at least we try.[1] Linking creative expression to society is hardly a novel venture. Literary scholars of Russia have worked this vein with brilliant results. But then, print culture is only one form of expression. In a still largely illiterate servile Russia, its resonance was demographically slight — although its filter effect over the generations has been enormous. If we look for lower-class participation in culture through the lens of published fiction, we will have to squint. Broadening the lens to include art, music, and theater catches the serf violinist, the cook-turned-ballerina, the small-town painter, the actor from the urban depths. Thousands of men and women got their lives entwined with Mozart and Molière, Ostrovsky and easel painting. Where are they to be found in standard accounts of Russian history?

The title of this book, *Serfdom, Society, and the Arts in Imperial Russia*, roughly indicates what it contains, and the best way to explain it is to parse the title, in reverse word order. "Russia": while I venture occasionally into Ukraine and the Western Provinces, the bulk of attention is on European Russia. The Russia outside the capitals — the Russia of landowner estates and of provincial towns—looms large in the story as do the "two capitals," St. Petersburg and Moscow. The significance of the provincial story lies not simply in filling out a picture, but also in charting the many lines and links connecting the two tiny dots of St. Petersburg and Moscow to the infinitely larger population in the rest of Russia. "Imperial" in the title denotes chronology: the book covers a period from various points in the late eighteenth century to a sharp terminal date, 1861, the end of serfdom. It seemed to me that the triple turn in cultural history of the 1860s—the "revolt of the fourteen" at the Academy of Arts, the schism over the conservatory and "national" music, and the innovations of Ostrovsky in the theater—lacked an illuminating prehistory. I chose the preceding period because the cultural world of serf-era Russia formed the essential background to the great transformation. The history of the early nineteenth century's art worlds is relatively unknown in comparison with the age that followed—the era of the Itinerant painters, the Mighty Five composers, and the theater of Ostrovsky, Chekhov, and Stanislavsky.

"The arts" and their makers that I treat here belong, with some exceptions, at the high end of culture: classical music, theater, and graphic art—mostly painting. This omits folk culture, an altogether different universe, which features in this book only as it was employed by elite creators to add "national" flavor to their works. Similarly, local custom comes into play from time to time in scenes of public reaction to certain kinds of performance. I have gained valuable insights about the social dimensions of the other arts from non-dramatic literature, the most celebrated arena of cultural expression in Russian society of that era. Though they do not play a central role in this work, the literary canon, critical studies, and the now-forgotten fictions illuminate problems in ways not found in conventional historical sources. The history of the three branches of creative art forms a constantly shifting isosceles triangle with occasionally equal legs. The state-owned Academy of Arts and the Imperial Theaters provided institutional structure which the musical world did not possess. The first two also dealt in narrative forms and social codes. Since I have regretfully omitted opera, ballet, and most popular genres from this account, the musical world presented here consists mostly of art music in the home and instrumental concert performance where story line was rare. Yet, like theater, the "music world" that flourished in salons, orchestras—private and public, serf and free—upheld by concert societies and choirs and by foreign and Russian virtuosos required performance and thus audience, a fact that differentiated them both somewhat from the realm of painter and client. Underlying all the arts stood their varying social organizations and the social order itself.

I have endeavored to capture culture as it was experienced at the time; and so the ephemeral, the mediocre, and the once popular but now doomed-to-oblivion play a role. As Dostoevsky among others noted, the taste of the masses rules in their own time; the geniuses rule a bit later. Theater scholars, musicologists, and art historians draw from an arsenal of technical expertise and naturally tend to focus on their own disciplines. With some notable exceptions, they are attracted to master works and their creators and performers. In the critical idiom in which the winner takes all, one often finds the phrase "deservedly forgotten" applied to works of culture. Literary critics rightly praise works of transcendent value and eternal truths and consequently dismiss as unimportant those of "merely historical interest." This is as it should be. But in the fight for cultural memory, historians can recover what was once important to people without descending into antiquarianism by examining works that display the atmospherics of the moment when they were produced.[2] In examining art worlds[3] together, I am also concerned with the relationship of a broad range of expressive art to the people who made, performed, and consumed it. As a study of culture as process and experience, the book embraces not only works and their creators, but the life surrounding creation: career pathways, institutions, management, power grids, social attitudes and taboos, juridical categories, patronage, among other things. Thus the spread of pianos and sheet music, domestic art collecting, and backstage politics make up part of the story. The history of culture is, in and of itself, a worthy and important topic in *history*, and not simply a vehicle for illuminating larger issues. The study of the arts, when driven by a social perspective, provides multiple entry points into seldom explored aspects of people's lives and values.

"Society," a crucial component of the book, refers to the mutual relations between art practice and its products; and among those who engaged with the art worlds. This is not a reductionist attempt to explain the art itself strictly by its social environment. "It was certainly an error," wrote Raymond Williams, "to suppose that values or art-works could be adequately studied without reference to the particular society within which they were expressed, but it is equally an error to suppose that the social explanation is determining, or that the values and works were merely by-products."[4] The most important social conditioner of cultural life in this period revolved around the relationship of class and status to the arts. For a long time, pupils enrolled in the Imperial Theater system came from the lower classes. Those in the Academy of Arts collectively represented a more complex and pluralistic social body. Few social restraints inhibited upper-class men from completing an education in the fine arts; and painters, architects, and sculptors stood several notches higher socially than theater people, a situation not unique to Russia. Since no analogous institution of musical training existed in Russia until the 1860s, the status of musicians remained fluid and linked to other social determinants.

The huge popularity of amateurism among the privileged classes resulted both from the dearth of professionals and from the immense cultural attraction of creation and especially performance. If one could find little Byrons and Lamartines amid the forests and steppes of Russia, one might also encounter there would-be Chopins and Viardots. Amateurism came near to being one of the "accursed questions" in cultural debates before and after the Great Reforms. One view, floated by Anton Rubinstein and his archrival in matters musical, V. V. Stasov — the only issue that brought them near to agreement — saw amateurism as an aristocratic amusement that had nothing to do with serious art. Stasov thought it harmless, but Rubinstein held it to be a brake on professionalism. Yet the dilettante patrons and performers of the early nineteenth century contributed enormously to the promotion and spread of serious art music in Russia. Homespun music-making allowed for a free mix of players — titled amateurs, professionals, and serfs — who performed string quartets and even big symphonic works. And, despite the derivative and superficial quality of Russian amateur composers contemporary with Mikhail Glinka, some of their music was well-thought-of at the time and still deserves a hearing.

I begin the title of the book with the word "Serfdom" for several reasons. In the first place, serfs, freed serfs, and children of serfs appeared in numerous capacities almost everywhere in the late eighteenth and early nineteenth centuries where the arts were produced and performed: as painters, actors, orchestral players, singers, dancers, and even conductors and composers in gentry town houses and country manors; as individuals or entire troupes and orchestras sold to the Imperial Theaters; as trainees at the Capella or Court Chapel Choir, the Theater School, the Academy of Arts, and provincial art schools; as performers rented out on the provincial stage; and as spectators. The lives of real serfs crossed paths continuously with colleagues, managers, entrepreneurs, gentry families, the state. Their represented lives appear on canvas and as characters in drama and comedy. The interplay between the reality of serf and peasant lives and their imaging in the arts makes for one of the most arresting social-cultural phenomena of the time.

Russian belles lettres of the early nineteenth century and the myriad studies of it tell us something about the educated public's attitude towards serfs and other lower-class members of society, and even some details about their actual lives. Print culture, however, had little impact on the majority of the population. It is quite another story with the performing and the graphic arts. Theatrical companies all over Russia, serf orchestras, and art schools at various times were filled with the nonprivileged, including the unfree. Many more remained locked on their masters' estates. A struggle, marked by pathos and personalized politics, emerged during the final six decades of bondage that grew out of the social system of organized culture. The fight for freedom for serf artists offers a picture seldom encountered in studies of the institution which naturally concentrate on the far more numerous agricultural peasants. The protagonists of the fight included talented house serfs trained up in the arts while still in a state of unfreedom; their masters; and their sympathizers and patrons who tried to organize their emancipation so that they could live creative lives unfettered by the whims of their owners.

Serfdom also had an indirect impact on the relationship between society and cultural life: as a system, it intruded into almost every aspect of life and molded the mentalities of all classes. Ascription, making people live and die in a specified social cubicle with no hope of themselves or their heirs escaping, affected not only the lower orders. Society's hierarchical practices and juridi-cal norms reinforced the hermetical preferences of merchants and other classes. Courtiers who experienced malaise in salons attended by commoners inhibited, without fully preventing, a dynamic fusion of talents from all classes. The code that forbade aristocrats from exhibiting their skills in a public space further impoverished the cultural landscape. Subordination and deference at every level sprouted naturally from the patchwork of juridical estates. Russian serfdom underlay a vast system of unequal relations, personal and public: autocracy, bureaucratic hierarchies, employment practices, seigniorial authority, military regulations, family and gender bonds. Each displayed numerous forms of everyday personal expression in speech, posture, language, dress, manners, forms of address, and self-presentation. Class prejudices learned at home or in the garrison or chancery carried over to the theater school and backstage, to the Academy of Arts, and to the manor house. When some of the social barriers threatened to erode, snobbery and condescension often slammed the gates even tighter.

Expressive culture generated pleasure as it deployed power, and these became the central nexus between serfdom and the arts: the pleasure given by the material; the nuances of that pleasure among creators, performers, and audiences; the pain sometimes endured by those who were abused as free and unfree artists; and the framework of authority in which the culture was produced. Superimposing this thematic template over the social organization of the arts unavoidably highlights the social pathologies of serfdom. In exploring the fluid and sometimes ineffable connection between the light and the dark sides of the picture, I have tried to strike a balance between two familiar narratives: that of creativity and the sensual, esthetic, and enriching consumption of the arts; and that of the price some people had to pay for it.

Certain matters not present in the title thread throughout this book: private and public space, the growth of professionalism, and the emergence of national content in the arts — roughly corresponding to audience, artist, and the created work. In a recent collection of essays, several Russian scholars have attempted a synthetic and multidisciplinary approach to cultural space: "a representation of culture as an integral system, a definite sphere of social life, the patterned development of historical-cultural phenomena, and the forces shaping this development." Like the late Yury Lotman, from whom they draw some inspiration, they scan the environment of creativity and its reception — particularly "cultural information systems as an element of cultural space."[5] In plainer language, they examine the social context, over time, of shifts in cultural-social perception and the obstacles and accelerators that determined those shifts. In my schema, private space indicates the domestic sphere, hearth and home, the locus of family life, joined from time to time by relatives and friends. Public space, where everyone or almost everyone has access, may be either unrestricted and free of charge (fairgrounds and folk fairs) or open only to those with tickets (commercial theaters). This kind of arena, with a different name, has been called a "sphere of broad and largely unplanned encounter" among unequals, a place to "make diversity agreeable."[6] The public and the private represent the ends of a continuum between which lay a third sphere that I call social space — sites of private association such as Gentry Club, officers' mess, regular salon, large-scale home entertainment — broader than family but still restricted. Kinship, law, and money are the determining and differentiating factors in these spaces. The private is set by institution and biology and cemented by affection. The social is created by invitation of one's peers, often juridically defined. The public is unrestricted or defined by the market and sometimes by dress codes.

Applying elementary social-spatial concepts yields complex combinations and variants over time. To take one development, when the owners of a domestic serf theater or orchestra regularly invited neighboring gentry into their home as guests and spectators for extended visits, private space escalated into social space. The proliferation of such cultural-social spaces under serfdom — that is the manorial theater or musical ensemble — indirectly constricted public space. As manorial entertainments became more lavish in the late eighteenth and early nineteenth century, lesser gentry flocked to the big houses for diversion as well as to district and provincial Gentry Clubs (Noble Assemblies). As a nearly closed caste, the gentry, except on certain feast days, needed no "public space" in which to disport themselves. Well before the end of the period here studied, however, public space began to expand, much more so in the provinces than in the capitals. The incursion of commercial theater troupes (ironically often staffed by serfs) and visiting virtuosos opened up constantly growing venues where a mixed public could assemble. How this and other modulations of cultural space worked out in detail is unrolled throughout the chapters; and its implications for the emergence of a public sphere will become clear.

Recent literature has recounted the constant struggle for professionalism in the late nineteenth century against many obstacles. The question of who had it, how much they had, and who else could get it persisted up to the Revolution of 1917. In the pre-reform era, the term was hardly used. The struggle in the arts for professionalization — the legal and social-psychological recognition of trained practitioners as accepted members of the community — varied greatly, from the entitled academic artist to the unrecognized musician to the shady denizen of the stage. At the Academy of Arts, even serfs could work their way to freedom and status. The Academy designation for its graduates, Free Artist, became a watchword for other cultural occupations bereft of that honor. Russian performers of the Imperial Theater system had steady employment, regular (if mostly low) salaries, and retirement benefits. Trained musicians and composers in the capital (unless employed by the Imperial Theaters) had few of these things. Lacking the equivalent of the Academy and the Theater School, musicians had to await the opening of the conservatories before attaining something like the status and consciousness of being professionals.

Needless to say, serfs who remained unfree could never gain anything like the status that the word "professional" implies: independence, respect, guild membership. Beyond the capitals things were not much better for those — free, unfree, or semifree — who toiled in the world of art. Except for the few scattered art schools with ties to the Petersburg Academy, almost no professional training centers existed. The classical music scene was dominated by gentry amateurs, and the provincial theater by serfs and other lower- or middle-class elements. In one sense, serfdom and amateurism formed a vise that constricted the growth of strictly professional actors and musicians during the early nineteenth century. And yet, the enormous spread of serf and amateur performance and its audiences laid the foundations for the astonishing explosion of the arts after the emancipation of 1861. The distribution of private and social versus public space made the amateur-serf combination prevail in music and theater. Once provincial theater spread and grew, actors' isolation from the private and social spaces of estate culture proved to be an advantage: performing for mixed audiences of "their own kind" (merchants, townspeople) as well as gentry promoted the use of a vernacular delivery and thus fed into an increasingly "Russian" theater culture.

The emergence of Russian national consciousness in social thought and literature from the eighteenth century onward is familiar scholarly territory, usually seen through the lens of literature, the salon, and the thick journals of the intelligentsia. The national and social narratives contained or implied in canvases, stage plays, and musical works have their own stories to tell about what it meant to be Russian. National consciousness is an awareness turned into self-definition via the imagery of difference, affinities, essentialism. It can be, among other things, an ideology with philosophical underpinning, historical perspectives, and mythologies. It can also begin with self-discovery. That moment arrived in the eighteenth century when Russians found the vocabulary to set themselves off from the much-too-emulated French.[7] The Napoleonic wars widened and reinforced an identity fashioned from a reverse image of a hated enemy. But the imported culture had become too entrenched by 1812 to allow its overthrow. Accompanying the political reaction of the latter part of Tsar Alexander's reign came a resurgence of French cultural hegemony, though diluted by other European inflows. The cycle turned again in the reign of Nicholas I.

As national impulses emerged in public discourse, the monarchy sought to control, deflect, or sublimate them into dynastic ideology, finally shaping up as Official Nationalism under Tsar Nicholas, a doctrine that accommodated the European elements in the self-image of the Russian monarchy. During his long reign (1825–1855), a process of renationalization took place at several levels and at different tempos. At the top, the tsar required speaking Russian at court, effected symbolic linkages with "the people" at ceremonies, presented a family image at odds with the loose court morality of the eighteenth century, built Orthodox churches in what was seen as a Russian style, and promoted the Church itself which had suffered somewhat at the hands of the Protestant-mystical policies of Alexander I. Tsar Nicholas' Minister of Education, Sergei Uvarov, articulated the doctrine of Official Nationalism in a triune formula of Autocracy, Orthodoxy, and *Narodnost*. At the base of its rather vague elements, lay specific implications: absolute rule, Russia as a European monarchy in the tradition of Peter the Great, the supremacy of the Orthodox faith, and a spiritual union of tsar and people. These themes were taken up with alacrity by painters, playwrights, and composers and reached their apogee with the historical-dynastic dramas of Kukolnik and Polevoi and with Glinka's opera *A Life for the Tsar* in 1836.[8]

At that very moment "a shot rang out in the dark night": Pëtr Chaadaev's famous philosophical letters which threw down a challenge to Official Nationalism and at the same time created a schism between two other national voices. The Westernizers sought patriotically to turn Russia more steadily toward the West, not that of European dynasticism but of modern legal and political forms. Their friendly Moscow adversaries, the Slavophiles, rejected much of the European baggage of Official Nationalism and harked back to Muscovy, projecting a vision of Russia as an organic, spiritual community, the product of a unique national development. No sooner had Slavophilism reached a certain maturity in the late 1840s than it began to merge unnoticed with Official Nationalism, both of which were transformed and subsumed in yet a new vision of Russia — Native Soil conservatism. Needless to say, these ideological formations, so often reified beyond recognition, were in continual flux and never achieved the kind of coherence suggested in writings by and about their leading figures.

By the 1850s, several streams of cultural life were flowing together: "realism" and increasing national thematics in art and theater, a quest for an authentic Russian musical style, and a merchantry that began to patronize Russian art. In the background, a chorus of voices sang the newly synthesized Russian ideology and fused it with the changing relationship among the arts, their institutional setting, and the social and geographical background that shaped a national tone. Literature, drama, and painting fed each other native and popular motifs. Artists bridled at the constraints of the academic style. Serfs arrived on stage and on canvas draped in a gritty realism and a touch of menace. Provincial actors, including ex-serfs, brought their modes of small-town stagecraft and speech inflections to the Imperial Theaters. And Moscow emerged as the center of what seemed to contemporaries to be both "real" and "Russian" — concepts eventually conflated with the notion of artistic "truth." The process owed much to personal inspiration and the curiosity of individual creators. The widening of the social ambit of all the arts from the 1830s onward, reaching a long apogee in the subsequent decades, generated a parallel breadth of vision and self-discovery by individual creative figures of inner forces, ambivalences, and psychological tensions that laid the foundations of Russia's greatest era of artistic creativity.

The opening chapter contains a panorama of socio-cultural space followed by two chapters on music (at home and in public), three on theater (capital and provincial), and two on art (academic and otherwise). The final chapter takes up the convergence of social and cultural developments on the eve of the Great Reforms and looks forward to what is to come. The bibliography will give a sense of where I have found my material. I have shared the interest of the scholars of the Moscow-Tartu school in hard surfaces, material things, dance steps, apparel, even meals in reconstructing the semiosphere of an age.[9] I have often found myself arguing with Soviet scholars about their readings of culture that displayed political correctness, overblown and retrospective Russian nationalism, esthetic elitism (often contradicted by a democratic populism), and the moralizing traditions of the nineteenth-century intelligentsia. Yet many of them, even those who wrote in the Stalinist years, made meticulous use of the sources and managed to retain an accuracy and decency in their interpretations under very difficult conditions. Two often coexisting tendencies in the literature have painted the picture in contrasting colors. The nostalgia school tends to exalt the beauties created and the refined pleasures enjoyed in aristocratic homes and palaces, provided by the talent of their human property. The victim school dwells on the pain induced by seigniorial power and unfree labor. Both elements are essential to the story and indeed both pervaded the rich Soviet historiography of serfdom and culture, creating a tension between a veneration for high culture and an ideology that stressed class exploitation.

PART I

Cultural and Social Terrains

Town and Country

Every manifestation, every kind of utterance in social life, belongs to the boundless historical domain.
— *Adam de Gurowski,* Russia as It Is *(1854)*

Cultural tours of cities like St. Petersburg and Moscow, valuable and necessary though they be, all too often resemble a museum visit. The galleries themselves are hung with paintings by periods, genres, or themes constructed out of modern museum ideologies. The opulent palaces no longer house residents but are the haunt of curators and visitors. City tours focus precisely on the edifices where organic life has ceased to exist, buildings with no function other than visual instruction. The places that still work in many ways as they did in 1830 or in 1860 are theaters, concert halls, and art academies. The first two are accessible to the modern public but only as audience in the front of the house. The "innards" of the performance centers are never the topic of a historical-cultural lecture. The former Imperial Academy of Arts, standing resplendent on the banks of the Neva, is still an art school but not a part of any city tour itinerary. Those seeking to get the feel of how people lived amid the surviving cultural artifacts usually consult guidebooks, though these also reflect a modern sense of what is historically and aesthetically important. Almost all Russian-produced evocations of past urban life — particularly of St.

Petersburg—draw upon the words of contemporary writers to summon up for us the ambiance, the life force, the details, and the mystique that have long ago passed from the scene but live on in the minds of the intelligentsia. Dozens of works on such themes as Pushkin's Petersburg and Griboedov's Moscow are built around these and other central figures in Russia's glorious literary canon. But the literary-biographical allusions all too often obscure or ignore the experience of others who lived at the time and the place.

Two Dots on a Map

The coming chapters will, I hope, bring to the reader some sense of what private and public cultural places meant to the people who lived, worked, studied, painted, and performed in them in those decades between the reign of Catherine II and the end of serfdom.[1] St. Petersburg, with a population of a half-million in 1858, ranked after London, Paris, and Istanbul.[2] Every capital has another capital somewhere inside it. Petersburg's capital-within-a-capital, not wholly defined by geography, formed an archipelago of power, cosmopolitanism, an interacting social elite, and the headquarters, so to speak, of high cultural production in the Russian Empire. Petersburg consisted of two concentric circles. The inner one formed the core of production and consumption; the larger, embracing most of the city, served as one of the great objects of early nineteenth-century visual art. The size of the inner circle is surprisingly small: a strip of Vasilevsky Island across the Neva River from the main part of town; and a rough triangle formed by the northern bend of the Neva; the Nevsky Prospect, St. Petersburg's main thoroughfare; and the Fontanka Canal, with an outlier at Theater Square. The island's embankment held the Academy of Arts, founded in the eighteenth century; and the university, slightly to the north, founded in 1819 and home of a well-known concert series in the 1840s. Across lay the Winter Palace, home of the royal family, of a private theater, and of a picture gallery—nucleus of the world-famed Hermitage (fig. 1). The residential rooms of the palace also played host to musical performance by the dynasts themselves and their courtiers. A few yards away, in a courtyard off the Moika River, stood the elegant Capella, the court choir.

St. Petersburg's major cultural zone lay along and near the Nevsky, with its center on Mikhailovsky Square. The Soviets renamed it Ferdinand Lassalle Square after the nineteenth-century German socialist and renamed it again in 1940 Square of the Arts. The land was planted in the eighteenth century with thousands of maples in rows, but used as a dump heap until 1823 when it was chosen for Grand Duke Michael's new palace and gardens, designed by Carlo Rossi. The Mikhailovsky Palace, now the Russian Museum, served as a musical venue under Maria Fëdorovna in the reign of Tsar Alexander I and Grand Duchess Elena Pavlovna under Nicholas I. Elena Pavlovna engaged Anton Rubinstein as her house pianist in the 1850s; together they helped launch Russia's first conservatory of music in 1862. Across the street, on the western edge of the square appeared in 1833 the then least Russian of the capital's theaters: the Mikhailovsky, later Maly, now the Musorgsky Opera Theater. Opposite, in a two-story flat (it is now a school), lived a key figure of art music in the first half of the century, Mikhail Vielgorsky, who held there a grand musical salon. A few steps away, across Italyanskaya Street, stood the Gentry Club or Noble Assembly, completed in 1839, which now houses the St. Petersburg Philharmonia. Three blocks to the east, on Karavannaya Street, General Alexei Lvov, a major mover in the musical world under Nicholas I, ran his own salon and private concert venue. In the other direction from the Gentry Club, around the corner on the Nevsky as it crosses the Catherine (Griboedov) Canal, is located the Glinka Small Hall which, as the Engelhardt House, played host to the most prestigious concert music of the first third of the nineteenth century.[3]

Of the two remaining zones, one lay nearby, off the Nevsky a block east of Sadovaya Street on the corner of which stood the Imperial (now Russian National) Library. Looming over a square that separates it from the Nevsky, the Alexandrinsky (later Pushkin) Theater still proudly stands, a monument to the mastery of its architect, Carlo Rossi. Behind the theater, southward toward another square and the Fontanka Canal, stretched Theater Street, also designed by Rossi, with matching edifices on either side. Inside the buildings on the east side were nested the illustrious Theater School and the management of the entire Imperial Theater system, the Directorate. The school remains and the main theater library has been added on the corner. Gostiny Dvor (Merchants' Arcade), then and now the city's largest shopping center, and Apraxin Dvor along the Sadovaya stood one and two blocks respectively from the Alexandrinsky Theater, a fact that accounted for the large number of merchants in that theater's audience. Theater Square, hardly a zone at all, emerged near the intersection of the Moika River and the Kryukov Canal, a few kilometers below the Nevsky. It included only the Bolshoi Kamenny or Great Stone Theater, the imperial system's oldest and its major opera and ballet theater until replaced by the Marinsky in 1860. St. Petersburg's three imperial theaters, together with the two in Moscow, constituted a state theater monopoly in the capitals; no other public theater could function in these two cities until the 1880s.

Intermixed among these zones, lay a multitude of private cultural sites. A few blocks from the Great Stone, the apartment of the Kukolnik brothers hosted the Brotherhood—composer Mikhail Glinka, playwright Nestor Ku-kolnik, and painter Karl Bryullov. Like the flats of Vielgorsky and Lvov, it served as an important private music-making center. Many schools offered music training, including the newly founded Law School on the Fontanka Canal which fostered the talents of Alexander Serov, Vladimir Stasov, and Peter Ilich Tchaikovsky. But classical music performance, unlike art and the-ater, lacked not only a professional conservatory but even a permanent con-cert venue. Space had to be rented; musical leaders had no state-sponsored institution (except the Capella and the theaters). They met at salons; and later on—as in the case of the Balakirev circle—at the university or through word of mouth. Interlacing all these special sites, a tangled archipelago of aristo-cratic homes served as music salons, gathering places for theater enthusiasts, and privately owned art collections. Carriages manned by liveried servants, usually serfs, linked the entire system together day and night.[4]

Beyond the central core lay the palatial suburban houses on the islands in the northwestern part of the city, and seasonal festive sites like Ekaterinhof, a few miles west of Petersburg proper. The most famous suburban entertain-ment center, Pavlovsk, possessed a resort-like park with a "Vauxhall" or enter-tainment center and a ballroom. About thirty kilometers from the capital, it was connected to it by Russia's first railroad line in the reign of Nicholas I. Johann Strauss, among others, offered the city's commuters the light music entertainment for which he was famous.[5]

Social life at the top in this glorious capital—where smoking; an unbut-toned uniform; or wearing a flower, glasses, or beard in public (by one in government or military service) could be fined—revolved around highly ritu-alized receptions at court, private balls, theatergoing, and the fashionable round of visits and soirées. In the aristocratic weekly "at homes," wits were expected to hold forth in nimble conversation—usually in French. The related soirée (and its larger cousin, the "rout") was more kinetic than the salon. As the size of a gathering increased, serious talk tended to give way to lighter conversation. The grandest upper-class social occasion, the ball, emulated the court in formality and order of the dance. Women here displayed not only their physical charms and sense of fashion, but also the *bon mot* and the correct social skills. The sociability of the ball included status striving, flirta-tion, and matchmaking. The novelist Ivan Goncharov in the 1840s wrote of social lions who prided themselves on *savoir faire* and *savoir vivre* in matters of table, wines, and effortless drawing-room behavior—all without excessive enthusiasm; and dandies, so obsessed with outward appearance that some were known to starve themselves in order to purchase finery. Russian dandies, whose hour peaked in the 1820s, emulated London beaux and Parisian *flâ-*

neurs whose costume, lisping speech, and balletic movements underlined their devotion to leisure and pleasure. Such attitudes among the highest ranks of society tended to inhibit the ardent pursuit of a creative life or career.[6]

Since aristocratic sociability put so much stress on form, contemporaries took note of its desiccating effect. "It is at social gatherings," wrote Nikolai Karamzin in 1790, "that one enjoys friends least. Such occasions are not designed for discussion, conversation, or display of sentiment. Each person must say only a word in passing, and then move aside so as to yield the stage to others. Everyone is uneasy lest he say something indiscreet and thus reveal his ignorance of good form. In short, this is a perpetual vicious comedy that goes by the name of social necessity, a comedy without meaning and above all without interest." A lady-in-waiting at the Russian court, Anna Tyutcheva, declared that "inflated ritualism is a vast emptiness, a profound boredom, and complete lack of serious interests and intellectual life." Even body language and facial expression felt the bonds of politesse. Sofiya Khvoshchinskaya (1828–65) who spent a half-dozen years in an aristocratic boarding school, told of her classmates' "restrained grimaces" reflecting the institute's "*manière d'être*" and the mechanical perfection of "good breeding." In polite society, the effete mannerisms and the "languid gaze and drawling tone" of dandies could drain social contact of natural expression and sympathy.[7]

The segment of the capital's population living in the triangle and on the islands essentially dominated its cultural output, but only indirectly — as managers, patrons, and audiences. Gentry folks, lofty aristocrats, or simple landowners could perform for whomever they wanted at home. But a mantle of taboo covered public performance, contaminated as it was by its association with money, professionalism, deference, and exposure to public opinion. The powerful social prejudice — shared by other European upper classes well into the twentieth century — curtailed for a long time the potential pool of creative talent that could appear in Russian public life. None the less, the aristocracy basked in the reflected light of St. Petersburg's cultural offerings. Pierre Bourdieu speaks of space in terms of cultural capital: prestige accrues to those who live in the capital and at its center with access to power and culture: theaters, university, museums, and each others' homes and salons. This capital is cumulative since the pleasure and privilege and the psychic benefits of the space are multiplied by the additional access to knowledge.[8] The capital as cultural and intellectual magnet and the brain drain from the provinces are hardly an earth-shattering discovery. After all, in Balzac's novel, when Rastignac climbed the heights of Paris, he vowed someday to conquer it and not Dijon. The magnetic power was not the exclusive possession of St. Petersburg but of its sister Moscow as well. Provincials were constantly coming into the capitals through will and wealth, promotion or reassignment, peasant temporary work, or a chance relative. A surprising level of economic mobility combined with relative social immobility meant that poor folks often had rich relatives in the capitals. The confrontation of the provincial with the big city has rightly been called the "great central myth of the nineteenth-century realistic novel: the solitary ambitious or underprivileged hero face to face with the corrupt and impersonal metropolis."[9] The theme was played with several variations in the Russian theater as well as in real life by artistic Rastignacs.

Around the enchanted circle of St. Petersburg, sometimes living among it, another population toiled and served — a universe of merchants, lower officials, free and unfree servants, ordinary townspeople, and the denizens of the lowest depths of crime, beggary, and prostitution. The terms *raznochintsy* and *meshchane* have spurred thousands of pages of analysis and contention and have often been used interchangeably. *Raznochintsy* ("people of various ranks"), a huge, porous, and ill-defined population and the core of Russia's middle social layers, could include the "clerkish legions" who toiled in government offices, educated commoners, and some members of the urban lower class (*meshchane*), depending on who was using the word. The taxable *meshchane* or townspeople belonged neither to the merchant, peasant, nor gentry estates. The vague term included porters, dredgers, coachmen, sales clerks, shop assistants, hawkers and vendors, and all kinds of humble laborers; as well as children of priests, déclassé gentry, the offspring of army doctors or estate stewards, and those who fit nowhere else in the order of social estates. Together they far outnumbered all other town residents and yet remain the least studied of all Russian social categories. In practice, *raznochintsy* and *meshchane* often overlapped. Much has been made of the plight of the victimized urban lower middle class, Dostoevsky's poor town folk, including a motley assortment of penniless students and various educated but impoverished types who lived in dingy flats or rooms without running water. Some writers pitied them and others assaulted their alleged *meshchanstvo*: crudeness and vulgarity of taste and behavior, a philistinism lower than that of merchants. Yet these sectors of the city population played their own role both as subjects and audiences of urban drama on the Russian stage and of graphic caricature.[10]

At the bottom of the social heap lay a world far removed from the showy homes of the elite, a dark-hued underground of pungent smells and bustling humanity; of taverns, brothels, tenements, lodges, and flophouses. Here and in other Russian cities, crime, alcohol, and prostitution raged long before statisticians began to lament their "emergence." Artists and feuilletonists began exploring the "back alleys" of St. Petersburg in the 1830s and 1840s. Vsevolod

Krestovsky entered this dank world with *Petersburg Slums: A Book About the Well-Fed and the Hungry* (1864), set in 1858, a close imitation of Eugène Sue's *Mystères de Paris* of the 1840s, but with a Russian setting. Dostoevsky followed in 1866 with *Crime and Punishment*. Both novels were set in the squalid Haymarket Square.[11] The denizens of the lowest depths never became characters on stage in this era and few ever gained entry even to the gallery of the Imperial Theaters. Yet some of the poorest and weakest urban dwellers — orphans and abandoned children, sons and daughters of serfs — made it into the theater school and the Academy of Arts as students who were set on a path of potential professional success.

The Russian imperial capital served then, as it still does, as an infinite urban tableau for depiction by visual artists. Its breathtaking panorama combined with a heartless sterility were captured in Pushkin's great poem, *The Bronze Horseman* (1833); its ghostly menace was celebrated throughout nineteenth- and twentieth-century literature by Gogol, Dostoevsky, Bely, and many others. A dominant paradigm in St. Petersburg's cultural history has been mythic and metaphorical, a celebration or lament about the city's aura and mystique. St. Petersburg has long generated philosophical and literary vistas, whereas Moscow has more often been approached as a "local study" (*kraevedenie*).[12] As a visual city, the northern capital, with its empire style, reached its zenith in the reigns of Alexander I and Nicholas I, with the General Staff on Palace Square, St. Isaac's Cathedral, the Admiralty, the Stock Exchange, the Senate and Synod buildings, the Imperial Library, and the buildings noted above. Luxuriant gardens, parks, squares, and broad avenues that divided and connected great mansions added further luster to a magnificent city, as did pleasure craft with liveried oarsmen, merchant barges, watch boats, and canal taxis that plied the many waterways of the capital. Artists at the Academy were drawn to the opulence of the capital, its architectural beauties and the sumptuous interiors adorned by crystal chandeliers, parquet floors, fine furniture, urns, and clocks. Especially admired was the "dynastic zone": the shores of the Neva and the Admiralty, the Kazan and Spassky Districts, the royal and grand ducal palaces, the grand cathedrals. Interspersed, as if on guard, stood government and military ministries and the barracks of the Guards Regiments.

Aside from the built environment, a prominent feature of Petersburg life that caught the eye of painters of the academic tradition was the military review. Extraordinarily flamboyant uniforms, worn even off duty, identified each unit. The northern sunlight glanced off metallic casques and lances as patrols trotted along the Nevsky or the streets near the Admiralty, the only paved thoroughfares in this period. Tens of thousands of soldiers and elite Guards officers, garrisoned in specially named streets, squares, and neighborhoods, provided the cast for the regular spectacles of coordinated movement. The obsession with geometric formations of tsars Peter III, Paul, and Alexander I came to full fruition under Nicholas. Inspections, maneuvers, changings of the guard, and mounted escorts gave the capital the countenance of an encampment. What came to be known as paradomania so offended the (easily offended) visitor, the Marquis de Custine, that he called Petersburg "a military camp converted to a town." The city's public, however, did not share Custine's sniffy attitude. People of all classes swarmed around the Field of Mars or Palace Square to soak in the visual performances. Graphics show pie sellers hawking their wares to the onlookers. Painters trained in composing group postures, battles, and urban perspectives had a field day capturing the contrast between the orderly ranks of the marchers, the flashing sabers, and the restless crowds.[13]

Academy painters and others reared in the European tradition naturally clung to the enchanted circle for a long time as a cityscape suitable for artistic representation. Street vendors and other humble urbanites made up the often stylized extras in the theatrical oil canvases that privileged a long perspective and grandiose squares filled with ladies and gentlemen enjoying leisure. Eventually, artists took on the grittier realities and picturesque scenes of the daily round in courtyards, back streets, dockyards, market squares, and town taverns. Organ grinders, stonebreakers, and washerwomen on the canals entered the world of urban representation. Even before Dostoevsky began peopling Haymarket Square south of the Nevsky with his unforgettable characters, that place, the source of feed for the thousands of the city's mounts and cart and carriage horses, was captured in graphic art, with all its energy and earthy tumult.[14] However, in pictures, only gradually did building sites begin to sprout once invisible laborers exerting their bodily strength in the innumerable construction, post-fire rebuilding, and repair operations that kept thousands busy throughout this entire period.

Evenings at the Russian opera or drama in St. Petersburg in the first half of the nineteenth century offered viewers luxuriant sets of Carthage, Athens, sixteenth-century London, the seventeenth-century countryside of Kostroma, and a host of other locales, but seldom of the Russian capitals, aside from standard drawing-room sets. The cityscape itself had yet to make an impression on playwrights whose Petersburg settings were generic. Fashion shops and merchant arcades appeared, even in play titles, but exterior — as usual in drama — remained subordinate to character and plot. In the course of the half-century, those plots began to expand their social content from the eighteenth-century gentry-and-servant genres to plays about merchants and other non-noble urban classes engaged in commerce or apartment hunting.

It was often said that a journey from Moscow to St. Petersburg could be like a trip to Europe, and the reverse journey was more like a trip to "Russia." In terms of national imagery and cultural geography, Moscow differed from Petersburg in almost every way. As an ancient city founded in 1147, and the older capital once the hub of the great Muscovite state, Moscow exuded tradition (fig. 2). Fëdor Glinka called it "ancient city, city of the heart." Russian emperors lived in Petersburg, but had to be crowned in Moscow. The Kremlin and Red Square summoned up memories of hefty boyars, barbaric executions, tsarist pomp, and what some foreigners called Asian (or in those days "Asiatic") splendor. Narrow lanes twisted through old neighborhoods that bore a strong sense of place in memoirs and fiction, such as the Arbat, Kitai-Gorod, Old Equerries, and Zamoskvorechie districts. The ring boulevards of Moscow seemed to encircle a rotund old lady, in contrast to Petersburg, whose ramrod character was suggested by linear streets. Moscow looked outward in every direction into the vastness of Russia; its northern sister gazed across the seas to the outer world. The older city's hundreds of Orthodox churches and twenty-nine monasteries (to St. Petersburg's four) marked a density of pious observance contrasting with the secular look of the Petersburg baroque and neo-classical skyline. Merchants and gentry lived in both capitals, to be sure; but thousands of Moscow's population of about one third of a million in 1840 engaged in trade, as opposed to the hundreds in Petersburg. Retailers overwhelmed street life in their outdoor markets or covered stalls and one was much more likely to see in Moscow rows of carts bearing goods to the shops than a smart military detail on parade. *A Modern Guidebook to Moscow* of 1833 spoke of its "rustic simplicity and pleasantness," where there is "fresher air, cleaner and healthier than in other European cities."[15] As a minor artifact of local boosterism, the book endowed Moscow with a rural "Russianness."

Moscow was no Geneva, Amsterdam, or Hansa town. Though merchants and tradespeople outnumbered the gentry in Moscow, the old aristocracy still dominated its cultural and social life. The conflagration of 1812 reduced the city to an ashen landscape of "great burnt out houses without window frames or roofs, tumble down walls"; and rebuilding went on into the 1820s.[16] Great noble houses used space lavishly, replicating country estates with extended wings, outbuildings, stables, and gardens right in the middle of town. The two-story home on Strashnaya Square of Mariya Rimskaya-Korsakova's husband had twenty rooms, stables, and a carriage house. A typical salon hostess of the 1810s and 1820s, she circulated among the Obolenskys, Golitsyns, and Tolstoys and regularly hosted large dinner parties and balls for a hundred guests.[17] The Moscow Gentry Club boasted a Columned Hall—where Tsar Alexander II scolded the gentry in the late 1850s for their reaction to emancipation plans, and where Stalin held his show trials in the 1930s — which could accommodate five thousand persons. It hosted a weekly ball during the winter months.[18] In the early nineteenth century, the club catered only to gentry members and their gentry guests; wealthy merchants gained admittance on special occasions such as a tsar's visit, but had to sit behind the columns, view the doings from a distance, and not mingle with the gentlefolk.

The wealthy merchant princes toiled over accounts in their offices and planned elaborate delivery and pickup journeys to the great fairs and beyond to India or China. Many of the thousands of merchants of Moscow and elsewhere rose from humble beginnings, including serfdom, to great wealth; many also fell back into the lower classes due to bankruptcy. The high risk factor made them conservative and often ready to swindle a competitor or customer. Since the bazaar retailers were especially notorious for sharp practices, they helped stamp this image upon those titled as merchants, partly accounting for their shady reputation among the rest of the population. In any case, many merchants deserved the sobriquet *arshinnik,* a cheat who cuts corners on the product. Like merchants in other societies that marginalized them, they tended to protect each other, give generously to charity, and take care of their own.[19] The Russian merchantry found it hard to shake their image among the intelligentsia as a "kingdom of darkness." Indeed many lived in poorly lit homes cluttered with heavy furniture and icons on the walls. But the darkness metaphor was also applied to their way of life: patriarchy, mercenary marriage deals, tyranny over lowly clerks. Since most merchants were religiously observant Orthodox or Old Believers, skeptics charged them with obscurantism, superstition, and hostility to culture and modern ways.

Shunned by high society and inward-looking, the Moscow merchantry, except for the very rich, thus largely lived its own life, partly due to ascription and partly by choice. The traveler in Vladimir Sollogub's 1845 novel, *The Coach,* noted in the merchants he met a sense of identity that was linked to "integrity" of national character. Their morality valorized sharp dealing with those outside the professional clan but not within it. Authenticity implied a refusal to climb upward, shave the beard, don the "German" wardrobe, or marry into gentry. For in doing so one lost personality, character, identity, and true self — and one became two "halves," both of inferior quality. The bulk of the merchantry limited their socializing to other middle groups of society. In the Moscow Merchant Club, founded in 1786, members mixed regularly with teachers, professors, physicians, other professionals, intelligentsia, figures from the art world, and occasional gentry guests. Until banned in 1859 by a reactionary governor of Moscow, even *meshchane* and artisans were admitted. Ordinary merchants made little effort to "gentrify" in everyday life. They invited their social betters to banquets, but the gesture was rarely returned because most merchants lacked foreign languages and gentry-defined social skills. Despite many exceptions, club rules, social practices, and even sumptuary laws kept class lines in place.[20]

The exceptions, wealthy merchant and manufacturing families, made or tried to make a transition to European culture or gentry-like ways. Even the humbly born founders of great merchant fortunes in the early nineteenth century were, in the words of a scholar, already adopting some aspects of Western "dress, manners, and hygiene, and . . . forms of entertainment."[21] They sired a generation, born roughly between 1830 and 1850, which finished high school but not university, traveled to Europe, and dipped more deeply into the well of Europeanized Russian culture. A Russian-speaking foreigner in the 1850s found a wealthy merchant's home decked out like a gentry mansion. The family wore imported clothing and the males were clean-shaven; the daughters sang Verdi arias for the company; and they all dined on French cuisine as they spoke French.[22] Gentrifying merchants and those who dealt on a national or international scale of business had an enormous range of contacts from all kinds of social layers and were far from being hermetically sealed prior to 1861. Growing ambivalence and variety of outlooks best describe merchant views of self and others. Subtle changes in identity and self-presentation were reflected in costume. Traditional merchants favored dark double-breasted suits, with beard, hair, and boots in a peasant style. In the 1840s, by one account, three variants of merchant facial appearance could be detected: fully bearded, a trimmed beard, and clean-shaven — the last among the merchant aristocracy who emulated Russian gentry and European men. The less adventurous retained the caftan and boots, but made of fine cloth and good leather. The uneasy mixture of European and traditional garb was matched among merchant wives.[23]

Given the social dynamics of a class as visible and tension-generating as the merchantry, it is no surprise that their lives intersected with the arts. In painting, this came in three forms: merchant as target, as sitter, as collector. The graphic artists, notably Fedotov, were happy to enlist merchants and their families as objects of satire along with other social types. Merchants themselves, from the eighteenth century onward, commissioned portraits, in oil and later in photographs, the history of which vividly illustrates the gradual modulations in self-image. In the 1850s appeared the first generation of merchant patrons of Russian art that went beyond family portraits and set the tone for the famous merchant collectors later in the century. In stage representation, Moscow merchants were, right up to the early plays of Alexander Ostrovsky in the 1850s, depicted monotonously as cheats and patriarchal interferers with a daughter's love interest. On the other side of the curtain, Moscow merchants joined their colleagues all over Russia in patronizing the theater on a regular basis, though some of them boycotted it as an immoral institution. Any number of merchant sons and daughters, with or without family blessing, made a career for themselves on the Russian stage.

The Moscow topography of cultural production and support also marks it off from that of the capital. Like Petersburg, it had its cultural salons and private performance venues. In the realm of public concerts, Moscow lacked anything like even the Engelhardt House and had to negotiate performance events with the often haughty Gentry Club or the Moscow branch of the Imperial Theater Directorate. There existed no powerful, court-affiliated amateurs or concert societies equivalent to those in St. Petersburg. An embryonic art school grew into a major institution from the 1840s onward. Although it remained fully dependent on the Academy of Arts until the 1860s, it spawned its own practitioners of realism in art. Public exhibit space was severely limited. The two major theaters of the imperial system with a continuous history at one location in Moscow appeared only late in the reign of Alexander I: the new Maly (1824) and the Bolshoi (1825). The mini-Directorate in Moscow, though subordinate to St. Petersburg, began to achieve great power and dynamism in the 1830s and 1840s, not only as the headquarters of Moscow performance art but as a staging area for musical virtuosos and theatrical tours to the provinces as well.

Moscow developed certain kinds of public and semipublic spaces that had no parallel in St. Petersburg, and led the way particularly in extending the reach of theater into public conversation: university, coffeehouse, and an actors' hiring hall. Moscow University, the country's oldest, had its own jail; and yet radicals like Herzen recalled the democratic atmosphere among students. The serious ones revered the best professors and eagerly discussed their ideas in a favorite tavern, the Brittania Club, across the street from the university on Mokhovaya Street, site of the present-day Manège complex. Amidst the general conviviality of song, drink, and food, students aired their current views on Moscow theater life, among other topics. One recalled that Muscovites, lacking the Hermitage and the Academy of Arts, saw the theater as their city's cultural focus.[24] Indeed some actors who graduated from the university retained strong ties. Another student hangout, Pechkin's Coffeehouse on Hunter's Row, across the street from both imperial theaters, played host to a much wider clientele: actors, playwrights, critics, members of the intelligentsia, and merchants. Pechkin's, the closest thing to the cafés and restaurants that sprang up in the theater districts of European cities, acted as a hatchery of taste. A few blocks away, Barsov's Tavern became the site of a theatrical agency where managers, theater owners, and performers sought each other out for short or long term engagements in the provinces. Barsov's, unlike anything in St. Petersburg, came to be the hub of the fast-growing provincial stage. Indeed, Moscow played a crucial role in provincial culture through the density of musical and theatrical estates nearby; a Russianness shared with the provinces; and a web of roads (and later railroads) leading to central Russia, the Volga, and Ukraine. Moscow became the focus of national intellectual currents such as Slavophilism and Native Soil conservatism and eventually the virtual capital of a Russian national theater.

A word about the capitals' foreign population who played an important role — both positive and negative — in Russian life and culture and its representation. Most important by far were the French, who deluged Russia during the Revolution and the Napoleonic era. Not all, like Prince Polignac, could enjoy a Potocki estate, complete with servants and serfs, for their use. Nor could all receive court appointments or ranks in the military or civil service. Some got work as teachers, tutors, owners of food and fashion businesses. Those reduced to an unfamiliar humble status anticipated in reverse the emigré Russian counts and princes who became valets or taxi drivers in the Paris of the 1920s and 1930s. Though members of an archenemy nation for two decades, the French stamped their language, manners, fashion, taste, and culture upon Russians through teaching and social interaction. Many a fake Frenchman assumed that identity for panache: it was widely believed that the Swiss restaurateur Branger was the cousin of the song writer Jean-Pierre de Béranger. In Moscow, a kind of foreign quarter, including many French-speaking Russians, lay near the French church and the Kuznetsky Most. The resident Irish pianist John Field lived there most of his adult life and never learned a word of Russian. Germans from the German states as well as Baltic and other Russianized Germans inhabited both capitals and held a dominant place in the world of instrumental music right up to the 1860s. Italians and other invaders of 1812 often stayed on and some were hired by Moscow aristocrats as majordomos.[25]

The Seigniorial Abode

With the emancipation of the nobility from obligatory service in 1762 and a vast giveaway of estates into private hands under Catherine II, the socio-cultural space of provincial Russia became animated. Many nobles deserted the capitals and settled into manorial nests (fig. 3). The affluent and ambitious created the cultural universe so eloquently described in Priscilla Roosevelt's volume on the Russian country manor. Of the roughly estimated 886,782 nobles in European Russia at the end of the period, a top layer of 2,000 to

3,000 wealthy magnates owned five hundred souls or more.[26] Well below them, as many as two-fifths of the gentry landowners were considered poor because they possessed only a few dozen or fewer souls — male serfs, the unit of measure. Rich lords maintained homes in the capitals; the country seat, their main source of income, provided either a seasonal or a permanent retreat. Serf villages provided them with unpaid labor (*barshchina*) or cash and/or goods (*obrok*). In short, the serfs fed their masters. Between them and the lord, stewards of various social backgrounds managed the estates. As buffers, stewards often got depicted on stage as villains out to cheat the lord, harass the peasantry, seduce a serf girl, or send a love rival into the army out of turn. The more enterprising gentry opened spas, distilleries, factories, or commercial theaters. A few "improving landlords" won success in adopting European crop systems, animal husbandry, and technology. The Free Economic Society in the 1830s opened agricultural exhibitions that brought together landlords and merchants who shared a common interest in the economic progress of their region. Such societies remained underdeveloped.[27] Old-fashioned conservatism, fear of state interference, lassitude, and popular Slavophilism played their part. One other factor might have been in play: "improving landowners" were roasted on the Russian stage. The playwright Alexander Shakhovskoi coined the adage "Even Russian bread won't grow in the foreign manner."[28]

In their fond memories, the Russian gentry overwhelmingly associated the estate not with business but with family and social life. The manor house as home marked the family's identity (fig. 4). One rarely encounters field serfs or stewards in estate memoirs. What comes through the mist of recollection most vividly is everyday life, often seen as an idyll: parents and siblings, tutors and house serfs; the porch, the garden, the nearby forest and brook; family and seasonal rituals, home entertainments, sleigh rides, and guests. The middle and lower ranks of the gentry in particular, those who could not afford lavish upkeep in the capitals, came to identify their lives with the countryside — their manor, the neighbors' estates, and sometimes the provincial or district town — an identity that varied from one region to another. The gentry of Tver Province, for example, looked upon family and estate as the emotional focus of life and tended to flock with their own kind. The well-off offered charity to some of the poorer gentry without mingling socially with them.[29]

With the exception of the few recluses who preferred to take their pleasures privately, the more affluent landowners in town and country shared their cultural treasures with friends and neighbors. Since estates were far-flung and isolated, hospitality and generosity became hallmarks of home living in the countryside for those who had the means. In a flourish of symbolism, retired artillery officers, when moved to entertain, would fire a cannon as the signal for a general dinner invitation to the neighbors. General Nashchokin greeted his guests with musicians on a tower. Alexandra Shchepkina, the sister of the short-lived promoter of German romantic philosophy Nikolai Stankevich and the daughter-in-law of the great serf actor, Mikhail Shchepkin, recalled that on the steppes of Voronezh Province, any gentry family who lived within twenty to thirty miles was considered a neighbor. Guests spent the night and the host's children would watch in the morning as the carriages disappeared over the flat horizon. In Ekaterinoslav Province during the same period, a landowner hosted a wedding and, since his home could not accommodate all the guests, he had built on the spot a temporary structure with a wooden dance floor.[30] In a land with relatively few stopovers, the socially active estate whose owners could afford to entertain guests on a regular basis became a hotel without a concierge and without a final tally. It could contain separate guest rooms or even suites as well as valet and catering services. Both guests and owners could live a life apart from the servants and from the service area while fully enjoying their social space at dinner, tea, shows, the hunt.

Throughout the period, landowners amplified their pleasures by means of artistic display and performance. The countryside attracted more and more noble families, including those exposed to foreign places, wars, and new knowledge; and students who shuttled between home and Moscow and the new university towns. From the 1820s, the estate as a fictional setting proliferated and historians have often singled it out as a hothouse of daydreams about beauty, social harmony, or liberation. But manor houses were more often showcases of power and pleasure than staging areas for the budding intelligentsia. For every Herzen or Bakunin — privileged sons of the gentry mansion — hundreds of landowners and their families took the servile order as a natural condition and translated their overlordship of other human beings into pleasure-giving institutions of art, music, and theater and into schools of culture. Catherine II encouraged the spread of culture to the countryside; she claimed to believe that people who sang and danced could think no evil. Gentry culture flowered in this period: in the wildernesses sprang up an archipelago of culture created jointly by lords and their serfs. Nobles who created cultural estates became *Kulturträger,* bearers of civilization into the backlands. Though their outreach remained largely limited to friends and neighbors, there is abundant evidence of cultural interaction between gentry and town folks.

Aside from commissioning architecture, sculpture, landscaping, and decorative arts, culturally aspiring landowners sought portraits of themselves and their families and pictures of their estates. Those unable or unwilling to pay professionals had their own serfs turned into artists via home training by a hired teacher, apprenticeship to a local icon painter, or a stint at the Academy of Arts or one of the half-dozen provincial art centers. Training serf musicians mostly followed this pattern. But since no conservatory existed, wealthy lords sometimes sent their serfs to Europe for professional training. Serf actors and other stage performers usually got the least training. Needless to say, any serf artist or performer could, at the whim of a master, be bought and sold or returned to manual labor. These staffing strategies eventually blossomed into serf choirs and full symphonic orchestras; serf painters of every degree of talent; and hundreds of serf theaters that spread their way across rural Russia. The principal content of these arts was European: portraits and landscapes in the academic mode; ballroom, chamber, and symphonic music; and the imitated or copied repertoires of the Imperial Theater system in the capitals, itself largely European in origin or inspiration. For most owners of cultured estates, Western art was seen as a marker of attainment and refinement which in no way conflicted with national identity.[31]

The notion of a "socio-cultural environment," floated by some recent Russian scholars, involves not only the place where people live but a cultural space that transcends it. It encompasses those regions where the inhabitants of estates have traveled physically and mentally: their books, memories of things learned, past life — the plays and music they have seen performed, the pictures they have viewed and still view. The recollected experience of nobles in a well-endowed manor house who had been to or lived in the capitals and abroad, had read widely, and knew foreign languages, formed as much part of their cultural space as their cultural furniture: piano, library, theater, or orchestra. The social imaginary of the cultivated estate residents stretched outward and backward in time through texts, classical gardens, family portraits, music, and exotic scenes on stage. The accumulated and recalled impressions or mental learning or artistic enjoyment extended the closed arena of home out into the world and deep into the past. Put another way, in the period of its richest flowering, "the manor house was tied by a thousand threads to the artistic culture of the epoch."[32]

Motivation for building cultural worlds on the estate took on many shades: good taste, a craving for distinction, slavery to fashion, the spell of luxury, and a show of authority. And all along the continuum prevailed extreme variations in the human treatment of the artistic servants. Critics have rightly highlighted vanity or vainglory, pride in showing off a string quartet, a vaudeville, or an opera. But there are nuances in pride: of property, of power, of refinement. of generosity, of organizational ability. Among the cultural magnates, genuine connoisseurs attended to every detail of training, rehearsal, and artistry; spared no expense; and often plummeted themselves and their family into poverty and debt. Some masters cast a benevolent net of kindness over their serf artists. For others, whim, caprice, and fancy led to abusive behavior and the display of uninhibited "feudal" powers. The estate, a universe of cultural and social tension until the release of the serfs, often rang with blows and shouts that alternated with the lines from Molière or the strains of Boiledieu. Fear, guilt, masking, speaking French in front of the servants, punishment, and resistance were all part of the story. Sadly, the combination of lash, harem, drill, and stage constituted a mode of expression for some masters in the servile order. The theater, garrison, and harem estates were miniature polities where an otherwise nearly functionless gentry wielded domestic power. Polarities sprung from concrete differences in juridical status and from the contrast between the bondage of serf artists and the fabled sense of "freedom" felt by nobles who built and lived in their own physical world, unencumbered by duty and service to the state. At the same time, many lords viewed the maintenance of estate culture as a mode of "acting European" though, ironically, some outsiders saw it rather as Asian barbarism, especially on those estates which offered glittering superficiality above the dirt and rust, stink and ruin beneath the surface.

Prior to the 1850s, the arts had little to say about the deeper levels of manorial culture or serf artistry itself. Only rarely did graphic art assault the life-styles of the gentry. Playwrights did so regularly, though always within limits of a nonsystemic critique. Individual "sinners" among the nobility felt the sting of satire in the eighteenth and early nineteenth centuries for excessive foreign emulation, corruption, failure to serve the state, abuse of serfs, sentimentalism, extravagance, and even agronomic experimentation. The miscreants were treated as exceptions; in plays about a nobleman's abuse of underlings, another nobleman would step in to restore justice — thus supporting the axiom that absolute monarchy, serfdom, ascription, and indeed the Russian social order as a whole were themselves God-given.

The seignior-serf world of culture eventually collapsed, though not fully until February 19, 1861. Among economically rational gentry, serf artists could be profitable. Landowners sent off individual artists, musicians, singers, or actors on *obrok* (temporary labor, with part of the wages due to the master) or on loan to the town, to a neighbor, to another theater. Sometimes whole companies were traded, rented, or sold together with families. The Imperial Theater system frequently purchased serf performers from cash-strapped owners. When public advertisement of serf sales without land was officially forbidden in 1801 (though the law was rarely observed), sellers frequented the fairs to do their transacting. Whenever patrons sought to purchase the emancipation of talented serfs, serf owners who knew the market value struck hard bargains. The price range for a creative serf ran from about two thousand to eight thousand (and on occasion as high as ten thousand) rubles while that of ordinary serfs ran to the hundreds of rubles. But the training and trading of serf artists as an investment was more than overbalanced by the enormous drain on seigniorial finances; many of the bankruptcies of this era were caused by those who simply invested too heavily without consideration of the costs. Estates of the grandees flourished until the ravages of war, inheritance laws that fragmented estates, the wages of squandering, and even an antiserfdom sensibility made their inroads into the system.[33] Yet, as Priscilla Roosevelt rightly observes, economic decline, with all its pain, did not define the life of the rural gentry. In fact that life was defined as defiance of the decline. In something resembling the active creation of social oblivion, some landowning families stubbornly maintained their patterns of life.[34] Even so, the creation of great cultural centers and elaborate manor houses declined from the 1820s onward both because of financial pinch and because some gentry began to prefer smaller-scale residences. Extravagant gamblers and prodigal spenders on luxury eventually had to take out a mortgage or face the auctioneer's hammer.

Slaves of Art

Creating nests of cultural life required more than money. Only about 2 to 3 percent of nobles could afford to build and maintain the two hundred or so staff required, say, for a large house, church, planned garden, and other amenities; and to hire foreign conductors, musicians, ballet masters, and set designers. The middling and poorer Maecenases of art had little alternative but to deploy their serfs on the front lines of creativity and performance. But even the grandees drew on their serf population for rank-and-file performers. The belief, just starting to erode in other parts of Europe, that artists were hardly better than artisans or servants remained intact in Russia; playing a violin or dancing on stage seemed only a step away from craft skills or household and farm chores. Owners of large estates could draw from armies of field hands, drivers, under-stewards, and various technical workers. For more modest landlords, household serfs made up the recruitment pool: cooks, scullery maids, butlers, and valets. Serf artists of all kinds could be differentiated and segregated from field serfs and domestics in treatment, apparel, and even housing. Just as often, they shared the status of stable boys, millers, blacksmiths, and domestics, even alternating in these roles on a regular basis. An ex-serf recalled in his memoirs how owners inhibited initiative and pride of work by shuttling serfs from farm to house, turning cooks to coachmen, lackeys to clerks or shepherds.[35]

The *dvorovye* (household serf) category, including *obrok* serfs as well as house serfs proper, provided the majority of serf artists. Based on the incomplete and approximate data of the revisions (a loose form of population counting) in the reign of Nicholas I, their percentage of all serfs rose from 4.14 in the eighth revision of 1835, to an estimated 4.79 to 4.85 in the ninth of 1851, to 6.79 in the tenth revision of 1858–9. This translated into a total of 1,035,924 serfs in 1851, and of 1,467,378 in 1858–9 in a serf population then estimated at 20,158,231.[36] The conversion by landowners of field serfs into house serfs accelerated in the 1850s. Tsar Nicholas I, who with his advisers considered house serfs both lazy and dangerous, took a few measures, mostly moot, to prevent their increase, but would not forbid conversion of village serfs into house serfs.[37] But by the late 1850s it became clear to the authorities that landowners, fearing emancipation, were increasing the relative number of house serfs, to whom owners would not be obliged to give land in any settlement. So on March 2, 1858, conversion was forbidden.[38] Figures for the provinces reveal clearly the human foundations of provincial culture in that the provinces with the highest numbers of *dvorovye* were for the most part those that had a high density of orchestras and theaters.[39]

How much did serf owners intrude into the lives of their serfs, aside from their latent right to punish miscreants with beatings, reassignment to the army, or even exile to Siberia? One form of "playing" with serfs, psychologically related to their use as actors, took place on "regimental manors," which, though more common in the eighteenth century, could be found right up to the end of serfdom. Retired officers trained as parade martinets retained their drill-ground spirit and attempted to transform serfs into toy soldiers with elaborate uniforms and constant drill. The power to move human beings around in an endless display of dressage appealed to ex-officers who had no other outlets for their energies. The state-run Military Colonies had the peasant-soldier alternate farming with parade drill. Playing with the intimate lives of serfs went far beyond the colonels' games. The ex-serf N. N. Shipov recalled that early in the nineteenth century an absentee landowner of the Saltykov family prevented his serfs from marrying out of their class, even though a few of them had enriched themselves in trade. The nobleman D. N. Sverbeev noted that in the 1820s widows and maidens were sold into marriage to landowners who owned villages where intermarriage was impossible due to tight kinship relations. Peasants themselves on a Smolensk estate married by lining up and casting lots in the late 1830s. Landowners sometimes punished servants with an unwanted marriage and gave away serfs to priests and merchants who legally could not own them. Elizaveta Vodovozova, a gentry woman of Smolensk Province, recalled that her neighbors believed strongly in controlling serf marriages; and they resented her father, who did not, as a bad example. A later account claimed that even good folks controlled the lives of their house serfs, including sex and marriage, and attempted to keep lovers apart for various reasons.[40] Against this must be put the finding that among female landowners, it was "common practice to manumit serf women who wished to marry on neighboring estates." Another study argues convincingly that serf marriage was not widely controlled by owners, though it deals only with village serfs.[41] Playing the colonel or the matchmaker were deviant forms of that game-playing and play-acting that characterized so much of Europeanized Russian gentry life.

House serfs, living or working in proximity to the masters, were ideal objects of manipulation. The everyday life of servants in Russia has not received the same attention as that of servants in the West (fig. 5).[42] The picture is so varied as to defy generalization. Bigger homes provided wings or outbuildings for their servants, but in most others gentry families and their servants — unlike the upstairs-downstairs partitioning of English upper-class homes — lived together. There were rarely servants' quarters as such, and domestics normally slept on the floor or in some makeshift resting place. In modest homes, servants had little privacy, except the interior privacy of their thoughts. Overstaffing meant that even in the large manor houses servants were under foot. Yet the worlds of servants and gentry diverged in almost every way. The juridical inequality was reinforced by way of life, values, clothes, deportment, language — and punishments.

Adjacent to virtually every elegant manor house, with its ornate formal gardens, stood a stable to which errant house serfs — including artists, actors, musicians — were regularly sent to be beaten. Fëdor Bobkov (1831/2–1898), a house serf, remembered details of relations among the fifteen to twenty house serfs who were, he relates offhand, sometimes beaten. But of atrocious abuse, he knew only by hearsay. Tsar Alexander I's right-hand man, Count Arakcheev, portrayed by contemporaries as a backwoods barbarian, beat and abused his serf architect I. S. Semënov, later a professor. Thrashing, sometimes severe, became a regular part of the life of musicians and performers of both sexes. Baron Nikolai Wrangel, a man learned in the arts, left a gripping memoir of a childhood that coincided with the last years of serfdom. While loathing serfdom, he tried to be fair to his fellow gentry, most of whom he thought to be humane. Yet he recounted numerous tales about the cruelty of his neighbors and the murder of masters by serfs. His most famous and much-quoted anecdote concerned the lord who forced a male and female serf to stand nude for hours in the garden posed as Hercules and Venus. In a rage, they jumped from their pedestals one day and brained him. Callousness also led to the sale of serfs without land (though forbidden since 1801), gambling them away, and the rending of family ties. The renowned painter Vasily Tropinin, to note only one instance, was given away as part of a dowry.[43] An even more abhorred practice, one treated gingerly on the stage, was the breach of recruiting norms — selling serfs as inductees or putting them into the ranks out of turn.[44]

Though landowners' sexual use of female house serfs was fairly common (fig. 6), establishing a seigniorial seraglio overshot the norm. Harem masters were able to enjoy the carnal favors of scores or even hundreds of women. A few masters filled their beds simultaneously with a cluster of serving girls. Herzen spoke with scorn of his uncle's serf harem. In the 1820s, landowner Pëtr Kashkarov (Koshkarev), in addition to wife and mistress, had a dozen young girls sleep in his bedroom, attend his weekly bath, read to him, and play cards. Yuri Lotman characterized this style of life as a mix of European secularism and paganism, typical of a large segment of the Russian gentry. It suited perfectly the tastes of those lords who blended carnality with a flair for music and theater. General Izmailov, owner of eight hundred servants, kept about thirty girls locked up in his home. Viktor Sinelnikov, an elderly bachelor and in-law of Avdotiya Panaeva, owned about two thousand souls and maintained a two-story stone building housing a harem of dozens of serf girls. For this, the local authorities eventually took his estate in trust. Such sanctions remained largely a dead letter although one landlord who had ravished some sixty young serf girls was punished. Peasants sometimes acted on their own to beat or murder the guilty party. There were also cases where girls' parents happily provided them to the lord in hopes that their offspring would have a better life. On rare occasions, the lord would take a serf girl as a bride.[45]

It is difficult to separate the abuses of household serfs from other kinds. In notorious cases of a landowner's mistreatment of his or her people, the state would intervene by taking the estate into official guardianship for oversight. In 1838, 140 estates were so handled and in 1854, 193. But these interventions arose only in response to outrageous cases. The tribulations of house serfs were less liable to public notice. The Decembrist leader, Colonel Pavel Pestel, in his revolutionary program *Russian Justice,* explicitly named household servants as the worst-off of all serfs. Alexander Nikitenko (1804/5–77), a serf who became a highly educated government censor, wrote in his diary in 1851, referring to recent years, that "ignorance and unlimited power made most Russian nobles behave cruelly in those days." As the author of a statistical study writing on the eve of emancipation understated it, the great majority of house serfs "have lived right up to today a life that poorly corresponds to the strict demands of civil societies."[46]

To be sure, the bad cases made good stories and caught the attention of writers then and later. In many a normal gentry home, the power of the master or mistress was often tempered by the capacity of the house servant — like the impudent lackey and the wily maidservant of comedy — to "resist," up to a point. As master and lackey grew old together, a kind of coupling could develop — reminiscent of Don Quixote and Sancho Panza — such as that of the mutually grousing fictional pair, Oblomov the lazy lord and his servant Zakhar, in Ivan Goncharov's celebrated novel, *Oblomov* (1860). The very presentation of their names — family for the master; first name for the serf — set the relationship of this matched set that generated entropy rather than synergy, a twinned image of the institution of serfdom in which servants everywhere usually were — and were depicted as — both lazy and loyal, even under frontier tyrants such as Sergei Aksakov's grandfather.[47] Though one must allow for a sterilized nostalgia in the elegiac pictures of "old-time life" that color so many gentry memoirs, one cannot ignore their overwhelming emphasis on the remembered kindness of their own parents towards serfs and their own fond recollection of beloved servants and nannies and "happy peasants."[48] Without joining that sometimes idealizing chorus, it is necessary to remember that the life of the average house serf in no way entailed the kind of physical toil, danger, and generally harrowing existence endured by soldiers, factory workers, miners, or railroad conscripts.[49] The less-sentimentalizing observers noted that homes were overpopulated with servants who could and did often avoid work.

Among the house serfs and others recruited from the villages, thousands managed to get some kind of education or training in creative artistic work that raised them above their ascribed station. Serfs attended the primary schools established by Catherine, resulting in the social mix described by the serf painter Tropinin and the serf actor Shchepkin. By an 1827 decree, they could go no further into *gymnazia* or university. When the bright young Nikitenko discovered that he was barred from further schooling due to his serf status, he contemplated suicide. The less well-known serf Savva Purlevsky (1800–1868) related his feelings of impotence in the face of sudden changes of fortune: transfers; the death of the master; the sending of young serfs to St. Petersburg, Siberia, into the mines, or to the army. Having witnessed both kindness and cruelty, he experienced self-discovery and desperation simultaneously when, as he learned to read, he said to himself "I am a serf" and found that reading and travel had generated new thoughts incompatible with serfdom. The revelation led him to take flight. This reaction resonated with those of the contemporary American Black slave, Frederick Douglass, who wrote: "I would at times feel that learning to read had been a curse rather than a blessing. It had given me a view of my wretched condition, without the remedy." Serf artists, on constant display, had to honor their lords in performance or product. They could suffer, in ways unknown to tillers of the soil (though these knew suffering enough of their own), from exposure to a world of high culture and refined tastes. Possessing talent, they were ever subject to the arbitrary will of the owner who could and did send an artist to the kitchen or a musician to the plow. Unlike field serfs who had various collective modes of everyday resistance, disobedience inside the manor house was wholly counterproductive and could lead to physical punishment or worse.[50]

A system that allowed the development of literate and artistically talented men and women and then kept them in bondage made a mockery of Tsar Nicholas's stated policy for landowners: do not mistreat serfs, but do not give them too much education. M. P. D. de Passenens, a French expatriate who had lived in Russia from the 1790s to 1812, published in Paris in 1822 a raging but well-informed indictment of "Russian slavery" and its negative effects upon every phase of life — including creativity. He argued that serfdom "stifles the embryos of genius and arrests the development of talent." Granting that the state offered some scholarships to artists, he personally observed that the majority of talents were ignored and that desperate artists fled the muses and fell into the arms of Bacchus. Although no comparable book appeared inside Russia during the existence of serfdom, the pathos of artists in servitude generated among Russians stories and conversations about underdogs and villains. Before 1861, tragic tales about serf artists circulated widely among the intelligentsia and some made it into print as fiction or observation. Shchepkin and Tropinin were fertile in producing anecdotes about their own and other's lives, a bit embellished for effect, but essentially true. Accounts of sexual abuse and harassment, beatings, and the depressed serfs' descent into alcoholism or suicide made their way into the public consciousness, and got magnified in the decades after emancipation by memoirs and treatments of the issue at the hands of the Russian intelligentsia as part of their retrospective glance at what had just been abolished. Ekaterina Letkova's 1883 canvas of abuses was the first to use the term "serf intelligentsia."[51]

After the Russian Revolution, Soviet scholars who focused on serfdom as part of their demonization of the old regime took up this appealing issue with determination. Elena Kots in 1926 synthesized the anecdotal literature published since Letkova and put a Marxist gloss on it in a still useful book entitled *The Serf Intelligentsia*.[52] Other Soviet scholars enriched the investigation with great detail on the individual arts and argued about the meaning of a serf intelligentsia in the economic-historical interpretation of "feudalism" and its decline. Subsequent Soviet approaches, while retaining the sweeping condemnation of gentry exploitation, in time partly diluted the assault by an elitist perspective and a certain ambivalence that forced to the surface almost unwittingly a pride in the achievements of the grandees whose serfs built such wondrous places as Kuskovo and Ostankino and Marino, to say nothing of the exaltation of serf-owner geniuses like the composer Glinka.

In recent times, the question of the Russian gentry's role in culture in the high age of serfdom has elicited widely divergent judgments. As in the case of St. Petersburg, the micro-world of estate and manor house has long been mythologized by nostalgic memoirs, idealized images in the arts, and all sorts of elegiac appreciations. Prominent among them were the often uncritical encomia of the first-wave emigrés of the 1920s and 1930s, now echoed in the post-Soviet gentry press. Typical of the latter is a well-meant but misleading homage to old-time gentry life published in the post-Soviet Petersburg journal, *Gentry Club,* which skips over this period of Russian history entirely, ignores serfdom, and focuses only on the undeniable glories of the gentry class.[53] A new generation of scholars, without demonizing it in the old Soviet way, have recognized the more complex realities of that life. Recent Western and Russian investigators have tried to evoke both the genuine accomplishments of the past and the exploitative base that allowed them.[54]

The climate for manumission at any level was never hospitable before 1861, in spite of the many aborted efforts to address the abolition of serfdom as an institution. Yet since tsars Alexander and Nicholas abhorred serfdom in principle and since no proserfdom ideology ever appeared publicly, hope always hung in the air. Between 1816 and 1819, serfs were freed in the Baltic regions without land. Before, during, and after these proceedings, several schemes for full or partial emancipation surfaced, some requested by Alexander I, some hatched by the revolutionary Decembrists. Nicholas I formed a committee to examine the question. The sporadic if never dead reform discussion has been laboriously reconstructed from the record by a number of historians who all note that very little came of government efforts. Private manumission was permitted by laws dating from 1803 and 1842. Only about 140–150,000 serfs were freed under both laws — the vast majority being field serfs. An 1847 law on auctioning indebted estates led to an estimated 964 male peasants redeeming themselves at an average price of seventy-six rubles per person. A few liberal landowners freed some or all of their serfs. Composer Nikolai Rimsky-Korsakov's father opposed serfdom, freed his servants one by one, and then took some of them back as hired labor. Serfs who managed to enrich themselves could buy freedom. One serf entrepreneur in the eighteenth century paid Count Sheremetev 130,000 rubles for his freedom, one of several examples. But the vast majority could not afford even a modest redemption fee. For various reasons, the government occasionally forbade manumission. The State Council was the court of last resort for voluntary freeing of serfs and sometimes owners were turned down. Finally there was the reluctance and inertia of the serfs themselves: the reform-minded A. M. Unkovsky offered to liberate his house serfs in the 1850s, and only a few accepted.[55]

Tracking the fruitless legislative plans at the top, a cryptic abolitionist literature in the reign of Nicholas I began to tap readers' humanitarian sentiment and private sensibility. Some of it is canonical. Nikolai Karamzin's *Poor Liza* (1792) deals with an innocent serf girl who drowns herself after being jilted by a young man of the gentry. Dmitry Grigorovich's "The Village" (1846) presented a "physiology" of rural life — that is, rich in realistic detail — and its suffering peasants. His treatment of village woes in this and "Anton Goremyka" (1847), won praise for its naturalism from the influential critic Vissarion Belinsky and drew sympathetic tears from society ladies. Ivan Turgenev's *Notes of a Hunter*, published serially from 1847, is seen by many critics as the first well-rounded depiction of peasants in Russian literature — and thus indirectly an indictment of serfdom. His "Mumu" (1854) criticized cruel nobles and serfdom itself more explicitly.[56] Aside from these familiar works, a lesser-known body of fiction, discussed in the coming chapters, dealt precisely with serf artists, musicians, and stage performers caught between the pride in their art and the demeaning position they held in society. Together they formed a literary discourse whose main theme went beyond that of the suffering peasant in Grigorovich or the noble peasant in Turgenev to the specially gifted and creative serf who endured the unendurable or escaped into personal tragedy.[57]

While officials wrestled with reform and writers published stories about talented men and women held in bondage, another relatively little-known discourse arose in conversations and correspondence among nobles, statesmen, and artistic institutions that bristled with entreaties, threats, negotiations, and contracts of purchase, transfer, and manumission of serf artists. Prominent individuals such as the poets Vasily Zhukovsky and Kondraty Ryleev, the painters Karl Bryullov and Alexei Venetsianov, courtiers and patrons such as Mikhail Vielgorsky, and many others lobbied and raised money to free particular artists who caught their attention. Venetsianov agitated for the release of Taras Shevchenko, who did get his freedom; and for Grigory Soroka, who did not. Landowners, bureaucrats, courtiers, and sometimes members of the royal family engaged in similar activity through pressure, letter-writing, and money-raising by lottery. Magnates and art patrons organized precisely for these purposes. The Society for the Encouragement of Artists and the Academy of Arts negotiated with landowners about freeing certain talented serfs in order to allow them further study. Those creative serfs lucky enough to achieve liberation perhaps shared the sentiments voiced by Nikitenko who wrote, after a difficult struggle for freedom: "I can only say Glory to the Almighty and proclaim my eternal gratitude to those who helped me to be born again."[58]

Needless to say, efforts to secure freedom for serf artists met with resistance from those landowners, later called "planters," who defended serfdom on principle or who declined to free individual serfs. The Tver Province gentry in this period displayed a pattern of paternalism coexisting with a fierce defense of serfdom and a loathing to grant freedom.[59] During the reign of Tsar Alexander I, some serf owners feared any kind of tampering with the system as a dangerous signal, an invitation to pretension and false hopes. Seigniorial anxiety put serf artists aspiring to freedom in the bind of setting a precedent. Baron Korff, advisor to Nicholas I, opposed giving too much help to house serfs, lest it cause resentment in others.[60] Some nobles perceived that their exclusive rights, status, and freedom were at stake. Timofei Prostakov (1748–1854), a serf architect belonging to an earlier Rimsky-Korsakov, gained a reputation among rich nobles for his fine work. But their intercession for his freedom had no effect. Rimsky told Tsar Alexander I that he would give up anything but not free his property. The widow who owned the serf butler and lackey Bobkov, citing the gospels, told him that "slavery was established by God," though she eventually offered him freedom which he declined. A gentry woman in Turgenev's *Notes of a Hunter* exclaimed in anger: "O Lord Jesus Christ! Am I not free to use my slaves [*kholopyakh*] as I wish?" Her friend agreed that moving serfs was "harmful for an orderly household."[61] This anecdotal evidence supports the generally held view that the attitude was widespread.

In cases of refusal, elements of spite sometimes surfaced. Kropotkin observed that serf owners, including his mother, reacted angrily to any kind of real or perceived airs and pretensions on the part of servants and serfs such as the "too gentlewoman-like manners" of a serf girl. The gratuitous malice exhibited by landowners resembled, at least in the telling, the exaggerated villainy of melodrama. Personal animosity drove more than one stubborn serf owner's refusal to release a talented serf, and not only in the art world. The ex-serf N. N. Shipov (b. 1802), whose father was a literate and wealthy serf cattle dealer on *obrok*, recalled a serf who offered the unheard-of sum of 160,000 rubles to redeem his family. The owner declined because he had once felt shame, envy, and regret at the huge success of one of his freed serfs who had become a prosperous Moscow merchant. Conversely, in 1839 a British visitor met landowners who prided themselves on allowing their serfs to accumulate as much wealth as they liked. But, far from rewarding that success with freedom or even profiting from a redemption fee, they enjoyed showing them off as waiters.[62]

How much more might the serf artist's skill have generated tension? The sleazy character Skotinin in Denis Fonvizin's *The Minor* says: "How can I feel kindly towards servants? They are so clever compared to me" (Act V). Untalented art-loving landowners may have suffered from inferiority and envy at the artistry displayed by underlings in a society where power, virtue, and accomplishment supposedly resided exclusively at the top. Fragmentary and elusive evidence suggests that some landowners, offended by what they deemed the "ingratitude" of serf artists who sought to better their condition, punished them for it. As Nikitenko recalled: "The ugly, unvarnished unjustness of my social status [as a serf] would hit me in the face. It had locked me out of high school and continued to close off future paths toward knowledge, toward the light. But meanwhile, my rebellious mind did not cease to evoke the seductive mirage of the university." His master's uncle, a general, turned against Nikitenko as soon as he unveiled his aspirations to education and freedom, and Nikitenko's life became a roller coaster of euphoria and despair. He recounted the familiar scenario of high-born arrogance as a drama, with near misses and cliff-hanging moments; dangers, dark villains, and virtuous protectors—as in the freedom tales of Shevchenko and other emancipated serfs. To the masters, the very entreaties for a serf's freedom by those in high places increased his value and thus stiffened their refusal to free a man with "audacious pretensions."[63] Other serf owners clearly resented efforts of fellow nobles to persuade them of the public value of the human beings they possessed and to pressure them into freeing a serf. The epic struggles of actors like Shchepkin to gain freedom from their masters were prime examples of this obsession with the ownership and deployment of human skill and art as well as the artifacts themselves, a near-atavistic throwback to classical slavery. No mechanism ever came into being that could overrule the serf owner and liberate his serf.

If nobles were sometimes gently mocked on stage, their right to own serfs went unchallenged. Serfs, whether in the field or in the household, provided little more than comic relief. Like their counterparts in landscape painting, they acted as mere extras or staffage, background shadows unendowed with much intelligence or character, except for the occasional wily servant of drawing-room comedy. Peasants as real people had even less visibility than merchants, and came into play only in the 1850s, toward the very end of this era. Peasants on canvas graduated a bit earlier from the status of stick figure near a manor house to their representation as tillers, artisans, housekeepers, dreamy children, carousers, and—eventually—even as menacing, impious troublemakers. Real serfs, at the same time, continued to serve their masters, sometimes as "slaves to art" and always as slaves in art.

Provincial Space

A young Europeanized Russian aristocrat stationed in the town of Orël in the 1820s, Count Mikhail Buturlin, found the amenities there rather thin after years in Moscow and Florence and on his cousins' estates. All businesses were concentrated in the Gostiny Dvor, he noted, but there were few good shops and no bookstore. The only hotel was at the empty far end of town. Government offices, residences, the manège, and the Gentry Club occupied the central square. Along a boulevard stood the stables and garrison. Dirty taverns near the river were hung with misspelled signs such as "City of Odesta" and "Keev." Yet later on in the account, Buturlin lingers over the many hours he spent at Count Kamensky's once famous serf theater. Another traveler, Mikhail Zhdanov, visiting Tver on the Volga a few decades later, saw a Vauxhall where the locals met, especially during the folk fair. All the beau monde appeared, he noted, and the place teamed with hussars and uhlans who made the dance floor swirl with uniforms. But, he complained in metropolitan accents, there was little in the way of conversation or good society. Alas, only four or five homes in the town were worth a visit, since the gentry lived on their estates and preferred to visit each other.[64] Zhdanov was tacitly comparing Tver with the capitals and their elaborate ballroom conversations and late-running dances and suppers. In that same year, Tver was recorded as having two monasteries, thirty-two churches, eight schools, a hospital, an alms house, and a prison. Its two-storied Gostiny Dvor held 455 booths. An annual fair, eighteen taverns, and twenty-two public houses served a population of about twenty thousand residents. For a traveler like Zhdanov, the place held no charms. Such impressions of provincial towns could be multiplied indefinitely.

Towns did not do much better at the hands of information gatherers. A pathbreaking handbook compiled by Prince Gagarin in 1843 is revealing about what he considered worth enumerating. A review of the data in these volumes on about twenty towns, mostly provincial capitals, shows that not a single hotel was listed as such, although public houses, inns, or eateries abounded as did vodka shops and taverns. Most of these towns possessed one or more monasteries, several churches, a hospital, an almshouse, and a jail. A Gostiny Dvor was present in over half, some with hundreds of booths; the others had dozens of shops and market days twice a week. Virtually every town had at least one annual fair, most of them more than one. Big places like Kazan and Kharkov could boast universities and stately bridges and squares; or, like Smolensk and Tula for example, turreted kremlin walls. There is no mention of a theater anywhere in this survey even though many of these towns, including all those mentioned, had regular or temporary theaters or permanent companies. The thirst for data that tormented the imperial statisticians at midcentury was limited: no mention of brothels (made tentatively legal the year after Gagarin's volumes appeared). In this otherwise handy survey, interestingly enough, no government building is listed either, no governor's mansion, no municipal council, no merchant or noble club, and only rarely a military complex — cadet school or barracks.[65]

Sole reliance on such a source gives a distorted picture of the provincial town, one not balanced by any romanticized versions; these, on the contrary, reinforce the then widespread belief that all Russian provincial towns were hollow shells with so many buildings carefully counted, and with lots of people doing nothing in public except perhaps eating and drinking in taverns, shopping, going to church, and occasionally landing in a hospital ward or a jail cell. Literary treatment captured the vibrancy of their noise and scandal, particularly the works of Saltykov-Shchedrin, who knew the lay of the land, and Gogol, who had little personal experience with provincial life.[66] Yet the cultural experience of many provincial towns, while no match for the great capitals, had its own coloration that was a part of the texture of life for its inhabitants — and not only the gentry and the wealthy merchants. Ironically, some of the most sarcastic travel accounts unwittingly reveal the vivid palette of life at the despised margins. Provincial towns were an integral feature of the entire cultural system, a network of performance for Russian and foreign artists, a source of future stars, a marketplace of audience choice, a testing ground for talent, a first entrée for lucky youngsters into the artistic life.

In the system created by Catherine II in 1783, each of the fifty provinces of European Russia (the number wavered) possessed provincial and district town capitals. In the 1840s the authorities, who knew little enough about them, began to count and catalogue the towns, officially numbered at 693, excluding those in Finland and Poland. Few towns had reached the size of fifty thousand. Many were marked by standardized forms: a central square, government buildings, church, markets, straight streets, sometimes named after the class who lived or operated there, such as Great Nobility Street or Lower Middle Class Street. The regime's dictated models for buildings and façades and the frequent comments by haughty visitors from the capitals reinforced erroneous impressions of the provinces as an undifferentiated backland. In terms of environment, climate, appearance, and function, provincial towns varied enormously: perched on a cliff, like Smolensk on the upper Dnieper; centered on a square kremlin, like Tula; bisected by a deep ravine and river, like Orël; sprawled over seven hills and three rivers, like Kursk; or surrounded by the Don and other waterways, like Voronezh — to say nothing of the great Volga cities set on the high bank, from Tver to Astrakhan. These towns, spacious and verdant, were a far cry from the images of a townlet tucked away in a forest or the middle of the broad steppe. Smaller, newer towns, creatures of the state, served as administrative centers or garrison posts with undeveloped institutions. Still others played specialized roles, such the spa resort Lipetsk where some families spent an entire summer,[67] or seaports and border towns where smuggling was common. Urban life could be suddenly transformed by a royal visit or the appearance of an "inspector general" from the center. When cholera or the plague struck, normal social intercourse was suddenly ruptured. Authorities set up quarantine stations and police cordons around afflicted neighborhoods and forbade public gatherings, even church services. Sometimes riots, murders, executions, and deportations ensued. Quarantines could swell the population by thousands, or strand and kill traveling performers.[68]

Given the diversity, one must be cautious in generalizing about ordinary town life in the prereform era. Yet the provincial capitals, where most of the nonmanorial cultural activity occurred, certainly showed certain patterns. Their populations were greatly reduced versions of the capitals: clean-shaven officials and gentry and their families; bearded merchants and clergy, as well as most other townsmen; and a wide assortment of peasants and servants and sometimes quartered troops. The governor, aside from presiding over the administration of the province, possessed social and cultural sway as well. He could license or close a theater, promote amateur performances, host visiting artists-or persecute them. He and the marshal of the nobility, an unsalaried elected figure, stood with their wives at the center of the local beau monde and sometimes competed in that realm. The headquarters for the social round of the gentry — urban or manorial — was the Gentry Assembly or Club. Originally a mere legal entity in the eighteenth century which had to rent or purchase a headquarters, furniture, and decor, it graduated almost everywhere into a focus of politics, socialization, and courtship; and in some cases into a cultural center. Some noble families maintained homes in town and country, but most lords commuted. The density of resident nobles and the frequency of their inflow from the estates became markers of a town's social vivacity for high-born visitors seeking their own kind. One of the virtues of town life, for those who disliked living in far-off estates, was sociability. Even a distant frontier post like Ufa in the midst of Bashkir country served as a magnet: Sergei Aksakov's grandmother could hardly wait to leave the countryside and get back to the streets and social life of her town.[69]

Visits by the military enlivened small-town life. When an army division was assigned to a province, one regiment was quartered in or near the provincial capital and the others in the district towns. For townspeople, the drill and the rituals of reveille and retreat offered a charming spectacle. For officers, when not hunting, drinking, or dancing, local theater productions and concerts offered relief from the tedium of peacetime garrison duty. Most of all, dashing officers provided male partners and fresh faces at the ball. To the traveler Zhdanov, Saratov in 1839 was a boring town except when artillery officers were stationed there. The appearance of a bivouacked unit could produce all kinds of unexpected results. For the serf boy Alexander Nikitenko, stuck in Ostrogozhsk in the 1810s, the stationing of young dragoon officers, fresh from European adventure and bursting with literary and political ideas, was an intellectual stimulus to his quest for emancipation. In the same town, the painter Ivan Kramskoi much later found a job in photography in the 1850s due to the presence of a garrison forming up for the Crimean War. The sordid side of army life intruded also into the local landscape. Fiction and memoirs attest to the debauching behavior of garrison officers. In Orël Province in the 1820s, hussar officers organized "Athenian Nights" featuring a "Patagonian Dance" in which some local beauties cavorted in a half-drunken state and then dined with the officers in the nude. Officers sought out local courtesans. Simon Karlinsky has pointed out how Gogol distorted reality in his eccentric picture of a garrison party in the unstaged piece, "The Carriage," depicting a bachelor affair without the presence of a lady of the evening. Townspeople, priests, and merchants found less enchantment in the billeted soldiers who often ate them out of house and home because they themselves had been mulcted by their commanding officers.[70]

In almost all the provincial and district capitals that I have "visited" — via the sources — the gentry ball represented the most important social event.[71] In Tambov in the 1850s, the marshal of nobility, governor, prominent magnates, and organizers of charity benefits took turns hosting. The triennial winter gentry elections, often the scene of corrupt lobbying and pressure, made a perfect occasion for a ball, since the bulk of the landowners came into town to vote. Dressed to the nines, the families arrived in carriages at the Gentry Club where noble misses made their debuts and junior officers flirted or courted. With music provided by a governor's or a landowner's orchestra (serf or professional), couples swung to the noble strains of the mazurka and the waltz in an established order of dances, as in the capitals, while others conversed about politics. In the wee hours of the morning, a late supper was served by lackeys. Some of the more imaginative governors arranged ornate amusements: Governor Kochubei of Orël Province in the 1840s had two horsemen and a bear appear in the ballroom.[72] The ball, in the minds of provincials, was far more of a social event than a cultural one. Yet Gentry Clubs in various places served also as centers of self-entertaining amateur theatricals and recitals and eventually as sites of public concerts and commercial theaters.

In a contrasting world, small-town merchants, arrayed in guilds like those in the capitals and free of military and certain other obligations, constituted the lifeblood of the town, which they helped to run. Beneath them socially and juridically, the townspeople, ranging from 66 to 90 percent of the provincial urban population, were like their capital equivalents, a mixed bag of artisans, small businessmen, ex-priests, children of certain soldiers, small farmers, and freed serfs. They paid taxes, provided recruits, and were subject to other obligations. Though women and serfs did not vote, townsmen did so and joined the merchants in local administration. The market square played a central role in socializing, commerce, and exchange of information for men and women. As early as the 1790s, 513 towns were offering 722 market days per week. In Rostov, for example, near the church and the kremlin, stood a Gostiny Dvor packed thickly with rows of indoor and outdoor market buildings and stalls, some of them run by women. Flatboats on the river overflowed with wares; nearby stood shops filled to the brim with goods, a tea house, and a tavern. On market days, these places came alive with commerce and conversation. Alexander Artynov, a peasant-turned-merchant, recalled how he and his colleagues did business and chatted all day long and, on off days, gathered again to talk and play checkers.[73]

In the tavern, a venue for male and sometimes female conviviality, conversation and singing were lubricated by spirits, followed by salty snacks to assuage the effects of the alcohol. Cheating and watering of drinks were common. A dense concentration of taverns prevailed in the Western Provinces of Lithuania, Belorussia, and Ukraine: about 53,000 licensed taverns, as opposed to 10,000 in all the provinces of Great Russia. Yet the Russian drinkers had wide access to the abundant bottle shops and stalls and to illegal premises and home distilleries. Thus towns or large villages of two thousand people had on average one tavern in addition to other outlets. In Kaluga Province in the late 1850s, of the 614 liquor outlets, 274 were taverns; the provincial capital had twenty-nine taverns; and the fourteen district capitals roughly averaged ten outlets each. In these haunts — as in village feasts — the oft-noted extremism in peasant and urban lower-class drinking could lead to a rapid leap into oblivion or to fights and rowdiness. In the "vodka riots" of 1859 in fifteen provinces, troops were brought in to quell the disturbances in half of them. The cause was the sudden, arbitrary, and illegal rise in vodka prices; the form was tavern smashing, destruction of stock, and oaths of abstinence. The great bulk of the rioters were peasants, *meshchane*, and soldiers on leave.[74] The taverns served as socializing headquarters at virtually every whistle-stop for touring theater people and other performing artists; and, as houses of temptation, they became the scourge of troupe entrepreneurs and the ruin of many an actor. Long ignored in the world of art, when genre painters began to include them on their canvases, the uproar was instantaneous.

Provincial and district towns had both socially ghettoized fraternization and mingling across classes — depending on the place and the moment. Churches, for example, were open to people of all classes. Though it was customary to stand, gentry sometimes sat up front and had servants bring velvet pillows for kneeling. Monasteries, which graced many provincial capitals, also brought all kinds of people together. In Tikhvin in the 1820s, women used the local monastery, with its religious festivals, as a social meeting place. The monastic stables at Rostov could hold as many as six hundred horses. Certain monasteries combined the sacred and the profane: Korennaya, Troitskoe, Kirillo-Beloozersky, and the Makarev offered festival, holiday, pilgrimage, and fair all at once. Outdoor church processions through the town or around the walls took place on holy days. Classes also mingled temporarily at the folk fairs (*narodnoe gulyane*) held on saints' days and at Advent and Easter time. These mammoth celebrations in towns big and small, with their puppet booths, rides, food stalls, and general revelry lent a carnival atmosphere to town life, after which the normal hierarchical social relations were resumed. The folk fair came to have an extraordinary attraction to educated Russians of all classes, served as a subject for huge canvases, and — in moments of patriotic fervor — was stylized on stage by professional performers long before it was adopted into the great ballets of the early twentieth century. In contrast, an equally omnipresent feature of town life on festive days, the wall-to-wall fist fight, got no attention from cultural creators. Hundreds, and sometimes thousands, of young townsmen from various trades, neighborhoods, or ethnic groups would line up and rush at each other fists flying, and then repair to the nearest tavern to toast victory or drown defeat.[75]

The fair, familiar in provincial life as a site of mixed social gathering, attracted whole towns whose people devoted themselves to commerce, sociability, and entertainment. In the 1790s, 864 urban fairs and 3,180 rural ones have been counted. By 1860 the total number had reached about 6,000 in European Russia, about a fifth located in provincial and district capitals. Though under the jurisdiction of the Department of Internal Trade in the Ministry of Interior, fairs suffered little from bureaucratic interference. In 1822 at the trading town of Khislavichi, owned by Count Saltykov, the annual summer fair included a gentry ball with merchants in attendance. At Dorogobuzh, a district town in Smolensk Province, the weeklong fair was studded with evening ballroom affairs attended by officers of the nearby regiment. At the Romny Summer Fair, considered one of the best, attendees bought and sold while their children enjoyed the amusements. The fair came alive with horses and all manner of conveyances. A visitor in 1803 observed the enthusiastic faces of the commoners tented in the fields like a bivouac preparing for war. The annual fair at Nizhny Novgorod, successor to the Makarev Fair, surpassed them all in scope and variety. Like the folk fair which it partly resembled, the fair became a suitable subject for painters of provincial genre.[76]

The archipelago of provincial towns fit into the Russian cultural system as a whole on several levels. Artists living in or traveling to the provinces began to break away from established landscape and move into genre scenes of provincial life. In terms of portraiture, the capitals may have provided the template, but local variations appeared as well in studies of gentry and especially of small-town merchants. Entire schools of portrait painting had already emerged in the eighteenth century in certain provinces and continued on as a "primitivist" local counterweight to the polished and often static parade portraiture taught at the Academy of Arts. Indeed the outreach of the Academy itself expanded by accepting the affiliation of a half-dozen non-Petersburg schools where local styles sometimes took root and where serfs and other lower-class pupils learned their art and even won medals. Long before emancipation, an inpouring of peasants and other rural dwellers into the cities[77] multiplied urban types and generated new representations of them.

The stark facts of geography in the early nineteenth century dictated the thinness of "capital culture" in the lands of northern and eastern Russia. The predominance of state peasants, the paucity of an implanted landlord culture, the low population density, the sparsity of towns, and the climate kept these regions relatively free of the cultural traffic that enlivened the seigniorial provinces. The "two nations" created by the gulf between gentry and serfs was cross-cut by the geographical gulf between private and state lands. The vaunted reforms on state peasant lands of the 1830s which introduced some schools and medical points did nothing to bridge the gap. Siberian settlements lagged well behind the European heartlands. The exiled Decembrist Baron Andrei Rosen wrote that Kurgan, his place of exile in Tobolsk Province in 1832, had not changed since 1800 when another exile, the dramatist August Kotzebue, had been there. Eventually the Decembrist exiles and their redoubtable wives brought culture to Siberian exile in the form of schools, libraries, newspapers, musical circles, chamber groups, and amateur art.[78] For mobile artists of any kind, travel could be a nightmare. Not much more than fifteen hundred miles of first-class paved roads existed, leading Tsar Nicholas to say that "Russia suffers from space." Mud, snow, back roads, and springless vehicles evoked the complaints of foreigners such as Custine, Berlioz, and Balzac. Byways were choked at times by an endless stream of peddlers, pilgrims, military men, couriers, officials, merchants, peasants off to trade or work, traveling cooperatives of workmen, gentry huntsmen, voyaging families, or convicts. Checkpoints at intervals on the highways were guarded by veterans with halberds. The Petersburg-Moscow railway opened in 1851, but few cultural stopovers lined this route. Getting from Moscow or Vladimir to the Nizhny Novgorod fair and its theaters before the advent of railway lines there proved hazardous, and the roads around the Nizhny Novgorod Fair were still infested with bandits and thick with forests and swamps. Early in the century, pirates sailed the Volga.[79]

Despite hazards, music and drama flowed through many channels in provincial Russia. Early in the nineteenth century there emerged a kind of entrepreneurial network operated by socially exalted figures close to the court and theater administrators in the capitals. They invited the best-known musical virtuosos of the day, from Franz Liszt to Henri Vieuxtemps, to play for Russian audiences in many towns. Stars of the musical system also included those born in the Russian Empire who had made a European reputation, such as Henryk Wieniawski and Anton Rubinstein. Thus the genius of foreign artists (the first pair) and those of Jewish background (the second) were made available to audiences of the interior who had little or no access to the great halls of the capitals. The Imperial Theaters also sent their stars to tour the provinces. In parallel, but on a much larger scale, a chain of commercial theaters with casts made up of all social classes developed into a circuit of troupes moving from town to town, producing hundreds of stage works largely copied from the capitals' repertoires. The audiences were socially diverse as well; and, as memoirs attest, far more interaction between actors and the public — in the house, backstage, and in the town — took place in provincial towns than in the state-run theaters of the capitals.

In approaching the prosaics of the provincial town, much is often missing from those literary studies that screen reality through belles lettres, particularly canonical works. In a recent collection entitled *The Russian Provinces: Myth, Text, Realities*, the "myth" and the "text" clearly predominate over the "realities." This filtering approach has its limits for historians of cultural events, realia, people, and places. One does not always get a completely accurate picture of the Russian provinces from Gogol, of French village life from Balzac, and of English court practices from Dickens. Yet these authors offer much about the mental sets of the people of their times and places. Here the theoretical and literary perspectives of the above-noted collection throw useful light on the mutual images of capitals and provinces. Concerning provincials' self-image, one of the contributors to the collection sets up a dichotomy between "provincialness," the blissful ignorance of backwardness; and "provincialism," a self-conscious inferiority complex vis-à-vis the capitals.[80] Real-life conversations and stage treatments are full of wide-eyed admiration of St.

Petersburg. Performed in the 1840s, N. I. Kulikov's vaudeville, *Mischievous Girl,* had a young provincial woman, returning from a visit to the St. Petersburg theaters, deliver a breathless account of its fashions, acting, ballet, and singing. Self-effacement even operated between district and provincial capitals. The local characters in A. F. Veltman's 1838 novel *Heart and Head* are made to wonder if a visitor is bored after having lived in a provincial center.[81] Conversely, snobbish disdain of capital residents for the provinces led many to equate their city with good manners, cultivated behavior, and of course, real culture. Mikhail Zagoskin's comedy *Mister Bogatonov, or a Provincial in the Capital* (1817), one of many such warnings, declared, à la Molière, that one could not simply acquire the garb of urbanity by "arriving" in the capital. All this is familiar, but, as a recent scholar argues, people of the capital also felt anxiety that both they *and* the real provinces were provincial vis-à-vis Europe. This combination of contempt and unease clearly paralleled the social malaise of the insecure and the wonderment about national identity of Russians poised between Europe and the empire's "eastern" hinterlands.[82]

Notwithstanding barriers set up by cultural images, self-images, neuroses, and stereotypes, social and cultural threads gradually tightened the bond between provinces and capitals. From the center came ideas, artifacts, and practices brought by royal entourages, educated travelers, landowning families, regimental garrisons, returning students, touring actors, and musical virtuosos. Local gentry, steeped in Petersburg fashion, came to town for social events and sometimes built town houses. They also spread cultural activities from the capitals to the provincial towns, either by visiting Moscow and St. Petersburg regularly or by adopting what they read in journals. In 1803, a visitor to Romny Fair in Poltava Province was astonished by the lavish women's costumes in the latest French taste. Another observer, deep in Kursk Province in 1831, noted the unsuitability of the gentry's foreign raiment to the climate.[83] A more dramatic instance of metropolitan invasion of distant towns came with the mass egress of noble families from Moscow to the provinces in 1812. Nobles without estates congregated in remote towns in central Russia, the Volga, and Ukraine. Many of these high-born refugees had traveled in Europe but never in the interior of their own country. They brought with them news and information, ideas, manners, and styles.[84] Much of Moscow "society" was transferred to Nizhny Novgorod by wartime exigencies. The memoirs and letters show a shock to the system — the longing for Moscow's Tverskaya Street as well as their own homes. A natural reassembly of the "noble assembly" was effected through balls and visits, the invitation list defining who had been who in the deserted Moscow. Clad in wigs and ball gowns, they reconstructed the card tables of Tverskaya and hurled curses (in French) at the French.[85]

The state played a crucial role in communication by establishing in 1838 provincial gazettes, bearers of laundered news items, book reviews, and fragmentary cultural coverage.[86] The thickness and effectiveness of the town networks depended heavily on proximity to the capitals or to dense clusters of cultured landowners. The difference in exposure between a place like Perm and one like Kursk or Nizhny Novgorod was enormous.[87] Conversely, Petersburg and Moscow readers learned of provincial doings from the coverage in "thick" journals such as *Son of the Fatherland, Readers' Library, Contemporary,* and a few others, however jaundiced that coverage sometimes was. Just as central organs of St. Petersburg were enlarging their own knowledge of Russia's interior by means of statistical studies and geographical surveys (discussed in chapter 9), the educated denizens of provincial Russia were learning more about themselves and how they fit into the empire as a whole — within, of course, the limits of censorship and the stingy need-to-know policies of the state.

The arts filled in the colors and shapes by presenting and representing topography and various elements of the population on stage and on canvas or in printed feuilletons or sketches. The provincial intelligentsia (an under-studied subject),[88] interspersed among or leading local salons and other groupings, played a crucial role in cultural life and its links to the capitals. This sector of small-town society, a scattering of gentry and *raznochintsy*, maintained two-way communication with the capital. Writers, journalists, self-appointed critics fed the thick journals of the capital with a constant stream of news and comment about local goings-on in the realm of music and theater and, to a lesser degree, fine art. They also found outlets in the few local journals and papers and occasionally in the provincial gazettes. They sat in audiences, made judgments in print (and often vocally) on what they saw and heard, mingled with visiting artists, and tried to impose their own notions of what constituted genuine or refined or simply "Russian" culture. Occasional accents of local pride, a mild version of postemancipation provincial boosterism, could be heard, presaging the time when that cultural giant of the capital V. V. Stasov would laud the provincial origins of national composers. The process of self-revelation was gradual and uneven across the vast empire; but one can say with confidence that, from the late 1830s and early 1840s onward, the provinces of Russia were on a slow but continuous trek toward cultural integration with the rest of the country.

PART II

Music of the Spheres

2

The Domestic Muse

Really, a man of forty-four, a paterfamilias in this out-of-the way dis-
trict, playing on the violoncello!
— *Ivan Turgenev,* Fathers and Children *(1861)*

Medical student Evgeny Bazarov, the original nihilist and one of the great characters of Russian fiction, felt both surprise and contempt for a middle-aged landowner and serf owner fiddling his life away on a country estate. The cello that found its way out onto the steppe to the modest gentry mansion of Nikolai Kirsanov made him an apt emblem of the myriad real-life serf-owning "fathers" who took their pleasure in the arts and brought the arts into the countryside. But Bazarov and his friend, the cellist's son, as students and "new people" of the late 1850s, had no time for silly pleasures — especially ones so remote from the raw life of the peasantry. The words quoted above from the novel *Fathers and Children* — quietly menacing in their quizzical tone — prefigure those hurled forth during the Russian Revolution when radicals promised to liquidate the "landowner culture" (which is where Lenin deposited opera). To Bazarov, the older man's cello playing seemed more scandalous than his begetting a child with a youthful serf mistress. Bazarov aimed his dart not at the exploitation of humans to gain pleasure in music, for Kirsanov did not own a serf orchestra, but at the act of taking solitary high cultural enjoyment deep in the provincial backwoods.

How differently resonate the atrocity stories about serf musicians of the period. In one oft-cited account, a serf owner sent his serf violinist to Italy for further study and the violinist returned a virtuoso. At an evening party, the master had the musician play a Viotti violin concerto; but as each guest arrived, the host commanded the violinist to begin from the beginning. After three hours of continuous play, the violinist asked if he could rest. The master, outraged by the "capriciousness" of the serf, threatened to have him whipped. The unfortunate man fled to the kitchen, took a hatchet and chopped off his right index finger, uttering the words: "Maudit soit le talent qui n'a pu me mettre à l'abri des traitemens d'un esclave." The story was retold and embellished many times. One version relates that the serf was actually flogged in front of the guests, and chopped off all the fingers of his left hand. But in any version, the focus is on the misuse of power rather than on misbegotten exotic pleasure.[1]

The vignettes may serve to remind us that in the twilight years of serfdom, music was very much part of Russian life, though many Western, and even Russian, accounts of culture ignore it. "In the first half of the nineteenth century, music practically did not exist in Russia," wrote an official of the Russian Musical Society in 1909.[2] The frequent invocation of Peter Ilych Tchaikovsky's opinion of Mikhail Glinka's *Kamarinskaya* as the acorn from which the mighty oak of Russia's music grew reinforces the myth. Russian and Soviet music scholars knew well the "missing story" of Russian music in the Glinka and pre-Glinka eras, but they often deified icons such as Glinka and read all culture through a star-shaped prism. The works and the tastes of common folk and the "progressive" intelligentsia were worthy of attention, while alleged "reactionaries" and obscurantists — tsars and magnates — got short shrift.

The Russian Ear

Music functions in a social field: audience, "ideology," a distribution system, the critical establishment, the works, their creators and performers, and the physical setting of performance space. The story of the fluid and changing relationships between private, social, and public spheres of musical life begins with the smallest space within the private sphere — the home, haven to family and the domestic muse. One might get the impression from textbook coverage of the last decades of serfdom that educated Russians heard only drill-field commands, salon gossip, poetry, chancery talk, and some underground political discourse. Melodic sounds have been somehow filtered out of history even though towns, villages, and estates resonated with church bells, chimes, sacred choral singing, folk songs, romances, and classical music of every sort. Machine music erupted from the hurdy-gurdy; the Viennese Physharmonium that played simplified overtures, marches, and symphonies; and a Kalaidaccousticon on which one could "compose" a million waltzes. Soviet popular treatments stressed the ubiquity of music in early nineteenth century Russia — workplace, humble cabin, highway, drawing room, and lofty salon — but often ignored two great sites of musical life: the imperial court and the village church.

Alain Corbin has evoked the rural bells of France as an engine of memory, an auditory sign of community and the solemn punctuation of the everyday. What he calls the "campanarian sensibility" partook of the "social circulation of emotions." In Russia, the feelings evoked within an "auditory landscape" fed the extraordinarily wide taste for musical sonorities that marked burials, weddings, alarms, victories, or moments in the sacred calendar. Village bells also melded "country" associations with elegiac longings — the familiar Russian *toska,* whether linked to a dying love, a lost way of life, or faded youth. Emanating from sleigh or church tower, bell-like images and rhythms informed a great many folk tunes and composed songs in this era, and formed a key element in taste formation and in the community of pleasure among Russians of all stations.[3] Inside many gentry homes, one could hear European art music. Since the symphonic classical canon that charted a line of greatness from Haydn to Mozart, Beethoven, Schubert, Schumann, and Mendelssohn was not yet in place, composers now rarely heard such as Hérold, Spohr, and Spontini still competed with the giants. The music found its way to homes through a dazzling array of piano arrangements, variations, transcriptions, fantasies, improvisations, and other adaptations of symphonic and theater music — Russian and foreign. To this must be added Russian genres of folk song adaptations and "folk song" compositions (including some by foreigners), Ukrainian and Gypsy melodies, military marches, and the patriotic songs of 1812 and after.

The song genre known as "romance" (*romans*) that ruled in home and recital room embraced a wide range of styles, some approaching the quality of art song or lied, others marked by greater emotional self-indulgence. Specialists call the Russian popular or urban love song of the time a *bytovoi romans* — a song about everyday life. Of the dozen or more best-remembered practitioners of this genre, only the major composer Mikhail Glinka is generally known outside Russia (fig. 7); but his output — though of high quality — enjoyed less repute than that of now more obscure figures: Verstovsky, Alyabev, Varlamov, Gurilëv, Dubuque, and the Titovs.[4] Like other cultural freight that rolled into Russia all through the eighteenth century, the romance quickly took on native coloration.

Free with grammatical rules and generous with diminutives in lyrics emulating peasant speech and singing, the Russian romance of nature or of love is gentle, sentimental, a bit elegiac — and seldom cruel or vulgar. The principal pool of verse drew from folk forms or from the poets of the day. Thomas Hodge has eloquently described the musical-literary intercourse: the poet writes, the composer sets, the song is published, performed, and adapted. The great poets of the Golden Age — Pushkin, Zhukovsky, Lermontov, and the rest — had their works set to music; and their verses helped to shape the lyrical beauties of the music itself. A few who preferred "real" poetry scorned the romance genre as dubious fluff for the society woman of low taste. Pushkin initially vowed not to write verses for a composer — even the admired Rossini — but then softened and wrote for Glinka and other composers.[5]

The variegated body of music moved around the country through the agency of people, pianos, and print. Sheet music began flowing out of the notation typographies at the beginning of the nineteenth century. The flood of song sheets, books, albums, and notes appended to journals offered arranged folk music and composed "Russian" songs side by side with such works as Giovanni Paisiello's *Miller's Wife*. Voice, piano, guitar, and violin arrangements in every style and genre appeared in shops on St. Petersburg's Nevsky, Malaya Morskaya, and Millionaya streets. Troubadour du Nord, Odéon, Minstrel, and Northern Lyre became, like bookshops, centers of conversation about music and theater. Though a few provincial towns had music shops — Voronezh among the oldest — Petersburg remained the hub of musical distribution. The poet Pëtr Vyazemsky wrote from Moscow to a friend there: "Send my wife everything there is for the piano from the opera *Der Freischütz*: waltzes, marches, overtures, and so forth." Paralleling the oral transmission of folk songs, the urban print network made works available to taverns, road houses, merchant and artisan quarters, as well as wealthy gentry homes. In 1831, a baron commissioned from the Bernard shop waltzes for his musically inclined fiancée. The demand rose for martial, court, funeral, and dance music — polkas, gallops, waltzes, and ballroom steps. Romances and Italian arias proved to be more marketable than the sheet music of Glinka.[6]

German piano makers arrived in the middle of the eighteenth century; many settled on Petersburg's Vasilevsky Island and established businesses on or near the Nevsky. One of the first opened in 1809 in Engelhardt House, a site of symphonic concerts. Early keyboard forms and designations — clavecin, virginal, spinet, claviciterium, cembalo, clavicimbal, *Flügel*, harpsichord, clavichord — gave way to the pianoforte which could control volume and sustain notes. In modern Russian parlance, the grand or royale came in three sizes —

home, salon, and concert; the upright is called *pianino*. Imported Viennese instruments came into fashion in the late eighteenth century, priced from two hundred to a thousand rubles. Ludwig Köstner advertised his products by quoting Mozart who endorsed them as "the most perfect pianos." The Russian public could buy instruments in music shops, piano makers' shops, and furniture stores. Russians and foreigners opened piano factories starting in the reign of Alexander I. The renowned Liechtenthal fled to Russia when crowds wrecked his business during the Belgian revolution of 1830.[7] The Italian composer, performer, and entrepreneur Muzio Clementi, who traveled through Europe demonstrating his piano models, became one of their most effective marketers in Petersburg. He arrived in 1802 with a young Irish pianist in tow — John Field — who soon abandoned the demonstration bench and took Europe and Russia by storm as a virtuoso. One of the best ways to sell pianos was to perform in public, and this Clementi and Field did in elegant Petersburg salons. Their sojourn had a dual effect: Clementi made piano sales rise; Field's huge popularity caused a rush of European and Russian pupils to the capital which a musical wag dubbed "pianopolis."[8]

Keys to Intimacy

"My pupils," wrote a piano teacher at the Maidens' Institute in the distant Siberian town of Irkutsk, "fanned out all over eastern Siberia, bringing with them to these nearly empty wastelands a love of refinement."[9] Long before it intrigued and annoyed Turgenev's Bazarov, the "love of refinement" in "empty wastelands" had become a feature of the inner life of educated Russia even in places remote from "society." The network of instruments and notes that radiated outward from the capitals paralleled the thick literary journals as a shaper of cultural identity, and musical performance became an instrument of emerging civility. The everyday practices of music *en famille* exposed people, mostly gentry, to a variety of musical experiences, encouraged their training, and attuned them to the wider social sphere of musical salon and club and to the public sphere of concerts and musical theater open to all. The home, as the nucleus of musical experience in nineteenth-century Russia, also had a narrowing effect on musical life. The privateness of performance and listening fortified a view of the household as the center of cultural life among those who could afford to sustain it. An otherwise comic episode during a Franz Liszt concert of 1843 makes sense in the light of this persisting attitude. After wining and dining the great Hungarian virtuoso and hearing him play in their homes, a group of music-loving grandees in Moscow took him to the concert hall and tried to sit on stage with the pianist as he played and to do so without paying.[10] Their essentially personal and proprietary view of the pianist as their guest and friend made them loath to sit with the public.

One normally thinks of the royal court as the site of monarchical spectacle rather than as a domestic cultural milieu. It was both of these and a center of musical activity — however socially exclusive. Richard Wortman has described in detail the genuine emotional intimacy of the court and family scenes of Nicholas I,[11] resembling in its bourgeois piety that of other mid-nineteenth-century families — royal or otherwise. The new sensibility matched a partial and complex shift away from eighteenth-century "classical" values and styles in fashion, art, literature, and life. General Alexei Lvov (1798–1870), composer of the tsarist national anthem, attests to the sometimes exalted character of this private sphere in his recollections of musical moments in the vast eleven-hundred-room Winter Palace. About twice a month in the 1830s, Lvov wrote little pieces for a chamber ensemble, with the empress at the piano, Tsar Nicholas on cornet (he did not read music but had a good ear and lip), and various accomplished amateur courtiers: Matvei Vielgorsky on cello, one of the Apraxins on bass, and Lvov on violin, with the voices of courtiers Mikhail Vielgorsky, a Volkonsky, a Bartenev, and a Borozdin. These performances ceased in 1837 after a palace fire. Lvov accompanied the royal daughters' voices on violin and put on miniature choral performances. Once, soon after the composition of "God Save the Tsar" (1833), the empress invited Lvov and a small gathering to sing it pianissimo. When the tsar descended to the small chamber and heard it, tears of joy began to flow. This expression of intimacy in art is worth stressing since the general image of Nicholas is that of an iron drillmaster who as a child preferred the drumbeat to music and the dance.[12] Nicholas never became a great concertgoer, but as an adult his musical interests transcended the regimental band.

The Winter Palace and its appendages served as important sites of music performance, aside from the extravagant musical shows begun in the eighteenth century. Pavlovsk, the last of the great suburban palaces after Gatchina, Oranienbaum, Peterhof, and Tsarskoe Selo, was given to Paul by Catherine the Great in 1777 on the birth of his son, Alexander. Paul preferred Gatchina which he ran like a military base, but his widow Maria Fëdorovna (Sophia Dorothea of Würtemburg) turned Pavlovsk into a center of solo and chamber music played by professionals and amateur courtiers in the years 1801–28. A keyboard pupil of Dmitry Bortnyansky, she held concerts in the elegant Grecian Hall of the palace and patronized musical training for aristocratic girls. Tsar Nicholas I's wife, Alexandra Fëdorovna, had as court pianist the renowned Adolphe Henselt. Although these lofty places were altogether closed to the general public, their owners enriched the musical scene by patronizing foreign and Russian musicians, some of whom were willing to teach and to concertize. Out of a dynastic environment of the 1850s came the first feasible impulse for the professionalization of music: the court of Elena Pavlovna, patron of Anton Rubinstein.[13]

As elsewhere in Europe—aristocratic or "bourgeois"—the gendering of musical performance meant that a young lady's voice and piano playing could entertain guests and enhance courtship potential, in addition to adding cultural glitter to the home. Few Russian novels about the gentry failed to feature a piano performance or song by a young marriageable girl. "In every family with girls they play and jingle the piano without mercy," wryly commented the *Northern Bee* in 1852. "In such families, they dance to the piano. Consequently, everywhere 'from the walls of Moscow to Peking' they must have sheet music." Like the ball, home performance nourished chaste interaction between the sexes, the compliments and blushes being as much a part of the performance as the movement of the hands or the vocal chords. For their daughters, mothers preferred preludes, nocturnes, and songs over excessively complex pieces. Performing Beethoven's Hammerklavier Sonata might violate the cult of domesticity which stressed piety, purity, submissiveness rather than complex creative activity. The view of playing the piano at home as something less than intellectually serious both gendered that art and demoted it.[14]

A social historian of Russia wrote that the "exaltation of the female domestic sphere derived from an idea of the family as an oasis of purity, a source of civility, and a refuge from official society."[15] In this fertile site for social and cultural interplay, private playing—as opposed to performance in concert—served as the lesser vehicle of musical expression analogous to the literary album, a private genre of largely feminine expression and the pendant to the male universe of belles lettres. Gitta Hammarberg has shown how the home album enlivened a flirtatious play with people and with literature; and how the sentimentalized content of albums—private communications, poems, reflections—implied a female reader of "idylls, eclogues, elegies, and songs," the intimate lyrical genres. Musical albums with romantic titles such as *Erato*, *Jasmine and Rose*, *Gift*, and *Lyre of Grace* offered tender love songs directed to the "fair sex." In the musical parallel, the piano bench offered a fine base of coquetry not only with men but also with "serious music." A minor 1833 novel about Tula provincial life makes a character primp her daughter specifically for courtship with the piano.[16]

In the complex gendering of piano playing, mostly males became the composers and public performers, but the private/public line remained sufficiently blurred that women could sometimes appear in "society" at the keyboard without losing face: Catterino Cavos — imperial music director early in the century — once had teams of pupils of the Catherine Institute for noble girls perform on multiple pianos an arrangement of Rossini's *Barber of Seville* overture. In a public concert of 1853, at least nine of the sixteen pianists on eight pianos doing a version of Rossini's *Semiramide* overture were female. The fact that out of this widespread piano training emerged virtually no concert careers for women derived not from lack of talent but from social conventions and expectations. Well-born girls should reach a skill level matching social position; to go beyond this required a measure of physical exertion (through practice) and creative power that would challenge both gender and class norms. Thus, in the musical economy, learning and attainment were diverted into the home rather than into the public domain. Males had it both ways. Smitten by the idea of playing as an intimate social art, gentry boys of both capitals scurried to take lessons after the luminous Russian debut of John Field. Army officers of all ranks could be found playing socially. The aristocrat Mikhail Buturlin described the vice governor of Orël Province playing four hands with the brigadier of an encamped garrison. And a relative once said to Mikhail Glinka: "Besides enjoying [music] itself, your piano playing may help you meet pleasant, indeed useful people." Glinka catapulted far beyond the relative's dreams: the piano greatly enhanced his social position and his love affairs — though not his married life.[17]

The piano in early nineteenth-century Russia acted like a technology of diffusion equivalent to radio, television, and the internet in our time. Original pieces made famous on the boards of a recital hall or opera stage by foreign or domestic stars were marketed to the provinces where they fed an interest not just in the instrument but in the whole literature of concert hall and theater. The traveling governor and littérateur I. M. Dolgoruky in 1810 claims to have found pianos even in the remote corners around Pskov, Smolensk, Crimea, Nizhny Novgorod, and Perm. Pianists on the provincial town circuit always had a pack of arranged highlights from the current Italian or German opera in their bags.[18] Most people who heard symphonic or opera music heard it first, or only, in piano transcriptions.

The presence of music in the home thickened the atmosphere of sentimental romanticism that infused literature at the time. So did travel, an activity that often involves an emotional reaction to new experiences. "There is nothing more touching," wrote the literary traveler Prince P. I. Shalikov in 1805, "than the languid sounds of a piano played by a tearful woman during the quiet and tender moments of the evening in a secluded chamber bathed in pale moonlight." We moderns may need to take a breath after this, as did most of Shalikov's contemporaries. Shalikov (1767–1852) heard in the music's blend of joy and sadness an echo of the human condition. The assimilated son of a Georgian prince who had fought in the Turkish wars developed in retirement a lavish affection for the tender beauties of "nature, spring, innocent love," and all things sentimental. He published *The Ladies' Journal* in Moscow in the 1820s and 1830s, a light miscellany of Paris fashions, fiction and poetry, album entries, and songs — all done up in the idiom of kindness, tender love, devotion, mercy, and charity. Shalikov reported sometimes gushingly on recitals, feuded regularly with other music commentators, and soon became the target of ridicule for his ultrasentimentalism. The crueler ones also mocked his hunchback, wand-like thinness, green spectacles, and picturesque apparel. Shalikov, a musical amateur, wrote verses to be set by the ex-serf composer Daniil Kashin; and he published the earliest songs of Alexander Alyabev. The formidable critic V. F. Odoevsky, a much more learned amateur, considered Shalikov musically illiterate.[19]

Shalikov's reading of musical affect resonated among many of his generation. The stirring power of music in the home brought nostalgic reminiscence in old age to the noblewoman Alexandra Shchepkina. Her father, sometime marshal of the nobility in Voronezh Province, purchased a small serf ensemble of six musicians who played dinner music and truncated versions of opera overtures at holiday parties. Shchepkina recalled her sister's piano proficiency in large-scale classical works and the sweltering atmosphere induced by sentimental music in the early 1830s. The sister once triggered the tears of a recently widowed young cousin by playing elegiac music that offered consolation and release. To the memoirist, domestic music meant an initiation into "the sorrows and fate of life."[20] Such testimonies to the effect of music do not abound in print, but some visual evidence suggests its emotional role: for example, P. A. Fedotov's 1849 portrait of the young Nadezhda Zhdanovich at the piano (fig. 8). A regimental comrade of the painter had two daughters who loved literature and art. Nadezhda, presented as a model of delicacy, warmth, and intimacy, is clearly posed, almost as in a photo sitting. She is also poised — full of quiet dignity, and ready to turn and strike the keys with a captivating blend of assumed solemnity and a childish lightness of being. Out of the picture comes an unmistakable note of serenity, comfort, pleasure — and the special aura of one partaking of art in the sanctuary of the home.[21]

The guitar, less versatile than the keyboard but portable and cheap, enjoyed the widest use of all musical instruments in Russia. By the nineteenth century it had almost lost its vulgar association with the Gypsy camp, and made it to the concert stage as well as to homes, salons, and taverns. The guitar did not escape criticism: A. A. Vetrov, writing in *Repertoire* in 1853, called it the instrument of southern climes, appropriate to Don Juan, Count Almaviva,

and serenades beneath the moon with a summer breeze in the rose garden —
but not to the concert stage. And indeed, after the great flourishing of high-art
guitar music by Fernando Sor and Carl Maria von Weber, the guitar stayed
mostly on the popular stage and at home. There it served as ideal accompaniment for that era's romances, folk imitations, and urban popular songs. The
guitar flourished more openly in Moscow than in St. Petersburg and came to
be seen as a man's instrument. Apollon Grigorev recalls passing the guitar
from hand to hand at his gatherings. Guitarists in the old capital, S. N. Ak-
sënov and M. T. Vysotsky, taught princes, counts, students, merchants, and
even Gypsies how to play it.[22]

The first private music tutors of the mid-eighteenth century, Germans and
other foreigners, included a few women. Demand exceeded supply by the early
nineteenth century and Russian music teachers multiplied. A Russian woman
of noble birth announced her skills in 1805 in the *St. Petersburg Gazette*. Live-
in governesses and tutors often doubled as music instructors. Piano tuners,
builders, and salespeople gave lessons on the side, as did composers such as the
serf Daniil Kashin who advertised lessons for people of all classes, without
charge for the poor. How-to books included a fraudulent item called *Masha's
Secret, or How to Play the Piano*. Pupils of the most celebrated teacher of the
time, John Field, included professionals and ordinary enthusiasts: Glinka,
Verstovsky, Dubuque, the serf Finogen, the Pole Antoni Katski and dozens of
gentry sons and daughters — but not, as legend has it, Maria Szymanowska,
Anton Rubinstein's teacher Alexandre Villoing, or the playwright Alexander
Griboedov.[23]

Aside from students in the Theater School and the Academy of Arts where a
certain level of professionalism ruled, pupils took music lessons in almost every
kind of school, from the military Cadet Corps to the aristocratic Smolny
Institute for young ladies. Less well-placed children in orphanages took up
music in order to become teachers and governesses in service to the upper
classes. The poets Lermontov and Zhukovsky dabbled in music in their school
years. At the noble pension attached to the Petersburg Pedagogical Institute
Glinka took his first serious lesson. Moscow University and its attached schools
abounded in musical education, offered by Kashin and several Italian teachers.
At the Law school, the Prussian pianist Henselt taught the budding composer
Alexander Serov and the future cultural critic Vladimir Stasov. (Tchaikovsky,
who entered the school later, missed this great teacher.) Training spread to the
new universities and to small-town schools. The pension of Nezhin where
Gogol studied had its own symphony orchestra. An observer in Nizhny Novgorod noted few society homes where girls did not play piano. Music and musicians found their way into the back regions. Around 1825, an ailing conductor

from St. Petersburg, who had come to Tikhvin Monastery a hundred miles away to pray and recover, gave violin lessons to a peasant boy and then presented him with the instrument (soon ruined from road travel). The Smolny graduate Varvara Bykovaya, who taught music there from 1836 to 1855, became that proud teacher mentioned above who saw her pupils transformed into *Kulturträger* in the Siberian wild.[24]

If later in the century, as Marcia Citron has pointed out, the domestic milieu occupied a lower plane on the musical-spatial hierarchy than public concert spaces, the reverse held true in early nineteenth-century Russia. And if, with Bourdieu, we agree that residence provides geographical capital, and that habitus—a predisposition to certain behavior connected with the habitat itself—then the noble women's seat at the keyboard reflected both. Music and foreign languages were not merely educational outcomes or social skills. For some women all through the century—and even beyond—they were vital elements of identity as well as survival mechanisms after the Revolution by gentry families who, living under the Bolsheviks, were unable to perform any other kind of work.[25]

Orpheus in the Salon

Yury (Georg) Karlovich Arnold (1811–1898), Russian composer, theorist, and critic, has been described by a Soviet writer as "one of the first Russian scholars to attempt to clarify the connection between musical art and social life."[26] Arnold—of nonnoble Russified German stock—got a jolting experience in this line when he first arrived at the musical salon of Prince Vladimir Odoevsky in the late 1830s. Announced by the butler as "Mr. Arnold" into a company of princes and counts, he was greeted by Princess Odoevskaya not with the usual proffering of the hand but with a frosty nod. Arnold silently decoded this gesture quite bluntly as: "you are a nobody." He then stepped into the next room where Odoevsky and other musicians gathered on a friendly and lively informal footing. This was hardly class struggle in the drawing room, a theme often extracted from the awkward behavior of such nonnobles as Dostoevsky glowering in a corner or Belinsky fuming over an elitist social perspective. Yet an undeniable tension between guild and beau monde, creative enthusiasm and social rigor, often filled the spaces where music-making met polite society. Ardor and intensity were among the principal markers that distinguished the outward behavior of members of the intelligentsia and would-be artistic professionals on the one hand from the avatars of high society on the other.[27]

Among the legion of culturally eclectic salons, several possessed a distinctly musical orientation. In regular gatherings, performance alternated with talk about current musical life. Vocal and piano music predominated, though the wealthier salon hosts could mount chamber recitals and even symphonic concerts. The salon expanded musical experience from the intimate family to the social sphere of invited company. As *intelligenty* and *raznochintsy* began appearing in aristocratic salons more often in the 1830s and 1840s, space tended to divide socially into constituencies, or "fronts" in Erwin Goffman's terminology.[28] The "outsiders" and their socially superior sympathizers could retreat into an adjoining room and turn the conversation from "society" (beau monde) to society (*obshchestvo*) and to intellectual topics such as music or literature. In doing so, they would raise the emotional temperature of their speech and deploy a more expressive body language. When the subcircles overlapped or mingled, discomfort arose like the kind experienced by Yury Arnold.[29]

In later years, the critic V. V. Stasov spoke caustically but accurately of "aristocratic arbiters in matters musical — two counts (Vielgorsky), one prince (Odoevsky) and one general (Lvov)."[30] General Lvov's socially exalted salon dedicated to music met in his Petersburg home on Caravan Street off the Nevsky, in the cultural heart of the city. Because of his proximity to court circles, his talent, and his fanatical dedication to symphonic genres, Lvov figured large in the musical life of his time, however reactionary he seemed to more liberal contemporaries. An accomplished amateur violinist, Lvov played privately for friends, since he was not permitted to perform in public due to his high rank. In the 1860s, deafness set in for Lvov, a decade before he passed away. From 1835, he presented weekly string quartets at home in a small music room with his fellow amateurs and aristocrats, the Vielgorskys, the fledgling Alexander Serov, and a few professional musicians (fig. 9). Using trained players in amateur groups — known in England as "stiffening" — was a common practice. By one account, an atmosphere of reverence for the music prevailed, paralleling the passionate talk in literary and philosophical circles. Fragmentary information on attendance suggests that this salon differed in social makeup from the elegant soirées that Lvov would normally attend as a high-ranking official and courtier. When Lvov mounted symphonic concerts for a broader public in the grand hall, Tsar Nicholas sometimes appeared in the same room as lowly clerks.[31]

The brothers Vielgorsky (the preferred spelling; originally Wielhorski) resembled the better-known Faddei Bulgarin and Osip Senkovsky in being wholly assimilated and successful men of Polish origin. Their father had served as a diplomat at the court of Catherine II. Both brothers achieved some distinction in music: Matvei (1794–1866) as a cellist; Count Mikhail Vielgorsky (1788–1856), a high-ranking court dignitary, as an amateur singer, violinist, and composer of romances, a symphony, and an opera (fig. 10). He had studied harmony, counterpoint, and organ with foreigners in Russia, and composition with Luigi Cherubini in Europe. Mikhail as a young man had befriended Beethoven to whose music he was fiercely dedicated. Tsar Alexander I banished him for a time due to his Masonic activities and a secret marriage to his sister-in-law soon after his first wife's death and he spent some years on his estate near Kursk. When Tsar Nicholas pardoned and befriended him, Vielgorsky returned to a brilliant court career. Mikhail Vielgorsky cast a broader social and musical net than did Lvov. His public outreach is revealed in a welter of diplomas and records of memberships and honors bestowed by Russian and foreign learned and artistic societies — including the Academy of Rome. Among other things, Vielgorsky belonged to a relatively unsung circle who raised money to free talented serf artists and musicians.[32]

Through the 1830s and 1840s, the salon and music center in the magnificent Vielgorsky home on Mikhailovsky Square (fig. 11) played host to the most celebrated musical visitors to mid-century Russia: Liszt, Berlioz, the Schumanns, and Pauline Viardot among others. Vielgorsky, as a patron who booked European talent into Russia through personal connections, played an unpaid role that was enriching the impresarios of the era such as Johann Peter Salomon in London. (Vielgorsky did however receive at one point an annual fifteen-thousand-ruble state subsidy to entertain and audition foreign artists.) According to the violinist N. Ya. Afanasev, Vielgorsky's salon was the only gateway to a musical post in the capital. As a locus of major musical events, Vielgorsky's home was an unofficial concert hall of the capital. There as many as three hundred guests could hear the works of the classical Viennese symphonists of the eighteenth and nineteenth centuries — including the Russian premiere of Beethoven's Ninth Symphony in 1836. There Glinka rehearsed parts of *A Life for the Tsar* in 1836 with the help of Prince Yusupov's serf orchestra. And there Robert Schumann conducted one of his symphonies in 1844. Because of the attendance of Gogol, Zhukovsky, Vyazemsky, Lermontov, Odoevsky, Glinka, Dargomyzhsky, and Bryullov, a contemporary dubbed Vielgorsky's home "a lively and original multifaceted academy of the arts." Berlioz called it "a little ministry of fine arts."[33]

According to the suspiciously precise estimate of Vielgorsky's son-in-law, the writer Count Vladimir Sollogub, 75 percent of the time spent in social occasions in the salon was devoted to musical performance two or three times a week. Although conversation was almost always conducted in French, all sorts of people gathered there for the music, the billiards, the talk. Sollogub, in a bit of instant sociology, divided the company into "the two elements: society people and art people." Vielgorsky's snobbish wife remained oblivious to the lower-ranking visitors. Acting as what sociologists now call "gatekeepers," female heads of aristocratic households held sway over etiquette. The host himself moved easily among all the guests. Returning from a formal court function, the count would doff his dazzling uniform embellished with sash and stars, don a simple coat, mingle with everyone, and charm them all. Though very close to the royal presence, he was known to comport himself equally to people of all classes. A certain egalitarian atmosphere noted in some memoirs prevailed.[34]

Vladimir Odoevsky (1804–69), descended from Kievan princes on his father's side and from peasants on his mother's, studied music at a Moscow lycée and busied himself in law, education, and charity. While he delved into numerous intellectual crannies, Odoevsky's passion for music made him one of the first generation of Russian music critics as well as an original writer. Patrician friends smiled ironically at his versatility and encyclopedic knowledge. Odoevsky, aware of his "otherness" in society, put it into his fiction. He consorted with nongentry intellectuals and artists "of various ranks" who visited his home in a near alliance — so to speak — of the noble superfluous man and the emerging creative intelligentsia. His musical and literary Saturdays on the fashionable Millionaya Street near the Winter Palace and later on the Fontanka ran from 1826 to the late 1840s. Though he avoided high society balls, Odoevsky remained very much the prince who went around town with liveried lackeys on his coach.[35] The issue is not consistent social identity or style, but the high-born amateur's skill at negotiating through social ranks and so helping to fashion a musical community. Avdotiya Panaeva observed that the blue bloods at the Odoevskys gathered in the salon room around the tea table where the hostess was serving; in the study huddled the host and the intelligentsia. The members of the less exalted classes awkwardly crossed the salon on their way to the study and were followed by derisive smiles and glances through lorgnettes of counts and princes.[36] This was the social minefield that Yury Arnold walked through. Once out of it, he found a more congenial harmony and more or less equality in the musical enclave.

In this era, literature, ideas, and music could pull people of different social standing together in salons. Their well-meaning hosts were "conciliatory" as opposed to "exclusive" aristocrats, in the terminology of Ernest Bramsted's discussion of nineteenth-century German society and fiction. The former were men of title open not only to science and the arts as serious endeavors but to their purveyors and creators as well. But it was not easy to bridge the chasm of social mores and the contrast of manners, dress, and even topics of talk. In Russia, the nongentry's malaise in the midst of "good society" is well documented. Wealth alone was no ticket to acceptance. A high-society figure, on seeing the son of a rich tea merchant family, V. P. Botkin, at his mother's soirée, expressed surprise: "Are you buying tea from him?" he asked. "No," she replied," I am serving him tea." Vielgorsky, Odoevsky, Lvov, and other musical patrons were caught between their genuine love of music at its root—performance and composition—and the strongly entrenched belief in their circles that for ladies and gentlemen art was something to be consumed and not created or performed, since these acts were considered labor or service. And, as in other societies, a certain aura of unmanliness might have lingered around serious engagement in the arts as well.[37]

The Kukolnik "musical-literary evenings" that began around 1836 take us to a different world from the salons described above, though there was some overlapping attendance. Vielgorsky, Lvov, Odoevsky, and other salon grandees lived and entertained within the magic residential triangle noted in chapter 1. Their gorgeous homes, mansions, and apartments invited a certain restraint in social intercourse. At the Kukolnik brothers' large but not opulent flat on Lantern Lane down among the city's twisting canals, revelry ruled. One of the hosts, Nestor (1809–1868), gained much fame in his day for patriotic plays, novels, and tales. His evenings (and all-nighters) became notorious in musical history for allegedly pushing the composer Mikhail Glinka into decline. Called by one scholar "a Petersburg Bohemia of the 1830s–40s," they offered guild pleasures to a guild of artists: ritual, excess, male bonding, and conviviality that sometimes turned into drunken orgy. The first cellist of the opera, Franz Knecht, encountered at the Kukolniks an atmosphere of musical frenzy: "Aber diese Russen! Aber so Enthusiasmus."[38]

Even rowdy bunches have hierarchies. At the center stood the troika or Brotherhood (fig. 12): dramatist Kukolnik, composer Glinka, and painter Karl Bryullov, already famed for his 1833 canvas, *The Last Day of Pompeii*. They saw themselves as embodying the arts of Russia and were so depicted in a cartoon of the time. The formulation probably derived from Théophile Gauthier's anointing of Victor Hugo, Hector Berlioz, and Eugène Delacroix as the trinity of the arts in France. To put it kindly, history has not been as good to Kukolnik as to the other two. An outer circle included Kukolnik's brother, Odoevsky, Belinsky, Bulgarin, and others. The bigger parties pulled in dozens of regulars and newcomers. People like Osip Senkovsky and even the policeman Leonty Dubelt would appear, along with a motley assortment of editors, hack writers, professors, artists, publishers, and booksellers. The Kukolniks' flat combined a fluctuating marketplace of inspiration with a whirlpool of social intercourse, gossip, intrigue, and gargantuan drinking. At the twice-weekly gatherings, Glinka sang in a much-admired voice. The Brotherhood was a male refuge for Glinka who was on the verge of divorce. He claimed that his wife thought more of ball gowns and carriages than music, and resented his waste of expensive notation paper when he was writing his first opera, *A Life for the Tsar*. Such anecdotes all originate from Glinka and his male friends. Soviet scholars repeated them and passed lightly over the multiple sexual liaisons of the father of Russian music.[39]

At one of the evenings in 1842, attended by Mikhail Vielgorsky, Sollogub, the composer Alexander Dargomyzhsky, and a large crowd on hand to honor Franz Liszt, Glinka made a little speech explaining that the artists of this world "are one big family, a Gypsy Bohème, and that the king of this Bohème in our time is none other than Liszt."[40] Glinka's remark, often quoted but little examined, throws some light on the social context of music-making in midcentury Russia. The reference to Gypsies was not simply metaphoric. The Russian public at that moment had a craze for Gypsy songs and the spirit of freedom and abandon they seemed to represent. At the Brotherhood, the guitar assisted the flow of Gypsy music. Glinka himself instructed one of his singing pupils on the "intonation of the steppe" or Gypsy inflection. But in his tribute to Liszt, Glinka was also alluding to the figurative urbanized "Gypsy camp," the Bohemia of artists, marginals, and members of the underlife of Paris and other European cities. Liszt, who mingled with kings and princes, seemed to represent precisely the freedom which allowed both disreputable revelry (or the look of it) and the anchor of beau monde respectability. The Brotherhood was more open than the salons of the upper spheres; but it was also selective, and the inner circle expelled other guests prior to its own midnight performances and carousing. Kukolnik's literary chauvinism and his closeness to the trinity of conservative journalism (Bulgarin, Grech, Senkovsky) gave him a coloring of middle-class patriotism, a rather crude cultural version of "official nationalism." Glinka, a court appointee at the Capella and a celebrity of upper circles, could find release in the relative social freedom and high-temperature uproar of the Brotherhood. How and if this environment affected Glinka's creativity remains an open question. The common belief that it damaged him as a composer cannot be taken at face value.[41]

This brief tour in no way exhausts the musical salons of St. Petersburg in this era. The poets Anton Delvig and Vasily Zhukovsky, the younger Gedeonov (his father headed the Imperial Theaters), and Fëdor Tolstoy of the Academy of Fine Arts all offered music in salons or soirées as part of their cultural life, as did the composer Dargomyzhsky and Ekaterina Karamzina. John Field dominated in personal appearances at musical evenings. Close behind came the sparkling figure of Maria Szymanowska-Wolowska (1789–1831), daughter of a Warsaw brewer, whose own daughter married the poet Adam Mickiewicz. Szymanowska, though patronizingly dubbed "a Field in skirts," was a prolific composer in her own right and introduced Polish motifs to St. Petersburg audiences. After touring Europe and Russia, in the late 1820s she played Petersburg salons attended by literary and musical notables. The child prodigy Anton Rubinstein launched his career in private salons.[42]

Moscow musical salons developed their own shape. The most brilliant of them belonged to Princess Zinaida Volkonskaya, daughter of a distinguished diplomat. She formed a "close friendship" with Tsar Alexander I who took her with him to Europe during his wartime and postwar travels. In the 1810s and 1820s she managed to study music with François Boiledieu in St. Petersburg and Paris and befriended Rossini. Volkonskaya, a cultural phenomenon in her day — poet, composer, contralto, courtier, and salon hostess — wrote an opera, *Joan of Arc*, recited Racine, and was dubbed "the Corinne of the North" (from Mme. de Staël's 1807 novel). Her social rank prevented her from becoming a successful professional performer. Tsar Alexander reprimanded her for her ventures into the world of opera — although at the Congress of Verona, he was delighted by her staging for an elite group of *La bella molinara* by his favorite opera composer, Paisiello. In 1829 she emigrated to Rome and became a Catholic.[43]

In the late 1820s, the elegant Volkonskaya assembled the Moscow beau monde, the local intelligentsia, and creative artists in a brilliant blend of readings, concerts, and opera. In her friend Buturlin's words, she ruled Moscow. On first meeting Pushkin, Volkonskaya sang one of his verses set by composer Osip Jeništa, a form of artistic coquetry that she brought to perfection. Fellow aristocrats and a few Italians joined her on stage, assisted by some choristers from the theater in a performance of, among other things, Rossini's *Tancredi*, an opera then much in vogue. Her success stemmed in part from the presence of a large Italian colony in Moscow, many left over from the 1812 invasion. A somber shade fell over Volkonskaya's salon after the suppression of the Decembrist revolt of 1825. Her sister-in-law, Maria Volkonskaya, came to visit on the eve of her departure for Siberia to join her convict husband, Sergei Volkonsky. It was the last high cultural soirée that she ever saw, but not the last time she would hear classical music: Zinaida had a small clavichord strapped to the vehicle that would convey her to Siberian exile. Adam Mickiewicz, a regular at the soirées, was one of the few to note the enormous contradiction between their atmosphere and the fact that the hostess was the owner of thousands of serfs.[44]

The violinist Afanasev claimed that no less than fifteen Moscow homes hosted chamber evenings in 1828, a practice that grew with the decades. In the early 1850s, Evdokiya Rostopchina's Saturdays welcomed casual visitors

from "the lower classes" and at her evenings could be seen the circle of budding Moscow writers known as the Young Editors of *The Muscovite*. In that
decade Moscow began to witness a vibrant cultural flowering among the
wealthier merchants, a class still despised by aristocrats and intelligentsia as
vulgar and retrograde. Scholars have written at length of the generous patronage by some of the more enlightened merchants of schools, publishing,
theater, and most famously art. A remarkable memoir by another violinist,
V. V. Bezekirsky, describes musical Moscow, with regular quartet evenings in
the merchant homes of A. A. Karzinkin, an amateur violinist, M. M. Varen-
tsov, and F. V. Perlov, with playwright Alexander Ostrovsky as one of the
regular attendees. But Moscow had nothing like the *Tafelmusik* enjoyed regularly in the homes of the merchants of Frankfurt, Hamburg, and other German cities of the time; or the myriad middle-class musical salons in London,
Paris, and Vienna.[45]

Scattered references to provincial salons give few details. N. Ya. Afanasev, a
native of Perm in the far north, named a half-dozen families together with
exiled Poles who in the 1820s held musical evenings in a little town of four
streets in the middle of forests and fields. Of a different magnitude was the
home of the Nizhny Novgorod critic, composer, dramatist, translator, and
patron, A. D. Ulybyshev (1794–1858). Raised in Germany, he served in many
ministries and retired at age thirty-six. While a member of the Green Lamp
society—a satellite of the Decembrist movement—Ulybyshev wrote a utopian
sketch called "The Dream." His later years were devoted almost wholly to
music. An autodidact violinist and musicologist, Ulybyshev published one of
the first serious analyses of Mozart's music. His obsession with music and his
sharp tongue apparently rubbed off on his protégé, Mily Balakirev, founder of
the circle that became the Mighty Five. Ulybyshev's Nizhny Novgorod home
hosted a vigorous musical life—part salon and part concert hall where large-
scale works got a hearing.[46]

What did salons do for musical life in Russia before the great transformation of
the 1860s? As a larger version of the family music circle, the salon perpetuated the
private consumption of music—by invitation only. But, to a greater extent than
purely domestic gatherings, salons reverberated with self-conscious collective
musical discussion and enthusiasm. They inspired budding composers and performers. One Russian scholar not given to excessive piety has recognized the
musical salon of this era as a site for the "celebration of life," a hothouse of
romantic sensibility that actually melted icy social forms. The social composition
of structured musical evenings made them into sites, to borrow language from a
social historian, with "porous and indeterminate boundaries," full of ambiguity
springing from the persistence of "hierarchical relations and socioeconomic dis-

parities." Even in the most tight-lipped drawing rooms, blunt-edged music lovers "from below" found expressive scope. Gentry-intelligentsia salons were thus Orphean in the mix of social psychologies, the mythological Orpheus having blended the restraint of Apollonian reason with Dionysian energy.[47]

Salons represented an important phase in the transition from private to public spheres in the musical life of the country. From them sprang initiatives for concerts in a public sphere which attracted multicolored crowds—a pluralistic milieu that generated its own tensions. Given the absence of a conservatory, the metropolitan salons, musical evenings, and schoolroom learning together constituted an archipelago of musical culture and a vast clearing house of musical talent and pleasure. However amateurish their coloration, Russian salons—like those in Vienna, Berlin, and elsewhere—constituted a musical infrastructure, one might say a collective "night school" or "adult education" class where elites and their *raznochintsy* protégés and friends studied, talked about, performed, and gained a taste for serious music. Not the least of its functions, the salon provided the milieu for alliances and conversations that sometimes led to the manumission of talented serf musicians. The misplaced contempt for upper-class dilettante music-making, though from differing perspectives, voiced by Anton Rubinstein, V. V. Stasov, and others would long obscure the legitimate value of the music salon for Russian culture as a creative bridge between the domestic sphere and the public arena of concert life.[48]

Serf as Musician

Beyond the salons stretched a vast sea of serf-made music. Ranking very high in the spirit of domestic theatricality that possessed so many gentry lords stood Count Pavel Skavronsky, a well-known patron of the arts, Italianophile, and music lover—nay, worshiper. In St. Petersburg and in Italy where he spent most of his brief life, the young count—whom the gossipy homosexual Vigel called effeminate—forbade spoken conversation beneath his roof and required his house serfs to address him in operatic recitative which he composed for them! One must imagine them-in the manner of Bellini, Donizetti, or Rossini—singing him such lines as "would the master like to have the samovar put up for tea?" or "Your excellency's carriage is here." Skavronsky's grotesque musical regimen, aside from being the quaint practice of a Russian eccentric, vividly demonstrated to what extent cultural pleasure could be intermeshed with proprietary power. The dress ball and manorial theater in the eighteenth century brought instrumental ensemble music into the countryside. The shortage of trained Russian actors, musicians, singers, and dancers led to the practice among the great magnates on the more opulent estates and in lavish town mansions of deploying trained serfs for musical and theatrical entertainment and for their own and their neighbors' cultural enrichment. Starting in the capitals, domestic theater and music spread to provincial towns and estates from the last quarter of the century to the abolition of serfdom in 1861, reaching a peak in the decades before the Napoleonic invasion of 1812. Serf orchestras and choirs, small or large, could be found even in some modest manor houses. One estimate of the serf orchestra total counts more than 310. Solo singers and players sufficed for landowners unable to afford ensembles.[49]

In small private salon settings, amateur performers, visiting professionals, and listeners, though of divergent social backgrounds, could act, talk, and perform as equals, or at least play at the fiction of egalitarian social intercourse. The language of music possesses no class inflections, and playing it requires a unified set of gestures where manners and mannerisms hardly counted. The farther from the arena of politesse and the less prominent the verbal exchange, the lower the tensions among the men and women of different stations. As in any human activity involving disciplined cooperation — war, labor, performance — those of rank must adapt to the leveling it creates. Once we introduce serfs into the social equation, however, the rules change drastically. On hundreds of estates in town and country, serfs were very much a part of that equation — as performers for and sometimes with their owners in "orchestras." The Russian word *orkestr* could denote anything from a large ensemble to three players. Prince Dolgoruky applied the term to the violinist, cellist, and cymbalist in the home of a Polish landowner in Ukraine in 1817; and Lermontov in 1840 complained about a "featr" (theater) in Cherkassk that featured an "orchestra" of four clarinets, two double basses, a fiddle, and a drum.[50]

Similarities between serf musicians and serf actors in their cultural, social, and moral milieux will become apparent in later chapters. But important differences remain. A certain amount of technical training was essential for instrumentalists and singers, more so than for actors; and musical ensembles, more numerous than theaters, were cheaper to maintain. Owners occasionally loaned their players to a landowner who had a serf theater but no musicians. Practically all serf instrumentalists — solo, chamber, or orchestra — were male. This suggests that if a master pursued sexual contact with them, he would probably try to hide it. I have found no example of homoerotic relations between serfs and masters, though a number of highly placed homosexuals are on record in this era. Nor do the annals reveal a Russian Potiphar's wife or a Lady Chatterley seeking the favors of a male serf musician. It would be unwise to exclude these possibilities, given the power possessed by serf owners. The famous ex-serf actor Mikhail Shchepkin related a tale of an orphaned general's daughter who fell in love with a serf violinist in the quartet at her gentry foster home. Unable to marry, they attempted a double suicide by shooting each other: her gun misfired, his killed her, and he died under the lash.[51]

Russian estates abounded in enserfed men and women born with natural talent or genius regardless of education: architects, painters, sculptors, musicians, singers, dancers, actors, and even engineers. Owners identified gifted house serf children or, like the owner of the serf Savva Purlevsky, pulled the most promising village youth into house service as musicians or lackeys. Accomplished trainees were bought and sold. A landowner advertised the sale of a fifteen-year-old bassoon player with a bass voice, in a batch with other servants. The training varied according to the wealth of the owner: at home with Russian teachers (including serfs and masters) or resident foreigners; or study in a provincial town, the capitals, or even Europe. Few could, with Count Orlov-Chesmé, bring two artists and a clarinettist to Leipzig with him for lessons. Most settled for home tutors. Like missionaries following assault teams, German music teachers had begun infiltrating Russia in the eighteenth century and the fleeting references to "music schools" indicate no more than teams of teachers assembled for the musical training of serfs. The sourpuss German music teacher joined the various light-headed or light-fingered foreign tutors as types in Russian literature. A peasant character in Turgenev's *Notes of a Hunter* recalls a German teacher of olden times who had "pretentiously" and unsuccessfully sought to dine at the table with the master and was put in his place. In the same author's *Nest of Gentry,* set in 1842, self-image and social identity became blurred for the melancholy Saxon music teacher, Christoph Lemm. In a bizarre allegedly real-life case, a Polish musician hired in the 1790s to train the house serfs of a Kostroma landowner instead incited them to a revolt which was suppressed. The vengeful owner had the teacher jailed and his stringed instruments destroyed for good measure. In the face of arrogant owners, music masters had to play humble or risk being fired, like the tutor in a brilliant 1859 tale by Karolina Pavlova who is dismissed precisely because he shows his erudition.[52]

Some serf boys, tired of rote instruction, would ask to be returned to the plow. The father of Prince Kropotkin, the prophet of modern anarchism, had a twelve-to-fifteen-piece band composed of servants who played music in the evenings and were often loaned out to neighbors in the Old Equerries Quarter of Moscow. When one of the kitchen serfs refused to learn an instrument, the father sent him into the army. Teaching by the stick—a natural mode in a culture of corporal punishment—might transform a peasant or lackey into a passable musician in a few months. The great war hero General Suvorov strictly supervised by mail the instruction of the serf singers and musicians on his many estates. When a serf was earmarked for training with no consideration of talent, he was sometimes beaten regularly until mastery was achieved, a fact reported by a foreign visitor at a provincial estate in 1829–30. A village priest related that a Saratov seignior had the habit of calling out the name of anyone who sang off key during the serf choir dinner serenade: the serf would redden, report to the stable for a whipping, and then return to the choir. The rod continued to hover long after training. Afanasev, on being lured from the Imperial Theater orchestra to the Shepelev estate, promptly ended the existing practice of corporal punishment in his orchestra of fifty and chorus of thirty-five to forty members, retaining only fines and the seigniorial jail.[53] By contrast, no female domestic servant was ever harmed for any misstep at the Kireevskys' Dolbino estate, where music and dance were common.[54]

A few landowners breached the dignity barrier by conducting their own ensembles. But learning and displaying this skill before company was a bit too close to creating the déclassé effect of acting on stage. When the eighteenth-century magnate N. P. Sheremetev played in the orchestra alongside his serfs and under a serf conductor, his guests did not like it and told him so. Russian servants, like those elsewhere, performed according to social cooperation and rules; their owners consumed according to conviviality and etiquette.[55] Rich owners could employ a foreign conductor — thus replicating a pattern familiar in estate management, the army, and the bureaucracy (and later in many factories): an outsider — often foreign — mediating between privileged and unfree or lower-class Russians. Manorial conducting could be a stepping stone. One German serf orchestra conductor later founded several orchestras in around Kazan Province. Ludwig Maurer (1799–1878) worked for V. A. Vsevolozhsky; and the Austrian, J. J. Johannis, for Prince Yusupov and Alexander Panchulidze, Saratov governor and passionate patron of the arts. Maurer and Johannis later led Imperial Theater orchestras.[56] But the position of the typical German conductor was ambiguous. Even among the grandees of central and western Europe the kapellmeister long felt the weight of informal servitude. The great Haydn served for a generation as a live-in composer and conductor who wore livery and slept in servants' quarters on the estate of the powerful Hungarian magnate Count Esterhazy. In Russia, many an estate conductor dined alone — too lofty to eat with the servants, too lowly to sit at table with the gentry folks.

Opinions about the skill of serf players ranged from pretty awful to mostly mediocre with some brilliant exceptions. A few ensembles attained great proficiency and the Imperial Theater more than once purchased troupes of singers, dancers, and musicians from landowners. In a story by Ivan Panaev, a rural gentry host surprises his guests, newly arrived from St. Petersburg, with a hidden orchestra playing the overture to *Le Calife de Bagdad* and says to them: "Admit it. You did not expect, I think, that there could be such surprises among country bumpkins." Grandees such as the Sheremetevs and the Yusupovs could mount entire ballets and operas with first-class orchestras. Prince Potëmkin in the eighteenth century bought from Field-Marshal Razumovsky a superb fifty-piece orchestra for 40,000 rubles. Another landowner allegedly purchased one violinist for 20,000 rubles. In the early nineteenth century, the Chernyshevs had a serf orchestra on their Orël Province estate conducted by a foreigner, which Buturlin ranked with the best theater orchestras in the capital. At the Yurasovsky estate in the same province in 1828, a forty-four-piece serf orchestra, costing 37,000 rubles (including the families of the players), performed opera, ballet, and choral music. In the neighboring province of Kursk, Prince Ivan Baryatinsky, an amateur composer, kept a well-trained classical orchestra of forty to fifty players at his palatial manor house, Marino, backed up by a library of over five hundred scores with works from Mozart to Donizetti. The wealthy P. G. Galagan at his Degtyar holding in Ukraine heard Beethoven rendered skillfully by his serf orchestra led by a German and assisted by a serf as first violinist who had trained in Dresden.[57] G. S. Tarnovsky's Chernigov Province serf ensemble, considered poor by one visitor, was apparently good enough to rehearse Glinka's *Ruslan and Lyudmila*. But visitors to estates all too often complained about substandard craftsmanship, particularly excessive volume which was apparently seen as a virtue: a noble recalls dining in the 1850s to a loud ensemble of "violins, drummers, and *dukhobors*" — the last being a pun combining a religious sect with players who fought with their wind instruments.[58]

In the late eighteenth century, a market of over one thousand serf musicians provided hire for as many as fifty monthly balls in Moscow. A commercial sanatorium on a Moscow Province estate advertised in 1817 that guests would be serenaded daily by music played by serfs and conducted by a German. P. I. Yushkov, a big landowner, had three homes in Moscow; another in St. Petersburg; ten thousand serfs, including two hundred house serfs; and a well-trained serf orchestra, choir, and horn band. Legendary for his midnight balls, all-night music, and three-day galas, in 1811 he held eighteen balls in three weeks. Glinka heard Yushkov's serf orchestra in St. Petersburg in the 1820s as part of his musical education. P. A. Sobakin, an old-time landowner dressed in the mode of Catherine II, owned estates in Novgorod and Orël. In his Moscow residence, he maintained a superb serf orchestra. The more serious manorial music lovers offered irregular private concerts with outreach to neighboring gentry. A. A. Pleshcheev alternated concerts and operas with cello recitals on his Orël estate. The Vielgorskys mounted a great Beethoven marathon in the middle of Kursk Province in the winter of 1822–23 consisting of thirty-three concerts during an intense four-month cycle. Performing were the hosts, neighboring gentry, hired German professionals, and serf musicians from the Chernyshev, Teplov, and Baryatinsky orchestras. This highly miscellaneous crew performed—in addition to works by Mozart, Boccherini, Cherubini, Méhul, and Rossini—seven Beethoven symphonies.[59]

Choral music occupied an important place in the Russian musical land-scape, quite aside from what was sung in regiments and churches. It has been claimed that in Tula Province, every landowner had at least ten or so musicians, including choristers, and that nobles joined in with folk choirs. Ukraine had become the traditional recruitment region for boys' voices from the time of Empress Elizabeth when grandees from the south brought them to the capitals. Well into the nineteenth century, scouts—including Glinka—would comb Ukrainian provincial estates, towns, and churches for boys, mostly serfs, to be bought for private manor houses and the Court Capella. Most serf choirs were little more than simple clutches of peasants brought in to serenade the guests with folk songs for hours while standing in the doorway during dinner. In Ivan Krylov's mocking fable, "Musicians," the serf chorus produces noise like screeching animals. Manor house guests liked dinner music and often sang at table themselves if nothing else was available. More ambitious classically trained ensembles took on opuses of great complexity. High-ranking families such as the Sheremetevs, Golitsyns, Yusupovs, Vorontsovs, Volkonskys, Kurakins, Lopukhins, Galagans, and Tarnovskys maintained choirs that sang a capella or with orchestra in works ranging from folk to liturgical and opera. The last two landowners regularly took their serf choirs to the Contract Fair in Kiev. In the 1830s, Prince Pavel Lopukhin, at his luxurious castle in Korsun, directed and composed, and sometimes shamelessly inserted Italian arias into his compositions.[60]

Among the earliest of the grandees to indulge in this musical form, the Sheremetevs of Moscow ranked high. Nikolai Petrovich's huge pool of estates and serfs provided singers who, when their voices changed, were sent home with a bonus or made clerks on his various estates. The chorus, comprising mostly Ukrainian serf recruits, was led by such eminent figures as Antonio Sapienza and the serfs Stefan Degtyarëv and Gavriil Lomakin. Lomakin (1812–85), the son of the steward on a Kursk estate of D. N. Sheremetev (or by some accounts Sheremetev's natural son), went to St. Petersburg as a boy soprano soloist in 1822 and was later freed and appointed conductor. A key figure in the founding of the Free Music School—the "anticonservatory" of the 1860s—Lomakin eliminated Sapienza's Italianate style, corrected the choir's accumulated errors, and turned it into a marvelous instrument of sixty voices which earned plaudits from Liszt, Berlioz, Viardot, and the Russian critic Vladimir Stasov for its performance of Russian liturgical and eighteenth-century European choral music.[61]

Unlike the Sheremetev choir which remained inaccessible to the public, that of Prince Yury Golitsyn (1823–1872), originally composed of serfs and eventually of hired professionals, performed in England in one of the first international displays of Russian culture on the concert stage. It began with a chorus of thirty men that grew to a force of 150 men and women. At age nineteen, Golitsyn, who had studied with Lomakin and with European teachers, organized his serf ensemble and conducted it publicly in the capitals and other Russian cities. This body was among the first to make folk music adapted for choir available to a wide public. An inveterate spendthrift, Golitsyn squandered huge sums on his chorus. When he went bankrupt and failed to sell the choir to the imperial court, he dissolved it in 1857. Because of his closeness to Alexander Herzen, the revolutionary exile, Golitsyn was expelled from the capital and fled to London in 1860 where he conducted concerts of Russian music in St. James Hall. There he also produced a Herzen Waltz, an Ogarëv Quadrille, and, as the new age was dawning in 1861, an orchestral fantasy entitled *Liberation* to mark the freeing of the serfs that year.[62]

The Russian horn orchestra (fig. 13) illustrated remarkably how theatricality and the display of power often intermixed with love of music and entertainment. Its popularity began in the extravagant era of Catherine II among big magnates such as Razumovsky, Potëmkin, Stroganov, and I. M. Dolgoruky who possessed both a horn band and a symphonic orchestra. The landowner Naryshkin's early nineteenth-century horn choir had forty-two live "keys," players with horns, the longest of which was about four feet. Though each player blew only one note, they could perform overtures to Boiledieu's *Le Calife de Bagdad,* Rossini's, *Semiramide,* Méhul's *Joseph in Egypt,* Cherubini's *Les deux jours,* and Spontini's *Fernand Cortez.* These works of the first decades of the century were all written in what may be called the Paris-Italian style, by no means simple band music that one would expect horn players to take into their repertoire. Rossini's alternating staccatos and lentos and his accelerandos and crescendos are well known. Boiledieu's overture is a translucent piece of music, elegiac in spite of its comic subject, with a gauze-like tracery that seems unplayable except by strings. The largest horn band on record consisted of ninety-one instruments of varying length, covering four and a half octaves and played by forty players. It is staggering to think that such a band could seriously render this kind of music. Yet the Russian musicologist Yury Arnold and the German composer Ludwig Spohr admired the astonishing musicality of the players.[63] Other observers were less kind. De Passenens asserted that only slaves could be brought to play a single note; and the poet Derzhavin scorned the bands as a low entertainment of overindulgent aristocrats. The horn band declined along with estate theater and disappeared after the introduction of the valve trumpet.[64]

Those noblemen who organized and watched with sheer amusement as dozens of men alternated their notes in a complicated score clearly enjoyed a certain sense of power and command. In this sense, the horn orchestra resembled the human toy soldiers on drill parade estates — a nostalgic surrogate for real power. Though he had no horn band, the military martinet and chief administrator of Tsar Alexander I, Alexei Arakcheev, maintained a serf orchestra and choir at Gruzino, his utopia-like estate where geometric order reigned supreme. The players presented dances, marches, serenades, Russian songs, overtures, arias, and operas — including Martin y Soler's *The Tree of Diana* and Mozart's *Magic Flute*. All the servants, dependents, military personnel, and other subordinates fell under the eye of this strictest of taskmasters who oversaw their manners and costumes. He and his mistress displayed inordinate harshness to their underlings for which she paid with her life in a brutal act of murder. The eccentric whim of a master sometimes verged on madness: the Kursk nobleman P. A. Denisov, when in a bad mood, had his entire orchestra perform on their knees or had them pull his sleigh.[65]

Pleasure-inducing music had its price for the owner as well. The labor of house and field serfs cost nothing of course, but some owners paid wages to their serfs as an incentive and gave gifts to favored players and singers. Instruments, notes, and training had to be paid for. The more elaborate establishments with concert chambers and theaters found their musical offerings much in demand by neighbors and friends, and their hospitality thus expanded: their owners invited guests or transported entire serf orchestras to a friend's estate for extended periods, as did a landowner in Orël and Glinka's uncle in Smolensk. The practice of maintaining serf orchestras and choirs could be ruinous. Prince Odoevsky, financially squeezed, sent his orchestra players as serfs on *obrok* to support him. Others took them to fairs and charged admission. Insolvency commonly resulted in dissolution or sale. Chronicles in the first third of the century contain purchase records detailing the unloading of singers, dancers, and entire orchestras onto other landowners or the Imperial Theater complex. A lord's profligacy often caused misery for his serfs who might be sold, split up, or sent as soldiers. As early as 1806, long before the general dissolution of serf orchestras, they were already being mocked in Alexander Shakhovskoi's opera, *The Love Post*, which satirized all kinds of manorial productions. Remarkably, serf orchestras continued right up to the end of serfdom itself and long past the point when owners were disbanding their serf theaters.[66]

Serf musicians paid in a different coin. The fact that orchestras and quartets sometimes mingled serfs with landowners in performance did not affect the relationship between master and servant during the twilight years of serfdom. Masters used their musicians in various ways. Prince Vyazemsky, for example, in order to economize, had his fiddlers and flutists double as buffet waiters and attendants. At Koshkarev's estate in Nizhny Novgorod Province, lackeys, huntsmen, and musicians rotated their jobs. Field-Marshal Suvorov sent his musicians into the fields when harvest hands were needed. A story by Mikhail Zagoskin poked fun at some landowners who assigned instruments to men according to physical qualities: the double bass for a tall serf, the bassoon for one with a good set of front teeth. The oft-cited French expatriate, de Passenens, recounts that masters would select serf children and simply say to them: "you, you'll play bassoon, and you clarinet." In the 1820s on one of the Kurakin estates in Orël Province, musicians and singers worked also as servants and laborers in the manorial garment factory. Doubling was common: Prince Baryatinsky had some of his serfs trained as musicians and as floor polishers—human tools who skated across the parquet with brushes tied to their feet (a token of demeaning labor highlighted in the Soviet film of 1934, *Chapaev*).[67]

Like other serf artists, musicians experienced a variety of fates. In a minor success story, the first violinist of Strakhov's band, after his master's death, made his own career as orchestra leader in Kazan and Simbirsk.[68] Better known is Daniil Kashin (1770–1841), an energetic pioneer of Russian music, though his early life is still shrouded in obscurity. One of G. I. Bibikov's serfs, he managed to study in St. Petersburg with Giuseppe Sarti. In Moscow, Kashin became the conductor of Bibikov's serf orchestra—all the while in bondage. At age twenty, he was already the versatile author of overtures, concertos, choral works, romances, and opera; at thirty he was freed with the assistance of the poet Sergei Glinka and two actors from the Imperial Theater system. Kashin concertized, conducted, and composed as a freed serf after 1799. Long before the advent of Mikhail Glinka, Kashin turned his ear to coachmen's songs of the high road, peasants in the fields, and Gypsies in performance; he gathered folk songs, arranged them into romances, wrote patriotic occasional music in 1812, and did variations on folk songs—all of which endeared him to Russian nationalist intellectuals. Like most of the composers who collected and arranged folk material, Kashin reworked it in the European musical vocabulary in which he been trained. This versatile man was one of those few who emerged from estate bondage to breathe the air of freedom.[69]

The more complicated case of the violinist I. I. Semënov illustrates the ever-present tensions inherent in the process of liberating talent from serfdom. Vyazemsky and Mikhail Vielgorsky made an agreement with the violinist's owner, Prince Alexei Kurakin (d. 1829), to release him for a fee. But, irritated at all the buzz in Moscow in 1824 about this event, Kurakin changed his mind and returned the ten thousand rubles paid for Semënov's freedom. This was one of several cases where the owner interpreted public knowledge of such transactions as pressure and became indignant that other people could influence the disposal of his personal property. Semënov was freed in 1834, a few years after his master's death, and soon became the concertmaster of the St. Petersburg Imperial Theater orchestra. In 1836, he appeared solo on the Engelhardt House concert stage. The public delayed applauding for a moment before releasing a stormy ovation and — breaking with custom which encored only actors and singers — brought the ex-serf back to play again. Although a dozen or more ex-serfs had performed in public by that time, the public was still apparently rhapsodic over the spectacle.[70]

Since memoirs of serf musicians are rare, information about them is found largely in second-hand observation by outsiders. A serf flutist, Alexei Chemerovtsov, who deserted his master and lived for eighteen years in Europe, left a deposition describing the unbearable humiliation of his parents. In 1814, moved by patriotic impulses, he gave himself up and was returned to Russia to an unknown fate. The literature on the suffering of serf musicians is affecting, but not very large. Atrocity stories were recycled many times. But the fact remains that their protagonists suffered a particular psychological agony. By training and occupation they were pulled out of one environment and placed in another, from kitchen or field or stable to a world of high culture and refined taste. This could, if the landowner chose to reverse the path, result in arrested development or the enchainment of talent. Alexander Herzen, one of the preeminent foes of serfdom, reported the case of two highly trained serf brothers, a cellist and a violinist, on the Smolensk estate of P. K. Vonlyarlyarsky. When the cellist attained some notoriety in the capitals, he was peremptorily recalled by his master and forbidden to leave the estate (as was his brother) on pain of exile. The owner, hearing rumors of an offer to buy the cellist's freedom, declined any offer. The murder of the elder Count Kamensky of Orël Province in 1809 has been attributed to two of his violinists whom he sent to Leipzig for training where they enrolled in a curriculum of freedom as well as music. On their return, according to hearsay, Kamensky still beat them for minor infractions. They stole into his bedchamber by night, and reproached him for wresting them from their natural environment into the free air and then plunging them back into slavery. The two serfs then chopped their master in pieces.[71]

The gentry memoirist Elizaveta Vodovozova (1844–1923) has left an account, full of dismal irony, of Vaska (no other name) a serf musician belonging to her father, the landowner Tsevlovsky. Vaska once heard a gentry woman playing a Chopin nocturne, memorized it, and played it on the violin. His owner loaned him to a neighbor (probably N. B. Golitsyn) whose wife, a foreigner, deepened his musical knowledge and offered to purchase him for further education. But Tsevlovsky declined and ended the serf's musical training by putting him to work in his estate theater as prompter, actor, soloist, and musical director. When in 1848, cholera took away the master, his widow had to retrench and put house servants on either *obrok* or field work. Vaska, aged thirty, no longer suited for either and mocked by his fellow peasants, sought release from the plow. Vodovozova's mother became annoyed by Vaska's "pretensions" as a musician and by entreaties couched in the high rhetoric he had learned in her husband's theater. Vodovozova indicates between the lines that her mother was taking out her anger at her husband's theatrical extravagance on an innocent participant. She threatened to send him to the army but instead made him a coachman. Vaska's only sympathizers were the children of the manor, including the narrator. Eventually, Vaska was purchased for fifteen thousand rubles by the neighbor's widow who took him to Moscow and freed him. Vaska worked for a time in a Moscow theater orchestras, then went abroad and disappeared. Vodovozova's mother, despite the enlightened atmosphere of the household, simply could not fathom why her neighbor would buy and free a serf. In a remarkable passage, Vodovozova recalls the tearful farewell when Vaska and his wife departed into freedom, to the equal astonishment of the other serfs.[72]

The house serf Finogen, son of a cook, had trained on piano with John Field and Daniel Steibelt, spoke four languages, and served as pianist, conductor, and teacher on the estate of a Smolensk landowner and music lover. Neighbors paid Finogen well for the private lessons he gave, but he was isolated both from society which did not receive plebeians and from his fellow serfs. The humiliation of Finogen, an avid reader, reached the limit when he had to seek permission from the mistress of the house to borrow a book from the manor library and was punished for breaches of the rules. Then came a familiar episode: the master agreed to free the serf upon his death, but his executor colluded with the widow to suppress the document. The suit went to court and Finogen had to pay five thousand rubles of his savings to free himself. Ruined financially, he turned to drink, and died in poverty and obscurity in Moscow.[73]

The father of the literary historian and censor Alexander Nikitenko was one of N. P. Sheremetev's Ukrainian serf boy singers whose overexposure to high culture turned into a source of constant agony once he was returned to a menial job on a provincial estate. Alexander, who eventually won freedom and became a government censor, described Sheremetev as a despot corrupted by wealth, sated and bored, and "drowning in luxury." Out of the same milieu came the composer Stepan Degtyarëv (Degterev, 1766–1813) who, though living in bondage until he was in his thirties, built for himself an impressive musical career. Born in Kursk Province, at age seven he sang in the Sheremetev choir and became choirmaster and conductor of his private orchestra. Degtyarëv trained with Sapienza at the Sheremetev estate school, and, like Kashin, with Sarti. Called the Russian Haydn, he won renown as a composer of mostly choral works, the most famous of which was *Minin and Pozharsky, or the Liberation of Moscow* (1811), the first oratorio on a Russian national theme. It cleverly invoked the early seventeenth-century Russian heroes who had rallied an army to free Moscow from an invading Polish force — an early example of "restaging the Time of Troubles" for patriotic effect that took hold in drama at the same time. Degtyarëv's composition, ornate and triumphant in the manner of his teacher, alluded to the current Napoleonic menace and foreshadowed the imminent occupation of Moscow again after two centuries. However great Degtyarëv's renown, his master continued to tyrannize over him and keep him enserfed for most of his life. When Degtyarëv's longing for freedom was stalled, he turned to drink.[74]

In these, and in victim tales about serf actors and painters, ruination by alcohol recurs as a frequent theme. Its conveyors simply take it as a given that bondage and mistreatment caused destructive drinking among creative serfs. But how does one determine that causation? Drinking strong spirits was endemic in rural Russia among free peasants, state peasants, and serfs alike — as well as the urban lower and middle classes and many among the upper reaches of society. Further complicating the problem is the fact that performing serfs (and performers in general) were especially prone to drink. In one example among many, the governor of Vyatka Province, Kirill Tyufyaev — notorious in Herzen's vilifying memoirs — once planned a grand ball in honor of the visiting tsarevich (later Alexander II). In order to keep the musicians from becoming drunk he had them jailed on the day of the ball, taken from their cells directly to the Gentry Club, and locked in their seats for the duration of the ball. Herzen saw this as social atrocity; the governor as a sensible measure based on experience. The terms "abuse" and "overuse" of liquor are elastic terms and hard to evaluate; it is even harder to measure the role of drink in the disappointments and personal sufferings (and triumphs) of serf musicians and other artists.[75]

But it is not just the number of abused victims or their level of self-indulgence or even the mechanism of their exploitation that marked serfdom as a scourge. It was embedded in the very culture of unfreedom, the dark shadow of uncertainty, whim, or malicious decision by a lord who could alter—and ruin—someone's life. Of all the forms of servitude, domestic serfdom, in the view of the great reformer-in-exile Nikolai Turgenev, was "the most hideous and repulsive." The historian Michael Confino ranked household service along with removal to another village and recruitment into the army as the great disasters of peasant life (though evidence suggests that factory servitude was worse). Serfs in the manor house lost their previous economic identity and mentality. They produced nothing and were relatively unproductive in their service. Uprooted from the village and planted among aliens—their masters—musicians and artists were thus doubly alienated: as house serfs estranged from the village; as trained artists, from their fellow domestic servants to whom they often felt superior. The Tsevlovsky serfs, who had loved Vaska the Musician when he played folk tunes at peasant weddings, mocked his "sawing on the violin" when he became a domestic musician.[76]

The lush flowering of sentimentalism in literature, often associated with humanitarianism, coexisted with serfdom because the machinery of teary empathy for the wronged worked best when the victim was far away. With a flash of clarity rare in such memoirs, Shchepkina declared that people of her class in the 1820s and 1830s, though governed by sentiment and love, failed to extend these feelings beyond their own family and close friends. Only a Christian sense of charity for the poor tempered their severity to underlings. Kropotkin, though often subjective on these matters, rightly noted how members of his class could be reduced to tears over a French novel and in the next minute punish a serf. Karamzin and his readers who wept for the fate of "Poor Liza" mistook the tale as an aberration rather than as an almost unavoidable offspring of servile relations. The sense of inflated pride in owning somebody else's talent could blind a master to another's pride or sensitivity. Prince Dolgoruky, writing in 1817, described a serf-owning acquaintance who appeared promptly at 6 P.M. in the hall of his home, greeted his female dancers by name, struck up the band, and sat in leisure, "dreaming himself to be some kind of Elector of the Holy Roman Empire." Pride in a sense became a commodity, an object of competition, and in that struggle, the self-pride of the serf artist had to defer to the landowner's pride of ownership.[77]

It is fitting to recall that one of the most affecting treatments of bondage in all of Russian literature revolved around a manorial serf musician. The author Nikolai Pavlov (1803–64), known best as the husband of the writer Karolina Pavlova, was a literate "insider" who lived his first eight years as a serf, son of a house serf. As a free adult in 1835 Pavlov wrote "Name Day"—a narrative with a shocking final twist—to describe how enslavement brought psychic pain when its bearer encountered book learning, musical art, and love. The house serf protagonist can find no character resembling "himself" in the books that he chances to read; they are all free. Trained to entertain the master, the serf reveals a musical talent that is doomed by a cramped existence. His woe is exacerbated by a hopeless love affair with a neighboring gentry girl. The cruel mechanisms of fate lead him to dreams of cutting the throat of his master who gambles him away to another lord, in real life one of the great anxieties of peasant existence. Instead he flees, is captured, and sent into the army. *Mirabile dictu,* he finds there a haven from the unbearable inner conflicts of private servitude and indeed finds success on the battlefield, honor, and promotion.[78]

Out of the Forest: Glinka

"The people create the music," wrote Mikhail Glinka (1804–1857), Russia's first recognized secular art music composer of greatness; "and we [composers] merely arrange it" (fig. 14). These words are inscribed in metallic letters in the lobby of the Glinka Museum of Musical Culture in Moscow; they are uttered as a theme (though never demonstrated) in the tendentious 1952 Stalinist film, *Glinka, the Composer,* a movie that helped shape subsequent popular Soviet discourse about Russian composers;[79] and they have been repeated with nauseating regularity in virtually every Soviet treatment of Glinka. The composer certainly stood at the confluence of several Russian musical and social rivulets of the time. Domestic playing fed the musical life of the nation and was in turn fed by the circulation of a large and diverse body of genres through tutoring, sheet music, instruments, visiting artists, salons, and serf orchestras. In and out of the home, one could hear solo or group singing of folk songs. This environment shaped not only Glinka's creative life, but also the lives of Russian composers who grew up in this era but became famous only near the end of it or in the decades following serf emancipation in 1861: Dargomyzhsky (born 1813); Serov (1820); Anton Rubinstein (1829); Borodin (1833); Cui (1835); Balakirev (1836); Musorgsky (1839); Tchaikovsky (1840); Rimsky-Korsakov (1844). The oldest, Dargomyzhsky was close to fifty and the youngest, Rimsky-Korsakov, seventeen when serfdom and the creative system around it came to an end.

The genius of the composer Glinka found nourishment in an entire range of musical sounds and forms from peasant songs to European orchestral works. As a child on the family estate of Novospasskoe in Smolensk Province, he apparently could distinguish the bell ringing of every church in the vicinity which alternately used the dominant chiming modes (*raspevy*) of the time: Smolensky, Tikhvinsky, and Vladimirsky. Bell sounds were especially audible and evocative in the hushed surroundings of the countryside: Novospasskoe lay, as it still does, very deep in the woodlands. And, like Pushkin, Glinka supposedly absorbed national folk culture from his peasant nanny, though there is little notice of it in his memoirs. Glinka recounts that as a child he drank in the tunes of Smolensk Province and that they helped shape his musical consciousness. He clearly drew from folk songs sung by serfs and the road songs of coachmen, but the process of "imbibing" the music of the *narod* (the popular masses) was not as unconscious or mystical as the mythology would have it.[80]

The memoir of one of Glinka's serfs, Alexei Netoev, dictated a quarter-century after the composer's death, offers some insight into Glinka's mode of adaptation — the conscious borrowing of peasant tunes by an already accomplished composer. Though containing errors and crudities, Netoev's account convincingly describes — in the accents of a loyal servant in old age — the cultural exchange between educated master and talented servant. He recalls how the young Glinka loved to watch and join in peasant dances, songs, and revelry (there is no mention of him carousing with the peasants — though he became a prodigious drinker as an adult). On returning from Petersburg as a grown man, Glinka befriended his serfs, the Netoev brothers: Alexei, a violinist, and Yakov, a cellist and contrabassist. Glinka took Alexei to the capital for further musical training and Yakov remained Glinka's valet. The composer borrowed songs, phrasing, and styles from the serf and in return paid for music lessons to increase his skills. On his visits to Smolensk Province in the years 1828–47, Glinka mingled with peasant musicians from other landed estates. He went round the villages, and invited peasant girls to his home where he transcribed their singing into piano arrangements. He also formed serf choirs and orchestras. Ethnographic research reveals that most of the folk songs that Glinka incorporated into his choral and orchestral work — and even his songs — were simply copied directly by him when he was already an adult composer.[81]

Glinka has never been accused of plagiarism, any more than has Beethoven, who used Russian folk themes in two of his quartets, though Glinka has often been presented as a lone figure in a more or less deserted field. There is nothing surprising about Glinka's musical sources in the backwoods of Smolensk; after all he drew also from the environs of St. Petersburg, Finland, Orël Province, Ukraine, and the Caucasus as well as from Poland, Germany, France, Italy, and Spain. Some commentators saw folk structure — sharp contrasts of mood, tempo, volumes — in Glinka as opposed to mere copying of folk songs. But, as Gerald Abraham pointed out many years ago, Glinka and others of this era did not use folk harmony. Though the early influence of village folk songs on Glinka is undeniable, so are many other sources, including classical music that he heard at home. His mother played Mozart on the harpsichord. He heard barcaroles and "the mighty peal of heavy German waltzes." He was also thoroughly trained by Siegfried Dehn and other European masters and was thus wholly familiar with the music of German, French, and Italian composers of the age.[82]

What astonished Glinka most and clearly shaped his later work were the styles and repertoires of his uncle's serf orchestra. Shmakovo, the uncle's home, was one of those magnificent piles of the Catherinian period—at the zenith of gentry luxury—immense and ornate with galleries, ballrooms, dining halls, a theater where plays and concerts where performed. During Glinka's childhood, it retained only a remnant of fading grandeur, the serf orchestra, which the uncle would bring to Novospasskoe about twice a month, sometimes staying over for days at a time. If the acoustics were as good then as they are now in the wooden manor house, the experience must have been a revelation. The programs included overtures and symphonies by the Parisians Cherubini and Méhul; the Germanic masters, Haydn, Mozart, and Beethoven; the noted German cellist Bernhard Romberg, and the Russianized German conductor, Ludwig Maurer. When they played classical music and orchestrated folk songs, the young Glinka would join the band and learn to play different instrumental parts. For Glinka, who jokingly called a collection of canaries his "serf orchestra," serf musicians supplemented in childhood the auditory richness of church bells and peasant singing on his estate. Glinka's first spark of inspiration came from the serf orchestra and then from folk song. He needed both to achieve greatness; otherwise, surmises Ugo Persi, he might have become another imitator of Western music or a romantic folk song collector. Glinka's childhood exposure to orchestral music was not exactly a model for other future composers of greatness. The young Rimsky-Korsakov heard only piano and a few instruments of itinerant musicians in the quiet little northern town of Tikhvin. But when he heard in St. Petersburg the works fully orchestrated that he had played again and again in childhood, he was enraptured and later became one of the paramount symphonic orchestrators of all time.[83]

The British scholar Stuart Campbell aptly speaks of the "fragmentary quality of musical life" in this era, the awareness of which accelerated concertizing.[84] The conditions were vastly improved by the establishment by Anton Rubinstein of the Russian Musical Society in 1859 and the St. Petersburg conservatory a few years later. Campbell's comment applies to the public sphere, particularly concert and theater performance of serious music. But fragmentation is a relative thing and is not the same as weakness or absence of musical life. The public symphonic concert scene was indeed modest, compared to that in the German states and other European countries of that era; but opera and ballet flourished grandly in the capitals and the provinces. All genres were constantly expanding, and this expansion owed much to the constant sustenance of music in the home, where musical sounds not only sensitized the minds of composers such as Glinka but also trained the "Russian ear" to the rich possibilities of music that would come in the following generation to conquer masses of listeners all over the world.

3

In Search of a Concert Hall

All the arts have their own magical effects on us, but not a single one of them reaches into the innermost feelings of our soul so deeply as music, and especially music cleansed of any adulterations, music without verses, without dances, without spectacles, music powerful in itself, in the romantic sphere of the ideal, that is — music expressed in the symphony!
— *M. D. Rezvoi, 1841*

Mikhail Glinka broke the barrier to Russian secular art music; it fell to Anton Rubinstein to build a permanent institution on which it could rest. This required concert facilities, a public attuned to musical masterpieces, and a central educational establishment. The last named, in the form of a conservatory, arrived last. The other two unrolled slowly, beginning at the turn of the century three decades before Rubinstein was born. But, if the evolution of public musicality beyond the private sphere of home and salon walked a vexed and uneven road, that road was rich in musical experience and, for the historian, full of stories about how it intersected with society. To the extent that the concert hall served as a training ground for the musical ear and an instrument of cultural identity, listeners gradually learned to shed visual, dramatic, and other extramusical associations integral to song, opera, ballet, and melodrama in order to experience the relatively abstract instrumental music of symphony and chamber concerts and solo recitals. James H. Johnson has shown that among Paris audiences in this period, listening habits shifted from scenic and textual guidance to an engagement with sonorities, forms, and harmonies, from "thinking of hunts, battles, and queens to focus on purely musical logic." The social dimension of this shift saw an increase in audience etiquette and a reduction in coughing, conversation, and movement in the hall. Johnson shows how this shift simultaneously made for a more individualized consumption and a new sense of shared aesthetic experience—amounting almost to piety. The concert milieux in Paris eventually ceased being minicourts or houses of fashion and became "temples of art."[1]

How soon did Russians heed the words of army engineer, amateur painter, composer, and cellist M. D. Rezvoi, who in the quotation at the head of this chapter praised "music without verses, without dances, without spectacles"?[2] Though not wholly answerable, the question is worth pondering. A study of concert programs, reinforced by contemporary observations, indicates that through most of the early nineteenth century, quiet reverence and concentration on the "long line" offered by entire symphonies did not come easy to most Russian concertgoers. The operatic voice soared in popularity over the orchestra, as did shorter instrumental works over longer ones. People tended to talk more during instrumental playing. To put it another way, public space long remained beholden to the habitus of private space; the concert programs —though grander in scale—still partly matched the mixed-genre evenings of salons and other home performances. Yet toward the end of the period, some evidence emerges of a mood change. Glinka, well aware of old habits, showed delight at audience reaction and attentiveness to his *Kamarinskaya,* an early example of orchestrated Russian thematics. Odoevsky, at an 1847 concert, noted with glee the public's keen reception of a Berlioz program. In 1859 he claimed that "the artistic sensibility of our public is growing more and more." The composer Alexander Serov, who could be haughty as a critic, in 1856 happily reported a postconcert conversation with a merchant who, in spite of some confusion about genres, had become a great enthusiast.[3]

It would be useless to attempt to reconstruct a hierarchy of listening modes such as that proposed in a rather schematic way by the twentieth-century social philosopher and musicologist Theodor Adorno, with its "structural listener," "good listener," "cultural consumer," and so on. Critics then and now bemoaned audiences' eclectic tastes. Lamenting hybrid performance practice, Eleanora Fradkina in 1994 reprinted the program of a Philharmonia concert of March 1859. The first half: Beethoven's Fifth Symphony, an aria from Mendelssohn's *Elijah,* the first movement of the Beethoven Violin Concerto, the "Sanctus" from his *Missa Solemnis,* an excerpt from Wagner's *Tann-*

häuser, and the finale of Glinka's *Life for the Tsar.* The second half: the last two movements of the Beethoven concerto, an aria from Glinka's *Ruslan and Lyudmila,* a solo piece for the Ophicleide, an aria from Halévy's *La juive,* and the finale of Mozart's Jupiter Symphony. Fradkina, reflecting both a twentieth-century elitism and a Russian purist version of it, shudders over the division of the violin concerto, the little "doses" from opera, and the intrusion of a "dessert": the Ophicleide, a popular brass instrument invented in 1817 (not 1821, as she says). Fradkina is dismayed that such a serious conductor as Carl Schuberth (1811–1863) offered this pot-pourri. But Schuberth could feel the pulse of his audiences. This meant getting them to the hall, and pleasing while "uplifting" them — a strategy that has been used by conductors, when suitable, right up to our own time. Schuberth may have shared the tastes of Glinka and Odoevsky; but he also knew the tolerance level of the public.[4]

Russian concert audiences hardly differed from those of Europe at midcentury. They could noisily request the encore of a movement or section, and the conductor could accommodate or not.[5] Only rarely did scandals erupt. The most serious, and hilarious, occurred in Petersburg in 1855 or 1856 at a Gentry Club Philharmonia concert of the music of Alexandre Lazareff, conducted by himself. Lazareff, billed as a "noted Russian composer," but one unnoted in the annals of Russian music, issued calling cards with the device "ami de Rossini"; he later wrote a book comparing himself with Beethoven. After the first set, Odoevsky, choirmaster Gavriil Lomakin, and the composers Serov and Dargomyzhsky were up in arms. Serov mounted a chair and shouted angry words at the conductor-composer; the two men hurled things at each other; the audience — divided in sympathy — howled, and the orchestra engaged in cacophony. The police arrested the combatants and a half-dozen others and the concert ended in infamy.[6] This and a few other minor skirmishes constituted exceptions in the otherwise placid progress of symphonic performance in public. The Lazareff affair — in no way comparable to the radical premieres of Victor Hugo's *Hernani* or of Stravinsky's *Rite of Spring* — resulted simply from the disgust of musical esthetes at apparently bad music played by a very bad conductor. The problems faced by lovers of symphonic music in Russia ran much deeper — even to the lack of a permanent venue or fixed orchestra. The present-day Philharmonia, firmly anchored to its home and fully attended, is a far cry from its ancestor.

Philharmonia and Capella

The Great Hall of the St. Petersburg Philharmonia is among the most photogenic concert sites in the world. Documentary and feature film makers have for decades panned across the symmetrical seating of the parterre, the Corinthian columns, the great organ behind the stage, the balcony. The interior geography has not changed much in a century and a half, and the civic austerity introduced in Soviet times cannot hide the fact that this was once a ballroom. Its balcony — where Liszt, Shostakovich, and Stravinsky have stood — was designed for a dance orchestra. Old woodcuts and photos capture the former versatility of its private and festive character: potted palms, garlands of flowers, chairs removed for dancing or a charity bazaar (fig. 15). These pictures eloquently depict the Great Hall as the spatial heart of collective gentry life.[7] When the Gentry Club of St. Petersburg in 1836 first rented the hall to the Philharmonic Society, that hall — which in 1943 would serve as a virtual emblem of the city's wartime spiritual survival — was the playpen of aristocrat pleasure. The power of the capital's corporate gentry class at mid-nineteenth century and the grandeur of its headquarters stands in contrast to the then relative insignificance of the Philharmonic Society that would some day give the hall its name (fig. 16).

The St. Petersburg Philharmonic Society or Philharmonia, no latecomer on the European scene, emerged in 1803, a decade before the British Philharmonia and several decades before those of Vienna and Berlin. But the chronology is misleading. A "Philharmonia" is an organization that offers concerts to the public (or part of the public) on a regular basis. In this, Russia lagged behind Europe. The long haul in establishing regular concert life in western Europe began in the 1670s and was mostly complete by 1800 in all but official nomenclature. Russia — in the familiar telescoping process of late borrowing and rapid adaptation — squeezed through this stage in the half-century between the founding of the Philharmonia in 1802 and of the Russian Musical Society in 1859. Russia borrowed European patterns that had emerged ad hoc. Christian dogma prohibited theater productions during the Lenten season, theater being seen as a sensuous pleasure — like meat and sex. Since music was not so vilified, Lent became the original concert season. Jean-Baptiste Lully in Louis XIV's France pioneered in nurturing the public's appetite for nontheatrical music. His followers in eighteenth-century Paris began the *Concerts spirituels* in 1725. Concertizing took place at the Leipzig Cloth Hall (Gewandhaus), in Vienna, and in Britain from the 1760s onward. Imported into St. Petersburg from these traditions were the absence of a permanent location and a regular conductor, a preponderance of amateur musicians, and the rarity of rehearsals. As the century turned, figures such as Spontini, Weber, Mendelssohn, and Spohr in various ways infused their orchestras with discipline and professionalism. Control and standardization via metronome and a podium conductor gradually eroded improvisation. All over Europe, audiences of courtiers and magnates widened to include a large urban public. Groups that were broad in terms of repertoire, audience, and the use of professional musicians challenged the older elitist societies dominated by aristocrats.[8]

In addition to the customary shortages plaguing European concert life — of skilled players, interested audiences, and available space — Russia faced a particularly heavy foreign domination of its orchestras and the absence of those European musical infrastructures created in previous centuries. At the start, the St. Petersburg Philharmonia was an outpost of Germanic musical culture in terms of patrons, musicians, and repertoire. It hardly differed from music societies in Riga and other Baltic German centers. With little outreach and no chain of local singing and orchestral societies and schools to feed it, the Philharmonia did not act as a central nervous system of early nineteenth-century Russian concert life, for there were few outlying limbs with living nerves connected to the center. But it certainly launched the enterprise from which other efforts grew. Petersburg's and Moscow's public concert life in the 1770s began modestly. Prior to that, performance of classical music was almost strictly confined to court circles and the aristocracy. The prerevolutionary historian N. F. Findeizen cites only a handful of public concerts from the 1740s to the 1760s in St. Petersburg. During the last quarter of the century, gentry clubs, musical "kloby," and private theaters grew apace — especially after the gentry reforms of Catherine II. Some of the antecedents were elaborated private salons turned into concert space: a Musical Club in St. Petersburg, founded in the 1770s lasted until the end of the century; a Musical Society met at the Buturlin family home in the 1790s. What the listeners heard in these places was the kind of serious music sweeping Europe at the time: symphonies by German masters, and oratorios and masses written by now relatively forgotten Italian and German composers, together with such canonical masterpieces as Pergolesi's *Stabat Mater* (1736), Mozart's *Requiem* (1791), and Haydn's *Creation* (1798).[9]

One the eve of the Philharmonia's founding, the musical scene in the Russian capital came under the scrutiny of the German Ludwig Spohr (1784–1859), ranked in his day alongside Beethoven, Kreutzer, and Viotti as a major composer for the violin. A popular conductor, said to be the first to wield the baton, Spohr made contacts mostly with foreigners — Germans from Baltic towns and Petersburg, as well as Clementi, Field, and the crowd at the (French-speaking) Bürgerclub. But Spohr was present at the *Creation,* so to speak; he played in the inaugural Haydn concert of the St. Petersburg Philharmonia in March 1802. In the previous autumn, a banker to the court of Tsar Alexander I, Baron Alexander Rahl (Rall), held one of his regular music evenings, where a recent returnee from Europe described the enthusiastic notices that Haydn was getting. So great was the reverence in this circle for Haydn, then at the peak of his European fame, that the St. Petersburg Philharmonic Society was launched that night in his honor. A Haydn concert was planned and its organizers — mostly Russian Germans — became the founding members of the society. Composed of musicians from court theaters and patrons, including Yury Vielgorsky — father of Mikhail and Matvei — the society's twofold mission was to awaken in the public an interest in classical music; and to assist financially the widows and orphans of deceased musicians. Thus the motto: "To Comfort the Living."[10]

The four performances of Haydn's *Creation* on March 24 and 31, 1802, formed a landmark in Russian musical history. The receipts financed the initial activities of the Philharmonia. The performances took place in Engelhardt House which established that place as the main site of Philharmonia concerts up to the 1840s. The orchestra of Petersburg's Bolshoi Stone Theater included some outsiders. Spohr's participation in the first violin section had no further resonance (he claimed, by the way, that the orchestra had seventy violins, thirty contrabasses, and doubled winds). But it helped make fourteen-year-old Mikhail Vielgorsky, who played second violin, into a supreme musical patron and amateur impresario of the early nineteenth century. The chorus in these performances was the Court Chapel Choir or Capella. The impact of its magnificent voices and the genius of Haydn's music on Russian musicians and music lovers was tremendous. *Creation* became an annual event of the Philharmonia along with other choral works. In terms of listening experience, it may well be — as in Paris — that audiences new to large-scale works of this sort were enticed at least partly by the programmatic elements in Haydn's work: the orchestral mimicry of primeval chaos and the successive creation by the deity of day and night, the earth, the seas, and living creatures. By 1807, the society had hardened into a real institution, with an imperial prefix, state patronage, a charter, and about a hundred members.[11]

The pale blue mansion on the corner of the Nevsky Prospect and Griboedov Canal, Engelhardt House, has from 1949 borne the name Maly Zal or Small Hall of the Philharmonia (fig. 17). Visitors to Russia are hardly aware of it, as indeed are most Petersburgers who know the building only as a subway entrance. Yet for over half a century (1789–1846) the second floor of this house was the capital's main concert venue. For about a decade after 1789 its hall was rented out for concerts and balls and was dubbed the Sâle Lyon after the Frenchman who leased it. It passed first to a merchant and real estate magnate in 1799, and then in 1828 to his son-in-law Prince Vasily Engelhardt who gave it a new decor and a long-lasting name. The gorgeous columned foyer with ornamented mirrors lent optical depth to the interior space. In the spirit of cultural versatility, the place served as a favorite scene of testimonial dinners and of masques in the 1830s for Petersburg high society. It is best remembered by literary scholars as the setting for Mikhail Lermontov's *Masquerade*.[12]

By the 1840s, the Engelhardt House was suffering from poor upkeep. The visiting Clara Schumann noted its cold, dark squalor. The last concert there in the nineteenth century was held in 1846. Merchants bought the building and turned it into a shop. The Philharmonic Society and other concert organizers had to move around to the homes of rich patrons, though these had difficulty accommodating the growing audiences. Enter the St. Petersburg Gentry Club. The architect Carlo Rossi and his colleagues finished the Hôtel Péterbourg (later named l'Europe) in 1834 across the square from the Mikhailovsky Palace; and by 1839 they had built the new Gentry Club in matching style across the street. In 1846, its Great Hall became the new, though irregular, home of the Philharmonia. Troubles arose on both sides: some in the society considered the hall acoustically unsuitable due to the thick stone columns; and club administrators sometimes showed reluctance to host concerts except when foreign celebrities were on the program.[13]

In the early decades, the Philharmonia offered the towering choral and symphonic works of the German and Italian masters, excepting of course Bach who was only revived by Mendelssohn and others in the 1820s. From 1802 to 1860 it gave 127 concerts, usually in January and March, and sometimes in November or December — averaging a bit more than two a year. The repertoire of the 1800s — Haydn, Mozart, Handel, Johann Nepomuk Hummel (1778–1837), Giuseppe Sarti — was extended in the following decade to Luigi Cherubini, Tepper, Beethoven, and Pergolesi. On March 26, 1824, Beethoven's *Missa solemnis* had its world premiere in St. Petersburg, the only time it was performed in the composer's lifetime; the next full versions came in Cologne, Leipzig, and Bonn in 1844. Beethoven's Ninth Symphony got its first Russian performance in 1836. But the rather purist classical profile was somewhat modified by the inclusion of Rossini's *Thieving Magpie* overture played by two hundred musicians from a Guards regiment, and of Beethoven's *Wellington Symphony* (*The Battle of Victoria*, 1813), a military potboiler which made Beethoven admirers such as Mikhail Vielgorsky hold their noses. Under Nicholas I, the offerings became more secular and contemporary, but still largely European, with a glittering array of foreign composers and virtuosos. By the end of the era, Italian opera selections held center stage at the Philharmonia concerts, a fact loudly lamented by certain critics.[14]

Who came? In the eighteenth century, according to one account, the aristocracy paid what they wanted at concerts, a practice that reflected its enmity to the cash nexus in general, and as applied to pleasure in particular. Here we have the same social mentality — anchored in a domestic universe with its tight circles of friends—that induced noble hosts to "tip" musicians (as did the tsars) rather than paying them a fixed fee; an outlook that led the Moscow hosts of Franz Liszt ticketless onto the concert stage to hear "their friend" perform. When concert tickets emerged, they were pricey enough to keep away the poor. Sketchy data suggest that they ran to about fifteen paper rubles under Alexander I and from about one to ten under Nicholas I. Early in this period, concerts started at 9:00 P.M., which would tend to inhibit the lower classes from attendance, and would fit perfectly into the leisure-driven clock of high society where late night balls and suppers were commonplace. Faddei Bulgarin afforded a fleeting glimpse of nonnoble concert attendees in the 1830s. Speaking of the public who came to Engelhardt House for music, he cautiously applauded the mingling of classes. This certified villain of Russian literature and journalism preached a little sermon to high society about its duty to mingle with the merchants and tradesmen who were constantly at their service in shops and businesses. Bulgarin was not speaking of the urban masses. During this era, one still had to pass through two gates in order to attend elite concerts: one of money, one of class. Yury Arnold observed that it took a long time for the Russian public to become attuned to serious symphonic music. Aside from the rarified art, other forces retarded its growth in Russia in the first half of the century. Neither Alexander I nor Nicholas I attended concerts on a regular basis. Fashionable circles tended to follow monarchs to their entertainments. The rage for foreign divas and virtuosos dictated a repertoire of short pieces and crowd-pleasers rather than the longer, more complicated works.[15]

The "German" coloration of the Philharmonia remained in place throughout the period. People with names like Grimm, Fuchs, Haberzettel, and Meinhard still ran it a quarter-century after its founding; and in 1852 a letter to Mikhail Vielgorsky from its board contained ten signatories, only one of which was recognizably Russian, the rest being mostly German. With a letterhead in gothicized Cyrillic, the document is a real artifact of interethnic culture in Imperial Russia—a Germanic body writing in French to an ethnic Pole high in Russian service. After the death of Guillaume-Alexis Paris (1756–1840), a Belgian who had came in 1799 to St. Petersburg to conduct opera and who regularly conducted the Philharmonia concerts, Russian Germans—Ludwig Maurer, Karl Albrecht, Carl Schuberth (1811–63), and others—took the podium. Arnold noted that the players, drawn mostly from the theater orchestras, were 90 percent foreign and mostly German.[16] The Teutonic dictatorship in Russian concert music was only a bit more thoroughgoing than that in Britain. Indeed, most European countries of the time were "occupied" by foreign musical forces: Italians, Germans, and Frenchmen. Invaders, though rarely in coalition, descended upon their objectives to conquer musical markets, audiences, and jobs. In the first decades of the century, they were joined by the detritus of war and revolution — refugees seeking shelter and a living. What sociologists call coping strategies led them to teach or perform in whatever skills they possessed. German hegemony in Russia was more socially complex because part of it was based on the large presence of German-Russians, native or permanent residents or people of Baltic origin. As Tsar Alexander I had put it in 1806 in justifying, though lamenting, the use of "well-known foreigners of proven talent": "can we postpone events until our nationals become masters of every function that they have to perform?"[17] From a musical point of view, the German hegemony proved advantageous in the early years of the Philharmonia due to its members' familiarity with the newest and best German and Austrian music.

Like symphonic societies elsewhere, the Philharmonia had been formed under the inspiration of a particular composer or composers. In England and America, it was Haydn and Handel; on the continent of Europe, Beethoven. The symphonic genre and the large-scale choral work created the need for space: for the orchestra, the audience, and acoustical reproduction. Such spaces transcended the "narrow sociability of noble society for the broad performance space of the modern concert hall." Within a very short time, however, those spaces in Europe proliferated and the performances in them multiplied far beyond the experience of Imperial Russia (Vienna put on 111 concerts during the 1826–27 season; London at about the same time mounted 125). Concert life in the Russia of serfdom thus became another of the many markers of how fast a public sphere could grow.[18]

The word "Capella" denotes both the Imperial Court Chapel Choir (*Imperatorskaya Pridvornaya Pevcheskaya Kapella*) and the exquisite hall housing it, presently known as the State Academic Capella of St. Petersburg. This architectural gem spans a courtyard off the Moika River, with an interior of modest dimensions and magnificent acoustics. Like the Engelhardt House, it is less-known to the world of visitors than the famous Philharmonia Hall. The oldest professional choir in Russia was founded in 1479 in Moscow as an adult male ensemble for the Uspensky Cathedral and court functions. Under Peter the Great, it moved to St. Petersburg, traveled with him in Europe, and was designated the Imperial Capella with eventually over a hundred men and boys. With the incursion of the music of Corelli and Telemann in the 1720s followed by wave after wave of Italian masters and teachers and composers, the Capella alternated between sacred music and service on the opera stage. As a result, the choir achieved a European level of vocal brilliance, technique, and suppleness. The price was the Italianization of style. A churchman complained in

1799 that when the doctored "melodies were sung the church was more like an Italian opera house than a house for reverent prayer to the Almighty." Various efforts to Russianize the music were launched in the early nineteenth century.[19]

Unlike some of the Italian states which employed castrati up until the middle of the nineteenth century, the Capella used boy sopranos. From the 1730s onward, grandees from the south began bringing talented youths with them to the capitals. For real or imagined reasons, Ukraine henceforth became a recruitment region for young voices well into the nineteenth century. The Capella maintained from 1738 to sometime before 1773 a permanent base at the inaptly named town of Glukhov (meaning "of the deaf") in Ukraine where the far from tone-deaf boys, aged six to fourteen, got preliminary training. Among Ukrainian recruits who achieved renown through the Capella were the composers Bortnyansky, Varlamov, and Stepan Davydov, the painter Anton Losenko, and any number of lovers of empresses Elizabeth and Catherine. Though the Capella, all male until the Revolution, has been called "the only professional academy of music in Russia" until 1862, it offered instrumental training only sporadically. When their voices changed, boys with the best voices were kept on as adult singers, given rank XIV on the Table of Ranks, and freed if they were serfs. Thus the Capella, like the Theater School and the Academy of Arts, was another little-noticed agency of recruitment into freedom. Those not selected, also ranked, went to monastic choirs or theoretically got jobs as clerks in government service.[20]

Of the Russian directors who came after the Italians, Dmitry Bortnyansky (1751–1825) achieved the greatest distinction, and his music still looms large in the Russian choral repertoire. A Ukrainian son of a military man, he was born in Glukhov, which probably accounts for his early recruitment into the Court Capella, at age six or seven. Scholars say little about his parents or how they gave him up. In Petersburg, he studied with Baldassare Galuppi and traveled to Italy. After minor posts, Bortnyansky served as Capella director from 1796 to 1825. By 1817, the choir had twenty-four boys and men. Bortnyansky partly succeeded in "de-Italianizing" the choir. His successor from 1825 to his death in 1836, Fëdor Lvov, was a dilettante known for the concerts at his home in the 1810s.[21]

The European reputation that the Capella acquired in the early nineteenth century is largely attributable to its director from 1837 to 1861, General Alexei Lvov, who succeeded his father. Until 1859 the Capella's participation in the annual Philharmonia concerts made it integral to the musical life of the city. Hector Berlioz, in an oft-quoted remark about the choir which had sung his own music, wrote: "to compare the singing of the Sistine Chapel choir in

Rome with these glorious singers is like comparing a miserable little bunch of scratchers from a third-rate Italian theater with the orchestra of the Paris conservatory." The ensemble that Berlioz actually heard was the Capella amplified for his needs by voices from the Imperial Theaters. But the judgment still stands. Robert Schumann likened its octave basses to the low tones of an organ and its tenors to female voices. Lvov tried to enhance the musicianship of his singers in instrumental classes, in order to prepare them for jobs in orchestras, then held mostly by Germans. The theater musicians opposed this and the Imperial Theaters director lobbied to gut the program, even though some of it was financed out of Lvov's pocket. Lvov also waged a musical struggle that went beyond the bounds of his own ensemble. From 1816 onward, the director of the Capella had been ex officio arbiter of church music throughout the empire. By the time of Nicholas I, many liturgical choirs had succumbed to "bad habits" which Lvov campaigned against. An ambitious man, he won the authority to approve all liturgical music performed in Russia, and he promoted his own compositions freely, along with those of Bortnyansky and a few others. Lvov even forced all choir teachers to take training at the Capella in order to keep their jobs.[22]

Despite his impressive accomplishments and dedication to choral music, Lvov suffered at the hands of later historians, especially in the Soviet period, because of his contentious relationship with the cultural hero Mikhail Glinka. After the success of his opera *A Life for the Tsar,* Glinka served at the Capella under Lvov in 1837–39 as kapellmeister, which came to mean teacher, composer, arranger, and rehearsal conductor. In addition to these duties, Glinka went on recruiting singers in Ukraine, an experience he enjoyed. According to a Soviet editor of Glinka's memoirs, the appointment was suggested by "the musical reactionary and personal foe of Glinka, A. F. Lvov," as a way to tame a man who had too much popularity in society. This story is confirmed by other accounts. Lvov clearly envied Glinka and used his power to deflect glory away from him. It is generally believed also that Lvov relied heavily on the talented ex-serf Gavriil Lomakin who had moved from the Sheremetev choir to the Capella in 1848 as assistant director for rehearsals and training, but took the baton himself for public concerts. All this must be balanced by Lvov's major contribution to music-making at a high level, at home, in the Capella, and in the concert hall.[23]

Evenings with the Orchestra

The year 1812 called into being many institutions, long- and short-lived, to help those widowed and orphaned by the war. One of them became a useful partner of the Philharmonia: the Society of Patriotic Ladies (later St. Petersburg Women's Patriotic Society). Founded by Empress Elizabeth and a group of aristocratic women in November 1812, it created among other things a girls' school that became the Patriotic Institute in 1822. The society, a perfect blend of the patriotic and the patrician, viewed music as the natural coinage of charity and began in 1815 hosting fund-raising concerts. As an august sponsor of charity, the society could enable people to perform who were otherwise restricted from public appearance due to rank, such as the foreign celebrity Henriette Sontag and the Vielgorskys. At an 1837 concert, Matvei Vielgorsky performed a cello concerto and his brother played in the orchestra while titled male and female amateurs with illustrious names sang in the chorus. Throughout the period, charity served as an ideal link between private effort, upper-class performance, and public service. The garrulous prophet of sentimentalism Pëtr Shalikov commented transparently on the intimate tie between philanthropy and philharmonics. "Talent," he wrote in *The Ladies' Journal*, "is all the dearer when it is used to succor our neighbors," and music served two impulses: friendship among equals and benevolence to the poor.[24]

Although classical music performance still partly depended on the imperial purse or a princely Maecenas, it continued to flourish in the capital. The Imperial Theaters Directorate ran its own concert series during the Lenten season in order to keep the revenue flowing when plays, operas, and ballets were banned. The Directorate got around the ban on "theater" partially by luring audiences to concerts accompanied by *tableaux vivants* composed of ballet dancers and actors. Of the forty concerts given in the Lenten season of 1839, the theater orchestras gave seventeen. Of the rest, twenty-one were private or amateur affairs; only two were given by the Philharmonia.[25]

The concert scene got a boost in 1842 with the launching of the Musical Exercises of St. Petersburg University Students (the term was adapted from the Paris Conservatoire concerts), commonly known as the Musical Mornings, presented on Sundays in the three-hundred-seat university Ceremonial Hall where generations of Russian and foreign students right up to the present have received their diplomas. The amateur violist A. I. Fitzthum von Eckstedt (Fitstum fon Ekshted), a retired army colonel and a popular inspector of students, inaugurated student music evenings and formed an orchestra. This assortment of, at its peak, about fifty-sixty amateur students and nonstudents performed without benefit of rehearsal and got help from some distinguished participants. Carl Schuberth of the Philharmonia regularly conducted; Mily Balakirev made his St. Petersburg debut there as a pianist; and Anton Rubinstein, though no friend of amateurism, debuted as a replacement conductor there in the 1850s and generously praised the orchestra in his memoirs. The composer

Alexander Serov gave one of Russia's first lecture courses on music history at the university in 1858. The Sunday morning performance time allowed a varied audience which reflected a growing interest in concert music among those not admitted to the high altitudes of salons and the more exclusive concerts — students, high school pupils, minor officials, members of the non-gentry intelligentsia.[26]

Soviet historians have with some justice seen the university concerts as the "first swallow" of democratic concert life in terms of the mixed audience. The journalist and children's writer of the 1930s M. Ilin (Marshak) went further and found democracy even in the musical programs. He cited the attendance of the young Alexander Borodin at the university concerts, which he contrasted with the "elitist" programs of sweet arias by visiting Italian divas and the acrobatics of virtuoso instrumentalists.[27] But in fact visiting soloists such as the singer Pauline Viardot also appeared at the Morning Concerts from time to time; and it is doubtful that its audiences, including Borodin, would have shunned other virtuosos. The largely symphonic offerings of the Morning Concerts were in fact elitist by both European and Russian standards of the time. If nationwide university enrollment figures are a guide, the frequency of these concerts and their growth in orchestra size and quality coincided with a rise in gentry enrollments from 1843 to 1848.[28] The influx of home-trained student players suggests their gentry origins. Thus the Mornings presented young people from the gentry and other social groups who possessed amateur music skills performing in a professional setting. The musicians (though unpaid) faced a large socially heterogeneous paying audience in a public space and were led by and accompanied well-known professional musicians in serious symphonic music. The university expanded the offerings of classical music in a city where these were still limited. From 1849 onward, the number of annual concerts jumped to ten a year. The university concerts ended in March 1861 after student disorders, just as new Russian musical establishments were being founded and at the moment when disturbances were ushering in an age of rebellion. Concert life within the university walls virtually ceased until 1883. But by then an entire concert network had been well established.

The Vielgorsky brothers and Alexei Lvov, major figures in the creation of musical life in the Russia of Nicholas I, floated their own concert organizations. The Vielgorskys and M. V. Rezvoi formed the Symphonic Society of St. Petersburg (1839–50) which played about fifteen times a year on Saturdays during the winter at the university or the Capella. Its amateur players performed Haydn, Mozart, Beethoven, and some now forgotten composers. It apparently ended for financial reasons. Mikhail Vielgorsky had spent much of his adult life advancing the cause of serious music in Russia, particularly

through the Philharmonia which celebrated its fiftieth jubilee in 1852 by playing his Second Symphony. Matvei (1794–1866), a cellist, had both a domestic
musical upbringing and exposure to the best in European classical music (fig.
18). During the last campaigns against Napoleon, he traversed Europe in a
Ukrainian cossack regiment and commanded a cuirassier division. Like many
poets, dramatists, and painters of the age, Vielgorsky combined the warrior
with the art lover; and he acquired friendships with master composers, including Luigi Cherubini. After retiring as a colonel in the mid-1820s, he pursued
his avocation as a cellist and composer, and played with visiting musicians
such as Liszt and Vieuxtemps.[29]

Opinions vary on Matvei Vielgorsky's musicianship. His friend, the Decembrist Mikhail Lunin, rhapsodized about his playing of Beethoven by quoting
from the *Russian Primary Chronicle:* "We didn't know whether we were on
earth or in heaven." Anton Rubinstein, also a good friend of Vielgorsky but a
stickler for professionalism, privately had a low opinion of his virtuosity.
Soviet musicology, while always exalting Glinka above his contemporaries,
rendered a different judgment. Vielgorsky's surviving scores show a high technical level. At Potsdam, he played Mendelssohn's Cello Sonata, Op. 56, with
the composer himself at the piano and won his praise. Since Mendelssohn's
cello works demand great virtuosity to retain the lyrical spirit in rapid passages, the respected scholar Boris Shteinpress, writing in the 1940s, gave Vielgorsky high marks as a musician. Another distinguished musicologist, L. S.
Ginzburg, hailed the cellist's technique and composition, basing his judgment
on Vielgorsky's fingering and bowing instructions. The music itself is derivative and slightly Schubertian. Judging from the performance of a surviving
theme and variations for cello and piano, Vielgorsky had a light and charming
touch, anticipating Tchaikovsky's famous *Rococo Variations*.[30]

The Concert Society (1859–80s) owed its birth to Alexei Lvov. Gifted with
a musical ear, he had taken up the violin on the family estate, played in
domestic orchestras, and studied with several German tutors. At age nine,
Lvov debuted with a concerto by Viotti, still a reigning favorite. Like other
high-born amateurs, Lvov alternated his lifelong passion for music with more
prosaic concerns. As a graduate of the Institute of Transportation, he worked
for General Arakcheev in the Military Colonies and eventually rose to become
an adjutant to Tsar Nicholas I. While abroad, he became friendly with Mendelssohn, Schumann, Spontini, and Meyerbeer, the last of whom gave him the
theme for his duet for violin and cello. Lvov performed his own violin concerto with Mendelssohn at the Gewandhaus in Leipzig and with Liszt in Dresden. In European musical circles, the Russian was judged an accomplished
dilettante violinist. In time Lvov received honors from academies in Rome,

Bologna, and Berlin. In Russia, though not permitted to perform for the general public, he could do so without fee to select audiences and at charity events. If the recital was reviewed in print, Lvov could not be named.[31]

Lvov's violin concerto of 1840, subtitled "Three Movements in the Form of a Dramatic Scene," lasts about twenty minutes. Haydnesque in places, it also echoes Beethoven's *Egmont* music in the first movement, though as a whole it is clearly in the Italian school where Lvov had begun. Ever the admirer of Mendelssohn, Lvov seems to have indulged in what Charles Rosen has called "religious kitsch" in a movement marked *andante religioso*. The result is pure and sweet but without any notable generalized piety. Lvov first played it in Russia at the Vielgorskys in honor of Liszt's visit in 1842. Although an eminently pleasing concert piece, this concerto was apparently never again performed afterwards until 1987. Given the relationship of Lvov with the musicians who dominated concert life in the late nineteenth century—especially Anton Rubinstein whose conservatory plans Lvov opposed—this is perhaps not so surprising. The Soviet neglect is even less so.[32]

Lvov's surviving reputation in Russian music, despite all he did for it, is almost solely as the composer of the tsarist national anthem in 1833. Prior to 1816, neither nation nor dynasty possessed an official hymn. In that year, Grand Duke Konstantin, Alexander I's brother, ordered the music to "God Save the King" (the British anthem) to be played for the tsar's arrival in Warsaw—a custom continued on and off until 1833. When Tsar Nicholas voiced a desire for a Russian hymn, Glinka, Vielgorsky, and others tried their hands. Lvov, after many attempts, came home one night and within minutes wrote it out. He asked Zhukovsky to set the tune, at first entitled "Prayer of the Russian People." Zhukovsky wrote an apostrophe to God seeking his protection for the tsar—the latter a synecdoche for the nation: "God Save the Tsar! / Mighty, autocratic / Hold sway to glory, / To our glory. / Strike fear in our foes, / Orthodox tsar. / God Save the Tsar!" Lvov tried, in the melody, to combine the spirit of Church, people, and army. In November 1833 the Capella first sang the new hymn with two military bands, Lvov's father conducting. Tsar Nicholas demanded three more playings after which he shook the composer's hand, kissed him and said: "Thank you, thank you, marvelous— you have understood me completely!" Later the composer had the words "God Save the Tsar" inserted into his coat of arms.[33]

The first large-scale public performance of the new anthem took place at the Moscow Bolshoi Theater on December 11, 1833, in the rather irreverent company of one-act vaudevilles and ethnic dances. By one account, the four-hundred singers, including a dramatic troupe, students, and several orchestras and bands were greeted by an audience that rose to its feet. In the capital, the public first heard the hymn in 1834 at the Alexandrinsky Theater. Henceforth, the imperial anthem became routinely heard at the conclusion of concerts, sometimes with amplified musical forces to enhance its emotional power. A biographer quotes Lvov saying that "in a flash it was known in every regiment, all over Russia, and all over Europe as well." Already in December 1833, the notes were circulated throughout the army and then spread to provincial towns. After the rise of a network of provincial orchestras in the late nineteenth century, the national hymn was heard everywhere — and, in the Russian manner, repeated several times after all kinds of performances. Ironically the British, who had supplied the predecessor to Lvov's work, now adapted and sung his melody in churches. Lvov's anthem was adapted to the concert stage as a concert piece for cello in the 1870s.[34] With its use in Tchaikovsky's *1812 Overture* and *Marche Slave* the world has long been familiar.

Lvov's Concert Society, the last important musical body formed before the advent of the Russian Musical Society, was created with the help of Rezvoi, the Vielgorskys, and Odoevsky, and was prompted by a schism. As Capella director, Lvov had regularly offered its sumptuous hall and its singers for Philharmonia concerts. When that body began featuring Italian opera excerpts, Lvov ended the collaboration and launched his own organization of three annual Lenten concerts. Primarily designed to further European symphonic music, especially that of Beethoven, they occasionally enlisted the artistry of singers Rubini, Tamburini, Mario, and Viardot — though this contradicted Lvov's alleged reasons for the break with the Philharmonia. Lvov programmed his own *Stabat Mater,* a work very much in the tradition of Haydn, Pergolesi, and Rossini, and made a few solo performances. The society catered to a select audience, including the royal family. Ticket prices, ten rubles for men and six for women for the three annual concerts, would not alone account for the attendance at these "aristocratic concerts."[35] Invitation lists or other forms of clearance used in Europe were doubtlessly employed. But the real proof of the privateness of these events was the fact that high-ranking amateurs could face an audience of social equals such as they would meet in each other's homes. Lvov may have had multiple motives in creating the Concert Society, but the result was the reprivatization of musical space at a moment when it was expanding elsewhere. General Lvov's position, both as "victim," unable to perform to a broad public, and as agent of audience restriction, illuminates perfectly the artistically impoverishing power of the prevailing socio-cultural system embedded in an ascriptive society.

Unlike the amateur university concerts, neither the Symphonic Society nor the Concert Society paid much heed to Russian composers, except for occasional works by Lvov and the Vielgorskys. Under Alexander I and his predecessors, Russian instrumental music rarely made it into the concert hall — as opposed to the opera. A compilation of mentions of composers in the journals, 1800–1860, gives a sense of the dominance of European over Russian music in the news — even more so if one subtracts the mentions of operas by Glinka and others. A few neglected composers should be noted. Jozef Kozlowski (Osip Kozlovsky, 1757–1831), a Polish nobleman, had been working in Russia since 1786, first as a cavalry major and then as musician for Prince Potëmkin. He produced a wide variety of solo voice, choral, and instrumental works — particularly versions of the polonaise of his native land. A recording of two of these performed by a chamber ensemble gives a sense of his elegant style — polished and stately, without the furor later associated with that form in Chopin. In the late eighteenth century, dance pieces (allemande, écossaise, mazurka) adhered to rhythmic control for the sake of coordinated dancers.[36] Alexei Zhilin (1766–1848 or later), a composer and pianist from a Kursk gentry family, blind from childhood, in 1808–18 taught and conducted at the St. Petersburg Institute for the Blind and made at least one appearance, in 1811, at the Philharmonia. Surviving in recordings are romances, piano pieces, and a waltz for viola and piano written in a carnival spirit like barrel organ music — the mark of many early waltzes. His elegiac Variations on "Doves Sitting on an Oak" for piano contains passages reminiscent of Beethoven.[37] The music of Kozlowski and Zhilin, thoroughly European in construction, sometimes contained Russian themes. Kozlowski went to popular sites to listen to folk and urban songs. These composing and performing noblemen, perhaps because of background or handicap, stand as special cases, as do the few serf composers who also appeared in public.

In the 1850s, Vladimir Odoevsky, who also adored European symphonic classics, set out to correct the rarity of Russian pieces in concert programs. "A *Russian* concert," he wrote in 1850, "consisting *exclusively of the work of Russian musicians,* until now seemed an impossible cause." The reason, he argued with some venom, was the interminable performance of Italian opera music, which he called "macaroni." Odoevsky had been lamenting Rossini worship since 1824 when he entered a fleeting debate over the virtues of that composer versus Mozart. Though not an operaphobe, Odoevsky nursed a major grudge against the tyranny of Italian opera and the grand opera of Giacomo Meyerbeer. Consumers of symphonic music everywhere constantly decried the "popular" or "vulgar" taste for opera. This charge might sound strange to our ears, because opera got canonized alongside symphonic music all over the Western world in the latter part of the nineteenth century, except for Italy where it was long "popular" as well as "serious." As concert organizer of the Society for Visiting the Poor, Odoevsky mounted in 1850 the first (apparently) all-Russian concert, with works, mostly instrumental, by Glinka,

Dargomyzhsky, Vielgorsky, Rubinstein, Alyabev, Lvov, and two minor figures. The society's lavish sponsorship allowed for a large orchestra and five weeks of rehearsal. This concert, and the impulse behind it, can be seen as an early instance of musical nationalism, but a nationalism lacking the aggressive ideology of the spokesmen for the Mighty Five that would soon emerge. No chauvinist, Odoevsky, in his report on the next Russian concert of the same year, identified Rubinstein, Henselt, Maurer, and John Field as essentially Russian by birth, upbringing, habit, or simply "love for Russia."[38]

In comparison to Vienna, Leipzig, Berlin, or Paris — the Petersburg concert offerings seem thin. Monika Lichtenfeld counted about twenty-five classical music concerts in the Austrian capital each season (excluding chamber music) in the years 1850–56. Yet Petersburgers had access to many venues where good music was played: New Hall on the English Embankment, the Passage (a shopping complex on the Nevsky), the Yusupov and Stroganov palaces, the Imperial Theaters, and suburban resorts. When in 1856 Johann Strauss took the baton at the Vauxhall in Pavlovsk, previously a venue for restaurant and ballroom music, he offered symphonic works. Particularly active were the German Lutheran churches, with their singing academies and instrumental groups. In the 1850s, Balakirev performed on piano in symphonic concerts at the Commercial Hall on Kronstadt and at Myatlev Hall, a hostel for foreign guests. And the growing public interest in music is attested by a study of the available press which showed the number of items dealing with music tripling from the time of Alexander I.[39] While many so-called amateur gentry musicians got serious training from accomplished teachers, what Russia lacked was a permanent public society with full resources and an orchestra fed by a truly professional training center — to whit, a conservatory.

Listening Around the Empire

The word "concert," first separated (in English) from its other musical meaning (concerto) in the early eighteenth century, still possessed fluid properties. Almost everywhere in Europe it could mean an evening or afternoon of music of almost any kind and in any blend of solo recital, arias, chamber music, or large-scale choral and orchestral works. In that sense, Russian concert life was far more vibrant than what was suggested by the limited schedule and repertoire of the concert societies. Virtually everything musical in St. Petersburg was repeated in Moscow — salons, clubs, German singing societies, ad hoc concerts sponsored by private families, charity groups, the university. Odoevsky, the Vielgorskys, John Field, and others moved back and forth, bringing their musical interests with them.

Moscow University, Russia's oldest, became that city's epicenter of nontheater music during the reign of Alexander I. Its energy source, the ex-serf Daniil Kashin, began while still in bondage to organize Moscow's first open concerts, sometimes with an orchestra of two hundred. On gaining freedom in 1799 or 1800, Kashin anchored the musical life of the university for three decades as pianist, conductor, composer, teacher, and folk song collector. The story is told that when the French entered Moscow in 1812 and asked Kashin to produce some music for them, he declined, uttering the words of Tasso: "I now feel humiliated in my heart." Amid the riot of musical patriotism that erupted after the Russian victory, Kashin produced stirring war-related works such as *The Don, The Vanguard,* and *The Defenders of St. Petersburg,* which achieved instant popularity at folk fairs, shows, and concerts. The regular orchestra of thirty to thirty-five players reached out to the Moscow public; at an 1823 performance, a professor counted eighty carriages and 150 sleighs arriving at the hall.[40]

The shift of the epicenter of concert life from university to the Moscow Imperial Theater organization during the reign of Nicholas I owed much to the shrewd management style of its musical director, Alexei Verstovsky (1799–1862), a popular Russian composer and a powerful bureaucrat. Before his appointment in 1826, a few theater concerts had been organized by the Silesian Friedrich Scholtz (Fëdor Sholts, 1787–1830), who had come to Russia in 1811. Once Verstovsky took over, his self-promotion in concert life revolved around large-scale productions, or "monster concerts." He scored for four harps and large orchestra his own choral hymn set to N. M. Yazykov's "Great Sovereign," which is full of gushing gratitude to Tsar Nicholas. In 1831, Verstovsky conducted it in the Moscow Gentry Club at a Lenten benefit concert for victims of the recent cholera epidemic. The imperial family attended the concert which featured a hundred voices, a 150-piece orchestra, and eighty horns. Verstovsky masterfully combined amateur gentry participation, philanthropy, and patriotism in his musical events. Patrician ladies of the Sheremetev and Bartenev families, in singing to a limited public at the Gentry Club, were merely extending the domestic setting to a wider assembly of their peers. On one of the programs was inscribed the now familiar motto: "Art has always been the friend of charity."[41]

As musical arbiter of orchestral forces, voices, concert space, and fees, Verstovsky received a steady stream of letters from Russian musicians and visiting performers such as Catalani, Pasta, Berlioz, Viardot, and Clara Schumann. The polite epistolary discourse evinced a natural desire to please a powerful administrator; and the tone occasionally descended to unctuousness. Most letters came from Petersburg musicians seeking paid engagements in Moscow. In 1834 Ludwig Maurer wrote such appeals on behalf of himself and his sons.

Verstovsky's opera *Askold''s Grave* became a totem of flattery for those dependent upon his good will. In the early 1850s, the Polish violinist Apolonary Katski (Kontskii, 1825–79) thanked Verstovsky, "My general and illustrious maestro!" for his assistance, praised *Askold''s Grave* which he had seen excerpted in Simbirsk, and requested concert engagements in Moscow. Letters from more exalted figures — the Vielgorskys, Odoevsky, and the political policeman Leonty Dubelt — reflected their power. The files are full of their recommendations and letters of introduction for friends, clients, and foreign guests. Their coded language of persuasion was embellished with ornate rhetoric and subtle hints. The grand patrons of St. Petersburg, as the hosts and semi-impresarios of musical life, saw Verstovsky's satrapy as the Moscow branch of their hospitality.[42]

Vasily Bezekirsky (1835–1917), a violinist, minor composer, and son of a piano maker, cast some garish light on the musical operations of the Moscow Theater Directorate, which, he claimed, once cheated his father in a business deal. Bezekirsky himself, after studying violin in Moscow and abroad, debuted in 1850 and eventually entered the patronage network of Grand Duchess Elena Pavlovna. Through competition, Bezekirsky gained first chair in the Imperial Moscow Theater orchestra. But his boss Verstovsky held the violinist's salary down for a long time. Germans in the orchestra were eligible for a pension after ten years as opposed to Russians who had to wait twenty. Other minor grievances marked the clash between the two men.[43] Bezekirsky's lament points up to the recurring problem of unequal wages and the privileges enjoyed by foreign-born or "foreign"-named musicians, one that became an issue for reform minded figures as different as Alexei Lvov and Anton Rubinstein.

Music-making in Moscow remained very much in the social sphere: a clubby setting of semiprivate space for members only. Aristocrats invited each other to their homes or to hired places such as the Gentry Club. When the internationally renowned diva Giuditta Pasta (1797–1867), for whom Bellini had written the title role in *Norma,* came to Moscow in 1840–41, she asked her friend and host Mikhail Buturlin to sing with her at a public paying concert. But Buturlin's superior, Moscow governor D. V. Golitsyn, told him that it was not acceptable for "members of high society to participate in a public concert of professional artists." The position of a well-born person performing in front of an audience suggested "serving"; and this put the function of critical judgment through applause in the wrong hands. Though Buturlin believed rightly that the attitude had attenuated by the 1870s, in some quarters it persisted right up to the Revolution.[44] But since high-ranking figures constantly performed for some publics, the notion of "public" was fast becoming fuzzy and the walls around private space sprang holes. It was one thing for the master of an estate to join a serf ensemble for a few hours in front of friends. It was quite another for him to appear in the guise of a professional. The notion of honor had always resided exclusively in the noble spectator, not in the performer. This notion got diluted as performing music grew more popular among the high-born.

In the two capitals of the Russian empire some subtle shifts had occurred in thinking about and organizing the realm of public space and social participation in the arts. Charity remained a key that opened the door to wider public performance for the upper classes. As long as noble performers received no fee, other commercial arrangements became acceptable: ticket sales, paid musicians, profit. In a sense, the philanthropic ticket buyers, in addition to supporting a favorite charity, were subsidizing the musical backup to gentry performers in a legitimized setting. The piano bench, long an artifact of courtship, was occupied by pianists from the gentry, such as Balakirev, in public display. During the rage for opera in the 1840s, owners of lustrous voices (real or imagined) wanted to show off beyond the closed circles of club and home. Charity concerts offered ladies and gentlemen of noble origins the chance to perform in a wider but still respectable milieu and for a worthy cause. Noble dilettantes were unknowingly narrowing the distance, dictated by the tribal mores of the aristocracy, between private and public space.

By the eve of the 1917 Revolution, Russians had created a wide network of provincial concert halls — institutionalized sites of nontheatrical musical performance, usually backed by a local symphonic society and a permanent orchestra. All this had been made possible by the Great Reforms of the 1860s, the rapid spread of railroads, and a host of cultural and social changes set loose by these. In the early nineteenth century, the regions that lay beyond the capital were by no means empty of cultural enterprise. But the bulk of non–folk musical performance in the provinces remained on the private estates or in the town theaters where audiences flocked to opera, ballet, and vaudeville. Concert life as such remained fragmentary and episodic, hardly surprising in light of the vastness of the land, the underdeveloped means of communication and transportation, and the sheer novelty of the concert format.

Classical music was brought to provincial towns for the most part by artists on tour. The combined itineraries of only four of the many soloists who toured the empire's towns in the 1840s and 1850s — Henri Vieuxtemps, Apolonary Katski, Henryk Wieniawski, and Franz Liszt — included Revel, Riga, Dünaburg, Vilna, Novgorod, Tver, Vladimir, Tula, Orël, Voronezh, Tambov, Penza, Nizhny Novgorod, Kazan, Simbirsk, Saratov, Kiev, Kharkov, Poltava, Kursk, Ekaterinoslav, Taganrog, Novocherkassk, Kremenchug, Elizavetgrad, and Odessa. Verstovsky helped set up some of these engagements. In the

1840s, the Russian violinist Afanasev made seventy-eight appearances in four years, cutting a huge swath in every direction from Moscow, including the Jewish Pale. He claimed to have been the first Russian virtuoso to make an extensive tour of the empire. His account offers insight into how tours were arranged for artists such as himself who did not possess the luster of the foreigner or the sponsorship (apparently) of a Verstovsky. Afanasev and his cellist brother always needed recommendations in advance to local notables who would usually book them into the Gentry Club and try to whip up a modest audience of two to three hundred. The governor sometimes bought up fifty to a hundred tickets and distributed them to friends. The rest were passed downwards from officials to the police chief to constables who would place them in merchant stalls.[45]

These itineraries make it clear that concertizing took place in far-flung corners of the empire, though the offering was diverse and the term "concert hall" (*kontsertnyi zal*) had yet to gain usage. Gentry Club, private mansion, or theater provided stages, and artists would often play after or between theatrical presentations. In the 1820s, a Tula merchant's house doubled as a concert venue for musicians from the capital. The concerts of professional virtuosos, noble amateurs, and serf orchestras hosted by the Kursk Gentry Club from the 1840s onward were regularly chronicled in the provincial gazette. Although provincial capitals were the main centers, one finds solo recitals even in tiny district towns, such as the historically famous Uglich in Moscow Province and in the Voronezh provincial townlets of Zadonsk in 1856 and Pavlovsk in 1861. In that province, charity began to harness the concert medium in the 1850s with the arrival of such stars as Wieniawski and the pianist Nikolai Rubinstein (Anton's brother), Yury Golitsyn's serf choir, and Elizaveta Khristiani [Christiani] (1827–53), the cellist who allegedly inspired Mendelssohn's *Songs Without Words*. These Voronezh occasions were interspersed with local amateurs and occasional performances by the theater orchestra. A Soviet chronicler found that the two to four annual concerts were poorly attended due to high performance fees and expensive tickets. He also claimed that only the rich went to concerts, but in the same breath said that they were indifferent to real art.[46]

In Saratov, an 1853 concert of Weber, Rossini, and Haydn's *Creation* organized by nongentry folk evoked malicious accusations by aristocrats at not having been consulted, and the dispute was aired in the provincial gazette. In an attempt to tie music to politics in a direct way, a Soviet student of the city's musical life dutifully recorded that the soon-to-be revolutionary N. G. Chernyshevsky was moved by listening to Rossini's *William Tell* overture. Such nuggets in the literature served ideological correctness and also to fill in the rather thin story. Yet Saratov is interesting for other reasons. A few clues demonstrate that audiences were treated to a broad range of experience. The appearance of the internationally renowned Wieniawski in 1853 represented the reach of mobile impresarios. But the concert stage was fed from interior resources as well, including serf orchestras. The marshal of the nobility, N. I. Bakhmetov, an amateur violinist, played with his own serf orchestra at public concerts in the years 1848–51.[47]

In the spotty record elsewhere, the "spots" offer a few insights on town life. Civic pride displayed itself in 1833 when the *Ladies' Journal* printed a report from Ekaterinburg that attempted to deflate the myth of "wild Siberia" by describing a charity concert there in the brightly lit hall of government house, where the women in the audience wore the latest Paris fashions. An orchestra of twenty played Weber's *Der Freischütz* overture and music of Hummel, Mozart, and Herz. Deeper in Siberia, Governor General Yakoby brought a forty-piece orchestra to Irkutsk in the 1780s. Tobolsk offered an example of how musical life in distant places depended on the presence of a particular person, in this case Alexander Alyabev, the most famous popular song composer of the era and a convicted murderer living under sentence of exile. The governor in Tobolsk had been a comrade-in-arms during the Napoleonic wars, and in 1831 he provided the composer with an orchestra. Alyabev left an autograph program of a piano recital by the visiting Zintl sisters from St. Petersburg. The pattern repeated itself in Orenburg on the edge of Central Asia, a bleak military frontier town with a population of only fifty thousand. In 1827, Vasily Verstovsky, brother of the composer and an amateur musician, arranged concerts with other local amateurs. When Alyabev was transferred there in 1833, he found congenial company: Verstovsky; Governor General Vasily Perovsky, an 1812 veteran of enlightened views; and his secretary, Vladimir Dahl, guitarist, lexicographer, and poet. Together they organized the musical life of the town.[48]

Kiev had a small city orchestra of sixteen players until 1852, and a Symphonic Society formed in 1848 gave concerts at the university. Kukolnik in the 1850s described a symphony orchestra in Taganrog on the Sea of Azov. Wieniawski, while concertizing with his pianist brother Jozef, told Verstovsky that the take was excellent in diminutive Kremenchug, even though the audiences at the district Gentry Club had to bring their own seats and lanterns; and that in Kharkov, his five concerts won him a lavish reception, bouquets, and further concert invitations. Though the violinist was ingratiating and self-centered, there is little cause to doubt his success there or anywhere else.[49]

The two most interesting musical cities outside the capitals — Nizhny Novgorod and Odessa — showed contrasting tastes. Alexander Ulybyshev's musical salon expanded into concerts with a repertoire of classical German symphonic offerings and works of Liszt and Chopin. Ulybyshev's Thursday and Saturday evening concerts in 1841–1855 drew art figures, writers, and intellectuals, as well as the young Mily Balakirev, future luminary of the Mighty Five. Polish exiles and foreign visitors were on hand. For Mozart's Requiem, the Beethoven symphonies, and choral works of Bortnyansky, the host marshaled the town's musical resources: amateurs, theater musicians and singers, wind players from military bands, and singers from the archdiocesan choir. To a greater extent than in the capitals, provincial towns like Nizhny had to gather a variety of social types and roles together for large-scale works such as a symphony or cantata. A reporter in the *Neue Berliner Musik Zeitung* in 1850 expressed amazement that this music was being performed in the middle of the immense spaces of the tsar's empire, halfway to Asia. At the great Nizhny Novgorod Fair, classical music could be heard at the Main Building. In the 1850s, Rubinstein, Balakirev, and many others appeared there. Programs were not only eclectic but set in a holiday atmosphere that was socially and psychologically distant from the solemnity of the capital concerts.[50]

Odessa, among the most musical cities in the empire, had a long love affair with operatic music, even in concert. A surviving program at the Odessa theater directed by an Italian in July 1836 featured orchestral pieces by Sarti; Rossini; Mercadanti; a local violinist-composer, Leonid Gold; and Alyabev's Grand Symphony "Farewell to the North." When the trained dilettante P. D. Seletsky arrived in Odessa to teach in the 1840s, he discovered that opera so consumed musical taste there that his own passion for German instrumental music "produced a marked effect, like a news item" in that city. He joined a quartet and from his cello seat launched a brief unhappy affair with the musical host's wife. In addition to the foreign virtuosos noted below, Odessa hosted dozens of lesser known artists from the Russian empire such as Yuliya Grünberg (Grinberg) of Kharkov and Guillaume of Estland. Two local Jewish soloists offered recitals and chamber works: the pianist Yakov Weinberg, physician and brother-in-law of Anton Rubinstein; and Leonid Gold, who had studied in Vienna, concertized in Europe and Russia, and founded the city's first violin school. This was one of the early markers of a city that would produce some of the finest violinists in the world in the nineteenth and twentieth centuries — the American Nathan Milstein and the Soviet David Oistrakh among them.[51]

The Vanquishing Virtuoso

Ire and indignation among European art music critics — never in short supply — grew particularly harsh in the second third of the nineteenth century, when two great currents of music competed and colluded: serious "classical" music and what the Germans call *Trivialmusik*, the lighter genres, particularly as rendered by divas and virtuoso soloists. The death of Beethoven in 1827 spread a veil of pious solemnity over the classical forms, especially the symphony. At the same time, the intrusion of the nonaristocratic classes into the concert hall audiences of Europe, reinforced by advanced modes of commerce, print culture, travel, and communications, pulled the glittering arts of the virtuoso onto the stage. Eclectic, crowd-pleasing concert programs were tailored to the deftness of professional performing artists: variations, fantasies, bravura solo works, romances, arias. William Weber, in his discussion of the struggle between the two currents, notes correctly that taste publics often overlapped. He quotes a French diarist speaking of those who "swoon in the morning with Beethoven and in the evening with Rossini." Although mixed genres in concert rooms or halls had also been common earlier, critics poured venom on the swelling of variety and the blend of light and heavy, or of light masquerading as heavy.[52]

Adventure, romance, fortune, and fame—keywords in the modern cult of celebrity—hovered around the professional soloist who emerged in the early nineteenth century. The European supervirtuoso, beginning with Paganini and Liszt, rode the commercial highways to wealth. Performers and their agents carefully cultivated an aura of supra-artistic prowess—demonic and orgiastic. For the star, planned international appearances replaced the passive drift from court to court, from salon to salon, or to badly managed concert venues. Fame had certainly heralded the arrival all over Europe of pianists such as Moscheles, Kalkbrenner, and Hummel; but the repute of Niccolò Paganini and especially Franz Liszt translated into status and social power. In a great leap of uneven development, a virtuoso pianist could consort with monarchs in a Europe where court soloists were just a few notches above the lackey. Though extramusical flourishes were part of the game, musical technique was at the heart of virtuoso appeal. In the words of Richard Sennett, sociologist and practicing musician, the performers employed "passes, retards, rubato" and "the immediate attack, the sensuous tone, the stunning chord"—all building blocks in the personal charisma that created a celebrity-attuned audience. Virtuosos followed the erotic trails blazed by the mythical and mythicized Don Juans and Casanovas. Women fainted over Paganini, clusters of females arrayed themselves on stage when Liszt performed, and males fashioned whole cults around opera divas. The virtuoso was equally hounded everywhere in Europe by the critics, purists, and lovers of the symphonic classics.[53]

In Russia, where "uneven development" ran strong, the virtuoso experience took on a variety of meanings in terms of the artists' status, popularity, aura, and earning power. "Foreignness," a mark of distinction for most of them, could apply to the visitor from abroad; a performer from the Baltic or Poland; or a Russian who had won recognition in Europe. In a concert hall where virtuosos played, two hierarchies prevailed: one applied to the artist on stage who towered above his worshiping public; the other to the listeners divided by seating. The two loftiest status points stood opposite each other: center stage and the imperial box. Early in the century, a hailstorm of concert tickets rained from the sky in St. Petersburg for seats to see ubiquitous singers, pianists, guitarists, violinists, and clarinetists — including foreign artists of high quality and show-off virtuosos of little talent. Engaging artists in a concert circuit did not become regularized in this period due to an absence of professional impresarios. But the well-placed Vielgorsky brothers, Lvov, and Verstovsky assured a steady stream of performers. Mikhail Vielgorsky, sometime elder of the Gentry Club, board member of the Imperial Theaters and the Visitation to the Poor Society, had a particularly long reach and could lure visiting virtuosos into his home in addition to putting them on public stages.[54]

Russian audiences saw Irishman John Field, a permanent guest who never learned Russian, as a French-speaking nonnoble foreigner — something between a visiting virtuoso and a native performer (fig. 19). His regular shuttling between home recital and concert appearance tells us something about the persisting distinction between private and public musical space. In the homes of grandees, Field had to contend with the boorishness of noble patrons who "tipped" him like a servant. A proud and sometimes mischievous man, the pianist would hand over the none too generous fee to a lackey and then leave.[55] Once Field established himself as a celebrity, he took to the concert hall and became a regular at the Philharmonia. In Moscow, where he settled for a decade in the 1820s, Field's drinking habit caught up with him: several times the governor had to send the police to find the drunken pianist and bring him to the hall. At the peak of his career, Field was earning five thousand rubles for a soirée, and usually ten thousand for a public concert. *Fildanstvo,* the cult of Field, reigned in piano music. Following his return from a European tour, Field gave his last concert and died in 1837. He had taken Russian society not so much by storm as by tears. Liszt, the emperor of frenzy, disdained Field's style as "inert" or "flaccid," but it won the hearts of Odoevsky, Verstovsky, Apollon Grigorev, and dozens of budding concertizers who printed the device "pupil of Field" on their posters. Glinka, who loved to "weep sweet tears of emotion," wrote of John Field that "his fingers fell on the keys like drops of water."[56]

Field's music gave rise to a belief in a stylistic continuity between him and Chopin.[57] The musicologist Patrick Piggott has demolished the myth by demonstrating the differences between the two pianists. Some of Field's phrasing and ornament will remind listeners of Chopin in spite of the deeper differences. The myth was fueled by the role of the nocturne in both composers. Field applied the term to some of his piano pieces. In contrast to earlier forms, *notturno* and *Nachtmusik*, Field's resembled romance, serenade, pastorale, all of which names he used—a wordless love song, first named nocturne by him in 1814. The romantic and atmospheric music suited both the intimate salon and the large recital. Unlike some of his contemporaries, Field did not win audiences with muscular passages and bravura. Though most of the nocturnes are written in the major, they have an elegiac quality perfectly suited to the Russian sentimental ear. A century later, theater director Vsevolod Meyerhold thought Field's music was the perfect reflection of the hollow decrepitude of Russian society of the time, and he used the Nocturne No. 5 in a 1928 production of Griboedov's *Woe from Wit* to illustrate the point.[58]

Maria Szymanowska's salon successes led to bookings in larger public sites such as the Philharmonia where she played solo and with Field. She was appointed the "first pianist of Their Majesties Elizabeth Alexandrovna and the Empress Maria Fëdorovna." An 1823 tour took her to Kiev during its annual Contract Fair and then deep into the Ukrainian provinces—to Tulchin, Zhitomir, Dubno, Kremenets, Lvov, Vinnitsa. These names resonate with the memory of the old Jewish Pale but the sources are mute on the relative make-up of the audience as between Polish gentry, Russian garrison forces, Ukrainian, and Jewish residents. After a European tour, Szymanowska was back in St. Petersburg in 1827, more popular than ever. A reviewer emphasized her European success—still the major marker of prestige among performing artists. Yet Szymanowska could not escape the stereotype of female (thus inferior) version of Field. Her gender was underlined when she participated in an "all-female" concert in the Engelhardt House in 1830, performing side by side with relatively unknown women pianists.[59] Clara Schumann attracted the public attention usually reserved for the male player or the female vocalist. Although women pianists probably outnumbered men all over the world (just as cooks outnumbered chefs), the gendering of the piano did not extend to virtuosity. Female pianists in this era avoided the flamboyance affected and perfected by male artists. Nevertheless, Clara Schumann easily impressed the music lovers of the Russian capital in 1844 by her sheer force and intellectual quality in the rendering of the works of the German masters, including her husband. Robert Schumann had come along but limited himself to conducting his First Symphony at the Vielgorsky home.[60]

The male European violin virtuoso as a cultural type asserted both his virility and his virtuosity by dazzling pyrotechnics on the instrument. Among the first to cause a sensation in Russia, since Paganini only got as far as Warsaw, was the

Norwegian violinist Ole Bull (1810–80) who played there in 1838 and 1841. After a St. Petersburg concert, the conductor at the Italian opera, Heinrich Romberg, wrote that "Bull is simply a charlatan, a bad imitation of Paganini," an opinion echoed in the next century by the scholar Boris Schwarz who called Bull a "calculating showman." Romberg's comment did not harm Bull's success in Petersburg. In Moscow, the governor arranged a concert at the Gentry Club and the artist endeared himself in the customary way by playing his newly composed *Homage à Moscou* based on Russian folk material. Ole Bull impressed audiences by his august stature and his unusual techniques adapted from Norwegian folk playing of the Hardanger fiddle whose low bridge and long bow allowed quadruple-stop chords. Those critics who admired him employed the cloying habit of interpreting music as a reflection of the topography of the composer's homeland. Yet although the mountains and fjords of Norway which he evoked may not have been depicted in the music itself, native musicians from those hills were certainly the source of Ole Bull's style. And it was this exotic element rather than the quality of his compositions that accounted for warm reception in Europe, America, and Russia.[61]

Belgian violinist Henri Vieuxtemps (1820–81) as a child prodigy conquered the salons of Europe. During a tour of 1837–38, Matvei Vielgorsky invited Vieuxtemps to Russia and for two years he garnered success on the heels of Ole Bull. Vieuxtemps returned to Russia in 1846 as Court Soloist and teacher at the Imperial Theaters. Between duties at the theater, he managed to tour a dozen cities including regular trips to Moscow. His letters to Verstovsky contain ritual thanks for engagements and requests for advertisement in the press and posters of his upcoming appearances. Employing a tried and true device of musical celebrities, flattery, Vieuxtemps played violin adaptations of Russian popular songs such as Alyabev's "Nightingale," and of themes from Verstovsky's *Askold's Grave*. Vieuxtemps left Russia in 1852 (to return only once in 1860). A Russian biographer hints at a breach of contract which he blames on tsarist despotism. The more likely cause lay in Vieuxtemps' heavy burden of playing incidental music for the theater, concertizing, and teaching. A European biographer cites a letter in which Vieuxtemps in later years recalled having "vegetated" in Russia, "this land of fraud and elegant society — refined and captivating." Another source claims that Vieuxtemps thought Russia a fine place because audiences were generous, hospitable, and deferential to artists. As an artist and state employee who navigated a career in theater, concert halls, and gentry homes, the Belgian violinist may have been accurate on all counts.[62]

Another child prodigy, Henryk Wieniawski (1835–1880), would one day succeed Vieuxtemps as professor of violin at the Brussels Conservatory (fig.

20). Boris Schwarz called Wieniawski — a Polish subject of the tsar and the son of a Jewish physician in Lublin — "the romantic virtuoso par excellence." He won first prize at the Paris Conservatoire at age eleven and became widely known as "the Chopin of the violin." For his 1848 Petersburg début, thirteen-year-old Wieniawski enchanted audiences at the Mikhailovsky Theater and the Gentry Club by playing a Viotti concerto and his own "fantasies" on *Lucia di Lammermoor* and Lvov's national anthem. During a later sojourn in Russia, Wieniawski composed *Souvenir de Moscou* (1853), a bewitching rendition of two Varlamov romances for violin and piano which combines the flavor of the originals with the brilliant Wieniawski pyrotechnics; and his best-known piece, *Légende* (1860). A vigorous concertizer, Wieniawski made 194 appearances in the capitals and provinces.[63]

Around 1852, a curious and revealing incident occurred at the Moscow Gentry Club when Wieniawski appeared together with the thirteen-year-old Czech violin virtuosa, Wilma Neruda (Vilemina Nerudová, 1839–1911). Vieuxtemps, who was present, gave Neruda a bouquet and the audience broke out in a great ovation. Perhaps a Pan-Slav sentiment surfaced at the sight of a Czech and a Pole — symbolizing friendly and hostile Slavs respectively. More likely it was simple courtesy. But the seventeen-year-old Polish performer, angered by Neruda's triumph, tactlessly offered to prove his superiority. Outraged, audience members mounted the stage to remonstrate. Wieniawski prodded a Russian general with his bow and asked him to be silent. Insulting a general in the reign of Nicholas I was no light thing, but next day, the all-powerful Governor-General Zakrevsky — long famous as an overbearing administrator — merely ordered Wieniawski out of Moscow within twenty-four hours.[64] Yet the reaction was moderate and the little scandal did no harm to Wieniawski's career. In spite of occasional spurts of temperament — by then almost obligatory in a virtuoso's professional profile — he became a regular at the musical evenings of Grand Duchess Elena Pavlovna and Grand Duke Konstantin. Wieniawski's prestige as an international virtuoso protected him from the usual rules. In the 1860s he gained appointment as Court Violinist and professor at the St. Petersburg conservatory before taking up the Brussels post. Though preceded by generations of Polish Jewish fiddlers, Wieniawski became the first model for a career that was to be taken up by scores of young compatriots for the next hundred years and more.

Among the big guns of European performance in the 1840s, Hector Berlioz employed as his instrument the mammoth orchestra which he tinted with lavish colors. As one of the earliest of the virtuoso conductors, Berlioz magnetized audiences with his tall frame, gaunt face, and flaming red hair which added visual spectacle to the auditory show. When news of his music in Russian journals excited interest, in 1841, years before Berlioz arrived, Heinrich Romberg mounted a performance of the composer's *Requiem* at Engelhardt House, employing instrumental and vocal forces from the theaters, the Capella, and two Guards regiments. Unfortunately both the hall and the musical forces were insufficient to do the work justice — 150 singers and 100 musicians in a room with a 300-seat capacity. Berlioz wanted more, and when he arrived in Russia after a harrowing trans-European journey in 1847, he got them. Within hours, Lvov and the Vielgorskys mobilized the Capella, the Imperial Guards regimental band, and an amplified orchestra of the Imperial Theaters for a total of 160 players, 180 singers, and 50 military musicians. For the two concerts at the Gentry Club — a much larger venue than the Engelhardt — Berlioz conducted the *Roman Carnival* overture, an incomplete version of *The Damnation of Faust,* and excerpts from the *Symphonie funèbre et triomphale.* Though reviews were mixed, public acclaim was loud.[65]

Berlioz repeated his triumph in Moscow though with a few glitches. When the marshal of the Moscow nobility was asked for the use of the Gentry Club, he became confused because he thought the word "concert" meant concerto (the words are the same in Russian) and that Berlioz was the performer. The idea of a symphonic concert was apparently new to him and he looked upon Berlioz as merely another virtuoso. He invoked the rule that in return for the use of the hall for a public performance, the artist would mount a free one exclusively for the membership — yet another effort to keep separate the public paying environment from that of the private. But in this case, the marshal required that Berlioz play on an instrument in his home. The great composer was proficient only on the kettledrum and the guitar. After some pleading, he was excused from the personal appearance and allowed to mount his concert. Berlioz returned to St. Petersburg several more times at the Capella and at court and left Russia in May 1847. The reception of his concerts had been phenomenal. Though Russian audiences were noted for their responsiveness, they were not attuned to modern music. It seems likely that some of the enthusiasm was generated by the composer himself, the sheer scale of his works, and their brilliant orchestral palette.[66]

What Berlioz could do with a huge orchestra, Franz Liszt tried to match with a grand piano. Some have claimed that the Czech Jan Dussek (1760–1812) was first to sit sideways to the public when performing on the piano, but it was the Liszt profile that turned a pianist into a star performer. Both Paganini and Liszt came late to the practice of commercial promotion and both created a sensation. Heinrich Heine coined the word "Lisztomania" to describe the furor that swept Europe. Liszt, with the help of a modern professional manager, Gaetano Belloni, invented the modern piano virtuoso. While in Rome in 1842 at the peak of his fame, the Hungarian pianist was invited by D. V. Golitsyn, governor general of Moscow, to perform in Russia; Mikhail Vielgorsky organized the visit. Liszt's début there on April 8 at the St. Petersburg Gentry Club drew an unprecedented audience of about three thousand people. On an island stage in the middle of the hall, surrounded by the public on all sides, stood two pianos on which Liszt alternated so as to give full force to his visual presentation. The pianist strolled arm-in-arm with Mikhail Vielgorsky around the balcony before descending for his patented entrance: as he walked through the crowds towards the piano, he stripped off his white gloves, threw them beneath the piano and sat down to pound out the complex adaptations for which he was renowned. The censor Nikitenko observed that "the instrument vanishes beneath his hands." In the audience, the budding composer Alexander Serov reached a state of "inexplicable ecstasy, of blissful rapture." He and the influential critic Vladimir Stasov — in a musical version of the exalted revolutionary pledge made a dozen years earlier by Alexander Herzen and Nikolai Ogarëv on Sparrow Hills — "took a vow that thenceforth and forever, that day, 8th April, 1842, would be sacred to us."[67]

In Moscow, Liszt, unable to book the Gentry Club, turned to Verstovsky who offered him a deal: for three concerts at the theater, the house would take all the receipts for one concert or half the total of the three. At a benefit concert, Liszt improvised a fantasy on the Russian Gypsy songs he had heard that same evening at a Moscow tavern. He was persuaded to give still more concerts which were labeled Final Appearance, Another Final Appearance, and the Absolute Final Appearance. By participating in charity and benefit affairs, Liszt endeared himself to the musical public of Moscow, even when he was naughty. On one occasion, the pianist was out feasting with friends, failed to appear on schedule, and had to be searched for. Arriving unfazed, he mounted the stage, and cast his gloves into the audience — a more elegant anticipation of the modern rock star tossing a sweaty garment to the female fans. It was at Liszt's first concert in Moscow that his friends from Rome and Moscow, Alexei Golitsyn, Prince Dolgorukov, and others tried to sit on the stage. The enraged Verstovsky, after some hot words, finally managed to get them off. The reporter of this episode claimed that the arrogant blue bloods wished to avoid buying tickets and also to display their closeness to the celebrity. In fact the intruders, far from being stingy, had lavished money on dinners, suppers, and picnics for the visitor. But they resented having to pay to hear their friend perform in company with everybody else at a public affair.[68]

Liszt's last appearance in Russia also marked his swan song as a public concertizing pianist. In 1847, he arrived by sleigh from the Moldavian capital of Jassy at Kiev for appearances at the Contract Hall and at St. Vladimir

University where he improvised on themes sung out to him by the audience. After concerts in Odessa at the Bourse, the largest hall in the city, Franz Liszt literally ended his paid concert career in the small southern town of Elizavetgrad. At the early age of thirty-five he announced his retirement from the concert stage.[69] Numerous anecdotes — some dubious — surfaced about the tsar and the pianist: Liszt allegedly stopped playing when Nicholas arrived late and began talking (in fact Liszt once silenced Queen Victoria this way); the emperor did not care for Liszt's hairstyle and inadvertently insulted him by mentioning that he had a Russian regiment currently stationed in Hungary.[70] The brightness of socially nondescript stars in the firmament where majestic dynasts and dazzling aristocrats had shone was a potentially disturbing marker of instability. Liszt, a gargantuan upstart, rejected as a member by the Paris Conservatoire and the Magyar nobility, had a persona that combined, in one scholar's phrase, spectacles of the mind and the body.[71]

The great littérateurs had yet to be wrapped in veneration, and they were rarely seen by the public at large. Performance celebrity was self-made, and its agency was enhanced by heretofore unfamiliar hordes of fans and fanfare, media coverage, and seductive propaganda. Its extramusical content — personal lives, love affairs, scandals — resonated as much as the talent displayed on the stage. Star quality and role expectation, normally associated with the age of mechanical reproduction, functioned smoothly through most of the nineteenth century. Audiences became inquiring and curious about social advancement, geographical mobility, artistic fees, and other qualities of the European entertainment market, all of which challenged the culture of ascription. The result was a burbling mix of condescension, envy, admiration, ambition to emulate — all lapping against the traditions of upper-class hospitality and expectations of deference.

The foreign virtuosos cut and healed, wounded and caused joy — in different ways for different people. Some of the readers of Dostoevsky's "Netochka Nezvanova" (1849) must have felt the thrill of recognition in his evocation of a demonic spirit inside an aspiring Russian violinist crazed by the success of a foreign virtuoso rival. Herzen and other intellectuals despised the public's "slavishness" to Liszt.[72] But a positive image also came into focus. The sheer range in national background of the virtuosos helped create a kind of "Euromania" which diluted the exclusivity of the Francophilia already attenuated by the 1812 war. Even for rock-ribbed Gallomanes, all the "monsieurs" — whether French, Polish, German, Hungarian, or even Jewish — spoke French and could be elevated to the status of gentlemen or lady guests. For the Euromanes, such visitors may have created temporary social, emotional, and esthetic alliances and even acted as a reassuring force in an age when Russian foreign policy hummed with tension over the Eastern Question, British Russophobia, the tsar's high-nosed treatment of the July Monarchy, and the recurring repressions of Polish freedom. The constant presence of foreign artists from potentially hostile nations may have acted—as it did during the late rivalry of the United States and the USSR in the three decades after Stalin's death—as a signifier of hopeful mutual accommodation. If so, this would partly account for the great astonishment of educated Russian society upon the outbreak of the Crimean War in 1853.[73]

Less speculative is the effect Liszt and Berlioz's personal appearances had on Russian musical life. The onslaught of foreign virtuosos exposed Russians to a wide range of music. Of all the manifold reactions by musicians and music lovers—lifelong cults, temporary infatuations, ambivalent resentments, or just plain rejections—the most poignant was that of Vladimir Stasov, the great prophet of Russian national music and the foremost designer of the myth of the Mighty Five. In his exuberant first-hand observations of 1843, Stasov told of Liszt's arrogance and conceit, but then bristled (silently) when he overheard a few unflattering remarks from Glinka about Liszt's playing. "I was absolutely scandalized!" wrote Stasov later. "What! How dare some 'mediocre' Russian musician, who had not yet done anything in particular himself, talk like this about Liszt, the great genius over whom all Europe had gone mad!" Stasov's love of Liszt grew into hyberbolic worship, and he became a friend and admirer down through the decades of that monumental pianist. In a pious exegesis written after Liszt's death, Stasov laboriously canvassed all the quotations he could find in print or in letters to prove how much Franz Liszt—and Berlioz as well—had championed the Russian national school of composers.[74]

It can be argued, of course, that Liszt, for example, banefully influenced audiences with his meretricious repertoire—the infamous flashy improvisations and transcriptions with which he won fame and fortune. But once again, we must consider the pedagogical function of such performances which are often gateways to more "serious" music and to the performance site itself. Just as symphonic pops and promenade concerts and children's programs in the nineteenth and twentieth centuries initiated untold numbers of young people into the pleasures of great music, so Liszt and his fellow virtuosos generated or sustained interest in that kind of music by popularizing the more exalted forms. The adventurous cultural historian Richard Leppert has offered some broader suggestions on the "meanings" of Liszt in his time, some of which apply to the Russian reception. Among other things the pianist represented extravagant individualism, blatant sexuality, the market, the subject, agency, the body, physicality, the reversal of the performance gaze of desire, spontaneous expression as freedom, and "enthusiasm"—a virtual taboo among the highest ranks of society but a trait that the middling classes were beginning to see and emulate in public places. Though the few scorned showiness as vulgar, the many found it irresistible and perhaps contagious. As Robert Schumann wrote at the time, "the sight of any virtuosity elevates and strengthens." Finally, it is clear that the growth of Russian public musical venues and performances in the capitals and around the empire, and their loose linking by touring virtuosos, helped bring about the release of art music from what T. C. W. Blanning has called, for eighteenth-century Europe, "the thralldom of representation" — that is the adornment and artistic projection of courtly power.[75]

Out of the Pale: Rubinstein

In the Paris of 1790, getting to a recital by the violinist Giovanni Battista Viotti required its aristocratic audience to climb five flights of stairs in a private home. James H. Johnson has suggested that this very concrete episode may have been a turning point in the emergence of the musical professional.[76] Surely other, especially foreign, artists were able to do things like this in pre-revolutionary France; and certainly the musician as servant lingered long after 1790 — under whatever regime. But the point is well taken. In western Europe, the full-blown independent professional conductor and performer visibly emerged in the first decades of the nineteenth century. Around 1839, Anton Rubinstein (fig. 22) became the first keyboard titan — excluding Chopin — to come out of the Russian empire which would eventually generate a flow of distinguished performers such as Serge Rachmaninov, Ignac Paderewski, Arthur Rubinstein, Alexander Brailowsky, and Vladimir Horowitz, to name only the best-known.

The career of Anton Rubinstein can best be understood in the context of the foreign domination of orchestras and the virtuoso invasion. His Jewish origins had no significant effect upon his early successes. Jewish performers, actors, and singers — converted or otherwise — had become a familiar sight in the slow dawning of Jewish emancipation and assimilation in post-Napoleonic Europe. Moscheles, Herz, Ferdinand David, Giuditta Pasta, Rachel, and many other Jewish names glittered in the public arena. Two composers of Jewish origin reigned supreme in musical capitals: Meyerbeer in Paris and Mendelssohn in Leipzig and Berlin. Wieniawski, a subject of the tsar, a Pole, and a Jew, apparently suffered no grief about his ethnic background. Rubinstein, a Muscovite since age six, fit easily into the familiar tapestry. He offered no comment on his Jewish background in his autobiography, but he never hid it and was offended by Wagner's anti-Semitic diatribe, *Jewishness in Music*. As a child prodigy, Rubinstein rode the wake of such fashionable wunderkinder as the five Katski children of Cracow whose music-loving father took them on tour to Russia in 1829–30 and then on the European circuit. The violinist Apolonary Katski went on to a successful Russian career. The thirteen-year-old Rubinstein was among the last of the child prodigies to dazzle St. Petersburg audiences in this era. In addition to his performing genius and enormous technical skills, youth, royal attention, and European celebrity assisted Rubinstein's rapid climb in Russian musical life. A true virtuoso, he deployed both his own style of frowning when playing and of laughing when taking applause, as well as a version of the Lisztian manner of flying hair and plunging hands.[77]

Examining the take-off point of Russian musical life at midcentury places two sets of brothers — the Vielgorskys and the Rubinsteins — in illuminating opposition: active dilettantes versus the professionals who founded Russia's first two conservatories. The contrast between Anton Rubinstein and Mikhail Glinka is clarifying as well. The Vielgorskys, however much they contributed to the musical life of their country, were marginal figures. Glinka and Rubinstein were — in their different ways — giants in the mainstream. The striking polarity of their social and geographic backgrounds set against the musical contexts of their lives reveals much about the cultural topography of music in this era: Glinka, the pampered child of a noble landowner, raised deep in the forests of backwater Smolensk Province; Rubinstein, the pampered child of Jewish converts from the edge of empire. Both were richly endowed with talent, had musical mothers, became roving cosmopolitans, and achieved fame in their lifetimes. Glinka's world reputation, slower in coming but far more lasting, rests on his compositions. Rubinstein's music even at its best pales by comparison. Radios and recital halls all over the world up through the 1940s, long after his death, continued to ring with his Melody in F and the song "Desire" ("Zhelanie"), both written in the 1850s; but by then he was being constantly confused with the Polish-born pianist Arthur Rubinstein. Though nowadays Anton Rubinstein is rarely heard, his importance to the musical culture of his time is unassailable. Wherever the musical canon may put him, the historian must place him at its very center alongside Glinka.[78]

Anton Rubinstein's grandfather hailed from Berdichev, a shtetl set amid the swirling currents of pious Judaism, Yiddish culture, and the Haskalah or Jewish Enlightenment. He rose through energy and hard work to be a rich merchant who won and lost fortunes, sat in jail for a time, and fought legal battles with the magnate Radziwill family over land titles. Two sons later went to university; Anton's father Grigory settled in the village of Vykhravatinsky on the Dniester, in the Balta District of Podolia Province on the border of Bessarabia — a classic site of Hasidic Jews and the scene of ghastly pogroms before and after the nineteenth century. There Anton was born in 1829. Before he was five, the family had made two crucial steps: conversion to Orthodox Christianity and removal to Moscow. The mass baptism on a single day of sixty Rubinsteins in Berdichev in 1831 was not unique to this family. Converts acquired exemption from the 1827 laws on double taxation of Jews and the recruitment of their children. By purchasing substitutes for the army, Jewish converts could avoid the scourge of the brutal cantonal system. Since they could also move from the Jewish Pale and take up residence in Russia proper, Rubinstein *père* took his family to Moscow in 1834.[79]

Grigory Rubinstein set up a pin and pencil factory in Zamoskvorechie district, at the heart of the Moscow merchantry. By all accounts a jovial and generous person and a good family provider, he welcomed a socially diverse company to his home: Russian merchants, petty nobles, workers, and a circle of intelligentsia — teachers, officials, and his brothers' university student friends. Groups of them would travel in a bone-rattling cart up the Ordynka Road and across the river to the Bolshoi Theater. When music dawned in the household, the circle widened to include J. J. Johannis, conductor at the opera, among others. Home music was provided by Anton's mother and then by the budding pianist-composer himself who in later years said "apparently I was never young," in reference to the rigor and regimen of piano lessons that began at age five. His mother Kaleria, née Clara Löwenstein, came from Prussian Silesia and had met Grigory in Odessa. With her musicality she combined energy, practicality, and ambition for her children, and a domineering will that reached — according to a son-in-law — the point of despotism. A stern teacher, she subjected the sleepy child to finger exercises in the dark and cold of early mornings.[80]

In 1837 after seeing a performance of the ten-year-old Kharkov piano prodigy Yuliya Grünberg, Anton's mother engaged her teacher, the noted pianist Alexandre Villoing, the son of a French cook in refuge from the Revolution. Within a few years, he turned the talented boy into a child prodigy who débuted publicly in 1839 at Moscow's Petrovsky Park. The pretty little boy with the long curls whom a journalist affectionately dubbed a *monstre musical* performed at the university and evoked rave reviews from the nationalist literature professor Stepan Shevyrëv. After a brief stint in Paris with his teacher, where he concertized and met Chopin and Liszt, he returned to Russia on the death of his father. In Petersburg Rubinstein's fame brought him an engagement with the Philharmonia at the Engelhardt House. Tsar Nicholas, hearing of the boy's European repute, had him perform at the Winter Palace. Rubinstein recalled in his memoirs how he brought the tsar to laughter by imitating Franz Liszt's signature hair-tossing body language. The next venture to Europe, this time with his mother, included study in Berlin with Glinka's old teacher Siegfried Dehn, and more than two hundred appearances. In spite of his earnings, the young Rubinstein felt pangs of hunger and was even brushed ever so slightly by radicalism in 1848. On his return to Russia, he was searched thoroughly at the frontier and nearly arrested. Like Dostoevsky, he attended briefly the utopian socialist circle of Mikhail Petrashevsky in 1849 but certainly had no interest in a revolution. A few years later, he collaborated on an operetta with one of the Russian radicals of the 1860s, M. L. Mikhailov, but this had no political overtones. Yet Rubinstein was on the verge of playing some very important personal and professional politics that would change the shape of Russian musical life in his time.[81]

Rubinstein's name began appearing at the Philharmonia and university concerts and he toured Russia in 1849. In 1852, an early opera caught the attention of Grand Duchess Elena Pavlovna. Born Princess Charlotte Marie of Württemburg, she had married Mikhail Pavlovich, youngest brother of Nicholas I. She came to St. Petersburg in 1823, became Russianized, and retained a German accent as well as a vague admiration for "la liberté" — a certain freedom and scope for the individual within a conservative enlightened monarchy. In the 1840s, Elena Pavlovna's salon evolved into *soirées morganatiques,* her term for socially diverse musical evenings on Thursdays. Barenboim, bowing to Soviet historiographical constraints, wrote that she was thereby co-opting unranked guests for the goals of autocracy. In fact the grand duchess was keenly interested in the arts and in artists. Like some of the earlier salons, and at a loftier level, the evenings of mixed company were — like morganatic marriages — not quite acceptable in the highest circles but necessarily tolerated. The site of Elena Pavlovna's gatherings, the Mikhailovsky Palace, lent enormous social prestige to the assembled company.[82]

In 1852, the twenty-three-year-old Rubinstein, strikingly handsome, immensely talented, well traveled, and fluent in several languages, won appointment by Elena Pavlovna as Court Pianist or Accompanist, a post that had been occupied by distinguished European artists. Essentially a high-toned servant, Rubinstein referred to himself sardonically as the imperial family's "musical furnace attendant," playing at dynastic residences in and around Petersburg. Rubinstein was the ultimate stiffener at the musical evenings as he accompanied the tsar's son, Grand Duke Konstantin Nikolaevich, a talented amateur. Rubinstein dedicated several of his pieces from this period, including the Melody in F, to Elena Pavlovna. Some held Rubinstein's elevated connections against him. In 1918, one writer claimed that Rubinstein had loved the luxurious court surroundings. Barenboim rightly refutes this. Rubinstein found Elena Pavlovna capricious and autocratic, blowing hot and cold on Rubinstein's push for more serious music. Although Rubinstein's Jewish origin apparently played no role, he was after all the son of a Moscow businessman. The young and self-confident musician knew how to play the courtier, but his discomfort occasionally shows through in the autobiography. Playing at court was a job that he could eventually use to advance his professional ambitions and his larger vision about musical life in Russia. In this regard, the young pianist differed sharply from the transient colleagues at the Mikhailovsky — Vieuxtemps and Wieniawski. Rubinstein's wunderkind reputation faded into partial oblivion, and the emoluments from the palace hardly sufficed for him to live on. He taught and concertized, but detested the still common practice of making the rounds in society to sell tickets for his appearances. High officials in the cultural world continued to call him, now a grown man, by the familiar form of "you" (*ty*). Anton Rubinstein felt more or less at a dead end.[83]

Rubinstein's escape from the dead end, a new European tour from 1854 to 1858, almost sunk him. He had proposed opening a conservatory of music in St. Petersburg as early as 1852, and when this failed, he continued to build up his prestige abroad. But while in Vienna in 1855, he wrote what became a notorious article on "Russian Composers" for *Blätter für Musik, Theater, und Kunst,* a sharply negative survey of the Russian musical scene. He conceded that the Russian people were musical, but claimed that their "melancholy and monotonous" folk tunes did not suit adaptation in opera. While praising Glinka's genius as an instrumental composer, Rubinstein disparaged the operas. Actually Rubinstein had very little knowledge of folk material. He grew up amid the German classical idiom and as a boy heard urban romances, dance music, and some Moldavian Jewish tunes. In his Moscow neighborhood, he had occasionally seen round dances of peasants turned workers, but had never lived in or near a village or been exposed to peasant music. Much of his own music is diluted Mendelssohn and Schumann, weak in harmonic and melodic innovation. His essays in "national" opera uniformly bombed. The tactless polemic evoked a storm of hostility in Russia and Rubinstein regretted it to end of his days. Glinka, who had always been polite but cold to Rubinstein, informed a friend that "the Jew [*zhid*] Rubinstein has undertaken to acquaint Germany with our music and has written an article in which he flings mud at us all, touching rather arrogantly my old lady, *A Life for the Tsar.*" Glinka then referred to Rubinstein as "an impudent Jew [*zhid*]." Barenboim, quoting the letter, omitted with ellipses references to the term *zhid*.[84] Though the word *zhid* was still a neutral ethnic term for Jew, Glinka's usage was clearly an anti-Semitic slur. Anton Rubinstein, unlike his father, was never particularly at ease with people and vented his intolerance of views and practices associated with "amateurism" — at least among his peers — which he wrongly conflated with a misplaced "national spirit" in music. Rubinstein was by no means alone in his assault on the dilettantism that continued to dominate the Russian musical world. And his dismissal of the folk idiom in Russian music eventually led to the harmful and much overinterpreted schism between two allegedly opposite schools of music in the latter part of the century (see chapter 9 of the present work).

But a kind of salvation arrived during Rubinstein's sojourn in Europe. Elena Pavlovna, wintering in Nice in 1856–57, invited Rubinstein to come and play the musical furnace man again in the lavish villas of the elite where Matvei Vielgorsky was also on hand. The three of them spoke at length about Russia's musical future and the need for better professional training. Though the topic was not new, it was apparently here that the seed for a conservatory was planted in the right soil. It is highly doubtful that the courtier-dilettante Vielgorsky, for all his love of music, could or would have carried the idea to fruition. Rubinstein, a man bristling with ambition and possessed of great self-discipline and organizational energy as well as talent, reputation, and connections, was poised to convert the still amateurish musical scene in Russia into one of professional dedication.[85] Returning to St. Petersburg in 1858, he began the process that would establish the musician as "free artist" on the cultural landscape just as the mass of the enserfed population was being turned into free subjects of the tsar.

PART **III**

Empire of Performance

Inside the Capital Stages

By now, the house is full; the boxes blaze;
Parterre and stalls — all seethes;
In the top gallery impatiently they clap,
And, soaring up, the curtain swishes.

— *Pushkin*, Eugene Onegin

The transition from musical life to theatrical life in prereform Russia adds two important elements to the picture: "story" and institution. Unlike the scattered and roughly structured musical world, theater was firmly anchored in the Imperial Theater complex of the two capitals. In common usage, especially in Anglo-Saxon countries, theater has come to mean almost exclusively stage drama. A New Yorker will speak quite distinctly about going to an opera, the ballet, a musical, or the theater. The usage arose partly out of increased specialization in roles, métiers, genres; and partly from the efforts of dramatic practitioners to identify their work as art and their workplace as a temple — thus the deification of legitimate "theatuh" as drama and its sharp and sometimes nasty divorce from other stage genres. But in early nineteenth-century Europe and America, drama shared stages, direction, and very often casts with musical and entertainment genres. The Russian theater fit that pattern as well as European styles of theater architecture, royal monopoly, censorial control, audience scandals, fights over profit versus art, and the overflow of theater into journalism, literature, gossip, and everyday life. Russian theater shared other things with "marginal" states and emerging nations of northern, southwestern, and eastern Europe which took their models from the core: France, Italy, Britain, and the German lands (though feelings of marginality sometimes emerged within the core itself). Actors emulated Talma, Garrick, Mars, Georges, and Rachel just as much as writers copied Molière, Voltaire, or Metastasio. In time, wavelets of revulsion erupted in the periphery against Gallomania or other foreign "tyrannies" and the international styles of classicism. National expression took a multitude of forms, from the deployment of folk culture on stage and native historical plays to critical demands that naturalistic acting replace "unnatural declamation." The story of Russia's theatrical life brought not merely a gradual emancipation from foreign repertoires, but a whole drama of changing power relations, native styles, and provincial-capital interchange.[1]

Laurence Senelick has aptly described the wellspring of Russian theater, the eighteenth-century court, as a "performative" environment. Richard Wortman has rigorously reconstructed its elaborate theater of power, housed in splendid edifices, lavishly decorated, choreographed by masters of the court, and finely ritualized for the role-playing monarchs and courtiers. Contemporaries dubbed Tsar Alexander I "the Talma of the North"; and the eternally mordant Marquis de Custine commented in 1839 on the court of Nicholas: "I see it increasingly as a theater where the actors pass their time in dress rehearsals. No one knows his part and the first night never arrives, because the director is never satisfied with his subjects' performance. So both actors and director spend their lives in ceaselessly preparing, correcting and perfecting an interminable social comedy, entitled 'On the Civilization of the North.' If this is tiresome to watch, just imagine what it must be to play."[2]

In the narrow sense, Russian theater itself started at the top with buildings and institutions. The Russian court was among the first to put on secular scripted performances, though at first spectators other than tsars and tsarinas had to stand in the wings. School dramas and mystery plays long preceded the coming of a Russian theater establishment in the middle of the eighteenth century, as did puppet shows, carnival acts, dance routines, and folk dramas. Some of their forms gradually folded into the fixed conventions of the imported European stage. The ragged history of theatrical institutions from Tsar Alexei to Elizabeth has been thoroughly tracked. The Romanov court eventually maintained four exclusive royal stages in the Winter Palace's Hermitage, Tsarskoe Selo, Gatchina, and Peterhof. Some seventeen theatrical companies —French, Italian, German, and British—appeared at the Russian court between 1730 and 1783, bringing the glories of Racine, Corneille, Molière, and a galaxy of operas and ballets. Amid these foreign incursions, the stepson of a merchant, Fëdor Volkov (1729–63), organized a comedy troupe in Yaroslavl in 1750 and performed at merchant homes and warehouses. Empress Elizabeth invited the Volkov troupe to Petersburg and in 1759 brought it under court administration. Although minor theaters had sprung up earlier in the provinces, Volkov was canonized as the father of Russian theater since his was the first professional, public, continuous state theater. Catherine II quickened cultural importation, took a personal interest in the theater, and wrote a number of works for it.[3]

In Moscow, after several failed public theaters in the 1750s and 1760s, the famous Petrovsky or Maddox Theater arose. An English magician, mechanic, and set decorator of Jewish origin, Michael (or Menkol) Maddox (1742–1825), worked as a magician in Petersburg in 1767 and founded a troupe in Moscow in 1776, based on actors from ruined companies and the serfs of his associate, Prince P. V. Urusov. In 1780 he moved the troupe to a newly built stone theater on the broad Petrovka thoroughfare, near the future site of the Bolshoi Theater. The theater, a commercial entertainment venue, mounted Russian operas and comedies. The premises also hosted balls and masques in their rotunda for as many as two thousand guests, many of them gentry seeking grooms for their daughters. The ambience of costume and intrigue is captured in Mikhail Zagoskin's tale "Concert of Demons." A Moscow aristocrat, Elizaveta Yankova, the "granny" of a famous memoir, combined elitism with anti-Semitism when in old age she recalled Maddox as "a Jew [zhid], a charlatan, and a speculator" because of his massive popular entertainments, attended not by "important people" but those of the middle ranks and by idlers and spendthrifts. When Maddox complained to the government about unfair competition from the private Sheremetev Theater, its owner is said to have commented: "I do not sell fun and good times." Bankrupt, Maddox was forced out in 1801 and the theater was taken over by the Board of the Moscow Foundling Home. After a fire swept the theater in 1805, the Imperial Theaters took over the troupe.[4]

A Soviet account stressed the Petrovsky's progressive repertoire of Voltaire, Lessing, Beaumarchais, Schiller, and Russian works mildly critical of serfdom and "tyranny," and also attributed that theater's humanitarian impulse to its serf actors. Aside from lack of evidence, the argument seems odd in that the management continued to keep its actors enserfed, whereas the tsarist government that took it over immediately freed them. Prior to the takeover in 1806, the Petrovsky Theater was Russia's rare example of an urban privately owned public commercial theater (as opposed to a manorial theater) staffed by serfs.

Maddox and Urusov started with a cast of about thirty and a band of about thirteen musicians. The corps of serfs and wards of the foundling homes was expanded by purchases of serfs including Alexander Stolypin's entire seventy-four-member serf theater company bought for 32,000 rubles. S. F. Mochalov, a serf from the manorial theater of N. N. Demidov, entered the Petrovsky troupe in 1803 and by luck got his freedom three years later when the imperial system took over. He played major roles in Shakespeare, Molière, Kotzebue, and Ozerov with an electricity that was noted by contemporaries. His serf actress wife bore one of the most famous actors in Russian history: P. S. Mochalov.[5] Thus at the dawn of the nineteenth century, a pattern was in place. Foreign companies came and went, the dynasty possessed an embryonic theater system, serf theaters multiplied and were already feeding the capital stages. Private commercial theaters in the two capitals would not reappear until the 1880s.

Imperial Playhouses

Aside from the exclusively private theaters for royalty and guests and some short-lived wooden playhouses, St. Petersburg came to possess three imperial public theater buildings: Bolshoi Stone, Alexandrinsky, and Mikhail-ovsky. Each had its own character. The Bolshoi Stone (Bolshoi Kamenny) Theater, the first permanent one, was completed in 1783 on the site of the present St. Petersburg Conservatory across Theater Square from the Mariinsky Theater (fig. 23). The first to match European standards in grandeur, it had three tiers and a capacity of two thousand spectators. Rebuilt in 1802–4, consumed by fire in 1810, and restored in 1818, in 1836 the house was again renovated by Albert Cavos, son of the composer, with five tiers and a new stage. By that time, the Bolshoi Stone Theater had come to be the major opera and ballet stage. Glinka's *A Life for the Tsar* premiered there in 1836. In 1860, the venerable house lost its preeminence to the new Mariinsky, also designed by Cavos. The Bolshoi Stone saw its last performance in 1886; it was demolished soon after and its walls used for the St. Petersburg Conservatory, erected in 1896 and still occupying the same site. In the early years, the Bolshoi Stone had a wooden "sister," the Maly or Small Theater on Mars Field, then known as Tsaritsyn Meadow. It fell victim to the arbitrary Emperor Paul who, seeing it in the middle of a usable drill field in 1796, said to the governor-general: "Let that, sir, not exist." In one night about five hundred laborers aided by torches dismantled the structure. Revived in 1802 on Catherine Square, it served as the capital's main theater during the rebuilding of the Bolshoi Stone, 1810–17.[6]

The Alexandrinsky and Mikhailovsky Theaters still stand. The former, an architectural jewel crafted by Carlo Rossi in 1832, separates Theater Street and Catherine (now Ostrovsky) Square, just south of the Nevsky. On opening, it was named after Tsar Nicholas's wife, Alexandra Fëdorovna (fig. 24). The theater proper occupies a modest part of the building, which is elegantly adorned in the imperial style. Along with the usual tiers of boxes, a tilted amphitheater offers ideal sight lines to the stage. The stage itself is so vast that the house must have looked small, as it still does, when looking out into the foreshortened space of the audience. Behind the curtain, stage hands worked their magic without the electricity that now powers the elaborate visual and aural effects, trap doors, and flying contraptions. In 1836, the dramatic troupe from the Bolshoi was relocated there and the Alexandrinsky became the primary dramatic stage of the capital.[7] A year after its opening, A. P. Bryullov, brother of the painter, built a house for French and German productions: the Mikhailovsky Theater, on the square of the same name (fig. 25). The state-supported foreign troupes played on alternate nights. The French company clearly dominated this house and it was considered de rigueur for the diplomatic community, the court, and the upper circles of the aristocracy to attend. When the tsar appeared, society followed suit. It was joined, in less exalted seating, by the French emigré community, from shop owners to tutors and serving maids. Grand Duke Mikhail Pavlovich, who lived a few feet away, was a frequent visitor. Although merchants' sons also came to mingle with the quality and students to perfect their French, the tone was restrained and there was no gallery.[8]

Moscow, in the two decades after 1805, experienced the most turbulent period of its theater history until the Revolution of 1905. The theater company migrated to several private homes until the conflagrations of 1812 forced it to evacuate the city. Moscow was in ruins — an estimated 2,626 remained of its 9,158 wooden and stone structures. After the war, a reassembled troupe returned to perform in the homes of the Moscow magnates. The Moscow Imperial "Theater," then, consisted of a troupe of wandering players forced to move at least six times in twenty years and to cease working for two years during the war with France. The troupe catered to the aristocracy and mounted French and Italian operas and ballets as well as vaudeville-operas with Russian themes and patriotic pageants. Moscow theater had difficulty competing with the numerous balls and shows where the gentry could do theater for themselves and by themselves.[9]

In the meantime the burned-out ruins of the Petrovsky rotted away to the sound of the birds and frogs who had settled in swampy vegetation that grew within its ravaged walls. It took more than a decade for a new theater to replace the Petrovsky as a permanent home on the same site. Known ever since as the Moscow Bolshoi Theater, it opened its doors on January 6, 1825. The building, with its clean classical lines and eight-columned Ionic portico atop which Apollo rode his chariot, was made to face Petrovsky (now Theater) Square (fig. 26). The grand opening featured a classically inspired "Prologue: a Celebration of the Muses," with music mostly by Verstovsky and Alyabev. According to Boris Shteinpress, the reported success of the performance, long attributed to Verstovsky's music, belongs to Alyabev. It is easy to see why Alyabev's music would have charmed the audience. His miniature oratorio with strings, harp, and a largely female chorus with some vocal solo and trio passages, was done up in eighteenth-century harmonic and instrumental vocabulary with a wide dynamic range. The declarative and triumphant cadences of its finale make it a cousin to Mozart's Jupiter Symphony. In mood and structure, the music fit nicely with the classicism of the performance motifs and of the newly unveiled edifice.[10]

After a devastating fire in 1853, Cavos rebuilt the Bolshoi in the form that it now has and it reopened in 1856, an immense and spectacular building with marvelous acoustics. At the time of its reopening, Cavos reported the new theater's dimensions to an English visitor who noted that, in magnitude of stage and proscenium and diameter of the ceiling, the Bolshoi surpassed San Carlo in Naples, La Scala in Milan, and Covent Garden in London. On the *bel-étage*, each loge was a suite of "so many little drawing-rooms furnished with sofas, mirrors, and damask hangings," a place amply suitable for rest, entertaining guests, and refreshment. Below the loges and the two imperial boxes were arrayed five hundred stalls seats for a total capacity of two thousand. As had been the case for about a century, women displayed themselves in the frame of the box during performance. But now, their servants stood outside the boxes instead of inside them or on the outer porches of the theater.[11]

The Moscow Maly Theater (fig. 26), the city's oldest dramatic theater, has been mythologized in Soviet literature as the House of Shchepkin, and thus an escape hatch from serfdom; as the House of Ostrovsky, and thus the cradle of realism; and as the "second Moscow University," and thus a rallying point for the intelligentsia and other progressive forces in Russian life. There is truth in all these claims. The Maly Theater opened in 1824 a few months before the Bolshoi and was rebuilt in 1840. Another gem of early nineteenth-century theater architecture, the Maly's huge structure stands long and proud beside its more famous sister, the Bolshoi. Its size is deceptive, for the theater proper occupies a modest part of it. The Maly conveys a sense of intimacy by the reduced proportions of the imperial box and side boxes, the small parterre, an even smaller amphitheater behind it, two flanking open spaces resembling a *baignoire*, and three tiers above that. Yet the theater is capable of mounting large-scale productions. Beneath a very deep stage lay the vast machinery room full of monstrous iron contraptions that moved the stage above and created special effects. The backstage is still a labyrinth of staircases, glistening foyers, dressing and makeup rooms, and the offices of the Directorate.[12]

Front Office

The engine that ran this theatrical empire for over a century, the Imperial Directorate, came into being officially in 1766. With its Moscow branch (founded in 1806) it fell in 1826 under the newly formed Ministry of the Court, and in 1842, the Moscow houses rejoined the central Directorate in St. Petersburg. The Directorate comprised the Chief Director and three members (one for Moscow in certain periods), each heading an "office." At various times it held sway over the Russian, French, and ballet troupes of both capitals, the Petersburg German troupe, and the orchestras and schools. Often "assisted" by powerful outsiders, directors made policy and brokered art, money, work, and sex. The Directorate leaders, as serf owners and owners of serf theaters, tended to transfer the social hierarchies and disciplinary culture of regiment or estate to their serf-like underlings. In an interlock of state and manor house, performers flowed from the seigniorial home to the imperial stage and back again, blurring the distinction between a public and a private sphere.[13]

Chief Court Steward A. L. Naryshkin, the first director to keep his post for any length of time (1799–1819), came from an old boyar family. A witty and boisterous Maecenas, he became a legend among many such legends for his gargantuan hospitality and lavish spending. Unlike other ebullient old-time aristocrats, Naryshkin was one of the few imperial directors to display politeness to his actors. But generosity weakened his financial management. Naryshkin, who naturally looked upon the Imperial Theater complex as his personal fiefdom, freely borrowed its artists for his vast domestic entertainments. Since Tsar Alexander I was Naryshkin's personal friend and often attended the festivities, misuse of office could not be invoked. Along the two-way street between theater and home, the director in 1807 sold to the Imperial Theater his troupe of serf actors; later, long after retirement, he rented it his chorus as well. The rented singers chose a deputy to petition the crown for freedom from Naryshkin's ownership in 1825 and the negotiations ended in the manumission of most of the original two dozen choristers for the redemption price of eight thousand rubles.[14]

When the Mongol Prince P. I. Tyufyakin (1769–1844), appointed Naryshkin's vice director in 1812 to restore fiscal responsibility, succeeded him from 1819, the wicked stepmother replaced the fairy godmother. This abusive tyrant regularly mistreated actors of both sexes, including an eight-year-old boy whom he struck with his opera glass. Mikhail Buturlin recounts that during a trip to Paris to inspect its theatrical riches, Tyufyakin earned the scorn of a French wit who said of "le prince Tioufiakine" that "tout faquin est prince" ("every fool's a prince"). His secretary Rafail Zotov got his job through connections and rose steadily to become Chief of Repertoire. He left a lengthy record of the Directorate's inner workings, including management cabals, artistic feuds, and a brisk traffic in bribes, medals, and the promotion of favorites. He claims that Tyufyakin, whom he admired, paid him to translate a play for his current mistress.[15] After several short-term directors came A. M. Gedeonov (dir. 1834–58), a man with court connections and, like many literary and theatrical people, a heroic war record from 1812. Throughout his long tenure, he and his subordinate in Moscow Alexei Verstovsky lorded it over the system. Bureaucratic corruption, a way of life in Tsar Nicholas's Russia, could hardly bypass the theater administration. Under Gedeonov, according to Avdotiya Panaeva, a hostile witness, the tsar's underlings pilfered, embezzled, and built themselves glorious homes. A friend of Panaeva called the administration a "Tatar invasion." A boss frequently described as a tyrant, womanizer, panderer, and arrant snob, Gedeonov nevertheless had his defenders. One, the violinist Afanasev, who worked at the Petersburg opera in the 1850s, maintained that Gedeonov was no more than a kindly despot whose bark was worse than his bite.[16]

An early Moscow director, F. F. Kokoshkin (1823–31), had been a prosecutor — not so strange in a system where officials constantly moved from one métier to another. A writer, actor, and theater lover, he also scouted the provinces to recruit future Moscow stars. His successor, Mikhail Zagoskin (1789–1852, dir. 1831–42), came from a Penza landowning family descended from Tatars. Connections led him into the theater system in 1817. Zagoskin's soft-handed manner with staff made him a weak manager. He eventually became a well-known historical novelist. Since Zagoskin knew nothing about music, the composer Verstovsky gradually became the real force, belying his modest titles of Inspector of Music (1825) and of Repertoire (1830). In the years 1825–59, he wielded enormous creative and administrative power in two of the five great imperial houses, the Bolshoi and the Maly. Verstovsky's promotion from Collegiate to State Councilor in 1853 followed his appointment as head of the Imperial Moscow Theaters. He dwelt among the elite in the heartland of Moscow, first on Old Equerries Street and then on Bread Lane, where Prince Kropotkin (b. 1842) and Konstantin Pobedonostsev (b. 1827), respectively, were growing up. Verstovsky kept company with conservatives, Slavophiles, and Official Nationalist ideologues who also happened to be ardent lovers of the arts—people such as Sergei Aksakov, Stepan Shevyrëv, and Mikhail Pogodin. A contemporary painting shows Verstovsky at the piano at Aksakov's Abramtsevo estate, with Gogol and the actor Shchepkin in attendance.[17]

Like many figures in an arena where creativity and management converge, Verstovsky has gotten mixed reviews from memoirists. Some Soviet commentators held his conservative friends against him, while others appreciated his contributions to theater as manager, pedagogue, and composer. Verstovsky has been called good-natured, stubborn, willful, sometimes cruel, demanding, hard-driving, and opinionated. His correspondence and other traces bear out this complex image. Verstovsky was forceful enough to marry a serf's daughter, actress Nadezhda Repina, against the will of his father who apparently thought that it was one thing to manage actresses, another to marry them. Verstovsky, like most other theater executives, addressed his singers and actors with the familiar "ty" form for "you"—thereby putting them in their place as social underlings. Yet, playwright Alexander Ostrovsky claimed that artists did not mind being addressed that way, especially when accompanied by praise. Verstovsky could make life hard for actors, yet one of them concluded that the good outweighed the bad in him. A conscientious man, he attended rehearsals religiously. At least one sign of loyalty and humanity was his continued correspondence and collaboration with the composer and condemned criminal Alyabev.[18]

Verstovsky and Gedeonov, bowing to aristocratic desires, smiled upon Italian opera and French plays and equally disfavored some of the best-known figures of Russian drama: Turgenev and Ostrovsky and the actors Shchepkin and Mochalov. Verstovsky's voluminous, detailed, and friendly but deferential correspondence with Gedeonov reveals a good deal about his pivotal role in Moscow theater life. Much of it concerned mundane traffic back and forth of artists and productions from Petersburg to Moscow, hiring and firing actors, the costs of foreign artists, scandals and insult-matches. One finds here and there a flattering note to an elevated figure such as cellist and courtier Matvei Vielgorsky. A report on the audition of a provincial actor, I. I. Lavrov, indicates the all too human side of the somewhat insecure Verstovsky as a composer. In 1853, Lavrov, then working in a provincial theater, tried out for the Moscow stage and cleverly chose as his number an aria from Verstovsky's opera *Askold's Grave*. As the composer's positive response shows, Lavrov's gambit paid off.[19]

From the front office to the stage and backstage of the Russian drama, opera, and ballet world, the distance in power and status was enormous. Serfdom provided an important pool of performers and support staff. Rentals and purchases of manorial serfs occurred from about 1800 to the 1830s in the Petersburg theaters (Moscow ceased buying in 1824). Around 1800, Naryshkin purchased a dozen performers from the defunct Zorich estate; other directors bought individual serf musicians from landowners. In 1822, when Vera Khlyustina sold the violinist Afanasy Amatov, he and the theater each paid her two thousand rubles for his freedom (for Amatov, the equivalent of more than two years' salary). Imperial choreographer Glushkovsky in 1824 purchased for the Moscow Bolshoi a ballet corps of eighteen serf girls from a Riazan landowner. Such transactions not only enriched the staff of the Imperial Theaters, but endowed the purchased serfs and their families with freedom from bondage. But the freedom was far from absolute: physical punishment, sexual exploitation, discipline, and heavy restrictions were all a part of the "serfdom of theater." Ex-serf performers still remained in the taxable classes and thus subject to disabilities, including incarceration, corporal punishment, switching to menial duties, or transfer to the army. Ex-serf musicians were treated little better than house serfs.[20]

Foreign actors appeared from the very beginning, some recruited by Russian theater managers on junkets to Paris to see Talma act and study French theatrical art. A French vaudeville of 1802, *Allons en Russie,* poked fun at mediocre Parisian talents who set their sights on good jobs in St. Petersburg.[21] Russian nonserf actors acquired by ascription, connections, accident, and a dozen other ways accounted for the remaining personnel, mostly foundlings, orphans, the children of serfs, servants, soldiers, and others at the bottom of the social scale, rarely the child of an impoverished noble. The Imperial Foundling Schools, in addition to training in more menial occupations, provided courses in performance and graphic arts to talented youngsters who might be drafted into the Imperial Theaters or the Academy of Arts. In Europe, foundlings and orphans had been a traditional source for performance skills. By the early nineteenth century, acting "dynasties" were shaping up. Serfs were officially excluded from the Theater School in 1817, though there is no evidence of any attending at that moment.[22]

The Theater Directorate tended to hire foreign players for orchestra first chairs and soloists and filled the remaining positions with Russians recruited from Theater School pupils, serf orchestras, and the Capella. A Pskov serf owner in 1829 sold thirteen male serf musicians to the Directorate in order to bail himself out of debt. The acquisition of a twenty-seven-piece orchestra from the Chernyshev estate in Orël — some of its musicians veterans of the Beethoven concert cycle of the 1820s — included instruments, sheet music, and the players' families who were immediately and forever freed by the transaction. The Inspector of Music supervised the musicians: from the late eighteenth century, the post was held successively by a Pole (Kozlovsky), a Russian cuirassier officer, an Italian, and two Germans. The last, Ludwig Maurer, spoke Russian badly. During his tenure (1841–62) the orchestra reached a high level of disorder. Musicians would go ill, skip work, pay the conductor to excuse their absences, refuse to tune instruments, make rude noises, leave the pit before the finale, play wrong notes, and miss cues. Some were arrested. The Moscow orchestra reached to over ninety in the 1840s. Players came mostly from the commoners, including serfs, trained at the Moscow Theater School, which also had a Noble Pension attached. They were conducted by a string of German and other European conductors one of whom, J. J. Feltzman, in the words of a contemporary, "led the orchestra with the cold-bloodedness of a true German." N. Ya. Afanasev, a first violinist in this orchestra in the 1830s, related that the lazy and miscreant musicians exceeded even those of Petersburg in absenteeism and in fights that broke out between the acts of an opera.[23]

Behind the scenes the regisseur or stage manager oversaw casting, reading, rehearsing, costumes, and physical plant. The most famous set designer of this period, the Italian Pietro Gonzago, worked in Russia from 1792 to his death in 1831 and was followed by the equally renowned Andrei Roller (Andreas Leonhard, 1805–91). Their elaborate machinery created the waves, storms, clouds, and thunder for the great stage spectacles. Writers — unlike in some other countries, all male — had little impact on the how their works were staged unless they worked in the theater. They received higher rates of pay for verse than for prose. Authorial status remained shaky due to favoritism, brittle contracts, and a lack of copyright laws until 1828. At one time a governor general of Moscow could stage a play of Sumarokov without his permission.[24]

Three celebrities of artistic direction emerged in St. Petersburg during the reign of Alexander I: Didelot for ballet, Cavos for opera, and Shakhovskoi for drama. Charles-Louis Didelot, called "the Byron of the ballet," served the Imperial Theaters from 1801 to 1829, with a break in 1811–16 (fig. 27). As dramatist, composer, choreographer, artist, director, mechanic, and teacher, he drove himself day and night. Isolated by language from Russian life and wholly obsessed with his art, fired and rehired several times and once jailed, Didelot waged a continuous war with the cast and Directorate and died a few years after retirement at his country home in Ukraine. At work, this strict disciplinarian struck and bruised pupils of both sexes and pulled the hair of soloists between curtain calls for performance errors. He frightened his young charges at the Theater School when he appeared at 11:00 A.M. each day to review the dancers who had been working out in the icy studio since dawn. School veteran Avdotiya Panaeva recounts that when Didelot was dismissed for a time in the 1810s, the pupils greeted the news with joy. But manager and writer Rafail Zotov claimed that Didelot, despite an "ungovernable temper," was "loved and adored by everybody," and noted that it was Didelot who turned from the practice of hiring French ballerinas to recruiting Russians from the Theater School.[25]

Didelot's own view of things is recorded in a memo of 1828 to the front office in which he explained in angry and puzzled tones that the ballet company, the most ornate and expensive element of the Imperial Theaters, failed to carry its clock-like elegance into daily life. A picture of the real-world looseness of backstage comes through palpably in the document: lateness, insubordination, and truancy from rehearsals. Didelot's staff of *maîtres de ballet* seem to have lacked power over the dancers; the summoning bells planted all over the theater and the graded fines for lateness could not ensure punctuality. *Coryphées* and *figurantes* constantly complained about their placement on the stage, and principal dancers appeared in costumes of their own devising. All of them, Didelot lamented, struggled to remain on stage until their dying day—however stout or decrepit they might appear to the public. Didelot made no bones about the need for early retirement of dancers because his esthetic required the display of youth and physical beauty. Having worked in the Imperial Theaters for nearly three decades, he could think of no more imaginative solution to his problems than increased discipline; and as an answer to the perpetual excuse for tardiness, "My carriage came late," he demanded more carriages.[26]

For the first three decades or so of the century, the crown of Russian operatic composing sat on the head of the Italian Catterino Cavos (1775–1840) who lived in Russia for forty-two years (fig. 28). Father of the theater architect Albert Cavos, the great-grandfather of the Silver Age artist Alexandre Benois (and thus an ancestor of actor Peter Ustinov), Cavos worked permanently in the Imperial Theater system from 1806 as, successively, conductor of the Russian Opera, Inspector of the Court Orchestra, and Director of Music. In the memory of the musician Yury Arnold, Cavos had the manners and tone of educated society, was friendly and decent, but lacked warm or intimate relations with his colleagues. To the end of his life, Cavos maintained iron work habits—morning rehearsal with singers, afternoon orchestra rehearsal, and evening performance. Cavos's greatest contribution was promoting Russian themes in opera and ballets in collaboration with Russian composers.[27]

The achievement of the central figure in the creative life of the St. Petersburg Imperial Theaters in this era, the playwright, manager, and teacher Alexander Shakhovskoi, has suffered neglect. Born in Smolensk in an ancient but middling gentry family, Shakhovskoi attended the Noble Pension of Moscow University before entering the military service which took him to St. Petersburg where personal contacts pulled him into theater life. About him, one wise and learned scholar wrote: "It is, perhaps, only in our own day [1953], when the art of the theatre has come to mean the sum of the play, actor, and producer, greater than any one of these single parts, that we can best appreciate the multiform, but happily coordinated contribution of one of the first great men of the Russian theatre." As director of repertoire from 1802, Shakhovskoi dominated the stage, with a break for the war of 1812, until 1826. His attitude toward money and professionalism resembled Anton Rubinstein's. Believing that only talent should be rewarded, he fought for an anti-star system which led to endless battles with the imperious would-be luminaries of the Russian dramatic stage. Shakhovskoi also promoted a Russian repertoire in an age when most "Russian" performances were translations. He wanted a national idiom to replace the "powder, embroidered coats and red heels from Paris."[28]

The Imperial Theaters Directorate abhorred competition and steadily upheld the monopoly which was reinforced by government decrees. Nor did it deign to administer according to sound accounting principles. No Meyerbeers worked in the Russian system to keep costs down and box office up. Expenses exceeded the combined total of ticket receipts and subsidies. So, in spite of the monopoly and a heavy state subsidy, the system ran on a deficit. The tsars continued to fatten the Imperial Theaters' budget for the extravagant outlays required. For them theater held equal value to the great palaces and imperial displays in terms of its political projection of majesty, power, and European cultural sheen. The spending was very uneven. An annual budget in rubles of around 1810 assigned 855,079 to the Petersburg theaters and 365,000 to Moscow's. In the breakdown (minus the cost of wardrobe and props) the budget allowed 54,600 for the Petersburg Russian troupe and 35,000 for Moscow's; 175,648 for the Petersburg French company, 66,340 for Moscow's; 85,620 for the Petersburg ballet, 32,093 for Moscow's; 148,930 for the Petersburg orchestra, 37,690 for Moscow's.[29] Thus, the state spent about a third more on St. Petersburg than on Moscow, and a great deal more on foreign companies than on Russian, some of this due to higher salaries for non-Russian performers.

Backstage Stories

In the era of late serfdom, theater presented not only dramaturgical works of the imagination but its own real-life backstage dramas whose plots throbbed with competition, humor, jealousy, and rage among the actors; the farces and burlesques of mischievous and drunken cast members; melodramas of villainous managers and vulnerable players; and tragedies of seduction and the ruin of actresses. The backstage scenario starred performers at every level, including walk-on roles for policemen who sometimes appeared to restore order in the wings. Within the vast backstage space, the behavioral dynamic remained largely invisible to the public. It was conditioned in large measure by the highly choreographed worlds that molded it: the stage itself where the actors played roles according to a plot; the front office which scripted their offstage deportment — dress, deference, discretion; and the theater schools which trained them. Tensions stored up in these arenas exploded in venomous rivalry and malicious gossip — as well as in tender attachments of friendship and love. Theatrical discipline, crucial to a good performance, requires a professional outlook in which personal problems and their attendant emotionalism are supposed to be left at the stage door. Managers tried to enforce it by reprimand, fine, flogging, arrest, dismissal, and assignment into the army. Some authorities exercised fair judgment and tried to fit the punishment to the misdeed, but the surviving sources naturally stress dramatic abuse over normal maintenance of order. In fact, all too often, those wielding authority failed to leave their own emotions and prejudices at the door, and introduced favoritism, sexual procuring, personal vendettas, and arbitrary and excessive retaliation. And, lest it be forgotten, all those possessing and exuding superordinate power were males.

The physical expression of displeasure on the part of superiors to inferiors grew out of the culture of Russian social relations. The closer a boss was to the daily labor, the more likely that blows would rain. A. V. Karatygin claimed that corporal punishment was not permitted at the Imperial Theaters in this period, but the violinist Afanasev said that it prevailed up to the 1830s and 1840s. Middle and upper management, whose dignity would not permit them to raise the hand, employed contempt towards underlings. When Tyufyakin tried to use the familiar "ty" to the eminent actor Yakov Bryansky (1790–1853), his daughter Panaeva recalled, the latter threatened to quit and was backed by the rest of the cast. Because of this, Tyufyakin's successor Gedeonov never tried it with Bryansky, though he did so with all other subordinates. When the equally eminent singer Ekaterina Semënova (not the tragedienne) corrected Gedeonov on this violation of her dignity, he banished her to Moscow. He ordered the withdrawal of back pay for pregnant actresses until they had "recovered," invoking the strictures on immoral behavior and debauchery of the cast. This in truth was a recurring problem, though hardly worse than the debauchery of the directors. Gedeonov also enforced the rule that actors had to memorize twenty-five lines per day. Shakhovskoi became known for his verbal abuse. According to his goddaughter Panaeva, he would say to his students: "You, my dear little bastard, keep hitting the taverns and you won't learn the role." He could reduce women to tears: "Use your voice, you whine! You, you sweet little idiot, are deaf! Where is the meter, you belong in a laundry, not on stage." He told Karatygin that he should be working in a fair booth.[30]

In prereform Russia, jail loomed as an occupational hazard for all kinds of people. Students, seminarians, professors, teachers, journalists, censors, publishers, officials, and other unlucky folks found themselves incarcerated as temporary punishment. The Directorate used a brig in the basement of the Bolshoi Stone Theater, the nearby guardhouse, or a cell in the Peter-Paul Fortress. Though most theatrical inmates ended up there for drunkenness and disorder, jail time could be earned in many ways. Gedeonov, for example, threatened to confine Panaeva's mother for walking on stage without permission. In 1810, the Moscow actor Yakov Sokolov, for refusing to take a role on short notice, got three days in a guardhouse where he fell ill. Hearsay has it that even the renowned set designer Roller was jailed for a few days on order of the emperor because of a foul-up in the scenery. A lapse in deference or simple carelessness could bring down the thunder of the bosses. In 1822, V. A. Karatygin failed to rise when the interim director A. A. Maikov, a man of vaulting arrogance, entered the dining room. Said Maikov: "one ought to feel the nearness of a director." Governor General Miloradovich put Karatygin in the fortress for two days. Miloradovich, known to historians as one of the defenders of the throne killed during the Decembrist Uprising of 1825, enmeshed himself in theater life by virtue of his office and through romantic entanglements. He came of Hercegovian ancestry and had fought in almost every Russian war since his teenage years. His brilliant career earned him the love of his men and a chest emblazoned with medals. Suffused with the culture of military discipline, this general despised actors, could not even comprehend their insubordination, and was known to threaten them with the madhouse for disobedience. The Maikov-Karatygin tiff acquired political overtones when Miloradovich interpreted the actor's rudeness to a superior as subversive and called him a "young liberal." Two years after an alarming 1820 mutiny in one of the tsar's favorite regiments, authorities everywhere bristled at the slightest sign of disrespect for the constituted order.[31]

Petty hurts to professional pride often sting the most. Actresses could be forced to play different roles in different theaters on the same day. One singer, made to perform while afflicted with bronchitis, lost her voice and her career. Vera Samoilova (1824–80) had running battles with Gedeonov in the 1840s over costumes. At one point, she refused to go on and was ordered to do so by the tsar from his box. Alexandra Kolosova managed to aggravate drama coach Shakhovskoi by switching to Pavel Katenin for acting lessons and going

to Paris to study under Talma and Mlle. Mars. Shakhovskoi, backed by Miloradovich, took away her roles and punished her for overstaying her tour in
Moscow where she had been warmly received. The actress then actually went
to nearby Tsarskoe Selo and got an audience with Alexander I who consoled
her and promised to rectify things. She was nevertheless suspended for going
outside the chain of command.[32]

Actors, who fomented conflict as well as being victimized, often engaged in
intrigue and gossip. Panaeva's mother Bryanskaya, for example, feuded bitterly with her rival A. M. Karatygina. Performers of both sexes upgraded their
public acclaim by buying bouquets to be thrown to them at curtain time.
Panaeva alleges that some Alexandrinsky Theater actresses even rented bouquets for performance and returned them to nearby Gostiny Dvor at half
price. Tales of inebriation and disorder abound. A former serf who behaved
drunkenly in the chorus of the Alexandrinsky Theater was sent to be beaten by
the theater's furnace attendant — just as estate serfs were beaten in the stable.
Some merchants who patronized male actors as jesters and imbibing companions would wine and dine them in return for their no doubt vivacious company — a custom that led to a lot of alcoholic excess among actors. During the
pre-Lenten merriment, actors sometimes had to be rounded up in the taverns.
Disputes among male actors occasionally turned physical: when one of them
hit an antagonist on the head, the victim was recompensed with the perpetra-
tor's benefit money. Afanasev described "coupling" backstage among actors,
students, and managers in the 1850s. A scandal erupted once when the curtain
inadvertently rose on the scene of a pair in a compromising position. Gedeonov, dallying with an actress in a dressing room, once delayed the orchestra
rehearsal. The virtuoso violinist Henryk Wieniawski, who sought the favors of
Adelina Patti, crushed his rival in a door jamb. Nor were executives above
scandal. Gedeonov and Rafail Zotov nearly fought a duel over the former's
request for housing for a vaudeville actress. To avoid losing Gedeonov, Tsar
Nicholas fired Zotov.[33]

According to the earliest theater rules published in 1784, the comportment
and moral makeup of the actors backstage had to be aligned with the noble
and elevated behavior of the characters on stage. But in practice, tsarist theater
— like many others — had all the makings of an erotic hothouse. Young actresses, ballerinas, and choral singers with great physical charms inhabited all
the theaters. They and all others were enveloped by the aphrodisiac ambience
of performance and rehearsal life: close quarters, the flimsiness or fancy of
costumes, the frottage of perspiring bodies, and the pure delirium and exhilaration of stage and backstage existence. It can hardly be wondered that sexual
affairs and romantic liaisons at every level bloomed in this libidinous environ-

ment. Some were more or less equal relations; others arose from a nexus between a performer's understandable desire for economic, creative, professional, and personal advancement on the one hand and the passions of a powerful admirer on the other. In the imperial houses, the males at the top were landowners, serf owners, officers, bureaucrats—some geared to the sexual pleasures made possible by that power. Rafail Zotov recounts that it was commonplace, even accepted, for those in management to take young mistresses from the cast. Males in the audience were enchanted by the genuine talent of stars and by the adulation shown them by the public, an attraction perhaps enhanced by the very distance between the stalls and the stage.[34]

Leonid Grossman, slightly exaggerating, wrote that Guards officers and high officials "looked on the female performers as a vast gynaeceum, differing from a serf harem only in brilliance, refinement, and range of choices." In stage romances and sexual liaisons, the techniques of approach varied immensely and differed from the relatively simple methods associated with landowner–serf girl sex. Courtiers and royals wielded the greatest power but also required certain discreet arrangements. When the time came, they gave their mistresses large dowries and married them off, as was customary in other European courts. Nataliya Apollonskaya was among the alleged mistresses of Nicholas I. The radical publicist of the 1860s Nikolai Dobrolyubov wrote an unpublished denunciation of the tsar as a "destroyer of virginal innocence." Working from rumors, he claimed that Nicholas routinely entered actresses' dressing rooms to watch them in deshabille and that Gedeonov pimped foreign female performers for himself, the tsar, and other dignitaries.[35]

General Miloradovich, who ex officio held sway over the St. Petersburg theater system, had a passion for female dancers and pupils of the Theater School, a passion not hard to satisfy, given his position. On December 14, 1825, the very morning of his death, the fifty-four-year-old Miloradovich breakfasted with one of them, the twenty-one-year-old ballerina Ekaterina Telesheva (1804–57). A soloist of the St. Petersburg Bolshoi Stone, she captured many admirers, including the governor general and the playwright Alexander Griboedov. The latter would go to Shakhovskoi's dacha where actress pupils were on hand, in order to "enjoy himself with a daring hand along the swan's down of lovely breasts." The erotic preference for ballerinas over actresses (including singing ones) was a classic case of seeking a sexual object devoid of too many complications. For certain kinds of males, the alleged lack of cerebral talent may have been precisely the attraction, in addition to the splendor surrounding ballet, the graceful athletics, and the scanty costumes. In any case, the preference lasted well down to the end of the dynasty and even increased.[36]

If the theater building itself was an erotic playground, the Imperial Theater School which fed it was seen by many as a training ground for its sexual culture, though this was by no means its intended purpose or main function. Theater manager Rafail Zotov noted that Paris Conservatoire pupils commuted daily at their own expense and that only about two hundred of its roughly four hundred annual graduates would get work in Paris theaters, while the rest went off to the provinces or became teachers. In contrast, the Russian school sheltered, fed, and transported its many fewer pupils and guaranteed graduates a post in one of the two capitals, an income, and a pension. In 1836 its elegant new quarters, which also housed the Directorate, opened as part of the ensemble designed by Carlo Rossi on Theater Street, made famous as the title of the much-admired autobiography of the twentieth-century dancer Tamara Karsavina.[37] Pupils, including females after 1757, increasingly came from theatrical parents. By 1800 the enrollment norm was about fifty of each sex who studied religion, languages, mathematics, geography, history, dance, fencing, singing, declamation, mythology, and music. A detailed memoir drew a somewhat mixed picture of life inside the walls. Its author, Alexandra Asenkova, an orphan girl, mentioned no sexual harassment or attachments, noted the rigorous schedule and the mediocre training, and recalled that the staff was mostly kind. Indeed, she remembered her school years as the happiest of her life. She graduated in 1815 with a dream in her heart to see her name on an *affiche*. Her debut in the popular *Shakespeare in Love,* alongside the famous Yakovlev as the bard, ushered this lower-class orphan not only into a career but into a state-owned apartment and into the high-toned society of the salons. Compared to seminaries, military academies, and most other schools where rote learning and corporal punishment ruled, the Theater School apparently offered a privileged refuge.[38]

Other accounts are not so rosy. A convent-like wall of rules surrounded the school to isolate female pupils. The tsar forbade shops and cafés to be built near it. According to Panaeva, admission policy sometimes favored sexual allure over talent. Girls who spoke no Russian and read no music were stood in the chorus as ornaments. Female pupils customarily sought a well-placed admirer who would have a carriage and apartment waiting for them upon graduation. A middle-aged official, infatuated with a beautiful teenage German pupil, set her up in a flat after graduation and married her. When he suffered paralysis, the young wife deserted him. Anna Natarova (1835–?), whose parents were freed serfs of the Sheremetevs, recorded a kind of mutual hazing at the school in the 1840s that had nothing to do with social origin: after the separation of the drama and ballet troupes in 1836, acting pupils began calling dancers "the brainless" while the latter called the former "the uglies." Dancers did better in the sexual patronage market than actresses, though this hardly guaranteed stability or happiness. Pupils would flirt with each other on the sly during lessons, but the real sexual energy came from mature men outside the school. The son of Rafail Zotov claims that the policeman Leonty Dubelt frequented the school's off-limits classes and dressing rooms with a prurient purpose. In 1853, a cause célèbre erupted over allegations by a discharged whistle-blower of officials pimping schoolgirls for persons in power. Vasily Insarsky, the investigator, found grounds for an indictment but, after some resignations, a cover-up cleared the major suspects, including Gedeonov. During the inquiry, the school director invited Insarsky to look at the practice classes of the seminude adolescent dancers, apparently as a bribe. Yet the very fact that a case was made reinforces the older Zotov's claim that public morality in the theater had improved since the early nineteenth century.[39]

Among fashionable officers, to be "in love" with a pupil at the school was considered de rigueur, and they would patrol Theater Street or ride horseback beside the school's well-known Green Carriage (fig. 29) to snatch some conversation with female pupils. Some admirers pursued this and other carriages on foot and even harnessed themselves to them. Yakubovich, the duelist who shot Griboedov, once smuggled himself into the school disguised as a peddler. Patrons worked hard to get introductions, devise modes of seduction, and organize the keeping of their mistresses. Natarova dispassionately explained why some dancers acquiesced so easily to "arrangements." They came from humble backgrounds with families in need. This and the familiarity in the school with a refined (though not luxurious) environment created a longing for security and made them easy marks for rich men. Pupils so inclined communicated with their beaux by secret letters, a coded system of gestures, a nod or a wave of a scarf, from the stage to the front rows — which Stanislavsky later dubbed the "mimetic telegraph." Once a favorite pupil had graduated to the stage, the admirer would court her through applause and claques consisting of his friends. Konstantin Bulgakov, a witty troublemaker, enraged his commander, Grand Duke Mikhail Pavlovich, by deserting his guard post on Haymarket Square to rush to the Alexandrinsky Theater a half-mile away to see his favorite. Ardent young men and rich and powerful older men each, in their different ways, formed their attachments by way of charm, money, position, looks. Some resorted to other methods. Prince Vyazemsky was put in a fortress for kidnaping a dance pupil who was, it was said, admired by Tsar Alexander.[40] Numerous male viewers with no access to female performers fell madly in love at a distance, a habit treated with great irony in Dostoevsky's *Poor Folk*.

Man-in-pursuit-of-woman dominates the tales of amatory life in the theater. Did gentry women find lovers on the Russian stage? Did same-sex love flourish in the shadows? The obstacles to the first kind of nexus were probably much greater than to the second. Since the sources are mute on both, we can only speculate. Homosexual conduct was a crime, and an 1832 law on sodomy could bring Siberian exile to offenders. Most of society seemed quite unaware of them or of transvestites: when survivors found a complete woman's costume in the closet of a deceased Italian male resident of Moscow, they could not figure out its purpose.[41.] Of lesbianism, I have found no traces, but homoerotic love was no secret in St. Petersburg literary and art circles. Serena Vitale's statement that "homosexuality was quite widespread in high society at the time" may be too sweeping, but several prominent figures are often named, including Prince Dondukov-Korsakov, believed to be the lover of the married minister of education Sergei Uvarov, and Ivan Dmitriev, poet and minister of justice under Alexander I. The only documented homosexual figure of the theater world, F. F. Vigel (1786–1856), left informative memoirs of theater life. Pushkin once wrote to him: "To serve you I'll be all too happy, / With all my soul, my verse, my prose, / But Vigel, you must spare my rear."[42]

The stories about power and abuse, intrigue, scandal, and harassment, however exaggerated, are too many and too consistent to be dismissed. When faced with injustice, actors found ways to resist. It is fashionable nowadays to employ the metaphor of the "backstage culture of resistance" in a nontheatrical meaning to denote general "social spaces" where dissent can be played out silently or otherwise.[43] In the present instance, it would be silly and pious to emphasize the physical backstage of the theater world as an arena of resistance against the state, as embodied in management. But theater people were as adept as any member of the lower orders at deploying the "weapons of the weak" in everyday life. Males and females used their contacts, appealed, went over the heads of their superiors, refused to perform, and generally made trouble in finely calibrated gestures deployed to get their way while avoiding dismissal. In at least one case, a kind of radical politics was invoked when the actor Mikhail Shchepkin, backed by the cast of the Moscow Maly Theater, threatened to inform Alexander Herzen's emigré revolutionary newspaper *The Bell* about managerial abuses. Some of the roughhouse, drunkenness, and absenteeism backstage and in the pit might be compared to the familiar modes of peasant resistance to landowner and steward, but it would be an error to romanticize it.[44]

The other side of the picture was displayed by the noted Soviet scholar Vsevolodsky-Gerngross. His prerevolutionary work, drawing heavily on Stepan Zhikharëv and Faddei Bulgarin, tried to sympathize with the problems of the Imperial Theater administration—a rare thing in the historiography. While granting the justice of some actors' complaints, he also noted that many of them went into theater only in order to get free of serfdom; and then abused their new position by making unseemly demands. The Directorate had to deal with lazy, opportunistic, stubborn, disruptive, drinking, lying, cheating, deceiving, and shirking actors. Theater personnel lived under a strict regimen, but in relative comfort too. A stage manager, S. P. Solovëv, had, among his myriad duties, the unpleasant task of imposing fines, transmitting reprimands from higher-ups to the cast, and marshaling everyone for the 6:00 P.M. "first bell." In his engaging and doleful memoir, Solovëv lamented his unpopularity, his lack of friends, and indeed lack of a life.[45]

What of actors' lives outside the theater? When in the 1790s Semën Vorontsov, the Russian ambassador in London, was asked to help recruit dancers of good morals for the Imperial Theaters, he replied that he "detested the society of theatrical people," who would compromise his noble birth and his position. The Russian public inherited the traditional European view of actors and entertainers. Performers, almost a caste, remained, in Rafail Zotov's words, "outside ordinary society." "Everyone" liked to get actors drunk, he said, but would not treat them as equals. Actresses who married officers had to quit the stage. The ballerina Anna Natarova once heard that a metropolitan of the Russian Church asked whether theater girls crossed themselves. Audiences admired stars but saw ordinary actors as vestiges from minstrel days, transient and shady. Some of those merchants who opposed the stage threatened to disinherit sons who went off to an acting career. The merchant's son Pëtr Plavilshchikov (1760–1812), who had been a student at Moscow University, was invited to good houses. But this was uncommon in the early nineteenth century. The theatrical parents of Panaeva (b. 1819) had wanted her to become a ballerina and so enrolled her at the Theater School. She managed to escape school, theater, and parents by marrying. But as a product of the theatrical world, Panaeva was coolly received in her husband's noble family and in high society.[46]

Class bigotry reinforced moral suspicion of actors among the gentry. The voracious theater lover Vigel occasionally alternated the term "world of actors" with "backstage riff-raff." The government made a dent in the class-based system in 1839 when Tsar Nicholas bestowed on actors of the first rank after ten years of service the title of Personal Honored Citizen; and after fifteen years Hereditary Citizen. These titles exempted holders from conscription, corporal punishment, and the poll tax, and theoretically gave them admission preference to certain schools. Untitled actors remained *raznochintsy*. Offstage, the profession enjoyed little in the way of prestige. If socially elevated musicians were prohibited from appearing before the general public in a professional capacity, how much more would this apply to acting? The prejudice was codified in an 1827 law by which a noble lost rank by appearing on stage, softened a bit a few years later by a directive which restored the rank to those who left the stage. Many nobles adored performing in any genre but not before a diverse ticket-buying public. This "social stage-fright," unlike the ordinary kind, was not an occupational disease but a status anxiety: the reluctance by men and women of the upper classes to put themselves in the power of an audience, to be judged, applauded, or jeered — just as they themselves were wont to do from their seats. Professional theater people thus suffered not so much for what they did as whom they did it for. Theater had yet to reach that moment in history when paid performers began to look down from their superior perch to a humble and imploring public.[47]

Star worship, fully in place by the late eighteenth century, had its limits. For example, the actor Alexander Martynov (1816–60) was beloved enough to be feted by Nekrasov, Ostrovsky, Yazykov, Shevchenko, Druzhinin, and other writers — forty in all — at a restaurant in 1859. When he died prematurely the following year, a huge crowd followed his cortege through the streets of St. Petersburg. But A. I. Saburov, a notoriously rude head of Grand Duke Konstantin's court before his appointment at the Imperial Theaters, wondered about all the fuss over a mere actor. "Pity!" he exclaimed. "Now ticket sales will drop off." This reflected an opinion in some quarters that awarding talent with celebrity status menaced the rank-and-serfdom system. Even foreign stars were not immune to snobbery. In Rafail Zotov's story, "Two Prima Donnas" (1842), one of them at an aristocratic evening mingles with the musicians, "crosses the line," and breaches the social barrier between guests and "staff." In real life, the diva Pauline Viardot, whose fame swept Russia like a gale, appeared at a ball of Countess Rostopchina in 1844 and was invited to dance. This met with negative gossip by mothers of eligible daughters. Though technically the married Viardot could not compete for a nuptial partner with those daughters, as a person of the theater, she was seen as a pretentious social intruder and a distraction.[48]

Lacking the lineage — to say nothing of the wardrobe, social skills, and income — needed to enter an enchanted social circle, actors tended to intermarry and socialize with each other as most professional people tend to do. The Lenten months and August set them free; some actors worked summer jobs in suburban sites to supplement a meager income. Salaries for most theater employees were usually three times lower than those of foreigners, though they did include housing, firewood, and a few other perquisites. Leading players cherished the benefit performance as a key boost to their income. The custom, originating in France in 1735, lasted in Russia until 1908 in the Imperial Theaters. On benefit nights, an actor or group of actors received a portion of the box office. The beneficiary had to follow a ritualized custom in order to advertise the coming event. Older actors with families often assumed silly costumes and wigs, painted up like clowns, and did folk dances on stage. The beneficiaries would then go round town begging high officials, society people, and merchants to come to their performance and they were sometimes received rudely or shown the door. These circus-like parades were said by some commentators to humiliate actors. Yet V. R. Zotov claimed that actors abused the system by demanding benefits consisting of poor plays that would attract large crowds at inflated prices.[49]

Imperial Theater actors had no right to leave town or marry without permission. At least one male actor was arrested for disobeying this rule. Marriage outside the profession was rare. A few well-known love matches catapulted actresses, but not actors, upward, a well-tested practice in the Latin world. The most famous Russian instance was that of the tragedienne, Ekaterina Semënova (1786–1849). Her mother, a serf of Smolensk Province, had been given to a teacher at the Cadet School in St. Petersburg who first sired her children and then married her off to a servant. The daughter Katerina entered the Theater School and became the star known as Semënova Bolshaya. She lived with Prince I. A. Gagarin, an art and theater enthusiast, bore him children, but refused to marry him until 1828, since as a titled princess she would be denied the public stage. Her sister Nimfodora cohabited with V. V. Musin-Pushkin in blinding luxury and proudly went about in her own carriage with liveried lackeys. A disaster awaited the singer Darya Bolina who tired of the theater at age eighteen and married a nobleman. Later appointed a governor, he turned this poorly educated and mismatched woman into a human wreck.[50]

In the Imperial Theater system, a classic battleground of social power, skirmishes broke out almost daily. In the long term, performers and musicians could win a battle for continued career and a pension, but almost never the war for dignity or status. Part of the problem arose from the very nature of the theatrical enterprise where self-pride is the almost inevitable companion of talent and success with audiences. When pride turned to pretension and demand for privileges, conflict was bound to arise and the actors' opponents almost always embodied a formidable combination of state authority, economic leverage, and social superiority. Any creative triumph under the footlights could be psychologically reversed backstage at the whim of an overseer. As with serf actors on private estates, the contrast between the temporary assumption of exalted roles and the permanent status of underling engendered acute pangs of double identity. Actors on the imperial stages understandably did not ponder the indisputable fact that their station in life was infinitely better than that of serf actors. So the record left by commentators on both sides, bristling with fictions and rumors as it is, leaves us with a real sense of theater life as a social landscape blemished by the kind of ascription, inequality, and abusive authoritarianism that prevailed almost everywhere else, and yet also as a very lively arena of extraordinary color, euphoria, and emotion.

Audience as Cast

On the other side of the stage unfolded quite a different drama, with the audience as cast playing very stylized social roles in a living seminar on class, gender, sexuality, the body, and cultural consumption (fig. 30). The nearly ascriptive character of the seating culture, only partly affected by the market, assured one's place in the audience geography. Costume, mannerisms, and language signaled status: satin-gowned misses with décolletés and lorgnettes; gilded youths glancing into the female sector of the second tier, signaling to their mistresses on stage, or hissing the "unfavorite" of the moment; rich merchants from Gostiny Dvor basking in an elevated milieu; destitute but animated students and government clerks straining to see both the audience and the stage from high up in the gallery. The drama here was played out in public space, with its sights and sounds — the buzz, the hush, the applause — and its placement amid the furniture and architecture in seating hierarchies. Every performance was tripled: backstage, on stage, and in the house. A rich and complex field of interaction arose each evening as the audience played to the players through silence, clapping, gestures and noises, and the awarding of flowers in the soloist wars; and to each other in an interior show of glances, flirtation, fashion, surveillance, and gossip. Promenading in the foyer, clustering at intermission, and courting at the stage door added side shows to the main event. In a famous scene in Tolstoy's *War and Peace,* the stage performance is reduced to insignificance as compared to the stalls-to-loge exchange of glances that launches an almost lethal courtship.[51]

The "look" of a theater, exterior and interior, played a large role in spectator consumption, particularly for those who had no other access to magnificent edifices. The palatial façade, intimidating in other settings, must have lent a sense of enormous privilege to the middle and lower classes entering for the first time. Performance space for audience drama was particularly ornate. Candelabra, oil lamps, and huge chandeliers suspended from the ceiling illuminated the plush and gilt of the loges, the symmetrical rows, the drapes and tassels in the side boxes and the imperial box, the carved wooden ornament, and the immense curtain that transected the stage. The journal *Dramatic*

Messenger in 1808 explained in rapturous tones that theater required spatial grandeur to gratify the senses, shake up the mind, and enhance the refinements of the performance. A European style of seating prevailed in Russia's Imperial Theaters from the outset. The "orchestra" meant the space behind the musicians, divided into stalls up front, whose first rows had expensive numbered seats, and an open pit or parterre behind it where patrons usually stood. Ringing the parterre was the baignoire (a row of boxes or loges), and above it the *bel-étage*, considered the choicest placement outside the two-tiered imperial box situated in the center of the half-circle. Above the *bel-étage* rose a few more tiers up to the galleries, at the top of which, near the ceiling, were the cheap seats of "heaven." The side boxes practically overlooked the stage.[52]

The stalls played a leading role in audience performance. Their nucleus, a masculine crowd of young dandies and Guards officers, set the tone and had the best "lines." At the Bolshoi Stone, the ten rows of stalls held a few hundred men, the young supplemented by a regular body of older officers and high officials who, in Pushkin's words, "arrived from their barracks and council chambers" weighted with worldly concerns. Although Pushkin could not read minds, literary scholars tend to quote as gospel his statement that the older crowd attended theater more "for form than for pleasant relaxation." Pushkin's own sector of the "left flank" of the stalls in the years 1817–20 included Yakubovich; Alexander Ulybyshev; Vasily Engelhardt; and the dramatists Griboedov, Gnedich, Katenin, Shakhovskoi, and Khmelnitsky. Though women rarely broke the unwritten gender rule for the stalls, a general's daughter with a secret protector began to transgress that rule in the 1840s.[53]

The loges, the natural abode for ladies and families, played a relatively reserved role in audience performance. Here a magnate could show off his eligible daughters or display a well-turned-out family in a replica of domesticity: comfortable chairs, refreshments, servants in attendance. Loges housed the prime target of masculine gaze—discreet and clandestine for some, bold and direct through a well-aimed rolled-up program or an opera glass for others. Conversely, the theater box constituted a prime showcase for the display of feminine charms, natural and sartorial. One bought a ticket or subscription to be seen as well as to see. Unfortunately for the performers, the house was kept dark before curtain time, so that the main fashion show had to take place during the action on stage. Subscribers welcomed guests into their loges, though filling them up was considered vulgar and stingy. Wealthy merchants who packed their boxes with the maximum complement of twelve viewers were considered to be in violation of good taste. Well-born ladies and gentlemen needed the extra space to stretch.[54] Social standing was clearly determined by social sitting, in form as well as location.

Many never sat at all in the Imperial Theaters. At the turn of the century, only six rows of stalls were set up, with as many as a thousand viewers, sometimes packed like sardines, standing behind them in the parterre throughout the performance. Early in the nineteenth century, the stalls were extended back leaving space for about four hundred standees. For Russians accustomed to be on their feet through a three-hour Orthodox Church service, this was apparently no great hardship, and in fact permitted a certain amount of freedom to move and socialize. Sources vary greatly on who stood. Grossman, writing of the late 1810s, roughly identified them as "teachers, journalists, youth, Guards officers, the most lively of all." One of those upright spectators, Nikolai Polevoi, later a dramatist, said that "we connoisseurs made it a point to go to the parterre." By all accounts, even early in this period, much of the standing audience comprised what Dostoevsky in *Crime and Punishment* would contemptuously call the "town criers": the urban middle, educated elements — teachers, writers, and journalists. This loose collection was amplified by the merchantry which had thronged the theater virtually from the start. In the mid-eighteenth century, Empress Elizabeth, noting the thinness of the audience, had ordained that prominent merchants and wives be invited to the opera and theater "on condition that they not be hideously dressed." The prosperous merchant Ivan Tolchënov made it into the court theater and home entertainments of magnates from the 1770s. Merchants packed the houses, coming and going in accordance with the rhythm of their trade.[55]

In a variant of Pushkin's observation, Rafail Zotov claimed that the socially variegated crowd standing in the parterre came to the theater for the art, as opposed to the seated public who came for the show. Although this opinion is impossible to verify, Zotov — a seasoned theater man — insisted that "the parterre is a crucial element in the theater. Without it, the passion of the middle classes [*srednoe soslovie*] for theater would not develop. . . . The life imparted by the parterre encourages actors and lessens their fear of the stern and informed judgment that is located there." Parterre wits tried to arbitrate success and writers often catered to them. Zotov's argument finds some basis in the report that, although the show normally ran from six to nine, parterre people came as early as three or four o'clock in the afternoon to get places. It may well be that Russia's parterre in the early nineteenth century resembled that of France in the previous century when it was pretty much the domain of the middle class: "lawyers, schoolmasters, writers, students, and schoolboys," all male and standing squeezed together. The French parterre also included upper-class men and writers who preferred it to the loge which they saw as a salon made up of distracting women who had no interest in theater. Commenting on the gallery — the cheapest places — the journalist Bulgarin in 1826 spoke of a "grateful crowd" of clerks, salespeople from fashion shops, lackeys, servant girls, valets, artisans, and customs guards."[56] The one certain thing about audience responses is that class did not necessarily correlate with public manners: the snobby stalls and the plebeian gallery made the most noise.

Commentators tend to speak of theater audiences in general terms; but the Imperial Theaters public in this era varied between the capitals, among the theaters, and over time, including seasonal time. In 1802 the Bolshoi Stone, in ordering preferential subscriptions in the first two tiers for people of high rank, solidified the familiar visual picture of privilege upside down: the aristocracy in the lowest tiers and the rest in diminishing rank rising to the gallery. Yet by the 1840s, journalists noted that merchants and midlevel officials had moved downwards spatially and upwards in prestige to the second tier.[57] A striking illustration of how social mobility could defy the hierarchical seating geography emerges from a light-hearted 1825 feuilleton by Faddei Bulgarin. This conservative Polish renegade, journalist, novelist, critic, backbiter, snob, foe of Pushkin, vigorous apologist for the monarchy, and one of the most popular writers of his time, read the pulse of a large segment of Petersburg educated society and theater audiences. His impressionistic and snide feuilleton subtly chronicles a man who starts out in the heavenly spheres atop the theater and then — as wealth, position, and family increase — works his way through the parterre and into the best boxes in order to demonstrate his status and display his marriageable daughters. Each stage of this once enthusiastic theater lover's social climbing increases his malaise and diminishes his real mobility.[58] This familiar lament in the literature of bourgeoisification insists that one's inner freedom (and innocence) evaporate along the corrupt highway of ambition with its ritualized gateways and checkpoints involving changes of apparel, habits, and diction.

The Alexandrinsky, primarily a drama theater, evoked its own brand of commentary. Contemporary observers, using such terms as "beau monde," "connoisseurs," "the better sort" (*chistaya publika*), "beards" (merchants), "students," and "the gallery," show a rough consistency about audience make-up. The main attendees at drama seem to have been middle and lower officials; merchants, sometimes with their clerks; visiting landowners with families; and newly graduated pupils (since enrolled pupils were restricted in theater attendance). The writer Nikolai Nekrasov in 1845 saw in the gallery "a remarkable variety and a multicolored mixture" of people, including masons, guards, cooks, retired soldiers, and domestic servants. In his own arbitrary division of the public, he saw those who came for entertainment, for art, and for the actresses.[59] These and other observations of maids, lackeys, and other underlings in the gallery, an exuberant pack of theater enthusiasts in the stalls, an array of ladies and gentlemen in the boxes, and a rich assortment of middle classes in various places, point to the Alexandrinsky's status as the theatrical gathering place for a broad cross-section of the urban population, excluding the clergy who were forbidden by Church law to attend.

Moscow had a harder time pulling in the aristocracy during the reign of Alexander I because of competition from private theaters and the constantly changing venues of the imperial company. "Granny" Yankova archly recalled that few in her social set attended the theater even after the hated Maddox house was gone. "Now every *kartuznik* [workingman, i.e. those wearing the *kartuza* or peaked cap], cobbler, corset maker, and modiste goes to the theater. But in our day, not only did many commoners shun theater as something shameful, but some in our own circle thought all that play-acting was sinful."[60] Yankova despised the system of tickets whereby anyone could gain entry; she preferred private theater, by invitation only and exclusive to "her crowd." And after all, her friends actually possessed opulent theaters of their own. With recovery after the disasters of 1812 and the erection of the new Bolshoi and Maly, these houses attracted audiences whose composition hardly differed from those in St. Petersburg.

In a public space where ushers wore imperial livery, personal appearance and comportment had meaning. The Marquis de Custine noted in 1839 that a uniform or civilian garb that accorded with one's station in life was required in the theater. The composer Alyabev, while in the military, spent a month in the Peter-Paul Fortress for wearing a frock coat instead of his uniform to the Bolshoi Stone in 1822. Count Samoilov, Herzen tells us, offended Nicholas I by wearing outlandish apparel to the theater. Rather than a reprimand, the tsar chose instead public ridicule from the stage. An actor was ordered, while playing in a vaudeville, to mock the count and his costume. Unperturbed, Samoilov rewarded his impersonator with a diamond. What is remarkable about this petty incident is that Count Samoilov had once reached for his sword when Nicholas, then a grand duke, harassed him on parade. Whatever had inhibited stern retribution at the time of the drill field incident, Nicholas as all-powerful autocrat reduced his postponed retaliation to the level of burlesque. Pushkin was disciplined for rude behavior and language to an official in the stalls; and later for openly showing people sitting nearby a portrait of Louvelle, the French assassin of the Duc de Berry in 1823. Pushkin's raucous "left flank" hardly differed from the fops, beaux, wits, and show-offs in eighteenth-century London theaters.[61] The aristocratic ordinances about self-control and good manners prevailed at soirée, salon, parade, and court reception. But when male bonding ruled, as at a stag evening or in the mess hall, the men let down their hair. In the theater stalls, personal assertion and showing one's colors in a bit of excess became a standard feature of audience role-playing. The natural ebullience of young men combined with social arrogance at times attained near-riotous levels. It is rather extraordinary how much buffoonery, playful shenanigans, and even scandalous behavior went on under an imperial roof.

Applause as a social and cultural act fell under the rules of comportment. Emperor Paul at his Gatchina theater enunciated a principle of audience behavior in an absolute monarchy: clap and laugh aloud only when the tsar does. The rule remained in force in all theaters whenever a monarch attended. At the very end of this era, Tsar Alexander II ascended the throne in Moscow and attended the Bolshoi Theater. During the performance of Donizetti's *Elixir of Love,* a very funny opera, the public had to hold in their glee. Modern audiences are largely shielded from direct contact with backstage drama, however much they may glean from magazines, novels, plays, and movies. Powerful figures in early nineteenth-century European and Russian audiences had access to the backstage world, were privy to its tribal conflicts, and joined in by means of claques and scandals. In Britain, claquers had originally been provided with noise-making boards, a practice which mercifully died out. The claque came to be employed mostly for or against performers. In Paris, during a drama about Cleopatra, when the serpent poised itself to strike the queen of Egypt, a claque member who disliked the actress portraying her cried out: "I agree with the asp."[62] Young Russian bucks happily emulated the practice. The aura of festivity, Eros, and adventure backstage led to duels, kidnaping, secret trysts, bribed servants, and even cross dressing — as if in mimicry of the comedies of manners acted out on stage. The "left flank" exhibited disdain for the — in their judgment — run-of-the-mill actress. Strenuous ovations for the "wrong" performer brought frowns from those in power. Miloradovich, offended by an officer claque, ordered their commander to have them cease applauding their favorites at the ballet. The commander cheekily requested from the general a list of whom to clap for and whom not. Audience members were not above taunting and insulting stars, especially females. At the Alexandrinsky in the 1830s, Guards officers threw men's underwear at an actress who was performing poorly. This widely known scandal spurred popular interest in the private lives of theater people and thus indirectly in the theater itself.[63]

The best-known scandals involved some highly visible theater people. When in 1822 Ekaterina Semënova brought her supporting actress Maria Azarevicheva on stage for a curtain call after a performance at the Bolshoi Stone, the poet and dramatist Pavel Katenin (1792–1853) shouted an insult. Semënova reported the incident to General Miloradovich, Azarevicheva's admirer, and the tsar ordered the expulsion of Katenin from the capitals.[64] (After three years in Kostroma Province, he was permitted to return.) A more complicated case involved Elena Andreanova (1819–57), Gedeonov's mistress whom the stalls frequently hissed because Gedeonov denied them access to the stage door. In 1843, Gedeonov had the disruptors removed from the theater with the help of police, and a few students were expelled from university. A big scandal erupted over Andreanova's rivalry with Smirnova who was hotly supported by the influential caricaturist Mikhail Nevakhovich, her lover and later husband. He constantly roasted Gedeonov and other theater officials, including his own brother, Alexander Nevakhovich. On a night when Andreanova was featured, he organized the public in a clangorous war of hissing at her.[65]

Interventions of another sort emerged from among the lower orders in parterre and gallery. When townspeople, recently urbanized peasants, and sometimes even merchants encountered staged fiction for the first time, they often reacted as if what they saw was real. As spectators at folk fairs, and other forms of outdoor entertainment where classes mingled and noise and show were the norm, they had jostled one another and voiced their opinions loudly about what was going on — at once interacting with and contributing to the spectacle. All over the Western world, the "civilizing" of boisterous publics played a major role in theatrical history, as did the parallel "hierarchization" of stage art. Apparently Russian theater audiences were very disorderly in the eighteenth century, but in the view of a British scholar, towards the century's end they "tended to settle down." He quotes the visitor John Carr who in 1802 spoke of the "silence and decorum" of a Russian theater audience and compared it favorably with audiences in England.[66] But an arch Russian observer, writing almost a half-century later, used the derisive term *okroshka* (a summer soup of assorted vegetables) for the crowd at the top of the Alexandrinsky. They wore loud clothes; merchants in their well-combed beards sat beside their daughters who ogled the uniformed men; sales clerks gawked at the opulence of the theater. Sweaty "experts" gossiped about the lives of the actors on stage; and all performed their own ballets, comedies, and melodramas.[67] What the reporter saw as simple vulgarity was in fact a colorful and vivid tableau of athletic enthusiasm, spontaneity, and engagement in varying forms with the stage, the rest of the house, and each other.

Lackeys and other enserfed menials had yet a different kind of experience in the theater. At least until the end of the eighteenth century, custom dictated that when gentry entered the theater, the servants were left outside at the carriage porch with the coats and cloaks. In wintertime, sleeping on the outer garments did not suffice to protect these servants from the bitter cold, so they tore off wood from the theater itself to build fires. To prevent disorder, a civic guard directed by army officers watched over the lackeys, a guard that at least on one occasion comprised as many as 180 men. Audiences inside the theater were sometimes distracted by the sound of shouts and the whips of the guards being applied to the backs of hundreds of waiting servants. No doubt because of the discomfort and even peril of this arrangement for the theatergoers, around the turn of the century lackeys were permitted to stand behind the families of their masters outside the boxes and sometimes inside them. Thus was created for the first time in a large public space the cultural anomaly of serfs-as-servants actually being able to watch actors (including recent serfs) playing idealized peasant serfs. Unlike the experience of workers watching workers perform as workers in the early Soviet period, reactions to this moment have not been captured in the sources. Lamentably, the greatest figure in Ukrainian literature, Taras Shevchenko, while still a serf laboring on the decor of Petersburg theaters, attended as a ticket holder performances at the Petersburg Bolshoi theater, but left no record of his impressions.[68]

Given audiences so socially differentiated, one could hardly expect to find within the huge spaces of the Imperial Theaters anything like a community or even common consciousness of what was going on. Each segment of the audience tended to replicate inside the theater its own quotidian haunts: family circle, salon, club, tavern — isolated private communities within a public space, a mosaic of ghettos. Thus from the 1830s onward, once all the permanent theaters were built, something on the order of seven to eight thousand urban spectators entered lavish edifices almost nightly from September to May (except for Lent) and fashioned within their walls a rough version of urban society at large. Situated sociographically between a church congregation and a crowd at a popular festival, it was an indoor assortment more spontaneous than the former and more restrained than the latter. The still relatively unsolemnized aura and constricted space of the theater allowed each segment to observe with admiration, envy, or both the social intercourse of other groups. Whether or not middle- and lower-class spectators did, as in eighteenth-century France, "learn social graces" there, they could, as it were, eavesdrop at a society salon, an officers' mess, or a noble family evening. And, though we have no solid evidence, perhaps the spectators of all classes could find in the audience space not only a "theater for themselves" but a school as edifying as the production on stage.[69]

The next chapter unrolls some of what audiences saw on stage in this period. As to how they saw it, a few general comments are in order. Vigel and Sergei Zhikharëv, important observers of theatrical life in these years, tended to patronize audiences; like many Enlightenment figures in Europe, they doubted the taste of the plebs. Zhikharëv considered merchant audiences primitive and uninformed, unable to understand much of what they watched and prone to garbling the names of actors, authors, and plays. After the curtain at an 1809 performance of Voltaire's *Tancred* with Semënova and Yakovlev — generally recognized as a supreme moment in the Russian neoclassical theater — a spectator demanded that the author appear on stage. A misinformed know-it-all in the audience shouted that "Racine" had been dead for fifty years. Spectators from all strata could be frightened or angered by the action on stage. When a cowardly villain from a Shakhovskoi play made his stage exit, according to a Vyazemsky epigram, whistling erupted not only from the parterre and gallery, but from the stalls as well. This was not a uniquely Russian mode of response. Urban folklore relates that at the 1816 premiere of Rossini's opera *Otello* in Naples, when Othello approached Desdemona in her bed, the audience shouted to the actress: "Watch out, he has a knife [*sic*]!"; and that a German viewer of Mozart's *Don Giovanni* shouted to the pursuers of Don Juan: "He ran away down the alley to the right!"[70]

Misreading a text or performance is not the same as not "understanding." Viewers of all classes added their own meanings based on life experience, previous attendance, present circumstance, seating, line of sight, audibility, and even the company seated near them. Politesse did not equate with comprehension, and intervention on the part of spectators often indicated their sharp attention to the performance. Remarks about the "loge ladies" and tired bureaucrats who came only to show off or conform and who understood nothing of what went on on stage are purely subjective. Even a failure to record in memory what one saw proves no lack of engagement at the time of performance. People often recall the experience of the theater environment better than they do the stage action. Pavel Medvedev, a small-time Moscow merchant, told his diary almost nothing about the plays he saw in the 1850s but rhapsodized about the male youth in the audience (he was bisexual). Yakov Kostenetsky, son of a landowner of modest means, went to the theater two or three days after his first arrival in Moscow in the late 1820s. What struck him much later about the ballet he saw, Cavos's *Prisoner of the Caucasus,* were the props and decor — an eagle flying over mountain peaks — a premonition of his disgrace and exile to the Caucasus. The serf lackey Bobkov, given theater tickets by an actor friend, understood nothing the first time he went, but then his appreciation widened through regular attendance.[71]

What did the lower classes get from theatrical performances? The only sure answer seems to be pleasure, excitement, and a sense of magic and wonderment, the aura of directness in live performance; and for some, a sensuous grasp of the nuances and richness of the spoken Russian language, a respect for talent, and scorn for its obverse. Ordinary folk had no means or inclination to chatter analytically in the manner of salon habitués about what they saw. But the commonality did serve as historical agents. In the decade 1836–46, the public at the Alexandrinsky underwent a social shift in favor of merchants, clerks, officials, students, and other nongentry spectators. The shift there and in other theaters effected a change in repertoires and styles of acting, and the resulting popularity of certain performers.[72] For nongentry audiences, occupying space for three hours with the elite and exposure to interior decor that most of them might never see elsewhere, may have engendered among them a feeling of being part of "a public," of sharing an emotional response to what went on on the stage.

For educated society, theater was designed by authors and adapters as a school of morals. To the extent that they imbibed the lessons taught from the stage, this part of the public engaged in what Elise Wirtschafter has aptly called "*civic* society," a prepolitical community of moral concern. Moments of a larger public solidarity clearly came when the performance struck a national chord. In 1807, during Ozerov's patriotic play *Dmitry Donskoi,* the actors had to stop speaking for five minutes as the audience exploded in approval. Many more expressions of national identity erupted in the era of the Napoleonic wars. This temporary and faintly carnivalic moment of solidarity, when social gradations were downplayed, by no means marked an embryonic civil society. The theater, notwithstanding rhetoric about its democratic nature, remained far from social leveling. Not only did certain groups shun theater and different publics sometimes attend different theaters, but within each house social, spatial, psychological, and cultural distances reinforced the hierarchical order of the outside world. What theater did do at various times was to serve audiences as a rendezvous for habitués, a fashion show, an incubator of culture, a school of manners, a site of social mimicry and contestation, an arena of competition for favorites, a festival, and a staging area for further action backstage or in the salons.[73]

Besides the performances in the house, backstage, and on stage, the Imperial Theaters of St. Petersburg provided almost nightly a fourth show, which took place outside the theater. Footmen, lackeys, and valets — most of them serfs — acted out their script on the porches of the building or on the adjacent square. Contemporary pictures depict coachmen huddled in animated conversation around the stove (*grelka*) in a half-dozen specially built shelters on winter nights on the huge windblown Theater Square. Having no transcripts of these lost dramas, we can only extrapolate speculatively from what we know about the life and work of serfs and servants in the entourages of Russia's aristocratic families. One need not take Pushkin's well-known verse, "and round the fires the coachmen curse their masters and beat their palms together," as a sufficient

summation of the outdoor scenario. In this nocturnal scene, with its props —
the icy wind, the frosty breath of the horses, the roar of the fire — minute social
markers would be on display in diction, apparel, and size of the drivers' conveyances; and one might well imagine that, amid the general grousing and
camaraderie, one could hear some one-upmanship rooted in the relative status
of the masters, gossip about them, and perhaps a bit of bragging as well. At
curtain time, the drivers rushed into their carriages. Since all four-horse carriages had to be filled before a two-horse conveyance could pull up, anarchy
worked in tandem with inequality in this final scene of a night at the theater.[74]

A Crooked Mirror?

As in other conservative European eighteenth- and nineteenth-century
monarchies — "enlightened" or not — Russian rulers forbade the stage presentation of pornography and the ridicule or criticism of monarchy, state officials,
army, and Church as well as excessive caricaturing of the gentry. Serfdom as a
system was out of bounds, though serfs were constantly impersonated on the
boards. From 1750, no dramatic portrayal of dynasty, clergy, or police was
permitted. Patrolling the zones of public expression led to the banning of
many works in the eighteenth century, even though Catherine II was tolerant
of plays featuring jibes at the gentry and even the priesthood. The French
Revolution led to harsher measures in Russia. The burning of Ya. B. Knyazhnin's *Vadim of Novgorod* in 1793 became the most celebrated case of political censorship of eighteenth-century drama. Though rehearsed at the Court
Theater in 1789, with Pëtr Plavilshchikov as Vadim, it never reached the stage,
allegedly because its ninth-century antityrannical polemic was thought to be
aimed at Catherine or at her own pro-autocracy play about Ryurik. And yet
Knyazhnin's Ryurik and his rival Vadim both get fair treatment, and Catherine
and the censors had permitted other "antityrant" plays to be shown. Some
scholars suggest that political misunderstanding or professional jealousy were
at work. In any case, the timing was bad: the French Revolution broke out
in 1789 and in the next year Alexander Radishchev's notorious *Journey
from Petersburg to Moscow* appeared, only to be suppressed and burned. The
empress commuted Radishchev's death sentence and exiled him to Siberia.
Knyazhnin was much luckier.[75]

When Tsar Paul ascended the throne, censorship interventions increased
drastically from the 340 in Catherine's long reign to 234 in his much shorter one
(1796–1801). Paul also posted NCOs in the theater, dictated an early curtain
time, and closed theaters for ten months to mourn the death of his mother. A
quirky and rare example of risqué opera, *Olinka or First Love* (1796), precipi-

tated a scandal. Called "pornographic" by some, it was no more than an updated *Lysistrata* which demonstrated the potential of women to withhold their sexual favors from men. During its performance at the serf theater of Alexander Stolypin, the outraged audience, after catching the main direction of the plot, began exiting one by one. When Emperor Paul got wind of it, the author, Prince Alexander Beloselsky-Belozersky, senator, diplomat, landed magnate, art patron, and the father of Zinaida Volkonskaya, barely escaped the tsar's wrath by means of a ruse. Tsar Alexander I eased the censorship and restored several works to the stage, but also standardized print censorship. Political sensitivity rose at the time of the Napoleonic menace. Even the remote town of Petrozavodsk felt the lash of the censors who railed at an 1809 performance of *Dido Inside Out* for its shabby portrayal of royal personages — the Queen of Carthage and a founder of Rome. The play was also condemned for offending decency, having no redeeming value, and being "insulting to the refined sensibilities of the noble audience." With the onset of reaction and officially promoted religious mysticism, the censors from 1817 on cracked down on any unflattering allusion to the faith in print, fiction or nonfiction, Russian or in translation. Serfdom as a topic was declared unacceptable.[76]

Under Nicholas I, the Ministry of Public Education censored publications including drama criticism, while the Ministry of Interior oversaw theater. Drama fell under dual control and the screws were tightened. In 1837, Sergei Uvarov urged the tsar to codify rules about putting Russian royals on stage: pre-1613 rulers were allowed if presented with suitable dignity (though in opera only with the tsar's permission); the Romanov tsars were taboo. By this time, only the lower and middle classes and the provincial gentry could be mocked, peasants had to be idealized, and colloquial language was banned. By 1842 the censorial regime had reached into the provinces. Enforcement, however, was another matter. Since moral message and satire were essential tools of dramaturgy, and since the upper classes most often appeared on stage, the playwrights had to walk a thin line. No formula ever solidified, and so a good deal of trial and error prevailed. Like playwrights, filmmakers, and writers in other times and places, Russian dramatists and directors either remained well within the bounds of propriety, however shady and blurred, or set out to test the patience of the authorities who always had a representative in the front rows. Through textual coding, actors' speeches and gestures, and audience responses, a theater of politics functioned continuously.[77]

Nicholas' fish-eyed censors often descended to absurdity in their efforts to keep high-born personages off the stage: in the 1840s, the eighteenth-century court figures Dashkova and Shuvalov were renamed in one play and Josephine Bonaparte became Mme. Leclerc in another. Church officials were no doubt pleased when the word "dieu" became "divinité."[78] The Slavophile Konstantin Aksakov's *Liberation of Moscow in 1612* was closed down by Governor General Zakrevsky, a poorly educated soldier with a coarse administrative style, after one performance at the Moscow Bolshoi. The alleged cause? An actor's reference to St. Petersburg as "a city with a foreign name" elicited a storm of applause by the Muscovite audience.[79] The biggest sin was holding up "society" to scorn, one that bedeviled a masterpiece of Russian theater, Griboedov's *Woe from Wit*, staged in a drastically cut version in 1831. Young people all over Russia memorized and recopied whole scenes from it that were cut by the censor for their offensiveness. When Gogol lampooned audience mentalities in the playlet *The Theater Lets Out After the Performance of a New Comedy* (1842), a censor saw it as "audacious in respect to civil servants, the government and the Russian people." Ivan Turgenev's *Charity Case* (*Nakhlebnik*) got censored because it allegedly depicted the gentry as cruel and heartless.[80] Russian rulers could despise the nobility and officialdom, but to allow the general public to do so might lead to the spread of impiety and disrespect for authority. Almost gone were the days when aristocracy and nobility, bursting with self-confidence, could laugh at themselves or each other in public. Needless to say, no Russian Scaramouche ever appeared on an imperial stage.

It took a while for theater criticism to join the plays as objects of attention. Under Tsar Alexander I, drama criticism, though spotty, flourished in journals for a time. In 1804 Ivan Pnin (1773–1805), a Radishchevite enlightener who opposed serfdom, declared theaters "a branch of public education"; and another journalist wrote that an actor is "a public figure, just like a professor who gives public lectures, and like orators of old." By 1815, the authorities, realizing that press notices had the potential to decode variant meanings in the theater, forbade even favorable commentary about it and its personnel in any periodical.[81] The ban was not enforced and in 1825 Alexander Shakhovskoi, responding to an attack on him, asked Miloradovich for stronger measures against theatrical criticism. These were imposed shortly after the general was killed in the Decembrist Uprising. Faddei Bulgarin challenged this harsh regime on the grounds that wild political talk in mansions, barracks, and merchant stalls would replace the careful scrutiny of the nation's only public arena. The authorities were convinced. Bulgarin was protecting his own turf as an editor, but other journals benefited from his victory. Critics could now speak out within certain parameters. This was much more than a technical victory for the press. The critic, as an intermediary between work and audience, personified the public character of theater and represented an independent force outside the private household character of the court and the manor house. This bothersome fact accounted for the constant miniwars between the authorities and the press.[82]

Bulgarin's *Northern Bee,* the most widely read privately owned popular newspaper, enjoyed a circulation in the 1830s of about seven thousand, which dropped in the 1840s and resurged to about ten thousand during the Crimean War. Bulgarin, an alert press man with plenty of adventure and travel behind him in France, Poland, and Russia, had a feel for the demands of the urban middle class of officials, lower gentry, clerks, merchants, and teachers; and he believed that printed matter had to match the taste of reader and spectator. He pioneered a continuous conversation that gave the reading and theatergoing public of the middling layers of the capital a sense of collective identity altogether different from that of the salons. The more specialized journals, *Repertoire* (later combined with *Pantheon* in 1841) frequently ran afoul of the censors for its sharp tone. V. R. Zotov, who worked for them, once received a scolding from a censor who asked: "Why do you gentlemen as editors assault our theater, plays, some actors, and almost all writers?" Cruelty and ridicule, he warned, must give way to fair and constructive criticism. *Repertoire* was closed in 1846 and the policeman Dubelt told Zotov that he was hated by the Imperial Theater people. When a journalist, on the basis of a rehearsal, foolishly filed a rave review of the singer Viardot in 1843 even though the actual performance had been canceled, he had to spend a week in the guardhouse; and his journal, *The Russian Veteran,* could no longer do theater reviews. An angry Gedeonov wrote that journalists knew nothing of art but filled their columns with inflammatory invective. He once asked a journal not to heap too much praise on an actress (Nikulina) lest it turn her head.[83]

Vissarion Belinsky commented on theater as an important and influential sideline to his literary criticism. More closely involved with theater, Stepan Zhikharëv (1788–1860) studied at Moscow University and, as a member of Friends of the Russian Word, the Free Society of Lovers of Russian Literature, and Arzamas, mingled with the best literary minds of the age. He ardently dreamed of becoming a successful playwright himself and actually wrote or translated about thirty pieces, none of them ever performed in public. A friend of many actors and playwrights and an enthusiastic theatergoer, Zhikharëv left rich and often emotional memoirs of theater life and personalities. Though hardly a reactionary, he worshiped Tsar Alexander I and distanced himself from those friends who became outright radicals. Shortly before his death, he was appointed chair of the Theatrical Literary Committee under the Directorate of Theaters. By the 1820s, Sergei Aksakov, father of two prominent Slavophiles and a supporter of the "Moscow school" of acting, from 1828 on added a drama section to his journal, *Moscow Messenger.*[84]

The ring of censorial protection widened when drama's social ambit expanded to search into the lives of other estates, particularly the merchantry. Until after Nicholas I died in 1855, no class could be honestly probed on stage if the treatment led to systemic critique. Many plays that passed the publication test could not be performed, a comment on general illiteracy and the growing accessibility of theater. The arts could thus mock the foibles of various classes only as aberrations from the norm, not as essential traits. Since the portrayal in public of Russian tyrants, priests, or bandits would undermine the trinity of Autocracy, Orthodoxy, and *Narodnost,* and since class derision was severely limited, foreign surrogates such as historical operas, romantic rescue works, brigand ballets, and unflattering scenes of Catholic Europe were sometimes read as Aesopian commentary.

Was censorship a crooked mirror that distorted real life by requiring false representation on stage? Yes and no. Playwrights in their texts and actors through grimaces and gestures, omissions and ad lib lines, often cut a path of truth through the censorial thickets. Censors could also fall asleep on occasion. And then of course much that was legally allowed possessed a certain social accuracy. If we speak of the stage's distortion of reality, then the censors were hardly more guilty than the producers of stylized classical tragedies, patriotic confections, and baroque fantasies that shared the stage with the plays that applied themselves to Russian life. Russian censors often overreacted but hardly differed from their European contemporary (and even later) confreres. In Madrid and Brussels, whistling, shouting, and calls for encores were forbidden. In Berlin, no new play could be reviewed before its third showing.[85] Napoleonic and Restoration France, Austria, Prussia, the Papal States, and the Kingdom of Naples provided their own little censorship absurdities and some that were not so absurd. Censorship, combined with repertoire decisions and public taste, allowed a blurred image of Russian life. The real value of looking into the mirror of censorship lies in its accurate reflection of the values, fears, and anxieties of the regime and the social imagery it rejected: corrupt officials, bad government, deep social tensions and class conflict, impiety, gross immorality, barbarous behavior, and liberal or radical political ambitions. It sought to protect privileged groups from public infamy and the decline in respect that it would surely induce.

A recent study of the Petersburg Imperial Theaters in the first decades of the twentieth century asked how much the court affiliation of these houses affected their role as public cultural institutions. The author's answer, amply demonstrated throughout the book, was that they were bifunctional (he uses the term "ambivalent"), serving both the monarchical ideology and its social manifestations as well as the broader public.[86] Oddly enough, the answer is the same for the era of serfdom. It could not have been otherwise. In spite of ticket prices, sartorial rules, and censorship, the theaters always remained public. And in spite of lavish state subsidies, their repertoires had to reflect public taste to some degree. In the early years, that public was relatively narrow, though never wholly exclusive to the aristocracy, and it then gradually expanded to include a wide variety of social categories. And as the scope of audiences broadened, the social content of the drama correspondingly unfolded.

Theater in the Round

Theater life did not begin and end with bell and curtain, entrance and exit. The imperial houses reached out to the surrounding world. Salons became extensions of backstage and audience where strong opinions were aired, works read and critiqued, performances vetted, plans hatched, and networks sustained — all of which helped to shape the workings of the theatrical bodies themselves. Alexei Olenin's salon became a cradle of classicism. In the reign of Alexander I, the Petersburg salon of Admiral A. S. Shishkov, who sought to preserve the glories of the ancient Slavonic language, attracted the critic Zhikharëv, the dramatist N. I. Gnedich, and the poet and statesman Gavrila Derzhavin to discuss drama and acting. Their ideas floated into the stalls where salon-critic became spectator-critic. Gnedich, a vigorous commentator on the roles of author and actor in creating a work of art, naturally argued on behalf of the former. The playwright, he maintained, was the key to success, not actors — even great ones. Displaying the hubris often associated with his profession, Gnedich protested that dramatists did not write plays for actors like "some kapellmeisters" who compose an opera on demand. In Moscow in the late 1820s Sergei Aksakov attended the salon of F. F. Kokoshkin, a theater official and translator of Molière and Tasso. At his home on the Arbat gathered actors, writers, and professors. Aksakov's own Saturday salon assembled theater figures and the Slavophiles Alexei Khomyakov and Sergei's son, Konstantin. Stage performers' salons were a rarity at the time, but M. D. Lvova-Sinitskaya held one in Moscow and surrounded herself with a pleiad of writers, actors, and composers.[87]

In Moscow, Pechkin's coffee house — or the Iron Tavern — stood on Kuznetsky Bridge near Theater Square. The owner, Ivan Bazhenov, was the actor Mochalov's father-in-law. Pechkin's served as a meeting place in the 1830s to 1850s for Shchepkin, Ostrovsky, other theater people, and their intelligentsia friends. Male actors of the Maly Theater, mostly *raznochintsy*, frequented its five rooms to play billiards, read the papers, and talk. Westernizing intellectuals such as Herzen, Belinsky, Katkov, and on occasion even that flamboyant prophet of anarchism, Mikhail Bakunin, came to Pechkin's. These and provincial actors, merchants, and petty officials created a colorful, noisy atmosphere unlike the restraint of the courtiers and high officials encountered in the salons. Their orality bristled with word games, jokes, verbal battles, acting gestures, and witty improvised verses about themselves and the critics. Sometimes there reigned at Pechkin's colossal drunkenness, and many of the habitués died relatively young, having proudly paraded their epic drinking bouts. The pianist and composer A. I. Dubuque blended — as creative and convivial people often do — an exceptional wit and an unquenchable thirst for alcohol. At the Brittania Tavern students also discussed theater.[88]

The amateur theatrical, a popular Russian pastime right up to the Revolution, formed a mimetic bridge between theater and life. On its modest platforms appeared cognoscenti, students, soldiers, servants, and especially gentry. Unlike serf theater or the modern amateurism of players with day jobs, this enterprise featured mostly noble families with unlimited leisure time acting before chosen audiences. The class taboo against the public stage and the related lowly status of professionals in no way inhibited the craze for private acting among many sectors of the gentry — whether urban officialdom or rural landowners. Unlike professional and serf actors, amateur gentry performers obviously harbored no fear of audience displeasure or punishment for muffing their lines. Home theater enjoyed a good deal more freedom and flexibility than did the imperial stage: families did the casting, chose their audiences of friends, family, and servants, and moved freely through languages and genres. Although sociability and self-entertainment probably prevailed as motives, Elise Wirtschafter is right in stressing moral pedagogy as an impulse for mounting plays at home.[89]

A 1750 decree of Tsarina Elizabeth allowing private home plays suggests not a beginning but recognition of an established habit. In the 1760s, graduates of the Petersburg Cadet school and the Moscow University theater under Mikhail Kheraskov had carried their taste for theater out to the estates and thus fed both amateur theatricals and serf theater. Grandees with serf theaters also performed on their own. In a truly wondrous reversal, P. B. Sheremetev, with Empress Catherine present, staged in his home Philippe Destouches's *Le philosophe marié* in 1765. His son played a lackey, while other noblemen in servants' livery impersonated ushers and ticket collectors. When these grandees transferred the court repertoire to their estates, they had their serfs play counts and princes. In 1774, the real-life counts Sheremetev and Razumovsky and princes Kurakin and Gagarin — owners of serf theaters — performed at the Little Hermitage theater in the Winter Palace. The most famous of the magnate actors, Prince Ivan Dolgoruky, acted at home, at court, and in Sheremetev's theater. In public he wore fragments of his stage costumes, mixing mufti with uniform dress. Starting in the 1780s, the noted Tula landowner and memoirist, Andrei Bolotov, fitted out an estate building with two hundred seats where he and his family acted before an audience of gentry, townsmen, and probably peasants.[90]

Amateurism blossomed in the nineteenth century. Grandmother Yankova recalled with glee how her aristocratic lady friend always forgot her lines and would walk over to the souffleur and cry *"comment?"* The father of the writer Natalya Grot and his circle did Molière at home in the original. Yury Arnold appeared as a child in Kotzebue's melodramas. Mikhail Buturlin, serving in a provincial garrison in 1827, attended domestic comedies on nearby estates as part of his duty. The Stankevich family — including Nikolai, one of the most influential thinkers of the 1830s — indulged their eclectic tastes in speeches from high-art drama and opera arias. In this household, as in many others, the drawing room accommodated wholly contrasting genres and levels of seriousness. Needless to say, as Alexandra Stankevich-Shchepkina reminds us, her family never even dreamed of going on stage, though her sister did and she herself married the son of Mikhail Shchepkin. Prince Pëtr Kropotkin, on seeing Fanny Elssler in *Gitana,* reenacted it at home for an audience of servants, with a serf girl dancing the Gypsy. His family even tackled Racine's *Phèdre.* The practice may have been accelerated by do-it-yourself literature such as an 1842 piece in *Repertoire and Pantheon* entitled "An Easy Method for Building a Domestic Theater" — a homemade rig made of boards that could be set up in minutes by two lackeys.[91] Bertold Brecht liked to distinguish between dilettantism, the copying of professional stage art, and true amateurism which creates its own art.[92] For noble theatricals, dilettantism would seem to be the operative term, and for the gentry imitation was the greatest form of flattery.

A variant on gentry amateur theater can be found in private galas that dealt in patriotic self-congratulation and dynastic praise. One mounted at a Moscow theater in 1814, celebrating the taking of Paris by Russian troops under Tsar Alexander, combined folk fair with aristocratic amateurism. The daytime popular segment featured Gypsy performers, carousels, and fair booths. Evening brought a performance of *Immortality, a Melodrama,* here meaning theatrical action accompanied by music. A chorus of aristocratic and court ladies who personified characters such as Russia, Europe, and Glory delivered verses lamenting the absence of the tsar-angel and offering him thanks from the liberated peoples of Europe. The language of exaltation and triumphalism was very much in the lineage of eighteenth-century panegyric odes and dynastic ceremonies from the time of Catherine II.[93] The organizers were thus able to include the "people" in the tribute to the tsar but exclude them from the more elevated proceedings.

Schools opened many avenues to theatrical penetration of society. Secular school theaters in the eighteenth century appeared in Novgorod, Kazan, Smolensk, Tver, Irkutsk, and, in the first decade of the new century, in Vyatka and Nizhny Novgorod. When playwright Mikhail Verëvkin directed *School for Husbands* at Kazan in 1760, he announced that "Molière is now known in Tartary." At the Smolny Institute, performance by aristocratic girls bred social self-confidence. By the nineteenth century, all kinds of educational institutions had regular amateur theatricals done by pupils, students, and faculty. An amateur student theater at the newly established Kazan University ignited Sergei Aksakov's lifelong devotion to theater. At the Nezhin pension, the young Gogol played Creon in Ozerov's *Oedipus in Athens,* an old woman in Krylov's *Lesson to Daughters,* and opposite his schoolmate Kukolnik in Fonvizen's *The Minor.*[94] In the 1850s, Petersburg Mining Institute students expended feverish efforts on vaudevilles, concerts, plays, and especially opera, since they were banned from the stalls at the Italian opera. K. A. Skalkovsky recalled their special relationship with actors who had attended this institute. Students fought over the virtues of a certain singer, her husband, maid, and dog, and held a mock requiem service when she left the capital. Skalkovsky staged his own opera, *Alonso, or a Villain Punished.* "In accordance with Russian custom," he wrote, "no one knew his lines and the orchestra howled mercilessly." As good eclectics and exuberant youngsters, the students also copied the cancan which they saw in the French farces at the Mikhailovsky Theater. In Moscow, a more permanent liaison opened between the university and the Maly Theater, often called "the second Moscow University."[95]

School amateurism grew out of an institutional environment. Relatively closed corporations — school, army, prison — contain important elements feeding the impulse to self-entertainment: a fixed locale, bonding, a captive audience (and cast), and the need for relief from the hard duty of regiment and classroom. Catriona Kelly has noted widespread soldiers' and prison camp performances whose repertoires resembled traditional folk drama which soldiers often performed for money at fairs. Officers in garrison or on bivouac killed time in self-entertainment. During the Russo-Turkish war of the late 1820s, Mikhail Buturlin and fellow officers put on French plays at a local estate in a persistent effort to keep life normal in wartime.[96]

Did theater-going help shape everyday behavior? Some contemporaries thought that it ought to. An 1849 etiquette manual, *Handbook for Young and Old of Both Sexes,* taught that the art of polite story-telling in company could be cultivated by "frequent attendance at the best dramatic productions."[97] Yury Lotman, going way beyond the overflow of theater practices into home and school, argued that theatricality was a principal molder of the aristocracy's identity. As "foreigners" in their own land, westernized Russian nobles played the role of Europeans every day. This view may be a bit exaggerated in so far as it implies a wide scope and the uniqueness of the Russian case, though its fundamental accuracy cannot be denied for the upper reaches of the nobility. In everyday transactions, the theater of power that E. P. Thompson called the "studied and elaborate hegemonic style" of the eighteenth-century British aristocracy comprised setting, manners, gestures, costumes, and habits that vividly set off its users from the lower orders. Some of the French philosophes, Rousseau in particular, censured the nobility's quotidian theatricality. They saw it as a perfect example of the fraudulence of aristocratic values and they denounced the stage as a schoolroom where society learned false role playing.[98]

Though generalizations need to be qualified even for Britain and France, theatricality as an expression of personal power applied to certain segments of the Russian elite. Petersburg court ritual was partially reenacted in some drawing rooms and reception halls where the grand "scenarios of power" fashioned at the top were transmuted into librettos of power at a lower level. French neoclassical tragedy in particular mirrored the order and culture of the court: rational, rigid, restrained, reserved. Litany and liturgy formed part of the structure of the classical performance: the three unities, the balletic movements of the actors, and declamation that echoed the annunciatory accents of official occasions. During the peak of neoclassical drama, c. 1760–1830, the behavioral style of high society became theatricalized; actors and aristocrats in effect imitated one another, and the affectation of theatrical costume was at full flood. Books like *Paris Theaters, or a Collection of Remarkable Theater Costumes* (1829) served a function similar to the fashion and screen magazines of our time. Dynastic court ritual could not provide librettos for all practices. Gentry "actors" in daily life acquired *emploi,* deportment, lines, and costumes from observing foreigners; from expressive patterns of the French language; from fiction; from news stories in the foreign press; and from theater attendance. As in Europe, where people looked to the stage for clues as to appearance and social identity, so in Russia the stage radiated outward certain forms and patterns of behavior.[99]

Long before theater took hold, the Russian elite went about in European apparel with the help of tailor or couturier in emulation not of actors but of foreigners abroad or in Moscow and St. Petersburg. By the early nineteenth century, theater had amplified the mimetic aspect of public life, and the influence of stage costuming had become continuous for both sexes. Acts of display on stage were replicated by the public both inside and outside the theater.[100] The public gaze and the role-playing response to it were taken home to the salons and soirées and to balls and receptions. For females especially, in the words of Helena Goscilo, the body became a "public entity."[101] Seeing a familiar object, personage, or situation represented on stage, in print, or on canvas causes the "shock of recognition." Even when, or especially when, the image distorts through malice or friendly satire and is subjected to a public gaze, it registers sharply in the consciousness of the onlooker. Spectators of the class or set portrayed on stage, depending on the nature of the work, identify with protagonists, laugh at them, or despise them. Those choices — whether accompanied by a thrill of pride, smugness, or a twinge of tension or guilt — reflect and even shape one's own self-image. Theater is a crystallization of what human beings are doing all the time: playing roles. In "real" life, the roles vary as does the level of self-conscious acting. In theater, only the roles vary, not the consciousness. Stepping "out of character" is a constant for people of the stage; a rarity among those in life. And in each generation, it all depended on what was being shown on stage.

5

An Unfolding Drama

Theater is not supposed to change the world. But it shows the world can change.

— Ali Fafii

In the 1790s, Russian actor and playwright Pëtr Plavilshchikov, who saw theater primarily in national and social terms, urged that Russian history be taken up in tragedy and the lives of merchants and peasants in comedy. Nikolai Gogol echoed the desire in an oft-quoted passage from 1836: "For heaven's sake, give us Russian characters, give us ourselves, our own scoundrels and cranks!" Sociologist Wendy Griswold correctly equates the importance of the political, social, and cultural context in connecting the theater of any era with the other corners of her "cultural diamond": author, text, and audience.[1] Russian drama in this era progressed through numerous stages, shaped according to fashion, foreign import, audience demand, censorial constraint, and factors hard to determine. "History" entered theater with a roar in moments of national stress, particularly during and after the Napoleonic trauma and more subtly in the successive political dramas of Nicholas I. But since the social system throughout this period remained rooted in serfdom and the human edifices built upon it, Plavilshchikov's "merchants and peasants" remained overshadowed on the stage for some time by long-dead kings, queens, and nobles. Slow shifts in their representation through plot, acting styles, sets, and costumes accompanied the multiplication of the common people in drama. "Schools and styles"—neoclassical, romantic, realist—became so elusive and intertwined that in time the lines became blurred.

Actors at Work

"The influence of the theater upon the social and spiritual life of [Russia] owed at least as much to the appearance of a constellation of brilliant actors as it did to the writings of any of the authors who are perhaps better known to history." This perceptive observation by Anatoly Altschuller reminds us that performers brought texts to life. Where did the actors come from and how did they work? In all ages and all nations, acting talent of both sexes has always been found in every social stratum and, where permitted, has gone on to the stage. For a while in Russia, the rule against women acting (as opposed to dancing and singing) persisted in some quarters, and even after the appearance of women became customary, men often played comic crones. The class taboo was more permanent: the unwritten law, later folded into an edict, said that living nobles, people of high rank, were not to be seen on the public stage. The law could be broken by those with courage and motivation, but the vast majority of performers came from the merchantry and the lower classes and their progeny.[2]

By 1800 or so, the Imperial Theater system had adopted the standard range of dramatic roles or *emplois* from Europe: male lead, young lover, second lover, father, comics and servants; female lead, young mistress and first co-quette, mother, and a variety of utility actors. For tragedy, certain actors were made to specialize as kings, queens, and so on. This roster persisted until 1882, though drastically modified for the new social types in the dramas from the 1850s onward. How did actors from the lowest classes manage to emulate great lords and ladies on stage? Bulgarin in 1825 advised actors to attend the French theater in order to observe the proper behavior of the upper classes — by which he meant not the French actors on stage but Russian society in the boxes. But observing and replicating social styles were two different matters. On arrival from their points of origin — Theater School, serf company, or a nondramatic background — actors had to learn or relearn the arts of acting. The playwright and actor Ivan Dmitrevsky (1733–1821) became a legendary teacher of the imperial stage who trained countless luminaries.[3]

Two of Dmitrevsky's successors advanced contrasting pedagogical styles. The drillmaster Alexander Shakhovskoi required slavish copying of his gestures and readings. Like Tsar Peter the Great who tied hay and straw to the feet of his soldiers to teach them left from right in drill, Shakhovskoi told actors which foot to stand or lean on for which line. Some of the human material he worked with was still raw. Unschooled players thought "Albion" meant "albino" and would point to heaven when referring to the underworld's River Styx. Shakhovskoi responded with a despotically applied coding system which some actors resented, preferring the methods of P. A. Katenin. Of partial Greek parentage, Katenin was a translator, teacher, and erudite classical scholar. After valorous service in the war of 1812, he saw the great tragedians Talma and Mlle. Mars in Paris. Revering Corneille and Racine, he tried to transfer to his pupils a feeling for classical learning in order to deepen their interpretations. From the classics, Katenin himself absorbed a sense of civic virtue and personal rebellion that led him to the margins of the Decembrist movement.[4] Did the teaching work? Contemporaries and scholars — even sympathetic ones — agreed that among rank-and-file actors and even some stars, a narrow vision encompassed career, role, and the play — in that order. Most had no literary pretensions, broad cultural background, or refined esthetic sensibility. Scholars have tried to attribute this situation to the humble, often out-of-wedlock social origins of actors. But acting was (and still is) a job, and in bygone days little recognition was gained by an actor of any social class with an academic understanding of a role or of the historical background of a play. The relation of run-of-the-mill actors to playwrights was like that of artists' models to artists. In each case, usually only the latter had some formal education in mythology and other literary and historical subjects indispensable to academic art.[5]

Social origin did not determine failure or success. Any number of superb performers of both sexes sprang from serf origins. Russian commoners who went on the stage certainly lacked an upbringing of listening to skilled homiletics, as absorbed by some of their European counterparts, for example.[6] But they did grow up in a particularly expressive population. Russian styles of conversation and oral narrative in all classes were richly animated and conveyed with an abundance of gestural machinery. Proper training and endless practice could convert these properties for those with talent into theatrical skills of a high order. Quotidian "theatricality" did not of course transfer automatically into good acting. On the contrary, the vocal style that predominated through the early part of the century — declamation — required very special training as well as skill and a good memory. This system, in full force on the Russian and European stage in both high tragedy and sensational melodrama, died a very slow death everywhere as is clear even from early twentieth-century silent movies, whether made in Hollywood or in Yaroslavl. Declamation arose from the nature of the poetic scenario and from the size and acoustics of the theater itself. In 1830, Rafail Zotov spoke of the need for projection and precise enunciation, since the gallery was 140 to 150 yards from midstage.[7] Central to the style was the tirade, a long, virtuoso recitation, usually in verse, designed to display the rhetorical gifts of the actor, the beauties of the text, and the pathos of its meanings.

Declamation employed a stringent code of gestures and body language, one of many visual elements that theater borrowed consciously from graphic art (fig. 31). Its poses and facial moves can be found in sculpture and in such pictures as fright prints, for example Cruikshank's depiction of the response of horrified spectators to a duel. A serious dramatic actor, Alexander Bantyshev, would often stand with arms asunder like an entertainer at a Russian folk fair. The clenched fist pressed to the forehead was a sure sign of mental anguish. The section "On Fear" in a Polish acting manual *Mimica* (1812) by Wojtech Boguslawski mandated four or five stages of revulsion and terror as an actor sees a friend being beaten to death, with speech and gestures attending each phase. Stage exits were signaled twice: by moving feet and by an outstretched right hand. Mikhail Shchepkin, who later mocked the style, was fond of recounting the story of an actor who forgot the hand gesture when exiting, returned to center stage, and then properly followed his pointing hand into the wings. The extended hand mode was still being parodied in Ostrovsky's late nineteenth-century play about provincial theater life, *Talented People and Their Admirers* (1882), in which the "tragedian" stalks around in high style bellowing irrelevant lines from *King Lear* and *Hamlet*.[8]

Russian actors developed their own modes of vibrato, volume, crescendo, modulation, and liquidity in order to convey pathos, terror, hatred, love, and any other emotion. Just as often, they copied from each other, from predecessors, stars, rivals, and foreigners. Codes could be dictated by directors, teachers, playwrights, powerful observers, and even the audience. The downside appeared when star performers subordinated plot and fellow actors to their own spectacular deliveries. Yet pedagogues and audiences both deemed declamation the only correct way to interpret dramatic material, certainly that of a high level. Greatness on stage mimicked "greatness" in social life. Stepan Zhikharëv observed that a magnate of Catherine's time displayed grandiloquence in gesture and gait and weighed each word in prolonged and enunciated diction. Such people, seeing a drama about exalted figures of the past, would certainly expect to see noble character adorned with the proper speech and gestures just as they would in portraiture. "The tone of everyday speech is not suitable for tragedy," said a critic in the 1810s. Audiences of the early part of the century apparently agreed and expected mountainous declamation and outward gravitas as signs of importance.[9]

Out of the vortex of competing genres that swirled after the Napoleonic wars came new actors whose versatility made them unclassifiable as mere tragedians or comic actors. They carried their individual styles into all genres, and what struck audiences and critics of this period was the contrasting stage-craft of St. Petersburg and Moscow. The cultural duel between the two capitals, often represented as an intellectual contest between Slavophilism and Westernism, was fought on many fronts, including the theater boards. The rivalry between adherents of Pavel Mochalov of Moscow and Vasily Kara-tygin of St. Petersburg stretched over decades. Mochalov (1800–1848) came from a Moscow family of serf actors, graduated from a pension, and debuted in 1817 in Ozerov's *Oedipus*. Working in European and Russian tragedy and comedy, Mochalov reached his peak in the 1830s and 1840s, playing roles in Shakespeare and Schiller. He did well in historical plays and melodrama, especially in the role of Meinau in Kotzebue's wildly popular *Misanthropy and Repentance* (fig. 32). Mikhail Buturlin reports that when the actor, burdened by a drinking problem, sometimes appeared shaky on stage and forgot his lines, the audience forgave him. A nervous playwright once begged him to leave the buffet and drink after the performance. Mochalov replied: "I'll drink now and after the play too." It is not known if, as often happened, the alcoholism was rooted in some deeper ailment,[10] but the defect was one reason why the Moscow theater director Verstovsky disliked him. Boris Varneke, in a Soviet edition of his book, implied that Mochalov was victimized by the nobility and the theater management, while in its 1914 edition, he had blamed Mochalov's woes on personal failings.[11]

Some contemporaries thought Mochalov plebeian, in contrast to Kara-tygin's "high" style. He was the darling of nongentry communities in the old capital. His success, like that of many performers, was conditioned by the intersection of his particular talent with the social environment: the growth of merchant audiences and the overheated intellectual-emotional atmosphere of student circles. The Moscow merchantry raved over his tragedies, financed his trip abroad, and closed their shops when he died.[12] A student recalled later that he and his fellows found in theater an ennobling and enriching experience that afforded a refuge from the "cold apathy" of the time. Philosophical excitement there was aplenty in classroom and student gatherings; but rational and hard modes of thinking could not satisfy emotional needs. Those were answered by Mochalov's volcanic force and deep creative powers. Students would buy two tickets on the same night: one to see a new production and one to see a few moments of Mochalov. They would weep and share the actor's soaring joyful moral victories—especially in Shakespeare. For these young spectators, that actor seemed to possess what they understood as a Russian breadth of spirit.[13] Mochalov also enjoyed success on the provincial circuit in no small way because he could speak from the stage in a diction accessible to those audiences.

In contrast, Vasily Karatygin (1802–53), the leading figure in a large dynasty of actors, allegedly personified the very essence of the Petersburg school of acting (fig. 33). The Moscow actor Shchepkin made the oft-quoted observation that "Karatygin is uniform-clad Petersburg, laced up, all buttons buttoned, stepping onto the stage as though on parade." A giant of a man, Karatygin, after some urging, once did a comic impersonation of Tsar Nicholas in the imperial presence and received from the delighted tsar a case of champagne. As a political conservative, Karatygin moved in high aristocratic circles, but when the Chief of Gendarmes suggested that he insert patriotic and prodynastic touches in his performances, he refused. The tsar apparently liked Karatygin's performances so much that he refused his request for early release from his contract with the Imperial Theater. According to Buturlin, Nicholas in jest told him that the only transfer he would allow would be into the ranks of the Preobrazhensky Regiment. Lofty patronage did not, however, shield Karatygin from the daily rigors of life backstage. He was imprisoned once by that keen jailer of actors, General Miloradovich; and, like many another, was insulted by his teacher Shakhovskoi. Through his common-law marriage to the temperamental A. M. Kolosova (1802–80), Karatygin got embroiled in feverish rivalries.[14]

Karatygin debuted in 1820. His brother's diary entries reveal the extraordinary number of parts that actors had to master. In 1822, at age twenty, the actor handled twenty-nine different roles, most of them major, averaging three to four different characters per week — some of them done twice. The management assumed that once a part was learned, it was fixed forever in the actor's mind. For Vasily Karatygin, roles in classical and historical national plays came to dominate. A favorite was Belisarius in Eduard Schenk's historical melodrama of that name dealing with the Byzantine warrior who regained territory in Italy and Africa from the Goths and Vandals in the sixth century. Falsely denounced, the blind veteran was reduced in old age to obscurity and beggary. The moment when one of his former soldiers recognizes Belisarius became the focus of literary and artistic renderings. Referring to Jacques-Louis David's painting on the subject, *Belisarius Receiving Alms* (1781), Hugh Honour called it "a poignant lament for the transience of human glory, the helplessness of age, combined with a meditation on moral heroism in adversity." One can easily imagine what a great actor could do with such a role, particularly at a time when sentimentalism was being so neatly welded to historical motifs.[15]

The Petersburger's fame grew out of his lofty roles and his monumental acting style: heroic poses, parade-like posturing, elevated rhetorical delivery. A meticulous craftsman and scholar-actor, Karatygin pored over textual and graphic sources for clues to authenticity. His stylized acting and studied movements found admirers in this age of ballet and opera frenzy. Literary critic Apollon Grigorev offered this colorful metaphor: "Karatygin is an exquisitely planned garden with clean allées, luxurious flowerbeds, and velvety lawns — nature bent to the needs of art, tidied up, neatly clipped, and well groomed. Mochalov is a dense forest: here you have an enormous pine tree, a weeping birch, and the giant oak growing alternately, with interlacing roots and twigs." Grigorev's figure is one of many claims that Moscow possessed a special personality that could be embodied in art. A minor culture war broke out among followers of the two actors. In 1833 and 1835, they appeared together on the Moscow stage. One suspiciously schematic review of their performance in Schiller's *Maria Stuart* claimed that the upper classes in the audience favored Karatygin, the middle strata were divided, and the lower orders were for Mochalov. The critic Vissarion Belinsky saw Mochalov's style as more democratic and realistic. Ever the "furious Vissarion," Belinsky did not limit his views to print: at an 1839 banquet held to celebrate the launching of the journal *Repertoire and Pantheon,* Belinsky engaged in a shouting match with Bulgarin and Karatygin. But, Buturlin noted in his memoirs, there were no victors in this theatrical war.[16]

Given the essential differences in the two cities and the fact that Moscow theater life came under imperial auspices fifty years later than St. Petersburg, a special style was bound to develop there. Mikhail Shchepkin (1788–1863), though not a direct participant in the duel with Petersburg, attributed his own success to Moscow audiences. Among other things, he was the most famous serf actor in Russian history and spent seventeen years in servitude working in provincial theater. While still a serf, Shchepkin first revolted against thunderous declamation adorned with gestures and verbal ornamentation. It was actually a nobleman, Porfiry Meshchersky, who introduced Shchepkin to a different style. Upon seeing an 1810 performance of the amateur prince in a Sumarokov play, Shchepkin recalled saying to himself: "he speaks simply, why, just the way everybody speaks. Really, what kind of acting can you call this?" It occurred to him that Meshchersky "wasn't acting, he was living." Meshchersky had abandoned shrieking tirades and other tools of the traditional kitbag. Though there remains some doubt about his sudden epiphany, Shchepkin came to abhor exaggerated gestures and lengthy recitations with no change in facial expression.[17]

Though Shchepkin got his freedom and a post at the Moscow Maly Theater in 1822, it took time before he could master the naturalness that he so ad-mired. He advised the soon-to-be-famous Prov Sadovsky never to look into the audience, thus critiquing the whole tradition of bravura performance and the well-entrenched habit of playing to the house rather than to each other. Shchepkin must have realized that, however elevated the content of the perfor-mance, such acting could degenerate into a series of orations. He thus went beyond the individualist approaches of Karatygin, Mochalov — whatever their differences — and their predecessors by concerning himself with the whole cast, thus anticipating the ensemble practices that were borrowed from Ger-man visitors in the second half of the century and adopted by Stanislavsky at the end of it. Stressing the need to react to one's fellow actors' lines, Shchepkin affirmed that "on the stage there is no complete silence." Though he denied it, his view of acting was "ethnographic" or "physiological" as those terms were used in the era. In 1848, he urged a pupil to "mingle with society as much as time permits; study man en masse." To another colleague he said "never learn a role without having read carefully the entire play. In real life, if you want to know some person inside out, you inquire about where he lives, his style of life, his habits, his friends and acquaintances — this is what we must do in our business as well."[18]

Shchepkin excelled in roles that unveiled the noble qualities and talents of the lower classes. He played the title role in Shakhovskoi's *Aesop the Slave* in 1826, a work whose irony is implicit in the subject but which was doubled by the performing artist's own life as a star risen from the swamp of serfdom. Nikolai Nekrasov celebrated the hard-won dignity of theatrical art in *The Actor* (1841), a vaudeville with a serious message in which an actor, modeled on Shchepkin, defends his humanity, his talent, and his profession to an igno-rant landowner. This little-noted tribute to Shchepkin was an early indication of the intelligentsia's growing respect for those who worked on the stage, and a challenge to the persisting view of actors as mere clowns and servants. One of Shchepkin's most memorable creations was the title role in *The Sailor* (trans-lated from the French). When a seaman returns home from an interminable voyage, he finds his wife married and a daughter grown up. Like Belisarius, he has lost his old identity and no one remembers him. By shedding tears on stage in this role, Shchepkin re-created the kind of pathos and suffering that the Russian audiences found irresistible.[19]

Shchepkin's work in Moscow turned him into a public figure. He frequented the English Club, Pechkin's coffee shop, and Moscow University where one of his free relatives taught and where students gathered round him, attended his plays, and brought him to their own rehearsals. Immune to the affliction of alcohol that ruined so many of his colleagues, Shchepkin mingled regularly in intelligentsia circles whose members got drunk more on ideas than on vodka. His friends included Gogol; Sergei Aksakov and his Slavophile sons; and the Westernizers Pavel Annenkov, Timofei Granovsky, Vissarion Belinsky, and Alexander Herzen. The last held a special place in Shchepkin's life as a confidant and conversationalist, though in the distant exile of London. Although he once actually told Herzen that the serfs did not wish freedom, Shchepkin loathed serfdom, recounted endless stories about its abuses, and rejoiced at its end and at the birth of a profession of free actors who could work with dignity. But he remained a devout monarchist who — despite his early life in bondage — refused to condemn the gentry as a class. In one of his numerous little lectures to fellow actors, he said: "You must observe all ranks of society without prejudging any of them. Then you will see that there is good and bad everywhere."[20]

Admirers often attested to Shchepkin's long-range influence on theater. He personally coached the grateful actress Glikeriya Fedotova (1846–1925)[21] and many others. Stanislavsky, born the year Shchepkin died, reveled in the stories he heard about the actor and filled the pages of his memoirs with quotations from Shchepkin's advice to thespians. Although many actors were noted for their realism before and in Shchepkin's time, he became the emblem of a new style of acting. Stanislavsky named him as the one who replaced false with inner emotion and thus "the first to introduce simplicity and lifelikeness into the Russian theater." Stanislavsky came to believe that Shchepkin's tradition had declined in the late nineteenth century, and he built his own fame on a rejection of his generation's theater.[22] Much of the Soviet scholarship on Shchepkin — and there is very little else — reeks of hagiography that makes him the prophet of Russianness on stage, of realism, and of a democratic and even radical sensibility; a fearless foe of serfdom, aristocracy, and classicism.[23] Stressing Shchepkin's "serious" roles, the literature often ignores his achievements in the lesser forms of farce, vaudeville, and melodrama. Shchepkin's engagements in the provinces won him many disciples there. He died in Yalta in 1863 while on tour.

The Terror and the Pathos

"In every landowner's library," wrote A. N. Grech in a moving obituary of the Russian estate, written in a Soviet prison in 1932, "could be found Racine, Corneille, Molière, Boileau, Fénelon," along with the Encyclopedists and the Greek and Latin classics.[24] The nostalgic exaggeration contained a kernel of truth. The classical tradition could be put to many uses. The "Greek" upbringing of Catherine II's grandson, Grand Duke Konstantin, was designed to prepare him to ascend the Byzantine throne of Constantine in Istanbul (Tsargrad in Russian) which Catherine hoped to wrest from the Ottoman Turks. The momentary fashion allowed many Russians to blend with blissful eclecticism the eternal Hellenic verities, imperial ambitions in the Balkans, and liberal sympathies for national revolt. But classicism also served a much wider audience and constituted a crucial link to European high culture. Virtually all the arts delved into the ancient past for inspiration: odic poetry, Anacreontic ballets, operas with antique settings, and academic canvases depicting scenes from mythology.[25] The classical theatrical repertoire, including Greek, French, and Russian tragedies and comedies, occupied a prominent position in the early decades of the nineteenth century.

Drama, "literature that walks," both reads and "walks" differently from one era to another. In 1800, tragedians still obeyed the codes of Aristotle and Racine: the unities of time, place, and circumstance. The teleological plot followed a long line of exposition, development, variations, crises, complications, and resolutions. As in a Renaissance painting or a classical symphony, the themes, plot, subplots, characters, action, and setting were canonically derived and formally constructed. Condensation, focus, tension, and the heightening and poeticizing of life's moments prevailed over naturalistic imitation. In the Greek heroic model, "great men of the almost mythical past were ultimately descended from the Olympian gods themselves — are kings, princes, royal leaders in peace and war, proud aristocrats whose life and pleasures were founded on wealth, display, prowess at hunting and fighting, and feasting among their equals." How marvelous, then, the tragic catharsis induced by the power of fate, the wrath of the gods, and the searing moral conflict between duty and love. Tragic heroes grow strong in defiance and opposition to adversity, however hopeless the struggle; and nobility flows from the muscular and moral exertions of that struggle. In early modern France, neoclassical drama had reached a level of unsurpassed perfection in the works of Racine and Corneille. The styles, rules, and even costumes of French drama captivated elite audiences all over Europe. At the end of the eighteenth century, Goethe and Schiller in Weimar actually struggled against emerging "realist" modes in order to promote stylized acting and high-art drama — especially tragedy. Goethe even used a baton and chalked squares on the rehearsal stage in order to choreograph actors. The plays of the two German authors were thus removed from everyday experience not only in time and place but in presentation.[26]

For decades, Russian audiences flocked to experience the tragedies of Racine, Corneille, Voltaire, and Metastasio, who at the time were considered virtually equal in artistic merit. Censors and state officials rarely had a problem with classical tragedy. From the very birth of Russian theater in the mid-eighteenth century, Russian playwrights such as A. P. Sumarokov (1717–77), M. M. Kheraskov (1733–1807), and Ya. B. Knyazhnin (1740–91) began to practice the art of classical drama. Sumarokov rode the theme of conflict between duty (usually in politics) and emotion (usually in love). He made his plays "remote in time and place as if to emphasize the essential and eternal in human behavior rather than the mere local and picturesque." In this regard, the aspirations of dramatists paralleled those of eighteenth-century landscape painters who sought through elevated perspective and panoramic scope to raise the viewer to exalted climes. The more daring Knyazhnin, Sumarokov's son-in-law, though remembered mostly for social satire and the politically charged *Vadim*, also took on the Virgilian triangle and the epic of the Carthaginian wars in his tragedy *Dido* (1769), which inspired many later versions, including a lavish 1827 ballet mounted by Didelot.[27]

At the dawn of Tsar Alexander I's reign, the sentimentalism that was threading itself into classical tragedy emerged full force in the works of Vladislav Ozerov (1769–1816). His poor Tver provincial gentry family entered him as a child in the Infantry Cadet Corps where he mastered French and acted in amateur productions of Racine. Like so many playwrights of his time, Ozerov served as an officer and then as a civil servant. He still held a general's rank during his literary triumphs. His retirement years were clouded by waning success as well as personal and mental problems. Ozerov, whom the great twentieth-century poet Osip Mandelshtam lovingly called "the last ray of tragedy's sunset," earned the sobriquet "the Russian Racine" in some quarters, even though he shattered the unities and sometimes omitted the mandatory tension between public and private life.[28] Ozerov read and rehearsed some of his most important works at the salon of Alexei Olenin, an exceptionally learned man who later headed the Imperial Library and the Academy of Arts. His home on the Moika and his estate at Priyutino hosted artistic celebrities as well as future Decembrists. One of the great incubators of Russian culture, Olenin's salon brought together Katenin, Kapnist, Gnedich, the fabulist and playwright Ivan Krylov, future education minister Sergei Uvarov, and painter Orest Kiprensky, among others, in an environment where classicism and patriotism fed each other.[29]

Ozerov's eminence at the time rests almost wholly upon three thematically unrelated tragedies that appeared in the years 1804–7. The first, *Oedipus in Athens,* came well armed with star power: music by Osip Kozlovsky, decor by Olenin, sets by Gonzago, and the main roles played by Yakovlev, Shusherin, and Semënova whose career was launched in this play. The entire troupe moved to Olenin's estate to rehearse. As a very free adaptation of Sophocles' *Oedipus the King,* Ozerov's version vented an emotional immediacy that contrasted with previous classical works. It also made a hopeful political statement. The character of Theseus, the wise and just king of Athens, was seen as embodying liberal ideas of a law-based state that arose with the accession of Tsar Alexander I and the emergence of the reform-minded "unofficial committee," ideas that the tsar later frittered away. Theseus is made to be a servant of his people rather than a tyrant. Spectators memorized lines from *Oedipus* and recorded them in that great artifact of sensibility, the album. In the 1830s, regimental officers billeted in the little town of Ostrogozhsk in Voronezh Province were still reciting whole passages from it in high diction. Taras Shevchenko, an art student at the same time, was inspired to make drawings of its scenes. One of Mikhail Buturlin's talented serf waiters could repeat tirades from *Oedipus*. On stage it ran until 1809 and in revival from 1816 into the 1850s, belying the notion that audiences only wanted "naturalistic" Russian speech, though Ozerov's other classically inspired works had little success.[30]

Ozerov moved easily from neoclassical tragedy to the mists of medieval Scotland in *Fingal* (1805). The object of an all-European rage, James McPherson's counterfeit Ossianic legends swept into Russia like a North Sea gale, though without displacing neoclassical drama. In fact the cults of Homer and Ossian reinforced each other, the latter seen as somehow the "northern equivalent of the Greek poet." F. P. Tolstoy of the Academy of Arts designed two ballets: the Ossianic *Golden Harp* in 1838 and one on Grecian motifs in 1842.[31] Ozerov's loose adaptation retains the story of Fingal, the poet-soldier —portrayed at its debut by Yakovlev—caught in the cross-hairs of love and hate as he slays the brother of his beloved and then sees her killed by her own father. Jagged caves and raging seas on stage underlined the bleakness of the plot as the action unfolded with the aid of chorus, ballet, and song. Though the play is no longer performed, it resonated at the time, as a recent scholar has convincingly shown, "as a proud statement of Russia's unique identity and superiority among the brotherhood of northern peoples."[32] One can get a feeling of what the music sounded like to listeners of the time from modern recordings. A monologue of Moine, Fingal's love, begins with declamation around which the composer Kozlovsky wove dramatic modulations, and concludes with a stormy aria matching the drama. This work in particular underlines the onset of the intimate bond of words and music in nonoperatic drama of the era. And though Kozlovsky's music is more restrained and lacks the lustrous quality of a later work inspired by Ossian — Mendelssohn's *Fingal's Cave Overture* (1832) — it certainly provided both the blood-and-thunder and the tenderness required by the Ozerov play.[33]

The third in the Ozerov trilogy, *Dmitry Donskoi* (1807), brought the action closer to home and made transparent comment on contemporary political issues. Possibly inspired by Orest Kiprensky's 1805 historical canvas, *Dmitry Donskoi and the Battle of Kulikovo*, Ozerov's play, like all Russian historical dramas of this era, gave fanciful treatment to a past event, the exploit of the fourteenth century grand prince, Dmitry "of the Don," so-called for his alleged victory over the Tatars near that river. *Donskoi*'s "two-thousand-odd hexameters, "writes a modern critic, "roll down the page now as they must have rolled out into the audience then, in tedious waves of unoriginal grandiloquence."[34] This is arguably true of the text, but not of the 1807 audience who still savored the rich music of declamation. The quasi-historical pomposity was balanced by the principals' dilemma of love versus duty which, though conventional, was infused with sentiment. In fact, the opening night brought a smash success. This stemmed in no small part from its performance at the time when Russian armies had just suffered a chain of major defeats in the wars of 1805–7 against Napoleon. "More fit to die in battle than bear a shameful peace!," Dmitry exclaims to his fellow princes. The tragedian Yakovlev's patriotically inflected utterance of Donskoi's language elicited a storm of emotion in the house as the audience, transforming the arrogant medieval Tatars into Frenchmen, was energized by the prospect of throwing off a new "Mongol yoke." Additional patriotic stimulation was provided by Semënova's performance of a Russian folk dance in stylized peasant costume as an encore. Tsar Alexander, not an avid theatergoer, saw *Donskoi* at the Hermitage and a few nights later at the Bolshoi Stone. After the stunning success of this play, Ozerov became the most popular dramatist of his time. His fresh, warm approach to tragedy and the performance of superb actors brought drama closer to the heart than had Sumarokov and other eighteenth-century tragedy writers.[35]

The Ozerov triumph belongs in the long list of public expressions of Russian patriotism and dynastic loyalty that broke out on parade grounds and in churches, public squares, and railroad stations, right up to the early years of World War I. It also made a big moment in theater history. Since the theater in Russia was created from above, it took a long time to develop an organic relation between audience and repertoire. Ozerov's tragedies responded to a national emergency and made what a prerevolutionary theater historian called "a temporary breach in the wall between stage and public," a moment when the theater resembled an assembly rather than a presentation.[36] That "temporary breach" also forged a temporary sense of community in the audience more powerful than that produced by the tears of melodrama, the laughter of comedy, or the shattering trauma and catharsis of classical tragedy.

The credit for Ozerov's success must be shared by the actors who realized his dramas on stage. Alexei Yakovlev (1773–1817), son of a Kostroma merchant, came as an apprentice to St. Petersburg where he chanced to attend the theater and became obsessed with tragic declamation. Working as a shop clerk in Gostiny Dvor, he would ardently recite lines from current tragedies to his customers. He came to the attention of Dmitrevsky who took him on as a pupil. After debuting in the 1790s, Yakovlev soon broke with his mentor's style in order to privilege emotion over reason. Though he first made a name in the sentimental role of Meinau in Kotzebue's melodrama, *Misanthropy and Repentance,* he performed best in plays of Shakespeare, Ozerov, and the Greeks. Audiences adored Yakovlev's rich voice, classical costumes, and majestic maneuvers alternating with feverish lurches. Convinced that reserve in the utterance of key lines did not work, he shouted certain passages which brought excitement to the hall and loud applause. This by no means unique habit led critics, Bulgarin among them, to lament Yakovlev's catering to the majority in the audience at the expense of refinement. Some claimed that, since Russian audiences were dull-witted, Yakovlev got a false impression of his talents from their enthusiastic applause. This was a familiar case of damning an artist on the basis of popularity. Like many actors of his time, Yakovlev was defeated by liquor (and by unrequited love); he declined into melancholy, attempted suicide in 1813, and died a few years later at the age of forty-four.[37]

Ekaterina Semënova (fig. 34), the most charismatic actress of her time, studied with Dmitrevsky, Shakhovskoi, and N. I. Gnedich (1784–1833) who fell in love with her. She debuted at age seventeen and began doing tragedy in the grand manner. In majestic postures, she presented a classical face and a sculpted figure in Greek tunics and Roman togas and deployed her stately and severe contralto voice in a singsong style of declamation. Semënova's performances, though emotionally spirited, were also rigorously disciplined. Gnedich "scored" her scripts with markings for emotional gestures. When, in Voltaire's *Tancred,* she threw herself on the corpse of Tancred as if to rouse him, she recoiled in horror and simply whispered audibly: "He is dead." The effect on audiences was electrifying; in Moscow spectators involuntarily rose from their seats. One actor recalled her in *Medea* as she confronted Jason, with her dagger bloodied from the slaughter of her children: "See how your blood—and my blood billows." Alexander Bestuzhev-Marlinsky, a Decembrist and later popular writer, wept over her rendition. Playwrights designed vehicles especially for her, and a close dramatic partnership with the playwright Ozerov brought Semënova to the zenith of success in his tragedies. People recalled the night of November 23, 1804, when Semënova played the role of Antigone in Ozerov's *Oedipus in Athens,* transporting herself back to ancient Greece and captivating the audience with a voice, a beauty, an expressiveness, and an emotionalism they had never seen or heard in Russian classical tragedy.[38]

Semënova engaged in a bizarre challenge at Moscow's Great Arbat Theater in 1811, an emotionally charged event that paralleled the fateful duel between Napoleon and Tsar Alexander I. Semënova's opponent, Mlle. Georges (Marguerite-Joséphine Weimer, 1787–1867), had achieved professional renown in Paris opposite Talma in neoclassical plays; and notoriety for her brief liaison with Napoleon, a fact that set society all agog (fig. 35). After her Petersburg debut in *Phèdre,* she enthralled the Moscow public with her physical attributes, a singsong drawl, and a trick of suddenly modulating the volume and speed of delivery. Since Georges and Semënova were each doing *Tancred* in their own languages but in different theaters, the idea of a duel came naturally. In Moscow, the two young actresses played identical roles on alternating nights in the works of Racine and Voltaire, including the former's *Phèdre* and *Andromache* and the latter's *Semiramis* and *Tancred.* Factions formed on either side — *zhorzhisty* versus *semënovtsy* — and the competition generated bulging box office receipts as well as minor scandals. On a night when the Russian actress was off, a drunk declared himself ready to throw a thousand rubles onto the stage for her presence. The police ejected him and made him sign a promise never to revisit the theater. Mlle. Georges's adherents conceded no more than a tie, while Semënova's faction claimed victory. Win, lose, or draw, Semënova's star rose ever higher among the theater public. Patriotic Gallophobes supported Semënova in this cultural prelude to the 1812 war. Once back in St. Petersburg Mlle. Georges was booed as a traitor and a spy.[39]

While most professional observers raved over Semënova, Zhikharëv thought her acting "unnatural." Sergei Aksakov responded wryly that all of theater was unnatural. Pushkin called Semënova "the sovereign queen of the tragic stage" and Kiprensky immortalized her in a magnificent portrait. The actress's private persona was not so glittering. Like the Hellenic princesses and European monarchs she portrayed, Semënova offstage proudly donned luxurious raiment and displayed a massive arrogance. She snubbed mere critics such as Zhikharëv and esteemed herself well above titled people. Self-indulgent and capricious, she expected only deference, reveled in scandals, fought with male leads, and ruthlessly persecuted younger actresses. Her thirst for adulation led Semënova to crowd-pleasing tricks such as the folk dance following Ozerov's *Dmitry Donskoi.* After her prime, when old and overweight, she often assumed inappropriate roles in comedies or vaudevilles. For this or other reasons, the actress was once called "a shabby old cat" by an audience member. In 1826, an angry Semënova retired under difficult circumstances from the theater but made several comebacks. In old age, she tried to relive her glory by performing at home, in what Buturlin called "archaeological dramatics," excerpts from Ozerov's *Oedipus.* To Buturlin, born of another generation, the declamation and gesticulation seemed affected. She died in 1849.[40]

Soviet critics long vacillated between admiration for the grand style of Russian classical theater and suspicion about its motivations. Since it was no great trick to learn from classical tragedy lessons about (among other things) the virtues of patriotism, enlightened monarchy, and class distinctions, one Soviet writer claimed that "the struggle against classical method was transformed into a struggle for the freedom of mankind." Yet opponents of serfdom and absolutism also drank deeply from the well of classicism. During this era, Decembrists and those near them began writing their own "freedom plays": Katenin's *Andromache* (1809–19, staged 1827); Fëdor Glinka's *Velzen, or Holland Liberated* (1808), on tyranny (Napoleon's, not Tsar Alexander's); and Wilhelm Küchelbecker's *Argivyane* (1820), on tyrannicide. Katenin translated Corneille's antityrannical *Cinna*. Few of these plays were performed. Future Decembrists read, studied, translated, and discussed works on ancient Greeks and Romans, focusing on the themes of tyrannicide, national spirit, noble sacrifice, heroic deeds, and the evils of slavery. Kondraty Ryleev and Alexander Bestuzhev memorized the Brutus speech from Shakespeare's *Julius Caesar*—Ryleev was later hanged and Bestuzhev and Küchelbecker exiled after the failed revolt in 1825. Yakushkin read the same speech to his friends. Cicero, Tacitus, and Polybius were scanned for suggestive ideas. It may well be that the very style of declamation in which these works were recited in the secrecy of political salons itself reinforced, by its pathos, the passions of opposition. There can be no doubt that the ideological polarities nourished by the Decembrists, made famous in the essay by Yury Lotman, were reinforced by their readings.[41]

Imported tragedy continued to grace the stages of Russia more or less regularly up to 1825 and then afterwards on a reduced scale. Russian hatred of Napoleon generated only a temporary hostility to French culture, and after 1815, it dissipated rapidly. It may seem odd to modern readers that the neoclassical idiom held on so long. As is well known, styles imported from Europe into Russia tended to become fetishized and often persisted long after they had disappeared in their place of origin. One must not underestimate the genuine admiration of audiences for the classical forms and their lofty ideals, the beauty of the versified language, the majestic delivery. Like the eighteenth-century French aristocracy, who prized characters of high station and birth and the *style noble*,[42] the Russian elite continued to prefer good tone and grandiloquent protagonists on stage rather than shopkeepers from Gostiny Dvor. The classical idiom, though almost wholly removed from the ordinary, in its own time entranced audiences, partly because the actors adhered to the canon and partly because they modified it. Even when the classics thinned out on the stage, reverence for them persisted in areas of everyday life. It was not only embryonic Decembrists who recited lines from the ancients or the French masters. The sheer elegance and majesty of Racine and Corneille were taken as the last word in refinement; aristocratic girls of the Smolny Institute and other finishing schools were still required to recite these masters in the 1850s.[43]

Nevertheless, a variety of forces eroded the power of classicism, Russian and foreign, in art and in theater, in form and in content. Neoclassical tragedy requires an accumulation of intensive emotional experience built up to a climax, involving an admirable and noble protagonist with a fatal flaw. The core of tragedy is what happens to the mind, not the body; in Aristotle's view, it is this that arouses the deepest pity and terror. After a lengthy sojourn in these depths and heights, much of the Russian public seems to have lost interest. The art itself had become infused with "alien" elements long before it passed into secondary significance. And the rules that had once been laid down for good esthetic reasons, when applied to lesser works, acted like a boa constrictor, crushing the life out of theater; and the tighter they squeezed, the greater the suffering of the victim. The upsurge of interest in Schiller and Shakespeare and new dramatic styles contributed to the process. Sentimentalist, romantic, melodramatic, Gothic, Byronic, and historical plays (à la Walter Scott) rendered forms and styles of "tragedy" so diverse as to make taxonomy almost meaningless.[44] A contemporary student witnessed in 1830 what he called the "death of classicism" at the dissertation defense of Nikolai Nadezhdin, one of whose *opponentus* was an advocate of classicism, Professor Alexei Merzlyakov. The student reported that he and his fellows in attendance supported Nadezhdin and romanticism but admired his opponent and witnessed how classicism died a brave and noble death.[45]

Theater of War

In a censorial culture like that of Imperial Russia, historical fiction about the country on stage or page virtually had to have a patriotic subtext, particularly if it reflected recent history or current events. In the eighteenth century, Sumarokov, Knyazhnin, and others had wrestled with semimythical Kievan themes, but plays set a thousand years ago could not generate much euphoric patriotism. The full tide of historico-patriotic drama broke onto the Russian stage only at the dawn of the nineteenth century: a decade of using history to face Napoleon; the ephemeral typhoon of 1812 chauvinism; and the longer-lasting swell in the reign of Nicholas I. In the Napoleonic era, Ozerov's successful use in *Donskoi* of the old trick of seeing today's events through the eyes of yesterday's was only one of many examples. Catchphrases about the Tatar or Polish menace sent audiences into raptures of bellicosity towards the current enemy, France, and loosed a paroxysm of applause whose real object was the Russian army and the tsar. Actors often had to wait out the clapping before resuming.[46]

From the battle of Austerlitz in 1805 to the victory celebrations of 1815, Russians cultivated a keen interest in the liberation of Moscow from the Poles in 1613 and other episodes of the Time of Troubles (1605–13). Ivan Martos's monument in Red Square to the heroes of that struggle, Minin and Pozharsky, was begun in 1807. Earlier stage treatments paled in comparison to the flood that began with *Pozharsky* (1807) by Matvei Kryukovsky, an infantry officer who followed hot on the heels of Ozerov. Prince Pozharsky, acted by Yakovlev, dominates the play; Kuzma Minin, the Nizhny Novgorod butcher who raised money and troops to liberate Moscow and who actually chose Pozharsky as commander, has only six brief lines. The tumultuous reception of *Pozharsky,* which won a "bloodless victory" on the scenic front, set off a fad that continued with Sergei Glinka's drama *Minin* (1811); Degtyarëv's oratorio of the same year, *Minin and Pozharsky, or the Liberation of Moscow;* and the Shakhovskoi-Cavos opera *Ivan Susanin* (1815).[47]

The capstone of the public-spirited mood came in 1815 in Cavos's 1815 opera, *Ivan Susanin.* In an age of raging patriotism, it was almost inevitable that someone would dredge up the semifictitious story of Ivan Susanin, the Russian peasant who allegedly saved the newly elected tsar, Mikhail Romanov, from the Polish invaders in 1613 during the Time of Troubles. According to legend, Susanin diverted the Poles deep into the forests of Kostroma, for which ruse they tortured him to death. Cavos and Shakhovskoi were inspired by a work of Sergei Glinka, a man of extreme anti-Napoleonic impulses. Cavos wove Russian folk melodies into the Cherubiniesque score and Shakhovskoi invented a happy ending. Just as the torture and execution by the Polish invaders of the Susanin family is to begin, Russian Cossacks arrive to save them. It was a colossal success.[48] Two decades later Glinka would revisit this legend with much superior music and the original tragic ending, creating what is generally considered Russia's first national opera.

As in Britain where the exploits of Nelson and Wellington were made into spectacles, Russian theater put news events on stage. In 1812, patriotism began to unroll in intermezzos, divertissements, ballets, and folk singing woven around military engagements, partisan raids, bivouacs, and triumphal celebrations. The best remembered of the war-related productions was Stepan Viskovatov's (Viskovaty, 1786–1831) *Universal Militia,* performed together with a ballet, *Love for the Fatherland* (music of Cavos), on August 30, 1812, over a month after the French invasion. The peasants in this drama have graduated from comic buffoons and idyllic shepherds to serious Russian patriots. When a village feast is interrupted by news of war, all the lads enlist and the older peasants donate their savings. For additional poignancy, the long-retired icon, Ivan Dmitrevsky, made a cameo appearance. Playing an aged war hero now unfit for campaigning, he donates his medals to the war effort, a gesture that unlocked a frenzy of weeping and clapping. At one performance, a spectator tossed his purse on stage and shouted "here, take my last seventy-five rubles." On the morning after the performance a large number of spectators enlisted.[49] This dramaturgical recruiting device suggested that everyone would serve — one of the many mystifications of that war. In fact, the militia formed in 1807 as temporary units evoked suspicion and unrest not only among landowners, but among some peasants who feared it would turn into regular twenty-five-year military service and argued among themselves as to who would be drafted into it. Needless to say, those from the upper echelons of society made their own decisions as to whether or not to serve.

The city of Moscow was understandably even more exercised by the war since it was taken into its very heart. After the Battle of Borodino, the commander in chief of the Russian forces, General Mikhail Kutuzov, decided to sacrifice the ancient capital. "By preserving Moscow," he said, "we do not preserve Russia." The unplanned fires that consumed the city were probably the work of released convicts who turned to looting and arson; nobles who torched their homes; and government agents. The fire destroyed half to two-thirds of the city. Russians blamed the French; the French executed alleged patriotic arsonists. The governor of Moscow, Fëdor Rostopchin, actually bragged about his role in the fire when traveling abroad but denied it at home. The governor's role in 1812 was far more significant that any alleged arson. In the view of a recent historian, the period 1807–12, so fraught with tension and confusion, allowed Rostopchin for a time to clarify and resolve the confusion by means of vulgar demotic patriotism — cultural acts, performances, and widespread writings expressing violent xenophobic emotions set in a popular idiom. He was backed by the tsar's sister, Grand Duchess Ekaterina Pavlovna. Like many in the elite, she spoke Russian badly and, to compensate, made a mad dash to abandon everything French and to "Russianize" herself.[50]

All this jingoistic show paralleled and reinforced an unprecedented assault on French ways and their Russian emulators in everyday life; and a corresponding exaltation of things Russian. While the Russian army was defeating the monster military power of Europe, Russians at home jeered French actors, boycotted their theaters, and mocked Gallomanes on stage with raucous public laughter. The Napoleonic invasion set off identity crises among many nobles who "discovered" suddenly that their Russianness was paper thin. They hastened to polish up their spoken Russian, don traditional costumes, and learn folk dances. Gentry women in Penza ceased speaking French and wore peasant sarafans and conical hats. Elsewhere men shifted from French tobacco to Russian rough-cut majorca and from champagne to cabbage soup. Theater and other arts drew inspiration from the deep wells of native history and folkways. The rustic figures on stage who had once been laughed at for their bumptiousness seemed for a time to represent the true spirit and soul of the land. Patriotic shows made many Russians self-consciously happy to be Russian.[51]

The wartime Gallophobia created a temporary and superficial national moment, not the beginning of a community of national spirit of the sort engendered and fed by the wars, rituals, and festivals of the French Revolution. No mass popular nationalism erupted during the struggle. Peasants made war on the battlefield under noble officers. Behind the lines, they fought French looters in the name of survival and vengeance and punished them the way they did horse thieves in peacetime — live burial, roasting, dismemberment. Civilian peasants were armed only as a last resort, after Moscow was occupied. The Moscow population evinced no ideological motivation in their untrammeled looting which paralleled that of the invaders.[52] The re-Russianization of the privileged and Europeanized classes in 1812, skin-deep at best, soon began to diminish and the outburst of wartime patriotism failed to reach the level of either Uvarov's Official Nationalism or the Slavophiles' demophilia. The deepest longings for a "national awakening" aroused by the war, those of the Decembrists, were at odds with official patriotism and thus never on public display. French cultural influence revived and continued long after the fighting stopped. Satirical swipes at imported ways and mores also continued but with no more venom than those of the eighteenth century.

In the decades after the victory over Napoleon, war drama traveled full circle back to the representation of Russia's past wars as national inspiration. It reached fruition in the reign of Tsar Nicholas I in a series of mediocre historical pastiches, the dramatic rendering of the ideology of Official Nationalism; and in Russia's first genuine national operas. Two principal forces behind the new nationalist wave were members of the Brotherhood: Kukolnik and Glinka. Nestor Kukolnik (1809–68), though born in Russia, was the son of one of many Carpathian Rus teachers recruited into Russian service in the early nineteenth century (fig. 36). The family became thoroughly Russianized and Orthodox. Nestor's father, V. G. Kukolnik (b. 1765), an avid monarchist, served the state in several capacities: at the German theater in the 1810s; on the General Staff; as a civil servant; and as a professor of law and philosophy. One of his pupils in home study, the future Tsar Nicholas I, recalled him as one of "the most insupportable pedants imaginable." In a family steeped in history, literature, and languages, Nestor as a child played Don Quixote in a family performance. He graduated from Gogol's alma mater, the Nezhin Gymnasium, taught in Vilna, worked in state service and as a Polish translator. In St. Petersburg Kukolnik became associated with several thick journals and during the years of the Brotherhood wrote scenes for Glinka's *Ivan Susanin*.[53]

In 1833, at age twenty-four, Kukolnik began his drama career with a big hit, *Torquato Tasso*. He was compared by some to Goethe and Byron, though modern critics call the play historical hash and cringe at its verbosity. His triumph was even greater with *The Hand of the Almighty Has Saved the Fatherland*, a play about the Time of Troubles which premiered in 1834 at the Alexandrinsky, with Karatygin in a major role. Benckendorff helped sponsor it and the tsar himself added a few touches at his desk in the Winter Palace. The title is a quotation from Ozerov's *Dmitry Donskoi*, thus linking the liberation from the Tatar Yoke with liberation from the "Polish Yoke." The main theme shining through the hazy historical spectacle is the relationship between leaders and people. In the opening scene, two citizens of Nizhny Novgorod discuss the news and set the story of the Polish army on the move. With the entry of Minin, who is gruff, manly, and therefore quintessentially "Russian," loyalty to the Romanov dynasty takes center stage. Critics then and later read this as hardly more than an excretion of conservative monarchism and chauvinistic nationalism, both projecting and reflecting the love of "true Russian people" for Tsar Nicholas I and a reminder that the recently suppressed Poles were a long-time danger to Russia.[54]

Like many plays of this era, *The Hand* is a colossal bore to read, and yet made a vivid impression on audiences. A Stalin-era critic saw it as mere pandering to the feelings of the "Russian conservative bourgeoisie," and sneeringly noted its great "success among the Apraxin and Gostiny Dvor [merchant] public"—a standard way for both nineteenth-century and Soviet literati to insult a work. Yet the merchants of those establishments showed enthusiasm for many different genres at the Alexandrinsky Theater—their "home stage." *The Hand* was an immediate favorite of the tsar who ordered an upgrading of the production and a command performance on February 18, 1834 after which the author was received into the imperial presence. Royal favor was so palpable that when Nikolai Polevoi attacked the play in his *Moscow Telegraph*, that journal was promptly closed. Kukolnik's work—and subsequent ones as well—really was the dramatic expression of Minister of Education Sergei Uvarov's notorious but hardly original triune doctrine of Autocracy, Orthodoxy, and *Narodnost* that was being circulated at just that moment. If, as Richard Wortman rightly says, Lvov's "God Save the Tsar" was the nation's new hymn and Glinka's *Ivan Susanin* (later *A Life for the Tsar*) its national opera, then Kukolnik's *Hand* was surely its national drama. Indeed, so closely was it associated with the dynasty that in 1866, in the aftermath of the failed assassination attempt against Nicholas's son, Alexander II, the play was revived by official order so as to arouse patriotic feeling.[55]

The extraordinarily prolific Kukolnik's other patriotic plays took up similar themes. *Prince Skopin-Shuisky* (1835) brings us once again back to the turbulent years of the early seventeenth century. According to legend, one of the powerful wives at the Moscow court assassinated the popular hero Mikhail Skopin-Shuisky in 1611. In Kukolnik's play, his avenger Prokopy Lyapunov forces her to drink from the same poisoned cup. This alone guaranteed public success and the thunderously delivered poisoner's line, "Drink under the knife of Prokop[y] Lyapunov! Drink under the anathema of the Holy Tsardom!" was especially savored by provincial actors.[56] Kukolnik's 1841 *Prince Kholmsky* dealt with a fifteenth-century Novgorod heresy known as the Judaizers. Kukolnik moved the action to Pskov and added a dubious love triangle involving a Russian prince, a Teutonic baroness, and a Jewish maiden. The incidental music to *Kholmsky* by Glinka includes a very busy declamatory overture with a graceful coda, a *marche funèbre* that rolls into maestoso, a pastorale alternating with the sound of menace, a triumphal piece dotted with timpani, and lots of Sturm und Drang — much of it resonating with the music of Weber, Schumann, and Beethoven (especially the Coriolanus Overture and the Egmont music), lightened by the funny rhythmic style of Rossini. This unfortunately neglected music is far more memorable than the vehicle it was written for, but it did not save *Kholmsky*, which was taken off the boards after three performances.[57]

Kukolnik has always had a bad press among the intelligentsia and fellow writers. His play on the life of Jacopo Sannazaro — poet of the arcadian movement of the 1490s and celebrant of pastures, shepherds, nymphs and satyrs — was considered the height of bad taste. Dostoevsky's despicable violinist in "Netochka Nezvanova" admired this particular play; and Turgenev, in *Zapiski okhotnika*, judged its admirers to be people lacking discernment in art. In 1847 Kukolnik abruptly departed the St. Petersburg literary scene and worked for ten years as a supply agent for the army in south Russia from Bessarabia to the Caucasus. After a brief return to Petersburg, he went south again — this time to Taganrog where he stayed mostly until his death in 1868. What little he wrote in these years concerned local patriotism and the promotion of railways. Like other dreamers — such as Fëdor Chizhov and the French Saint-Simonian *Père* Enfantin — Kukolnik apparently saw national salvation in the vistas of the iron road. Long gone were the heady days of the Brotherhood. Kukolnik outlived Glinka and Bryullov but unlike them was forgotten. The dramatist's near complete desertion of his former career in letters may seem odd. Possibly he realized his talent had dried up or that his moment had passed. As one dedicated to the monarch, Kukolnik seems to have had no regrets serving in a capacity somewhat less exciting than that of a famous playwright.[58]

Inspired by his friend Kukolnik's success in the early 1830s, Mikhail Glinka took up the theme of Ivan Susanin. The composer claimed to have heard the story as a child, and Soviet scholars held that he was inspired by the Decembrist Ryleev's piece about Ivan Susanin. But it was the romantic poet Zhukovsky, tutor to the heir apparent and a powerful figure at court, who gave Glinka the theme and insisted on the tragic ending as "the apotheosis of love for the fatherland." A minor poet, Baron Egor Rosen (Rozen), personal secretary to Tsarevich Alexander, wrote most of the libretto. In *Susanin*, Glinka illustrated musically the national and cultural polarity of the opposing forces. Russian solidarity and popular will resound in the chorus; and tender familial values are rendered in the folk-like arias sung in Susanin's modest peasant cabin. In contrast, a gala ball held at the castle of King Sigismund II of Poland depicts the would-be conquerors of Russia, arrayed in baroque costumes, as arrogant and effete courtiers dancing the polonaise, mazurka, krakowiak, and an anachronistic waltz. The same music is transposed into the sound of evil menace as the Polish invaders approach Susanin's village and shatter the tranquility of its life. In the finale, after Susanin is put to death, a triumphant chorus with words by Zhukovsky — the "Slavsya" — is sung to mark the ultimate victory over the Poles and the ascension to the Muscovite throne of Mikhail Romanov. It became Russia's national anthem for a few years under Boris Yeltsin over a century and a half later.[59]

Cavos, conceding Glinka's version to be superior to his own, conducted the premiere of *Ivan Susanin* on November 27, 1836, at the opening of the rebuilt Petersburg Bolshoi Theater. During the flamboyant scenes at Sigismund's castle, the audience remained silent, perhaps reflecting hostility to the Poles after the recent uprising of 1830–31. Some sources say that aristocrats scorned Glinka's use of folk tunes and called his work "coachman's music" — an epithet he allegedly accepted by saying that coachmen were more useful than lords.[60] True or not, the incident has been oversold as proof of Glinka's "democratic" character. *Susanin*'s triumph is not in doubt: salons buzzed about it for days, ballroom orchestras played its dances, and its songs made their way into homes and even the streets. Odoevsky wrote a week or so after the performance that "this is the dawn of a new age in the history of the arts — the age of Russian music." Intelligentsia and literary circles divided: Belinsky and Gogol admired the opera, Herzen and Stasov did not. The Slavophile Khomyakov applauded Glinka's national spirit.[61] The delighted tsar requested the opera be renamed *A Life for the Tsar*.[62] Soviet scholars complained that this made it an apology for chauvinistic Official Nationalism against the composer's intentions which were grounded in sincere popular patriotism. Glinka's "patriotism" eludes simple categories. Whereas his friend Kukolnik personified Official Nationalism, Glinka blew hot and cold on his own country, depending on how it was receiving his works. But *A Life for the Tsar* clearly constituted the expressive peak of national and dynastic mythology in this era. Glinka added to Orthodoxy and Autocracy a strong element of *Narodnost*, with its overtones of popular monarchy, through the glorification of Susanin, the first large-as-life tragic peasant hero.[63] This troubled Glinka's liberal admirers and so disturbed the Soviet establishment that editors were ordered to rewrite the scenario and to change the title back to *Ivan Susanin*, under which name it remained a permanent part of the Soviet opera repertoire.

Rivaling both Glinka and Kukolnik in the esteem of the tsar, Nikolai Polevoi (1796–1846) became the king of dynastic flattery on stage. He grew up in a wealthy merchant family of Irkutsk. At fourteen, he was struck by a performance of Kotzebue's plays at the Makarev Fair near Nizhny Novgorod. In 1825, Polevoi became editor of the *Moscow Telegraph*. Count Uvarov's closure of the journal in 1834, allegedly for an attack on Kukolnik's *Hand,* was an excuse to silence Polevoi, then deemed a dangerous revolutionary. After this episode, Polevoi turned rightward in politics and stageward in writing, and proved even more prolific than Kukolnik: some forty plays in the next dozen years. Like Kukolnik, Polevoi did better with the public than with the critics. If the claim by a modern scholar is correct that all of them were staged and garnered great popular response, Polevoi would have been the most popular dramatist of the time.[64] He also gained the approval of the throne, once the *Telegraph* affair had blown over.

Nicholas I especially admired Polevoi's *Grandfather of the Russian Fleet* (1838), the tale of a real-life Dutch gunner and shipbuilder of Peter I, Carsten Brandt (d. 1693). In the play, Brandt recalls in folkloric tones his clash with Stenka Razin's bandits on the Caspian Sea, intrigues against him, and his arrest on false grounds and descent into poverty and obscurity. At the end, Brandt, a model of the work ethic, is "rediscovered," honored, and rewarded by Tsar Peter, at which point the old shipbuilder predicts greatness for Russia under Peter and his successors. The premiere in 1838 won loud applause. Polevoi's own favorite, *Parasha the Siberian* (1840), with music by Verstovsky, is another mawkish retelling of a tale based on a real event, this one about a poor girl who walks from Siberia to plead successfully with Tsar Alexander I for the release of her father who has been exiled for a minor offence. The prototype, Praskovya Lupalova, had won release for her father from the tsar and had inspired sentimental treatments by Marie de Cottin and by Xavier de Maistre (in *La jeune sibérienne,* 1825) who had known the real Parasha in St. Petersburg. The "action" of the play — mostly long-winded speeches — takes place in Moscow but its highlight is Parasha's simple and naive farewell speech as she sets off on her mission. At the end, her dying father comes back to life as his daughter brings the news of his pardon. Both these plays, combining Biedermeier sentiment with historical pastiche, exalt a benevolent offstage Russian monarch concerned about characters who are both suffering in some way and totally loyal to him — thus reinforcing both the traditional "popular monarchy" of the peasantry and the doctrine of Official Nationalism. Herzen saw *Parasha* as an example of Polevoi's decline from civic virtue. Soviet scholars usually argued that Polevoi colluded in the imposition of a repertoire that exalted dynastic values.[65]

These verdicts need some qualification. It is true that of the five most frequently performed Polevoi plays at the Imperial Theaters in 1837–55, three promonarchist works — *Parasha* with 65 performances, *Grandfather* with 51, and *Igolkin, Merchant of Novgorod* (1839) with 42 — stood near the top. The others were *Ugolino* (1838) at 49, and Polevoi's 1837 translation of *Hamlet* (which was more Polevoi than Shakespeare) at 79. *Hamlet* — played by Mochalov in Moscow and Karatygin in Petersburg — topped the list of favorites and could easily be read as a warning against tyrannical and treacherous monarchs. *Ugolino* (1838), Polevoi's contribution to Gothic, was a thirteenth-century bloodbath drawn from a Dante theme with real historical characters.[66] Polevoi, like Kukolnik, certainly glorified the regime and won huge acclaim from the public as well as from actors who found in his lines an opportunity to use classical declamation. The "good monarchs of the eighteenth-century Russian stage" had grown into omnipotent and benign interveners in Russian life throughout history and into the present. But Polevoi did not simply imitate Official Nationalism. A subtheme in his work was the merchantry's support of the monarchy, as reflected in *Igolkin.* Although the author had given up his early radicalism, he continued a struggle against the aristocracy in the name of a *Narodnost* that was not that of the peasantry but of the class from which he had sprung, the authentic bearers of Russian culture. In his 1832 speech to commercial students predicting a glorious future for the merchant estate and in his merchant-based plays, Polevoi fashioned a key link between the Moscow merchantry and the Russian stage.[67]

Many of the historical dramas of this era centered around violent conflict — invasion, occupation, resistance, and a bloody dénouement. Much of this was fueled by the immense popularity of the historical novel — both the imported ones of Scott and the native ones of Mikhail Zagoskin, especially *Yury Milo-*

slavsky (1829), a blood-and-thunder tale of the Time of Troubles. An extreme example of theatrical chauvinism was *The Death of Lyapunov* by Stepan Gedeonov (1816 or 1818–1878), son of the director of the theater system. Staged at the Alexandrinsky and later in Moscow and in the provinces, it featured the historical figure Prokopy Lyapunov. The young radical Alexander Herzen at its 1845 premiere heard the bloodthirsty speech of the protagonist about the pleasure he would take in spilling Polish blood (this was only a decade and a half after the most recent spilling of that blood). Herzen claimed that the entire audience shared his revulsion.[68] To a liberal like Herzen, identifying the Russian national spirit with warfare and the belligerent sentiment it nourished denied the humanitarian sensibility of the Russian people. But one must finally ask how effective any of these post-Napoleonic works were in generating patriotic feelings, national identity, or monarchical loyalty. Pathos on stage does not always produce the intended effect. A half-century after this period, lower-class audiences in People's Theaters were heard snickering at emotional scenes on stage.[69]

The Time of Troubles as a historical event interested Slavophiles and Official Nationalists. For the former, the great heroic episode reinforced their reverence for the pre-Petrine past; for the latter, it ushered in their much-beloved Romanov dynasty. The period also provided a storehouse of rumors, legends, and stories that dramatists could work up. But why did the Napoleonic invasion of 1812 not catch on in theater and fiction as *the* great historical epos of national struggle and moral victory? One can easily imagine how much ideological capital patriotic writers could amass for the regime (and fame for themselves) by addressing this war, one that remained vividly in public memory. And yet, after the brief flurry of triumphalism in 1812–15, that theme virtually disappeared from the stage. And not only from the stage: Zagoskin's monumentally popular 1613 novel was followed by a disappointing reception of *Roslavev* (1830), which dealt with 1812.[70]

If the Poles and the French were twinned as primordial enemies of Russia in a mythologized web of ideology, the Jews of the Russian Empire were constructed in drama as a people worthy of casual contempt in time of peace and of alarm in wartime. Censorship policy actually prohibited the representation of the Russian empire's Jews as people with decent moral principles. This was balanced occasionally by the staging of sympathetic or at least complex figures in *Merchant of Venice*, Lessing's *Nathan the Wise*, Scott's *Ivanhoe*, Richard Cumberland's *The Jew* (a tract for toleration), Halévy's opera *La juive*, and a dramatic version of Scribe's libretto for that opera. Shchepkin, who played a nasty Jewish character in the provinces for its comic richness, also chose for his Moscow benefit performances Shylock and Sheva. The latter is Cumberland's good-hearted Jew, a "virtuous miser" who gives to the needy. The buffoon image of Russian Jews dominated, as in Pëtr Grigorev's *Postal Driver,* which took the stage at the Alexandrinsky and the Maly in the 1840s and 1850s; and in Nikolai Khmelnitsky's *Quarantine* (1820), a border intrigue in which Movsha, whose only strength is his "army of ducats," gleefully confesses his essential nature as a money grubber.[71] Kukolnik assigned a more insidious role to the Jews in *Kholmsky* where he tied Jewish greed to crime and treason, though even here the character of Rachel, a young Jewish woman smitten with a Russian prince, was drawn with sympathy. In the stage version of Gogol's *Taras Bulba* (mounted in 1852–53), audiences saw Jews acting as spies who betray the Cossacks,[72] — an eerie foreshadowing of the real thing acted out in Poland and the Pale in 1915 when the Jews, as "enemy aliens," were subject to Cossack pogroms. It is worth noting that in 1860 the censors about-faced and began prohibiting Judeophobic works on stage, a position that quickly became a dead letter.

Innocence and Evil in Faraway Places

One evening at his home in the 1820s, theater director Fëdor Kokoshkin held a theatrical duel involving himself reciting from Corneille's *Cinna* and Mochalov from Victor Ducange's *Thirty Years* in order to illustrate the difference between classical drama and melodrama. The Ducange was more immediately effective; the Corneille left a deeper mark of power, majesty, and honesty. Melodrama, like historical drama, profited from the decline of classical tragedy and helped displace it. Although classicism long resisted the barbs aimed at it, those barbs were numerous. In France, Beaumarchais in the eighteenth century had asked: "What possible interest could I take in the death of a Peloponnesian tyrant? or in the sacrifice of a young princess in Aulis?" Not much later, the Russian playwright and actor Plavilshchikov echoed the sentiment: "Of what use is it to a Russian that some Tatar Chinggis Khan was the conqueror of China and performed many good deeds there? Why do we need to see some Dido languishing for love of Aeneas and Iarbas possessed by jealousy?"[73] As if in response to these remarks, Russian historical plays brought the story to "here"; and the contemporary domestic melodrama brought it to "now." Although melodramas of effect (or action) were popular in Russia, melodramas of affect (or emotion) had a greater impact upon theater tastes, especially for women, and on acting styles. The most popular were the imported works of Kotzebue, Ducange, and Caigniez.

The king of European melodrama, August Kotzebue (1761–1819) is remembered almost exclusively as the victim of a student assassination in 1819 which set off a wave of reactionary decrees in the Germanies. During a sojourn in Russia, Kotzebue had been exiled to Siberia on false charges by the Emperor Paul. Upon release, his anti-Napoleonic writings under Alexander I won him a high rank in Russian service and the role of an adviser to the tsar on German affairs—one reason for his murder by the inflamed Karl Sand. Pushkin's 1823 poem *The Dagger* celebrated Sand's deed as a blow for freedom and was widely circulated among younger officers. To the broad Russian public, Kotzebue had a wholly different resonance. The author of about 230 plays, Kotzebue became for a while a European cultural phenomenon. His plays were translated into a dozen languages, gained wide acceptance in Europe and America, and made up almost half the pieces performed in Petersburg and Moscow in the years 1800–1820. The appeal of Kotzebue's works lay in their stageability, spectacle, immediacy of sentiment, and a sense of empowerment and agency that was almost absent in the neoclassical genre based on Greek models where the gods were in charge. Kotzebue's success arose partly from the exotic settings in South America, the Near East, on the high seas. Audiences gaped at the animated impersonations of pirates, Gypsies, slaves, Peruvian Indians, uprooted Asians, rebels, impoverished nobles, and misused women—to say nothing of kings, sultans, and pseudohistorical figures attired in colorful costumes and backed by elaborate sets. Interwoven into the spectacle was the open expression of "naturalistic" feeling, with an occasional hint of sex, and a down-to-earth sentimentalism. The socially expanding Russian audiences could readily identify with his works.[74]

Kotzebue's *Misanthropy and Repentance* (1788) became his greatest success in Russia. This lachrymose piece, devoid of violence or villains, offered emotional turbulence when an errant wife repents to her husband and is forgiven. Baron Meinau, the male protagonist, has spent years of bitter hatred of self and of the human race due to her infidelity. Kotzebue presents an affecting dramatic treatment of the protagonists' desolation. The icy Meinau is the hard man with a soft heart; his wife Eulalia, whose "heart bleeds and [whose] tears flow" at her fate, is endowed with kindness, charity, and chaste modesty. Their reunion is contrived and in the final moment of the play, after extended speechifying suspense, the afflicted couple are reconciled in the presence of their children.[75] During Kotzebue's Russian sojourn, Tsar Paul was deeply touched by a French production of *Misanthropy and Repentance* at the Hermitage Theater. Kotzebue's popularity thereafter grew apace. By 1806, he was filling theaters in Petersburg, and being presented on Russian provincial stages and in serf theaters and amateur productions; dozens of his plays were translated into Russian. *Misanthropy and Repentance* led the pack. Audiences and theater entrepreneurs adored it and certain actors found in it a natural vehicle for their talents. At Kazan University, Sergei Aksakov played the role of Mei-

nau in amateur student theater, and some of the most eminent professionals —
Yakovlev, Alexandra Karatygina, and Mochalov — made their mark in this
play.[76]

Not everyone shared audiences' admiration. The Decembrist Wilhelm
Küchelbecker (V. K. Kyukhelbekker), for example, not only detested the
"sentimental-German" drama of Kotzebue, but scorned "the ladies of the
Zamoskvorechie District [of merchant Moscow]" who raved about him.
Quite a different verdict was offered on the playwright and his public by Rafail
Zotov, the dramatist and spokesman for the seatless parterre. He wrote that
"our audiences were raised on exclamations, shouts, and turgid phrases. But
as soon as they were shown a domestic environment, the joys and sorrows of
ordinary life, as soon as they saw verisimilitude and naturalness, as soon as
they heard the voice of natural feelings — they joyfully jumped off the high
horse of Sumarokov [the eighteenth-century classical dramatist] and with all
their hearts attached themselves to the plays of Kotzebue."[77]

The melodramas of Guilbert de Pixérécourt (1773–1844), the "father of
French melodrama," and his Parisian rivals, L.-C. Caigniez and Victor Ducange, flooded into Russia in the 1810s and 1820s. Petersburg and Moscow
repertoires in the years 1813–25 featured ten melodramas of Pixérécourt, four
of Caigniez, and several of Ducange, including *Theresa, or the Orphan of
Geneva*, which by then had already played around the world. Its heroine, a
young orphan adopted by a noble family in the Swiss Alps, is actually of noble
birth, but has been fraudulently denied her birthright by the villain. In a
contrived accident, the villain murders Theresa's protector. When confronted
in court by the live Theresa who he thinks is dead, the villain is frightened into
confessing his crimes; the orphan is absolved, inherits her rightful fortune, and
marries her young lover. This silly and suspenseful piece electrified audiences
even in the exalted interior of the Imperial Theater. The sound effects and
music marked in the margins of a Moscow copy of the script indicate that the
dramatic tension could be further heightened by aural effects. Since actors on
the imperial stage had to play roles assigned to them, the Petersburg audience
could watch seasoned classical players acting out the shenanigans of melodrama. The classical star Ekaterina Semënova played the murdered woman,
with her sister Nimfodora as Theresa and the noted tragedian Bryansky as the
villain. The play ran for at least three decades in the capital and in provincial theaters from the Volga to the fairgrounds of Ukraine. *Theresa* possesses
neither psychological depth nor social message. Yet audiences who could delight in the "pity and terror" of tragedy, also wanted agency, action, spectacle,
and thrill. A murder plot twisted around the fate of a victimized young woman
answered the desire to perfection.[78]

The legend of the "thieving magpie," of obscure origin, was fashioned into a

French melodrama in 1815 as *La pie voleuse*. The plot involves a young maidservant accused of having stolen her mistress's silver plate which has actually been pilfered by a magpie attracted by its glitter. By chance the maid has quite recently sold one of her own plates in order to help her elderly father, an army deserter. A nefarious magistrate falsely accuses the maid because she has rebuffed his advances; she is convicted and sentenced to death. As in many melodramas, the innocent party cannot reveal the truth out of fear for another's fate. But when the magpie reappears and steals a bright coin, the stolen plate is discovered. The young woman is cleared and her father pardoned.[79]

The Russian version of *La pie voleuse, Soroka-Vorovka,* premiered in Moscow in December 1816, had three more performances that month, and in 1817 played nine times—a record run for that era. The most enduring treatment of the magpie was the delightful opera of Gioacchino Rossini, *La gazza ladra,* which premiered at La Scala in Milan in 1817. It opened in St. Petersburg in February 1821 in Russian also as *Soroka-Vorovka,* with Nimfodora Semënova singing the lead role. Like its model, *Gazza* had a long stage life in Russia. Pushkin saw it in Odessa during the 1823–24 season and borrowed for *Boris Godunov* the cleverly wrought scene in which the heroine deliberately misreads to the mayor the police description of the deserter. Thus for about three decades, and perhaps longer, the thieving magpie flew around Russia as *La pie voleuse* in the French theater; as *Soroka-vorovka* in Russian theaters; and as an Italian opera. Alexander Herzen's story "Thieving Magpie," inspired by a real-life episode in the provinces, illustrated the links between the magpie legend and the injustice of serf theater (see chapter 6 of the present work).[80]

One needs caution in assessing the emotional impact of melodrama, not least because of the tremendous variation among audiences in terms of wealth, position, estate, geography, gender, and age. Traditional Soviet readings of melodrama complained that its alleged concern for the poor and the weak was offset by an affirmation of the "bourgeois" order and a preachy message of class peace. The genre thus masked real, systemic social evils behind a war of abstract good and evil.[81] This familiar mode of Marxist explanation proclaims that "bourgeois" art is never innocent. If so, melodrama may have been guilty of a quite opposite "sin": Russian viewers who regularly saw legally permitted productions about the struggle of the poor and the weak against the rich and the strong in a secular setting may have become as attuned to social evils as did the far fewer readers of antiserfdom novels and essays. The intention of melodramatists, by all accounts, was precisely to wrench tears of sympathy for victims of injustice; and Russian audiences responded accordingly. The sentimentalism of the earlier "Poor Liza effect" from Karamzin's famous story was amplified by a "reality effect" which made the accumulation in fiction and theater of details about previously unobserved members of society part of what a historian has called the "humanitarian narrative."[82]

Melodrama also helped change acting styles. Acting did not become "realistic" overnight. Each generation, it seems, smiles at the "realism" of previous ones and experiences verisimilitude in its own terms. But melodrama clearly diverged from the high-style method of neoclassical verse drama. Melodrama sought illusion rather than stylized quasi-balletic performance, in order to drive the story and heighten suspense and sensation. In spite of all the flamboyance, the asides and soliloquies, it allowed a more "naturalistic" interaction of the players. The methods required to perform imported melodramas successfully were also those that made the plays accessible to audiences from increasingly broad social origins. Even actors on the capital stages found — or reinvented — themselves by acting melodrama. Melodrama and vaudeville — the least cerebral and seemingly the most lacking in messages — became, to the chagrin of critics, the most popular forms on the Russian stage by midcentury. And one of the many ironies in this story is that Vasily Karatygin, generally seen as affected and unnatural, was credited or blamed for deserting the refined diction of classicism and introducing a looser and more realistic style when playing imported melodramas; and he applied that style even while garbed in the robes and tunics of Oedipus, Nero, Fingal, and Donskoi.[83]

The Human Comedy

Russian comedy, though originally drawing shamelessly from Molière, Marivaux, Beaumarchais, and a dozen others, had much more to say about Russian society than did tragedy with its universals, history with its past, or melodrama with its exotic sites — all to various degrees remote from the viewers' quotidian experience. These genres captured moods, emotions, ideals, even some political attitudes, but in the voices of dead heroes or live ones in distant climes. As Laurence Senelick has noted, comedy was more congenial to Russian audiences than tragedy because it dealt with familiar conflicts and resolutions within a community setting.[84] Instead of archetypicality, timelessness, and eternal verities, Russian comedy offered topicality: local color, recognizable places and figures, recent news and gossip. Instead of a menaced or victorious "Russia" embodied in stylized heroes and foreign enemies, it offered something resembling live Russians facing domestic dilemmas. Instead of abstract victims and villains of melodrama, if offered slyly crafted versions of real people.

Comedy's people are in love, in debt, on the rise or on the downswing, enmeshed in sexual intrigue, or blindly infatuated with things foreign. Most of all, they are engaged in problems that resonate with audiences. The burst of laughter creates the flash of recognition. Playwrights' awareness of shared preoccupations and their keen sense of tension between order and change in the general consciousness enabled them to mount these matters on stage with little danger from the censors. Comedy compressed larger concerns and displayed them sparely — subtly in high comedy, broadly in vaudeville. Successful comic playwrights read a cognitive map of their audience and offered an invisible sense of common experience, however limited by class distinctions. Satirical exposure on stage of society's foibles could arouse a whole range of audience responses: animosity, embarrassment, shame, malicious glee, release, and pure delight — sometimes mingled in an uneasy blend. Generating laughter can also serve a variety of "political" functions: moral uplift, social criticism, and conformity. Russians inherited the well-established traditions of comic representation from classical and neoclassical comedy, puppet show, commedia dell'arte, school drama, and even masked balls. City slickers and country rubes, servants and masters, coquettes and cuckolds and nagging wives, ingenues, femmes fatales, boastful cowards, prodigal sons, strict parents, and pompous asses collided on stage in fictionalized microdramas of society.

How much did the representation of social types on stage change over time from the French Revolution to the emancipation of the serfs in 1861? The servant-master relationship in drama entered Russia from France where, in the first three-quarters of the eighteenth century, aristocratic values and tastes predominated. Servants appeared as bumbling fools, physically ugly, sometimes corrupters of their betters — all in contrast to refined noble masters. Servants functioned as the chorus or as go-betweens, offering comic relief, brazenness, wisdom, and occasionally social inversion. In contrast to the pomp, dignity, and aloofness of their betters, they tended to be base in speech and manners, loquacious, sensual in matters of food and lust, complaining, often pretentious — yet sometimes cleverer than their masters. Because of such complex representation, liveried servants were excluded from the audience in French theaters.[85] Russian servants were also presented as fundamentally silly and uncouth, though occasionally cunning as saucy soubrettes or impudent valets. Yet house serfs on stage, like their counterparts in life, often showed a superior attitude to field serfs. Around the turn of the century, when imperial stages were alive with actors playing servant roles, real-life servants of gentry spectators could actually see themselves thus portrayed. There is no cause to think their reaction was monolithic. Well-dressed and well-treated serf valets may have thought themselves lucky if they saw shabby ones on stage acting the fool, or been astonished to see clever ones advising the master. Badly abused ones might have hankered to change roles with those on the boards. And there were surely those who simply enjoyed the show without engaging in the slightest sociological rumination.

In eighteenth-century theater, peasants often walked the stage as no more than stick figures or as clownish types who spoke in elevated diction. Since real peasants often simulated stupidity in self-defense, they were so represented in theater. Peasants on stage, as in fiction, were the unwitting victims of city swindlers, as in the mid-eighteenth-century comic interlude, *The Hatter and the Peasant*.[86] Even when treated sympathetically, peasants were stereotyped as parts of a collective. They spoke in poeticized and un-individualized voices in settings of utopian villages where no real labor occurred. The reassuring image of Russian peasant contentment persisted until the mid-nineteenth century when it died a hard death; it revived as a national industry and state enterprise all over twentieth-century Eastern Europe. The theme of peasant patriotism in 1812 incorporated the rural population into the body politic, but only as long as the emergency lasted. Almost to the end of serfdom, the clichés prevailed. Since a taboo for a long time hung over acting in folk idiom and certain forms of everyday speech, lower-class representation was bound to be artificial. Thus while one could learn much about "the peasant's shifting visibility and invisibility (as well as his audibility and inaudibility)"[87] in pastoral literature and landscape, little of real village life was visible or audible in theater.

A few playwrights sought greater novelty. Vladimir Lukin and Plavilshchikov pioneered the scripting of Russian ways and manners and peasant speech. For them peasants became protagonists with Russian names in a Russian setting, though still subject to the vagaries of a safe plot, usually a collision between peasant boy, peasant girl, steward, and lord, benevolently resolved by a deus ex machina. In Lukin's *Wastrel Reformed by Love* (1765), one of the earliest depictions of a serf in a "naturalistic" setting, the hero actually declines the freedom offered to him by his owner. Plavilshchikov made a village romance the focus of his play *Bobyl* (1790). It contains a peasant drama played out on its own terms, contrasting a poor landless peasant (*bobyl*) with the wealthy but rude and cruel village strongmen. Matvei, the *bobyl*, is remarkably self-confident, almost a modern man. When his owner scoffs at the idea that a peasant in a gray kaftan could love, his paramour replies: "The muzhik has a heart just like the master's."[88]

Sentimentalism eroded the austerities of classicism even before the latter went into decline. Drawn from sources as varied as Ossian, Laurence Sterne's *Sentimental Journey*, Rousseau's *Nouvelle Héloise*, and Goethe's *Sorrows of*

Young Werther, it filtered into Russia through translations and imitations. Elegiac, travel, and epistolary genres celebrated chaste love, nature's glories, and easily triggered tears, offering what Sterne called "the joy of grief." The related theme, sympathetic treatment of the poor and the weak, appeared in many Russian genres of literature and theater, as Simon Karlinsky has shown, long before the canonical "realists" of the 1840s. Catherine II's *O, Time!* on the Moscow plague, the plays of Knyazhnin and Kapnist, the operas of N. P. Nikolev, and the prose of Nikolai Novikov and Radishchev dealt with the theme, though in stylized form. The romance between upper-class male and lower-class female offered a perfect vehicle for sentimentalist plotting. Nikolai Karamzin (1766–1826), who made *chuvsvitelnost* (sensibility) and *sentimen-talnost* (sentimentality) immensely fashionable in Russian life and art, had the story "Poor Liza" (1792) turn on the dalliance of a young nobleman with a poor peasant girl, ending in her suicide and revealing, amidst an abundance of tears, that "peasant women, too, know how to love!" The heart-melting pathos of "Poor Liza" magnified and popularized the sentimentalized peasant for early nineteenth-century Russian readers.[89]

But a real and tragic Liza never reached the stage. Karamzin's numerous imitators preferred happy endings. Nikolai Ilin's *Liza, or the Triumph of Gratitude* (1802) featured a sentimental cross-class romance that gets resolved by having his "poor Liza" revealed as the daughter of a nobleman, an ending that drew applause from audiences. In Vasily Fëdorov's *Liza, or the Consequences of Pride and Seduction* (1803), Liza is pulled out of the pond and saved. Ilin's sentimental play about recruiting, *Magnanimity, or the Selection of Recruits* (1803), was among the first play to have a wholly peasant (as opposed to merely rustic) setting. Its characters speak in lofty cadences, love their work, and revere the tsar. These and other frequently staged plays drew conflicting reactions to putting peasants on stage as more than cunning house serfs or buffoons. Ilin's critics charged that his peasants were unreal. Others objected that even the lame attempts to reproduce village speech and folkways offended the ears and had no educational value. The most revealing denunciation came from I. I. Dmitriev, aristocratic poet, courtier, and justice minister under Alexander I. He drew a cultural line between the nobility and all others when he wrote in *Messenger of Europe* that peasant life has no place on the stage since "the noble part of the public" had no interest in "taverns, in village markets and in the huts of *odnodvortsy* [smallholders]. . . . They have *their own* customs, *their own* prejudices, and *their own* weaknesses."[90] This antipopulist argument inscribed class lines in indelible ink. Behind the affirmation that it was useless to know the lower orders perhaps lay the fear that it might be dangerous as well.

If both field and household serfs abounded on the Russian stage, serfdom itself had to be approached with caution. Dramatists like Kheraskov in the eighteenth century idealized serfdom, while a few daring playwrights and librettists made a leap from social satire into social criticism that willy-nilly struck at one of the foundations of Russian life. In the plot of the first opera written by a Russian, *Anyuta* (1772), the peasant heroine's love for a nobleman induces her peasant suitor to defy the landowner with veiled threats.[91] It seems clear that this opera would not have reached the boards a year later when the bloody Pugachëv peasant revolt began. In Nikolev's opera *Roseanne and Lyubim* (1778) the master attempts to abduct a serf girl who is in love with a freed peasant lad. She is saved by the repentance of the noble kidnapper. On the general lot of serfs, the lord's huntsmen sing these astonishingly provocative words:

> The masters' joy is our bad luck,
> When they have sunshine, we have storm.
> When they sneeze, we catch cold,
> They have fun at our expense.
> Too good are they for bread and water,
> Yet bread and water make our fare.
> Amusement and well-being are the masters' lot,
> Our good life lies in precious freedom.

The first line is often cited as a deep critical comment on serfdom and inequality. In fact all the lines are set up as false assumptions and are followed by a rejection of their judgments ("Net, Net, Net") and an announced satisfaction with their lives. Even so, the initial litany itself must have been disturbing. In spite of his sly dance around the issue, Nikolev, by generalizing in class terms, broke the taboo on fundamental social criticism.[92]

The most famous treatment of serfdom was Knyazhnin's comic opera, *Misfortune from a Carriage* (1779). Yakov Knyazhnin (1740–91), a Pskov nobleman, led a stormy life which embraced gambling, a criminal conviction, and a death sentence reduced to service as a soldier in the ranks. After a miraculous exit from these woes, he spent over a decade in educational work. In *Misfortune,* the Russia-hating nobleman Firyulin, mindlessly enamored of all things French, displays absurdity and callousness with every word he utters. He yearns for a new and expensive Parisian carriage. Through a ruse, his steward Klimenty (whom the owner calls Clément [*Kleman*]) arranges to raise the money by selling as a recruit a serf boy who is the steward's love rival. To avert this disaster, a kindly nobleman teaches the serf a few French words, and the boy persuades the benighted master that he is fluent. In the lord's eyes, linguistic talent has made his human property suddenly precious, and all ends well.[93]

Prior to *Misfortune,* plays about recruiting abuses had illustrated the magnanimity of landowners or officials who intervened to correct the misdeeds of lesser beings — stewards or malevolent peasants. Knyazhnin blamed the serf owner himself and combined the accepted indictment of Francomania with a denunciation of the mistreatment of serfs. While some Europeans and Russians were identifying the evils of serfdom with an essentialist and barbarous Russia, Knyazhnin linked them to the European cultural impact: the need for the carriage stemmed from the Francophile nobleman's aping of foreign ways; and the salvation device stemmed from superficial knowledge of that culture. Conversely, the highborn character who shows kindness to the serfs is made to seem authentically "Russian." Yet we can wonder with Simon Karlinsky whether audiences did not see beyond the "abuse" to the injustice of the system itself. As all viewers would know, although this particular victim was saved from a lifetime of military service, someone else would have to go in his place in order to fill the quota. *Misfortune* was shown at court with Catherine II and Paul in attendance, performed eight times in St. Petersburg in the years 1779–91, forty-four times in Moscow, 1780–1800, and twice again there in 1810. It retained its popularity into the 1820s.[94] The authorities clearly saw only the main message: inane noble foiled by wise and kind noble. Knyazhnin exposed serfdom's capacity for ruining lives, but only its *capacity*, since on stage tragedy was always averted. In real life, the sale of recruits, the rupture of serf romances, and other cruelties were actually going on without the intervention of a fairy godfather. *Misfortune*'s appeal for fair and just treatment of serfs within the system can also be seen as an apology for the system. Knyazhnin and other writers were working within the constraints of political censorship. Only the individual misuse of serfs by lord, steward, official, or each other could be publicly aired, and thus no "serf tragedy" was ever performed until after the emancipation. Even in fiction, which had a freer scope than theater, serious canvassing of the peasants' lot did not surface until the 1840s.[95]

The peasant genre declined after the Napoleonic wars until the 1850s when something like real peasants appeared in staged villages with their own diction, stories, psychological profiles, problems, and — often unhappy — resolutions (see chapter 9). Literary interest in the subject that flourished in poetry and prose in the 1840s had no parallel on the stage, which was dominated by melodrama, vaudeville, and historical plays. In one of the most popular comedies of the reign of Nicholas I, Pëtr Grigorev's *Filatka and Miroshka the Rivals* (1833), a minor village official blackmails his desired bride and her lover by threatening to send the rival's brother into the army. Although the brother, a stout Russian patriot, is willing to serve, base villainy is thwarted by a benevolent noble who rights all wrongs. *Filatka,* as a rural courtship vaudeville and rescue comedy, said nothing new. Its success grew out of the use of peasant dialect and the acting by Grigorev and Prov Sadovsky. *Filatka* ran at the Alexandrinsky Theater for over fifteen years to audiences ranging from the imperial family to clerks and lower townspeople. It delighted the provincial public as well, including those in Dostoevsky's Siberian prison camp. The total unoriginality and lack of authenticity of this delightful piece indicated how far the theatrical stage had strayed from the peasant theme since the early nineteenth century.[96]

Needless to say, most comic drama and opera with domestic plots revolved around the life of the gentry. Of social classes on the Russian stage in this era, only nobles spoke in language which, even when versified, faintly resembled their own speech. But what could they say and do without offending the censors? Some comedies employed more or less politically neutral themes of European inspiration: cross-gendering, adultery, cuckoldry, coquetry, and mistaken identity. Some playwrights simply wrote panegyrics to their own social order, as Vasily Maikov seemed to do in the musical pastorale *Village Feast* (1777) which praises the landlord and unmasks a corrupt steward who oppresses the peasants.[97] Since such stewards were indeed a common type, this device neatly deflected blame from the master. Drama without conflict and flawed human beings ceases to be drama, and a wholly virtuous and noblehearted collection of characters is no fun. Comedy requires human frailty, even repugnant behavior that can be corrected or punished. But criticizing gentry required caution. The trick was to treat a noble's sin as an aberration condemned by the majority of the class. Most social comedies were morality tales with a minivillain who was neither a wrathful god of tragedy nor a melodrama monster—too bad to be true. Each age offered explanations for deviant behavior: poor upbringing, unpatriotic Gallomania—illustrated in Denis Fonvizen's great comedies, *Brigadier* and *Young Nobleman* (or *Minor*) —excessive sentimentalism, or boorish provincialism, each in varying mutations and often combined.

The catalogue of upper-class sinners had to be carefully compiled. Sumarokov's included "inept judges, soulless law clerks, vain fops, pedantic Latinists, misers, and compulsive gamblers." Vasily Kapnist's verse comedy *Chicanery* (1798) targeted corruption. The author (1757–1823), a Guards officer of Greek ancestry, left the army, served as marshal of nobility in Kiev Province in the 1780s, worked at the Imperial Theaters Directorate in 1799–1801, and then served for twenty years in Poltava Province. *Chicanery* exposed the fraudulent behavior of crooked judges who cheated fellow nobles amid bouts of drinking and festivity. Though it ended in the victory of honesty and probity, after a brief run the comedy was banned under Tsar Paul for still obscure reasons. It regained the stage and appeared thirty-six times in Petersburg in the years 1805–25, twenty-eight times in Moscow in the years 1808–25, and numerous times in the provinces long after its debut.[98] Avoidance of government service also became a butt of stage satire. Although the gentry were released from mandatory service in 1762, some nobles regarded service as patriotic. D. M. Volkov's *Upbringing* (1774) dramaturgically pits a Francophile spoiled brat who refuses to serve against a veteran colonel wounded in the Turkish wars who itches to return to battle. The play equated service with virtue and enlightenment. At another level it argued that the nobleman occupied an elevated position from which to do good deeds, in contrast to the poor who, though honorable, could never attain the highest pinnacle of honor.[99] Thus the nobleman, as master of land and people, sees and knows what others cannot, and is able to act high-mindedly. This notion, common among European nobilities, also drove an ideology of portrait and manorial landscape painting of the era (chapter 7).

Excessive emulation of foreign ways topped the list of vices most frequently pilloried in eighteenth- and early nineteenth-century Russian comedy which ridiculed Franco-Russian speech and the compulsive borrowing of foppish manners and clothing. Ivan Krylov (1769–1844), later renowned as a fabulist, wrote the anti-Gallomanic *Fashion Shop* (1806) to send up dishonest French shopkeepers who garbled the Russian language; and boorish gullible provincial Russian gentry women who worshiped all things French. Overpriced goods, smuggling, blackmail, and the fumbling of drunken lackeys are woven around a standard love farce. Towering above all the characters in brains and earthy common sense, Masha, the enserfed Russian shop clerk, juggles all the characters in the air in a hilarious plot that ends with her gaining freedom.[100] Most scholars agree that theatrical satires on the Francophile gentry offered no deep social or political critique of the social order. Even those linking foreignism and foppery to domestic inequities had a safety clause. There is not much evidence that the reception of social satire was characterized by a mixture of laughter and tears. Even so, the continual dramaturgical parade of privilege gone awry, asinine serf owners, vulnerable servants and peasants, and the blatant moral messages encoded in the plays must surely have had an effect on some gentry audience members, not to mention the middle and some of the lower classes in those audiences.

Krylov and Shakhovskoi broadened the indictment of gentry vices in the early nineteenth century to an assault on provincial estate theaters, agricultural experimentation, and the slavish adoption of European sentimentalism. Alexander Shakhovskoi — archenemy of political reform, modernism in language, and Westernism in general — vented his negative views for decades in the Imperial Theater (fig. 37). A man of great wit and self-irony, Shakhovskoi set as his goal "to refine taste, to soften manners, to eradicate vices, to rouse the spirit and a sense of patriotism."[101] *Semi-Lordly Amusements, or Domestic Theater* (1808) roasted the rustic indulgence in serf theater. Roughly modeled on Molière's *Bourgeois gentilhomme,* the hero, Avdei Tranzhirin (spendthrift), is a tax collector of indeterminate class origin and a man on the rise. On becoming a landowner, he establishes a manorial serf theater which stages a performance of (presumably Knyazhnin's) *Dido* to honor the landowner's relatives. All the elements are in place for a successful production: serf girls as Minerva and Juno, a ballet, a double chorus, and even a horn band. When liquor flows backstage, trouble begins: missing props spell disaster to the scenic gods, a real dog bites into a stage bear, and the roof of the theater collapses.[102] This spoof was not wholly exaggerated. In provincial serf theater, far advanced as of 1808, one could find many examples of bizarre productions — including some of *Dido. Semi-Lordly Amusements* remained in the repertoire until 1837, with Shchepkin often playing Tranzhirin; and it inspired several sequels and imitations. Griboedov, in Act II of *Woe from Wit,* took a passing shot at a "ballet troupe of serfs," made up of children ripped from their families.

Shakhovskoi and Krylov aimed their shafts at another species of the provincial gentry, the improving landowner who sought fiscal salvation in books, journals, and foreign experts on agronomy. Most fell victim to a naive reverence for European science and technology unmatched by an understanding of them or of the peasant mentality. Peasants, though skilled in making their own adaptations, nourished, in the words of Michael Confino, "a deep scorn for any initiative coming from the landowner."[103] An offstage character in Krylov's *Fashion Shop* purchased Dutch cows, English rams, and Spanish lambs which perished in the unsuitable Russian climate and brought him ruin. In 1819, just when the Moscow branch of the Free Economic Society was founded to promote agricultural innovation, Shakhovskoi staged his *Prodigal Landowners,* one of the funniest plays of the era, which mercilessly mocked the innovators. The hapless landowner, Prince Rainbow, builds factories on his "plantation," imports merino sheep, introduces sugar beets, and deploys machinery and irrigation technology — all of which fail miserably. The peasants resist newfangled ways, managers cheat him, his wife overspends, and his "expert" relies on the philosopher Kant for guidance.[104]

Shakhovskoi's *A Modern Sterne* (1805) broke new ground in social comedy by showing the fatuousness of the sentimentalism that was sweeping over Russian literature and life. He fashioned a wicked caricature of the "modern Sterne" in the nobleman Pronsky, who romances a sturdy peasant girl already enamored of a village lad. Comic disaster results on several fronts. In the manner of Don Quixote, the master miscommunicates with his servant and other lower-class people whom he has totally idealized. He speaks in the sentimentalized conventions that are as inappropriate as the feudal imagery of the lord of La Mancha. Pronsky refuses to serve in the army and makes grandiose verbal love to a poor peasant girl whose simplicity he adores. But he blanches at the thought of being the brother-in-law of his lackey who is courting the maid's sister. Shakhovskoi insisted that "sentimentalism" and rigid social snobbery went hand in hand. The obtuseness of the hero is heightened by the fact that he is a Russian noble-playing-the-European-playing-the-peasant.[105]

A Modern Sterne was put on the boards two years after the publication of Admiral Shishkov's antimodern treatise on the old and new styles of Russian literature and language. Shakhovskoi became close to Shishkov's circle of "archaists" which eventually included Derzhavin, Krylov, Katenin, and Griboedov, among others. They were ranged against the "moderns": Karamzin, Zhukovsky, Batyushkov, Vyazemsky, and Zhikharëv. Lesser Karamzinists, Pëtr Shalikov and Vladimir Izmailov, were the prime targets of *Sterne* which derided the sentimentalist trope of a love between nobleman and peasant girl and the saccharine travel traditions launched by Laurence Sterne. Beneath the transparent assault on Shalikov and other sentimentalists lay an attack on emotionalism's corrosive effect on the social order. In Simon Karlinsky's view, Shakhovskoi's antisentimentalism was rooted in a conservative, quasi-racist belief in the inability to communicate between classes. The play underscored the abnormality of class transgression by having "patriarchal" figures from opposing classes (a general and a serf) converge in their hostility to it. Shakhovskoi's farcical expression of antisentimentalism was all but inevitable; whenever a Sterne appears, a Richard Brinsley Sheridan is bound to be not far behind.[106]

Shakhovskoi unleashed another offensive against gentry sentimentalism in *A Lesson for Coquettes, or the Lipetsk Spa* (1813). Its huge success issued partly from the scandal inspired by its heavy-handed satirizing of some prominent literary figures. A minor character in the play, the gentry poet Fialkin, mischievously caricatured Zhukovsky. While the character strums a guitar and solemnly improvises verses on Homer, the peasant girl he is serenading cries "what nonsense" as an aside and a maid says "Great! The blind leading the blind," in reference to the Greek bard. The all too recognizable Zhukovsky sat in the audience, side by side with Vigel and Zhikharëv. For a performance of *Lesson for Coquettes* at court, the role of Fialkin was cut in order to protect the feelings of Zhukovsky who had a secure place with the imperial family. The waters of the spa resort overflowed into a torrent of abuse and factional polemics that Zhukovsky called "the Lipetsk flood." The wrath of several writers descended upon Shakhovskoi, and the famed Arzamas Literary Circle (1815–18) — Zhukovsky, Uvarov, Batyushkov, Karamzin — was founded in reaction to *Lipetsk*.[107] Although the pastorale still lurked as background to many a noble adventure, Shakhovskoi here used a different chronotope or space-time setting — the spa — which, like its European prototype, served as a potential curative site for romantic, matrimonial, or sexual needs as well as medical ones. Imported coquetry, one of the playwright's satirical objects, found a natural habitat in a foreign-inspired place which, like any holiday resort, offered relative freedom from the constraints of home. The elite segment of the play's audience could well connect Shakhovskoi's chauvinistic lesson to the setting they knew so well. The Lipetsk spa itself declined soon after the play appeared in favor of German spas and Caucasian mineral water centers.[108] But Shakhovskoi, followed by Griboedov and a few others, had opened up one more social venue for stage action, setting the scene for the use of the ballroom and salon in the prose society tale of the 1820s and 1830s.[109]

Shakhovskoi and Krylov represented more than a harmless brand of satire aimed at gentry foibles. Their barbed wit seemed to be aimed at all "useless" gentry who retired from service, got bored with nothing to do, and indulged in extravagant hobbies such as estate theater and experimental agronomy; or in Gallomania and mawkish deference to foreign literature. The acerbic Shakhovskoi especially seemed to be transcribing the old device of shaming the cuckolded husband into a scorching indictment of Russian rural life where naive gentry allowed themselves to be duped by false foreign ideas and dishonest employees. Indeed the linking of sexual and foreign intellectual seduction was suggested in Russian comedy long before its darker version, the antinihilist novel of the 1860s.[110] Nicholas I and his censors became more stringent about offending the social estate upon which the throne rested. The dramatist Alexei Potekhin was warned during the 1850s that it "was not permitted to represent a nobleman on stage in comic form." Though Potekhin exaggerates the effect of the warning, the episode shows how much things had changed since the time of Shakhovskoi and Krylov.[111] In 1845, an interesting "class-neutral" sideshow carped at signs of an emerging women's independence current, known in the 1840s as "zhorzhzandizm" after the French novelist. *The Emancipated Woman,* an unsigned "caricature in two acts," featured a gentry wife who rode horseback, hunted, smoked, played billiards, bossed her hubby around, and addressed men with demeaning diminutives. For her "assertive tone" she was dubbed "a Russian George Sand."[112] With literary opponents like this, the gentry could relax, at least until the 1850s when harsher themes in the landlord-peasant nexus were mounted on stage (chapter 9).

Like their real-life counterparts in the audience, merchant and other urban characters made their way gradually onto the stage. Mikhail Matinsky's *St. Petersburg Gostiny Dvor* (1779), the eighteenth century's most original and popular comic opera, led off by situating merchants in their own workplace — Gostiny Dvor, the famous arcade of shops on the Nevsky Prospect that still bears the name and fulfills its functions. Actor, composer, and writer Matinsky (c. 1750–c. 1820) was a former serf who had been freed and sent to Italy to study music. In an interesting social juxtaposition, this satirical opera by an ex-serf writing about merchants for the delight of an audience including the aristocracy was done up in a Russian national style and inhabited by city people — merchants and clerks in a shop setting where "sacred truth" wins out over cheating. Although the plot device and resolution were adapted from contemporary comedies of gentry life, the novelty of the milieu and characters gave *Gostiny Dvor* an immense success that lasted well into the nineteenth century.[113] Matinsky's *As You Live, So Are You Judged* (1792) contains more somber tones. Virtue wins again, but the mercantile villain, a "heartless creditor," surpasses the petty cheats of Gostiny Dvor by preying on rich and poor and by reveling in his squalid methods. An honorable nephew appears to establish a moral balance and to allow proper space for honest business practices in the social order.[114]

An equally common vice attributed to merchants, social climbing, evoked frequent sermonizing on the stage from the eighteenth century right up to Alexander Ostrovsky. Wirtschafter discusses two works that underline the lesson. Osip Chernyavskoi's *In the Company of Merchants* (1780) warned merchant daughters to beware of ensnarement by noble suitors who turn out to be swindlers. V. A. Lëvshin's *Mr. Voldyrov's Wedding* (1793) reverses gender roles in a tale about a foolish merchant who meets disaster when he falls for the charms of a corrupt gentry widow. The focus on merchant gullibility and gentry rascality of course is presented as exceptional, a moral failing rather than a fault in the social order.[115] Plavilshchikov, who lamented the general neglect in drama of merchants, clerks, workers, peasants, servants, and seminarians, tried to devise comedy plots which depicted their inner life. Anticipating Ostrovsky's vaunted "kingdom of darkness" by half a century, his *Shop Clerk* (1804) unfolds in a murky world where a merchant attempts to frame the poor and virtuous clerk whom his daughter loves, and to marry her off to a rich man — a theme addressed many times in the coming century.[116] Playwrights taking up the merchant genre told their audiences mainly two things: cheating, a natural side effect of the business profession, can be overcome by moral fiber; attempts to marry out of one's class invariably result in failure or worse.

Scholars seem to agree about the long hiatus in the merchant theme on the Russian stage in the first decades of the nineteenth century, but have no plausible explanations for it. Undeniable, however, was its resurrection in the 1830s. A Soviet writer, dealing with performances at the Alexandrinsky Theater, with references to Moscow, offered unconvincing theories about the rise of the Russian bourgeoisie, the advent of the "bourgeois monarchy" in France, and the efforts of Official Nationalists to rope in all classes for the monarchy. A more likely answer is the turn of playwrights, as with graphic artists, to a broader panorama of society, and the continuous growth of merchant theater audiences. In any case the output, not great in either quantity or quality, floated two subthemes that drew on older plays: the historical merchants, Minin among others, who help save or are saved by a tsar; the stubborn daughter who aspires to marry upward out of her class or who wants to marry downward for love. In the historical genre, one new note was sounded — the serf who becomes a rich merchant (Polevoi's *Igolkin, the Novgorod Merchant,* 1835). Plays about marital squabbles provided a bridge between those of the eighteenth century and the upcoming work of Ostrovsky. Indeed one of them strikingly anticipates Ostrovsky when the father, opposing his wife's search for a gentry son-in-law, asks: "Why get into another's sleigh?" In these ephemeral works of the Nicholas period, the critic Nikolai Dobrolyubov would have found ample material for his withering commentaries on merchant life that were triggered by Ostrovsky in the next reign.[117]

P. G. Grigorev (1807–54), born three years after the appearance of *Shop Clerk,* took up the theme in the 1830s. From 1831 he acted at the Alexandrinsky Theater, a veritable hangout for merchants. Grigorev excelled in merchant roles and wrote over thirty comedies and vaudevilles, including the popular *Merchant Polka* and *Once Again the Merchantry.* The merchant milieu of Nikolai Gogol's *The Marriage* (1842) was suggested to him by Shchepkin in order to draw a contrast to gentry courting habits. The female protagonist, daughter of a deceased tyrannical merchant, seeks a gentleman groom but finally chooses a midlevel official. Her initial fussiness was a motif echoed in Pavel Fedotov's 1849 painting, *A Choosy Bride.* Simon Karlinsky argues that the play showed a new "social and erotic interaction" between merchants and gentry and that it reflected Gogol's own revulsion at marriage itself, largely because of his homoerotic disposition. But *The Marriage* was seen by many contemporaries as a negative comment on social pretension. The perception was in the long run more relevant to the history of cultural attitudes than was the real motivation. More important is Karlinsky's observation that Gogol's play "contributed to the emergence of a more realistic mode of staging and acting."[118]

Vaudeville, one of the genres that flourished from the 1820s onward, occupied a blurred space beside comedy. The term has been traced to the fourteenth-century French poet Olivier Basselin's *Chansons de Val de Vire,* though the first modern vaudeville theater appeared in 1792 in Paris where it served as a cruder successor to French comic opera. Unlike American vaudeville — essentially a suite of show numbers without a connecting narrative — original vaudeville involved a brief situation comedy devoid of ideas or dramaturgical harmony. The plot was subordinated to wit, dialog, songs of banter and charm, couplets (actually quatrains), dances, funny business, horseplay, schtick, sight gags, virtuosity of performance, and often direct interaction with audience. The brevity of the form allowed vaudeville to be presented as an added attraction before or after a main performance. Vaudeville enlivened the stage and introduced or sharpened new themes, particularly satirical broadsides at the current butt of ridicule. Many critics, notably Belinsky, hated vaudeville as a pure exemplar of trivial commercial culture, without recognizing or caring about its social effect as a vehicle for presenting novel situations and new places of human interaction.

Hundreds of vaudeville adaptations or originals appeared on the St. Petersburg stage alongside full-length comedies. In the 1830s and 1840s, vaudeville flooded the boards of the two capitals to the sound of clapping hands and clinking coins at the box office. Actors took up the pen and added their own sense of a visibly changing public to their pieces. In terms of content, the "wider social purview of Russian vaudeville from the late 1830s on" took in city folk, clerks, the lower middle classes, country bumpkins in the city, and provincial actors, with a pronounced shift in setting from gentry estates and metropolitan drawing rooms to clerks' lodgings and merchant shops. Though most vaudevilles were adapted from foreign works, the social content suggested a new way of looking at Russia and at the notion of who was Russian. Under the influence of Eugène Scribe, vaudevilles presented scenes of everyday life, paralleling the physiological sketch, feuilleton, genre picture, and urban song. In the 1840s, as the term "natural school" was emerging, vaudeville kept pace.[119]

Critical interest in social verisimilitude on stage was sparked in 1817 by a comedy that mocked the rustic who comes to town: Mikhail Zagoskin's *Mister Bogatonov, or a Provincial in the Capital,* another adaptation of Molière's *Bourgeois gentilhomme.* Molière's hero was hardly needed as a model for the wide-eyed provincial. In 1812, Konstantin Batyushkov had described a rustic on his first visit to the capital: "a lucky fellow who, having just galloped in on a post coach from the shores of the Sekvana River in light-blue pantaloons and an unsightly wide frock coat, is devouring the sights." Zagoskin's Bogatonov travels through three different identities: from bourgeois to noble landowner, from Russian to Gallomane, from rustic to urbanite. He fails the final rite of passage and is swindled outrageously by city folk and foreigners. *Bogatonov* ran in Moscow and St. Petersburg for a dozen years or more and had become a hit in the provinces by the 1820s. Critics at the time argued that Zagoskin lacked social realism. One claimed that a provincial as ignorant as Bogatonov could not have been found in St. Petersburg even twenty years earlier, a doubtful proposition. A Russian biographer of the playwright found the character of Anyuta to be not at all Russian, citing her boldness: "In our country, maids do not converse so openly with the master." Bogatonov offered little of interest about urban life, but the brief flurry over it indicated a growing interest in the issue of accurate social reflection and how it was distorted by obsolete characterization and excessively slavish imitation of foreign models.[120]

In the late 1830s and 1840s, as painters and journalists were exploring the obscure corners of urban life, the comic stage began to present a more or less believable cross-section of the capital's population to the public gaze in the form of landlord-tenant relations, apartment hunting, dachas, and contrasting neighborhoods. Pëtr Karatygin's *House in the Petersburg District* (1838), a vaudeville with an undercurrent of urban blight and heartlessness, appeared in *Repertoire and Pantheon* at the moment when Eugène Sue's *Mysteries of Paris* was being serialized there. Karatygin offered a stock villain, female victim, and hero. The villain is a greedy urban landlord in the northern part of the city, Mr. Pennypinch (Kopeikin), who engages in rent gouging, eviction, confiscation of furniture, and insulting language. The hero poses as a criminal, punishes the landlord, and saves the tenant. In a mock-Gothic touch, he torments Pennypinch by having his accomplices sing the satanic chorus from Meyerbeer's opera *Robert le Diable* which was at that moment frightening and thrilling Petersburg theater audiences. The landlord must recompense his victim but remains as deaf to moral principles as the street in the Petersburg District known as Deaf Alley. When the hero asks Pennypinch if he understands that "a noble person must be lenient to the less fortunate," the latter replies that he does not. This piece of dramatic migration from the familiar climes of manor house and gentry town home to big city neighborhoods marked a major turn in stage representation that put ordinary denizens of the capital into the limelight for all to see.[121]

Comedy writer Fëdor Koni (1809–79), father of the famous Russian jurist, moved in liberal gentry intelligentsia circles in the 1840s. Yury Arnold was impressed by the enormous social range of his characters and his grasp of their customs and speech in plays that captured the lives of the poorly defined but dominant sector of urban society: merchants, townspeople, impoverished landowners, and various lower-class people. *St. Petersburg Apartments* (1840) featured a newly promoted official out to display his success in a lavish apartment. His quest takes him from his home in the respectable Kolomna District near the Bolshoi Stone Theater to Gorokhovaya Street (later notorious for Rasputin's flat at one end and the Cheka at the other), to Mudflats and Goat Marsh. Along the way he meets an aging French actress, an opera regisseur, some journalists, and assorted shady characters. Theater people and mercenary journalists (including Zadarin: read Bulgarin) are mercilessly caricatured. At one level, *Petersburg Apartments* works as a bedroom farce, at another it denounces petty bourgeois values. Money infects everything and, like some of the tiny flats visited, it constricts life, relationships, and horizons. Neither Karatygin nor Koni delved into the lower depths in the manner of Dostoevsky or Vsevolod Krestovsky. But their plays and others like them offered new X-ray pictures to be added to the growing image of the body social, new crannies and corners of the urban landscape that theater writers and audiences were willing to explore.[122]

Other sites of Russian life came into the theatrical purview to join the estate, the town, the spa, and the quarantine station. Among these, the backstage of provincial theater inspired a work that, though rarely mentioned in literary histories, became one of the most enduringly popular comic vehicles in the annals of Russian theater and one of the few works of this period — along with Griboedov's *Woe from Wit,* Gogol's *Inspector General,* and some Ostrovsky plays — never to have left the stage: the 1839 vaudeville *Lev Gurych Sinichkin* by Dmitry Lensky (1805–60). Lensky (fig. 38), one of those theater folk who frequented Pechkin's coffee shop and the Moscow Merchant Club, lamented his lack of success as actor, his life's dream, and denigrated his fame as vaudevillist.[123] The French prototype of *Sinichkin, Le père de la débutante* (1837) by M. E. G. M. Théalon and J. F. A. Bayard, and an early Russian adaptation were both performed with no great success in St. Petersburg in spring 1839. The following autumn the premiere of Lensky's version, with music by Verstovsky, met a resounding response in Moscow, repeated in St. Petersburg in 1840, and it was performed in seven different provincial theaters in the first two years alone. The provincial actor, Sinichkin — like Noël Coward's "Mrs. Worthington" — wants his daughter on the stage and will stop at nothing. Among the obstacles are an aging female star and a womanizing gentry "patron" of the theater. The action revolves around a rehearsal of "Borzikov"'s *Pizarro in Peru with the Spaniards,* a droll conflation of two popular European melodramas: Kotzebue's *The Spaniards in Peru* and Pixérécourt's *Pizarro, or the Conquistador of Peru,* both well known to Russian theater audiences.[124]

As in the take-offs of serf theater, the rehearsal-in-the-play explodes in chaos. The timpani player is at the tavern, the unprepared actors are fined, and the orchestra plays too loud. When an actress "faints," a cast member calls out the immortal line — first used by Alexandre Dumas *père* in another backstage drama, *Kean* (1836), and still being repeated in Anglo-American radio and film comedy into the 1940s — "is there a doctor in the house?" Riotous action predominates and the couplets offer slashing commentary on actors, owners, critics, writers, and theatrical Lotharios. When the vaudeville opened at the Moscow Maly in 1839, the entrance of the famous comic actor Zhivokini as Sinichkin brought prolonged laughter even before he opened his mouth. Verstovsky's wife, Nadezhda Repina (1809–67), who had been purchased as a serf by the Imperial Theaters, premiered the role as Liza, the hopeful theater debutante. Several characters made playful reference on stage to themselves and other real actors, including Lyubov Mlotkovskaya, from one of the best known provincial theaters in Kharkov. Lensky, with his "half-Kalmyk" features, refined manners, and fluent French,[125] took the role of the slimy seducer.

Lensky, playing to an "in" audience, shrewdly offered familiar situations and "talking names." Moscow and Petersburg audiences who had attended theater in the provinces could recognize his version and perhaps feel the superiority of being a "capital public." They were reminded that provincial audiences' "wits are blunt," and all the worst that they had seen or heard about provincial theater was on full display: a blaring orchestra, inappropriate quotations, mispronounced foreign words, and awful acting made worse by wild gestures and ponderous archaic declamation which Lensky took pains to parody in action and words: "Hands are stretched now up, now down / As would act a foolish clown." What the spectators might have heard about backstage life — jealous rivalry, drunkenness, fines, police actions, directorial tyranny, authors' claques, and sexual politics — was gleefully embellished. Though pure farce was the main concern, bits of social reality shone through as well: the landowner Prince Vetrinsky (Windbag) took actresses to his estate, Revelry Hall; uncooperative ones he could ruin by working hand in hand with the manager, Pustoslavtsev (Vainglory), who was modeled on a real manager, Vysheslavtsev.

Lensky let out all the stops. In a fashion later to be called "zany" and "screwball," he shattered all logic of plot through slapstick, and never gave the audience a chance to think about absurdities — or much about the unjust practices unveiled. Serious critics, appalled at the success of vaudeville, attributed it as usual to the twin demons of an unversed public and entrepreneurial greed. Gogol denounced vaudeville, along with melodrama, ballet, and opera. The literary historian and Official Nationalist Stepan Shevyrëv, writing in 1851, distinguished between ephemeral farce and enduring comedy. Leaping to the defense of the genre, Koni, writing in *Northern Bee* in 1840, insisted that vaudeville's purpose was not to enlighten or "to embody an idea," but to entertain an undemanding audience. A modern scholar has rightly stressed the "nonlinguistic codes," the acoustical and visual aspects of the genre in Lensky's work: choreography, decor, music, and the actors' bodily and vocal mimicry.[126] *Sinichkin* was widely imitated and has persisted up to our time. Ostrovsky's *Talented People and their Admirers* (1882) is not only a slightly grim picture of stage life and morality, but a homage to Lensky's brilliant exposé of some of the silliness of theatrical conventions. Tsarist censorship, however, did not allow *Sinichkin* in popular theaters in 1905 — a time when grand dukes and other worthies had their theater mistresses — because of its "ludicrous" insinuation that privileged people sexually exploited actresses! The Soviets put on *Sinichkin* in the 1920s in modern dress and setting at the Vakhtangov Theater, and a 1956 film, starring the eminent Nona Mordukhova, tried with only modest success to recapture its original buffoonery.[127]

In the eighteenth century, theater had offered, in the words of Elise Wirtschafter, "a conversation about Russian society." Resolutions in drama sought not a change in society but reconciliation and individual moral reform via a conservative Enlightenment which preached preservation of the natural order — including autocracy and serfdom. Theater as a whole represented a civic society of association and mutual moral instruction — in fact preaching — not a civil society devoted to structural change. In other words, theater acted as one organ of the larger educated society devoted to bettering Russia by bettering Russians (and not institutions) for the general good. In the early nineteenth century, the didactic element weakened.[128] But what changed most was the social content and audience composition. Drama can do no more than offer modern readers a blurred glimpse of those worlds. But in its own time, the unfolding drama of society gradually produced for the consumption of a wide public a panorama of sites and personalities, both familiar and new. Some have seen literature, others theater, as the surrogate parliament and bearer of Russia's political and social conscience in the preparliamentary age. This may be an exaggeration, but it seems clear that the social exploration and representation of Russians on stage awakened curiosity about "the other country" that lay within the borders of the Russian state, particularly those of the semi- or nonprivileged estates. Widening the lens to various parts of the human terrain uncovered novel situations. The "gentry nests" did not disappear from audience view in this era or indeed until after the Revolution. Yet while audience attraction to social comedy and vaudeville was spurred by sheer boldness and humor, there can be no doubt that that genre's commentary on everyday life and social relations in the Russia of Nicholas I had reached a level of candor that was equivalent to revelation.

6

Playing the Provinces

To perceptive eyes music, scenery, and novels must look different with every three-degree change in latitude.

—*Stendhal,* La vie de Henry Brulard

"Provincial drama theater," wrote one of the sterling historians of the Russian stage, "reflected more clearly than the other arts the characteristic features of the inner spirit of society." And, she reminds us, the provinces, plus the two little dots St. Petersburg and Moscow, *are* Russia.[1] Was she arguing that, in order to get the biggest gulp of cultural understanding of serf-era Russia, one must desert the capitals and move into Gogol's and Saltykov-Shchedrin's stinking marshes of corruption; to realms that possessed, travelers warn us, no charm, no society, no intellectual life; regions that historians often call simply the periphery? What out there could possibly await and reward the patient seeker after Russian cultural life? If one reads "society" as a demographic indicator, the provinces loom as the largest spatial and human arena where culture "happened." Leaving aside religious ways and folk art, theater ruled provincial cultural life; it reached out to many more consumers than did literature, classical music, or fine art. Illiteracy and underdeveloped institutions accounted for this. In the pre–reform era, the stage graduated from an elite engine of amusement and enlightenment in the capitals and on rural estates to a network of public entertainment centers open to all in scores of provincial and district towns. Yet though Russian and Soviet and a few Western scholars have been publishing material on it for decades, this socio-cultural domain goes unnoticed in general treatments of Russian culture and the arts, to say nothing of works on Russian history.

As in Britain and France, Russian provincial audiences tended to be noisier than those in the capitals—thus the "civilizing process" had to work its way geographically outwards as well as downwards through the estate or class system. Theater lovers in those two countries looked to London and Paris; just as—via a similar mechanism—their American counterparts looked to Europe. Naturally the expectations of many provincial Russians were set by the Imperial Theater system. Theatergoers and actors who traveled from the capitals to provincial houses were often appalled at what they saw. The by-product of this reaction is that theater history has been largely written not only from the top down but also from the center outward. In Russian histories of theater —pre- or postrevolutionary—the treatment of provincial theater often reeks of condescension. Yet provincial Russia—almost universally pictured as a vast cultural wasteland—contained a multicolored world teeming with life. Its theatricality comprised manorial serf theaters, itinerant or permanent town theaters, domestic amateur theatricals in town or country, folk drama, fairground shows, and performances of all kinds, in gentry and merchant clubs, barracks, schools, and universities. That world invites us to ponder the words of Laurence Sterne in *A Sentimental Journey:* "I pity the man who can travel from *Dan* to *Bersheeba,* and cry, 'tis all barren. And so it is; and so is all the world to him, who will not cultivate the fruits it offers."[2]

Manorial Stagecraft

When in 1910 the folk ensemble director Mitrofan Pyatnitsky brought the Voronezh and Ryazan peasants he had gathered onto the stage of the Moscow Gentry Club and directed them to "sing your songs and dance your dances,"[3] older people in the audience may have remembered a long-gone private version of what they were seeing now in public: serfs on stage, playing sometimes peasants, but more often Carthaginian queens, Byzantine admirals, orphans of Geneva, Spanish barbers, Muscovite heroes, or classical cupids. From the reign of Catherine II to the emancipation of 1861, serf actors trod hundreds of stages all across Russia. Theatrical serfdom lay along a continuum of entertainment that ran from manorial to urban theaters. In the former, the setting ranged from serfs in impromptu performances at home right up to formal scripted stage presentations in built theaters. The Soviet

investigator Tatyana Dynnik defined serf theater as one with a regular repertoire and audience, a trained cast of serfs, some technical equipment, and an
owner.[4] But an important distinction must be made between private manorial
serf theaters; public gentry-owned serf theaters; and "free" public theaters
hiring serfs on *obrok*. The crucial feature of the latter two can be summed up
in a word: "ticket." In town theaters, the public entered with a paid-for piece
of paper. In the manor house, entrée was gained by face, person, family, name.
Estate theaters served a private audience, the seigniors and their guests, sometimes entire families of neighboring gentry, with retainers, servants, and dependent relatives.

Certain rural practices contributed to the growth of estate theater. The
eighteenth-century nobility had a fondness for watching their villagers "sing
their songs and dance their dances" inside or outside the manor house. A print
of the late eighteenth century shows a gentry family and their guests ensconced
in a loge-like veranda enclosure. Below on the stairs, musicians are playing.
Further down, on the ground, serfs perform folk dances as others in festive
costume await their turn (see the dust jacket of this book). Scenes like this were
represented in prose and graphic arts right up to the end of the period. P. E.
Zabolotsky's painting, *After Harvesting* (1822), has serf women dancing to a
folk instrument, the *domra*. The master looks on admiringly from the stoop,
but his wife seems to glare at him (fig. 39). During Church festivals such as the
twelve days of Christmas, masters and serfs sometimes reveled together in
song and dance and feasting. Although many varieties of Russian folk dances
such as the *barina* or *golubets,* a flirtation narrative, required grace, supple
body language, and precise timing, the folk dance could also descend to vulgar
licentiousness, especially at public celebrations such as fairs. For this and other
reasons, the gentry — while often joining in the song — seem to have been ambivalent about emulating their social inferiors, at least until the brief outbreak
of imitative folkish patriotism in 1812 when nobles actually took folk dance
lessons from peasants and others. This is the background that gives such force
to the scene in Tolstoy's *War and Peace* where Natasha Rostova, a noble miss,
executes a folk dance.[5]

A much greater impulse for serf theater was the desire of cultivated nobles
to harness the Western art forms flowing into Russia in the eighteenth century.
After 1762 many nobles freed from obligatory service chose a life of leisure to
absorb and adapt that imported culture. The delights of amateur theatricals
led some families to expand the experience into full-scale serf theaters. The
most affluent among them, with ancestral holdings of lands and serfs (or
newly enriched by Empress Catherine's generosity), set about building for
themselves miniature rustic paradises. The shortage of trained actors, musi-

cians, singers, and dancers led the gentry to utilize their serfs, a practice that originated in the capitals and provincial centers and spread to rural manor houses. The movement peaked in the years 1800–1812 and dwindled thereafter. Owners began to rent, sell, or put out on *obrok* their serf artists to theaters, or sell entire troupes to the Imperial Theaters. Estate "theaters" are hard to count and even to define. Yu. V. Sobolev claimed forty-five for the eighteenth century; a drop to twenty-six in 1800 due to Tsar Paul's interference; and sixty-nine in the reign of Alexander I. In the 1920s, V. Vsevolodsky-Gerngross listed only about seventy-five sites (see below). Dynnik's study of serf theaters, manorial or otherwise, counted 173,156 of them in known locations. Of these, fifty-three were rural manorial stages located in twenty-three provinces. A recent count, based on a looser definition, brings the tally to eighty-six manorial serf theaters in twenty-seven provinces and one unplaced.[6]

Since most manorial theaters are marginally documented in memoirs, only a sampling of the more interesting ones can be offered here. A few rivaled the great court theaters in St. Petersburg in luxury of design and quality of performers, though most were modest efforts created to accommodate holiday productions for family and guests. The great houses in or near the capitals set the tone for most provincial theaters. The Yusupov palace on the Moika, later notorious as the murder site of Rasputin, had a luxurious theater which can still be seen by visitors. The Shuvalovs and Sheremetevs had theaters on the Fontanka, and Sheremetev had one on the Millionaya as well; Prince Potëmkin's nested in his Tauride Palace, future site of the Duma and the Petrograd Soviet in 1917. At Varfolomei Tolstoy's theater in Tsarskoe Selo, Pushkin as a boy first became enamored of theater. One Petersburg nobleman, noted for his outlandish self-authored scripts, performed only in the role of animals, coming out on all fours as a ferocious tiger. Vsevolod Vsevolozhsky, a rich patron of the arts, maintained a dacha in the Petersburg suburb of Okhta where, on his name day, some five hundred guests would watch performances of his serf troupe, chorus, and orchestra — transferred from his Urals estate — followed by the evening ball.[7] In Moscow, S. S. Apraxin, in his home on Arbat Square, put serfs and aristocrats on stage in an opera which featured live deer and dogs cavorting to the sound of hunting horns. P. A. Pozdnyakov, who was wont to dress as a Persian or a Chinese at masquerades, ran an estate theater that mounted magnificent opera performances. His serfs were treated well and, it was said, acted better than some free actors, a tribute no doubt to teachers from the Imperial Theaters. The Moscow elite eagerly turned out for his presentations. The French destroyed the theater in 1812. N. A. Durasov transported huge parties of Moscow gentry to his estate, treated them for weeks at a time to opera and ballet, and provided tutors for their children. Grandmother

Yankova claimed that one of Count Orlov's estates possessed almost five hundred serf musicians, actors, and painters.[8]

Moscow and its environs formed a dense center of estate theater. A magnate of the Catherinian era, Pëtr Sheremetev (1713–88), built an outdoor wooden theater in 1787 at Kuskovo near Moscow where plays could be performed in summer to thousands of spectators, including commoners if properly dressed. The indoor theater, built earlier, ranked with court theaters in magnificence. Foreigners played beside serfs in the orchestra, and the serf Ivan Argunov worked as scene designer. The lavish productions impressed Catherine II but offended the conservative moralist Mikhail Shcherbatov who railed against Sheremetev's extravagance. The Sheremetev heir Nikolai (1751–1809), a musician who had studied in Paris, built the Ostankino palace and serf-designed theater north of town. He established a major school of performing arts, with Imperial Theater actors as teachers. The theater staff of 170 included about a hundred paid serf actors. Females — given names like "Garnet," "Pearl," and "Ruby" — learned proper etiquette and social dancing in order to mingle at the Sheremetev balls. The repertoire included comic operas dealing with the peasantry, three of which — *Anyuta, Roseanne and Lyubim,* and *Misfortune from a Carriage* — dramatized social tensions between lords and serfs. Yet the master permitted serfs to watch performances from the gallery — a practice illustrating how comfortable were grandees with public shows of bondage; and how little they thought about how their real serfs would react. After the peak of its fame in the 1790s, Ostankino declined and its troupe was sold or transferred to the Imperial Theaters where Sheremetev served briefly as director in 1799.[9]

Prince Nikolai Yusupov who, according to Alexander Herzen, "reduced love for women to a sort of voracious gourmandise," is always remembered as the magnate who had his serf ballerinas strip on the stage of his theater. While director of the Imperial Theaters in the 1790s, "the girls of the theater choir," housed in one of his Moscow homes, were nicknamed "the Yusupov seraglio." A gentry memoir of boyhood days tells a less well-known story about him. A. P. Milyukov, invited to the Moscow home of his classmate Kolya (Nikolai Nikolaevich) Yusupov, witnessed a huge ceremonial dinner with orchestral accompaniment. He then attended the father's theater where the audience stood and faced the host as he entered the loge with a ballerina. After the performance of *Zephyr and Flora* by an all-serf cast, "Flora" came to the prince's box and kissed his hand. Kolya told the surprised Milyukov that if she did not kiss the master she would be whipped. To Milyukov's expression of puzzlement that "such a great and beautiful star" could be beaten, his friend replied that "Well, she is a serf girl." Yusupov's family owned over 21,000 serfs. On acquiring Arkhangelskoe west of Moscow in 1810, he created a theater and an art school which over the years trained fifty-one male and twenty-five female serfs. After Yusupov's death in 1831, the school closed, and the company was freed and scattered. Some actors joined provincial theater companies.[10]

Outlying manorial theaters fit a rough geographical pattern. Rolled up in a corner of the Bakhrushin Theater Archives in Moscow is a huge crumbling wall chart crudely drawn in colored ink and entitled *Map of Serf Theater*. Produced in the 1920s by students in the eminent Professor Vsevolod Vsevolodsky-Gerngross's theater history seminar, its purpose was to indicate roughly the major manorial theaters and orchestras. Only about seventy-five sites are plotted and so the map was incomplete, given what was known even then. What is striking about Vsevolodsky-Gerngross's map is the blunt visual impression it gives of Russia as two distinct cultural regions. The map has fallen apart from age or careless handling. As it happens, the northern half is virtually empty except for the few theaters plotted around St. Petersburg and a few at the bottom. In this respect, the professor's map is entirely accurate. Manorial theater took hold where serfdom did, in the forest-steppe and steppe–black earth regions. The northern provinces, thinly populated mostly by state peasants rather than privately owned serfs, were virtually bereft of manorial theaters. In a rare exception, the magnate P. A. Mezhakov maintained in the early nineteenth century a forty-one-room castle in Vologda Province with a picture gallery, large library, symphonic orchestra, and serf theater which attracted practically the entire province's gentry. The vacant regions of Olonets and Arkhangelsk, with few estates, held no known manorial theaters except the probably short-lived one in Petrozavodsk that produced the scandal over *Dido Inside Out*. Pskov Province had one serf theater; Novgorod and Tver Provinces, two each.[11]

The provinces widely circling Moscow show a much different picture. At the end of the eighteenth century, theater caught on in the heavily enserfed Smolensk Province, where fifty-six families (1 percent of the landowners) owned 30.8 percent of all serfs. The Glinkas, Baryshnikovs, Brovtsyns, Nakhimovs, and a few others enjoyed the pastime. The Griboedovs had a Gypsy ensemble housed together with their serf actors. In 1827, town dwellers of Smolensk and Vyazma saw the serf actors of the Lopukhin and Bezobrazova estates perform melodrama and comedy. Of the half-dozen estate theaters in Kaluga Province, that of Princess Dashkova maintained one where in 1803, in the words of her Irish upper-class guest Martha Wilmot, "our labourers, our Cooks, our footmen, and *femmes de Chambres* [sic] turn into Princes, Princesses, Shepherds and Shepherdesses."[12]

In Orël Province in 1805, A. D. Yurasovsky made an unusually large purchase from another landowner of a choir and orchestra that accompanied performances of ballet and drama, with carpenters doubling as the cast. Yurasovsky and a brother provided a wide variety of entertainment. An oft-cited surviving *affiche* advertised Fëdor Scholtz's ballet *Barbary Pirates, or the Benevolent Algerian*. On the same bill appeared *Vaska and Filatka, The Berdichev Fair, or Recruiting a Jew,* and various other diversions.[13] Although sources briefly mention nine other manorial theaters in the province, details survive only on a few. Ivan Turgenev's mother ran a kind of theater school and sent her serfs on *obrok* to perform elsewhere. The Taneevs built a stone theater for guests and a wooden one staffed by serfs and free provincial actors for an unspecified "public." Connected to the manor house by a long road, the latter was equipped with machinery and with sets from Moscow. Almost daily during autumn and winter in the 1840s, it put on drama, ballet, and opera with an orchestra of forty-five players. The crowds grew so large that the owner deployed mounted huntsmen to maintain order. In 1848 the estate was auctioned off.[14]

The Orël theater of Field Marshal Count Mikhail Kamensky (1738–1809) gained notoriety because of a story, "The Makeup Artist" (1883), by one of Russia's greatest writers, Nikolai Leskov. Kamensky had been a comrade in arms of Suvorov and a favorite of Tsar Paul and Arakcheev. The retired count was murdered in his bed by serfs: in one version by two musicians; and in another by his serf mistress and her fifteen-year-old lover. In Leskov's story, the lord has his maiden serf actresses dress up as St. Cecilia, "the virgin and martyr," for his rituals of defilement. The makeup artist, a young serf in love with the master's next victim, flees with her. The horror piles up as in a Gothic romance, with torture chambers and bestial acts. The lovers are saved from death to live out other miseries. But the murder of Kamensky is unrelated to the central plot. Though highly fictionalized, the Leskov tale is among the most arresting of many backstage atrocity stories, and the atmosphere of private tyranny, blighted love, and permanent fear is captured in high melodrama.[15]

Though one scholar speaks of the spread of Tula Province serf theaters, only one lordly owner is recorded in the eighteenth century and two in the nineteenth. Notable among the latter, P. M. Yablochkov, though austere in his personal life, gave his wife big sums to produce her own plays, acted by serfs. In Ryazan Province, landowner Rzhevsky, a ballet fanatic, maintained a dancing school for his house serfs; like many a prodigal noble, he eventually had to give up his expensive pleasure and in 1829 sold his company to the Imperial Theater system. In the provincial capital, a barely literate ennobled former pie hawker and liquor agent, Gavriil Ryumin, ran a theater in the 1820s that, rumor had it, set him back ten thousand rubles. All properly dressed townspeople were permitted entry.[16] In Vladimir Province arose a half-dozen estate theaters. Field marshal Suvorov issued from distant battlefronts meticulous instructions about roles, acting styles, and personnel in his serf theater. Near the end of his life, the eminent diplomat of the Catherinian era, Count Alexander Vorontsov, in 1794 moved his theater from a Tambov estate to one in Vladimir Province. His serf and free paid performers — forty-eight males, seventeen females, thirty-eight musicians — put on works to full houses thrice weekly in a plain wooden building. Three-fourths of the ninety-three-piece repertoire were drama, including Fonvizen, Krylov, Molière, Goldoni, Kotzebue, and Sheridan — an unusual assortment in estate theater, which tended towards spectacle. Vorontsov, a witty, brave, and independent-minded figure, who remained a friend of Radishchev even after his sentence, was the only serf theater owner to show Fonvizin's *Minor* and *Brigadier*. When Vorontsov passed away in 1805, the theater died with him.[17]

In the remote back country of Nizhny Novgorod Province stood the holdings of the Tula manufacturers, the Batashëv brothers, owners of the Vyksunsky Iron Works, other factories, extensive lands, a multitude of serfs, and an enormous manor house. Andrei Batashëv (d. 1799) tyrannized weaker local gentry and bribed officials, and, according to one story, he had some miners, who were illegally minting money for him below ground, buried alive to prevent government inspectors from discovering them. Ivan Batashëv (1741–1821) in 1806 erected in the park behind his ninety-room three-story palace one of the finest theaters in the Russian empire. Mikhail Zhdanov, a friend with a critical eye, reported a splendid orchestra of forty players. Ivan's granddaughter inherited all this and married D. D. Shepelev, a hussar general who aspired "to live by effect." Shepelev invited an entire regiment to bivouac on his grounds and enjoy his gargantuan feasting, and invited "all Moscow society" in winter to attend his theater. His truly eccentric son, I. D. Shepelev, grandfather of the dramatist A. V. Sukhovo-Kobylin, became a railroad magnate who owned eighteen thousand factory peasants. Dressed up as an Ottoman sultan, the son would lounge among the cushions and divans of an "oriental" tent attended by black-faced lackeys. In the serf theater he inherited, the actors put on drama, comedy, ballet, and operas such as Weber's *Der Freischütz* and Hérold's *Zampa* in which Shepelev himself sang baritone.

In the 1840s Shepelev hired as a conductor N. Ya. Afanasev at thirty-five hundred rubles from the Imperial Theater where he had been getting only eight hundred as a first violinist. Afanasev immediately abolished corporal punishment in the orchestra. As ballet master, Shepelev hired the famous Moscow dance teacher (and a character in Tolstoy's *War and Peace*), P. A. Jogel (Iogel). The set decorator installed gas lights at a time when the capital was still using oil lamps. The grand theater on the Vyksa River gained wide renown. Forestry and mining officials and neighboring landowners were admitted free, except for benefits to which the owner made his guests subscribe. Shepelev was, like many landowners, robbed blind by his serfs and had the son of a steward flogged in his father's presence for imagined cheating. Since the master tutored his cast with the stick, females wore cushions under their garments to soften the blows. He punished musicians with fines and incarceration. For receiving a note from one of his favorite female actresses, his choir leader landed in a dungeon and perished during the night. Yet Shepelev paid the serfs and artists whom he imported from Moscow and Petersburg and protected his female performers by having their carriages guarded by jaegers to and from his music school. Given the outlay for a theater of this scale, it is hardly surprising that in 1846 the Vyksa estate was mortgaged.[18]

In Saratov Province on the Lower Volga lay the estate theaters of the Bakhmetevs and Kurakins. A theater mounting comedies and operas appeared in the provincial capital in the 1810s under the auspices of Governor A. D. Panchulidze (1762–1834), a Georgian prince in Russian service. When the governor was fired for embezzlement in 1826, his successor helped faltering attendance at the theater by pressuring Old Believer merchants into buying tickets, though their religion prevented them from attending. In Simbirsk Province, the Tatishchevs, Ermolovs, Stolypins, and a few others owned serf troupes. A former house serf described a performance at the estate of Prince Gruzinsky at the end of the eighteenth century. In a pastoral scene inhabited by a dozen young serf women, daughters of the landowner's weaver and huntsman, sang verses of love and praise to the prince in a gesture common in everyday manorial culture. In Penza Province, inland from the Volga, the Gorikhvostov troupe specialized in opera and Italian music. Vasily Kozhin and his wife ran a modest serf troupe that did comedies at the Gentry Club for "the quality." They had one professional actor; and Kozhin's wife taught one of the serfs a role she had played while a pupil at the Smolny Institute. According to Dynnik, serf theater ended in Penza province in the 1830s.[19]

In the south, a half-dozen magnates of the fertile province of Kursk owned thousands of serfs. In the years 1820 to 1826, Prince Ivan Baryatinsky on his Marino estate had serfs do Russian plays and tutors and governesses do French ones. I. O. Khorvat, author of the opera *Martha of Novgorod*, entertained nobles, officials, and hussar officers from the nearby encampment, occasionally feasting his guests for weeks and months. He maintained separate quarters for his serf actors, addressed them courteously, and acted side by side with them.[20] Out of the theater of Count Wolkenstein (Volkenshtein) emerged Mikhail Shchepkin. The Ukrainian provinces of Poltava, Kiev, Volynia, and

Kharkov each had one or two recorded manorial theaters, and Chernigov had three. The estate known as Buda, alleged to be the richest in Ukraine, stood on an island in an unspecified province. The owner, D. I. Shirai, organized nightly spectacles and balls for his numerous guests in an effort to make his home a new Athens. The effusive Shalikov, who attended performances around 1803, noted a scale of production matching Sheremetev's theaters. In his usual saccharine tone, he reported on the beauty of the serf women performers and praised the master for raising up his "children" (i.e. peasants) from nothing.[21]

The marshy and thickly forested Belorussian provinces have left few traces of Russian manorial theater. A notable exception was the mini-court and theater at the Shklov estate of the magnate Semën Zorich (d. 1800) in Mogilëv Province. Positioned at a gateway to the interior, Zorich, a Serbian-born officer in Russian service and one-time lover of Empress Catherine, lavishly entertained travelers entering Russia; and he welcomed as house guests incoming artists who, in return for his hospitality, performed together with his serf troupe. This protean company of cadets, serfs, professionals, and amateur aristocrats performed for Empress Catherine II and Emperor Joseph II of Austria in 1780. The spendthrift Zorich left debts of more than a million rubles and his heirs sold some of the dancers to the Imperial Theaters. But due to financial complexities in the sale, these remained in serfdom for another twenty years.[22]

Motivations for most founders of manorial theaters excluded monetary gain, an impulse that went against the ethos of lordly hospitality and reeked of loathsome commerce. Yet repugnance to moneymaking in public was by no means universal, and strapped or profit-seeking landowners from time to time took their troupes to town and opened up shop. The notable gentry owners of ticket-selling serf theaters all appeared between 1798 and the early 1820s. Prince N. G. Shakhovskoi of Nizhny Novgorod Province, possessing a hundred performers, ran two theaters, to one of which he invited the peasants. In 1798, he moved the troupe to the city of Nizhny Novgorod and converted it from a manorial to a public theater, the first in provincial Russia to leave important traces. By 1811, Shakhovskoi's profits and some gentry subsidies enabled him to rebuild the theater and maintain drama, opera, and ballet troupes in daily performances. Shakhovskoi took his troupe to the nearby Makarev Fair every July up to 1817 when that fair closed down. He then built another theater which survived until a fire took it in 1853. Since the owner disliked plays about everyday Russian life (except for Alexander Shakhovskoi's comedies), he offered Shakespeare, Calderón, Schiller, Kotzebue; Russian neoclassical and historical plays; and operas of Mozart, Boiledieu, and Martin y Soler.[23] Mikhail Zhdanov, historian Mikhail Pogodin, and other observers gave Shakhovskoi's theater high marks. But the opinion of I. M. Dolgoruky, amateur librettist, actor, and all-round theater enthusiast, is shaded with ambiguities. The costumes were marvelous and the acting sometimes good, he thought. It was "lots of fun to have the chance three times a week to mingle with people in this public place." Dolgoruky's *Love's Magic* with music by D. Ya. Davydov opened there in 1813. In a much-quoted report, Dolgoruky described hilarious errors in the production: the violinists' beards caught on their strings as they cranked their bows in a frantic effort to catch up with the conductor; the prompter screamed audibly to change the set; and the set man, foaming at the mouth, forgot to move away the "forest" at the right moment.[24]

Although critics mocked, Shakhovskoi's house as a rule filled up three times a week in season and every night at fair time with local gentry and their families and servants in boxes, merchants clapping loudly from the stalls, and the lower classes on benches. The proprietor, bewigged and powdered, attended all performances. For a visitor like the roving official Gavril Gerakov, the Nizhny theater in the 1820s was a special treat. There is no reason to contest aesthetic judgments on the quality of the performances by connoisseurs like Dolgoruky. But pleasure derived from attendance clearly did not always depend on the quality of the piece or of the acting, as the prince himself admitted. A visitor found it odd that the actors tried to do tragedy, which was beyond their talents, when ordinary people came to enjoy comedy and light operetta. Gatsisky recalled the childhood thrill of being in the theater itself and peeking through the curtains at the people backstage. In the early 1820s, V. V. Selivanov sat entranced in his aunt's loge in the yellow wooden theater with its white painted columns and five gendarmes in the lobby. The public knew the serf actors by their familiar names only — Yasha, Ivanushka, and Minai. Fans adored Minai the comic long after his decline, a familiar habit of Russian audiences whose attachment to personalities was so strong that it forgave the faults. In the calculus of pleasure, power, and art, Shakhovskoi scored high on the first two.[25]

Down the Volga in the port city of Kazan, landowner P. P. Esipov founded a town theater in 1803 with a troupe from his nearby estate. Some sources claim that he kept his actresses in a harem. When Vigel dined there, the host, in a breach of custom, sat them between the male guests at table, together with actors and musicians who rose to serve and then dined with the guests. After some kissing and flirting, the guests repaired to filthy quarters and next day watched the serfs perform Martin y Soler's *Una cosa rara*. One of Esipov's serf actresses, Kuzmina, told Shchepkin that he was a kindly master and she made no reference to sexual matters. Though Esipov's Kazan theater performed poorly, it was animated periodically by visiting stars from the capital. Esipov, an improvident man, went broke and died in debt in 1814 and his troupe dispersed. Audiences had responded in different ways. Sergei Aksakov, a student in the newly opened university, thrilled to Plavilshchikov playing in Kotzebue's *Child of Love.* Students would cut class or leave early to get good seats in the gallery. For Muslim Tatars who attended, the effect was one of shock. At a performance of Voltaire's *Mahomet,* when the prophet's turban appeared on stage, the Muslims in the audience fell on their knees; some, fearing the wrath of Allah for mingling with infidels, prostrated themselves and threw off their shoes.[26]

In the city of Penza, landowner Grigory Gladkov maintained a serf theater from 1807 to 1821. The cast comprised female serfs and male stable hands, servants, and — by one account — clerks and seminary students, an extraordinary fact, since the last were prohibited from even attending theater. Combining a passion for theater art with a profit motive, Gladkov trained his actors in tragedy. Visitors commented on mediocre performances, lower-class audiences, and the owner's mistreatment of the cast. The poet Vyazemsky noticed bruises beneath the actors' makeup. One, Gladkov's recently beaten serf mistress, was unable to sit, lie, or walk. Vyazemsky even repeated a rumor that Gladkov had actors beaten to death in order to take out his rage at the poor performance of his dogs during the hunt. The alert traveler Vasily Insarsky spoke of watching two simultaneous performances: on stage, where serfs cavorted as kings and heroes; and in the front of the house, where Gladkov roared at actors, flew on to the stage, and struck them. After his death, the theater held on under his son until 1829.[27]

Sergei Mikhailovich Kamensky (1771–1835), the most notorious serf theater owner, brought his father's troupe to Orël, ran it from 1815 to 1835 and, like his father, found an unenviable niche in fiction. A decorated infantry general, he avoided war talk; a cruel martinet to his house serfs, he donated generously to the poor; a hater of theater spongers, he gave free tickets to those he liked; as the ruler of a legion of serfs to serve him, he lived in the midst of unspeakable squalor. This short, fat, bald dandy, the owner of seven thousand souls, created an elaborate complex on Cathedral Square with residence, church, theater, and actors' dorms — housing altogether about four hundred people.[28] Sparing no expense, Kamensky engaged a German ballet master; sold five hundred serfs to buy a few good actors; bought an acting couple and their six-year-old tap-dancing daughter for 250 souls; maintained a well-trained serf orchestra and horn band; and unsuccessfully offered twenty thousand rubles for Shchepkin, who appeared only in short runs. The serf cast doubled as tailors, shoemakers, and barbers. The leading actor alternately played a Spanish grandee, a Venetian gondolier, a Russian coachman, a Turkish pasha, and a Tyrolean huntsman. In a regiment-like operation, actors took their meals standing up and were marched back and forth to the music of drum and horn. A jail cell was on hand for infractions. Kamensky closely monitored actresses and had them flogged for leaving their quarters at night, corresponding with officers, or even looking at spectators. He dictated stage gestures as if from a lexicon, had actors memorize lines without a prompter, and beat them between the acts when they fumbled.[29]

Kamensky apparently did not fear suffering his father's fate. One of his serf actors allegedly killed himself after Kamensky refused an offer of a thousand rubles from the Moscow Imperial Theaters to buy him.[30] A more famous case inspired the antiserfdom story of Alexander Herzen, "The Thieving Magpie." Kamensky had purchased serf actress Kuzmina (or Kozmina; no other names in the sources) from Esipov's heirs. Orël audiences greatly admired her in such roles such as Cordelia in *Lear* and "Edelmona" in *Othello,* as well as in lighter genres. Shchepkin, a guest actor there in 1822, saw her in Caigniez's *Thieving Magpie,* the tale of a falsely accused servant girl. Shchepkin, interviewing Kuzmina, learned that Esipov had given her an education, training, foreign travel, exposure to a broad culture, and a promise of freedom which did not materialize. She was cheated of her promised freedom by Esipov's heirs. When the new owner Kamensky besieged her with sexual advances, she rejected them. Kamensky insultingly implied that she was selling her body in order to purchase costumes. Kuzmina replied that, though innocent, she would spite him by taking a lover. Her experience was in fact commonplace for actresses of the era—and not only serfs. But the pathos of her exceptional talent in thrall to such an unworthy master led to a sharp treatment of her case at the hands of Shchepkin who recounted it to Herzen. The latter, the most important Russian radical of the age, added extra force by having his heroine-victim die in childbirth. The role of the wronged female was constantly being played on stage by serf actresses, themselves subjected to all kinds of mistreatment and false accusations in their everyday lives.[31]

The poignancy of the magpie story and its resonance down through theatrical history should not obscure the contribution of Kamensky's theater to cultural and social experience. The Orël public was regaled, in one season alone, with eighteen operas, fifteen dramas, forty-one comedies, six ballets, and two tragedies. One production mounted simulated naval battles, shipwrecks, and live gunfire. Gerakov found the acting excellent, except for a few performers who were "obviously slaves"; and he praised the owner for providing a cultural service to the town. The owner's behavior was sometimes off-putting. When several generals and their ladies jeered at his productions, he barred them from the theater. He also tried to prohibit loud applause except when he or the governor signaled it, a ban constantly violated by the macho officers. Prince Dolgoruky noticed Kamensky's ambivalence toward money and class: he admitted the prince free of charge, but expressed annoyance that mere acquaintances were always expecting gratis tickets — a sign of social disdain for the impersonal mechanisms of the market, or just plain stinginess? The theater was rarely empty. The governor recommended it to visitors. Though as an opera lover, the Guards officer Buturlin, stationed in Orël in 1827–28, scorned Kamensky's singers, he saw the theater as a refuge from garrison life. Gury Ertaulov, as a young boy in a military family posted there in 1826–27, recalled the town's pride at having a permanent theater as opposed to touring troupes. The theater drew some fifteen to eighteen hundred spectators a week and all the proceeds went to Kamensky, though neither these nor his personal wealth could ward off the financial ruin caused by lavish outlays.[32]

The last known gentry-owned commercial serf theater arose in the 1820s when Kostroma landowner Vasily Obrezkov (Obreskov) brought his manorial company to the provincial capital and set it up in a tannery. Obrezkov's serf cast was supplemented by two professionals: Andrei Shiryaev, a former Maly actor; and Vasily Vasilev, one of the rare gentry career actors. Obrezkov also had the use of two choruses and a seventy-piece orchestra loaned to him gratis by retired general A. S. Kartsev, a wealthy landowner and patron of the arts. Cheap tickets brought in large audiences. The writer Alexei Pisemsky, inspired by what he saw there a child, organized his own shows at home and later as a student at Moscow University. In time Kartsev withdrew his people from Obrezkov's theater and set up his own, which became part of an emerging circuit involving several cities. Obrezkov died in debt in 1830.[33]

What happened on the stages of serf theater? Their repertoires were as diverse as those of the capital theaters, the principal source. Catherine II apparently feared the growth of estate theater, but did not limit it. Tsar Paul tried to control the content of performances by allowing manorial theaters to stage only what had been approved for the capital stages. Owners had to pay a percentage of the take — whether public or private — to charity, a device that soon faded into oblivion.[34] Alternative inspiration was occasioned by the visit of a literary or theatrical connoisseur who could recommend or even bring along a play or opera, by a landowner's exposure to other theaters, or even by reading reviews. Tatyana Dynnik's list of 297 vehicles performed in serf theaters contained 114 comedies, 94 operas, 28 ballets, 18 vaudevilles, 12 "dramas," 6 tragedies, 5 prologues, 2 patriotic pieces, and 18 of unknown genre. Thus comedy (including vaudeville), opera (mostly comic), and ballet dominated both the manorial and the public serf theaters. Tragedy and other drama made up only about 6 percent of the repertoires. As elsewhere, some of the works floated themes of social conflict. In Martin y Soler's opera *Una cosa rara* (1788), a virtuous Spanish peasant wife resists seduction by a haughty prince and is saved from dishonor by the queen's intervention. This stage display of triumph over sexual and class hegemony was performed by serfs (whose own triumphs were all too few) at, among other places, the Sheremetev, Kamensky, Esipov, and Gorikhvostov theaters. Luigi Cherubini's *Water Carrier* (1800) offered a comic reversal involving a spoiled upper-class wife who is transformed for a time by a fairy into the wife of a water carrier who beats her, a concept that has actually been called "democratic" by a noted music historian.[35] It is fair to conclude that, with a few exceptions, manorial theater repertoires remained conservative, unreflective of the broadening social ambit that was being explored on imperial stages.

The Russian national theme, as inscribed in folkish performances, fared better, though not for long. For the Saltykov outdoor theater on the Marino estate, Karamzin in 1803 wrote a stylized rustic comedy, *Only for Marino,* with himself, Vigel, and the owner in the cast. In the late eighteenth century, Count Razumovsky put on an annual "haying" tableau in his garden: as the serfs acted out mowing, they sang in chorus and danced in bright costumes. At the peak of patriotic feeling in the Napoleonic era, folkloric divertissements attained great popularity. Among a half-dozen productions, *Semi, or Funfair at Maria Grove* was the most enduring, and major variants of it are found later in Ostrovsky, Tchaikovsky, Rimsky-Korsakov, and Stravinsky. With staging by Isaak Ablets and music by S. F. Davydov, *Semi* first played at Ostankino in 1814, and then in the capitals and the provinces. It featured a chorus of Russian soldiers praising their army to the sound of old instruments, spoons, bells, and fifes. Buturlin's family mounted a variation on serf theater on May 1, 1816: they had the peasants perform *Semi* and then held a real folk fair with feasting, dance, and songs.[36]

The nationalizing pathos of Westernized Russian nobles, eagerly grasping at what they took to be the essence of village life and peasant sensibility, stylized their pleasant, harmless, and entertaining side and allowed nobles to enjoy peasant frolic without losing a semi-European identity. Even when — as in Razumovsky's tableau — they recognized that backbreaking work such as haying was also part of true Russian "peasantness," they embellished it. In this way, the gentry's journey of "discovery of the folk" took them barely a step closer to reality than when they watched serf actors performing as "peasants" on stage. The "labor" in folk entertainments remained mediated through the filter of spectatorship. In many ways, this resembled early Russian painters who idealized on canvas scenes of peasants at work in the fields (see chapters 7 and 8). The practice of alternating between the performances of folk material and that of European opera reflected the ever-present ambivalence about the national self.

Witnesses testify to the high level of performance art in the great estate theaters in or near Moscow, Petersburg, and at a few of the big rural complexes. At the other extreme lay stories of disastrous production. In 1811, the *Drama Journal* presented a pair of examples of the unintended farcical level reached on some manorial stages. One was an allegorical ballet in which a hefty Amour and a portly Psyche sashayed across the stage with a vigor that set the stage hands howling and sent the audience into raptures. The other concerned a performance of the comic opera *Two Hunters*, in which the hunters' "forest" consisted of peasant lads standing with birch branches in their hands. The host explained to his visitors that "we have no Gonzago here." During the opera, cast members kept bumping into each other, and a Great Dane began attacking an actor dressed as a bear. The enraged landowner shouted "Keep at it, idiots. We'll hang the dog, and let's see how the opera ends."[37]

Given such episodes, too numerous to recount, manorial theater as a cultural practice became an easy object of attack. From the capital issued the arch comments of critics who were used to metropolitan productions. From the pens of witty playwrights flowed the mocking send-ups: Alexander Shakhovskoi's *Semi-Lordly Amusements* which actually anticipated the bear incident, and Mikhail Zagoskin's *Noble Theater* (1827) were made popular in the 1830s and 1840s by Shchepkin and Mochalov. Zagoskin's piece concerned a theatrical production which included family, friends, house serfs, and a retired actor, to which "the whole town" was invited. The ploy — repeated endlessly in works about the stage — was a race against time to untangle love intrigues, elopement, mutinies, and other disasters before the high-toned spectators arrived. Posters advertised the admission fee as "friendship and indulgence," a clear signal not to expect too much. One of the subthemes is the constant bickering between the lord and his wife, and her all too prescient warnings that theater will ruin the family. On the central theme of marrying for money, one of the characters says: "ten thousand souls is but naught if you have no soul of you own," echoing a real argument in the host family. Indeed, when the play within the play proceeds, the stage audience does not even notice that it parallels what is happening in the household.[38] This touch embodied Zagoskin's dubious belief that manorial theater audiences made no connection between stage action and social realities. A strong sense of ascription and a dose of competitive scorn operated in the mocking of provincial theater, an argument that theaters did not belong "out there," lacked resources and talent, and posed financial hazards to those who kept them.

Impulses for establishing manorial theaters varied immensely among serf owners: family entertainment, love of stage art, imitation of the court, display of wealth, gargantuan hospitality, organizing human beings, creating an erotic hothouse, and in a few cases making money — many of them in combination. Pedagogy moved Andrei Bolotov to form a children's theater. In the 1840s, Elizaveta Vodovozova's father started a "theater" in his home in a Smolensk district town. In order to promote noble feelings in his family through the plays of Molière, Fonvizen, Griboedov, and assorted musical works done up in peasant costumes, he tutored the cast which included his children, a half-dozen serf actors, and five musicians. Though little investment was needed, the habit became ruinous because of the continuous flow of guests from a radius of thirty to forty versts who were fed and housed for days at a time. Despite financial drain and the malicious envy of some neighbors, the father persisted in sustaining the family's pleasure and enlightenment.[39]

Spurred by quite a different kind of motivation, one landowner, during a performance by his serf actors, exclaimed to his guests: "These are all my people, my servants!" Landowner A. A. Kologrivov, who still wore a wig in the 1820s, had his serf cast painted black and shorn like monks. On visiting Moscow, he would bring along a huge entourage of orchestra, actors, singers, and dogs because, as he put it, "at home in my own theater, when I arrive all the actors and choristers bow to me. I come to your theater here, and no one wants to know me or bow to me."[40] What we might see as gargantuan ego was in reality an almost unself-conscious arrogation of power and prestige. This quaint articulation of domestic grandeur, shared in varying degrees by many serf owners, reflected a deeply rooted revulsion against a public sphere that was enmeshed in unfamiliar social and cultural relations. The iron law of personal authority over property and chattel among the gentry intensified a cosmic sense of unresponsiveness to modern life among many privately empowered people. More subtle psychological mechanisms operated as well, such as theatricality and the compensatory deployment of "subjects" by otherwise powerless nobles.[41] In these blends of seigniorial pleasure and power — pleasure in consuming the product and power over the production — the lords had much greater sway than the managers of the imperial houses. Out on the landed estates, there were no contests among audience, cast, and management; no real backstage force; no appeals over the owner's head. The tsarist government refrained from controlling life inside the manor house and rarely prevented the abuse of serfs and other kinds of malpractice on far-flung estates.

Estate theater essentially committed financial suicide. With the few exceptions noted above, all revenue went out for expenses, and none came in. This accounts for the difference between the estate and the commercial town theaters and for the eventual decline of the former after 1812. Moscow Province, heartland of manorial serf theater, especially felt the blows of war: ruined homes and the lavish spending of landowners-turned-officers on the European campaign trail. Expenditures on education, travel, and luxurious appointments made it hard for all but the most affluent to maintain domestic theaters: in 1859 half of all nobles owned only twenty serfs; as early as 1837, those with one thousand or more accounted for only 2 percent. Hard times forced some noble families to sell their troupes to the Imperial Theaters. A few held on by taking their operations to a town and converting them into businesses, but even these eventually collapsed. Still others, adapting the institution of *obrok* labor, sent their serf actors and musicians for hire to public theater companies, thus feeding what was to become the major element of provincial theater.[42]

Serf as Actor

The lives of manorial serf actors differed from those of the Imperial Theater performers in several ways, aside from greater vulnerability to persecution. Those locked in like lepers, hospital patients, or convicts lived under a kind of social prophylaxis. Most were, like musicians, youngsters taken from the field or household serfs: waiters, cooks, cleaners, tailors, shoemakers, painters, carpenters, maids. At N. A. Durasov's estate near Moscow, Martha Wilmot attended a performance in 1806 with about a hundred serfs on stage and in the orchestra. Her host apologized for the poor showing since, he explained, most of the cast was at the harvest. G. I. Bobrikov had the children of his servants trained as dancers, taught French, and renamed as la Fleur, la Tour, and so on. He then invited the dance teacher Jogel to mount ballets at his estate theater. Those lacking Bobrikov's fortune often used the stick to turn a maid into a tragic queen.[43]

To a greater degree than serf musicians, actors had to deal with multiple roles and identities. Around 1812 or earlier, General Komarovsky, visiting Count Ilinsky's estate in Ukraine, observed that the Italian actors from Odessa, whom his miserly host had engaged, dressed as princes in the opera, but went around hungry and in rags when the show ended. These performers were free people. How much greater the swing for serf actors from the stage's world of noble birth, mighty deeds, courage, refined tenderness, regal bearing, and sweeping acts of mercy back to the real world of servitude. The German scholar Baron August von Haxthausen, observing what he wrongly took to be serf actors in Nizhny Novgorod in the 1840s, commented on the polarity between roles and reality: "What endless contrasts must this have produced in their feelings." Laurence Senelick aptly likened the serf's reversion to inferiority to the fairy tale in which, after a lofty dream, a peasant awakes in a "stinking byre." Serfs often appeared on stage with masters, family, and friends. Alexander Stolypin permitted his daughter to act in his troupe of seventy-four serfs. Serfs impersonating monarchs in tragedy or opera alongside a noble in the role of a subordinate created anomalies, especially if the serf's talent exceeded the owner's. The actor P. M. Medvedev recalled a wealthy landowner who acted alongside her serfs at home. When they reached a sufficient level of excellence, she took the troupe to Vitebsk. They flopped because she, devoid of ability, insisted on playing the lead beside her genuinely talented serf actress. For gentry, acting no doubt produced pleasure. But at curtain time, serf actors resumed a posture of deference, and might endure punishment or a return to field or pantry. Playing — and seeing other serfs playing — serfs or nobles, serf actors experienced "doubling": on stage before an admiring public; and as the character in the plotted role. Letkova, who coined the term "serf intelligentsia," remarked on the actor's multiple roles as performer, stage character, and servant — with the additional role of concubine for the actress.[44]

Stories abound of serf owners' manipulative use of their human chattels for theatrical effect. In a culture where dwarfs and fools could still be found on estates, where peasants were marched around in close-order drill for the amusement of a retired officer, where serfs were dressed up as counts and countesses for a mock court ball, and where nude girls were made to stand in the garden as living statues, this could be expected. Some of it was harmless, as when Herzen's servants, dressed as Turks for his birthday party, performed a puppet show. Dmitry Putilov of Samara, a rich and intelligent minor versifier and friend of composer Alyabev, went far beyond this when he gathered all the hunchback males and females in the district, married them to each other, and organized a Hunchback Ball.[45] Serf actors were subject to the same rhythm of physical punishment for lapses, or for no reason at all, as were musicians and other servants. A particularly observant village priest recounted how a seignior had an actress sent to the stable to be whipped by the coachman for showing insufficient dignity in her role as a countess; she then returned to play in another piece with the scars on her back, thus adding humiliation to the physical pain. All the evidence of abuse is anecdotal — direct observation or hearsay. I have found no litigation. But too many accounts from different kinds of people have come down to us to be ignored: traveling landowners and officials, journalists, serf and nonserf actors, literary figures, foreigners, a priest. Tatyana Dynnik, writing in the early 1930s, set out to "explain the historical role of serf theater in the class struggle of feudal Russia." But serf resistance was rare: at the Yurasovskys, in 1816 an enraged female dancer broke a rib and possibly injured the testicles of a French ballet master.[46]

Sexual exploitation of female (and probably male) performers in serf theater, subject to little or no control and thus more widespread than in the imperial houses, forms the nub of many victim stories. At Sheremetev's Ostankino, guests would mingle and dance with the artists after an opera performance. On some estates actresses were passed around from owner to guests. The owner could easily avail himself of "the glamour and sexual licence associated with the actor," show off the trophies of his sexual power, take pride, display generosity, or generate envy. Lyubov Nikulina, an ex-serf and provincial actress in the early 1840s, while visiting the home of a Tambov Province landowner, spent time with an involuntary member of his serf theater and a harem of ten women. Her informant told Nikulina how the master would take away young girls from their families for training as actresses, debauch them, and then marry them off to some brute. Villages were emptied of their young women, and helpless peasant men were bereft of their fiancées. Desertions, beatings, a wife murder, and attempted suicide ensued. One serf stabbed his wife to death for being "the master's paramour."[47] In this as in some other cases, "theater" was simply a ruse for maintaining a collection of concubines. The female body, in some cases, served multiple functions as an acting device, a sexual object, and a target for the knout. Aside from the concrete abuses, some serf actors must have felt the disorientation that comes from a change of life circumstances, especially if sudden, which often generates previously unused energy. That energy could feed either creativity or despondency and unruly behavior.

The literary assault on the social practices of manorial theater found expression in a now-forgotten novel by sometime playwright and amateur composer Prince Grigory Kugushev (1824–71). *Cornet Otletaev* (1853) combines some of the Kamensky-Herzen material with other examples of real-life kidnaping, fraud, and mistreatment of serf actresses. The married villain, a retired junior officer and landowner, lures away a recently freed servant from a good household with promises of marriage and then sets her up as an unfree actress in his serf theater. Housed in a separate building called Mon Plaisir, the troupe offers vaudeville performances. Obsessed with sex, money, and power — all of which he loses — the master rudely berates the players, calls them "things" and "toys," and furiously says to the kidnaped actress: "I am a lord. And you? a slave, the daughter of a lackey." The mark of a man, in his words, is "to serve, to love, to drink." In the end the young woman is rescued but soon languishes and dies of consumption. The villain, bankrupted by the extravagant entertainments he puts on for a nearby garrison, becomes a homeless and forlorn wreck who, on the last page of the novel, in an almost literal replication of the famous Pavel Fedotov painting *Encore* (1851–52), is presented as a miserable provincial officer amusing himself with dog and stick (see chapter 8).[48]

The fairy tale of maid into mistress and goatherd into prince rarely came true. Nowhere in Russia, apparently, did a prince steal into the sultan's harem and rescue the slave girl. Freedom for manorial serf actors, often promised, was rarely granted. The oft-told case of Zhemchugova resulted from a poignant love story that fitted the archetype of the rich boy–poor girl romance. Praskovya Kovalëva (Zhemchugova, or The Pearl), the diva of the Ostankino opera troupe, was born a serf in 1768, the daughter of a blacksmith on one of the Sheremetev holdings in Yaroslav Province (fig. 40). At seven her training in languages and music began and at eleven she debuted at Kuskovo. Nikolai Sheremetev fell in love with her and, in order to hide it, showered gifts on the entire female cast. Later he freed Praskovya, endowed her with a fictitious Polish genealogy, and secretly married her in 1801, a major violation of the social code. A Russian scholar justifiably speculated that Sheremetev and Zhemchugova got inspiration from the lines she sang or spoke from Paisiello, Grétry, and Voltaire that breathed the spirit of a love that conquers social prejudices. She died two years later, a few weeks after childbirth.[49] Serfs not lucky enough to marry out of bondage had to rely on kindly masters or on patrons and admirers willing to pay the redemption price. Ivan Sibiryakov, a serf actor who had served in the Napoleonic wars beside his master, won the admiration of General Miloradovich and other grandees, who sought his freedom. The owner demanded ten thousand rubles and the actor died in bondage. Agafiya Guseva, in a rare case, gained freedom while a manorial serf. As an actress on a Saratov estate in the early nineteenth century, she suffered the usual grief. When she displeased her master, he took her off the stage, married her to the coachman, and refused to free her. The arts patron Afanasy Stolypin raised the redemption money from Saratov society through a subscription. Guseva then joined a commercial troupe. In a rather daring act, she received her freedom publicly at a benefit performance along with her husband.[50] But the escape route from serfdom for most bonded actors lay only through the purchase of bankrupt seigniorial troupes by commercial troupes or by working in the latter as *obrok* serfs on loan where they might gain notoriety in public performance.

In being exposed to rich theatrical and musical art, was the serf actor in the manor house the servant of two masters, the muse and the lord? Did serfs attain a significant measure of creativeness in their work? Aside from Shchepkin, who spoke freely about his art, we have few articulations from serf actors. A Soviet scholar argued that serfs performed to a "socially hostile public" and lacked that "internal contact with the audience" so necessary for theatrical art.[51] There is some truth in this, though free actors often faced the same problem. I. M. Dolgoruky, speaking from wide experience, was blunt on the subject. After the 1813 production of his opera in Shakhovskoi's theater he made this comment:

What can you expect from a dense slave who can be beaten or sat on a punishment stool at a whim? And so [Shakhovskoi's] numerous actors perform just the way an ox pulls his load when goaded by the driver's switch. I will not go into the reasons why a serf cannot have exceptional talent. I simply say that the theater performances are quite good in Nizhny Novgorod for people of a certain rank. But to call [the performers] actors is almost impossible unless you avert your eyes from their bodily movements. They do not act but rather — to put it plainly — they pose. To repeat: this is no more than one can hope for from slaves.[52]

As Dolgoruky hinted, Prince Shakhovskoi's management of serf actors required an imposed schizophrenia. On the one hand, the owner tried to imbue them with the outward features of gentry style. His wife taught serf actresses the ladylike arts of conversation and needlework. Female stars were permitted to dance with guests at balls. To ready his actors for upper-class roles, the master took them all the way to Moscow to view performances at the Imperial Theater and afterwards had them sit in the gallery of a ball at the Gentry Club "in order to learn the manners of the beau monde." On the other hand, he subjected his crew to the lash and punishment stool, a device with three spearpoints held at the neck so that the victim could not move. He had them double as waiters at lavish dinners. If Kamensky chose the regiment as his model, Shakhovskoi, a pious husband and a puritan, preferred the nunnery. He never touched his charges, imposed strict monastic discipline through separate dorms, and forbade contact between actors on threat of punishment. He censored suggestive lines and prohibited physical contact between the sexes even when someone fainted in the play. Actresses were not allowed to read and write out of fear of billets-doux, and so they had to learn their lines by rote. Held in check by watchful duennas, they were married off at age twenty-five to other actors and given dowries. For Dolgoruky, Shakhovskoi's dual formula for actors — treat them as slaves but drape them in good manners — failed to have the desired effect.[53]

Dolgorukov accurately assessed what he saw in Nizhny Novgorod, Orël, and elsewhere, and others echoed his views. But he was wrong in generalizing that a serf could not be a real actor. Even the few examples of successful individual actors in bondage such as we have in these pages disprove the assumption, as do the convincing reports about the Sheremetev, Yusupov, and Pozdnyakov ensembles. A related argument concerns the moral and aesthetic balance sheet. In 1822, the poet Vyazemsky wrote that "to sanction by lawful authority the extravagant whims of a serf owner who wishes his slaves without talent or inclination to dance, sing, and act comedies is a civil enormity and should be prohibited by the authorities and the marshals of the nobility as an abuse of power." Yet, a few years after emancipation, he lauded the opportunities given to serf performers and their exposure to the great works of drama. Nikolai Evreinov, a noted theatrical figure of the early twentieth century, observed in 1911, fifty years after emancipation, that serf theater had often been used as evidence in the indictment of serfdom. He himself recounted the usual atrocities and conceded that in the final quarter-century of serf theater, it had lost its lofty and lordly (*barskii*) quality and had become a vehicle of petty tyranny and sexual exploitation. But he rejected the charge of unqualified evil by recalling the pleasure it gave and the culture it spread. Landowners were justified, he said, in their pride at turning "a raw peasant into some duke." Serf theater, he maintained, nourished many talents. A mid-twentieth-century scholar, Bertha Malnick, shared this sentiment by stressing the expert training, and in some cases the payment, that some serf actors received. "There can be no *apologia* for a serf theater," she wrote, "but indignation at serfdom must not blind one to the fact that some Russian serf theaters made theatrical history."[54]

The vaunted Russian peasant's gift for dissembling[55] may have helped on stage. But did the exposure to greatness enrich many performers? Did they, as actors must, leave their other identities in the dressing room when they stepped on stage? General Suvorov's serf actor Nikita may have never understood or felt anything spoken by the kings and heroes he played, and for this Suvorov threatened to box his ears and send him to the stable. One of Kamensky's serf actors, Evgeny Bystrov, a skillful performer, was almost illiterate. An old-time serf character in Turgenev's *Notes of a Hunter* tells the narrator about his life as an "akhter" in a "keyatr." They dressed him up, put him on stage, told him what and when to speak. The provincial actor Medvedev met an old serf actor in Tula who, when asked what his *emploi* as a *raisonneur* meant, said: "Forgive me, sir. I am a serf, they told me I am a *raisonneur* and so I say I am a *raisonneur*, but what the word means, the lord only knows."[56] Soviet historians may have tediously rehearsed the evils and abuses of power in serf theater[57] — manorial or otherwise — but their ultimate verdict must be placed against the argument for pleasure and art.

The Theatrical Circuit

In the eighteenth century, a dozen or so towns had semipublic stages. Under Catherine II, provincial town theaters distinct from manorial stages appeared on local initiative or from above. After the great Pugachëv peasant revolt of the 1770s, governors were encouraged to institutionalize gentry self-entertainment in their capitals. As part of the state-building process of linking provinces and society to the center through cultural institutions, in 1784 Catherine decreed the creation of theaters in selected provincial capitals. According to one source, this was to "bring people together for the spread of social life and politesse."[58] During her and Paul's reigns, theaters appeared in Tver, Smolensk, Kaluga, Tula, Kursk, Ryazan, Orël, Tambov, Voronezh, Penza, Kazan, Vologda, Tobolsk, Irkutsk, and Kharkov.[59] These early "opera houses" hosted balls as well as performances which favored comic operas and mythological shows over drama. Ill-defined admission policies ranged from invitation, to gratis opening for the public, to ticket selling. Nor had casting yet rigidified. In Smolensk, the governor's daughter played in Nikolev's serf-themed opera, *Rosanne and Lyubim*. A Tula nobleman, defying a class taboo, played the lead in a mixed cast before an appreciative public that included "the nonaffluent Tula inhabitants." The Tula theater had its roots in governors' celebratory occasions of 1777 that, by the 1780s and 1790s, had developed into regular performances. Visiting and local actors took to the boards in works by Molière, Beaumarchais, Sumarokov, and Knyazhnin, among others. Praised by Andrei Bolotov and directed by the enlightened writer P. S. Baturin, the enterprise was inspired by the remarkable cultivated musician and salon hostess Varvara Yushkova, grandmother of the Slavophile Kireevsky brothers. Yushkova's case, and the number of insistent "female legislators," wives and daughters who pressured men into opening theaters, suggests a much greater role of women in theater life than has so far been recorded.[60] Enforced mourning of deceased monarchs in 1796 and 1801 brought the curtain down on some of these theaters. Most of the others disappeared by the early nineteenth century due to fire, lack of support, the transfer of an enthusiast, competition from manorial stages, or Tsar Paul's rigid censorship.

The new provincial circuit of commercial town theaters in the early nineteenth century drew from both the governors' theaters and the manorial system, replacing the first around the turn of the century and outstripping the second in the reign of Nicholas I. This represented in various degrees a shift from manorial to public culture, from ascription to the market, from gentry to all-class audiences, from country to town, and in a few cases from serfdom to freedom. Seignorial serf troupes in the towns at first coexisted with and were eventually superseded by a commercial system of markets, fairs, and urban networks linked by rivers and roads. When railroads spread and rural freedom sprang up starting in the 1860s, the pattern for the late nineteenth-century provincial theater network was already in place, whereas the archipelago of estate theaters constituted a diagram for archaeologists. The new theater entrepreneurs (*antreprenër, soderzhatel*), a different breed from the manorial lord, included merchants, townsmen, government officials, retired officers, actors, foreigners, even serfs; and in one case, a barber and a prompter.[61] They bought, built, or leased houses; formed or hired troupes; and took them from town to town. Around the practice emerged an actors' bourse in Moscow, bargaining, bidding, star-hunting, pirating, and other mechanisms of a free market.

Remarkably, most of the casts on the commercial stages came from the serf estate. Some of the ex-serfs were those sold individually or in troupes by economizing landowners to nonnoble theater entrepreneurs and thus set free. Beside them on stage worked serfs on *obrok*. Itinerant actor Pëtr Medvedev observed that even in the 1850s the majority of the older circuit actors were serfs on *obrok* or ex-serfs, and that the younger ones were mostly children of serfs. Serf actors, though expected to bow low to their superiors, shared the lives of their free male and female colleagues. Playing a dual role, they performed as fictional free people on stage, and masqueraded in the relative freedom of their lives. Like serf entrepreneurs, they roved the country, earning money for themselves and their owners. An English visitor in the 1850s encountered the case of an *obrok* serf singer who had moved from a manorial theater to the Nizhny Novgorod stage and made much more that the mere ten to twelve rubles a year she paid her owner until his death. When his heir threatened to take the star performer back into the manor house, the local merchants paid a ransom to keep her.[62]

A tour of early nineteenth-century provincial town theaters courses through a little-known stretch of social and cultural relations that contrasts starkly with the world of capitals and manor houses. The survey of the three great regions where town theater flourished — the central provinces, the middle and lower Volga, and the "south" (Kursk, Ukraine, and the Black Sea coast) — begins in central Russia, moving in roughly clockwise fashion.

The town of Yaroslavl, on the upper Volga, had a continuous theater from 1819 when the province's official architect set up a troupe of serfs and ex-serfs who alternated between it and Rybinsk. After a few subsequent owners, the merchant's son M. Ya. Alexeev acquired it in the 1830s. He had deserted his wealthy family to act on stage, but finally got his inheritance and bought the troupe. He raised salaries and erected a new stone theater. In 1848, the traveler Zhdanov saw only ten persons in the stalls and a dozen in the loges — all draped in warm clothes. On stage, an actor who had been fired from the Moscow theater butchered *Hamlet*. On Alexeev's death in 1848, V. A. Smirnov, a serf musician and theater cashier turned actor, bought up his debts; then, like a melodrama villain, pressured Alexeev's daughter to marry him, with the theater as dowry. In the 1850s, Smirnov, an eager exploiter, upgraded the theater. A reporter for the provincial gazette spoke of a brilliant season in 1856: drama, vaudevilles, comedies, benefits for Crimean War victims, and patriotic pieces by the orchestra and the band of the local rifle regiment. Society filled the house and Yaroslavl burst with civic pride. Visitors spoke of "a second Moscow." The local paper, rhapsodizing about the physical charms of the city and its social happenings, praised the theater as a unifying site for the upper classes. "For the first time in quite a while," the newspaper reported, "the cream of high society has been concentrated in this place and has brought its members closer than ever to each other."[63]

The ancient city of Vladimir-on-the-Klyazma boasted medieval churches, cathedrals, a monastery, an active merchantry, and the Hotel at the Golden Gate, but it lacked factories, trade fairs, and a permanent resident gentry. Vladimir got a public theater only in the 1850s where the self-taught serf lackey F. D. Bobkov saw comedies performed. Though the boxes stood empty, the stalls and gallery were full in this small house which resembled a fairground booth due to the raucous and drunken crowd in the upper tier.[64] In Tambov Province a town theater built in 1815 by a local landowner left no traces and a new one had to wait decades. A reporter for *Repertoire and Pantheon* was negatively impressed by a performance there in 1842. By the time the actor Lavrov arrived in the spring of 1846, Tambov, a dirty wooden town of about twenty thousand with a public library of thirteen thousand volumes, had the usual assortment of churches, schools, shops, taverns, a few factories, a twice-weekly market, and two annual fairs. Lavrov found a creaky theater on a muddy street, leased by an entrepreneur from a merchant who refused to make repairs.[65]

The capital of neighboring Voronezh Province, center of the vast black earth region, boasted the broad Great Nobility Street, with governor's mansion, homes of wealthy nobles and merchants, and a theater. After the gentry stage disappeared in the 1790s, a dozen Moscow players arrived in 1802 to form the first professional theater in the city. Magic operas and works by Molière, Sheridan, Kotzebue, and a local dramatist were shown. The ever-present Vigel, commenting favorably on the cast's performance of Kotzebue's *Misanthrope,* remarked that it was the only one of that time composed of free actors (in fact some were ex-serfs), a rarity indeed. Troupes came and went, with several periods of closure from then until the late 1830s. From 1839, Voronezh theater experienced rejuvenation, full houses, and good reviews (fig. 41). The provincial gazette gleefully covered the visits of stars such as Shchepkin and Mochalov in the 1840s. According to A. V. Koltsov (1809–1842), renowned as a poet of the people, the eminent visitors "awakened our sleepy town." The drama repertoire expanded to Griboedov, Gogol, Shakespeare, Schiller, and the patriotic melodramas of Polevoi and Kukolnik.[66]

Tula hosted only visiting troupes in the decade and a half after the closing of its eighteenth-century theater. The Freemason and minor Decembrist S. D. Nechaev initiated a revival, and the theater's subsequent organizers included men of all free classes including an emancipated serf. By 1821–22, the I. F. Stein company performed there at a merchant's residence used as concert hall and theater. The next year Shchepkin appeared with great success. Gerakov around 1821 witnessed an opera followed by a troupe of Gypsies in a "bacchanalia" of dance on stage. The ladies in the audience stood up and left. From the 1830s onward, the Tula theater offered a rich menu of productions, eventually including French drama, comedy, vaudeville, and melodrama; Shakespeare, Schiller, and Kotzebue; and Russian works by Knyazhnin, Fonvizen, Shakhovskoi, Ozerov, Gogol, Polevoi, Lensky, Sukhovo-Kobylin, Pisemsky, and the ubiquitous Verstovsky opera, *Askold's Grave*. Tula broke the rules in 1829–30 by showing part one of the prohibited *Gentry Elections* by G. F. Kvitka (1778–1843), a raw indictment of the provincial gentry's card playing, bribery, election rigging, and place seeking. In 1849, when the actor Lavrov arrived, the theater was racked with problems. Though the owner enjoyed the protection of the provincial government, police were preventing free actors from moving, talent scouts had infiltrated the cast to recruit for their theaters, and an able but trouble-making actor fell drunk on stage in the middle of a performance. Furthermore, although in the 1850s this beautiful city of over fifty thousand people could boast numerous schools and religious institutions, merchant stalls, shops, taverns, two seasonal fairs, and a renowned arsenal, the dirty and run-down theater was in decline.[67]

Enter actor and entrepreneur N. K. Miloslavsky. Arriving in Tula in 1851, he refurbished the theater, imposed stability on the company, pocketed the lion's share of the take, paid good wages, but kept half of them in reserve to protect the actors and himself. By 1853, Tula had both a winter and a summer theater, with a fairly good orchestra and permanent troupe, amplified by visiting actors from the capitals. After one of the numerous times when the theater burned down, the company performed in district towns. Tula audiences of the 1840s and 1850s saw many an actor who earlier or later gained prominence on the capital stages, including Mochalov, Lavrov, Evelina Schmidthoff (Shmidtkova), Nikulina-Kositskaya, and Prov Sadovsky. In 1859, on the eve of emancipation, appeared the unusual Chernyshev troupe composed exclusively of gentry actors who had decided to defy social prejudice. A visitor in the 1850s said this about Tula theater life: "As a whole, it must be admitted that I left the Tula theater — which was almost always full — with a feeling of genuine satisfaction that among provincials a taste for elegance has grown so quickly and vigorously, and that the actors here give their all just in order to pay back the flattering attention of the public."[68]

Kaluga, Smolensk, and Tver had a spotty theatrical experience in the early nineteenth century. Kaluga, 188 versts from Moscow with a population of 30,475 in 1843, boasted large squares, numerous bridges, thirty-three churches, a monastery, nine schools, three hospitals, a jail, an asylum, a Gostiny Dvor, twenty-nine taverns, twenty eating establishments of various sorts, and twenty-five mills. But the aristocratic noses of Buturlin and of Anna Smirnova, the wife of a governor, turned up when recalling this town. Shchepkin played to a nearly empty house in 1846. Even as late as 1864, a reporter noted that Kalugaites scorned theater. The majority of its merchants hated it as a den of iniquity, and their sons attended only in great secrecy.[69] In turn-of-the-century Smolensk, theater appeared sporadically until the war of 1812, which reduced the city to ashes. The record shows amateur performances in 1813 and touring company visits in 1819, 1845 (from Kiev), and 1849 (from Vitebsk). Smolensk apparently had no market for a permanent theater. A half-dozen or more rich families had manorial stages and the poorer gentry visited them as guests or did without. By the 1850s well-off gentry finally decided to create a permanent town theater on the Blone — now Glinka Square.[70] The first touring companies came via the Volga in the 1830s to Tver, a third of the way from Moscow to St. Petersburg, and to Vyshny Volochok further north in the 1830s, both outliers of a Kostroma theater company. Yet a guidebook of 1847 mentions only the Vauxhall as a public culture site. This reinforces a picture, suggested in travel accounts, of a relative cultural vacuum along the chief *magistral* connecting Russia's two most important cities. Neither Tver nor Vyshny Volochok became stopover centers in the constant traffic between the capitals. When, starting in 1852, cheap third-class railway fares packed the cars between the two capitals, the Petersburg-Moscow line still did not feed the beaten paths of the theater circuits, though it did enable actors to entrain from Moscow to Tver and Vyshny Volochok.[71]

On the watery road from the middle Volga to the Caspian Sea, Nizhny Novgorod offered the biggest and the best shows. Over four hundred versts from Moscow, the fortress town grew in population from 14,000 in 1811 to over 41,000 in 1862 and the engineers who planned Russia's first railway dreamed of linking it to Moscow by rail. Its fair, which succeeded the Makarev Fair in 1817, was the largest in Europe, even surpassing the renowned Leipzig Fair. Fair season doubled the city's population which thronged its thousands of shops in trading rows, its dozens of churches, and its even more numerous taverns, restaurants, and inns. The theater stood a few feet away from the main center of trade rows. Multitudes from all corners of Russia and many parts of Asia, and the constant mix and brawl of fair life made Nizhny noted for public and private celebrations. Governors held a grand table with dinner music and a round of balls, and local magnates followed suit. The gentry came to the fair to shop, attend theater, and — from the 1840s — to dance to Strauss waltzes at the Main Building. The Nizhny merchants generously welcomed strangers to their lavish celebrations. Sociability boiled up in merchant inns and teahouses where tea flowed in such volume that it was called the "third river" after the Oka and Volga.[72]

A few years after Prince Shakhovskoi died in 1824, a remarkable thing happened. His heirs sold the theater company not to the Imperial Theaters but to private entrepreneurs for 100,000 rubles. As a result, the hundred or so serf actors gained their "freedom." One of the new owners, I. A. Rasputin, a petty official with no right to possess serfs, signed a contract with the actors, freeing them on condition of their remaining in the troupe for ten years under salary. One of the largest serf manumissions to occur in the world of the arts, this transaction surpassed the earlier bulk sales of serfs to the Imperial Theaters. The ex-serfs had to work off their redemption payment by performing at low wages. Gender differences prevailed: the comic Minai (Polyakov) earned 240 rubles a year and the rising star Anna Vysheslavtseva only 170. When the ten-year period ran out and Vysheslavtseva was free to move, Rasputin increased her salary. The market was clearly at work with other actors as well: when some were denied raises, they transferred to the theaters in Kazan, Simbirsk, and Saratov, thus making Nizhny Novgorod a feeder to the middle and lower Volga. A British traveler of the late 1830s, who mistakenly called the Nizhny Novgorod house "the most easterly theatre in Europe," described the full houses, expensive tickets, merchants in the pit, wits in the stalls, a few ladies, and a generally multiethnic audience. He also commented on a very condensed staging of an adaptation of *Othello,* without a Iago or an Emilia![73]

In 1838, Rasputin sold out to the Moscow actor V. I. Zhivokini. Mikhail Zhdanov, who called Nizhny Novgorod's theater the best in the provinces — a claim made for several other towns — was impressed by the full houses in 1843. Around the same time, Haxthausen recorded that on one occasion less than forty people attended an opera (Verstovsky's *Askold's Grave*) at the town theater, though the fair theater was filled each night in season. Neglect of opera had hurt attendance under the new owners and their immediate successors fared no better. The theater revived when taken over in 1847 by F. K. Smolkov, an ex–provincial official. He upgraded the troupe and restored opera to first place. A tightwad, Smolkov withheld wages and refused to buy an axe for the beheading of Mary Queen of Scots in Schiller's tragedy; he had the hapless queen executed on stage with a pistol. Smolkov was blessed by the presence in the company of the Strelkova sisters and the Vysheslavtseva sisters.[74] In 1850 the first Italian opera troupe descended on the city. Like many foreign touring companies in Russia at midcentury, it was second-rate and thinly staffed. By then the Nizhny Novgorod audience was sufficiently educated to notice its glaring faults. In the years 1846–53, the writer Pëtr Boborykin was attending gymnasium in Nizhny Novgorod where he and his schoolmates went to the theater in winter wearing fur coats and boots.[75]

Unlike Shakhovskoi's serf theater whose troupe became free, P. P. Esipov's in Kazan collapsed after his death in 1814 and the actors were bought up by various landowners. After decades of only occasional visiting companies, actor-entrepreneur P. A. Sokolov arrived in Kazan in 1833 at the invitation of the governor, bought a serf troupe from a landowner, freed the actors, and opened a theater which he ran until it burned down in 1842. Sokolov catered to the light entertainment tastes of a Kazan paying public where money flowed rather freely. A Soviet scholar made much of an alternate audience. Students of Kazan university demanded more serious fare, he claimed; especially a contingent from Vilna University, recently closed by the authorities for subversive activity. But the popular repertoire prevailed. By the 1840s, the multiethnic city had grown into a bustling center of commerce with numerous churches and mosques, almost a hundred factories, and a population of over fifty thousand. By the 1850s, the large, newly finished stone theater on the square near the Gentry Club seemed luxurious to Boborykin compared to the wooden one in Nizhny. Its audience comprised gentry and Russian and Tatar merchants. When the "Italian opera epidemic" broke out, opera audiences, like those in the capitals, quarreled over rival divas.[76]

When in 1842 Sokolov and his actors from the burned-out theater in Kazan set sail along the Volga, Kama, and Belaya rivers, they entered an orbit that diverged sharply from the Volga towns. The vast region lying between Perm on the Kama, Ekaterinburg in the mountains, and Ufa on the steppe throbbed with mining and metallurgical works and had a prehistory of theatrical activity. The Stroganovs and Vesvolozhskys, big factory owners, maintained troupes and occasionally brought them to the towns. In 1807 Count Stroganov founded a theater at his Ocherksky Factory. Perm audiences in 1821, in what was probably their first such experience, witnessed the Ocherksky players performing in a salt barn on the shores of the Kama. To that same building came Sokolov and the first professional troupe in the region. He offered a varied repertoire. Though he had only a few singers and a twelve-piece band, he put on Verstovsky's *Askold's Grave* and Rossini's *Semiramida*. Sokolov relocated to Ekaterinburg, the hub of a minicircuit in which his troupe moved from Ekaterinburg in February to the Irbit Fair, in the spring to Perm, and then back to the base. From the 1850s onward, permanent theater was on offer to Ekaterinburg, a mining and gold center of ten thousand people, dominated by industrial tycoons with money to burn, government administrators, and a large body of technicians. Sokolov fed them operas, vaudevilles, and a few performances of Gogol's *Inspector General,* but apparently fell out of fashion in the 1850s when he failed to pick up on the success of the new Ostrovsky corpus. Sokolov went broke in 1857 and the orbit of Perm-Ekaterinburg-Irbit continued under new management.[77]

In the 1840s and 1850s, Saratov had a commercial theater whose troupe, run by D. Zalessky, also worked in Samara and Astrakhan. During the 1858–59 season, some former serfs of Shakhovskoi were still acting in the Saratov house. In Penza, theater owner Ivan Gorstkin during the 1840s formed a vivid contrast with the brutish Gladkov earlier in the century. It was rumored that Gorstkin had been exiled to Penza for his associations with the Decembrists. A landowner who displayed the polished manners of an aristocrat, Gorstkin had some acting ability as well and opened a public theater in his home and later built one. No esthete, he specialized in vaudeville, comedy, and operetta, with an occasional opera—Verstovsky's *Askold's Grave* and *Anyuta.* A visiting troupe who performed at Gorstkin's was well treated by the owner, well paid, and even introduced socially to the local gentry who wintered in Saratov.[78]

Little is known of theater life in Astrakhan at the mouth of the Volga except that the much-traveled Ivan Lavrov was converted to being an actor there in 1843, and that the dramatist Alexei Pisemsky walked out of a performance in that city in 1855. Like Odessa and Kazan, this multiethnic port stood at a crossroads of the empire. But the dirty, sprawling semi-Asian city on the Caspian Sea never had the cultural energy of the other two. Taras Shevchenko in the 1850s found this alleged "southeastern Venice" of the Russian Empire "a large pile of refuse." Medvedev strode the boards in Astrakhan. Arriving in 1859 by barge, he did see a resemblance to Venice in this town with its ninety mouths of the Volga debouching into the sea. When he got into the city, however, his eyes met trash, mud, and dead dogs on the street.[79] The whole Volga subsystem, while continuing to grow, felt the constant blows of audience fall-off, fire, and the splintering of companies.

To the southern cluster of Ukrainian theatrical towns, adjacent Kursk Province in Russia proper stood as an outpost. Its capital, set on picturesque bluffs, was one of the loveliest provincial cities in Russia. Though hosting few gentry residents, by the 1830s Kursk's life was animated by occasional visits of a dragoon regiment,[80] and by its theater. The original theater, sited at the Gentry Club high atop a ravine beside the cathedral, had twenty-six loges and seats for 115 more spectators (fig. 42). From 1792, it operated during elections but had little success. So big landowners such as Khorvat, Wolkenstein, and Annenkov pooled their serf troupes and, some time before 1805, put them under the management of an unusual team of entrepreneurs: the Barsov brothers — Niko-lai, Pëtr, and Mikhailo — the first two Annenkov serf actors on *obrok*, the third a freed serf. The trio owned the scripts, music, and costumes, and they rented the troupe and premises at the Gentry Club. Aside from being one of the first commercial theaters in Russia, the Kursk theater, run by serfs in a gentry establishment, clearly displayed a growing, and still little-studied, habit of interclass entrepreneurship; and it offered space for landowners unable or unwilling to sustain private theaters. It also gave status to the serfs who ran it. Shchepkin was quick to observe that they were "treated differently" — in fact as freemen. He eventually formed a kind of partnership with them and later adopted Pëtr's children. The troupe moved to Kharkov in 1815 or 1816 and Kursk was absorbed in a Ukrainian theatrical circuit. Though its ever-broadening audiences were sometimes tormented by a scandalously bad *Hamlet* without skulls for the graveyard scene or goblets for the poisoning, the Kursk theater remained a key site on the circuit.[81]

Kharkov looked north toward Kursk, Orël, Eletsk, Tula, Ostrogozhsk, Voronezh, Ryazan, and Tambov as well as to Ukrainian towns and fairs. After several theatrical ventures prior to 1812, it became a vital theatrical center of commercial touring companies. In the 1840s, Shakespeare, Schiller, Fonvizen, Griboedov, and Gogol shared the stage with local Ukrainian favorites I. P. Kotlyarevsky and Kvitka and French melodramas. Its renditions won praise from Zhdanov, the historian Mykolay Kostomarov, and the Moscow actor Mochalov.[82] The university — founded in 1804 and the oldest after Moscow — had begun its role in theater life with riots in 1817 and 1823, involving dozens of students who threw fruit at the cast. In the quieter 1830s and 1840s, students and schoolchildren formed ties with the actors. In 1835, P. D. Seletsky, a fifteen-year-old gentry pupil, had to smuggle himself into the theater dressed as a girl — for which he was put on bread and water for a week in the school jail. The city's numerous schools, as well as its many squares and public gardens, attracted gentry visitors and residents. When a new theater was erected in 1842, Baron Rosen pronounced that it had "all the attributes of a capital theater." Officers stationed at nearby Chuguev lent tone to society. The city's intelligentsia had ties to Belinsky and to the stage. A constant influx of visitors to Kharkov's fairs enlivened the town whose population grew from about 10,000 to 52,000 between 1811 and 1862. The theater played no small role in leading Baron Haxthausen, with Kharkov in mind, to state that "these new Russian [provincial] cities are becoming the centres of national life, the parents of social development, cultivation, and progress."[83]

Prince N. G. Repnin, governor-general of Poltava and Kharkov, a hero of the Napoleonic wars turned theatrical autocrat, tried to make the town of

Poltava in the 1810s a major military center and the Athens of Ukraine. Repnin's theater was intimately tied to Mikhail Shchepkin's epic struggle for freedom. It closed for financial reasons in 1821. The dreamed-of Athens failed to materialize. Poltava—renowned for the historic 1709 victory of Peter the Great—long remained unimpressive and lacked even a hospital or an almshouse, things possessed by almost every provincial capital, for its nearly ten thousand inhabitants. But in the 1830s, a new theater in the City Garden became a regular stop for touring companies; and a stationary Poltava troupe worked there for a time while fanning out to nearby towns and fairs. In 1838, during the gentry elections held simultaneously with a fair, a troupe put on *Othello* and *Hamlet* (in Polevoi's translation) and Zhdanov got to hear the foremost male opera singer of the era, Osip Petrov, later of the Petersburg Imperial Theater. Additional delectation was provided by a ballet of children doing Cossack and folk character dances. The boxes were occupied by gentry families of two to three members each with their lackeys standing behind them. Zhdanov also mentioned, without comment, two daughters of a wealthy local Jewish merchant in the audience.[84]

On the right bank of the Dnieper River lay ancient Kiev, cradle of the Russian Orthodox Church, state, and civilization. In this town the Poles, who had previously ruled it for several centuries, played a visible role in public life. In the wake of the Polish rebellion of 1830, Kiev's autonomous civic institutions with their colorful flags, uniforms, and parades, were curtailed for a time, though the city remained a hotbed of Polish and Ukrainian nationalism and a center of vibrant social, cultural, and commercial activity. Throughout the period, Kiev's famous Contract Fair in February provided much entertainment and full houses. A permanent theater had appeared in 1806 or 1807 on Kiev's main street, Kreshchatik, where Polish, Ukrainian, Russian, and foreign companies played. Buturlin related that early in the century, when there were no balls or soirees, the theater was "the meeting place for society," and mentioned en passant the performance of a French vaudeville at the Polish theater. Gerakov saw a Kotzebue play done there in Polish around 1820. Indeed, all over Ukraine, the language of performance was so fluid in this era that the journal *Pantheon* praised an actress for speaking good Russian. By the 1840s, a Russian theater was functioning under the management of the actor-owner K. I. Vasilkov. The dancer Bogdanova performed at the fair and the university with great success. In 1855 one of the local magnates, an Engelhardt, bought the troupe and put on only vaudevilles because, as he said, "I like them and I play them for myself."[85]

Recently founded Odessa on the Black Sea—with its semitropical climate, huge multiethnic population, and spectacular staircase designed by Francesco

Boffo — possessed a theatrical character of its own. Russian, Ukrainian, Italian, Yiddish, Greek, and a half-dozen other tongues battled for a hearing all over the town. Its casinos, restaurants, and public entertainments made it more like New Orleans than any Russian town. Odessa's elegant theater, built in 1804–9 with seven to eight thousand seats, became essentially an opera house. Nowhere in Russia was the passion for this art so ardent and continuous. An opera news sheet actually preceded regular newspapers. When Italian singers arrived each spring, the house filled up with foreign businessmen and Russian merchants, landowners, high officials, Guards officers, and high-society women. Seletsky compared the audiences of the early 1840s to a colorful bed of flowers, and he offered lyrical and sometimes salacious descriptions of women's physical charms. An exceptionally vocal and diverse general public formed claques that usually pitted Odessa Italians and Greeks against the Jews. As in the capital, claque politics among the upper classes sometimes led to fights and duels.

Opera became the chief focus of Odessa civic patriotism. The garrison commander permitted the use of his troops for the Procession of the Empress in Rossini's *Semiramida*. After Bellini's *Norma* premiered, Odessa mothers had their daughters learn "Casta Diva," Around 1841, the Italian manager of both the opera and the quarantine service pumped the revenue of the latter into the former. Arias were sung in the streets; and guests at costume balls dressed up as Faust, Quasimodo, Bertram, and Leporello. Jews dominated the parterre by the 1830s; and by the 1860s some had graduated to the stalls. A Russian traveler was amused by their wild enthusiasm that deafened the audience. Opera helped enrich the cantorial traditions of the Jewish community, and — to the chagrin of some — got its members interested in what was called "lemonade music," popular songs heard in the numerous restaurants.[86]

The theater offered vaudeville, plays, and concerts; and touring virtuosos such as Liszt dazzled audiences. Opera frenzy inhibited the success of dramatic art in Odessa. In 1846, a performance of excerpts from *Inspector General* flopped because it lacked arias. The city was so opera-centric that two touring drama companies who came to town in the 1840s had to combine, and even then had to abandon the effort and leave town. Shchepkin's visiting performances of Molière, Gogol, and Griboedov could not break the spell. In 1847, he helped to found a Russian dramatic troupe in Odessa, partly staffed by his Moscow colleagues and pupils, which lasted until the shelling of the city in the Crimean War temporarily closed the theater.[87] Until the revival after the war, Odessa's main role in the theater circuit lay in its location as a stopover for Russian and Italian troupes who would then branch out into other Black Sea towns.

Beyond Odessa, a southern minicircuit was in full working order at the time of Shchepkin's 1846 tour. In the years 1836–52, Kishinëv in Bessarabia — a theatrical satellite of Odessa — received visits from ten troupes: four Russian, two French, two German, one from Jassy in neighboring Moldavia, and one ballet company. The southern towns of Nikolaevsk, Kherson, Sevastopol, and Simferopol were enmeshed in a network run by Danila Zhurakhovsky, an extremely mobile and businesslike ex-actor who hired the cheapest performers and was apparently ready to place his players anywhere, regardless of accommodations. Shchepkin, accompanied by the ill-tempered Belinsky, soon found out how primitive these could be when he departed Odessa for this circuit: bad supporting casts, an interfering governor, and other discomforts. Sevastopol audiences included a large and appreciative contingent of naval officers who had attended theater in the Hapsburg Adriatic ports of Venice and Trieste. At Simferopol, a Russian resort in a sea of Tatars, the composer Alexander Serov praised the performance of Shchepkin, while bemoaning everything else about the theater. In Taganrog, the theater founded in 1828 by the governor of Novorossiisk and Bessarabia, and subsidized with town funds, stood opposite the Gentry Club with a complement of about thirty well-paid actors and a fifteen-man orchestra, all Germans.[88]

References to theater in the thinly populated regions are scant. The northwest provinces of Novgorod and St. Petersburg (outside the capital) were apparently bereft of town theaters. In Vologda, the nobleman V. A. Kokarev created the first public theater in his home in the late 1820s or early 1830s, with house serfs for cast and an orchestra borrowed from a landowner. Kokarev later mixed his own house serfs with a visiting troupe. Still later, a theater building appeared in Vologda. Siberian public theaters came and went. In 1793, the Englishman John Parkinson in Tobolsk reported on "an opera in the evening at the theatre which did not go off ill. Their prettiest and best actress was a common girl taken from the Streets." Kotzebue found that people in Tobolsk and Kurgan knew his name and work, and the friendly governor offered to stage one of his comedies.[89]

Irkutsk in eastern Siberia experienced two eras of town theater. In 1787, the professional actress Tatyana Troepolskaya, who had performed in Moscow and St. Petersburg and then married a prominent official, organized a Theater of the Nobility there. The Livonian diplomat Jacob Sievers was impressed in 1789 by the acting and by the strong moral impression made on young spectators. "A theater? — I hear you ask. In this distant land? — Yes, indeed. You will be even more puzzled when I tell you that all the actors are local people who had never before seen a theater in their lives. Nevertheless, their performances are excellent." It remains unclear whether the actors were paid and the spectators ticketed. This theater ended in 1809 and revived only forty years later under the aegis of the vigorous Governor General N. N. Muravëv-Apostol who ruled the vast territory from 1847 to 1861. The demand had resurfaced: the population of Irkutsk had risen in the decades 1810 to 1860 from 10,000 to 23,000. Exiles worked on the local newspaper, and amateur theater groups had formed in the 1840s. In 1851, Muravëv established and oversaw a new theater. This stage mounted, in addition to the usual vaudevilles, the works of Shakespeare, Gogol, and Ostrovsky—including an illegal premiere of his *Family Affair* in 1858, two years before it was done on the Moscow stage. The theater burned down in 1861. Scattered notices show brief theatrical flurries in Eniseisk and Krasnoyarsk in the 1850s.[90]

The Don Cossack town of Novo-Cherkassk in 1857–58 played host to a touring company that played Shakespeare, Griboedov, Gogol, Kotlyarevsky, and Ostrovsky. The great provincial tragedian N. Kh. Rybakov played the small theater of Stavropol, operated in the 1840s by his brother-in-law, K. M. Zelinsky. Medvedev played Mogilëv in Belorussia in 1854. Vasily Obersky (Wassili Oberski?), the entrepreneur, had led many large Polish troupes before the uprising and repression of 1830–31. He then moved into Lithuania, Belorussia, and Russia. In Dvinsk, he acted as a front man for the real owner, N. I. Hagelström, a colonel of engineers and therefore not permitted theatrical activity. The colonel broke the officers' social code, not for profit but out of uncontrollable passion: on the sly he conducted the band, sang, and played as one of Schiller's bandits.[91]

The mighty A. M. Gedeonov, director of the Imperial Theater system, 1834–58, just before leaving his post, revealed an important fact about provincial life: forty-three public theaters were operating in provincial Russia outside the control of the Imperial Directorate in St. Petersburg. The estimate stands as roughly accurate. Dynnik's count of a hundred or so urban theaters included noncommercial manorial stages and long-gone governors' theaters. Working backward may help to assess claims about numbers, all of which hinge upon definition of provincial theaters—though all concern only urban, public, and commercial theaters, not manorial stages. S. S. Danilov in the 1970s stated flatly that by 1875, seventy-five commercial provincial theaters existed in Russia. Ira Petrovskaya, in a more recent and more complete tabulation, put the number for the 1860s at about a hundred. It is unclear how many of these arose after 1861. My own tally for the last two decades or so of Nicholas's reign, drawn from the sources and including those mentioned but not discussed in Petrovskaya, shows that at least forty-nine towns had theaters, permanent or visited regularly by troupes, but excluding most fair theaters except for Nizhny Novgorod. If one adds the makeshift barns at summer fairs that annually staged plays or operas as well as novelty acts, the number expands. Performers and managers on the provincial circuit were acutely aware of these refinements, but most of them had to be able to set up shop almost anywhere, from tent to lavish opera house. Thus stood the provincial theatrical map, constantly shifting and interlaced by circuits, around which human lives and livelihoods circulated in the era before emancipation.[92]

Lives on the Road

The inner story of provincial theater emerges from the wanderings among towns and fairgrounds where actors, musicians, stage hands, and entrepreneurs showed their wares, lived their lives, formed companies, split up, and moved onward. The epicenter of the provincial circuit lay not in St. Petersburg, but in the smoke-filled White Marble Hall of the tavern in Barsov's Inn near Theater Square in Moscow, the provincial actors' informal labor exchange (*aktërskaya birzha*). In autumn and during the Lenten off-season, actors and entrepreneurs arrived to seek work, start hiring, and court each other. Actors, deep into their acting mode while in search of a booking, turned the bourse itself into a stage. Lavrov and Pëtr Medvedev, writing of the mid-1850s, archly described how romantic leads strutted around in gaudy costumes, comics clowned and table-hopped with their success stories, and tragedians and Ostrovsky specialists held aloof. The rest comprised minor character actors and technical personnel. Bargaining styles ranged from pride to asperity, greed, contempt, and desperation — the level of confidence modulated by the amount of money in the actors' pockets. Owners proved more skillful at bargaining than their hirelings. Market forces hovered around each table: entrepreneurs watched and waited for days before making their skimpy offers until the actors' refreshments dwindled from sturgeon and vodka to cups of tea. By offering strong liquor to their prospects and listening to mendacious disclaimers about sobriety, owners tried to gage the dependability of the hires. Women, barred from taverns, waited in hotel rooms for news from husband or friend about job prospects. Once the deal was struck, the actors would pack up and head out with the company into the interior for a summer, a full season, or an indefinite spell. Entrepreneurs and agents of the Imperial Directorate also scoured the provinces for talent, negotiating backstage at some town theater or in a local drinking establishment. Pirating of performers and even entire troupes was common. Governors and wealthy landlords were not averse to prying talented theater people away from private companies by means of allurements or just plain force.[93]

The circuit map took shape from town audiences — population, class composition, wealth, and linguistic makeup. In Belorussia the swamps, and in the far north distance, scarcity of residents, bad roads, and climate accounted for low activity. Once on the road, actors had to face the formidable difficulties of Russian trável. Threading their way through a web of fairs and provincial towns, caravans of carts and carriages in summer and sleighs in winter, laden with actors, sets, props, and costumes bulging out of the conveyances, astonished villagers along the way. Actors carried everything with them — even curtains. Unattached actors such as the young Medvedev hoofed it or hitch-hiked in carts, wagons, or rowboats in order to reach a promising venue. Barge travel on the Volga could take whole companies from Tver to Yaroslavl, Kostroma, Nizhny, Kazan, and the lower Volga towns down to Astrakhan. The route from Yaroslavl to Nizhny Novgorod, almost impassable overland in winter, was easily managed along the Volga in summer. Yet, even with steam power the journey from Astrakhan up to Saratov took ten days in 1859. River traffic had its own hazards. Early in the century, a company, complete with costumes and props, sailed up the Volga to the Makarev Fair near Nizhny Novgorod along an established mercantile barge route. They were surrounded by a band of pirates led by an ataman who mistook them for wealthy merchants ready to be plundered. When the actors pointed their prop firearms at the pirates, the latter broke into laughter and allowed them to pass. Housing always presented problems. Actors were denied entry to some inns, or could not afford them and had to board with a family or even sleep at the theater.[94]

The wide range of provincial troupes owed a good deal to Russia's thousands of fairs, sites of trade and sociability. With a few exceptions, they clustered in relatively fertile and densely populated regions. A "broad swath of territory" from Ukraine through the Central Provinces and along the Volga, with numerous outposts beyond the swath, roughly matched the geography of town theaters. At special fair-like events, a theater could make a momentary appearance. In 1839, during military maneuvers at Borodino, Anton Rubinstein saw a troupe perform *Der Freischütz* at a nearby temporary theater. Fair theaters operated in an atmosphere resembling the folk fair — fluid, visual, kinetic, and plebeian.[95] I. M. Dolgoruky at the Korennaya Fair near Kursk in 1810 saw the comedy *Shakespeare in Love* and the opera *The Prince and the Chimney Sweep*. In a wooden shed jammed between merchant stalls, the performers — including the fledgling Shchepkin — aped the fair booth in broad raucous interchange between audience and stage. In Kremenchug, Dolgoruky heard actors, oblivious to each other, doing Molière in their own native tongues — "this one in Russian, that one in Circassian, one in Ukrainian, and another in Polish." When Shalikov squeezed into a barn in Ukraine around 1803 to watch acrobats, wire walkers, clowns, and mimes, he found it hard to believe that the public, including the gentry troupe owner, could actually enjoy such entertainment. Most fairground personnel sprang from the lower classes. Kirill Tyufyaev, the much maligned governor of Vyatka, originated among Tobolsk townspeople. As a fairground acrobat, he worked across Russia to the Polish provinces and ended up as a satrap in the half-empty regions of Vyatka, Perm, and Western Siberia.[96]

The fairground region with the greatest density and interlock with town theaters covered a northeastern Ukrainian quadrangle of Chernigov, Romny, Poltava, and Kharkov — with the Russian province of Kursk as an outlier. The cycle encapsulated eleven fairs in seven towns. Amidst these lay smaller urban and village fairs (roughly 425 in Kharkov Province and 372 in Poltava), usually based on feast days. The little Poltava provincial town of Romny came alive during the fairs, where the gentry congregated. Its theater and circus from early in the century was short-lived. When Shevchenko saw a performance of Kotlyarevsky's *Moskal the Sorcerer* there in 1845, it was probably at the fair. The Kreshchenskaya Fair in Kharkov, the biggest and most important, and three others in the vicinity, made the Kharkov fair scene second only to that of Nizhny Novgorod. Many of these fairs came to be dominated by Russian merchants who were more wont to travel longer distances than their Ukrainian counterparts. Some merchants managed to visit in the course of a year every one of these emporia in a crooked route of about 2,566 kilometers from Romny to Kharkov. Jews, despite official restrictions and local prejudice, entered the trading system, and for the most part maintained good relations with the Great Russian merchants.[97] This did not prevent the performance in the local theaters of coarsely anti-Semitic comedies.

The Korennaya or Root Fair near Kursk, one of many monastery fairs, formed a connecting link to the networks of the north and constituted a Russo-Ukrainian meeting ground and an assembly point for the local gentry. The Korennaya Monastery, built on a slope near the river Tuskar about twenty-eight kilometers from Kursk, got its name from the story of a peasant who found an icon at the root of a tree around 1300. During the annual two-day-long procession from Kursk to the monastery, the icon was passed from hand to hand among the thousands of pious marchers who included clergy, governor, city fathers, merchants, and townspeople, all animated by the doleful and joyful peasant voices in Russian folk songs. The tail of the procession was still in Kursk when the head arrived at the monastery. Ilya Repin later immortalized this procession in a famous canvas. For two weeks in June, visitors poured in from Kursk, Orël, Kharkov, Tula, Kaluga, Tambov, and Voronezh to purchase garments and other products, deal in horses, join the revelry, and attend the five-hundred-seat theater, the two-story stone Gostiny Dvor designed by Quarenghi, and the town's fifty-eight hotels and taverns.[98]

These southern regions formed the core of the first Russian commercial theater circuit for itinerant troupes, which did not so much blaze new trails as follow well-worn patterns of movement laid out by generations of merchants and mobile serfs. Millions of serfs moved over vast distances, seasonally and for long spells, in the well-established practice of legally working on *obrok* in all kinds of jobs.[99] This provided ample precedent for the wandering serf actor. From Polish and Ukrainian cultural zones came repertoires and persons. The works of the Ukrainians Kvitka and Kotlyarevsky filled the stages, and a local Pole named Piotrowski translated Molière. The territory attracted energetic figures, unencumbered by serfdom, from the Baltic and Poland proper. Antoni Zmiewski's theater company in Ukraine was one of a dozen provincial Polish troupes working Vilna, Grodno, Minsk, Lvov, and Cracow in the first decades of the century.[100] Russian companies there were long dominated by two men, Stein and Mlotkovsky. These pioneers differed sharply from earlier ticket-selling theater owners, such as Prince N. G. Shakhovskoi of Nizhny Novgorod or Count Sergei Kamensky of Orël, in that they hired all their actors — whether serf or free — and were ready to move wherever audiences could be found.

A German actor, Johann-Friedrich Stein (Ivan Fëdorovich Shtein, birth date unknown, d. late 1830s), had come from Silesia to play in the German theaters of St. Petersburg and Moscow in the years 1804–7. He fashioned fifteen purchased serfs into a ballet troupe which he later sold to Count Kamensky of Orël. Around 1814, he traveled to Kharkov, then the corner of a touring company run by a Pole, Józef Kalinowski (O. I. Kalinovsky), that played the fairs in a triangle which included Poltava and Kremenchug. Disorder reigned: one night, actors refused to perform the opera *Zemira and Azor* until they were paid back wages; Azor had to be brought to the stage from home by force. Stein joined forces with Kalinowski, brought discipline to the company, and in 1816 built a new theater in Kharkov under his exclusive ownership which inaugurated a period of continuous vigor in that town, and widened the touring circuit. Shchepkin joined the troupe. In 1817, he and a split-off group left Kharkov for Poltava but then returned to Stein in 1822 when the Poltava business folded. The Kharkov company now had forty actors and twenty musicians, serf and free. Aside from regular tours in the 1820s, the company sometimes divided, one group for Kharkov and one for Kursk which, with its Korennaya Fair, became a satellite of Kharkov. Stein's company was unequaled in the provinces at the time for its size, talent, and the scope of its circuit which came to include Tula, Odessa, Kiev, and other towns and fairs. The company played all genres: at Kiev, in 1831 it eluded the censors and put on *Woe from Wit*. Though most of the actors were free, this did not save them from harassment by the mayor, the police, aristocrats, and rich merchants, who punctuated their lives with abuse and intrigue. In 1835, after another schism, Stein retired. Out of his company emerged future entrepreneurs P. A. Sokolov, D. D. Zhurakovsky, P. P Mikulsky, and K. M. Zelinsky.[101]

Ludwig Mlotkowski (Lyudvig Mlotkovsky, c. 1795–1855), a Jesuit-educated Polish nobleman of Kiev province, broke with his family over his theater career. As an actor, he toured Poland, Bessarabia, and Ukraine with a Polish company until the 1820s when he joined Stein, shared the management with him, and oversaw drama while Stein directed ballet. In 1833 while playing in Kursk, a cohort of younger actors led by Mlotkovsky broke off from Stein and set up shop there while Stein's group went off to Kharkov and Kiev. Thus the "young" and the "old" troupes competed for venues as they criss-crossed the southern belt for a few years until Stein retired and Mlotkovsky absorbed his troupe in 1835. Mlotkovsky made Kharkov his base with out-stations in Chernigov and Poltava. After he built a new theater in Kharkov in 1842 with a school attached, Mlotkovsky reached the pinnacle of his success as actor and entrepreneur. Obeying his own taste — or, as a Soviet historian argues, that of the progressive Kharkov intelligentsia — Mlotkovsky intro-duced Shakespeare and Schiller and unleashed his more "realistic actors." He spent lavishly on production but always kept an eye on the box office which showed him that vaudeville and melodrama remained the staple favorites. Kvitka and Kotlyarevsky wrote for his company, university students sup-ported it, and fame raised its reputation so high that some called it the best provincial theater of the era. Yet in 1843, Mlotkovsky went broke and had to rent his theater to a Kharkov directorate composed of local notables and rich merchants. Mlotkovsky moved to Orël where he had little success; he acted and managed in later years in Voronezh, Saratov, Astrakhan, Voznesensk, and Nikolaevsk, and died in 1855.[102]

The grand provincial actor of the time, Mikhail Shchepkin, before gaining his freedom and moving to stardom in Moscow, spent the years 1805–22 on the road, mostly on the southern circuit (fig. 43). He was born into a serf family in 1788 in a village of Kursk Province belonging to the Wolkensteins. Although Shchepkin's grandfather had been tricked into servile status, Mi-khail's masters were relatively kind and never beat him. The boy heard about and witnessed abuse of serfs, but stood mute before these domestic dramas. Laurence Senelick, without in any way justifying serfdom, convincingly argues that Shchepkin's childhood status helped his formation as an actor. His "back-ground as a house serf, hovering unnoticed and silent at all sorts of gatherings, sharpened his observation even as it provided him objects to observe." His father, a steward, got Mikhail a primary education at a district school amid serf and gentry pupils. With his schoolmates, Shchepkin put on a play at the mayor's house. At home, the master, who owned serf musicians and singers, formed a theater composed of child performers with the purpose of uplifting them and entertaining the household. At fifteen, Shchepkin debuted there in Knyazhnin's *Misfortune from a Carriage*. Although Shchepkin later had much to say about the peculiar lot of serf actors, curiously enough he did not meditate upon this encounter with one of the best-known stage depictions of a system under which he and his fellow serfs lived; the more so in that he, still a serf, played the role of Firyulin, the flighty Francophile who nearly brings tragedy to his own serfs.[103]

In 1805, Shchepkin apprenticed at Barsov's Kursk Theater as prompter and stand-in, then in regular roles as the clever servant in sentimental comedies. He owed his debut to a common occurrence in theater life: the leading man had literally lost his shirt (and all other garments) at cards and could not appear. Despite his bondage, Shchepkin was virtually free to choose his place of employment. He moved with the Barsov company to join Stein and was thereafter involved in all the subsequent schisms and relocations. All the while Shchepkin engaged in a struggle for release from servitude. The chief patron of the circuit, Governor General Repnin, initiated proceedings to free Shchepkin by means of a redemption subscription. An irony of this process arose from the Jews of Romny who were avid theater goers. When the anti-Semitic *Success out of Failure, or Adventures in a Jew's Tavern* was presented there, the Jews were unable to buy it off stage, and Repnin even ordered a local Jewish community leader — openly satirized in the play — to attend. Yet although Shchepkin appeared in it, the Jews contributed to his subscription. The road remained rocky. When Wolkenstein died, a combination of his widow's asking price, her heirs' delaying tactics, competing bids, Repnin's own devious and lethargic role, and the lumbering red tape of the Senate turned the struggle into a saga of hopes and disappointments lasting from 1818 to 1822 when the actor and the family he had acquired got their freedom.[104]

Shchepkin's experience with serfdom and acting had been unusual. Aside from his debut performance in Knyazhnin, he had not been a manorial serf actor. Nor was he an actor on *obrok*, but rather a "free actor" — free to move and earn his own wages but still enserfed. In 1822, an official of the Moscow Directorate of Imperial Theaters went hunting in the provinces for promising material. On a visit to the Ilya Fair theater, he saw Shchepkin put on a dazzling quick-change display in seven roles including a soldier, a German woman, a Ukrainian teacher, and a matchmaker. Shchepkin stood out brilliantly in the barn-like structure amid tattered curtains and awful musicians. He was hired into the Moscow theater at one thousand rubles a year. Though he was getting six thousand rubles from Stein, Shchepkin clearly preferred the prestige of the Moscow stage. There he found himself doubling identities once again when he debuted in 1823, replaying his old role in Zagoskin's *Mister Bogatonov, or a Provincial in the Capital*. Following Mochalov's lead in touring the provinces, Shchepkin returned to his home grounds in the late 1820s, and subsequent excursions took him to twenty or so cities. Notable were an 1846 tour in the company of Vissarion Belinsky, and his final tour of 1863. Shchepkin had experienced all the modes of provincial theater: the schisms, the centripetal force which pulled actors into the capitals, and the centrifugal force which spun them out again, now as stars, across the country. Shchepkin embodied the interaction between manorial theater, the provincial circuit, and the imperial houses. His vertical rise to spectacular success and his horizontal trajectory outward to the provinces helped raise the art of actors by setting an example. Shchepkin profited from the tours because he could do roles there not allowed in Moscow. Not that provincial actors were always happy to see him in the outlands. Lavrov's troupe found Poltava "occupied" by Shchepkin at one point, leading one actor to call him "a locust from the capital" who ate up all the receipts and stole work from provincials.[105]

Nikolai Khrisanfovich Rybakov (1811–76), the actor who complained about Shchepkin, was the son of a Kursk estate steward. At age eleven he became enthralled by a Kotzebue melodrama at Stein's theater. At fifteen, while a government clerk, he worked for Stein as an unpaid extra; a few years later he quit his day job and joined the company. Later he worked with the Mlotkovsky group on the southern and Volga circuits. He failed twice to get hired by the Moscow Imperial Theater, and returned to the provinces. When Mlotkovsky's company dispersed, Rybakov became a floater, subject to the rigors of itinerant acting. Roaming the country brought hardship but also useful contacts and mutual learning. Rybakov came to value the freedom of movement and the eternal kaleidoscope of new audiences, faces, and places. The limited repertoire enabled the actor to play favorite roles over and over again. Employment in permanent town theaters, by contrast, required learning new roles every week and subservience to tyrannical managers and to the tastes of merchants and other patrons who preferred vaudeville and melodrama. Rybakov defined his style by critiquing other actors. He agreed with a reviewer's ridicule of a colleague who, while declaiming, pushed out his chest, cocked his head, extended his right arm, and thrust out his right foot. Rybakov rejected the wild shouts that alternated with silken whispers and the persistent habit of entering majestically rather than simply walking on stage. By the 1840s, he was considered the best provincial tragedian for his roles in Shakespeare and Schiller and his humanization of the grandiose Lyapunovs and Belisariuses. Rybakov sometimes ignited jealousy among actors because of his high salary. As a star, he bragged that he had once gotten through a city gate by showing the guard an *affiche* announcing him in the role of Skopin-Shuisky, thereby convincing the guard that he was a boyar.[106]

The career of actor-entrepreneur Nikolai Ivanov provides a perspective on provincial theater management, in this case in an Upper Volga circuit. Born in 1811, the son of a German factory owner, as a boy in Kostroma he changed his name, entered the Cadet Corps, and sang in the church choir. After landowner Obrezkov hired him to sing at his theater in the mid-1820s, Ivanov made the stage his career. In 1827, when General Kartsev created his own theater, he hired the teenager to direct it and teach his serfs. Ivanov found himself caught between two powerful rival magnates. Obrezkov had the governor arrest him; Kartsev got him released. When Kartsev died, Ivanov set out on his own in 1829. A canny businessman, he ran two or three theaters with the same troupe and made the most of each town's resources and character. In winter they played Yaroslavl to a small but stable audience. In summer they traveled to Rybinsk, a lively emporium of Volga shipping situated at a major junction of river systems. Its large transient population of merchants and clerks with money to spend filled the theater. Ivanov then offered winter showings in Tver and Kostroma and summers in Vyshny Volochok. When his enterprise entered the Lower Volga, the troupes switched monthly between Simbirsk and Samara. Aside from these, Ivanov acted in and managed, alone or in partnership, theater companies working in Vologda, Vyatka, Smolensk, Tula, Orël, Kazan, Saratov, and Orenburg.[107]

Swindles, scandals, intrigues, pirating of actors, and bitter rivalry with other entrepreneurs occupy many pages of Ivanov's memoirs. He also related how the gentry actor Vasily Vasilev was beaten to death in the late 1820s by the serfs of a landowner with whose wife he was having an affair. The landowner remained unpunished. Ivanov was able to hire temporarily such luminaries as Mochalov, Shchepkin, Zhivokini, and Sadovsky for his circuit. They not only earned extra money but also showed off their talents to local audiences. A famous dramatic actor, V. V. Samoilov (1813–87), actually began his career in one of Ivanov's productions. In Vyshny Volochok, Ivanov in 1855 ran into the all too familiar bureaucratic sandbagging over a technical matter involving the posting of *affiches* and the mourning period for Tsar Nicholas I. He was obliged to delay production for months. The earnings from provincial theater apparently compensated for the eternal grief: Gedeonov of the Imperial Theaters offered Ivanov six hundred rubles a year as an actor, whereas a rich landowner paid him fifteen hundred. Ivanov continued his life as a theater entrepreneur well beyond the emancipation of the serfs.[108]

Pëtr Medvedev (1837–1906) covered even wider ground. We have met him at Barsov's Inn in Moscow and on far-flung stages from Lithuania and Belorussia in the west to the mouth of the Volga at Astrakhan — with many stops in between. His original trajectory was unusual. Medvedev was born into a family of actors, and he breathed amateur theatricals at home, though his father was a minor official of the Senate. On his first visit to a theater, the youth was so excited by the religious scenes in Verstovsky's *Askold's Grave* that he stood and made the sign of the cross. In 1845, he entered the Imperial Moscow Theater School and at sixteen began life on the road in Tula. Medvedev provides a wealth of theatrical anecdotes: he was hospitalized for two weeks after being accidentally defenestrated during a performance of *Skopin-Shuisky*. But there is much novelty in this life on the road that began less than a decade before the end of serfdom. During the Crimean War, when he met two Piedmontese prisoners of war, Medvedev noticed that a straightforward propaganda play, *For Faith, Tsar, and Fatherland,* flopped while a naval spectacle, *The Battle of Sinope,* was a hit. Since the little town of Vyshny Volochok lay on the high road between Moscow and St. Petersburg, by the time Medvedev was working there in the 1850s — together with a ruined nobleman and two American-born actors, the Bravo brothers — he could take a train there from Moscow. Unique in his memoirs are his encounters with homosexuality and with Jews. In Tver, the young Medvedev experienced, and warded off, advances from one of the male actors. Throughout his travels in Lithuania and Belorussia, Medvedev, in contrast to the silence of other Russian actors who worked in the Jewish Pale, made frequent references to kindly Jews.[109]

The remarkable N. K. Miloslavsky (Friedeburg, 1811–82), a Baltic noble, retired hussar officer, and actor-manager, played briefly on the Petersburg imperial stage but returned by choice to the provinces. One of the mystery figures of the provincial theater world, Miloslavsky was said to be exceptionally unpleasant and was even accused by innuendo of burning down his own theater and leaving one of his colleagues to die in the flames. The episode found expression in a play by A. N. Samsonov, *A Provincial Actor,* and in M. L. Mikhailov's novel, *Birds of Passage* (1854). Many theaters did in fact burn down, and Mikhailov's novel contains a lurid scene of arson and theft perpetrated by a principal character. Otherwise the charge remains unproved. Mikhailov's fictional character does not fit with other things we know about Miloslavsky. Medvedev recalled him as a legendary thespian Robin Hood who played up his social background, exquisite manners, and knowledge of languages to thwart abusive authority and defend the dignity of actors. As one of the rare entrepreneurs received in society, Miloslavsky established excellent relations with the local gentry and governor by offering special performances where his actors mingled with the guests. According to theater lore, when local bigwigs tried to interfere with his business, Miloslavsky always seemed to outwit or intimidate them by his social bearing. He certainly won admirers for a perfectionist approach to acting, a broad range of roles, and a serious attitude toward rehearsals. Miloslavsky was the closest thing to a cultural knight that Russian theater history produced.[110]

The rich memoirs of I. I. Lavrov (Barsukov, 1824 or 1827–1902), *The Stage and Life in the Provinces and the Capital,* vividly recapture the theatrical circuit on the middle and lower Volga in this era. The son of a small shopkeeper deep in rural Tambov, Lavrov worked in all kinds of menial occupations. When he was six, the family moved to Nizhny Novgorod and lived in monasteries, where he began to read popular chivalry tales. When his father died, Lavrov was apprenticed to a Rostov-on-Don merchant and then worked in a factory where he was subject to a strict regimen enforced by bells, punishments, and mandatory church attendance. This gave him singing experience in the choir. In 1843, he began peddling goods at fairs along the Volga and served in a fisheries office in Astrakhan. There Lavrov saw his first play: Ducange's *Theresa, or the Orphan of Geneva.* The young spectator reacted exactly as had audiences all over the Western world for decades: he wept for the victim and felt a passionate abhorrence for the villain. Lavrov also witnessed something not in the script. When the villain denied his guilt on stage, a spectator cried out "You lie, you son of a dog, what a bandit! You killed [her]. Look, these good folks [in the theater] are witnesses." Stalls and loges erupted in laughter as the police took the man away. Lavrov, now hooked on theater, started in Zalessky's troupe as an unpaid apprentice. Initiation to backstage life in the dingy actors' quarters began with the greeting: "What kind of actor will you be, if you don't drink?" Lavrov entered that nexus of town and theater so common in the provinces where actors socialized with clergy, police, professionals, and officials of various ranks. Part of that mingling took place backstage in the form of what Lavrov called orgies.[111]

The troupe sailed up the Volga from Astrakhan to Tsaritsyn and then veered westward deep into the interior of Voronezh and Tambov provinces. By now Lavrov had gotten his first speaking parts. His major break came in 1846 as a stand-in when a famous singer asked too much money to play the lead in Verstovsky's *Askold's Grave.* Lavrov henceforth got regular roles in drama and opera. Tambovites at first shunned the impoverished actors. Merchants treated them as pariahs, not deigning to bow in greeting, and most gentry did not even know the theater existed. But a gentry patron invited his reluctant friends to see *Askold's Grave,* the house filled up, and Lavrov had a success. The patron invited the cast for supper where they socialized with the local gentry. Lavrov described how the ill-clad actors gradually shed their embarrassment. When the troupe divided in order to play two local towns, Lavrov went to Kirsanov which had no theater and whose people, Lavrov believed, had never seen a performance. In a makeshift building, by the light of oil lamps and candelabra, the actors improvised a production of Polevoi's *Parasha the Siberian* which entranced the audience and drew tears from its female sector. After a sojourn in neighboring Penza, the reunited troupe worked the fairs of the Don Cossack territory. At Taganrog, a plan to put on *The Plague in Milan* was forbidden by the authorities because an earlier production of it had seemed so realistic that many in the audience fled from the theater in panic. In fact, disease always lurked on the horizon for the troupe itself: in June 1849 at Rostov, the raging cholera took the lives of several actors.[112]

During his provincial days, Lavrov suffered constant scrutiny and harassment by the police because of his liability for military service. His remarkable tale of evasion illustrates how easily a wanderer could fall between the cracks of the system. Each time he was threatened with charges of desertion, his occupation gained him temporary relief. Petty interference from officials stalked the touring company. In Rostov-on-Don in 1848, the town prefect, perhaps unnerved by revolutionary events in Europe, bristled at seeing in Gogol's *Inspector General* a prefect (*gorodichny*) with two separate families, a situation that all too accurately paralleled his own domestic arrangements. When the directors explained that it was nothing personal, he threatened them with jail. At the Korennaya Fair, the profits were offset by the governor's demand that the Polish violinist Apolinary Katski play between the acts and get two-thirds of the take. Lavrov's colleagues generated problems of their own. Males lacked adequate costumes, especially when they pawned them for drink money after a performance. Actors had to dress the same way for all historical periods. Those without socks had their ankles painted black or brown. Obliging lackeys of local gentry would give actors garments stolen from their masters' wardrobes in return for theater tickets. Drink was a more serious scourge. A gentry actor in the troupe, Porfiry Aksakov, once got so offensively drunk on stage that the audience departed. Clever entrepreneurs would avoid stopping on the road where hard beverages were sold. At Tambov one of the actors, probably drunk, attempted to shoot a stage eagle in Weber's *Der Freischütz* and almost hit another actor, causing the audience to flee in terror. Lavrov himself was wounded by a bayonet-wielding actor on stage.[113]

For almost a decade Lavrov traveled with his company to thirty cities and returned again and again to previous ones, seemingly destined to a life on the road. In the 1840s, Lavrov had been approached at the actors' bourse by a Moscow scout, but had to decline because of his lack of the passport required of lower-class subjects. In 1853, while working in Ryazan, he sought and obtained a successful audition for the Moscow stage by singing a number from Verstovsky's opera, *Askold's Grave*. Verstovsky received Lavrov warmly, but the auditionee heard catty comments from other cast members about himself: "Really, how does all this provincial trash make it to our stage?" Verstovsky and other protectors helped him solve his passport and draft problems, and all was settled by the time of the coronation of Tsar Alexander II. Thus like Shchepkin, Ivan Lavrov, a man of humble background, managed — after performing for years in towns and fairs in eighty-two different works (sometimes in multiple roles) — to make it to the big time, to the Maly and the Bolshoi in Moscow.[114]

An outstanding theater figure on the middle Volga, Anna Vysheslavtseva (1818–95), has been lamentably neglected in the literature. Her trajectory took her through three distinct social roles: as the outright serf of Prince Shakhovskoi and his heirs whose Nizhny Novgorod theater they sold when she was ten; as an indentured servant who spent her first years on stage laboring under a binding contract; and as a completely free actress who rocketed to success not only in her own Volga stronghold but in a dozen towns of the Russian empire. Vysheslavtseva's wide range enabled her to triumph in roles as different as the doomed Desdemona and the resourceful aspiring actress in *Lev Gurych Sinichkin* where she essentially played herself. Her portrayal of underdogs brought the most acclaim: Theresa in *The Orphan of Geneva*, and Gudula, the Gypsy mother of Esmeralda in Hugo's *Nôtre Dame de Paris*. Like Shchepkin, Vysheslavtseva became known as one of the first provincial actors to speak lines in a plain manner. Born only a few hours journey upriver from the birthplace of Kuzmina who was destined to remain in bondage, Anna Vysheslavtseva gained her freedom. She owed her long career on the stage to her talent; but that life in freedom had hinged on the economic decision of her owners.[115]

As in any theatrical venue, provincial women had their own problems. In Lyubov Nikulina-Kositskaya's (1827–68) family of house serfs, her father was jailed by the owner and regularly beaten. The master and his brothers were so cruel, she records without further comment, that their peasants murdered two of them, one by crucifixion. After being sold several times, Nikulina's father managed to earn enough money in Nizhny Novgorod to purchase the family's freedom for two thousand rubles. Lyubov as a little girl worked in the home of a merchant's wife with cultural interests. This kindly woman took the child to her first theater performance where the vaunted Vysheslavtseva was playing in K. L. Bakhturin's *Red Veil,* a melodrama based on an "eastern" tale of Alexander Marlinsky about an innocent woman slandered, redeemed, and then married to an emir. When the stage-struck Nikulina declared her intention to act, her family waged a futile struggle against her aspiration because they identified theater with the devil and an acting career as literally a fate worse than death. Stricken by these objections, she fell victim to fever and loss of weight. Then, displaying a precocious sense of pride and self-esteem, essential for life on the stage, Nikulina surmounted all obstacles and, once ensconced in the theater, found that she could retain her religious piety as she learned the arts of the stage. At fourteen, she roamed the Volga circuit from Nizhny to Yaroslavl to Rybinsk, working in all genres: she sang the beggar's romance in *Belisarius*; danced in Mozart's *Magic Flute;* and played Agathe in Weber's *Der Freischütz,* Michaela in *Daughter of Charles the Bold,* and a maid in *The Orphan of Geneva.*[116]

Nikulina (fig. 44) later observed that the continuous peregrinations along the Volga circuit produced a psychology of homelessness among provincial actors. A few themes surface constantly in her memoirs: the Volga river which is invoked, often poetically, over and over—nine times in one paragraph alone; and her victimization as an innocent woman. Both may have been self-consciously inscribed in the memoirs from her later experience in acting the part of wronged Volga women in Ostrovsky's plays. The teenage actress encountered sexism at every turn: serf harems, stage door Romeos, and lethally jealous admirers. She was especially offended by the widespread male opinion that theater women possessed no moral code. The old roués in Bulgarin's novel *Ivan Vyzhigin* had put it bluntly about an object of their lust: "Too bad she is virtuous! Virtue in an actress is a luxury, it even ought not to be tolerated!" Nikulina in the 1840s heard almost the same words when a merchant in Rybinsk, contemptuous of her resistance to his advances and her allusion to a woman's honor, asked her "What's honor for an actress?" As with Lavrov, Nikulina's fortune was changed by *Askold's Grave.* In 1844, Verstovsky auditioned her as the female lead and hired her into the Imperial Moscow Theater in 1846. After she performed dramatic roles as Anna in Ostrovsky's *Poverty Is Not a Vice* (1854) and Katya in *Storm* (1859), the playwright created parts for her. She also starred in Pisemsky's *Bitter Fate* (1859). Nikulina eventually became the highest paid actress in the Moscow Imperial Theaters.[117]

The dancer Nadezhda Bogdanova (1836–97; fig. 45) came from a balletic dynasty: the Karpakovs—mother, uncle, and cousin—all danced for the Moscow Imperial Theaters, as did her father who trained her. After his wife died, the father, to test his children's skills, put them in front of the public. Nadezhda's first performances took place in a Moscow merchant club. She then went off with the family to the provinces in 1848–50 where she danced excerpts from romantic ballets. Vasily Insarsky, lodging at a Kursk hotel in 1850, saw the Bogdanovs who were rehearsing in the next room. They performed at gentry homes for a mere five rubles. The son played the violin while the father and Nadezhda danced. Lacking contacts, advance booking, or agents, they traveled to Yaroslavl in the middle of winter in 1848 where the theater owner treated them rudely during the bargaining. She or her father must have possessed some special charm: in Kostroma, through a letter of introduction from the governor, Bogdanova danced in a benefit concert for fire victims; and in Kursk she was assisted by the marshal of nobility. Her memoirs offer very little about her performance repertoire as she traveled through Kaluga, Tula, Kharkov, the Kiev Contract Fair, Odessa, Nikolaevsk, and Sevastopol. The rigorous circuit experience paid off. Bogdanova went on to Paris where she studied and successfully performed in a lead role at the Opéra. Her remaining career was studded with successes in major roles on the Petersburg and Moscow imperial stages from 1855 to 1864.[118]

Theater-Land

What meaning can we give to life on the theatrical circuit? A professional musician's verdict as of 1835 is fairly typical. Yury Arnold viewed provincial theater as an enterprise involving mostly *obrok* serfs and servants earning payment for their masters who leased them out from their serf theaters to replenish squandered wealth. Talented people were few in number, Arnold argued, and the best of them went off to the capitals. Those who did not make it frittered away their gifts in the harsh conditions of the backwaters. A journalist reporting from Tambov rendered a similar judgment in 1842. After describing how a troupe of forty actors had to tote the curtain and stage equipment from Voronezh to Tambov only to perform in front of twenty people, he wondered how they could even eke out a living in what he called this "ignoble and useless vocation." Much later, the Imperial Theater official Rafail Zotov looked back with contempt on the provincial theater "nomads" of this era on the grounds that commerce sullied the noble art of theater.[119] Although these judgments contain truths, they paint an exclusively dismal and dismissive picture of the provincial performance landscape.

The huge arc of travel flung the nomadic troupes over hundreds of miles. "Every provincial actor who has served Melpomene for ten years," wrote a reporter for *Pantheon* in 1852, "knows at least half of Russia as well as his own favorite role." This entailed physical exhaustion for the itinerants as well as a certain exhilaration for some. Geographical mobility, aside from whatever personal enrichment it brought, might have heightened observation of social types. It certainly enhanced actors' possibility of being "discovered." The entrepreneur Sokolov redeemed his wife, a serf actress, and several of her colleagues. Not many serfs on the theatrical circuit won their freedom, but for the brightest and luckiest, the endless travel could lead to auditions, invitations, freedom, and a career in a Moscow imperial theater — even though it might take years of wandering and subservience. Appointment to the Imperial Theaters did not end all the unpleasant aspects of stage life, but it did offer the chance of considerably reducing them. And, while the persisting provincial practice of requiring actors to play every genre may have developed versatility, the capital system of increasing specialization from the 1830s onward granted them an opportunity to hone their specialties and achieve celebrity.[120] There were of course actors who stayed in permanent town theaters or who moved in tight geographical circuits. These tended to marry each other, settle in one place, have children, and even raise livestock. Such "settlers" resisted all attempts by newcomers to replace them.[121]

Serfs on the circuit enjoyed a semifreedom unknown to manorial actors: they lived, as Bulgarin rightly put it, "on their passports," far away from the master's house where they could be enclosed, controlled, punished, and made to play to a limited audience. Although serf actors lacked an organized body of patrons such as serf painters enjoyed, they held an advantage over most other creative serfs: exposure to a large public. Those estate serf actors permitted to work in town theaters and touring companies in return for *obrok* entered the wider world and expanded their social ambience. They could sharpen their talents by watching fellow actors and visiting celebrities. Those who remained in bondage and in the provinces may have had to endure insults and indignities — the least of which was having their names listed on the *affiches* without a polite "Miss" or "Mister" in front of them; but at least they were able to take a gulp of liberty. That semifreedom should not be idealized. Even totally free actors felt the torrents of abuse that all the memoirs record. Like imperial actors, they suffered the double jeopardy of class and occupation. Local potentates were more arbitrary than those in the capital. Actors were often at the mercy of those whom Lavrov called "kulak-entrepreneurs." The men were additionally liable for the military draft and the women to sexual harassment. Merchants and tavern owners plied them with drink, but seldom food. Yet memoirs also tell of unexpected politeness from owners and local people. Medvedev recalled that in Saratov in 1858, the Gentry Club allowed his troupe to hold a New Year's ball downstairs; and that Astrakhan merchants in their stalls thanked the actors for the previous night's performance and offered them goods as tokens of appreciation.[122] It is surely not romanticizing to imagine also the sheer fun, high jinks, and mischievousness of backstage life, to say nothing of the euphoria that most actors feel performing in front of a paying public.

Fiction of the period provides a mixed picture of life on the road. Faddei Bulgarin's *Ivan Vyzhigin* (1829) introduces a Kiev troupe of the 1820s with a character's scornful words, "a troupe of wandering actors composed of under-educated schoolboys, expelled seminary students, semiliterate [serf] actresses from domestic theaters who were freed or living on their passports." The troupe displays éclat amid shabby conditions, stages benefits during provincial elections and hunts, and divides profits in each town when there are any. Bulgarin adds authentic details on the physical setting, interaction of character types, and repertoire.[123] Alexander Veltman (1800–1870) anticipated Gogol's *Inspector General* by a year in the amusing *Provincial Actors* (1835). During the performance of a visiting troupe, the actor playing Orlando Furioso in a vaudeville fails to appear. While the audience waits, the town constable searches for him behind the curtain. Meanwhile, a cry announcing the imminent arrival of a governor general empties the theater. As the owner apologizes for what he takes to be the cause of the egress—the absent Roland—the spectators fly home to don uniforms and take up their duties. The missing actor, drunk and quite mad, then arrives and is of course taken for the important emissary. The unintentional impersonator proceeds to scold the town officials with lines from *Julius Caesar* ("Et tu, Brute") which confuses them; and *Othello* ("I have killed my wife") which frightens them. In the end, the real general comes to town and sorts everything out.[124] Through all the fun and games in this story can be seen a fair depiction of the enormous tolerance of audiences for lapses in stage etiquette; the interference of town officials in theater life; and the ubiquitous bad boy who throws production awry.

A fuller and more somber reconstruction of that world is found in M. L. Mikhailov's engrossing novel about provincial actors, *Birds of Passage*. Mikhailov, though known mostly as a radical littérateur, also wrote librettos for Anton Rubinstein's shorter operas and knew the provincial theater intimately. The "homeless herd" of characters in the novel live turbulent lives on the road. In the mythical town of Kamsk, they play the popular opera *Rusalka* to a modest house with stalls, benches, and standing room. They spend their off-stage lives in small hotels and taverns, traveling from one town to another, looking for stardom and fighting a greedy entrepreneur who has risen from nowhere. Along the road, they squabble, fall in love, marry, graduate to entrepreneurship, languish and prosper, suffer and rejoice. The central dramatic moment—all too familiar in real life—is a theater fire which takes the life of their entrepreneur. Some give up, others go on. The main character, when asked "how we live," replies: "Well everyone knows how! We roam from place to place! We are nomads or, so to say, birds of passage." Mikhailov's novel, though full of harrowing scenes, presents rich complexity rather than dark simplicity. The memoirs of real-life actors reinforce his fictionalized account.[125]

What did the provincial public see? Until 1865, censors required entrepreneurs to order approved scripts from the Imperial Theaters library. On receiving a copy, they had to present it to the local governor who would send it back to the Third Section in the capital for approval, a process that could take months. Theoretically, only plays — and not all of them — already seen on imperial stages could be put on in the provinces. Enforcement was another matter. In 1842, the Ministry of Internal Affairs claimed that few city theaters obeyed the rules. Gedeonov was still complaining in the late 1850s that, despite numerous efforts, the Directorate and the Third Section were unable to catch everything. Local writers and actors often got their works performed sub rosa, and government officials could be made to look the other way. Scholars estimate that some forty thousand manuscript copies of Griboedov's *Woe from Wit* circulated illegally up to 1861 and that it was read aloud in private circles everywhere. In the first two decades of Nicholas's reign, *Woe from Wit* was performed in public illegally ten times. After an Irkutsk performance in 1852, exiled Decembrists engaged in a hot debate about its merits and the play was ordered off the stage by the police. Gogol's *Inspector General,* legally permitted, had immense success in the provinces by 1843 but, as we have seen, was closed down in some places by local authorities who feared that they were being satirized in it.[126]

Provincial audiences saw pretty much what the capital public saw, and, allowing for national works, pretty much what provincial Europe saw (fig. 46).[127] A vivid impression of the range can be gotten from the recollections of an inveterate provincial theatergoer, Alexander Artynov, born in 1813 in a freed peasant family on a Yaroslav provincial estate. After an itinerant apprenticeship, he became a wealthy merchant. He traded widely from the 1830s through the 1850s all over the provinces and the capitals, stopping at hotels and taverns, and recording his sights, including the public scourging of a convicted murderer. Artynov listed about fifty plays or musical shows that he saw in Yaroslavl, Moscow, Rostov, the southern circuit, and a dozen other locations. These included tragedies, historical works, comedies, melodramas, operas, ballets, and vaudevilles — works by Shakespeare, Schiller, Hugo, Mozart, Meyerbeer, Ozerov, Griboedov, Gogol, Kukolnik, and Glinka; and featuring such performing artists as Karatygin, Mochalov, Bryansky, Tolchënov, Zhivokini, Karatygina, and Taglioni. Artynov's catalog of things seen and heard, confirmed by other sources, attests to the astonishing variety and richness of the repertoire presented to virtually every social class among the nonserf (and sometimes serf) population of the provinces.[128]

Intelligentsia lamentations about the relative lack of serious drama notwithstanding, tragedies were always on offer in the provinces. Tragedians rated high in town theaters, and landowners often trained *obrok* serf actors in tragedy because they would earn more for their masters. The peasant hero of an 1852 Pisemsky story liked "unrealistic plays with 'foreign princes in bright clothing'." Though neoclassical drama was weak due to the lack of knowledgeable actors and to audience tastes, other tragic forms flourished. In the years 1846–53, young Boborykin and his schoolmates of Nizhny Novgorod savored Shakespeare and Schiller alongside Molière, Griboedov, and Gogol; and these alternated with French melodramas and the Polevoi and Kukolnik pageants. Everywhere, vaudeville, melodrama, and historical-patriotic plays led the field. In the late 1830s and early 1840s, Polevoi's *Parasha the Siberian* played on sixteen provincial stages, and Lensky's *Lev Gurych Sinichkin* and Kukolnik's *Skopin-Shuisky* each on seven. The melodramas of Kotzebue, Caigniez, and Ducange flooded provincial houses. Seletsky and his Kharkov classmates adored Victor Ducange's *Thirty Years, or the Life of a Gambler* (1827) which dealt with a degenerate gambler who kills a traveling companion for money to feed his gaming frenzy — and discovers that the victim is his son.[129]

A Soviet scholar argued unconvincingly that conservative ideology and social influence rather than genuine popular demand caused the constant showing of "lesser" genres; and he implied that the actors resented this. But he did make one indisputable point: that merchants loved melodramas, no matter how "unrealistic" they were. This may seem to contradict the fact that merchant audiences, in their love of realism, helped launch Alexander Ostrovsky's career in the 1850s. The simple truth, and the key to the great variety of the repertoire, is that, like most other people, merchants equally enjoyed and patronized the most extravagantly fantastic productions as well as realist plays. Spectators who may have felt rapture at hearing the ponderous classical cadences of Ozerov's *Dmitry Donskoi*[130] could also delight in seeing familiar Russian types on stage speaking in language closer to the vernacular. The taste for parody and farce also ran high, as it did on American stages of the same era. The popularity of Lensky's irreverent *Hamlet Sidorovich and Ophelia Kuzminishna* in Russia and *Hamlet and Egglet* which played the United States circuit testifies to that appeal.[131] Nor did the provinces seem to mind inferior production values. Eyewitnesses noted inappropriate costumes: African tribes in Spanish wigs, medieval women in nineteenth-century dresses, and Venuses in peasant sarafans. Critics saw visual anomalies on the imperial stage as well, but in reverse as when Anyuta, the peasant lass of *Filatka and Miroshka,* appeared in an opulent velvet sarafan.[132]

The rampant complaints about poor acting in commercial theaters were not limited to the printed page. In Nizhny Novgorod, Ulybyshev, an ardent theatergoer and arbiter of acting skill, would shout his judgments to the cast from his seat in the front row and the audience would follow his lead.[133] What kind of acting was it? The master narrative of how a Russian realist style emerged from the provinces and got taken to Moscow, though not wholly wrong, must be desimplified. Against the many stories of the few realistic provincial actors must be set, in Senelick's words, the "hoards of scenery-chewing hams . . . [who] clung to declamation and mannered gesticulation long after they had become obsolete in the capitals." Yet provincial actors owed at least some of their inflated style to veterans of the capitals. One of them admired Mochalov's ability to turn pale in the face of disaster. When, in Polevoi's bloodcurdling *Ugolino*, he discovered his stage wife dead, he zipped behind the curtain and poured flour over himself. An observer in Rybinsk in 1860 complained that actors from Petersburg had a harmful influence on the provincial stage; one tore his hair and beat his breast as he screamed the lines in Kukolnik's bloody potboiler *Skopin-Shuisky*. The entrepreneur N. I. Ivanov endlessly lamented the overacting, forgotten lines, ad-libbing, tampering with the classics, and audiences with "no sense of scenic truth." Yet his anecdotes show clearly that the audience loved the unrehearsed witticisms, one-liners, and interactions with the public. When naughty players in a historical drama had Ivan the Terrible say "merci" and make bows, the "none too keen" audience rewarded them with applause.[134]

Shchepkin, Pavlov, Ugarov, Vysheslavtseva, and a few others are often mentioned as pioneers of realism. The best-known of these, Shchepkin, is credited with spreading realism both from the provinces to Moscow and back again on his tours. Notions about what is realistic representation in stage, fiction, or graphic art vary greatly across time and space. Spectators exposed to examples of an alleged turn to realism, for example in cinema, will often be puzzled at what their elders considered true to life. We can never know exactly how Shchepkin or his contemporaries acted. Eyewitnesses, reviews, and recollections of the stage often contradict each other. We do know that Shchepkin, long considered the doyen of realism, was dubbed old hat at the end of his career; and his acting had not changed significantly. Shchepkin's repertoire helped gain him the reputation as a naturalistic Russian actor, particularly in vehicles that were not in the dramaturgical canon. Laurence Senelick aptly reminds us of the "the prejudice that entitles the art of acting to be an *art* only when it is linked to literary values," and especially to tragedy. Nevertheless, what contemporaries thought of as realistic stagecraft took root in provincial theater, where stage rules and customs were relatively fluid and where the neoclassical style remained weak. The kind of acting required for works on contemporary Russian themes began to appear. Gradually the Russian inflections and sensibilities nourished by lower-class actors trained in the outlying towns and fairs rose in value for directors and audiences and were occasionally brought to Moscow. That often despised center of patriarchalism and alleged merchant backwardness was the principal gainer from the influx of provincial actors to its stages. Theater became one of the main embellishments of Moscow's Russian face.[135]

Identifying agents of stylistic change is notoriously difficult in any art. Playwrights' "national" pride, actors' quest for novelty, trial and error at the box office, and sheer audience exhaustion with a particular brand of drama all played their parts. In many towns — not only university centers such as Kharkov and Kazan — a vocal intelligentsia of journalists, critics, teachers, and writers advocated realist acting and serious drama. In Novo-Cherkassk, capital of the Don Cossack Host Territory, the critic A. G. Filonov complained of the 1857–58 season that the troupe's actor-owner scanned the house as he "acted" in order to count his profits. Most galling was the glut of vaudevilles and non-Russian subjects. Speaking ironically for "[us] poor provincials," he warned visiting companies to respect the taste of the locals — meaning the intelligentsia. Filonov, drawing constant comparisons with the capitals, scolded the strolling players and their public for bad taste. From the 1840s onward, the voice of Vissarion Belinsky, promoter of naturalism in literature, was heard far and wide. Local critics sympathetic to the new wave formed a chorus of cheerleaders and denouncers. They deplored popular genres and nonrealistic acting. The Slavophile Ivan Aksakov admitted in a fit of candor that "in the stinking swamp of provincial life," disciples of his ideological rival, the Westernizer Belinsky, offered a breath of fresh air. Soviet scholars condemned popular taste, sided with the intelligentsia in their battle against it, and tended to exaggerate their power to shape repertoires. But those scholars were essentially correct in tracking the increase of press coverage which reflected an educated demand. The press intelligentsia spoke for itself, but may well have induced other readers to take a critical and respectable position.[136]

The intelligentsia aside, most provincial spectators had catholic tastes in theater. Boborykin believed that the eclectic offerings in that era helped common people and children to develop their imaginations and taught them concepts of nobility, fear of evil, and sympathy for heroes. Even vaudeville brought out the laughter and joy, he said, in those last obscurantist years of Nicholas I. Students and merchants everywhere, though sometimes devoted to particular stars, seemed eager to devour all genres of the stage. Unhappily, the voluble merchants Ivan Tolchënov of the eighteenth century and Artynov of the nineteenth, though ever ready to list what they saw, say little about how they reacted. The diary of Voronezh merchant Alexei Kapkanishchikov (b. 1800), mentioned his viewing experience in Petersburg but offered only an occasional reaction ("touching," "very touching"). Lower-class tastes are also hard to chart, since there were no theater surveys or questionnaires. The Kursk provincial gazette in 1840 printed an alleged reaction of a local peasant to a performance: "I see three noblewomen sitting before us talking about something; they talked and talked and then stood up and broke into song; they sang and sang and then, I guess, got tired and stopped. I see running around some long-legged fellow, not quite a lord, not quite a lackey. He must be a lackey because masters don't make such faces. . . . then those actresses leave and they send in some kind of barrel maker. . . ." Little can be learned from such fragments about audience understanding. Primitive though the peasant's observations may have been, he at least perceived the difference between the meaningless (to him) arias, the guffawing comedian, and the "cursed" wood goblin. However, audience reactions collected in the late nineteenth and early twentieth centuries for Popular Theaters catering to lower-class urbanites may offer clues to what went on in the preceding period. Popular Theater audiences brought certain expectations, moral judgments, and cultural baggage with them to the theater: experience with village rituals, calendric celebrations, folk drama, and fairground entertainments. Escape and entertainment were major motivations for theatergoing. Popular audiences could "like" a play without fully understanding it, show solemn respect for some genres, identify with certain characters, condemn others, and even display skepticism about implausible resolutions. By extrapolation, we can at least speculate that the known experience of 1900 or so did not differ much from that of 1850 and before. As with any audience, reactions to the stage gave no firm evidence on what new ideas or principles were taken out of the theater and applied to personal lives — except for those who became stage-struck. In our own day, even with a wealth of opinion technology, experts disagree about the impact of theater (and film and television) on people's behavior.[137]

Religious taboos on theater apparently had little effect, except for Old Believers. The Orthodox Church informally opposed theater and yet, to my knowledge, made no strong utterances in that vein, presumably because this would imply a critique of the dynasty and the aristocracy who supported the capital's theaters. The merchant Tolchënov (1754–1824/5) traveled widely in the capitals and provinces, attended theater, mingled with the aristocracy, joined clubs, and felt no conflict between his genuine Orthodox piety and his attendance at court performances of French comedies and ballets.[138] His son became a prominent actor. In the reign of Nicholas I, as the Church tried to enforce Orthodox social and cultural norms, the public went to the theater and attended mass as well. So did clergy. Travelers and memoirists routinely report the presence of priests at theatrical performances. Count Kamensky of

Orël once told a deacon that the theater was no place for churchmen, who ought to be singing hallelujahs and ringing bells. The deacon attended none the less. In the 1820s, the actor Andrei Shiryaev tried to sell a ticket to the bishop of Kostroma who told him that clergy did not attend theater because it distracted from pious thoughts. When the actor recited Derzhavin's ode, "God," the bishop bought a ticket (the price of which Shiryaev promptly spent on liquor). A story set in 1860 vividly contrasted the fanatical devotion to theater of provincial divinity students to the dire punishments they suffered when caught. We have seen Muslim Tatars in a Kazan theater. Jews, despite stringent restrictions of Orthodox Judaism and its Hasidic variant, made their way to the stalls and boxes from Poltava to Romny to Odessa, even though some comedies were salted with anti-Semitic remarks or even centered on an anti-Jewish theme.[139] Neither cultural and religious sensibilities nor a low quality of production sufficed to keep people out of the theater. What brought them in, mutatis mutandis, were the plays, the operas, the stories. It is hardly surprising that a paying public could feel joy and wonder and revelation in an amateurish and crude production. If theater did not always stimulate the brain, it could dazzle the eye and arouse the senses.

What did the theater circuit contribute to provincial life in the early nineteenth century? Most of all it created new publics. In Laurence Senelick's words, it "broadened the audience base, and began to create a theater public, made up not of aristocrats who continued to prefer French drama and Italian opera, but of the lesser gentry, the merchant class, the military, tradesmen and bureaucrats, and even the common people."[140] Since admission etiquette was laxer and ticket prices cheaper than in the great houses of Petersburg and Moscow, provincial stages afforded entertainment where few alternative modes existed. Aside from the church and the folk fairs, the theater was the only place where everyone could assemble: poor townspeople, merchants, gentry, priests, and even peasants and lackeys. Social intercourse may have been inhibited by the seating structure, but the shared experience was probably greater than in the imperial houses. As in the capitals, theater served as a site of mutual social inspection, and many visitors made pronouncements about local life on the basis of what they saw in the boxes, stalls, and galleries. The content of foreign and Russian dramatic fiction, the ways of theatrical art, varieties of acting styles, and a whole range of music performed by artists who criss-crossed the country became available to townspeople otherwise unexposed to such secular goods. While the bulk of the upper classes and the burgeoning intelligentsia took their literary pleasures more from texts than from the stage, lower-class audiences took theirs almost exclusively from "literature that walks," presented to them by provincial actors whose own literary culture was mostly confined to the roles they played.

In a broader sense, the network of provincial theater represented an expansion of public cultural space at the expense of the private sphere. As estate theater gradually gave way to town stages, private to public entertainment, and seigniorial power and largesse to market forces, tens of thousands of Russians over the decades publicly participated in a shared cultural experience. Increasingly, that culture filled up with themes from contemporary Russian life. Theater circuits created interesting opportunities and fed the daydreams of starry-eyed commoners with few exciting prospects. Indirectly provincial theater also seems to have enlivened civic life. From time to time, foreign observers, Russian travelers, and local papers reported a connection between the presence of a theater or a particular performance and town pride. Theater fueled lively local debates about its function, and it served in several places as a focal point for charitable activities. When fire ravaged a town, officials in some places had the theater mount a benefit evening for the victims.[141] Benefit plays and concerts assisted in aiding orphans and in school funding. In some towns, maintaining a theater generated a certain amount of self-organization and interclass collaboration. Market forces found an additional base. Both serf and free actors came and went, obeying the lure of higher salaries or more promising venues. Entrepreneurs bought and sold their troupes, props, costumes, and buildings. Rental contracts appeared; boarding houses and inns received actors. The most striking thing about the whole system of town theaters was the sheer variety of ownership and management, labor relations, repertoires, and audiences. The very entrance and departures of theatrical caravans and their hoopla around town preceding the shows offered a kind of people-friendly alternative pageantry to military reviews and the orchestrated ceremonies of visiting dignitaries such as the tsar.[142]

A final note. In surveying the empire of theater as a whole, Moscow pops into view again and again as a vital center of Russian performance life. Three buildings, within a block or two of each other, functioned as its collective headquarters: Pechkin's coffee house and the Maly Theater on Theater Square; and Barsov's Inn up the street. Petersburg, though possessing vibrant salons and theaters, had no equivalent to Pechkin's, where a socially variegated collection of actors and writers held forth together in a permanent discourse on letters and the stage. Across the square, deep in the interior of the Maly, Alexei Verstovsky (fig. 47) sat at his desk in the Moscow office of the Imperial Theaters Directorate. He and his staff, in addition to managing the two Moscow houses, handled bookings for actors going out to the provinces, recruited those it would bring in, and helped organize provincial tours for Russian and foreign singers and instrumentalists. The actors' hiring hall at Barsov's provided the hub of the provincial theater circuit. It is worth noting that the cultural capital, St. Petersburg, aside from designing buildings and training artists, played little role in organizing the public culture of Russia as a whole. Theater Square in Moscow became, figuratively speaking, the Rogozh-skaya Gate — the great stagecoach depot — of the cultural network, soon to be overlaid by the template of railway lines, many of which radiated from Moscow along routes already trodden by the nomads of a performing empire.

1. The tsar's residence, epicenter of Petersburg aristocratic life. V. Sadovnikov, *View of the Winter Palace at Night*, 1856. Massie, *Land of the Firebird*, following p. 128.

2. Moscow, late eighteenth century: Starikova, *Moskva starodavnyaya*, 303.

3. The glory of country living. Ya. Ya. Filimonov, *View of A. B. Kurakin's Estate*, c. 1794. Courtesy of the State Historical Museum, Moscow.

4. Gentry interior. L. K. Plakhov, *Portrait of A. S. Strumilov and His Family*, 1842–43: Courtesy of the Tropinin Museum, Moscow.

5. Serf as servant. P. Bezsonov, *Portrait of a Lackey Sweeping*, 1836. Courtesy of the State Historical Museum, Moscow.

6. Serf as actress. Nicolas de Courteille, *Anna Borunova in Rehearsal*, 1821: Roosevelt, *Life on the Russian Country Estate*, 149. Arkhangelskoe Museum, Moscow.

7. Domestic muse, ensemble: music-making with Glinka, mid-1830s. Khoprova, *Ocherki po istorii russkoi muzyki*, 60.

8. Domestic muse, solo. Pavel Fedotov, *Portrait of N. P. Zhdanovich at the Piano*, 1849. © 2004 State Russian Museum, St. Petersburg.

9. Music-making at General A. F. Lvov's: Fradkina, *Zal Dvoryanskogo Sobraniya*, following p. 199.

10. Courtier, composer, impresario: Mikhail Vielgorsky. Fradkina, *Zal Dvoryanskogo Sobraniya*, following p. 199.

11. The home of Mikhail Vielgorsky on Mikhailovsky Square. Stolpyanskii, *Muzyka i muzit-sirovanie*, following p. 128.

12. Evening with the Brotherhood, early 1840s: at the piano, Glinka; at table Bryullov (left) and Kukolnik (right). N. A. Stepanov, Wednesday at Kukolnik's. Courtesy of the Tretyakov Gallery, Moscow.

13. Serf as musician. I.-A. Atkinson, *Horn Orchestra*: Starikova, *Moskva starodavnyaya*, 309.

14. Out of the forest: Mikhail Glinka. Livanova, *Glinka*, 1: 168.

15. Ball at the St. Petersburg Gentry Club. Fradkina, *Zal Dvoryanskogo Sobraniya*, following p. 199.

16. The St. Petersburg Gentry Club, later the Philharmonia. Fradkina, *Zal Dvoryanskogo Sobraniya*, following p. 199.

17. V. Sadovinkov, *Engelhardt House*. Stolpyanskii, *Muzyka i muzitsirovanie*, following p. 128.

18. Aristocrat-cellist: Matvei Vielgorsky. Duleba, *Wieniawski*, 114.

19. John Field. *Pamyati Glinki*, 281.

20. Wunderkind: Henryk Wieniawski Duleba, *Wieniawski*, 18.

21. Petersburg concert. Stolpyanskii, *Muzyka i muzitsirovanie*, following p. 128.

22. Out of the Pale: Anton Rubinstein. Duleba, *Wieniawski*, 114.

23. Bolshoi Stone Theater, St. Petersburg. *Teatr Opery i Baleta imeni. S. M. Kirova*, 7.

24. Andrei Martynov, *Alexandrinsky Theater, St. Petersburg*. Lithograph, 1830s. Shevchen-ko, *Povest Tarasa Shevchenko*, 180.

25. Mikhailovsky Palace and Mikhailovsky Theater (left), St. Petersburg. Lithograph, unknown artist, 1850s. Lotman, *Velikosvetskie obedy*, 287.

26. The Bolshoi (left) and the Maly (right) Theaters, Moscow: *Gosudarstvennyi Akademicheskii Malyi Teatr segodnya*, 1.

27. Charles Didelot, ballet master. Krasovskaya, *Istoriya russkogo baleta*, fig. 10.

28. Catterino Cavos, opera director. Krasovskaya, *Istoriya russkogo baleta*, fig. 13.

29. The Green Carriage taking female ballet pupils to the theater. Deshkova, *Illyustrirovan-naya entsiklopediya baleta*, 182.

30. Audience at the Bolshoi Theater, Moscow. M. Zichi, 1856. Zarubin, *Bolshoi Teatr*, 48.

31. The gesticulating actress. M. Kirzinger, costume sketch. Starikova, *Moskva staro-davnyaya*, 291.

32. Moscow actor: P. S. Mochalov as Meinau in August von Kotzebue's *Misanthropy and Re-pentance*. Laskina, *P. S. Mochalov*, 179.

33. Petersburg actor: P. A. Karatygin as Hamlet. Laskina, *P. S. Mochalov*, 217.

34. A protagonist in a Moscow theatrical duel, 1811: Ekaterina Semënova. N. Utkin, woodcut, 1810. Starikova, *Moskva starodavnyaya*, 367.

35. The other protagonist (see fig. 34): Mlle. Georges. Starikova, *Moskva starodavnyaya*, 367.

36. National dramatist: Nestor Kukolnik. Shevchenko, *Povest Tarasa Shevchenko*, 69.

37. Master of comedy: A. A. Shakhovskoi. Laskina, *P. S. Mochalov*, 125.

38. Vaudevillist: D. T. Lensky. Laskina, *P. S. Mochalov*, 365.

39. Outdoor performance at a country estate. P. E. Zabolotsky, *After Harvesting*, 1822: © State Russian Museum, St. Petersburg.

40. A magnate's favorite. P. I. Zhemchugova-Kovalëva in costume: Starikova, *Moskva starodavnyaya*, 283.

41. Provincial theater in Voronezh, mid-nineteenth century. Anchipolovskii, *Staryi teatr: Voronezh, 1787–1917*, following p. 192.

42. Commercial provincial theater, Kursk, early nineteenth century. Bugrov, *Svet kurskikh ramp*, 1:11.

43. Up from serfdom: M. S. Shchepkin. Senelick, *Serf Actor*, 53.

44. Up from serfdom: L. N. Nikulina-Kositskaya as Katerina in Ostrovsky's *The Storm* (1860). Morov, *Tri veky russkoi stseny*, 198.

45. Out of the provinces: Nadezhda Bogdanova, ballerina. RB, 65.

46. A provincial performance, early nineteenth century. Zhikharëv, *Zapiski sovremennika*, 2: following p. 160.

47. Cultural power broker: A. N. Verstovsky. Laskina, *P. S. Mochalov*, 218.

48. P. Alexandrov, *View of the Academy of Arts*. Lithograph, 1827. Shevchenko, *Povest Tarasa Shevchenko*, 38.

49. G. K. Mikhailov, *The Second Antique Gallery at the Academy of Arts*, 1836. Shevchenko, *Povest Tarasa Shevchenko*, 150.

50. A. N. Ladurner, *Ceremonial Session, Academy of Arts*, 1839. Courtesy of the Tretyakov Gallery, Moscow.

51. Alexei Venetsianov, *Life Drawing Class at the Academy of Arts*, 1825. Fourth Version: © 2004 State Russian Museum, St. Petersburg.

52. Karl Bryullov, *The Last Day of Pompeii*, 1830–33. © 2004 State Russian Museum, St. Petersburg.

53. V. Timm, *Exhibition at the Academy of Arts of A. Ivanov's The Christ Appearing to the People*. Lithograph, 1858. Lotman, *Velikosvetskie obedy*, 298.

54. V. I. Borovikovsky, *Portrait of A. B. Kurakin*, 1801–2. Courtesy of the Tretyakov Gallery, Moscow.

55. G. G. Chernetsov, *Parade, October 6, 1831, on Tsaritsyn Meadow* (Mars Field). RKh, 673.

56. N. I. Podlyuchnikov, *Class at the Moscow Art School.* © 2004 State Russian Museum, St. Petersburg.

57. V. A. Tropinin, *Self-Portrait Against a View of the
Kremlin*, 1844. Courtesy of the Tropinin Museum,
Moscow.

58. Serf as artist. Grigory Soroka, *Threshing Floor*, 1842. © 2004
State Russian Museum, St. Petersburg.

59. *The Iron Foundry*. Unknown artist, early or mid-nineteenth century. IIRR, pl. 73. Vologda Regional Museum.

60. *At the Ale-House*. Unknown artist, mid 1850s. © 2004 State Russian Museum, St. Petersburg.

61. Provincial town scene. Evgraf Krendovskii, *Alexander Square in Poltava*, 1830s–1840s. Courtesy of the Tretyakov Gallery, Moscow.

62. Russian provincial merchant. I. V. Tarkhanov, *Portrait of an Unknown Person*, c. 1837. Kirsanova, *Stsenicheskii kostyum i teatralnaya publika*, 234.

63. A. Orlovsky, *St. Petersburg Winter Market*, 1820s. Lotman, *Velikosvetskie obedy*, 197.

64. An early photo of workers, Moscow: *The Zlakozov Brothers*. Daguerreotype, c. 1856. Courtesy of the State Historical Museum, Moscow.

65. M. M. Zaitsev, *Liberation: Peasants Discussing Alexander II's Emancipation Manifesto of February 9, 1861*. Nikitenko, *Up from Serfdom*, 201.

66. N. G. Dobrolyubov. Dobrolyubov, *Selected Philosophical Essays*, frontispiece.

67. Musical evening at A. G. Rubinstein's. Fradkina, *Zal Dvoryanskogo Sobraniya*, following p. 199.

68. Mily Balakirev of the Mighty Five. *P. I. Chaikovskii*, 60.

69. Alexander Ostrovsky. McReynolds, *Russia at Play*, 31.

70. Vasily Perov, *Easter Procession*, 1861. Courtesy of the Tretyakov Gallery, Moscow.

71. S. M. Tretyakov's Moscow mansion, later the Tretyakov Gallery. Buryshkin, *Moskva kupecheskaya*, following p. 128.

72. Passenger station on the St. Petersburg-Moscow Line. *Zheleznodorozhnyi transport*, following p. 160.

PART IV

Pictures at an Exhibition

Academic Vistas

*[The arts and epics of the Greeks] still afford us artistic pleasure and . . .
in a certain respect they count as a norm and as an unattainable model.
A man cannot become a child again, or he becomes childish. But does he
not find joy in the child's naiveté, and must he himself not strive to
reproduce its truth at a higher stage?*

— *Karl Marx*, Grundrisse

During the eighteenth-century shift from religious to secular art in Russia, European painting, with its canons, conventions, and hierarchy of genres, took up permanent abode in the Russian Empire. By mid-eighteenth century, a buzzing community of foreign and native artists of every sort catered to the symbolic needs of the state and of moneyed patrons. Eventually an energizing center of this activity arose as the Imperial Academy of Arts — both a training ground for an idealized realm of art, and the principal arbiter of taste.[1] When the gradual turn to naturalism or realism began, it involved and was partly shaped by a challenge to the social imagination and to the ideology of art that was created and sustained behind the thick walls of the Imperial Academy of Arts.

House on the Embankment

Like theater, the art world possessed a headquarters, a showplace, and a training center. The Petersburg Academy of Arts (fig. 48) remains to this day the same impressive piece of architecture on the vaunted Neva Embankment that Pushkin exalted in *The Bronze Horseman*. The character of an edifice — the distribution of space; the shape of its rooms, walkways and fenestration; and its entire visual system — can have a profound effect on the lives of its denizens and on what they create. The budding art student from the provinces, Ilya Repin, was transfixed upon seeing it for the first time in 1863. The Academy occupies a massive rectangle 140 meters along the river and 125 meters deep, with four square courtyards at the corners and a huge circular yard in the center, along which run three floors of galleries, offices, sketch rooms, classrooms, and attics. The cupolas on the front and rear facades sit atop, respectively, the Conference Hall, the administrative and ceremonial heart; and the interior Orthodox church, recently reopened after many decades. On the front or river side, twin staircases adorned with classical motifs connect elaborate lower and upper vestibules. The Conference Hall, designed in the 1830s by K. A. Thon, has a ceiling by the history painter Vasily Shebuev and is flanked by halls hung with copies of Raphael and Titian, done by Academy artists Karl Bryullov, Fëdor Bruni, and P. V. Basin. In this space, student work was displayed. Galleries of antique art offered ample space for pupils to copy reproductions (fig. 49). The library and administration have moved since then and faculty apartments are no more. But the present administrators — like those in the Academy of Sciences, Pushkin House, and the University — can still look out on the river Neva. In the basement beneath huge stone arches, the carriage drivers had their quarters. In 1834, Lavr Plakhov, in a rare example of a painter exploring the lower regions of the academic environment, portrayed the coachmen relaxing with pipes, conversation, and drinks.[2]

The Academy, though it had a long prehistory of art school proposals dating back to Peter I, emerged by Senate decree only in 1757 in the reign of Elizabeth. It was the brainchild of Ivan Shuvalov, whose still extant azure blue palace on the corner of Italyanskaya Street and Malaya Sadovaya contained a fine art collection. Empress Catherine II chartered it as an academy in 1764. When Shuvalov went abroad, the pedagogue Ivan Betskoi succeeded him as president and held the post almost to the end of the century. Betskoi, a pallid administrator, presided over a decline due to the budget drain caused by late eighteenth-century wars. The premises were moved in 1769 to several buildings on the Neva. Architects Jean-Baptiste Vallin de la Mothe (builder of the Gostiny Dvor) and A. F. Korkorinov launched the construction of a permanent home. As many as five hundred stonemasons and other workers were put to the task which lasted well into the next century, with many halts for financial reasons.[3] A British observer in the 1840s described the result as one of "those outwardly splendid piles, with ten times more space that in England would be allowed for the same subject, ten times more out of repair, and ten thousand times dirtier." The vastness had to accommodate as many as a thousand residents: professors and administrators and their families, students, painters, and servants, priests, and some models as well. The original nucleus of students from the Moscow University gymnasium and Petersburg soldiers' sons was amplified by children from the foundling homes. Later came a boarding school admitting pupils age five or six for a nine-year course of study. The first class of twenty graduated in 1767. Charter, procedures, and terminology for grades and academic rank were imported from France.[4]

A president, appointed by the monarch, operating more like a university rector than an authoritarian Imperial Theaters chief, was assisted by a vice president, a director (titles varied over time), and a council. One gets an intimate feel for this body from a painting by Adolphe Ladurner around 1840: a ceremonial session in the Conference Hall of about thirty members, middle-aged and elderly uniformed men with sashes, cloaks, and medals sitting solemnly around a long green baize-covered table, with a replica of Michelangelo's Moses in the alcove above them and spectators behind them (fig. 50). Pay and place in the Table of Ranks ranged from the president (rank IV), through the three rectors, six professors, six adjuncts, the conference secretary, and six councillors. Graduates were given rank XIV: they and all their descendants were forever "free and unencumbered people" with certificates expressly forbidding them to be enserfed. As president, Betskoi was followed by a Frenchman, several high-ranking Russian nobles, and, from 1843 onward, members of the royal family. Until Nicholas I, Academy matters were largely handled with little interference from on high.[5]

Normal squabbles among faculty, administration, and sometimes government marked the first two decades of the nineteenth century. The high-handed Count Marie-Gabriel Choiseul-Gouffier, appointed president by Tsar Paul, took over the apartments of the director, an assistant rector, and a councilor to combine into one big flat for himself. He was later expelled by Paul for reasons unknown. His successor, the learned and well-traveled millionaire and Maecenas of the arts Count A. S. Stroganov (1733–1811), ruled in 1800–1810. A great indirect contribution to the arts was the sponsorship of his serf and probably illegitimate son, the noted architect Andrei Voronikhin, whom he had sent to Europe to study and had freed in 1786. Voronikhin later designed the Kazan Cathedral on the Nevsky. Count Stroganov's largely friction-free

term allowed an influx of serfs and in 1803 secured the exemption of townsmen from tax and draft obligations, a notable boost to lower-class enrollments. Between the death of Stroganov in 1811 and the advent of Olenin in
1817, the Academy had no director and it came under the umbrella of the
Ministry of Education.[6]

Alexei Olenin, president 1817–43, a versatile figure, did not achieve distinction in any branch of culture. Yet his enthusiasm as an archaeologist and
antiquarian and his lofty connections enabled him to contribute to many
fields: as classical theater decorator, head of the Petersburg Imperial Library,
and director of the Academy of Arts. Since he was slightly deformed and a
participant in literary battles, Olenin became the butt of cruel jokes (Pushkin
called him a "cypher on legs"). His conservative stance on some issues guaranteed scorn from Soviet scholars, one of whom credited Olenin for reforms but
saw him simplistically as an exemplar of Tsar Alexander I's period of reaction.
Olenin cracked down on discipline inside the Academy and cleaned up the
mess he inherited: dirt, foul air and food, a poor clinic, and fiscal corruption.
He cut the number of pensioners sent to Rome for study, tightened the grading
system, and fired some faculty. Olenin's most embarrassing moment involved
the conference secretary and vice president Alexander Labzin (1776–1825),
who was also at the center of a swirl of Russian mysticism and Freemasonry.
When Olenin added prominent government and court figures to the roster of
honorary members and invited them to special dinners and exhibitions, Labzin sarcastically suggested at a council meeting that if the Academy sought
people close to the tsar they should invite his coachman. By not punishing
Labzin at once for this remark, Olenin fell into trouble for a time but eventually survived. Since Labzin was pleasant only to inferiors and liked to help
students during examinations, he was dismissed ostensibly for this also and
exiled to Tobolsk in Siberia. It was said that his pupils accompanied him to the
city gates when he left St. Petersburg.[7]

After Tsar Nicholas took the throne, the Academy was placed under the
Ministry of the Court. In 1843, the tsar's son-in-law Duke Maximilian of
Leuchtenberg (1817–52), son of Joséphine de Beauharnais, took up the presi-
dency, though he was constantly absent on military duty. His widow, Maria
Nikolaevna, who succeeded her husband as president (1852–76), usually did
not veto decisions of the council. When she tried in 1853 to get an academic
appointment for an architect without his taking an examination, she was
overruled. Yet her presence as a royal personage clearly affected decisions.

Tsar Nicholas intruded vigorously in the world of art. A fairly good drafts-
man, he had strong opinions on matters artistic. Contrary to received opinion,
as a child Nicholas spent more time drawing than with war toys. Not a day

went by without his sketching officers, high-ranking noblemen, houses, and churches. He apparently loved this activity at least as much as martial matters.[8] As emperor, Nicholas often bypassed the constituted authorities of the Academy as he advised, visited, preached, scolded, promoted and dismissed personnel, and ruled on admissions and curricula. He introduced an academy police detail and more stringent disciplinary punishments. Nicholas was in fact a petty tyrant of the arts, though his tyranny did not seem all that petty to those whose careers and even personal freedom were concerned. Art schools, almost by definition authoritarian, passed down a heritage from the great masters to a new cohort of practitioners. Innovation was discouraged until one had gotten hold of basic principles. Students who had innate talent and who were willing to work and to obey the rules could do very well. Under Nicholas, the Academy itself acquired more power in the art world at large: it now dictated the art curricula of the schools and replaced locals with its own graduates.[9]

Since Olenin's successors were relatives of the tsar, the real manager of the Academy became Privy Councillor Count Fëdor Petrovich Tolstoy (1782–1873), who served as its vice president, 1828–59. An aristocrat who declined a career as a naval officer to go into art, he was bitterly criticized by his family for dishonoring his social class by "consorting with who knows what kind of German and Russian professors." The comment reflects the scorn in certain circles of any kind of teaching or creative "work." Conversely, some artists and teachers looked askance at noble would-be artists. The sculptor Martos saw Tolstoy as someone aspiring "to be simultaneously a count, an officer, and an artist which" — in his view — was impossible for a nobleman. As professor of sculpture and engraving, Tolstoy specialized in reliefs, medals, coins, silhouettes, and patriotic medallions commemorating the events of 1812, mostly executed in a brand of lifeless classicism. But one of his silhouettes, *Taking a Recruit*, is as bleak as anything ever done on the subject, showing a cart driver turning away from the scene, the recruiter with raised fist, and the serf recruit kneeling and imploring.[10] A family portrait done by Tolstoy in 1830 shows a huge art-filled flat inside the Academy which became a nesting place for many a cultural figure of the age. Tolstoy's cultivated wife, who spoke many languages, presided over a salon that hosted his young cousin Lev Tolstoy, Pushkin, Alexander Nikitenko, Nestor Kukolnik, and renowned artists. On Sundays, he invited students who, his daughter relates, were grateful for the chance to mingle with great artists at his home. One of them recalled being "on a par" with the upper classes for the first time in his life: "you felt like you were somebody." An enlightened man of his age, Tolstoy ran a fairly open admissions policy and valued talent above rank.[11]

The faculty was a mixed lot, originally brought in from abroad, which included at least one Jew, Karl Lebrecht (Leberekht, 1755–1827). Stroganov recruited Russians from all classes except serfs, including the sons of an admiral and an ex-minister, a clockmaker, and a factory manager.[12] The best students went on to become faculty. In 1830, a professor of the first rank earned three thousand rubles per annum and one of the second rank, twenty-five hundred. These were lower than those of university professors but were supplemented by free accommodations and fuel, and with commissions for their work.[13] In the late eighteenth and early nineteenth centuries, some of the professors — including Borovikovsky and Levitsky — joined Masonic lodges. A Free Society of Lovers of Literature, Sciences, and the Arts founded in 1801 gathered a secret core of admirers of the exiled radical Alexander Radishchev. Later groups clustered loosely around the Decembrists.[14] But neither this nor any other cultural establishment, such as the Imperial Theater system or the concert societies, ever became a hotbed of radicals as would the universities some day. Throughout the reign of Nicholas I, the Academy of Arts remained remarkably stable — a stability that some would read as moribund rigidity.

Classes in Art

The most vexing issue facing the Academy in the early nineteenth century revolved around social class and admissions, particularly that of serfs. The Academy was not unique in this. In the new universities founded under Alexander I, it took most of two decades of conflicting resolutions and variant interpretations to resolve the issue. In practice, few serfs could apply to university since they required both permission to do so and an academic background for the examinations. University rules eventually allowed the admission of serfs only with prior promise of freedom from their owner which would be granted after completion of the full curriculum and with permission of the Senate. University students, members of the privileged classes, lived in and enjoyed a stipend. The nonserf obligated classes possessed a lower status, though they pursued the same course of study.[15]

But the Academy predated the new universities and thus already had serfs for training, though their status was ambiguous. In the eighteenth century, Shuvalov, in the first of many rulings against admitting serfs, argued that "since all the arts are free [he used words derived from both *volya* and *svoboda*], then serfs are not to be admitted."[16] This implied that art was an essentialized property unclaimable by the unfree — even though thousands of serfs were practicing music, theatrical, and decorative arts all over Russia. In practice, the long years and rigid course amidst cold and hunger, combined with social prejudice, did not greatly attract the upper classes in the early decades; and the student body comprised largely serfs, ex-serfs, children of serfs, petty clerks and clerics, soldiers' sons, peasants of all kinds, and orphans — all males. Under Stroganov, serf enrollment increased but faced contradictory rulings. Serfs were admitted only if their owners agreed to free those awarded a gold medal. Yet they could be pulled out by their masters at any time before the Academy authorities awarded them a medal or teaching certificate which automatically freed them — a frustration to the Academy and a personal tragedy for the unprotected serf artists.[17] As with some serf musicians and actors, the fall from euphoria and an exposure to refinement back down to the servile life led many serf artists to disillusion, drink, and sometimes suicide. Yet the inflow continued: serf owners with pretensions to culture had little need for university graduates; but they did need artists and they pressured the Academy to admit them.

The issue came to a head on October 23, 1817, when the tsar decreed through the Minister of Education that no more serfs were to be admitted to the Academy of Arts. Olenin justified the decree in an epistolary duel with the powerful General Arakcheev who had become virtual viceroy of Russia after 1815. Arakcheev depended upon serf artists and architects for the construction and decoration of elaborate buildings and grounds to satisfy the "dreamy poetic" and utopian side of his autocratic personality. Art and despotism held no contradiction for Arakcheev. An artist in one of his Military Colonies sketched a picture of the general descending into hell. Like other nobles, he supplemented the talent of hired specialists with that of serfs whom he sent to the Academy for training. Ivan Semënov, a serf architect at Gruzino, frequently beaten by his master, was enrolled in the Academy where he eventually won a medal (1859) and became a professor. Prior to 1817, whenever Olenin needed intercession on behalf of his artists, Arakcheev had assisted him.[18]

But in a letter of December 16, 1817, Olenin spelled out to Arakcheev why one of his serfs was being returned to him. Said Olenin: exclusion of serfs is good for the Academy, for its remaining students, for the serf owners, and ultimately for the serfs as well. To be an artist without a noble and elevated spirit is impossible, he wrote. Free students who at a tender age have to study and live with immoral people are denied that elevated spirit. Unfortunately, "the foulest vices are characteristic of the bonded or enslaved status, inherited down the generations." Keeping free students out of such company would preserve the Academy's reputation. By circumlocution, Olenin tried to tell Arakcheev that the Academy was not a vocational school for training merely skilled craftsmen. Echoing Shuvalov, he wrote:

> In the Academy, we are producing artists who — due to the very essence of their calling — must absolutely be instilled with ennobling thoughts and sensibilities for the pure enjoyment and exaltation of art; artists whose hearts and minds we must shape, to whom we must speak incessantly of freedom of thought, freedom in the choice of subjects, and of the free arts — for thus they have been called from time immemorial by all enlightened peoples.

A serf at the Academy, argued Olenin, had to work and reside for years with teachers and fellow students who were learning "about freedom, the concept of personal freedom, and its necessary connection to the free arts, and the rights of the artists." They are pointed to success, rank, and freedom of choice. But if the serf student has to go back to the dead end of unfreedom on the estate, despair and even hatred of the gifts he has acquired emerges, and he turns to drink, an evil fate for the serf himself (and of course — Olenin does not say it — a bane for his owner). Olenin clearly shared the views of his class, articulated in the eighteenth century by Mikhail Shcherbatov among others, that education for the lower orders was harmful to society. Olenin also played to Arakcheev's loathing of alcohol, to say nothing of his hatred of disobedience or revolt. Olenin's chief concern was to keep serfs out of contact with free students, though he was willing to allow serf pupils to study informally with Academy professors. His policy, he believed, would spread knowledge to the people, keep down vice, provide good craftsmen for the landowners, secure some monetary gains for the professors, and get the serfs to accept "the humble lot where fate has landed them."[19]

Olenin had a complex view of serfdom. In 1842, he himself possessed 1,845 serfs and his wife owned 420.[20] He recognized the need someday to abolish serfdom, but he publicly agreed with those who opposed any sudden or wholesale emancipation.[21] Historian Frederick Starr is right that Olenin's 1817 arguments and his enrollment policies were meant to upgrade art from a craft to a profession.[22] But the decision to exclude serfs was not his alone: his letter to Arakcheev, dated December 16, 1817, came months after the October decree and one day before an identical decision was taken in the Imperial Theater School — namely that all its incoming pupils had to be free. The ruling from the top was followed ten years later by Nicholas I's ban on admitting serfs into the universities. Olenin's views contained contradictions. Like Karamzin and many other nobles, he thought the peasants had been corrupted by serfdom and were thus unfit for freedom,[23] and some passages of the correspondence imply that the corruption was hereditary and unredeemable. Yet Olenin stated openly that he would be happy to accept talented serfs if their owners would free them: he could remold them if they were both free and subject to his discipline. Two ex-serfs became trusted assistants in his ethnographic and antiquarian expeditions: A. I. Ermolaev and F. G. Solntsev.

In 1817 Olenin asked all landowners who had serfs at the Academy to free them, and a few did so. The serfs of those who refused he expelled with the aid of police. Even those who had finished course work and were waiting for stipend announcements were returned to their masters, some to become house painters, cooks, and lackeys. Before long, under various guises, serfs began infiltrating the Academy again. Though it was strictly illegal, professors would take on serf pupils, give them access to the Academy services, and even get them into the Hermitage to copy the masters. Upon Olenin's death in 1843, the ban was reiterated.[24]

Olenin reduced the student body from about 300 to 160, lowered the number of nonserf lower-class admissions, and cut down the curriculum from twelve to nine and a half years. Courses in dance and music were made mandatory as a runway to gentility. Data on social origins from a limited but representative sample of graduates show that in the eighteenth century, a bit under 25 percent of Academy students were sons of officers, officials, or nobles (though the categories overlap); about 31 percent were sons of artists, musicians, merchants, and artisans; and about 43 percent were sons of serfs, state peasants, servants, clerks, priests, and (more than half of this category) soldiers and sailors. In the same period, the most successful artists in terms of reputation and commissions came from the lower two categories. Orphans abounded in these groupings, as they did in the early years of the Theater School. In the period 1800–1830 the top category jumped drastically, especially in the case of officials, from about 25 to about 44 percent. The middle group increased only slightly to over 33 percent; within it, the number of artisan children fell sharply and that of artists' children rose. The percentage of lower-class graduates fell sharply (from about 43 to about 22 percent) as admission requirements were tilted against them, although the number of serf children rose from fourteen to thirty-one. No soldiers' sons graduated. The pattern continued roughly from 1833 to 1839 (there is a gap in the data for 1839–50). For the years 1850–55, compared to the period 1800–1830, the top category fell by about 2 percentage points; the middle group fell from about 33 to near 26 percent; and the lowest group rose from about 21 to about 31 percent. In the lowest ranges, the townsmen swamped all the rest and the children of serfs were down from about 12 to about 5 percent.[25]

The Academy's student body resembled that of the Theater School only in the presence of art and stage "dynasties" — more for actors than artists — and in the release of obligated classes from government taxes, military service, and other burdens. The number of art students from the lower orders took a severe dip in the first three decades of the century but was on the rise in the early 1850s. Unlike the Theater School, the Academy always enrolled gentry. Their number grew significantly in the early nineteenth century, though middle- and lower-ranking officials outnumbered them. Like the universities, the Academy admitted only males. There were art courses for women in St. Petersburg in the 1840s and 1850s but I have found no details. One woman, Marfa Dovgaleva, managed to get a silver medal from the Academy. Sofiya Sukhovo-Kobylina (1825–67), sister of a well-known playwright and of the writer Evgenia Tur, received a silver medal in 1849 and a gold one in 1853 and 1854 for landscape, the first woman to do so. The Theater School grew increasingly Russian; the Academy was always mostly so. At least one Polish Jew, Samuel Mikhelson, a townsman from Kiev, was admitted to art classes.[26]

The Academy made a distinction, modeled on university statutes, between regular students and auditors. The former came up through the boarding school for pupils from ages five or six in a nine-year course of general education and art. Pupils wore a uniform of blue jacket, short pants, white stockings, and shoes with lyre-shaped buckles. The best of these were admitted to the Academy proper for a six-year course in painting, sculpture, architecture, or applied arts. The rest enrolled in what the French academy called *moindres métiers* — metal and woodwork and other manual arts. The school began with a triennial intake of about sixty. The admission age for the boarding school was regularly raised, and the length of study reduced; by 1830 the age was fourteen for a six-year curriculum. Regular students lived in, received scholarships, and followed a broad curriculum at the end of which they received a certificate, a government rank of XII (of the fourteen in the Table of Ranks), and became eligible for a pensionate to the Academy's branch in Rome. In 1798, the Academy opened a drawing school for auditors who lived outside the Academy and paid for their course work; they studied side by side with students but in a narrower curriculum. High-quality work could move an auditor into student status.[27]

The student round began at five A.M. with prayer and a Spartan breakfast of bread and Neva water, followed by classroom study, a hearty lunch of soup and meat, more prayer, rest, and classes. Misbehavior was endemic. One external student explained his constant tardiness by the melting ice on the Neva River that he had to cross. Olenin curtailed visits and socializing and ordered jail and expulsion for misconduct and for student protests about the food. In winter, an ice rink and slides were erected in the courtyards. Music and theater added light moments. Stag dancing was permitted, and amateur drama groups, using female relatives of the students, performed comedies and vaudevilles for the staff.[28] The gentry adapted with ease to the magnificent surroundings. Boarding students whose parents resided far away had to endure homesickness. Those from the lower classes faced the social tensions of studying with more privileged boys and probably felt the gulf between their station in life and the elevated ideals of the curriculum. To alleviate the situation, a later official, Fëdor Lvov, ran a salon at the Academy for student commoners, to replace the habits of the "country tavern" with good manners and social intercourse. As a whole, student life was more bearable than that in military academies or seminaries.[29]

The mixture of everyday bleakness and the light of opportunity may be illustrated by the experiences of a few lower-class art students. Lavrenty Seryakov (1824–81), son of a serf, suffered a rough childhood as a cantonist in the Military Colonies where he witnessed the brutal crushing of a revolt. A stroke of fortune got him sent to St. Petersburg for clerical work and he ended up in a topography office. Odoevsky and Kukolnik discovered his talent for wood engraving (as did Bulgarin) and he gradually moved into intelligentsia circles. When Seryakov requested permission to attend the Academy of Arts, his chief responded: "How dare you even consider it?" Kukolnik petitioned the minister of war who in turn got a favorable response from the tsar. In 1847, at the age of twenty-three, Seryakov was admitted. Through the veil of success, Seryakov later recalled the humiliating treatment serf pupils endured in the 1840s. One false move on their part, he claimed, and they could be sent home to serfdom or, worse, sent off to be soldiers. Seryakov himself won the status of Free Artist and from 1858 spent six years in France and Italy where he won some acclaim. He returned to Russia and was named an Academician.[30]

Fëdor Solntsev (1801–92), son of a serf from Yaroslav Province, had a knack for drawing from nature and copying popular prints. The low level of teaching in his village led him to aspire to the Academy of Arts. Luckily his father, granted freedom to travel and work by the master, served as cashier at the Imperial Theaters, and he used his connections to get his son into the Academy. Solntsev recalled being whipped for misbehavior, but said that gentry boys committed the wildest pranks. When Olenin became president, he noticed Solntsev's talent and hired him as an assistant in archeological work. Solntsev went on to become a scholar of antiquities and restorer of art and sculpture in Novgorod, Kiev, and the Moscow Kremlin. In his later years he was grandly feted by state and society as an archaeological pioneer.[31]

Taras Shevchenko, whose travails as a serf artist are related in chapter 8, got his freedom in 1838 and studied at the Academy until 1843 with fellow students who were mostly townsmen, merchants, peasants, and even serfs. The future poet recalled close teacher-pupil relations, especially with Karl Bryullov who had helped him gain his freedom and with whom he frequently dined. Shevchenko earned some money from portraits, though sometimes the client reneged on payment or offered food in stead of a fee. But the headiness of his newly won freedom led Shevchenko to carouse sometimes in various haunts on Vasilevsky Island. The Berlin Tavern and the restaurant of Carolina Jürgens were meeting places for students, poor clerks, and slovenly artists wearing long hair, beards, and wide-awake hats with ample brims who crowded in to see the celebrated Bryullov. For Shevchenko, basking in freedom, these were "unforgettable golden days." Having tasted the magic of life in the Academy, Shevchenko traveled back to his birthplace in Ukraine where the misery, injustice, and cruel treatment of serfs led him into radicalism.[32]

Gentry students suffered none of the corporal punishment or social discrimination of their humbly born classmates. The Guards officer F. F. Lvov, brother of the composer and later an Academy official, recalled that many of his fellow officers studied at the Academy in the 1830s. Their commander, Grand Duke Mikhail Pavlovich, brother of Tsar Nicholas, once told them that "Russia needs officers, not scholars and artists"; yet he encouraged drawing classes in the army. Lvov summoned up in his memoirs how the students crowded outside the classrooms in order to get good seats and how their ardor for the arts warmed them up in the drafty hallways. When not in class, they hurried off to the opera — a ferry or sleigh ride across the Neva — and on returning had to bite their tongues to stop singing arias from the then popular *Robert le diable* and *Fenella*.[33]

Painters followed a fixed progression: copying sketches, busts, and live models first, and then studying grouping and composition. The models, mostly peasants, received in the Olenin years a remarkable three hundred rubles a year plus clothing and meals for both modeling and clean-up duties. The Academy, like its French prototype, stressed draftsmanship, linear perspective, modeling, stereotyped figures, scrupulous imitation of small details, archaeological accessories, narrative, textual sources, and especially *fini*, the "finish" — with line dominant over color, no traces of brush strokes, no ragged edges.[34] The well-known master Alexei Venetsianov captured the atmosphere in the life drawing class at the Academy (fig. 51). Disobeying his instructions to offer a perspective study of the large semicircular auditorium where students were working with a nude model, and anticipating his eventual drift from academic procedures, Venetsianov offered instead cartoon surveys of a score of students, models, and professors talking, drawing, looking around, and loafing in a very informal milieu.[35] Venetsianov conveyed a real sense of place as the written sources rarely do: the large space as workplace, social gathering, and site of order, disorder, and hierarchy.

Graduates of the Academy could take a number of different routes, depending on their performance. All received a certificate of good behavior and competence from the conference secretary and the council. Major and minor gold and silver medals attested to the relative grading on the final examination. Students were assigned themes on which a sketch had to be made within twenty-four hours, followed by a canvas to be executed in one or two years without diverging from the sketch. The major gold medalist became an "Artist" (and after 1840 "Class Artist I"), with the government rank of XIV and the right to study for six years in Europe. Upon return, usually from Rome, those considered worthy could join the faculty of the Academy. The silver medallist, "Class Artist II," got no rank until he found employment. Those who passed without a medal became Non-Class Artists or "free artists," who, like all those above, were exempt from the military or compulsory state service and payment of the poll tax. They and their children were henceforth exempt from enserfment. All who received exemptions from obligations required a "class discharge" (*uvolnitelnoe svidetelstvo*) or release document from their home province governors and approval of the Senate. Graduates of all ranks were given preference over nongraduates in government commissions and public works. The Academy of Arts produced an estimated two thousand artists in all fields from its birth until the emancipation of the serfs in 1861.[36]

The Academy drew on the lower classes, as did the state, the army, and the landowners. Nicholas, though always ambivalent about educating commoners, in fact wanted an army of painters and ballerinas. Writing in the late Stalinist period, the Soviet art historian A. V. Savinov claimed that the Academy of Arts was the most democratic institution of higher education in Russia. By that he did not, of course, mean self-rule but rather the proportion of lower-class students and the relative lack of special patronage and favoritism.[37] There are two ways of looking at the social mobility which Savinov stresses. From the viewpoint of the rulers who owned the school, the Academy was a conduit from one kind of service (and servility) into another; from soldiering or serf labor into the ranks of artists, most of whom would teach or do pictures for the state or for gentry patrons. Their status varied from low-paid art instructors in the schools to professors and highly paid portraitists. Those in the higher range certainly possessed more social prestige, if not more fame, than actors. For example, Moscow merchant clubs in the 1850s included artists with Academy diplomas as regular guests along with professors and physicians — an honor that few actors enjoyed, Mikhail Shchepkin being an exception.[38] From the viewpoint of the talented poor lad who managed to win success, the training and the degree or medal were a ticket to a new life. The polarity and intermittent clash of these two perspectives shaped the social history of the Academy until the emancipation.

Of Gods and Heroes

What kind of art did students and professors produce for Russia? A fixed feature of the early Russian intelligentsia was their exposure to foreign ideas through reading imported materials and extended visits to Europe, especially the German university towns. Upon their descent from the exalted climes of Kant, Schelling, and Hegel and their return to Russia, the men of this generation virtually invented the main currents of Russian intellectual history. The esthetic parallel emanating from Russians in Rome has captured much less attention. Rome, because of its classical and Renaissance traditions, its landscape and light, had long before 1800 become a Mecca for European artists and creative people. The artistic road to Rome opened in seventeenth-century France and its status as cultural center achieved mythic proportions from the writings of Europeans who visited or lived there, such as Winckelmann, Goethe, and Byron, to name only a few. The aura of the Eternal City was enhanced by Mme. de Staël's popular *Corinne,* based on an 1807 tour. The novel is soaked in an atmosphere of art, architecture, ancient streets, historical figures, and active painters and sculptors such as Antonio Canova. The Russian Academy of Arts chose Italy as its principal source of artistic standards and it maintained regular contact with Rome from the late eighteenth century onward. Generations of creative Russian figures — painters and sculptors in particular — were shaped in the cultural crucible on the Tiber River.[39]

Aside from the few artists rich enough to finance their sojourns, the three roads to Rome for Russian students began with private patrons or owners; the Society for the Encouragement of Artists, a sponsoring organization; and, for most, an Academy pensionate. Awardees were assigned to a prominent local advisor, such as Vincenzo Camuccini or the Dane Berthel Thorwaldsen. Fëdor Matveev (1758–1826), the first Russian artist to take up regular residence in Italy, died there. F. Ya. Alexeev (1753–1824) gained fame by applying the techniques of the much-admired Canaletto's Venetian waterscapes to the Neva. A golden age opened with Orest Kiprensky (1783–1836) who lived in Rome from 1816 to 1822. Silvestr Shchedrin, arriving in 1818, become intoxicated with Italy. Then came Fëdor Bruni, Bryullov, and — eventually the most famous of all — Alexander Ivanov. In the salons of expatriates such as Zinaida Volkonskaya artists mixed with other creative figures. Almost all the painters executed landscapes and cityscapes in and around Rome and sometimes Venice and Naples. Although the usual pensionate was three years, starting in the 1820s some Russian artists remained a decade or more, steeping themselves in antiquity and the Renaissance. For them, Italy was a museum of the fine arts, the mammoth original of the reproductions they had studied in back on the Neva.[40]

One of the earliest Russian photographers, Sergei Levitsky, in 1845 took a group picture of the Russian art colony in Rome, Nikolai Gogol among them, wearing wide-awake hats, voluminous cloaks, walking sticks, and other paraphernalia of the era's romantic poses. The photo clearly suggests an atmosphere of bohemianism and emigré abandon that Russian artists at home did not possess. The writer Elizaveta Kologrivova applied the popular romantic theme of the eternal struggle between love and art to the life of a Russian artist in Rome in a short story, "Lady of the House" (1843), which pits personal romance against the worship of pure beauty. Real life was not quite so ethereal. Bryullov was having marital troubles and imbibing heavily. His friends led scandalous lives. The painter Orest Kiprensky drank too much, and the sculptor Nikolai Ramazanov caused such an uproar that he was ordered back to Russia under guard.[41] Tsar Nicholas, hearing bad reports about pensioners abroad, declared that if the miscreants had already shown signs of moral deformity at the Academy, then the council members who had endorsed them should repay the wasted money, including their return fares. In the 1840s, he established a committee to oversee the Rome pensioners, went there himself, and assumed the role of an inspector general, praising, rebuking, and commanding artists: "You [*ty*], Vorobev, your work could not be better"; "you Ramazanov, make your nymphs more modest."[42] The Italian romance peaked in the 1830s and 1840s and, as the Roman phalanx returned to assume academic posts on the Neva, had the result of reinforcing the classical-historical style of painting at the Academy.

The hierarchy of genres and a supporting ideology dated back to the Renaissance when *historia* stood as the highest category. By the mid-seventeenth century, the French Academy was ranking pictorial narrative above other genres. Mythic and real people of power, linked together by an idea, a story, a lesson, or a drama outranked the prosaic small beer of still life, trompe l'oeil, and landscape. Academic pedagogy ruled that perfection had been reached in Greece and Rome and that the Italian Renaissance had kept alive the eternal laws of the beautiful. The *style historique* gained further authority in eighteenth-century Germany from Winckelmann, Lessing, and Schiller, among others. That style in Britain revived when the Royal Academy was founded in 1769 precisely to train a school of history painting as the art form that conveyed public virtues displayed in classical postures of the great heroes and gods of antiquity. The terms "noble" and "heroic" were employed to stress the lofty character of this art. Art lovers revered those classical worlds — shrouded in myths and embellished by ancient drama — of Trojans, Athenians, Spartans, and Romans, locked in war, adventure, and tragedies of hopeless love and helpless struggle against nature and the gods.[43] Taras Shevchenko, in *The Artist,* quoted his friend and mentor Bryullov on Greek and Roman history: "Everything in it is simplicity and refinement."[44]

Three Russian historical painters achieved notoriety in their time. Fëdor (Fidelio) Bruni (1801–75), born in Milan the son of a Swiss artist, traveled to Russia with his family and entered the Academy of Arts. Sent to Rome in 1818, Bruni eventually garnered recognition from several Italian academies. Zinaida Volkonskaya had him do a portrait of her posing as Tancred, the doomed hero-king of Boccaccio, Tasso, Voltaire, and Rossini. Bruni's fame derived from classical renditions, the best known of which is the vivid *Death of Camilla, Horatio's Sister* (1824). Though Livy is the original source, Bruni may have been inspired by Corneille's *Horace* performed on the Petersburg stage in 1817, or by Fernando Paër's 1799 opera on the theme which was also well known in Russia. Horatio, one of the famous three brothers, has returned from war to find his sister lamenting the death of her betrothed whom he has just slain. Horatio responds to her grief by putting her to death. This canvas is a veritable textbook of classical composition with its coulisse frame, bas-relief treatment, perspective, positioning of groups, and use of the diagonal for narrative effect. The stoical Horatio occupies the center, his head is lighted, and the lines converge on him. Little sympathy is evoked for the hapless Camilla who lies in anguish at his feet.[45]

Alexander Ivanov (1806–58) executed classical studies before he began his more famous works. *Priam Begs Achilles for Hector's Body* (1824) is a startling psychological reconstruction of Achilles' ambiguous sexual orientation. Ivanov, himself a homosexual, embedded into a standard historical frame the kind of subtleties, complexities, and contradictions that abound in private spheres; and the painting's level of intimacy suggests realistic genre rather than history or myth. Achilles, modeled by a strikingly beautiful Italian boy, is presented sitting in victorious judgment as Priam in deep supplication requests that he may bury the body of his slain son, Hector. With lips curled in merciless contempt, Achilles beholds the father of the killer of his beloved Patrocles. One of his fists is clenched in rage, the other furled in an effeminate pose. The mixture of fury and desolation over a lost love is unmistakable. No greater contrast can be found than in the picture by A. I. Notbek on the same subject done in the same year, with its stiff posing of Achilles in a painfully uninteresting composition.[46]

The most renowned Russian painter of the age in his own time, Karl Bryullov (originally Brudeleau, 1799–1852), was descended from Huguenots who fled France and ended in St. Petersburg. His father taught at the Academy; and the student Karl's talent won him a stipend for Rome. During his first sojourn in 1823–24, Bryullov, Prince G. G. Gagarin, the architect Konstantin Thon, and one of the Dolgoruky boys performed Fonvizen's *The Minor* at home to entertain the Russian colony and to keep up their Russian. Later Bryullov fell into loose living, but his creative powers remained unhindered. He steeped himself in history, literature, and classical learning, devouring Scott, Schiller, Shakespeare, and the historian Leopold von Ranke. Moving with ease among an international aristocracy, this nonnoble painter illustrated how talent could sometimes transcend rank.[47]

Bryullov's masterpiece, *The Last Day of Pompeii* (1830–33), fused classical dignity in death with romantic terror (fig. 52). The painter chose a well-documented event in Roman history: the eruption of Vesuvius. Gagarin attests that Bryullov was inspired both by a visit to the excavations and by his friend Giovanni Pacini's 1825 opera, *L'ultimo giorno di Pompeii*. The Pacini opera, dedicated to his (and probably Bryullov's) sometime lover Yuliya Samoilova (née Countess Julie de Pahlen or Julia von der Pahlen), melodramatically re-created a fatal historical day. The libretto weaves an elaborate plot about ancient Romans that concludes with a fiery finale, the voices simultaneously and repetitively thundering the words "the last day of Pompeii is written in the heavens" and "we are fleeing, we are fleeing." Although Bryullov drew from Pliny, his canvas invokes no single narrative, and viewers are clearly expected to construct their own for the imminent victims of the mountainous explosion. Both the opera and Bryullov's picture are examples of disaster art, taking their place alongside the era's romantic treatments of floods, massacres, ship-wrecks, fires, giant battles, and mental agonies.[48]

Pompeii, going well beyond its Russian classical forebears, employs acting poses of the classical stage but also naturalistic gestures. However static it may appear to modern viewers, this canvas — the *Medusa* raft and the Chios massacre hurled back two millennia — took the Russian and European public by storm. *Pompeii*'s original commissioner is unknown, but it was sold to the Urals millionaire industrialist, Anatoly Demidov (1812–70), who presented it to Tsar Nicholas. Herzen subjectively read the canvas as suggesting the impending doom of the corrupt tsarist system in the aftermath of the Decembrist Revolt.[49] Viewers in the capital however responded with enthusiasm, not fear. *Pompeii* prompted a flood of history paintings as well as some popular cultural responses. In 1840, Nikolai Nekrasov in *Pantheon* anonymously satirized an imaginary provincial who thought the painting depicted a fire in Tula. Entrepreneur Christian Leman mounted a tableau on the theme at his Petersburg circus.[50] The painting now hangs proudly in the Russian Museum, still exerting its eerie spell on Russian viewers and foreign visitors, even those who prefer to hurry on to see the once-hidden works of the Russian avant-garde.

Bryullov's triumphant return from Rome in 1835 had a dual character. The success of *Pompeii* bolstered conservatism at the Academy where he taught until 1849, yet the painting's author tried to shift away from antique body studies which, he said, obscured the beauties of the living body and became a "lifeless" exercise. In 1836 he painted the twenty-seven-year-old Kukolnik at the peak of his theatrical fame. Savinov, perhaps driven by his prior opinion of the subject, stated baldly that Bryullov captured the "superficiality of [Kukolnik's] nature."[51] Superficiality there may have been, but surely this affectionate work shows no sign of it. Justly celebrated are Bryullov's several portraits of Yuliya Samoilova, one of which, with her foster daughter, stresses the "quasi-maternal civilizing role" of this eminent socialite.[52] Bryullov, as a European celebrity, raised the status of painters in Russian society. As a charismatic personality, he lived high, entertained lavishly, and assisted in the manumission of at least three serf artists. An admiring poet saw fit to record her single meeting with him in a verse full of tender admiration. The censor Nikitenko, who dined with him in 1840, was asked by a high official: "is he really a drunkard? They're all that way, these actors and artists."[53] Some contemporaries charged Bryullov, like his drinking friends Glinka and Kukolnik, with a moral decay that ruined him as an artist.[54] Bryullov suffered neglect for a long time after his death in 1852, but an 1899 jubilee marked a minor revival of his reputation. The composer Alexander Ippolitov-Ivanov wrote a cantata in his honor and a pious cult began to take shape.[55]

Biblical and mythological themes fell under the rubric of history painting and proliferated during the reign of Catherine II. Huge allegorical canvases of deities, nymphs, and satyrs flourished as part of the European rage for such subjects and because they could be folded into the panegyric utopia and "paradise myth" surrounding eighteenth-century monarchs. Savinov claims that after the great popular uprising of Pugachëv in the 1770s, mythology in art rose in significance, presumably to deflect attention from reality. He cites no evidence of intention. But deflection was certainly functioning via the classical pastorale or Arcadia, a dreamlike landscape inhabited by carefree humans and semihumans whose main business was pleasure—erotic, musical, or simply leisurely. Its key figure, the shepherd, was the most unlaboring laborer in all of art. As in theater, the systematic banishment of real toil in a rural setting, a major feature of eighteenth-century landscape painting, came to represent for critics the underlying falsity of that art.[56]

The biblical subtheme of the historical genre appealed to painters for its rich and pious narratives. But by the nineteenth century, the genre had declined in quality. A. E. Egorov (1776?–1851), the son of a Kalmyk prisoner of war, after passing through a foundling home, became a boy genius at the Academy and then attained great success as a professor of history painting. His most

famous work, the monumental *Torment of the Savior* (1814) won wide acclaim. In 1840, Egorov incurred the enmity of Tsar Nicholas I in his painting
of church images and was dismissed after nearly a lifetime at the Academy.
Bruni's late contribution is the grandiose *Brass Serpent*, which he worked on
in Rome and St. Petersburg between 1826 and 1841. By the time of its completion almost a decade after Bryullov's *Pompeii*, this anachronistic biblical canvas, though full of romantic horror, could no longer shock.[57] How utterly
different the fate of the masterpiece created by Alexander Ivanov, a seer and a
seeker who spent the critical years of his creative life in Rome, 1831–58, and
worked there on *Christ Appearing to the People* for more than a decade. This
awkward large-scale narrative canvas is more interesting as a psycho-religious
document than as art. Ivanov's Delphic utterances about its significance, the
lengthy and intricate process of its composition, and the constant stream of
talk about it prepared Petersburg audiences for an exceptionally exciting first
viewing in 1858. Shown at the Hermitage and then at the Academy (fig. 53),
Christ Appearing enjoyed only mixed success. Its numerous cryptic figures
puzzled many; and its "realism" applied to a sacred subject offended some at
the Academy. Virtually all shades of intelligentsia opinion, however, applauded Ivanov as the prophet of a truly Russian art: Herzen, Stasov, the
Slavophiles, Gogol, the emerging radical journalists, and later the Itinerants.[58]

As Werner Busch has succinctly put it, classical heroic pictures argued rather
than adorned. In the course of time, the universal moral hero drawn from
antiquity was joined by "national" heroes endowed with specific local virtues
and characteristics. Thus the abstract moral made room for the national political.[59] For a long time, Russian history could not compete with antiquity as a
source of painters' creativity. Foreign locales or bygone epochs outnumbered
Russian settings well into the 1870s. A typical Russian product of historical
classicism, the history painter Anton Losenko (Losenkov, 1737–73), came
from a merchant family and was brought to St. Petersburg as a choirboy in the
Capella. When his voice broke, he attended the Academy, received a pension
to Paris and Rome, and at home rose on the faculty ladder. Losenko, though
unoriginal, was the first Russian to execute a large-scale treatment in oil of a
Russian historical event, *St. Vladimir and Rogneda* (1770). The story in the
painting, drawn from the *Russian Primary Chronicle,* has Prince Vladimir of
Kiev courting Rogneda after he has just killed her father and ravaged her
lands. Losenko fell from grace due to intrigues and died in poverty, but the
Russian historical painting lived on.[60]

At the turn of the century, the Russian theme in historical painting received
a boost from Nikolai Karamzin, whose popular twelve-volume history of
Russia (1816–29) later fed the Russian national revival. In an 1802 essay on

suitable historical subjects for artists, he wrote: "Not only can a historian and a poet be agents of patriotism, but a painter and sculptor as well. If a historical character is presented strikingly on canvas or in marble, it makes even the [Russian] chronicles more interesting for us: we are curious to find out from which source the artist got his inspiration, and with great attention we read the description of the man's deeds, recalling what a lively impression his [deeds] made on us."[61] In 1804, Tsar Alexander I echoed Karamzin, ordered more paintings on Russian history, and named several themes. Vasily Popugaev, a commoner and a preacher of enlightenment, unlike Karamzin, condemned serfdom. In 1803 he demanded the depiction of popular-national heroes such as the lowly butcher of Nizhny Novgorod who is credited with saving Russia from turmoil during the Time of Troubles. Alexander Turgenev in 1804 suggested that the real heroes deserving artistic treatment were fighters against tyranny.[62]

Orest Kiprensky's *Dmitry Donskoi* (1803), executed amidst this discussion, exceeded in merit and interest most of its predecessors and successors. Dmitry Ivanov's prize-winning *Marfa of Novgorod* (1808) featured a political leader in Novgorod in the late fifteenth century who opposed Moscow's efforts to subdue her city. Savinov is surely right in saying that this canvas would have been unthinkable under Nicholas I because of its subversive message. In 1814, A. I. Ivanov (father of the famous Ivanov) produced *The Heroic Act of a Young Kievan*. The "young Kievan" is a classical nude on a tenth-century battlefield, with his Pecheneg adversaries draped in Roman garb. Neither this nor similar efforts did much to advance the genre of Russian historical pictures.[63] The French invasion produced a frenzy of national works in all the arts. From 1812 onward patriotic subjects were part of the Academy of Arts's examination process, with such assigned themes as a priest defying the enemy, the kindness of Russian troops to prisoners, and the valor of those Russians executed in Moscow by the French. The harrowing 1813 picture, *The Shooting of Russian Patriots by the French in Moscow in 1812,* has been attributed to Vasily Shebuev. As in the plays and odes of the early 1800s, distant struggles against Tatars and Poles were enlisted to illustrate the present menace.[64] Painters failed to range widely in Russian historical subject matter after the Napoleonic wars. N. Ivanchin-Pisarev, a pious monarchist, in the early 1830s listed many historical subjects and lamented the inactivity of painters who still busied themselves with Greek and Roman subjects. He ended by suggesting a depiction of the crushing of the Decembrist uprising on Senate Square with Tsar Nicholas as the hero. The Russianized German Karl Kohlmann, later a member of the Academy, had already produced in the late 1820s a canvas treating this event.[65]

History painting has long been out of fashion almost everywhere, though it can still excite the young who are seeing a large oil canvas for the first time. But even in its own time, the Russian product did not distinguish itself by great artistry or antiquarian accuracy. The works of eighteenth-century Russian painters especially reflect a poverty of research and a glut of abstract heroes and classicist idealization. Shebuev and Egorov, sheltered in the Academy from childhood, were enveloped by its system. The faces on their canvases lack a special character, the bodies and gestures are sculptural rather than painterly. Bruni, though a great craftsman, stiffened his figures into a tableau rather than forging a drama. Even works dealing with contemporary events seem false: the protagonists are often given gestures and poses from ancient Rome. Capturing a moment in historical narrative is normally done by means of a "dramatic closeup."[66] The Russian historicists rarely mastered the narrative conventions of battle, meeting, or confrontation; and they lacked knowledge of formula and stock detail that make historical canvases interesting and significant. This resulted partly from the constraints of the academic mode, but also from a still very weak grasp of Russian history and archaeology.

The Art of Elevation

In a remarkable kind of self-denying ordinance, the European and Russian arbiters of academic art, though closely linked to the aristocracy, forbade the two supremely class-serving genres of painting — portrait and manorial landscape — to take precedence over the more abstract genre of history. As late as 1829, the British Royal Academy counted it a special exception to admit John Constable, "a mere landscape painter," to its ranks. At the Russian Imperial Academy, portraiture was long held in low esteem, and it was a kind of insult to say "he is a portraitist."[67] But this branch of painting, along with landscape, had great appeal to the ruling classes; however idealized as art, those genres dealt with the world of the creator and his subject or patron.

European portraiture's conventions gave males strong character and females tenderness and delicacy. The privileged male subject must show dignity, stasis, and reserve — mirroring the restraint expected in polite society. The background, bathed in cool light, must reinforce that image with balance, opulence, and antiquity as signs of refinement and historical stability — even timelessness. The social order was incarnated in the poser and his setting. The full face, considered most effective for males, should be devoid of surprise, disgust, sadness, anger, or fear. Sometimes the tranquil enjoyment of riches, power, and pleasure got conveyed by "stylized informality" as in a cross-legged pose, but it was never cheapened by a smug smile. The portraitist, like a theater director, combined narrative, position, costume, props, and scenic background. The painter usually did the head at a live sitting and then added a background, with a well-established visual vocabulary of drapes, furniture, classical motifs, and a window to the outside world. Different rules applied for females, children, and family ensembles. Distance between figures, lighting, the body-face positioning, and the gaze were all arranged in a hierarchy of age, gender, and sometimes class.[68]

Family continuity occupied a high place alongside vanity in filling one's homes with portraits, old and new. A string of generational pictures on the walls of a domestic gallery or along a staircase formed excellent propaganda for genealogy and status. I. G. Galagin, a Chernigov landowner, had his serf execute imagined portraits of Bogdan Khmelnitsky, Ivan Mazeppa, and other Ukrainian hetmans of earlier times. The high-ranking official Viktor Kochubei (1768–1834) had his gallery of illustrious Cossack ancestors captured in a painting by G. K. Mikhailov. Landowner F. I. Glebov positioned images of the chronicles of Nestor and Pimen in his portrait gallery at home to suggest an ancient lineage.[69] Ancestral portraits formed one element in a visual system that included armorial bearings, obelisks, gravestones, and other markers of a "genealogical nest," though the nest might have been far newer than the family line. Seventeenth-century Russian pictures of tsars, metropolitans, and boyars had combined a secular subject matter with icon-like format. As European portrait styles made their entrance in the early eighteenth century, the "parade" or ceremonial portrait flourished with its key features of serenity and grandeur.[70] Portraits of adult males and of female rulers resembled the "swagger portraits" that Thomas Lawrence made for British aristocrats — images of vaulting self-confidence framed in antiquity, their subjects festooned with medals and sashes.[71] Stalin-era critics liked to mock the eighteenth-century portrait for its "military parade rigidity."[72] In fact, some of them were wrought with great sensitivity. Miniatures, half-portraits normally with a monochrome background and no props, were effective devices of family art. Rulers and great families delighted in seeing their images on tiny artifacts.

The great impresario of the Silver Age, Sergei Diaghilev, singled out among the giants of the Academy Levitsky and Borovikovsky as Russia's greatest painters. Dmitry Levitsky (1735–1822), was descended from a provincial priest in Ukraine and had an artist father as his first teacher. A visiting artist took him under his wing and in 1758 Levitsky enrolled in the Academy where he ended up heading the portrait faculty. Levitsky, though patronized by the very rich, retired poor and old with a miserly pension. To support his grandchildren, the seventy-two-year-old had to return to work at the Academy in 1807. Levitsky's well-known *Catherine as Lawmaker* (1783), set in the temple of Themis, the Greek Titan and goddess of law and justice, has no pretensions of subtlety in its symbolism. In a study of P. A. Demidov (1780s), a fabulously wealthy member of the famed merchant family, the subject, casual in a cross-legged pose, displays both the tools (watering can) and the creations (potted plants) of his horticultural hobby. Scholars have suggested that the plants served also as a metaphor for education and upbringing, of which Demidov was a promoter. Levitsky put his sitters at ease both as Russians and as Europeans. Undeniably delightful are his rendering of high-born women in action: separate studies of Alexandra Lëvshina and Ekaterina Nelidova (1773) dancing the minuet; and a Smolny pupil playing the servant girl in Giovanni Pergolesi's opera, *La serva padrona* (1733). In art historian George Heard Hamilton's only slightly exaggerated words, he "invented the character of St. Petersburg society for some time to come."[73]

Vladimir Borovikovsky (1757–1825), an unrivaled master of "virtuoso technique, the idealization of subject, [and] the ceremonial format," drew freely from European classical models. Born into a family of icon painters descended from Ukrainian Cossacks, Borovikovsky was discovered painting allegories at one of the many palaces where passing monarchs stopped. He eventually got into the Academy. The most important portraitist of the 1790s, Borovikovsky knew how to feed the ego. Alexander Kurakin, known as "the Diamond Prince" for his vanity, had himself painted many times, including Borovikovsky's 1802 portrait which is filled with luxurious accouterments (fig. 54). Like his brother who, as minister of internal affairs, a few years later admonished Venetsianov for his scathing cartoons about the gentry, Alexander Kurakin clearly preferred flattery to satire. The presence of Kurakin's recently murdered friend Tsar Paul is everywhere in the Borovikovsky portrait: his bust, the Maltese cross associated with him, and—glimpsed through a window—the Mikhailovsky Castle where that tsar had lived and died.[74]

Borovikovsky also excelled in the finely wrought intimacy of family scenes and in sentimental depictions of women, as in a portrait of Maria Lopukhina (1797). He displayed mastery in composition, directness, and individuality in the less common genre of "conversation pieces" with subjects of everyday cultural pursuits. He executed charming scenes of magnate families which combine graceful figures, domestic peace, and exquisite detail against a sentimentalized background of serene nature. Borovikovsky's 1802 study of the young aristocratic Gagarina sisters, fleshy and curvy in their low-cut Empire dresses against a pastoral background, has harmonious siblings sharing music: one with a guitar, the other languorously holding the notes. It is instructive to compare it to John Smart's 1806 watercolor, *The Misses Binney,* of two English sisters, also dressed in the Empire style, one looking on as the other plays

the piano. Both pictures are icons of domestication and essentialized femininity in which the music is marginalized and the instruments hardly more than
props.[75] In later years, Borovikovsky underwent a transformation, turning to
a more austere style. His participation in a mystical cult seems to have weakened his skills and he devoted his nights to drink and his days to prayer and
painting icons and crucifixion scenes for his religious friends. He died unnoticed in the home of a court chef adjacent to the Winter Palace.[76]

Orest Kiprensky (1782/83–1836), a figure of great contrasts and rather
alarming turbulence, was born a serf in the remote Cossack borderland around
Orenburg. The illegitimate son of a bachelor officer and landowner, he was
given to a foster father. In 1788, under the assumed name Kiprensky, the boy
enrolled in the Academy and graduated in 1803. He spent, on and off, the years
1816–36 in Italy. While there, he took a thirteen-year-old wife whom he
acquired, it was said, after murdering his mistress, the girl's mother, by pouring
turpentine on her. Kiprensky led a boisterous life in Rome and became known
for his boasting and conceit. One scholar called him corrupt, rich, greedy,
arrogant, and a sellout. *Donskoi* (1803), his first historical work, helped advance the vogue for painting Russian history. But, though seduced by Rome's
monumentality, Kiprensky ended as a superb portraitist. Among the earlier
studies, the 1804 portrait of his foster father, Adam Schwalbe (Shvalbe), stands
out for its realistic grimness. Kiprensky painted various statesmen such as I. A.
Gagarin, Sergei Uvarov, and A. M. Golitsyn. His portrait of Pushkin (1827)
became the standard likeness. A very original 1815 miniature of the poet K. N.
Batyushkov has the subject's head tilted upwards as if contemplating some
metaphysical problem. The brilliant facial color and the eyes make Batyushkov
seem both dreamy and creatively alert. When theater people came to be seen as
worthy of portrayal on canvas, Kiprensky pioneered with portraits of the
tragedienne Ekaterina Semënova and the ballerina Ekaterina Telesheva.[77]

Kiprensky's portrait of the Russian officer Evgraf Davydov (1809) — brother
of the famous partisan poet Denis Davydov — puts the dashing warrior of the
Napoleonic epoch in a cross-legged pose, indicating self-confident insouciance,
with a full-frontal head, eyes looking leftward. The serpentine pose suggests
grace, bodily strength, and suppleness. Complementing the flashy uniform and
the cavalry mustache, the artist painted in the accouterments of war: saber, map
case, and a huge helmet lying on the floor of a veranda with a garden background. The image of a gentleman-warrior is achieved by combining the domestic interior with the outward life of a soldier. Davydov's white breeches —
losiny (elk skins) — were donned wet and then dried tight to the skin. In the field
they were horribly uncomfortable as well as dangerous, due to the bright color.
But in parades and portrait sittings, the effect was both martial and sensual — a

key element in the attraction for women of officers of this type. Another feature that made male portraiture in this age so vivid was the shaven chin which allowed the face to come through on canvas — in striking contrast to the relative monotony of bearded visages later in the century. For hussars and uhlans (and after 1832 all officers), the permitted mustache added its own sparkle and dash. A decree of 1837 forbade facial hair except sideburns to serving officers and officials and, from 1848 to the end of Nicholas' reign, to any nobleman. Kiprensky's work — along with George Dawes's portraits in the Winter Palace Gallery of Heroes — must be credited with establishing a lasting public image of the noble and romantic Russian officer.[78]

Kiprensky's pair of self-portraits (c. 1808) — another turning point in the art of personal representation — seem to show two entirely different personae. One is of a wildly romantic and strikingly handsome young man with sensual lips and fierce eyes and paintbrushes perched behind his ear as he works. Although Sarabyanov described the portrait as "meditative," it seems more like the self-revelation of a killer and seducer and drunk. The other is of a quiet clerk-like man posing with a pink scarf.[79] It seems likely that the artist was attempting to show the various sides of his complex personality. Once known as the "king of painting," Kiprensky declined in the 1830s and few other portraitists arose to match the quality of the late eighteenth and early nineteenth century. Kiprensky's self-portraits, a rare genre before the nineteenth century, clearly betokened the growth of the artists' sense of — or search for — identity and self-worth. Kiprensky's social ambit was limited, but in going somewhat beyond portraying the elite in a restricted art of elevation, he took a small step toward something like an art of revelation. In any case, the artistic conventions and patronage mechanisms established for elite portraiture became easily adaptable to those in the merchant estate who began to seek their own special place in society worthy of representation and legitimation on canvas.

Not long ago, Britons could still get riled over attempts to "read" English landscape painting in political terms. In the last few decades, British art historians have been doing just that, with the principal focus on the ideological meanings of eighteenth- and early nineteenth-century landscape art. Though at odds about what the art means, they insist that the meanings transcend mere images of trees and ground.[80] Eighteenth-century British landscape artists, while bowing to esthetic and social conventions, divided over what were called occluded (or picturesque) and panoramic perspectives. The former took on specific localized scenes of nature such as a cottage in the trees, or natural events such as a rainstorm. Critics claimed that such views fit the taste of the vulgar to whom the larger view was inaccessible. Painting or viewing a picturesque scene was likened to a cramped political vision based on narrow self-interest. Conversely, the panoramic view, while suggesting scope and power, also indicated breadth of vision, a civic humanism reserved for men (and only men) of substance (landed property). The idealized panoptic perspective, which conveyed the sense of naturalness and permanence, unaffected by events, became associated with high social status, good taste, and wide learning. Thus, as in certain readings of classical drama, class hierarchy was explained by the ability of disinterested people of independent means to apprehend the abstract, the general, the universal, the essential. The art of elevation was another tool in the kit of honor along with lineage, service, patriarchy, and a willingness to duel.[81]

In manorial landscape painting, the "prospect" or high-angle perspective conveyed mastery — by the viewer of the picture and by the owner of the land depicted. Its archetype, Henry Hoare's *The Park at Stourhead* (1743–44), places the painter and viewer on one side of a body of water and a building on the other.[82] This arrangement became standardized throughout Europe, including Russia. There, some eighteenth-century landscapists simply copied European works directly; those who struck out on their own had to learn the rules of spacing and perspective and to deal with fore-, middle-, and background composition. They quickly became conversant with established styles, particularly those of Britain, France, and Italy. Claude Lorrain (1600–1682) long held sway over landscape both in specific devices — an arboreal "screen," a dark coulisse of trees on one or both sides of the picture; and in mood — a quest not for topographical exactitude, but for poetic and luminous scenes, tinged with nostalgia, and littered with classical remnants in a serenely receding landscape. The relative lack of a national signature appealed to the age in which it was born, but lost some of its force when the events and processes of the early nineteenth century released a flood of national expression.[83]

When the landscape involves property and people, organization and hierarchy, munificence and taste, then landscape art intersects with social history. The most striking thing about outdoor painting in Russia from Catherine II to Nicholas I is the relative absence of raw nature and the predominance of the manorial prospect — a privileging of landscaping over landscape. An ideology of "ruralism" came into play which self-consciously constructed the grounds of the manor house as an Eden where no one worked, or as a pastorale where real labor was concealed. Peasants were invisible; painted in as staffage, stick figures like extras on a theater stage; or occasionally seen as happy toilers like the haymakers of the theatricalized spectacles noted in the previous chapters. Painters, like the real and fictional landowners Thomas Newlin writes about, "aestheticized and pastoralized the act of labor" in order to create the "overall illusion of 'happy' rural life." The stillness of the garden became a metaphor for social peace. Painters again and again represented the estate as an island of freedom, reflecting the release from state service that the gentry had enjoyed since the 1760s. Highlighting the refinements of civilization, as embodied in manor house architecture and formal gardens set in the midst of bucolic nature, provided an aesthetic contrast and made a cultural statement. A striking reflection of the personal construction of reality are the written thoughts and the watercolor landscapes done in the 1790s by the eighteenth-century landowner and diarist Andrei Bolotov, which contained almost no peasants.[84]

It became customary for landowner patrons to invite painters in summer to their homes as, in a sense, artists in residence. Manorial painters ranged from renowned academy professors to serfs and unattached amateur artists, many of them now unknown. A socio-cultural compact emerged between patron and painter about how to re-create the manorial milieu on canvas. An early example of the genre is a 1794 view of the Kurakin estate in Saratov Province by Academy-trained Yakov Filimonov (fig. 3). In a classic elevated perspective, the viewer looks down at the seignior strolling with a guest in the foreground, pointing to his dozen buildings across a narrow river. He heads toward a boat being readied for him by retainers (probably the impoverished gentry who work for him).[85] From other sources we also know that dinner and a serf orchestra await him at the manor house. The familiar progress of pleasures is taking place: a walk in the country air, the proud display of land and property, a boat ride, repose, a grand meal served by lackeys, music played by his orchestra. All this was at the disposal of Prince Kurakin and his guests, thus adding to the host's sensual enjoyment the refined psychic pleasure of hospitality. In this respect, a host acted the impresario, deploying unpaid labor in the entertainment of his nonpaying guests. The pleasure of having his paradise on canvas was perhaps intensified by the fact that Kurakin rarely visited it.[86]

In the first half of the nineteenth century, painters replicated the pattern, adding variations specific to the particular locale: Maxim Vorobev's 1811 depiction of Arakcheev's famous militarized estate at Gruzino; an unknown artist's painting (c. 1830) of the Trubetskois' Akhtyrka estate in Moscow Province; Vasily Sternberg's of the Tarnovsky manor in Chernigov Province (1837); the Sheremetev serf N. I. Podklyuchnikov's of his master's Kuskovo and Ostankino homes (1839) in Moscow; Aleksei Voloskov's of Modest Rezvoi's Marienhof estate in St. Petersburg Province (1846); and Stepan Galaktionov's 1847 *Lake in the Park*. Anonymous undated works from the same period include a watercolor of the Bakunins' Raikovo estate; a painting of the Orlovs' Otrada in Moscow Province; and a canvas entitled *Lakeshore Road*. In all but one of these, the artists employ a high perspective and the Claudean frame and situate the manor house across a small body of the water (like fairylands across the sea in folk tales) — remote from painter and viewer, a place to be invited to and not to stumble into. The foreground varies: masters, family, guests, sometimes peasants or just cows. Even when highly idealized, touches of "realism" occur in the details (the tree leaves in *Lakeshore Road* could rival in verisimilitude the much-mocked pine needles of the noted Itinerant painter, Ivan Shishkin). Voloskov, a merchant's son, offers a rendering of Marienhof that contradicts the pattern in almost every way. The viewer looks up at the modest Dutch house which is set off to the side. The center and right are filled with huts, a mill, a stream, and two peasants building a raft. The privileged place of the manor has been lost and the painting has become a picturesque landscape and genre scene.[87]

The prevailing pattern in manorial painting presents a culture of pride and hospitality (pride even in the peasants at Otrada who are chopping firewood to warm the master's home). The manorial landscape is actually the portrait of a property, set in the center, well-lighted, surrounded by props and extras who augment its centrality in the life of the owner. The strong feeling of self-esteem derived from ownership is hardly surprising in view of what we know about the affluent rural gentry's attachment to their homes.[88] House and land, whether near or far from the capital, seemed to celebrate visually the emancipation of the gentry, to be a locus of freedom and a token of independent ownership by a lord unbeholden to the state. The apparent absence of commissioned paintings showing serf orchestras and actors on stage reveals another side of the picture. Serf owners' delight in their entertainers, at least as strong as that of home ownership, if displayed on canvas might transform serfs into much more than stick figures and thus make them compete with or even marginalize their owners. Lords could not prevent the satires of domestic theater on the imperial stages, but they could deny representation in the art they paid for. The practice of using chattels in such ways, though acceptable to like-minded guests, ought not to be inscribed as a boast on such a permanent document as a canvas.

Scenes such as those described above were hung on the walls of manor houses as comforting tokens of ownership. A guest would thus "see" the host's home twice, from the outside and on the inside. Except for Arakcheev's complex at Gruzino which had multiple purposes, gentry estates were represented as sites of leisure and pleasure and not of productivity. Although we have pictures of merchants' homes and of seigniorial and merchant factories, we have none — apparently — of the estate specifically devoted to the business of an improving landlord, even though the noted painter Venetsianov was one of these. Britons had added this theme to manorial depiction in the eighteenth century with the onset of the Agricultural Revolution, thus adding industriousness and enterprise to Arcadia — a visual account of how the gentry adapted to industrialization. The simple Arcadia gave way to a Virgilian vision of rustic life as healthy labor (regardless of who did the labor). The absence of this development in Russia can be explained by the relative paucity of modernizing landowners, the inefficiency of the few who ventured upon improvements, and the fact that such types were mocked on stage and in story.

Of course gentry outdoor pleasures could be recorded in other than a manorial setting: promenading on the streets of the capital, or on an outing in the suburbs. Ivan Khrutsky's (1806–1852) *Elagin Island* (1839) features two young ladies strolling a waterside path in this exclusive suburb of opulent palaces and mansions, near the bank of one of the Neva's branches. The two women are alone, undisturbed as if in the midst of an uninhabited wild, though they are probably denizens of one of the nearby private summer mansions or dachas. A rather rare scene in a watercolor produced in the 1840s by an in-law of the Poltoratskys in Kaluga Province has the family and a dozen peasants coming out of the estate church, each group going its own way. The juxtaposition is telling: the gentry move sedately in tight formation; the string of peasants pauses to hear one of the men engaged in an animated narrative, illustrated by broad arm gestures; in fact his figure dominates the entire picture. The treatment is indeed atypical as a portrayal of rural gentry; the artist, Ellen Southey Poltoratskaya, was an Englishwoman. A very different kind of outing is that shown in a provincial town with a fortress wall which a father is pointing out, and probably commenting on, to his two children.[89] All of this fell short of landscape in the larger sense. Once we move into a pursuit, dear to the gentry, that made contact with nature — the hunt — a "real" Russian landscape will surround and envelope them in pictorial form.

St. Petersburg has been celebrated throughout its three-hundred-year existence, among other things as the Venice of the North and "the most intentional city" (Dostoevsky), in innumerable works of poetry, prose, mythmaking, urban folklore, and graphic art. The literature on this subject is staggering.[90] St. Petersburg's very monumentality invited the representation of urban prospects, architectural ensembles, and ceremonial crowds. Among the most literal-minded of these, Alexei Zubov's (1682–1750) engraving *A Panorama of St. Petersburg* (1716) has even been called an example of imperial "socialist realism."[91] The initial entries in a collection of 231 plates dealing with the first third of the nineteenth century, *Pushkin's Petersburg*, reveal an overwhelming interest on the part of the mostly unidentified artists in space, parades, and linear design, executed in low horizon with an emphasis on perspective. The palaces, toy soldiers (the title of one), and princesses borne in gilded carriages drawn by six horses that were featured in some of them give the city a fairytale aspect. F. Ya. Alexeev, a veteran of the Roman pensionate, used angles, water, embankments, light, buildings, and vessels in much the same way Venetian painters had done for ages — particularly Canaletto and Guardi in the eighteenth century. In many a scene, the Neva has become the Grand Canal.[92] The ex-serf Vasily Sadovnikov's watercolors of the 1820s render majestic scenes of St. Petersburg in all seasons. The pink and blue skies and the pastels of the buildings soften and romanticize the cityscape which in many ways parallels manorial landscape, substituting the urban upper classes for the landowners, and the tsar's buildings for the manor house. The lower orders are represented by an occasional hawker and the military on parade. Sadovnikov's figures are more than staffage but less than group portraits or genre crowds. It is clear that patrons of this art did want it cluttered up with commoners; the viewer was expected to gaze with awe upon the beautiful (and beautified) Romanov edifices.[93]

The huge open spaces and ruler-straight prospects of the capital offered an exceptionally theatrical arena for the display of machine-like parades so beloved of the Romanov emperors. The squared-off phalanxes matched the geometrical lines of the inner city, and the colorful uniforms of the marching men enlivened the scene. Three artists known more for other forms of representation, Grigory Chernetsov, Vasily Raev, and Vasily Thimm, deployed their skills at perspective and crowd scenes from the 1830s to the 1850s. Chernetsov's *Parade, October 6, 1831, on Tsaritsyn Meadow* (Mars Field — 1832–37) (fig. 55), was inspired by a painting by the Berlin artist Franz Krüger.[94] Chernetsov presents a panorama of the ground between the Summer Garden and the barracks on the far side of Mars Field that makes this vast space look even vaster. As another remarkable demonstration of the city's and the tsar's powers of display, Chernetsov's canvas, in which some ninety thousand men and eighty-four cannons appeared in formation, captured the celebration of the recent subjection of insurrectionary Poland. Raev, while still a serf, also caught, in *Parade on Palace Square* (1834), the awesome symmetry of the rigidly packed formations on the huge space in front of the Winter Palace. In 1857, Thimm did a lithograph of the arrival of the bride of Grand Duke Mikhail Nikolaevich, son of the late tsar.[95] The retinue of the bride as it processes through Palace Square wears apparel from three historical ages: the mounted guards holding back the crowd are in contemporary uniforms; the foot guards in those of 1812; and the coachman in an eighteenth-century caftan, knee breeches, and tricorn. The closer to the dynast, the deeper the tradition. The onlookers, by contrast, are virtually excluded from the picture. Yet, though the crowds at parade time were subordinated to the main cast, they were willing enough to stand for hours in order to catch sight of the imperial splendor.[96] It is worth noting that these three artists, however much later historians stressed their nonacademic activities, were in fact children of the academic tradition and quite happy to alternate their genre studies with works of classical perspective.

Classical academic painters achieved social acceptance and even celebrity in their time. Sometimes the reputation was inflated: the popular writer Mikhail Zagoskin compared historical painter Vasily Shebuev to Raphael.[97] Bruni and Bryullov, called titans in their day, awed crowds with their historical canvases. The hierarchy of genre was reflected in ranks and salaries: rectors and professors had to be historical painters. Perhaps the Russian striving to emulate European standards of excellence lent compensatory force to rigid canonization of aesthetics. In any case, Academy president Olenin, a conservative on most matters, attempted a freezing of styles at the very moment when the upsurge of romanticism and realism were draining from classicism some of its power and resonance.[98] Classicism in the arts seemed to follow the pattern of a ball which loses energy and power with every bounce. Each new wave of revival or imitation promised permanence — from the Winckelmann aesthetic craze in the eighteenth century to the Jacobin-and-Bonaparte civic phase. But for Russia, Bryullov's *Pompeii* was one of the last bounces of classicism, even though the Academy pretended that the classical ball remained resilient. Ekaterina Yunge, living inside the Academy's walls and observing the ferment of the 1830s to the 1850s, argued — like a Hegelian — that passing through the stage of classicism was inevitable for Russia. Indeed the serf painter hero of the longest novel about art from this period, A. V. Timofeev's *The Artist*, a fanatical idealist, is obsessed exclusively by classical themes.[99]

The decline of academic style of course had many causes. In Europe, a fall-off in the market for large battle pictures and other historical genres partly stemmed from the growing lack of private manor house space to put them in — particularly large halls which offered perspective. This became true in Russia as well, where gentry fortunes were eroding steadily and sometimes dramatically due to mismanagement and prodigal spending. In a bleak setting of auctions, bankruptcies, mortgaged property, and deserted manor homes, the taste for shepherdesses and legionaries could easily evaporate. Conversely, new social elements with different values entered the taste public and became buyers. Artists appeared who were ready to serve new clients and express their own civic and artistic views as well. As in drama, the remoteness of themes, the excess of antique anecdote, and the lack of psychological relations among characters in classical art no longer met their needs. Ideology had turned into a sociology as well. A particular European type — whom Nikolaus Pevsner called "the academic dignitary" — was well placed, part of a powerful international caste, and suspicious of modern currents that challenged established rules. The American painter J. A. M. Whistler, voicing a growing resentment toward establishments, offered the following bon mot: "Whom the gods wish to make ridiculous, they make Academicians."[100]

The noted Russian art historian Dmitry Sarabyanov lamented the long classical hold on Russian art.[101] Its tenacity is partly explained by the fact that the great magnates in Russia, as in Europe, ordered and bought historical canvases because they reflected cultural capital — the owner's ability to "read" art at a high level of symbolic meaning. As with classical drama, catering to embodiments of ancient heroes implied both status and lofty moral character. On a more practical level, collecting such works generated a collective sense of status and cultural connections.[102] But the "decline" of the classical style, like that of neoclassical theater, was not a simple career downward while something else replaced it. In the last decades of prereform Russia, it was difficult to differentiate among classic, romantic, sentimental, or realist because they so often merged, mixed, or combined. Classicism bore many "alien" traits, and many classicisms existed side by side. Some of the European styles that simultaneously poured into Russia were themselves syntheses. Late classicism was loaded with storm and stress; romantics employed classical rules and realistic effects; the realists unwittingly employed idealization. Turbulent forces of nature such as raging seas, forbidding mountain peaks, terrifying abysses, dark forests, mysterious caves, sinister shapes, and picturesque ruins could serve as footnotes to antiquity or sites of danger from an alien past. The sheer eclecticism of the era was reflected in Odoevsky's 1839 tale "The Painter," whose title character is reduced to poverty and to painting only grocery signs. His tragedy, more subtle than that of victimized serf artists, stems not from social injustice: the artist, unable to master or synthesize all the imported images he has been learning, goes mad.[103]

The "academic vista," as critics have long pointed out, had a surfeit of blind spots. In obeying European conventions of high art, most of the professional painters for a long time settled on the received motifs of "historical" drama drawn from inherited stories and myths of the Hebrew, classical, and Christian past, largely neglecting themes of Russian history; on flattering parade portraits or scenes from upper-class family life, excluding most other classes as objects of representation; and on topographical works that exalted the palaces and the houses and grounds of nobles, ignoring for the most part the sweep and roughness of Russian nature and urban blight. A prominent Soviet critic of the academic mode, Savinov, even when writing in post-Stalin times, pronounced the Academy a powerful center of ruinous influence on art and its faculty for the most part mediocre, marred by adherence to unoriginal classicism and "sweet-salon" works. The Academy, he said, generated skills that often ended in lack of inspiration and a cosmopolitan style of interchangeable features. The judgment was not unique to Soviet critics. The learned Baron Wrangel was hardly kinder to the Academy which he saw as promoting neither national nor individual expression but rather as using an imported template when assigning students various genres and subjects.[104]

These verdicts, though accurate in the main, need some qualification. Even Savinov admits that one of the academicians he denounces was a justly popular professor who took teaching seriously and gave students some scope. Savinov aside, historians of Russian art — paralleling those of music on the issue of the Mighty Five — no longer accept the mythologizing of the Itinerants by their chief propagandist V. V. Stasov and countless other scholars who, in exalting the undeniable achievements of their favorite school, were led to an unjustifiable denunciation of the Academy in black-and-white terms. The Academy produced a great deal of good art and some great works as well. More important, it provided the needed discipline and training that helped launch the careers of those who would revolt against it. Already in the 1840s, even some conservative professors were allowing pupils such as Thimm, Rizzoni, and Fedotov to pursue their own inclinations toward genre and everyday life.[105] In later years, the Academy began to relax the rigid examination programs and their mandatory historical thematics and allow some genre subjects. None the less, the fact remains that because of the Academy's state attachment, its conservative faculty, its entrenched pedagogical traditions, and its excessive bending to Western models, it was inevitable that, to some viewers, the word "academic" came to mean mediocre, dry, cold, antiquated, irrelevant, uninspired, artificial, and historically detached from the creator and the place of creation. Artists in and outside the academy's walls would seek out other means of expression and would turn their eyes to objects closer to hand.

Seeing Art, Talking Art

If theater people exhibited themselves, artists showed — or tried to show — their art. Yet only a tiny proportion of the Russian population ever saw, bought, read about, or talked of fine art as then defined by the Academy, particularly oil canvases or watercolors. Some peasants could gaze for themselves at manor houses and garden sculptures; and house serfs could, as did the budding serf artist Tropinin, see the pictures on the manor houses' walls. The rest knew graphic art only through *lubok*, icon, or book illustration. The same applied to the urban lower classes. The gentry, educated classes, and burgeoning intelligentsia had vastly divergent viewing experiences, depending on when and where they lived. At one extreme, a literate official or landowner in a faraway provincial estate or town at the beginning of the century saw only the paintings he or his neighbors owned or those in the homes of wealthy friends whom he might visit in the capitals. Specialized publications on art were few. At the other extreme, a grandee in St. Petersburg could commission his own paintings, maintain a gallery, and visit the Hermitage, the Academy of Arts, and the private collections of other magnates. Only the select few had access to the opulent collections of the Yusupovs and Stroganovs. The Rumyantsev collection, donated to the state, was opened "to those of good background" from 1831. It later moved to Moscow. In 1846, Alexander Kushelëv-Bezborodko allowed public viewing of the picture collection in his home in St. Petersburg for two hours on Thursdays. It was not until 1862 that his son Nikolai bequeathed his part of the collection to the Academy on the stipulation that there be no restrictions or dress code for visitors. The Moscow Golitsyns established a gallery in 1810 that admitted the public except for peasants and "those shod in bast shoes." It lasted only six years. Zinaida Volkonskaya tried unsuccessfully to start a museum of copies of Western art at Moscow University in the 1820s. The Society for the Encouragement of Artists tried to found a Russian museum in 1824 but failed for lack of funds.[106]

The Imperial Hermitage collection in the Winter Palace had been established in 1764 by Empress Catherine II who sent purchasing agents to Europe. Russian rulers guarded the privacy of their residence, even though it contained eleven hundred rooms. By 1840 when the Hermitage was first opened to a limited public, it contained about four thousand paintings and thirty thousand engravings. Nicholas I made numerous purchases for the Hermitage from France, Italy, and Germany. Though Nicholas deserves much credit for the architectural masterpieces erected or begun in his reign, his record is mixed in regard to painting. A stubborn art lover, he clung to his own taste — intimate genre as well as battle and parade canvases — and would brook no correction from advisors such as Fëdor Bruni. The tsar's favorite painter was Franz Krüger, a major figure of German Biedermeier. Nicholas' manner of acquisition was idiosyncratic. As Baron Wrangel's 1912 archival study revealed, the tsar was also often destructive. In the 1850s he sold off at auction for a pittance hundreds of paintings, including valuable works by European masters. He also had paintings banished from the Hermitage collection and even burned. These included portraits of the lovers of his grandmother Catherine II, whose reign he detested; of the Decembrist rebels; and of anyone he did not like. Walking through the Hermitage one day and seeing Houdon's bust of Voltaire, he gave the order: "Destroy that ape." After suppressing the Polish uprising of 1830, the tsar had estates of the Polish nobility plundered and their art treasures, including fifty-five pieces from the Sapieha estate, brought to his palace. In 1834, as an act of revenge, he had many incinerated.[107]

Until 1840, only invited elites and vetted academy professors and students saw the Hermitage collections. When in 1840 the Hermitage did open to the public, it was to a limited public. A rule that ticket holders must wear black frock coats and white gloves automatically excluded the lower classes and many a notch or so higher. Taras Shevchenko needed a ticket and an escort to gain entry. In 1852, the Hermitage was declared a public museum, though an entrance fee remained. The well-known painter of the Itinerant school Nikolai Ge (1831–94) recalled that even in the 1850s he felt constantly watched, and he feared being thrown out because of his modest apparel. Only in 1863 was the public admitted free of charge.[108]

The Academy of Arts displayed hardly more generosity to the public than the other imperial institutions that were in various ways supposed to serve society. The Imperial Public Library, where Olenin presided from 1808 to 1843, opened only three days a week to well-dressed gentlemen and lovers of learning. Reader data for the first decades of the century are sketchy: in 1850, some 8,000, and in 1858, 35,000 visitors patronized the library. As for art viewing, the poet Konstantin Batyushkov left an amusing account of a "stroll through the Academy of Arts" in 1814 whose main point was to praise the Academy, its founders and leaders, and its Russian artists. The narrator, though learned in and respectful of European art, was quick to poke fun at those who saw beauty and grandeur only on foreign shores or in deep antiquity. As one of the characters asks: "is breathing the air of Rome indispensable for the artist, for the lover of antiquity?" Batyushkov's sketch left a somewhat exaggerated impression that the halls of the Academy were regularly visited by very engaged and well-informed people of various ages and tastes, and the scene suggested that the building was a natural venue for cultural debate in a public space beyond the salon.[109]

In fact, the Academy only mounted irregular shows every one to three years in September and October. Under Olenin, they were accompanied by the wining and dining of moneyed patrons who might contribute to his budget and buy paintings. Fragmentary glimpses suggest what the shows were like. One in 1820 was packed with lower-class people from the street. Apparently such visitors were segregated: in 1827 Nikitenko witnessed a crowd of "ordinary folk," since those of "good breeding" came in the morning. The Academy offering was far from brilliant. The traveler Thomas Raikes in 1829 saw "very few objects of interest or importance" and "few good paintings." Art students and professors had to visit other places such as the Hermitage to see the great masters. The sculptor Ramazanov recalled that up to 1833, the Academy was a closed institution divorced from the life of the great capital, with the artists inside and the public outside. The periodic showings generated large crowds and a flurry of discussion in society of the latest works. But then the talk would die away until the next triennial. In between came only a small trickle of foreign visitors and scholars. After the showing of Bryullov's *Last Day of Pompeii* in 1833, the doors swung open and public interest grew. The dawn of realism in the 1840s and the era preceding emancipation brought even greater public attention.[110]

Art museums, writes a modern scholar, provide "a way of seeing," and "the museum effect" turns objects into works of art. A museum can also turn "bad" art into art. Varying modes of hanging, lighting, and grouping—by genre, author, period, style, or school—will affect the way pictures are seen and understood, aside from what the public has read or heard about the paintings. The shows of the Academy functioned this way but on a very limited scale. As a school and not an art museum, the Academy offered mostly the works of professors and students. It thus lacked the symbolic (though not the physical) monumentality of a permanent collection. It was a place where judgments were necessarily conditional, lacking the long-range canonical power that a museum can endow upon its holdings. Yet, though the Academy was weak in the exhibition of art to the public, it reached out widely in other ways through its outpost in Rome, its staffing of ordinary schools all over the empire with art teachers, and its relations with the growing network of "independent" provincial schools (chapter 8). For the capital, the Academy offered a pool of painters, architects, and sculptors who built and decorated state and private structures—the palaces, lions, horses, and sphinxes that came to adorn St. Petersburg in that time and which gave the city its world renown.[111]

Thus seeing art remained for the most part the perquisite of those who could buy it, and of their guests. No real art market emerged in the preemancipation years, though certainly art was bought and sold. Churchmen such as Metropolitan Mikhail Desnitsky could order a portrait from Borovikovsky, but most orders came from court, gentry, and rich merchants. Though some grandees preferred European old masters, well-known families such as the Shuvalovs, Orlovs, Golitsyns, Kurakins, Gagarins, Lvovs, and Naryshkins were buying works of well-established Russian artists—Borovikovsky, Tropinin, and Bryullov, among others. In the 1820s, at least three art shops operated on the Nevsky, including Snegirev's, where Bryullov and others exhibited in the 1820s. But the buying usually took place by personal contact, at the Academy or through the Society for the Encouragement of Artists.[112] Inevitably some artists never made it at all or declined after the first flush. K. L. Pzhetslavsky's (Przeclawski, 1820–62) little-known painting, *The Poor Artist's Family and a*

Buyer (1857), bitterly depicted the pathos and humiliation that some artists felt about the market. On the canvas, the defeated painter appeals with a gesture to the kindness of a rich buyer, pointing to the destitution surrounding his mother, wife, and small child.[113]

One can speak of a journalistic discourse on art only in the reign of Nicholas I. Rosalind Gray's fine survey of the subject discusses the *Journal of Fine Arts* (1823–25) and the *Gazette of Fine Arts* (1836–41), which focused largely on European works. *Messenger of Europe* (1802–30), *Northern Flowers* (1825–32), *Annals of the Fatherland* from 1839, and other thick journals published irregularly on the arts. Nestor Kukolnik, editor of the *Gazette of Fine Arts* from 1836 to 1839, endeavored to avoid controversy and criticism, pointed aspiring Russian artists to Rome, and argued that Russian art was hardly more than a local variant of the Italian Renaissance as represented in the religio-Italianate works of Bruni and Bryullov, among others.[114] As of that moment, Kukolnik was essentially correct: the Russian world of art was a European world in terms of style, patronage, taste, discourse, public exposure, and pedagogical approaches. In this it paralleled opera, ballet, and classical concert music. Only in the 1840s did the discussion of Russian art come to maturity in illustrated journals and collections and in art criticism. By that time, the art world itself was turning a new corner.

8

Exploring the Interior

"Who would want to paint you when no one even wants to look at you?" an old epigrammatist [Antiochus in Anthologia Graeca*] asks of an exceedingly deformed man. Many an artist of our time would say, "Be as ugly as possible, I will paint you nevertheless. Even though no one likes to look at you, they will still be glad to look at my picture, not because it portrays you but because it is a proof of my art, which knows how to present such a monster so faithfully."*

— *Lessing,* Laocoön

Russian artists of the early and mid-nineteenth century set out on voyages of discovery: of their country's interior landscape; of the *intérieur* or domestic dwelling space of diverse social classes; of the "inner city" beyond the majestic squares of the capitals; and sometimes even of their own internal selves and those of their artistic subjects. The term "discovery" might well be replaced by "revelation" or "reinvention," since some artists were driven by various motives; and since they idealized what they "discovered" as did their predecessors, though in a new way.[1] No dramatic break with academia can explain the outward journey to the provinces and the inward gaze at everyday life and labor. Academy-trained artists, or those linked to it personally and intellectually, engaged in a slow and laborious process. The pioneers of discovery worked not by abandoning European traditions but by choosing which traditions to draw from and applying them freely.[2] One might even say that Europe provided them with a searchlight to hunt out Russia. While there is truth in the picture of students abandoning the gloomy recesses of the edifice on the Neva, they did not forswear all they had learned there. Rather they built on it.

As part of their discovery, artists moved into new genres and graphic media, including photography, and upgraded previously low-rated ones. And they moved physically into new art environments: dark spaces of the *urbs* and remoter corners of the countryside. The school of naturalism or realism that grew during the 1830s and 1840s, by offering representations of the here and now, led some people to visualize who they were and what they were in relation to others. By the early nineteenth century, virtually every province of Russia contained a swirl of painters and sketchers from the capital, roving artists, and artist colonies in places like Tver, Yaroslavl, Nizhny Novgorod, Arzamas, Saratov, Penza, Voronezh, Kaluga, the Urals, and Siberia.[3] New art schools — in both senses of the word: training centers and styles — arose in the provinces and in Moscow, which flung painters out of the studios into the countryside to gaze at the previously invisible, to see and represent what traditional artists were blind to. Art outside the capital was quickened by the ever-widening social perspective of the painters who worked there and of the human experience depicted. Paralleling these developments and partly related to them was the struggle for the liberation of serf artists and for an upgrading of the status of artists in general.

Counter-Academy?

A half-dozen art centers far from the Academy of Arts served collectively as minor vehicles for the spread of secular art in the countryside, promoted a new view of the world, and trained serfs and other lower-class artists. Provincial art schools arose in a dozen places, though those in Kharkov, Kazan, Tambov, Tiflis, and Feodosia were stillborn. Alexander Stupin (1776?–1861) opened the first private nonseigniorial art school in Arzamas. The illegitimate son of a nobleman, Stupin in the 1790s became an independent icon painter. Ambitious to be a teacher, he enrolled in the Academy of Arts in 1800, earned a silver medal, and, through the intercession of Director Stroganov, won gentry social status and received two hundred rubles for his journey back home to Arzamas. In 1802 Stupin turned his house into a school which he eventually furnished with thousands of books and pictures. He recognized a big demand for art in Arzamas, which stood at a crossroads in the province of Nizhny

Novgorod. Stupin's school enjoyed the official protection of the governor; and from 1809, when Stupin became an Academician, his institution was associated with the Academy of Arts. By 1830, of the seventy-five Arzamas graduates, twelve had entered the Academy (ten of whom won silver medals), and thirteen had gone into teaching.[4]

The Arzamas school offered Russian, geography, history, and theatrical art. Stupin taught classical painting and landscape, using purchased busts and pictures for copying exercises. His son, Rafael (b. 1798), who, while attending the Academy of Arts, had met the great tragedian A. S. Yakovlev, organized a school theater, open to the public, where Goldoni and Ozerov were performed. In art classes, he at first stood nude models in classical poses, and then shifted, in ways unthinkable at the Academy, to having them pose in everyday motions such as chopping wood and carrying bags, a method that exposed unfamiliar muscles and also was related to acts of labor. Students paid tuition for the six-year course and lived in a special dormitory. Out of this training came thousands of portraits as well as secular and religious works that were marketed in several directions. The school took orders for iconostases and sent its art works to the Nizhny Novgorod fair. Stupin called his institution the School of Historical and Portrait Painting in order to get gentry landowners to enroll their serfs and townsmen their sons. Open to all classes and without age restrictions, it attracted many serfs, 60 of the estimated 150 total enrollees.[5]

The serf painter Ivan Zaitsev (1805–87), a graduate, later recalled the kindness of the director and the staff. In contrast to other schools with lower-class pupils, a communal atmosphere prevailed. "There was no distinction between [serf and free]," wrote Zaitsev. "We lived—as they say—like soul brothers, each ready to die for the other." Like other serfs who received some education, Zaitsev looked back with bitterness on his servile childhood in Penza Province. His father had made erotic pictures at the command of one landowner. Another, a bachelor, would lie in bed, scan the latest list of his serfs, and summon one of the teenaged girls to his chamber. Under a new master, in 1824 Zaitsev was permitted to enroll at Arzamas where he experienced three happy years. When his master's estate was sold, Zaitsev, assisted by Stupin, won his freedom and entered the Academy of Arts from which he graduated in 1835 to become a teacher. Other Arzamas serf pupils got their freedom, including Vasily Raev, I. M. Gorbunov (d. 1837), Shevchenko's tyrannical boss in Petersburg, V. G. Shiryaev (b.1795), and two founders of their own schools: Kuzma Makarov and Afanasy Nadezhdin. Not all serf pupils were so lucky. A landowner declined the offer of two thousand rubles made to him by the Society for the Encouragement of Artists for the freedom of Grigory Myasnikov, an Arzamas serf pupil. Ordered into domestic service and denied aspirations to attend the Academy of Arts, in 1828 he killed himself and left a note containing the words: "Write on my tomb that I died for freedom."[6]

In 1836 Stupin passed the directorship to a pupil. Tension apparently existed with the local community. After Myasnikov's suicide, some police officials wanted to close the school. Stupin claimed that a fire that destroyed it in 1843 was started by evil-minded people out of either envy or a desire to plunder. We can only speculate about whether discontent was fed by the employment of nude models, a dormitory full of serf artists, the school theater where boys dressed up as girls, or the use of plaster statues, scandalizing at least one local priest who saw them as idols. Perhaps it was the presence of the one female student, Mariya Zhukova, later a well-known writer. In any case, in 1843 Stupin rebuilt the school after the fire. But by the 1840s, when Vladimir Sollogub had Arzamas art serve as the symbol of tradition in his Slavophile utopian novel *The Coach*, the school was already in decline due to change in tastes and the dwindling of interest in paintings "without ideas." So landowners stopped training their serfs in "useless" art and put them to work. Stupin died in 1861, having spent six decades promoting art education. His school ended in the following year. Arzamas, as the first provincial school, produced no outstanding painters. Its significance lies in the role it played as the earliest haven for serf painters outside manor house and Academy, the freedom it won for a handful of pupils, and the schools it spawned.[7]

The students of Alexei Venetsianov (1780–1847) at his Safonkovo school in Tver Province achieved greater notoriety. Descended from a Greek family, Venetsianov, the son of a Moscow noble working as a fruit dealer, moved to St. Petersburg in 1807. Though Venetsianov never studied officially at the Academy of Arts, he had connections to it. As a full-time civil servant for decades, he studied irregularly under Borovikovsky, used live models, and copied at the Hermitage. Venetsianov's 250 works include a large number of portraits, but in 1828, he wrote a goodbye note to portraiture and never did another.[8] Venetsianov retired to his estate in 1819 and began painting peasants. "I busied myself," he said, "with the production of the simplest and crudest of Russian subjects." "The art of drawing and painting itself is nothing more than a weapon assisting literature and thus the enlightenment of the people." Nature, "in its splendid guise," became his subject.[9] A Soviet work exaggerated only slightly when it dubbed him "the first in the history of Russian art to see the poetic content in scenes from surrounding life, in the Russian peasants and their labor."[10] For all his ruralism and protopopulism, Venetsianov always recognized the need for technique. He may have abandoned the philosophy of the Academy of Arts to strike out on his own, but he never repudiated it. In fact he even tried for a post there. After a profitable sale of a painting, he established a school on his estate in 1824 which lasted until his death in 1847. Venetsianov was the first who tried both to paint real serfs and to teach them as well.

Venetsianov's school did not emerge in a vacuum. He had debuted in teaching the lower classes at the literacy society of the Union of Welfare in St. Petersburg, a philanthropic body of the post-Napoleonic era that fed into the revolutionary Decembrist movement. From 1818 onward, Venetsianov spent summers at the Safonkovo school and winters in St. Petersburg, giving classes in his studio there. At Safonkovo, he tried some agricultural improvements[11] and surrounded himself with mostly serf and lower-class art pupils, eventually numbering seventy to eighty. Safonkovo resembled an artist's studio rather than an academy. The master paid the expenses, with some assistance from the Society for the Encouragement of Artists (see below). When he could afford it, he boarded pupils. The sociable Venetsianov regaled them at dinner with talk about art. "His family was our family," recalled one of his successful pupils, Apollon Mokritsky or Mokhritsky. The Venetsianov home also served as the "interior" that his pupils painted. Reflecting his desire for the pupils to see and paint familiar things, at Safonkovo the teaching began with objects, sculptures, and life studies before proceeding into the outdoors.[12]

By the master's estimate, about half his pupils became good artists. Some pursued genre; others "defected" to academicism. Art historian Alexeeva lists about fifty definite and probable disciples. Among the nonserfs were Alexander Denisov; Nikifor Krylov who won an Academy medal in 1827; Alexander Alexeev who later became a drawing teacher; Evgraf Krendovsky who attended Arzamas, Safonkovo, and the Academy; Lavr Plakhov (1810–81), who studied at the Academy and at Berlin and became a pioneer in urban scenes and photography; and Evgeny Zhitnev (1809 or 1811–1860). The last painted himself in 1833 in black tailcoat, pink waistcoat, white shirt, and black cravat — a complete European. Venetsianov assisted seven of his serf pupils to freedom by raising redemption money through lotteries and exercising his persuasive powers on serf owners. Among other onetime serfs who studied with him were G. A. Krylov, and Fëdor Slavyansky who gained freedom in 1838 and earned the title Artist at the Academy. Another, Grigory Mikhailov (1814–67), borrowed money from Venetsianov to buy his freedom and then switched over to study with Bryullov as a history painter and society portraitist. In a reverse direction, Sergei Zaryanko took Venetsianov's "realism" to great lengths as a professor at the Moscow School of Painting, Sculpture and Architecture, where he taught and inspired some of the Itinerants. With Venetsianov's death at age sixty-eight, the school vanished. The stylistic school of its pupils lived on.[13]

Two serf graduates of Arzamas founded provincial offshoots. Little is known about Kuzma Makarov (c. 1778–1862), a serf of the Gorikhvostovs (perhaps the Penza family who ran a serf theater). As a boy, Makarov was apprenticed to another serf painter, won his freedom on the death of his owner, enrolled at Arzamas, and earned a major silver medal in 1828. In the same year he founded a school in Saransk about which there survive few details, except that a fire destroyed it in the 1840s. In the early 1850s, he moved it to Penza in "a spacious house full of busts and pictures on a quiet street near the Church of the Nativity." To support his activity, he and his pupils painted frescos and icons for local churches. The Petersburg Academy began to sponsor the school, but another fire struck in 1859 and Makarov died a few years later. The serf A. D. Nadezhdin graduated from Arzamas in 1825 with a silver medal, and prior to receiving his freedom, around 1831 founded a School of Drawing and Painting in Kozlov, Tambov Province. The Academy of Arts, recognizing the quality of his students, began sponsoring it in 1836. Kozlov resembled Arzamas in its output of genre, portraits, and interiors as well as church iconostases and frescos; but the student body was socially broader than in other provincial establishments. Graduates included (of those identified by social class): a female landowner, Sofia Bekhtereva (two other women were not identified by social station); one merchant each of the second and third ranks; six townsmen; two free peasants; one state peasant; and eight serfs. Of the known career outcomes, nine became independent artists, eight district school art teachers, and five Academy students. Of the eight serf pupils, one was expelled, four were returned to their owners before finishing, one became a district school art teacher, and two won the title Artist. The director Nadezhdin, bemoaning the tyranny of patronage, stated that "splendor [in art] must be the fruit of freedom, triumphing over material things and not beholden to them," a notable case of shifting the discourse from juridical freedom to artistic freedom. Though racked with money problems, the school was still functioning in the 1860s.[14]

Even more striking in social makeup was the Public School of Painting Techniques, founded in Kiev in 1850 by Napoleon Buyalsky.[15] A man of means, Buyalsky studied in Berlin, Düsseldorf, and Paris with a specialty in history and portraiture. He won an unclassed certificate from the Petersburg Academy in 1846 and two years later built a school in Kiev. Since he could get art supplies only from St. Vladimir University, Buyalsky tried for a slot there and was turned down for lack of proper credentials. But the Academy endorsed his school and in 1850 it opened with permission from the Kiev civil governor. The class of 1851 contained eleven nobles (including one identified as a landowner), one "officer" (presumably nonnoble), and two townsmen — a major contrast to student bodies elsewhere.

Though Moscow hardly fits the term "provincial," it seemed that way as far as art was concerned to a visitor in 1838 who stated baldly: "There is almost no art in Moscow."[16] The visitor misspoke. True, until the 1830s, Moscow had neither an accredited art school nor public exhibition space; its picture collections were spread over the city in private hands. But during that decade the foundations were laid for the Moscow School of Painting, Sculpture, and Architecture (1843) which would make the old capital a major center of Russian art that rivaled the younger capital. The numerous Moscow amateur artists and graduates of the Petersburg Academy desired mutual contact. "Moscow is the center of our manufacturing activity," declared one of them; "it should also be the center of our efforts to establish and spread good taste and a love for elegance."[17] In 1832, E. I. Makovsky, an amateur and the father of four artists, formed the Moscow Art Society; Governor General D. V. Golitsyn, a cultivated art patron, secured a meeting place. The society launched the Moscow Life Class in 1832, which exhibited once or twice a week from two rented rooms. Its opening show in 1833 was the city's first public exhibition. A year later, the life class was renamed the Moscow Art Class (fig. 56).

Like a good many enterprises in Imperial Russia, the new school illustrated the tight cooperation possible between local government and private personages. Golitsyn organized a group of patrons who, for a donation of 250 rubles per year, could each enroll two pupils of their choice, free or serf. At a modest tuition rate, pupils of both sexes and all social classes took ten hours of drawing and eighteen of painting at a large rented apartment in the center of the city. Sixty-five enrolled in the first year. The first director, M. F. Orlov, ex-Decembrist and friend of Venetsianov, promoted an atmosphere less formal and more socially diverse than the Academy's. The Moscow Art Class trained artists, got them jobs and medals, and obtained freedom for a few serfs. In 1843, Orlov's successor, ex–civil governor of Moscow I. G. Senyavin (Sinyavin), appealed to Tsar Nicholas to make the class a branch of the Petersburg Academy. The tsar replied that there was no need for a second Academy of Arts, much less one in Moscow. But he did agree to permit the opening of a "school" (*uchilishche*) which eventually attained the title Moscow School of Painting, Sculpture, and Architecture.[18]

The major issues in the history of this school — its relationship with the Academy of Arts, its social composition, and the nature of the art produced there — together represent a case study of redefinition by rejection, a familiar feature in the growth of national cultural identity. Relations with the Academy revolved around Moscow's right to award medals and attendant privileges. The Academy permitted Moscow to grant only unclassed or Free Artist degrees to its graduates which afforded exemption from enserfment and from lower-class liabilities. In 1859, during the drafting of a new charter that would have made the Moscow School virtually independent of Petersburg, the sculptor Ramazanov argued that "Moscow has its own university, seminary, high schools, a self-governing architectural school, a Stroganov school with its own privileges — so why not an independent school of painting and sculpture? All enlightened Muscovites desire it." The charter was vetoed. The professional edifice of the Moscow art scene thus remained uncrowned and the school stayed subservient and unequal to the Academy of Arts.[19] The question of admitting serfs received a similar resolution. Earlier, when reviewing the charter of the Moscow Art Committee, Academy officials invoked Olenin's view that "the mixing of free and unfree pupils in the Academy caused among them all kinds of disorder and immoral behavior. And experience has shown that almost none of the serf pupils turned out to be well-behaved." When Moscow's charter came up for review in 1843, it allowed for equal education of free and serf artists. The Ministry of the Court removed the clause on serfs and reiterated the rule of 1817: no serfs to be admitted; exceptions required a declaration by the owner that, if the pupil earned a silver medal from the Academy, he would automatically be free. Olenin himself, now on the eve of retirement, was lukewarm to the Moscow School and viewed it as no different from all other provincial schools.[20] Thus any dream that some organizers might have had about creating a "school for freedom" faded, though it was not wholly expunged.

Moscow succeeded in retaining serfs (presumably with the required documentation) and many other members of the lower classes as well. In 1856, five years before the emancipation of the serfs, the 427 students constituted a body of great social and geographical diversity: townsmen, 195; officers of higher rank, 52; merchants, 43; freed serfs, 34; artisans, 23; serfs, 22; state peasants, 15; military and civil officials, 14; foundlings, 8; clergy, 8; foreigners, 6; house serfs, 4; Finns, 3; and one soldier on indefinite leave. Though place of origin is not tabulated for all, it is probably safe to assume that most students came from Moscow and the Russian heartland, though some hailed from the Solovetsky Islands, Siberia, Astrakhan, the Don region, Crimea, and Poland. Among the foreigners were one each from Mount Athos and Istanbul in the Ottoman Empire. No explanation is given for the categories "officers of higher rank" or "military and civil officials." The Moscow School was three-fourths filled with the lower classes studying together with over a hundred of the more or less privileged, a striking contrast to the Petersburg Academy where the lower strata at that time formed less than a third of the student body. In both schools, townspeople swamped all the rest, in the case of Moscow almost half the student body. Perhaps in response to this, Governor General Zakrevsky in 1858 attempted to limit lower-class enrollment.[21]

A mystical aura of Russianism informed the imagery around the school from the very beginning. The appeals for greater demographic democracy resonated with the rhetoric of the Slavophiles and Official Nationalists who adopted the school as an emerging center of national expression. Its opening in 1843 featured a student-faculty exhibition. In his inaugural speech as director, Senyavin dwelt upon the national spirit and character of the works displayed and spoke of the national face of Moscow, "where the physiognomy of the people, the monuments of antiquity, and historical memories all summon the fine arts to new discoveries." In a rhapsody reminiscent of the Official Nationalist Mikhail Pogodin's letter equating Russia's vastness with greatness, Senyavin exalted "Russian nature," which "combines all the world's climates, the translucent colors of the north, and the gently tinged hues of our natural vistas in the south. For our landscapists, there is available every kind of transition — from the frosty winter sky of the north to the sultry sky of the southern climes." For Senyavin, the subject of art was an eternal Russia that expected its children to capture its majestic beauties. With a lament far more typical of the intelligentsia than of a high-ranking tsarist official, Senyavin observed that "those Russian talents, of course, are latent in the Russian people, still hidden and lacking development."[22] In the wake of his rebuffed appeal for equality with the Academy of Arts, Senyavin's speech amounted to a manifesto exalting Moscow over St. Petersburg and Russian over cosmopolitan and academic art. His allusion to the native talents of the "people" (*narod*) clearly included the lower classes. Senyavin was no radical proponent of the critical realism that was unfolding in Russian art. Rather he was urging the expansion of a purely positive depiction of the beauties of the motherland and its people.

Moscow, the home of Slavophilism, had by this time also become the unofficial center of the Petersburg ideology of Official Nationalism. As such, it provided a natural hearth for the warming glow of Russianism. The Slavophile Alexei Khomyakov and the Official Nationalist Stepan Shevyrëv (along with his colleague Pogodin) were already eroding the differences that divided the two intellectual streams over some issues of Russia's future. Within a few years, they would forge their nationalist organ, *The Muscovite*, into a cultural synthesis around the new drama of peasants and merchants. In 1843, Khomyakov and Shevyrëv were serving on the board of the Moscow School. *The Muscovite* covered the opening exhibit on December 5, 1843, lauding national works on display, such as *The Russian Boy,* and thereby implying that a "natural" style equaled a "national" content. In a letter written the same year, Khomyakov advised artists to emulate Gogol and be inspired by "feeling, thoughts, and forms exclusively from the depths of their souls, from the treasure house of contemporary life." In 1845 Shevyrëv, in a lecture series on the lives of Renaissance artists, managed to weave national themes into his discussion of classicism.[23]

To what extent was the discursive tone of these inaugural anthems translated into art? They seem to have had little direct impact on the faculty, whose training backgrounds ranged from the smaller provincial schools to the Academy's branch in Rome. F. S. Zavyalov (1811–56), the history painting professor, executed biblical themes in cold, classical European style. The portraitist Apollon Mokritsky (1811–70), who had studied with Venetsianov, became a fierce disciple of Bryullov and financed his own way to Italy. In the manner of academics who identify intellectual vitality with refined nostalgia and the culture of their youth in sacralized places, Mokritsky filled his lectures at the Moscow School with reminiscences of Bryullov, Rome, and the "noble style." Vasily Tropinin, the most celebrated Muscovite painter of the time, now an old man, played a minor role at the school by advising in portraiture. Sergei Zaryanko (1818–70), another pupil of Venetsianov and of the Academy, taught in Moscow from 1856 to his death. His pupil, Vasily Perov, quoted him as saying: "Gentlemen, art in general is no more than imitation, that is, the attempt to imitate nature." The artist's goal is achieved "only by way of mathematical precision of copying." Zaryanko, though pedantic and intolerant of laxity and dreaminess — a Stolz to the school's Oblomovs — did not, as some believed, rigidly stifle the spontaneity of pupils. Landscape was taught by Skotti (Scotti, 1814–61), an Academy of Arts–trained painter of Italian ancestry who produced somewhat lifeless works on non-Russian themes; and by K. I. Rabus, a pupil of Maxim Vorobev.[24]

Though the senior professors followed academic values, their students carved out a divergent expressive path. Vasily Khudyakov, the only one in the 1840s to get a major silver medal, painted *Finnish Smugglers,* one of the first Russian purchases of the merchant patron Pavel Tretyakov. P. M. Shmelkov produced *Reading the Gospel in a Country Church* (1844) and a canvas depicting a soldier recounting his deeds, a theme taken up by other Moscow pupils. The big figure who radicalized genre painting was, of course, Vasily Perov (see chapter 9). The two most famous Moscow alumni who joined the later Itinerant school were Alexei Savrasov (1830–97) and Ivan Shishkin (1832–98), both of merchant families. The Moscow-born Savrasov as a youth sold landscapes, studied that genre at the Moscow School, graduated in 1850, became an Academician, and made a name by painting the dacha of Grand Duchess Maria Nikolaevna, then president of the Academy. In 1857, he replaced Rabus in landscape painting and was later canonized for his 1871 masterpiece, *The Rooks Have Returned.*[25]

Even more celebrated in his time, Shishkin was born in distant Vyatka

Province. On his arrival in Moscow, he saw oil canvases for the first time in his life, and was inspired to capture fields and outdoor scenes on the land the way Ivan Aivazovsky (Gaivazovsky, 1817–1900) was doing for the sea. Shishkin began in still semirural Moscow neighborhoods, sketching old churches and suburban parks, and then moving into the forests. While studying at the Moscow School under Mokritsky, Shishkin obtained permission from the Ministry of the Court to travel to his ancestral home in Vyatka to exhibit his works — the nucleus of the idea later developed by the Itinerants. On graduating in Moscow, he studied under Vorobev at the St. Petersburg Academy in 1856–60. Shishkin later made a reputation as the Knight Artist of the Woods and King of the Forest, though sarcastic critics would someday call him "the accountant of pine trees." These brief career sketches suggest that the impulse toward genre and naturalistic landscape came as much from within the artists as from any ideologically driven program of the Moscow School (Savrasov and Shishkin got their final training at the Academy, and the latter in Europe as well.)[26]

The historians Moleva and Belyutin correctly stressed Moscow's lack of lateral connecting webs and its dependence on the Petersburg Academy of Arts for sponsors, supplies, medals, admissions, and pedagogical methods. Dmitrieva, a pioneer historian of the Moscow School, honestly conceded the shortage of talented art students in the early years, but she did not exaggerate when she called it the cradle of realism and national art. Aside from Savrasov, Perov, and Shishkin, others who studied or taught there included such luminaries in Russian art of the later nineteenth century as Konstantin Savitsky (b. 1844), Vasily Polenov (b. 1844), Isaac Levitan (b. 1860), Konstantin Korovin (b. 1861), Valentin Serov (b. 1865), and Mikhail Nesterov (b. 1862). From 1865 to 1918, the Moscow School enjoyed an independent status with the right to award major and minor silver medals and to produce classed and unclassed graduates. In 1918, it was closed and its faculty flowed partly into the Soviet institutions, Vkhutemas and the Surikov Institute.[27]

As to public outreach, student art was exhibited irregularly along with the work of other Moscow artists. The shows began in 1839 and continued usually at two- or three-year intervals (but annually from 1849 to 1852). The tenth, in 1858, was the most successful up to that time in the quality of works, public attention, and profit — some 301 pieces done by pupils, faculty, alumni, and other artists. In the following year, the showing of Alexander Ivanov's *Christ Appearing to the People* became a major cultural event. The Moscow petty trader Pavel Medvedev, who with his friends frequented the art classes, noted that the pictures included some brought from St. Petersburg. The Moscow School was, for the vast majority of Muscovites, the only window to

Russian painting. The only other public venue was Moscow University where, starting in 1860, a new organization called the Society of Art Lovers showed mostly foreign works. In addition to the income from exhibit sales and lotteries, students received commissions. Among the purchasers, mostly gentry and merchants, were the future giants of merchant patronage, Tretyakov and Kozma Soldatenkov.[28]

Was there a counter-academy? Yes and no. S. Frederick Starr has correctly stressed the links, formal and otherwise, of the provincial art schools to the Academy of Arts. Venetsianov, Stupin, and his imitators in Saransk, Penza, and Kozlov all had close ties to the Academy. The Moscow School was more independent after 1843 but shared the Academy's general program. Starr correctly counters pious Soviet efforts to find budding realism and nationalism everywhere except at the Academy. Yet autonomous developments were inevitable at such distances from the guiding center. As Starr himself has shown definitively in his book on provincial administration, nominal chains of command or affiliations did not always translate into real power and influence at the local level. The schools' contacts with the masters in Petersburg were irregular. The surroundings and associations of local life — whether in Moscow or on a Tver estate — allowed a degree of drift from the hierarchical academic emphasis on history, portrait, and manorial landscape, and sometimes local versions of even these. Venetsianov trained his students at Safonkovo only in genre, never in historical painting. The thorough and balanced study of art education by Moleva and Belyutin, while granting that the template sent out from the Academy was accepted, shows convincingly that local conditions generated adaptation. The environment of the small country town and buyers' tastes conditioned new subject matter which in turn required different solutions in composition, light, and color. While new genre techniques had indeed first arisen in St. Petersburg, they remained marginal there whereas in the other towns they became more common.[29]

The modest proliferation of art schools somewhat modified the cultural space of the provinces. Though it is probably not true that outside Petersburg and Moscow no public gallery existed in the provinces until Aivazovsky opened one in Feodosia in the Crimea in 1880,[30] provincial showing remained weak until the advent of the Itinerants. Yet provincial schools in a limited way generated news and knowledge about art and sent artists out into the world. Their students interacted constantly with icon painters and did commissions for churches. Arzamas artists took their wares for public display to the largest fair in Russia, at Nizhny Novgorod. When audiences came to see the school's theater performances they saw art on the walls as well. Art schools beyond the capital helped open up space for viewing art and fueled new kinds of artistic expression. And the Moscow school became a major nursery for the painters of the coming generation.

Serf as Artist

Though an accurate count of serf artists at work in Russia in the last century of serfdom cannot be given, they far outnumbered serf musicians and actors. Thousands of serfs functioned as architects, decorators, craftsmen, technicians, builders, and engineers. Of serf painters, only a minority got on record: the very talented who worked in the fanciest palaces and estates, Academy graduates, and those who suffered a particularly cruel fate or who won their way to freedom — experiences that were not mutually exclusive. The rest left few traces. Innumerable amateur artists recruited from house and field serfs with little or no training painted for their masters, and — like actors and musicians — alternated artistic work with servants' duties. Some specialized in artisanry and folk art. Some of the clever daubers resembled amateur masters. The talented self-taught serf sketcher Beshentsev worked as a buffet waiter for the Buturlins. As cultivated and considerate masters, they never used corporal punishment or verbal abuse and remembered Beshentsev fondly for his family sketches and mocking cartoons of the mediocre art tutor whom the Buturlins had hired from the Academy.[31]

Unlike most of the grooms and maids who played on stage or in the pit with a minimum of tutoring, serf painters, to be worth something, needed serious training. Ephemeral performance blunders could be forgiven, forgotten, or punished. Flawed paintings left a permanent record. The capital and provincial art schools trained only a minute number of serf painters, many of whom returned to their masters. The poorest nobles would simply take a boy of whatever talent into the house and put him to work. For the more affluent, a common method was to apprentice the would-be serf artist to a local icon painter for a crash course in basic compositional skills. Art lessons for the gentry and their children were very popular, and their tutors were sometimes put to train serfs.[32] Many serf painters were "discovered" by their owners as icon painters. Grigory Ostrovsky, a serf of the late eighteenth century, carried his icon training over into domestic portraits.[33] Prince Nikolai Yusupov's training center at Arkhangelskoe taught decorative arts and painting from 1818 to 1831, using free and serf teachers and pupils. The steward would contract some of them out on *obrok* to other landowners, or to the estate's porcelain works. His reports complain about drunkenness, theft, and disorder among serf artists. After Yusupov's death in 1831, the school closed and the pupils dispersed to various estates or were put out on *obrok*.[34]

A few serf artists achieved fame in the eighteenth century. Ivan Argunov (1727–97), one of several artists in his family, did portraits for his master, P. B. Sheremetev, who freed him. Argunov, like many other serf painters, was often deflected by other duties, in his case as majordomo. His *An Unknown Peasant Woman* (1784), the first of its kind, probably had as its subject a wet-nurse from the common people — and not an actress posing for a formal portrait as once believed. Mikhail Shibanov, a serf of Prince Potëmkin (freed by 1783; died after 1789), worked for patrons all over Russia and was an early practitioner of the peasant genre. N. P. Rumyantsev granted freedom to Vasily Sazonov, later an Academician, "in homage to his talent." Most owners viewed serf painters as mere artisans but none the less held them to be more valuable than performers or musicians. The talented serf artist, even if still in bondage, could achieve renown. Owners obtained art free of charge and some collected *obrok* from a serf's own private commissions. In the 1840s, Baron Haxthausen met three serf artists in Arzamas — a father and two sons, one of whom had studied at the Academy of Arts. They paid 350 rubles a year *obrok* to their master so they could paint commercially and earned as much as 25 rubles for one picture. When a painter became famous, some serf owners charged high redemption fees for his liberation.[35]

Serfs who attained some technical skill with the brush were generally set to copying, making family portraits, or decorating interiors. Most of the two hundred pictures on one of the Obolensky estates in Tula Province were copies of masters. The skillful copyist Grigory Ozerov, with wife and daughter, was purchased for two thousand rubles. Owners cherished family portraits, even if executed by self-trained serf artists. The four hundred–odd half-portraits found on the Nadezhdino estate of the Kurakins, many done by serfs, ran the gamut from exceptional to mediocre. Amateur portraitists usually painted hands poorly and made the heads of their subjects too big. N. B. Yusupov at Arkhangelskoe hung on his walls engravings done by the pupils at his drawing school. The classical rage fed the desire for mythological ceilings, friezes, pilasters, gold inlay, and murals. Peasants or servants posed as models: in one case, a coachman sat for the figure of Paris and a dairymaid for Fair Helen. Adventurous lords had their serfs create imaginative wall art, depicting in primary colors palm trees, wild beasts, and figures of Chinese and Americans. For panoramas, the landowner would assemble prints and pictures and have his serf artist copy them onto a mural. Much of the surviving anonymous wall art, some of it possessing a *lubok* character, was done by serf artists. At some places, serf girls were put to work weaving carpets and tapestries depicting the owner's manorial park with ladies and gentlemen strolling around it. The master at the Zobnino estate near Tver in the late eighteenth century had his serf do a painting of the manor house, but since he did not do it from direct observation, the elevation was distorted.[36]

Serf painters did not escape corporal punishment. A priest told of a land-owner who had one of his serfs whipped to a bloody pulp for going to the village without permission, and then sicked his dog on him, whose bites proved fatal. Yet the suffering of artists seems to have stemmed more from psychological than physical abuse. Failure to get freedom was the bane of talented serf artists. In the 1830s a serf painter who belonged to one of the Orlovs had to leave the Academy of Arts when his master brought him home to paint iconostases and copy masters. He was freed only in old age. The historian Semevsky told of a painter who lived in virtual freedom until the death of his owner, at which point the artist was sold and his status was reversed by the new master. "Cases of suicide were a very common thing," wrote Letkova, "and the chronicles of serfdom are full of them." Yet she mentions only a few, including one who drowned himself in the master's pond because the recalcitrant owner made him paint floors and roofs and herd swine.[37] A painter named Polyakov or Palyakov (no surname given; not A. V. Polyakov) learned art from the father of Academician E. Ya. Vasilev, began to move in educated circles, and did portraits in St. Petersburg society at four hundred rubles each. Polyakov's owner encouraged the belief that he would free the painter and then reneged. He recalled Polyakov, and made him a liveried footman on his carriage as they drove to gentry homes where the serf's art was hanging and where he had been received as a talented artist. Polyakov took to drink and disappeared.[38]

For art historians, Vasily Tropinin (1776–1857) heads the list of notable serf artists in the way that Shchepkin does among serf actors for theater schol-ars (fig. 57). His protracted struggle for freedom generated lachrymose stud-ies. A 1956 Soviet children's book on his life, *Serf Artist,* typified the approach by heroizing and simplifying the subject and inventing conversations and scenes.[39] Tropinin, born a serf of Count A. S. Minikh in Novgorod Province, was given as part of a dowry to Count I. I. Morkov. Tropinin's father won freedom for his work as a steward, but the boy remained enserfed. The father, noting his son's talent, tried to have his owner send him to study in St. Pe-tersburg. Morkov instead sent Tropinin as an apprentice pastry cook in the home of Count Zavadovsky in St. Petersburg. The young serf constantly ne-glected his kitchen duties in order to observe a hired professional artist at work. He began to draw for himself and was finally allowed to attend the Academy as an auditor from 1798 to 1804. Tropinin's teachers tried to secure his freedom, but the stubborn Morkov had him sent back to one of his estates in Podolia Province to paint walls and carriage wheels as well as family portraits. Tropinin was too good a teacher and portraitist for Morkov to give him up.[40]

On one occasion, a story goes, when the count took a visiting French scholar to watch Tropinin at the easel, the guest was loud in his praises. That evening at dinner, seeing Tropinin in livery among the serving lackeys, the Frenchman brought up a chair and invited the artist-waiter to sit down at table. Both master and servant registered astonishment at this gesture. The oft-told episode, recounted by a contemporary of Tropinin and probably originating with the artist himself, resonates like a fairytale about the discovery of secret nobility or imprisoned virtue, with its innocent victim, heartless jailer, and benevolent unmasker. Though the tale may have been embellished in the telling, there is no reason to doubt its substance. Discovery and deliverance form the core of all the stories about how well-disposed and highly placed people secured freedom for talented serfs. And the deliverance actually came for Tropinin, though later in his life. In 1821, the Morkovs moved to Moscow and Tropinin with them. The campaign to free him launched by Apollon Maikov, Pavel Svinin, P. N. Dmitriev, and others became a hot topic at the English Club. Morkov finally consented and on Easter Sunday 1823, at age forty-seven, Tropinin received three kisses, a colored egg, and his warrant of freedom. Tropinin was elected to the Academy for his celebrated canvas, *The Lacemaker*. He gained fame as a highly paid portraitist: in his lifetime, Tropinin painted about three thousand portraits including those of Pushkin, Karamzin, Gogol, and Bryullov.[41]

The best-known of the unfreed serf painters, Grigory Soroka (real name: Vasilev; 1823–64), was born of serf parents on the estate of P. I. Milyukov in the Vyshny Volochok district of Tver Province. Around 1838 the boy become the property of the oldest son, N. P. Milyukov, whose home stood near Lake Moldino, a body of water that Soroka painted many times. Around 1841 Soroka met Milyukov's neighbor Venetsianov and studied on and off at the latter's school while working as a house serf, gardener, and actor for Milyukov. Soroka was not permitted to go with Venetsianov to St. Petersburg. At the Milyukov home during the 1840s and 1850s, he painted the study with its Napoleon statuette, skull, book, and candles. Soroka portrayed his master's father hunched over with downcast eyes and an unhappy visage and, more sympathetically, the master's little daughters. Soroka's self-portrait, though hardly a swagger, seems to project the serf artist into a different world: he is clean shaven, bright of face, and dressed in gentry-style white neckband, cravat, and high side collar covered by a frock coat.[42] Although serf owners expected certain male servants to be beardless and dress somewhat in a European manner inside the house (and sometimes in livery), Soroka's self-image seems to suggest not that of a house serf who happened to be a painter, but of an independent artist.[43] The natural pride embodied in the picture became the source of Soroka's special pain when confronted with arbitrary seigniorial power.

Soroka, an original painter, could never exhibit his work. Serfdom defined his anonymity for a long time, and his paintings were resurrected in Soviet times. The later notoriety derived partly from his fate. In 1818, a few years before Soroka was born, the elder Milyukov, who had driven his peasants to work a six-day week on his demesne and freely used the lash and forced army service, had been beset with peasant disorders.[44] The son apparently brooked no impudence or pretensions from peasants or house serfs. A spat with Soroka in 1842 led Milyukov to convert the painter to a gardener for a spell. Bad blood led Milyukov to deny Soroka freedom even though he did set free a less-talented serf painter who went to the Academy in 1857. Venetsianov, who had helped free Shevchenko in 1838 and was on good terms with Milyukov, intervened. In letters he stressed Soroka's virtues and his rapid progress in painting. But the master denied every request. Venetsianov accused him of raising up the serf painter to the delights of art, which was worse than keeping him in the dark.[45] Unfortunately, Venetsianov died in a freak sleigh accident in 1847 and Soroka lost his protector. In 1852 Soroka married a servant girl and in 1860 moved into his own home, thus removed from domestic service but still a serf. After emancipation, Soroka lodged a complaint against the former master, was sentenced to be whipped, and hanged himself in 1864. The unhappy painter acquired so much hagiographical reverence in later times that a pre-revolutionary silent film was made on his life.[46]

Milyukov, like his counterparts who kept their musicians and actors in bondage, was not atypical, but not all serf artists failed in their quest for freedom. Aside from the cases of those few who fled, the commonest path was simple manumission by a sympathetic owner or by redemption. Sheremetev freed N. I. and Ya. I. Argunov and the former became an Academician. The renowned Vasily Sadovnikov (1800–1879), a serf of Princess N. P. Golitsyna (the model for Pushkin's countess in *Queen of Spades*), was possibly born on her Kaluga estate but grew up in St. Petersburg. After the princess died, he was freed in 1838 by her son, D. V. Golitsyn, the Moscow art patron. Sadovnikov's training remains a mystery but he was named Perspective Artist by the Academy after his freedom, though he achieved Academician status only in 1852 in spite of the fame he acquired from his views of St. Petersburg.[47]

The state, which purchased actors and musicians in wholesale lots, did not do so for painters. Artists belonging to reluctant masters had to get their freedom through personal struggle, often with the help of private patrons. However, the Academy of Arts and the Society for the Encouragement of Artists lent their weight to the emancipation process by lobbying, politely requesting, and sometimes pressuring stubborn serf owners. The Academy artist as champion of freedom became a familiar enough figure in Russian life that it entered fiction in A. V. Timofeev's overwrought novel *The Artist* (1834) about a retired provincial Academician who redeems a serf painter with his last ruble and sends him to St. Petersburg. The process generated a loose structure of "public opinion" or collective moral judgment of peers. Dmitry Malyarenko, a serf of the widow of General Musin-Pushkin from Ekaterino-slav Province, in the late 1830s and 1840s revealed his skills while copying at the Hermitage. Academy vice president Tolstoy got the Duke of Leuchtenberg to ask for Malyarenko's freedom from the heirs of Musina-Pushkina. His letter of 1845 appealed to their kindness and to the contribution they would make to the arts of Russia. While waiting for a reply, Malyarenko informally attended the Academy and even exhibited his work there. The signature of the august in-law of the tsar carried sufficient weight and the request was granted in 1848.[48] The solution was rarely so neat. When the Academy collected three thousand rubles from well-wishers to redeem another serf artist, the owner raised the price to five thousand. Grand Duchess Maria Nikolaevna inter-vened with a royal request and the landowner relented. But when the serf artist delivered her letter, his master ordered him given twenty-five lashes for his uppity behavior. In another case, the Academy asked landowner Captain Bryanchaninov of Yaroslav Province to release a serf who was studying at the Academy. After a long delay, the captain, pleading poverty and a heavy mort-gage, requested a reimbursement of twenty-five hundred rubles. The outcome of the case is unknown. For these and other reasons, the Academy remained circumspect, reluctant as it was to cause a stir in remote provinces over the rights of serf owners and to arouse the wrath of recalcitrant lords, especially since a request to free a serf could backfire.[49]

A few Moscow serf pupils benefited from Academy intervention, both the two known cases resulting from the personal interest of Karl Bryullov. While visiting the Moscow Art Class, Bryullov arranged to free I. I. Lipin, a serf belonging to the Zubovs, and the event was enacted officially at a banquet. Bryullov dubbed him "my little son," and took him to the Academy as an external student where he won a silver medal. Kirill Gorbunov (1822–93), a serf of the landowner Vladykina, met Vissarion Belinsky who hailed from the same region and took Gorbunov under his wing. In 1836 Gorbunov entered the Moscow Art Class. His freedom resulted in 1841 from letters written by

Bryullov and Zhukovsky to Vladykina. After graduation from the St. Petersburg Academy, Gorbunov worked as a portraitist, later well known for his studies of Herzen, Gogol, Granovsky, and Belinsky.[50]

The more active and influential Society for the Encouragement of Artists (originally "of Art") had no analogue in the social history of music or theater. Originally a private organization, it was born in 1821, a few years after the official ban on serf students at the Academy of Arts. Its purpose was to support artists from all classes, including serfs, who had no other patronage. The founders met on November 30, 1821, in the lavish Petersburg home of Senator I. A. Gagarin on the corner of the Moika River and the Winter Canal. Gagarin, who had married the great tragedienne Ekaterina Semënova, herself of serf origin, created an exalted atmosphere by alluding to his wife's career. As she rose to leave when the men arrived, her husband intoned the words: "the servant of Melpomene will illuminate with her light the first gathering of those who seek to serve the god Apollo."[51] Founders included the first president, brigadier general, state secretary, and imperial aide-de-camp P. A. Kikin (1775–1834); Colonel F. F. Schubert; Lieutenant Colonel A. I. Dmitrev-Mamonov, a noted battle artist of the Napoleonic wars; and Captain A. I. Kiel (Kil) — all Freemasons except Kikin. The Society set dues at two hundred rubles per year or two thousand for life. In a few years, it began receiving government subsidies and in 1833 was renamed the Imperial Society for the Encouragement of Artists. Membership grew steadily to 160 by 1845; it came to include Academy officials such as F. P. Tolstoy; the writers Venevitinov, Gogol, Zhukovsky, and Odoevsky; and art lovers M. S. Vorontsov, A. G. Kushelëv-Bezborodko, D. N. Sheremetev, and V. A. Perovsky.

The society's organizers — courtiers, magnates, and patrons of culture like the founders of the Philharmonia two decades earlier — bore the progressive spirit and sentimental patriotism lingering from the 1812 war. Early membership included veterans of the proto-Decembrist benevolent unions, Freemasons, Bible Society members, mystics, enlighteners, and philanthropists whose causes were at flood tide before the crackdown of the mid-1820s and the failed Decembrist revolt. They brought a missionary tone to the society's discourse on artists, and they played on the romantic trope, then fashionable in European literature, of the poor and youthful artist embattled against adversity. The founders stated baldly that neither the state nor the Academy could bridge the gulf between talented artists and the public. This "had to be done in the public [sphere]." Since, as they put it, "the channel between [the public] and artists does not exist," the society would have to create it.[52] The language bordered on subversive in an ascriptive society like Russia's. To some it seemed as though this organization was impinging on the business of the state as arbiter of taste and controller of the art world. No wonder that the conservative Academy professor A. I. Sauerweid (Zauerveid), a man close to court circles, complained that "the Society for the Encouragement of Artists is in opposition to the Academy of Arts"; he denounced its members as "False Dmitrys who wish to undermine the Academy and make themselves powerful."[53]

In fact, although clashes occasionally arose, cooperation with the Academy prevailed. The society donated equipment to the Academy in return for special privileges for its subsidized protégés. It supported eight artists who went to Rome in the 1830s and 1840s. Its most famous pensioner, Karl Bryullov, broke with the society in 1829 due to a delay in getting his money. The society endowed gold medal prizes, set up special life classes inside the Academy for its own artists, and organized the release of townsmen's class obligations in order to gain them admission. It wheedled the Academy to bend its rules over and over again to accommodate pupils who were otherwise ineligible. It ran the Petersburg School of Drawing which had been founded in 1839 on Vasilevsky Island by Finance Minister Egor Kankrin to train the lower classes as draftsmen for industry and to train poor youths as artists. When a successor tried to withhold the school's funding, the society took it over and expanded it to one thousand pupils. Ivan Kramskoi taught and Ilya Repin studied there.[54] A prominent society member, Colonel Alexei Tomilov (1779–1848), on returning wounded from the 1812 war to become an art collector and patron of young artists, invited them to the private collections in his home, and maintained a guest center for artists at his estate near Staraya Ladoga on the Volkhov River where they worked even after Tomilov's death.[55]

From the start, the society, on its own and in cooperation with the Academy, engaged in freeing serf artists. Its motivation sprang from charitable and humanitarian impulses rather than from legalistic notions about civil rights. Yet it went beyond philanthropy and patronage in helping any talented artist — not only favorites of patrons. Since all transactions of the society were based on the permission of the owner, the process was completely legal. All manumissions had to be approved by the Senate. The state kept a watchful eye on the society's activities. Count Benckendorf, chief of the political police or Third Section, in checking that freed artists were really talented, inquired about them from the serfs' owners, the local governor, or both. Most landowners approached by the society agreed to manumission. According to sketchy data, the society helped to liberate the following artists: Pantaleimon Stepanov, a state peasant from Pskov Province, 1828; A. A. Alekseev, serf of Kuzminova, 1832; N. V. Lifanov, serf of S. V. Panina, 1834; Andrei Bezlyudny, serf of D. N. Sheremetev, 1835; the Arzamas pupil Vasily Raev (1807–1870), freed in 1839 for five thousand rubles; I. I. Konobeevsky, serf of E. D. Naryshkin, 1840; Anton Ivanov, serf of O. Ya. Domashneva of Kostroma Province, 1841: F. Belov, serf of S. I. Mestr [de Maistre], 1846; and an otherwise unidentified Konchalevsky.[56]

The case of Moisei Dikov, a serf of Poltava landowner G. Vishnevsky, produced narrative language that bore telltale signs of intelligentsia ideals of freedom and art and probably the standard mode of expression in such processes. In his letter to the society asking for assistance, Dikov wrote (or had written for him) his "story." Noting his "strong passion for drawing," his father had sent him to Kiev to work under an icon painter from whence after two and a half years he was brought back to the master's home. Dikov implored the society for its assistance "to achieve . . . what I cannot even live without. Granting me freedom, you will thus give me the strength to pursue the path designated for me by fate." Dikov's owner demanded six thousand rubles, which the society could not pay, and the painter's fate is unknown.[57]

Two serf artists whose liberation was associated with the Society for the Encouragement of Artists have left fuller traces. A. V. Polyakov (1801–35), a house serf of Lieutenant General Kornilov, was sent in 1825 to St. Petersburg to work under George Dawe. This English artist, commissioned by Tsar Alexander I to do portraits of the leading officers of the Napoleonic wars for the Gallery of Heroes in the Hermitage, ran a virtual portrait factory. A cheat and an exploiter, he had Polyakov and others copy his originals; he then signed them and sold them at a thousand rubles each to friends and relatives of the august subjects while paying his workers a pittance. Kornilov refused to free Polyakov. The publicist Pavel Svinin, a self-appointed champion of vulnerable artists, exposed Dawes's fraud in the pages of his journal *Notes of the Fatherland* and created a scandal in which Faddei Bulgarin defended the Englishman. In 1828, the Society for the Encouragement of Artists, outraged that a foreigner was exploiting the labor of Russians, took Polyakov's request for freedom to Tsar Nicholas who granted it — the sole case, to my knowledge, of his intervention for the freedom of a serf artist. The society got Polyakov admitted to the Academy as a pensioner some time before 1833 when he was named a Free Artist.[58]

The most famous serf artist of the Russian Empire, Ukrainian painter and musician Taras Shevchenko (1814–61), though renowned in the world for his poetry, won his freedom through art. Shevchenko experienced almost daily the sting of humiliation as a serf for half his life, and as a convict and private soldier in his final years. Born in Kiev Province on the estate of the lordly Senator Vasily Engelhardt, Shevchenko was orphaned at age eleven and worked variously as a swineherd and a kitchen boy where he was beaten by the chef. On the death of old Engelhardt in 1828, Taras became the personal servant of the son, Pavel (1798–1849), a civil servant known for misusing his serfs. When not filling the master's pipe and cleaning his boots, Taras surreptitiously copied the art that hung on the walls. Accompanying the master to his military posts, he got his first art lessons in Vilna and Warsaw. Engelhardt sent Shevchenko to Petersburg in 1831 to study art. Pavel's brother, Vasily, owner of Engelhardt House, apprenticed the young man to an ex-serf guildmaster of painters and decorators, V. G. Shiryaev, a graduate of the Arzamas Academy. Shiryaev had learned no moral lesson on the road from bondage to freedom except brutality toward his workers. Lacking sympathy for his underling's aspirations, Shiryaev assigned Shevchenko to decorating work at Petersburg's three theaters.[59]

In his spare time, Shevchenko read, looked at pictures, and copied statues in the Summer Garden (though serfs were not permitted there). He was befriended by fellow Ukrainians Evgeny Grebenko (Evhen Hrebenka), composer of the noted romance *Dark Eyes*; and Academy professor Vasily Grigorovich (Hrihorovych), who was also secretary of the Society for the Encouragement of Artists. In 1835 they got him into society-sponsored classes and the Hermitage. Serfs were in no position to return slights from their owners, but Shevchenko managed to get at least a bit of revenge on a nobleman who was not his owner. P. D. Seletsky, who once tried to collaborate with Shevchenko on an opera, tells an otherwise undocumented story about Shevchenko in his days as a budding artist before he got his freedom. A general commissioned a portrait of himself by Shevchenko for a fee of a hundred rubles; on seeing the finished work, he would pay only fifty. Shevchenko kept the picture, repainted it on a barber's sign, and hung it up in full view. Before the furious general could manage to purchase the serf artist in order to wreak vengeance on him, Shevchenko won his freedom.[60] True or not, the anecdote certainly reflects one aspect of the artist's rebellious character.

The "discovery story" or "freedom narrative" of Shevchenko comes in several versions. In one, an Academy student became his friend and protector. In another, he met his savior while sketching in the Summer Garden, a tale that Shevchenko may have borrowed from another artist's actual experience. In any case, the boy made the acquaintance of Venetsianov, Zhukovsky, Bryullov, and Mikhail Vielgorsky who, impressed by him, determined to win his freedom. One by one, supporters approached Pavel Engelhardt. Bryullov, though at the peak of his fame and influence, got a refusal to release the "indispensable worker." After his visit, Bryullov called Engelhardt "a swine in slippers." Venetsianov spoke to Engelhardt as one landowner to another and then discoursed on philanthropy and enlightenment. Engelhardt interrupted him in order to get to the price: of twenty-five hundred rubles. The desperate Shevchenko was close to suicide at one point. But the money materialized when Zhukovsky and Vielgorsky organized a lottery in which Bryullov's portrait of Zhukovsky was sold and the proceeds were used to free Shevchenko in 1838. The twenty-four-year-old ex-serf shouted "freedom, freedom!" and kissed the attesting document signed by Bryullov, Zhukovsky, and Vielgorsky. On the following day, Shevchenko enrolled in the Academy of Arts.[61]

After graduation, Shevchenko returned to his homeland where he produced literary masterpieces, engaged in radical nationalist politics in the Cyril and Methodius Society, and was arrested and sent as a soldier to the frontier region of Orenburg. In this new serfdom, which lasted from 1847 to 1857, the poet-artist was forbidden to write or draw. When the tsar denied Shevchenko's appeal to revise this ban, the artist in him suffered more than the writer. In time Shevchenko defied the ruling and even secretly sold some of his pictures through friends. Beyond Orenburg lay the broad Asian steppe and the shores of the Aral Sea. While posted to these regions, Shevchenko encountered Kalmyks, Tatars, Bashkirs, and Kirghiz. A decade earlier, these peoples had attracted the artist V. I. Sternberg (Shternberg) who had set out as a volunteer to Khiva with the ill-fated Perovsky expedition in 1839. Sternberg produced in that year a set of lithographs, *Peoples of the Orenburg Region,* and an oil painting, *Kalmyk Yurts.* These works, displaying painterly conventions in composition, coloring, shadow, and foliage, were among the earliest Russian graphic representations of the natives of this region. Shevchenko went beyond Sternberg in both content and style. His watercolors of what looks like a desert fire and of scenes on the bleak Aral Sea are original and disturbing. On an expedition into the steppe and the Karakum desert, Shevchenko sketched headless corpses of fallen warriors decades before Vasily Vereshchagin (b. 1842) built his fame on this kind of material.[62]

A few observations may be made about Russian serf painters, freed or otherwise. They worked in every form, not only genre and landscape which came to be associated with native "Russian" art; but in portraiture and, in a few cases, even history painting. Except for Tropinin and, to a lesser extent, Soroka, few produced masterpieces. Shevchenko's poetry by far outstripped in quality his graphics, charming as they may be. Yet serf artists as a whole not only enriched the everyday visual world of Russian homes but provided the painters themselves with an expressive outlet unavailable to the bulk of the population. The efforts of the Society for the Encouragement of Artists, limited as they were, brought freedom to some artists and undreamed-of career success to a few. As the Soviet scholar Golubeva noted decades ago, the society's contribution to the world of artists has been underrated by historians. It could never develop into a large-scale abolitionist movement. But by legally helping to free talented human beings from the chains of serfdom, it added a thread to the growing narrative of antiserfdom in literature and to the private conversations about freedom in drawing rooms of town and country. A prevailing view of art among the gentry put patronage and consumption of art at their end of the social scale and its creation or performance further down. Art was what the gentry bought or got free of charge from inferiors — including serfs; and their training of artists was strictly instrumental and personal. By institutionalizing "encouragement," the leaders of the society asserted a collective respect for art, and, by implication, for the artist. This constituted a further step along the way to a new social imagery of the art world from an ascriptive hierarchy to an open ladder on which people of talent could climb the heights of art made by themselves.

Peasants on Canvas

Paralleling the social activists who worked to free serfs from bondage came painters who sought in their canvases to free serfs and other rural denizens from anonymity or invisibility. For such painters this meant leaving the studio at least for a time. Artists engaged in outdoor art had traditionally used crayon and pen on location and then finished their works in a studio. This handy device lacked the direct confrontation of painter with the changing colors and light of nature. European plein air artists in oil or watercolor appeared in the seventeenth century and came into their own in the eighteenth. In Paris, the influential Pierre-Henri Valencienne exalted landscape as the equal of any style or genre, though only if done in plein air in a quest for "reality." He allowed for a distinction between the intellectual "historical" landscape and the emotional "rural" (contemporary) landscape. British artists "went to the countryside" also. Watercolor and sketching societies in the early nineteenth century made rural excursions to study natural detail and to depict the occupations and dress of its inhabitants in "natural" rather than "pastoral" physiognomy. It had become absurd, said one painter, to picture "a race of gods and goddesses, with scythes and hayrakes."[63]

Academic artists everywhere had to rethink certain key components of pictures when they embarked for the countryside. The Roman steed became a draft horse, the chariot a cart, the temple a village church, the grand plaza a market square, and the balletic and declaiming characters of Hellenic myth — ordinary people. Work habits changed as well. Traditional European painters often executed a landscape wholly from memory or imagination within a studio or in a mix of plein air sketches pieced together indoors. Painters also needed to learn new techniques to capture gestures, poses, muscles, body rhythms, strain, energy, and sweat, not to mention real people, crops, barns, land forms, and dirt—as opposed to studio models, sculptural figuration, backdrops, and props.[64]

The move to "observed landscape" in Russia came slowly.[65] Its artists faced a number of obstacles in turning to the land for inspiration. A strong impetus for British landscape painting in the late eighteenth and early nineteenth centuries was the intrusion of industrialization, which seemed to threaten nature and thus to render it more precious. No such threat loomed on the Russian horizon in these decades. The alleged lack of picturesqueness in the Russian outdoors noted by Karamzin still held sway in academic opinion and foreign commentary. The Marquis de Custine spoke of the landscape around St. Petersburg as "a soggy moorland, low-lying and scattered as far as the eye can see, with birch trees which appear scanty and meagre."[66] The Academy of Arts held the Russian land unworthy of serious representation. Silvestr Shchedrin was among the first Russian painters, in the 1820s, to go outdoors. But, though he executed masterly studies of the Italian countryside, his work paled when he applied his brush to Russian scenery. Some academic artists were unable to break with pastoral traditions. V. G. Khudyakov (1826–76), who had studied in Moscow, Petersburg, and Rome, as late as 1849 painted a *Shepherd and Peasant Girl*, (GRMFZh, 3545), complete with a stylized leering male who, though attired in Russian costume, held a panpipe, wore a wreath, and was shod in goatlike footware.[67] Then, of course, Russian distances and poor travel facilities and amenities discouraged traversing the deep interior. Those who began to work exclusively out of doors had to have physical stamina and to face the elements. It is not hard to see why an unknown Russian landscape painter on the outskirts of Moscow at midcentury painted himself at work, set up as comfortably as possible with easel, palette, chair, and umbrella.[68]

Russian artistic explorers, varying enormously in professional competence, shared an outlook sharply different from the painters of estate grounds. Indeed the fashion of big panoramic manor house canvases was fading, reflecting the decline both of the manorial economy and of the inclination to display one's manicured acres. The picturesque or occluded landscape came into play in painting and in fiction. Turgenev's *Notes of a Hunter* (1848–52), for example, contains only one or two descriptions of panoramic views.[69] The bulk of the outdoor scenes are bathed in more intimate nature. Early Russian realists, long neglected and marginalized as primitive, provincial, and subcanonical, were later and are now recognized as being more than makers of "quasi-art." In addition to the pupils and disciples of Venetsianov—Slavyansky, Nikifor Krylov, Soroka, Krendovsky, Zelentsov—many of the outdoor realists were lesser-known and unidentified artists from Novgorod, Pskov, Yaroslavl, Kostroma, Smolensk, Tver, Saratov, Nizhny, Tula, and other places. Their combination of European technique with native styles produced a body of work that was on the whole bright, charming, and direct. In spite of some stiffness, they lack aristocratic disdain, aloofness, and distance; and they are marked by affect, emotion, and openness. Color predominates over correct linear perspective, and landscapes lack the Arcadian tranquility of convention.[70]

Maxim Vorobev, a favorite of Nicholas I, an Academy man to the core and a veteran of the Roman pensionate, seemed to stand for all that later critics would complain about. Yet he exerted a great influence on the new landscape painters who moved outdoors. Some of his pupils ventured into the immense steppe, elongated by the unrelieved emptiness of a road, as in Alexei Savrasov's *Steppe in Daytime* (1852) and V. I. Sternberg's *Mill on the Steppe* (1838).[71] Others braved the frost. Nikifor Krylov (1802–31) executed his *Winterscape* (1827) at the Tosno River about twenty-five or thirty kilometers from St. Petersburg where the painter spent a month boarding with a rich fuel merchant patron. The landscape shows the river, a stand of evergreen trees dividing the whiteness of sky from that of the snowy earth, and frozen water beyond to add depth. Though conventional in composition, Krylov's canvas has abandoned Arcadia in favor of a bleak Russian winter.[72]

Undeterred by distance, two other Russian painters, the brothers Grigory and Nikanor Chernetsov, Academicians both, roamed Russia and the Caucasus in the 1830s. By decade's end, they were ready to carry out their dream of traversing the entire course of the Volga River and capturing it and the adjoining landscape in art. They sought and won the support of the Society for the Encouragement of Artists, and official permission from the Ministry of the Court via the Academy. In May 1838, the Chernetsov brothers, accompanied by serf artist Anton Ivanov (1818 or 1811–1865), set out on their voyage. In a specially designed floating studio, they sailed down the great river from Rybinsk to Kostroma, Nizhny Novgorod, Kazan, and almost to Astrakhan, facing sudden storms and ice floes on the way. During the voyage, the brothers, each doing opposite river banks, produced hundreds of sketches, prints, and paintings as well as a panoramic canvas of the entire voyage, later exhibited in Petersburg by unrolling it through two windows in a way that suggested the movement and noise of a ship. Selected works from the trip later shown at the Academy created a flurry of interest among the Petersburg public; and their success enabled the brothers, through the society, to gain freedom for their serf artist traveling companion Ivanov, who depicted the voyage in his painting *The Brothers Chernetsov on the Boat on the Volga*. The Chernetsovs produced no impressive landscapes on their journey. Rather they captured towns, skylines, historical and archeological sites; picturesque vignettes of river banks, waterways, and vessels of every sort; and people at work. By treating in their notes and pictures the Volga in all its drabness as well as in its glorious variety as a national icon, these Russian artists were seeking the "prospects for a nation" in a way rarely attempted in the polished studies promoted by academic art.[73]

Charting the limitations of some of these early practitioners, Christopher Ely, in his study of the evolving imagery of Russian nature, notes that "new aesthetic approaches to the depiction of Russian landscape scarcely registered until the 1850s."[74] This is true in regard to the rendering of physical land forms and the overall reading and construction of a "Russian nature" in art. The novelty came in works of provincial genre, often including or overlapping with landscape, representing people — indoors and outdoors — who came alive on canvas in new ways: peasants, workers, merchants, townspeople, and nobles.

How were peasants represented in art? Painters had a wide choice of treatment: grotesque and vulgar, nearly invisible as staffage, poor and miserable, wracked by physical labor, joyous, or possessed of noble dignity. The choices were conditioned by the conventions of one's era, the accessibility of real peasants, personal attitudes, or a reigning ideology — among other things. The grotesque peasants sometimes found in medieval and early modern European art, with their short, fat bodies and vulgar gestures, became rare by the eighteenth century when peasants were mostly reduced to staffage. Eventually, they graduated into close-up treatment; in Linda Nochlin's words, from "picturesque background figures" to the foreground, with attendant visual, social, and psychological implications in images devoid either of the "patronizingly picturesque charm" of previous imagery or of "elevated, transcendental rhetoric." This was a gradual and irregular process. Early nineteenth-century European artists studying in Rome tended to "nationalize" their Italian models; by the 1840s, they had turned to their "own" peasants to paint. The peasant genre spread throughout Europe in the wake of the ethnographic romanticism that flowered between 1806, when Clemens Brentano coined the term *Volkskunde*, and 1846 when W. J. Thoms invented the word "folklore." In the same era, European literature made its own discovery, combined with idealization, of a real and sympathetic peasantry. Alessandro Manzoni drew criticism for making peasants the protagonists of *I promessi sposi.* (1825–27). The vogue was taken up by George Sand in France and by Berthold Auerbach in Germany. Peasants thus entered the problem novel — and public consciousness — alongside workers, slaves, orphans, and the generally downtrodden or neglected.[75]

But what kind of visibility did painted peasants acquire? In England, paintings of the poor always fell under social and aesthetic restraints when produced for the rich. If properly rendered, they were welcome in gentry homes even though their real-life models were not. When rich and poor shared a canvas, the latter were usually painted in darker colors, thus making the chiaroscuro of landscape a metaphor of stratified society. "Negative" village types rarely appeared on canvas, and the late eighteenth-century paintings of George Morland (1763–1804) offended good taste by showing the poor in their poverty. Rural squalor and the uprootedness of country life brought on by a massive enclosure movement seldom appeared in British art.[76]

Peasants, except for those in popular prints, appeared in Russian art only in the late eighteenth century. Grotesquerie, when apparent, was reserved for drunken figures at fairs or taverns, and early manorial landscapists used peasants as mere stick figures without character. But Ivan Tonkov and Mikhail Ivanov produced a few scenes of village life and peasants at work.[77] As the landscape began to fill up with more kinds of figures in the early nineteenth century, the peasantry also assumed a natural place. No Russian Morland appeared until Vasily Perov in the 1850s. Till then, almost at the end of serfdom, the rural landscape rarely showed the drudgery and never the abuse and social conflict of "real villages."[78] As with other social representations, rural ones were bound up with the various relationships between art and power: those of production (patron, artist, model), of figurative content, and of the effect upon the spectator, real or implied. At the Academy, aesthetic conventions long discouraged coarse images of the "lower orders" from interloping into Arcadia. Peasant figures for the most part continued to be classicized, pastoralized, idealized, and romanticized. Although tsars Alexander I and Nicholas I both purchased paintings of peasants at "work" from Venetsianov, pictures depicting the harsh reality of village life could not appeal to gentry. Hung on the wall of the manor house, they would violate the myth of a cultured estate, serve as a daily reminder of peasant realities, and create political uneasiness.

Peasant life none the less crowded onto canvases continuously from the 1820s, in the form of work, leisure, domesticity, worship, revelry, and recruitment. Showing peasants engaged in actual labor proved to be a problem everywhere. In Britain, the transition from "happy husbandmen" to the "laboring poor" in art came in the late eighteenth century and it took some effort by painters and public alike to witness the "exchanging of the shepherds of Arcadia for the ploughmen of England." The Arcadian poor still persisted, but came to be balanced by Georgic husbandry. Here, peasants rested only after work, and not in an ale house. The resultant "half-image" continued to obscure the harsher realities of rural life but seemed to project a more honest picture. In France, Jean-Francois Millet's *The Sower* (1850), which offered viewers a glimpse of unadorned backbreaking toil, was harshly criticized by some as "provocative and socialistic."[79]

The prime painters of peasants in this era, Venetsianov and his pupils, proudly eschewed pastoralism. But most of them still idealized the peasantry and imputed a serene peasant universe which reflected a sympathetic and spiritual admiration for village people, but certainly not for the life they were constrained to lead. Though few have ever noticed it, the Venetsianov school strikingly anticipated and reflected the values of Slavophilism which also hailed the harmony of village life and the spirituality of the peasantry, while often downplaying its crudity. Venetsianov himself was the first to devote the bulk of his productive life — almost three decades — to Russian rural subjects: house serfs, shepherds, sowers, harvesters, and threshers. Richard Hare called Venetsianov's Russia a "dream-like agricultural utopia" based on a vision of loyal peasants and benign landowners. Most of his peasant studies recall the sentimentalized peasants of Radishchev and Karamzin. In the words of Alison Hilton, Venetsianov's "innovation lay in realizing that the classical ideal of harmony could be achieved through a new vocabulary of observation rather than imitation of antique models." He employed academic ideals not to marginalize his subjects but to elevate them to human dignity. That dignity, it turns out, was rooted not in labor but in repose.[80]

As to peasants at work, in the 1870s the Russian nationalist and social-minded critic Vladimir Stasov reminded viewers that a dusty road in a painting by Shishkin formed the route that real peasants took on their way to labor in the fields.[81] Apparently commentators in the earlier period did not feel the need to fill the viewer's mind with the "missing agriculturalist." During this entire period, not one Russian artist represented backbreaking field work. The regnant myth of Russian pastorale in manorial practices, poetry, and art implied that "work practically did itself on Russian estates."[82] In Venetsianov, one hardly ever finds someone actually working. Most of his studies are static portraits or depict some cart-pushing and leading of horses. Only in *Peeling Beets* (1822) does Venetsianov get down to real labor in a grim indoor scene about readiness for the winter, a reminder that field work was only one aspect of the labor that peasants — especially women — had to perform through the year. Even though the actual peeling is suspended for conversation in the picture, this is probably the closest Venetsianov ever got to a realistic representation of people at work. Despite its relative harshness, Tsar Alexander I bought the painting for one thousand rubles and hung it in the Winter Palace.[83]

Venetsianov's other peasant studies, more idealized and more appealing as art, exude a sense of the timeless rural world. Three pre-1827 canvases treat women in the field. In *Harvest: Summer,* a young mother with an infant on her lap dominates the foreground. The nearby sickle tells us that she will soon go back to reaping. The toil of the indistinct harvesters in the middle ground is only suggested. The comforting composition contrasts warm and dark colors with the bright sun-splashed fields. *In the Hayfield* combines the work-rest theme with that of the family. A peasant woman near a haystack nurses her infant and listens to her small daughter who will no doubt mind the baby when her mother picks up the rake at her feet and rejoins the farmers in the background. The repose is temporary, the nurturing takes place, and the figures seem in perfect harmony with each other and with nature. For the celebrated *In the Field: Spring,* Venetsianov has another young peasant mother in bare feet leading a team of horses pulling a cultivator while her baby sits nearby on the ground.[84] Instead of showing exertion, her body language closely resembles that of a Russian folk dance in the position of feet and outstretched arms. The dance had been a frequent source for figure composition since the early Renaissance.[85] A peasant viewer of the painting may have seen something else, a "live" version of a common motif in folk art: a peasant woman flanked by two horses, usually ridden by armed men.[86] The artist surely meant to indicate the naturalness of the peasant. For viewers, the treatment was bound to mask the arduous work being performed in the heat of the sun.

Venetsianov edged his way gradually into painting rural life. A piece from the early 1820s shows a dreamy little shepherd boy sprawled on the ground by a fence with a Russian *dudka* (pipe or fife). Is Venetsianov mocking the pastorale with a prop in the hands of an all too human peasant boy? A later picture, *The Sleeping Shepherd* (1824–25), clearly marks a transitional moment for Venetsianov between the mythic shepherds of his academic training and the peasant lad he sees before him. The boy is drowsing against a tree beside a stream, with a few figures and a barn or hut further on. The peasant lad *Vasyutka* (1820s) sits and rolls strips of bark into balls. *Parania* (1817–18), a very young girl, reposes beneath a tree in a forest with a basket of mushrooms. Boys and girls and women abound in Venetsianov. We never see anything like a strong, young, adult peasant male at work. There was as yet no room in this psycho-cultural space for such social imagery. Children were sexually neutral. Male artists liked to paint young women; and these were all too often available to serf owners, including Venetsianov himself who "sinned" with one of his peasant models. Venetsianov's sleeping boys and tranquil madonnas of the fields, with children asleep or at play nearby, is another world from Taras Shevchenko's bitter poem of the 1850s, "The Dream," in which a mother with her baby boy naps in a field and has a golden dream of freedom and happiness for her son. She then awakes still locked in bondage and facing heavy labor.[87]

Close-ups of peasants grouped in collective labor are rare in Venetsianov. In *Threshing Floor* (1822–23), a skillful exercise in deep focus, he painted his own peasants and barn. Two of the seven figures are "working" (one pushing, one pulling a wagon). The others, male and female, are sitting or standing, indifferent to anything that is going on and staring away from each other. Though some of them are relatives, to judge from facial features, there is no sense of family, much less of a devotion to the job at hand. Here, Venetsianov is exalting neither his peasants nor their daily burdens. Galina Leonteva's 1980 book on Venetsianov draws a somewhat unfair comparison of *The Threshing Floor* and Bruni's 1824 historical canvas, *Camilla*. One might as well set up a contrast between David's *Oath of the Horatii* and a Courbet or Millet field scene. But her point is unassailable. Bruni offered classical figures and poses that are theatrical rather than painterly, with artificial light emanating from nowhere, perspectives converging on Horatio, and a flat staging in the foreground. Venetsianov used deep perspective, a clear and natural light source, no dramatic center, and something like real people. Even though his peasants are obviously posed, they are posing for a picture rather than acting in a play. Commenting on Tsar Nicholas I's purchase of *The Threshing Floor,* Leonteva tartly remarked that the sight of happy hard-working peasants probably pleased him. Yet the picture suggests neither happiness nor hard work.[88]

For all his occasional "realism," Venetsianov almost always stops his peasants on the verge of performing a job. In *The Spinner* (1820s), a mature peasant woman faces us with the instrument of her labor in hand. Venetsianov virtually replicates the pose in *Pelageya* (no later than 1825), a young woman with a scythe — an odd thing since women normally used sickles.[89] They are all ready for but not engaged in physical action. In Venetsianov's *Morning of a Country Lady,* the tasks of the two serf women are anticipated, not shown. The mistress of the manor house — modeled by the artist's wife — looks down at a kneeling serf and points to a bundle of flax. The peasant women are wearing naturally wrinkled but clean sarafans. The kneeler looks up at the lady at an angle, accented by the rod held by her companion who looks at the viewer, her face possibly showing some trepidation. *Morning* is the only example in Russian painting of this era in which the serfs are face to face with their owner inside the house.[90] The only genre picture I have seen showing a servant at work inside the house was done in 1836 by P. Bezsonov, a pupil of Venetsianov. A well-dressed, good-looking young lackey is sweeping up a modestly furnished room with one of Venetsianov's pictures on the wall (fig. 5).[91]

Like Venetsianov, his serf pupil Grigory Soroka treated peasants in land-scape as autonomous figures. In *View of a Dam* (pre-1847), the manor house and park lie across the water, as in "prospect" paintings. But the foreground is populated not by the lord or his guests but by full-sized peasants, a lad and two women. In Soroka's well-known *Fishermen* (1840s), we have two peasant boys in the foreground—one on shore and one in a boat. Across a broad lake lie the estate buildings, church, and village. In these and similar works by Soroka about peasants enjoying leisure near the water, the recessional prog-ress of peasants, pond, and manor suggests a social narrative.[92] In Priscilla Roosevelt's words, *View of a Dam* "symbolizes the divide between the world of the peasant mowers and their landowner."[93] The viewer knows that this is not a village scene but gentry turf where serfs are essentially servants or farm-ers and not residents or guests. The painting also reveals Soroka's decision not to put his peasants to work: the boy holds a scythe and a rake lies on the ground, but he and his companions are having lunch.

Soroka also addressed one of his teacher's themes in *Threshing Floor* (1842) (GRMFZh, 5180; fig. 58).[94] Soroka's barn is bathed in darkness, with a few figures barely discernible in the rear. But the diminutive young peasant girls in the foreground tell the real story: the colorful local costumes of Venetsianov are replaced by dark and shabby garments, work coats called *balakhony*.[95] The figure on the left holding a bag of grain gives a faintly sad and ironic smile to the viewer; the other, lifting a basket, looks at the first with an expression hard to read. Nothing has changed from Venetsianov's treatment of labor; hardly any is in sight. But the indifference and quiet resignation of Venetsianov seems to have given way to Soroka's darker vision. Even if we did not have the artist's depressing biography at hand, this and his other canvases convey a somber mood about country life that one could never find in previous works.

Venetsianov's other students and contemporaries come no closer to the depiction of the strain and sweat of labor. In the foreground of Krylov's *Winter-scape* mentioned above, we have stacked lumber and employees engaged in not very strenuous work. Horses and peasant men and women are pulling firewood on sleds and bearing water; those in the middleground are chatting. Lavr Plakhov's haying cycle of 1840–45 (GRMFZh, 147–48) has a group of peasant farmers going to the field, haying, drying, and returning home. On the march to the field, peasants on foot and horseback brandish their rakes and flails like the weapons of a *bogatyr* about to engage in battle. P. Gruzinsky (1837–92), an Academy graduate who did battle paintings, tackled the same theme in *Haying* (1860). Peasants can be seen at work only in the far background. In the fore-ground father and son sit in a cart as the father gazes into the distance like a Byronic figure staring at Fate across the Alps (GRMFZh, 1403).[96]

This (non)representation of peasant work seems to fit a code emerging elsewhere about the relationship of the natural and the social order which implied an alternation of toil and rest. In British art, the juxtaposition has been interpreted, with the support of intertextual reading, as a Virgilian celebration of the normative daily life of the rural lower classes: physical toil followed by brief spells of regenerative rest as in Thomas Gainsborough's *Wooded Landscape with Peasant Resting* (c. 1747) and dozens of others like it all over Europe. But there may be a simpler explanation of all the sitting or reclining peasants. Venetsianov and his pupils often used studio models dressed in peasant costume whom they posed indoors; landscapes were painted in separately. We have direct pictorial evidence of this in A. A. Alexeev's 1827 canvas *Venetsianov's Studio*, where the "peasant" girl poses among copies of ancient statuary. There was nothing dishonest or unusual about this practice. European and Russian landscapists often built up their pictures from a combination of studio work, imagination, and plein air painting. Working in Italy, the French painter Léopold Robert posed local brigands as peasants in the 1820s and 1830s. It was much easier to paint a subject in repose than to capture one in the act of toiling. Practical considerations might have been as important as aesthetic or "ideological" ones in keeping work sufficiently far into the background of Russian rural painting.[97]

Things were different with handicrafts and metalworking in village smithies or industrial foundries. Plakhov's *Workshop* (1830s) shows a craftsman at work at a substantial worktable with his tools — vice, hammer, awl, hatchet, saw, glue pot. A few other paintings of the period have similar themes: men and boys as masons, carpenters, sweepers, blade sharpeners. Fëdor Baikov's *At the Blacksmith's* (1844), a rough and simple picture, sets the brightly lit smithy deep in a countryside arched by a big sky (GRMFZh, 3823). Plakhov's better-known *Smithy* of a year later is especially striking. Done in various shades of brown and red, it evokes the blazing heat of the workplace. Anvil, buckets, horseshoes, a vice, a sledgehammer, and other tools dominate the foreground. The bearded blacksmith with leather apron is in the act of shaping a wheel rim with his hammer as a younger man melts iron for the molds in the red-hot furnace.[98] Hard work, the laborers' dignity, and the equipment make the painting one of the most important treatments of labor in the realistic mode. The same holds for K. S. Pavlov's *Carpenter* (1838) (GRMFZh, 5258) whose brawny-armed subject is a real worker doing real work against a somber background.

Most factory workers belonged to the peasant estate, and many were serfs. Aside from Petersburg shipyard scenes, few factory paintings were set in big cities during this period, Vasily Sadovnikov's *Foundry Yard in St. Petersburg*

(1830s?) which I have not seen, being an early example of urban industry in art.[99] Although in 1800 Russia was the largest producer of iron in the world, plants and mills were often found in rural settings, particularly in or near the Ural Mountains, which by the end of the eighteenth century housed 176 metallurgical factories, mostly private, using serf labor. Their owners tended to spend lavishly on buildings rather than on reinvestment,[100] and these buildings — more often than the workers within — became the subjects of canvases commissioned by the owners.

Anatoly Demidov, the notorious profligate and art lover, resided in Florence and owned a vast metallurgical works at Chernoistochinsk in the Urals, built in 1729. In 1836, he hired the Academy graduate and provincial art teacher Pavel Vedenetsky to do a canvas of this industrial complex. Vedenetsky employed the manorial perspective: an elevated angle with the host in the foreground pointing out to his guests the vast network of factory buildings across the stream. A refreshment table and tent for the guests occupies the foreground and the workers' settlement stretches into the distance. The palpable inequality is softened by the peasants or servants sharing the foreground. As in manorial scenes, the painting is all about ownership and not about the labor going on inside the factory buildings. Another Demidov property was captured in the 1830s by I. Khudoyarov, a Demidov serf artist. His view of the Nizhny Tagil Metal Works, built in 1725, is another vast panorama with elevated angle. The foreground is crowded with officers, nobles, and ladies on a high bluff overlooking the factory and workers' village and a lakeside town. On display is the holiday promenading of the gentry, the men in European clothes, the women in local peasant costumes. The workers are completely invisible. The Demidov canvases, unsurprisingly, seem to have been the norm in what little there was of painting of factory complexes in the early nineteenth century.[101]

When a painter stepped inside an industrial worksite, the scene changed drastically. In *The Iron Foundry* (midcentury) by an unknown artist the viewer beholds the deep interior of a foundry, the red glow of the furnaces, and the allied machinery (fig. 59). The boss wears heavy merchant garb; workers are fully dressed, despite the searing heat, in peasant costume; and there is none of the sweaty brawn of Soviet foundry paintings. The workers here lack the grime-encrusted mien and the setting of dirt, oil, melting iron, molds, castings, bleeding rust, and belching flames whose sight and representations brought such rage to Dickens and Carlyle in the England of that day. Even so, the painting's soot-blackened walls, red faces reflecting the blaze, and overall suggestion of a prison-like inferno are enough to evoke the unpainted reality of gloom, misery, barbaric din, and acrid smells. This disturbing work shows another world from that of Vedenetsky and Khudoyarov and is indeed among the very first, if not the first such representation in Russian art.[102] Of the same period, the serf Vasily Raev's *Workers at the Demidov Factory* (GRMFZh, 6185), has the sparks from the foundry illuminate two workers. One seems posed and prettified, the other wild and almost bestial—like some of the Siberian types bonded to such factories, or escaped convicts and drifters.

Life inside the peasant cabin, though frequently described by gentry visitors in fiction and travel literature, is almost absent in painting until the 1820s. The eighteenth-century artists Ivan Eremenov and Mikhail Shibanov offer interesting exceptions. Their scenes of peasant mealtimes invite divergent interpretations. Eremenov's watercolor *Dinner* (1770s), one of a series entitled *The Poor*, shows two men, a mother with infant, and two children at table with a bread loaf and a common bowl of soup into which the family dips. The cabin is dark and the diners' garments are coarse. Rosalind Gray writes that "the child reaches aggressively for the bowl on the table, suggesting one who does not know when his next meal will be." These peasants are obviously shown to be "poor." But the meaning of the boy's "reach" is arguable because the bowl is further from him than from the men and his arm is shorter; the presence of a large dog near the table expecting to be fed somewhat weakens the notion of the specter of starvation. *The Peasants' Midday Meal* (1774) by the serf Mikhail Shibanov shows the head of household, his wife, son, and daughter-in-law who is nursing an infant. The rather raw realistic treatment of the males is offset by the women's ceremonial headdress. It is, as Gray rightly says, unidealized yet lacking in social conflict. Fifty years later, Fedor Solntsev produced *Peasant Family Before Dinner* (1824) which has the grown son cutting bread, a young boy inspecting the contents of the pot, and the mother and the father, who is mending shoes, looking at each other in less than a cheery manner. Gray reads the painting this way: "the tension between the old woman and the man on the right indicates an internal, domestic conflict brought about by the difficulties of their lifestyle, while the disaffection of the younger man carving bread on the left suggests that he may exacerbate the situation by leaving the familial home to seek his fortune elsewhere." Since the author cites no external evidence, this judgment remains speculative.[103]

Beyond field and cabin, the chief sites of peasant encounter (except for the meeting of the village commune which, I believe, was never depicted on canvas in this period) were the church, the tavern, and the festival. In the era of serfdom, paintings with religious scenes were reverential. Aside from being aware of the official ban on disrespectful imagery of the church, painters before Perov viewed peasants as naturally religious. An artist known for his popular and sometimes devastating genre scenes, Ignaty Shchedrovsky, became starry-eyed when capturing rural devotional life. His *At the Icon* (1835) uses bright coloring to render joyful peasant men and women revering an icon of the Virgin Mary at a roadside chapel (GRMFZh, 3730). G. K. Mikhailov in 1841–42 painted a beautiful, devout-looking young woman placing a taper in church.[104] F. A. Goretsky's *Easter Kisses* (1850) simplified and prettified the happy act of peasants exchanging the kisses and salutations required on Easter Sunday of Orthodox believers (GRMFZh, 3744). Grigory Chernetsov completed in 1851 a work that may have been sketched out during his and his brother's Volga voyage: *Transfer of the Icon of the Vladimir Virgin*. It is an impressive panorama of a river town with peasants standing at various distances from the icon and bowing (GRMFZh-3608).[105] Late in the period F. K. Zhukovsky pictured a *Baptism in a Village Church in Orël Province* (1859; GRMFZh — no number). The ceremony is attended by peasant villagers — immediate family, relatives, friends — decked out in their best attire, the women in particularly elaborate costumes contrasting with the young father in a recent bowl haircut. The painter has carefully put in all the artifacts of a church service — crucifixes, vestments, candles — to add solemnity to the occasion.

The tavern (*traktir*) served as a quite different, but equally important, site of peasant community. A fairly cheap eating and drinking place, it could often be found at a hotel or a post house. Less fancy ones stood in or near many villages.[106] Upper-class travelers came to the tavern occasionally, as described in Turgenev and Gogol. As a center of male conviviality and group activity that regularly led to drunkenness, the tavern could hardly be held by artists as an appropriate site of peasant life. And yet at least two surviving works vividly portray what it must have been like. The tavern in I. M. Tonkov's (1739–99) *Village Celebration* (1770s) sets up a very fanciful background in front of which we see fighting, shawl dances, a balalaika, and drunkenness (GRMFZh, 7643). The anonymous *At the Ale House* (*U piteinogo doma*, 1850s; fig. 60) offered an exceptionally animated scene containing about fifty figures: soldiers, cavalry officers, nobles, and people of almost every class sit or stand (or are collapsed). A Gypsy dances to the tune of a guitar player. A hurdy-gurdy man with his wife, dogs, and monkey stand nearby. Pairs of drunken men embrace each other. Others harangue, talk, listen, snuff tobacco, smoke pipes, flirt. An arrest for drunken rowdiness is imminent. A mounted officer accepts wine poured by a soldier; another listens to a one-legged veteran. The crowd inside the huge wooden tavern is barely shown through a window. A sorry landscape rears up behind the revelers — a few scraggy trees and a near absence of vegetation, suggesting the shores of the Gulf of Finland near St Petersburg. No moralistic judgment by the artist is in ready evidence (GRMFZh, 2637).[107]

Turgenev perhaps provides the reason why tavern interiors were rarely painted. It was not only the conventions of social restraint. Taverns were usually very dark, even by day, as was the case in Turgenev's story "The Singers" from *Notes of a Hunter*.[108] Combining a reading of Turgenev with the near contemporary *At the Ale House* offers a pretty good account of the tavern milieu. Both include figures of vague class origins — ex-serfs, lower-class townspeople, peasants, and workers. But the painting exposes a broader social scope. "The Singers" contains two narratives. One — the singing contest — has become part of the canon of great literature due to its poetic account of rapture and naive art accompanied by the anxiety, embarrassment, and ambition of the singers and the sheer delight of the onlookers. The other, devoid of literary value, is a documentary sketch of that part of everyday life that is so hard to find in other sources: the layout of the site itself, the interaction of people in a drinking establishment, and a concise chronicle of the rapid road to alcoholic oblivion.

Pavel Rizzoni (Ritstsoni, 1823–1913) caused a stir with his renditions of revelry in taverns and wineshops. Son of a Bolognese veteran of Napoleon's army, he was born in Riga, attended the Academy, and eventually won a pensionate to Europe. Like a few others, he was encouraged to follow his own inclination which led him to post stations, taverns, and low life. In 1845, having been assigned the theme "domestic life," Rizzoni produced *Interior of a Kharchevnya,* a very grim study of an eating and drinking establishment in a cellar and its three drunken, drinking, and flirting customers. Around the same time, Rizzoni did a large canvas called *Interior of an Ale House* (*Piteinyi dom*), a free-for-all of alcohol, dancing, and carousing. In 1853, he exhibited *Interior of a Wine Shop,* a compact picture of lowdown revelry. The Academy at almost every stage heaped medals and other awards on Rizzoni's works. Not all professors were happy about this. One wrote to a friend in 1853: "And Rizzoni again with his taverns . . . and all the nastiness . . . . Well-painted but repulsive and awful; he is no aesthete." At one Academy exhibit, the poet Apollon Maikov overheard viewers who exclaimed "What kind of subjects are these, there is nothing noble about them"; and who lamented the showing of filth, vulgarity, and drunks. Tsar Nicholas disliked Rizzoni's *Wine Shop* and grumbled at an 1853 Academy exhibition about the "monotony and poetic licence in his subjects."[109] The tsar, who liked pictures of "the simple folk," turned against low genre that featured simple folks who were drunks. The abstract and state-sponsored notion of *Narodnost* was hard to sustain in the face of graphic (in both senses of the term) depictions of the real *narod* in some of its less idyllic moments.

Hard drinking and reveling were common also in family and calendric village festivities. An anonymous and undated picture from this period of a folk fair, *Trinity Day at Krasnoe Selo,* is set near Moscow on a village street, densely packed with humanity in intimate contact, reveling and dancing near the stalls. Though mass inebriation is not evident, the kinetic abandon and spontaneity associated with the lower classes is on full display as peasants arrive from neighboring villages on an array of conveyances. Another festival, at Alekseevsk near Moscow (presently the site of the Exhibit of Economic Achievements), features folk dancing, and it contrasts the vigorous peasant body motion, gesticulation, and face-to-face male embraces with the restraint of a few nobles in the right foreground. Sternberg's *A Fair in Ukraine* (1836–38), a huge panorama in watercolor, brims with ox carts, tents, kegs, and crowds in colorful costumes and hats, including several Hasidic Jews among the fairgoers. A. A. Popov's (1832–96) rather stiff painting, *Folk Scene at the Fair in Staraya Ladoga* (1853), takes place on the shore of the Volkhov river near art patron Tomilov's manor. The tone is restrained — only a dozen figures, dancing, a balalaika, some storytelling and flirtation, and a hint of drink. Gruzinsky's 1861 *Village Celebration* (GRMFZh, 780) is a winter scene set around the time of emancipation but with no allusion to it. Three peasants and a driver on a troika are being seen off by their women. The men look happy and perhaps a bit inebriated as they set out for the next village.[110]

Several scenes indicate that people from neighboring villages were as welcome to a festival as were the far-flung neighbors of the gentry to their entertainments. An excess of drinking was expected in peasant feasts which often lasted for days. Higher forms of disorder, of course, were not shown in art or in any public forum. Russia was not that different from the rest of Europe in setting up rules and tacit understandings about the limits on expression. Arson, village murders and beatings, seigniorial punishments, religious dissidence, acts of resistance, witchcraft accusations, military reprisals, and arrests were naturally beyond the pale, though some of these were regular features of peasant life.[111] As to the last, it was again Perov who broke a rule in *The Arrival of the Police Inspector* in 1857.

The only violence in a peasant's life permitted on canvas was combat, and here the masses locked in battle were often indistinguishable from officers. There were no courts martial, executions, or running the gauntlet. Presentation of the peasant's military experience was limited to recruiting scenes. Frederick Starr cites among the permissible genre subjects at the Academy in the 1810s "A Recruit Parting from his Family." In 1839, Venetsianov did a pair of recruit paintings, showing departure and return, a common device in European art, though I have not seen them. Felitsin in *Sorrowful Tidings* (1851) offered a somewhat prettified picture of a mourning widow of a Crimean War soldier.[112] The literature suggests that recruitment from among village peasants was treated as equivalent to a death sentence — which indeed it was for an exorbitantly high percentage of Russian soldiers who perished from war and disease. Recorded cases of self-mutilation were fairly common as were other less dramatic modes of evasion. Corrupt exemption practices often favored well-off potential draftees. After a twenty-five-year term in the army, if he survived, the ex-soldier entered a kind of "homeless class," unwanted in the native village. Married life for an active soldier was extremely difficult to maintain, and the burden of it fell just as harshly on the wife.[113] None of this was reflected in the art of military or any other kind of painters.

Although a newspaper (*Russkii Invalid*) was partly devoted to surviving veterans, they played a humble role in Russian society, often as gatehouse or road guards,[114] just as in Soviet times they were used as hotel doormen. G. I. Bortnevsky (b. 1828), himself a veteran of the Moscow Bodyguard Regiment, won the title Artist at the Academy 1859 for his *Dinner of Invalids* (GRMFZh, 3759) which shows a vast dining hall with the gray-haired ex-soldiers, mostly peasants, seated side by side at mess. It is a moving snapshot of this usually neglected corner of society: seasoned old men of the ranks sitting erect for their picture proudly painted by one of their number.

A Provincial Gallery

For painters who lived in or visited the lands beyond the capitals, the provincial town as a topographical subject held less interest than did its residents, particularly gentry and merchants who could commission portraits. But a pair of paintings of each of two very different towns — a spa and a provincial capital — offer a few clues about how Venetsianov's pupils Krylov and Krendovsky saw small-town life. Two studies of around 1824, attributed to Nikifor Krylov, show patients taking the curative waters in the town of Bezhetsk in Tver Province. The first foregrounds what looks like a family of peasants or townspeople. A couple is helping a faltering man from a cart down to the waters of the spa; in the background, citizens of various classes stand on the shore and watch the patients bathing. The second centers on a local landowner, named in the title, who is about to undergo treatment as well. In the distance, boats, a church, banners, and town buildings seem to suggest the common enterprise of this town and perhaps a touch of civic pride.[115] Both pictures give the town a fairytale quality, implying, perhaps, the miraculous nature of its curative powers.

The Ukrainian provincial capital Poltava was put on canvas by artists of different periods, both focusing on Alexandrovsky Square, the town's symbolic center. Academy painter F. Ya. Alexeev's 1808 version might be called an official urban portrait: a panorama of grand Empire-style edifices with the governor's palace off to the right and an Alexander Column in the middle of the square. The vast, frigid, and nearly empty space overwhelms the few figures converging upon the column as if in pious deference to their emperor. With Evgraf Krendovsky's *Alexander Square in Poltava* (1830–1840s), the "bourgeoisification" of the town becomes palpable. At the rear stands the same complex of white stone neoclassical buildings with Corinthian columns, balcony, and archways for vehicles. To the left stand a chapel and a few simple but substantial houses. Ukrainian peasants guide a caravan of ox carts through the square in whose huge expanse are seen clusters of officers, officials, and gentry; a female water-bearer, a delivery boy, families, livestock, and conveyances of all sorts. Although the figures in the middle distance are still dwarfed by the immensity of the square, that space, rendered forbidding in 1808, is now a busy site where work and leisure cross each other. The earlier monumentality has been diminished by the buzz of town life (fig. 61).[116]

Lower-class provincial townspeople inhabit canvases mostly as a supporting cast for topographical studies, as in the works mentioned above, and in genre scenes of popular festivities. Aside from a few priests, only the nobles and merchants of provincial towns sat for portraits. Beginning in the eighteenth century, portraits of merchants, their wives, petty officials, and traders appeared in Russia by the thousands, most of them by unknown artists. Though often labeled "primitivist," their approach, unlike the neoprimitive schools of the fin de siècle, was unself-conscious and derived from both the skill levels of the artists and the accumulation of conventions. A stylized art that drew on iconography and folk art forms, provincial portraits were stiff three-quarter parade studies of prominent local figures and some family ensembles. Already by the mid-eighteenth century, in the words of James Cracraft, "such portraiture, however rusticated, had become a fixture of the cultural life of provincial Russian society."[117]

The Yaroslav provincial school of portraiture emerged among a half-dozen artists of the early nineteenth century. I. V. Tarkhanov (1780–1848), the son of an Uglich priest, in the 1820s through the 1840s painted gentry, officials, townspeople, and merchants; the merchant patronage far outnumbered that of all others combined. They and their wives were dressed slightly upscale and posed in the traditional manner with head and eyes turned in opposing directions. Tarkhanov in 1837 painted an unknown subject sitting at a window in the town of Uglich, holding a paper with books nearby (fig. 62). The familiar folds of a curtain provide background; beard, hair style, and shirt (*rubashka*) sticking out from under the vest reveal his merchant identity. Nikolai Mylnikov (1797–1842), who signed his portraits in French, presented his subjects as good-looking people possessing dignity rather than arrogance. In his badly cracked self-portrait, Mylnikov is indistinguishable from a metropolitan-educated noble of the 1830s. An anonymous family portrait puts a patriarchal father in the center and ranges the others according to place in the family; the artist is lost when it comes to realistic limbs, body postures, relative size, and perspective. Soviet editors of the Yaroslav collection claimed that these pictures represent a "democratic tendency" rarely found in the capitals — again referring to the social origins of the subjects.[118]

A good sense of provincial portrait imagery can be gained by viewing, alongside the 134-piece Yaroslav collection, that of Nikolai Mikhailovich Romanov, whose approximately one thousand pictures, mostly of the noble estate, include many from the provinces. Portrait subjects from the provincial gentry, officialdom, merchants of different guilds, and factory owners have all spent time and trouble preparing for the sittings, and the poses are clearly organized with little trace of spontaneity. Merchants and their wives display a spectrum of social and national self-imaging. At one end stand the stiff and traditionally-garbed *kupets* and *kupchikha* directing a kind of uneasy glower at the viewer and the painter. Some resemble stout boyars in nineteenth-century dress. At the other end, merchants from the neck down are hardly distinguishable from the gentry. Mylnikov in particular has his male sitters dress in a socially nonreferential manner, but topped by the easily recognized "merchant" head with bowl haircut and some kind of facial hair. The male, in dressing "upward," resorts to a European look, while his wife, though arrayed in very expensive garments, remains completely Russian in appearance. Thus, social mobility, status striving, and a certain amount of "denationalization" are strictly gendered. Among all these types, one stands out like a sore thumb: what seems to be a quintessential provincial *intelligent* in a portrait entitled *Man with a Book*.[119]

The modified parade style in merchant portraits by the now better-known painters reflected the same kind of social mimicry.[120] G. A. Krylov's *Portrait of a Rzhevsk Merchant* (1830s) recalls once again an increasingly ambivalent self-image. The merchant appears uncompromisingly "mercantile" in his beard and haircut, his ample torso, and the plain green fabric which endeavors to contain it. The unbuttoned look and the uneasy pose bespeak a contempt for elegance. And yet the awkwardly placed elbow of this captain of commerce rests beside two expensively bound books.[121] Tropinin's portrait of the merchant's wife Kiselëva (née Lazareva) in the early 1830s lacks the conventional furniture of an eighteenth-century formal portrait, but the subject is clothed in a luxurious bright red dress under an opulent green velvet gown with fur collar. Clues to her merchant status are seen in the clenched hand, the intense outward gaze, and the bizarre hair style.[122] But the same painter's 1842 portrait of I. I. Kiselëv of Shuya,[123] a wealthy merchant and presumably her husband, makes him almost a double of the elegant Victor Hugo as painted by Achille Deveria in 1829.

The imaging of provincial and Moscow merchants in portraiture had little resonance in society at large. Few people ever saw the portraits with their positive and ambiguous messages. They were in any case rendered irrelevant by the critical depiction of the merchantry on stage, in print, and on canvas. The genre paintings of the 1840s by Pavel Fedotov (1815–52) reversed the conventions of portraiture and bombarded the merchant with ridicule. Fedotov, like the playwright Ostrovsky, eagerly investigated the social interior. In preparation for a work, he would associate with merchants for weeks at a time in order to study their habits. As he put it in 1844: "Very little of my work — about a tenth — takes place in the studio. My most important work is on the streets and in strange houses. I study life." Fedotov's satirical canvases enlivened bourgeois interiors with episodes from merchant life. *The Choosy Bride* (1847), based on a story by Ivan Krylov, opens on the latest chapter in the implied narrative of the courtship experience of a merchant maid who has rejected too many suitors and is now being proposed to by a kneeling elderly hunchback. *The Major's Marriage Proposal* (1848) seems to blast both the merchant bride and the gentry officer who is nervously proposing. The bride coyly turns her back to the suitor, the family remonstrates with her, and the major, like a melodrama villain, twirls his waxed moustache. Social types were clearly recognizable to contemporaries in this easy-to-read domestic narrative: the matchmaker wears a short jacket or *katsaveika,* used by elderly common people to help hide corpulence. The bride is attired in a dress called "St. Gêne" after a then popular Victor Sardou play about the Napoleonic era.[124]

Fedotov enjoyed a brilliant success at the Academy exhibition of these pictures, although it soon turned against him and the government made his life difficult. The public was delighted and no one at the time seems to have objected to or even noticed the cruelty and misogyny in these works, intended or not. A few years after Fedotov's death a friend related that a real-life army major had come to thank the artist for *The Major's Marriage Proposal* and described his own happy marriage. Socially minded Russian critics then and in Soviet (and post-Soviet) times celebrated what they saw to be Fedotov's justified attack on the hypocrisy and vulgarity of the middle classes. In 1997, while standing in front of *The Major's Marriage Proposal,* I overheard a Russian guide at the Tretyakov Gallery tell a group of school children that the quality of clothing and goods in the bride's home acted as a superficial lure for the major into a union that would eventually lead to disillusion and divorce! Another treatment of merchant marriage, Adrian Volkov's *Breach of Promise* (1860), had a reneging groom exposed and shamed as the jilted bride faints and the bearded merchants express indignation.[125] Fedotov's and other satirical slams at merchant life made no dent in the market for merchant-patronized portraits which flourished and grew right up to the Revolution. But the satire did foreshadow the kind of merchant-bashing that the radical intelligentsia would unleash in a steady stream.

Though always visible in high art, the nobility began to appear on canvas in guises that went well beyond those found in panegyric portrait and manorial painting. The eventless paintings of palatial halls, galleries, and ceremonial staircases of the eighteenth and early nineteenth centuries declined in favor of more intimate interiors. But even many of these retained the academic use of enfilade, deep focus, doorways, and perspective. That quintessential Academy figure, F. P. Tolstoy, painted a conversation piece set in his flat at the Academy, *Family Portrait* (1830), that shows off its big enfiladed rooms extending deep into space. The classic severity of the composition is relieved by the living beings — Tolstoy in Byronic garb, his wife in Restoration style, the daughters in matching gowns; a dog in the central room; and bashful servants peeking around the door in the distant background. Interior painters beyond the capital employed the enfilade approach, and the inhabitants who filled the rows of rooms thawed out the chill of purely spatial representation and created an appealing mix of order and disorder. As Rosalind Gray has aptly put it, human activity in these works overshadowed "the glory of the architectural surroundings." When seen indoors, in settings less formal than the pompous backgrounds of the parade portrait, unposed figures in motion or action appeared more relaxed and human.[126] The renderings were of course sanitized, and rarely did the viewer behold the real dirt and shabbiness of some gentry households, frequently recorded in the provinces by the fastidious Filipp Vigel.[127] In the resulting vernacular interior genre, though often inspired by the early Dutch and Flemish works and contemporary Biedermeier, the tone was native.

The gentry's self-regarding outlook is still evident in paintings that included the family pictures on the wall so as to double the viewing pleasure.[128] Amateur nobles with a flair for drawing made album sketches of their families.[129] N. Kh. Karsten (Carstén), a Swede from Finland and a Russian citizen, painted *The Polovtsov Family* (GRMFZh, 5820) on their estate near St. Petersburg in the 1830s or 1840s. The elaborate conventions of family grouping by age, gender, costume, and pairing of spouses are on full display.[130] *On the Balcony* (1851) by Fëdor Slavyansky has his mother-in-law, his wife, an infant, two children playing, and himself standing at the door of the balcony in a remarkably modern manner and with an almost photographic picturing of conversation among these obviously wealthy people.[131] Although paintings of domestic scenes in France and England, even in the eighteenth century, possessed a much greater range of situations, narratives, characters, and relationships,[132] the Russian equivalents were coming into their own. As John Bowlt has rightly observed of this neglected genre, the interior study offered the everyday life of families in a Russian "domestic art movement."[133]

Although the dinner table played an important role in the life of gentry families, it is rarely depicted in art about that life.[134] Instead we see family members reading, frolicking with a dog, dancing, working. Artists have gone beyond the self-portrait to group studies of themselves. In Tyranov's *The Chernetsov Brothers' Studio* (1828), the brothers have put aside the palette and are relaxing in an intimate setting, one playing a guitar. In Zelentsov's *Studio of P. V. Basin* (1833) four painter friends, with a bearded old man as the model, happily avail themselves of ample studio space and abundant light.[135] V. I. Sternberg, a friend of the composer Glinka, was present at the Chernigov estate of Grigory Tarnovsky. Sternberg's remarkable 1838 painting has Glinka at work with a colleague on his opera *Ruslan and Lyudmila*. Sternberg is at the easel. Obviously a place of work, this gray-walled, austere, even grim interior with high ceiling looks out onto an equally colorless landscape. The whole atmosphere suggests seriousness and professionalism, and indeed the first full rehearsal of the completed *Ruslan* took place in Tarnovsky's serf theater.[136]

Though nobles got gently panned often enough in fiction and drama,[137] they remained relatively exempt from hostile treatment in portraits and genre works until the 1840s when the iconoclastic Fedotov began roasting them. His *An Aristocrat's Breakfast* (1849) rudely debunks an impoverished noble caught by an unexpected knock on the door while consuming his modest repast. His renowned *Fresh Cavalier* (1846) takes on a newly decorated official flaunting his self-importance in a theatrical quasi-Roman pose in the midst of domestic squalor which includes a drunken policeman under the table. Gogol's "Medal of St. Vladimir," a tale that deals with lobbying for a decoration, inspired this painting. As if to emphasize the lowly manners and taste of the subject, Fedotov has him ranting at his cook-concubine; and makes him out to be a fan of Bulgarin, one of whose books lies on the floor. The sympathetic critic Apollon Maikov, echoing things said about the theater of the time, announced that "the ire of a clerk at his cook is as worthy of attention in art as the wrath of Achilles." But this work was excluded from the exhibition of 1851 and forbidden to be lithographed until the medal was removed and the painting renamed *Morning After a Party*.[138] Fedotov's *Encore, Encore!* of 1851–52 made a more subtle and much sadder comment on gentry types. A retired officer — Fedotov knew the type very well — is enwrapped in futility and boredom in a provincial hole, lying in bed and putting his dog through its tricks over and over again in a taut compression of the type known in literature as the "superfluous man."

Outdoors we find gentry, who had always featured prominently in battle and parade scenes or on their estates, also expanding their roles. Fedotov, himself an army man, caught a detachment of officers in the watercolor *Bivouac of the Pavlovsky Regiment of Life Guards* (1841–42).[139] Resting on the march to maneuvers or an encampment, these men, though bearing a kind of collective identity through their uniforms and their obviously common enterprise, are individualized in actions and poses in a way that contrasts sharply with the familiar parade scenes of St. Petersburg. Though just barely an outdoor scene, A. F. Chernyshev's 1850 *Departure (Farewell of an Officer to His Family)* can be fruitfully compared to a real-life serf recruitment with its dirgelike quality. At a modest gentry home in a village, a priest stands in the door, and a young friend or brother offers the departing officer a bottle. The mother hovers by her son, who kisses his wife while keeping a foot on the axle of the coach. The coachman, true to form, waits patiently. On the right, older men chat, perhaps about their time in the service. Peasants, children, servants, and assorted figures fill in the row of people which stretches from the little manor to a village hut and, behind it, a church — seeming to depict an emotional solidarity that binds the whole community.[140] Chernyshev's departing officer shows no sign of resistance — after all, officers were not "recruited"; but the point is how greatly this gentry officer has been reduced from earlier representations in the parade portrait, the miniature, the manorial landscape. Now he — like the peasant — seems to have lost agency and elevation.

Among the most lively of male gentry pleasures was the hunt. Unlike England with its hunt clubs, balls, costumes, and other forms of ritualized social practice, Russians tended to hunt alone or in small groups.[141] The largest ensemble that I have seen on canvas is Evgraf Krendovsky, *Gathering for the Hunt* (1836), a tiny interior showing four men with their guns, dog, and boots.[142] The twenty-four-year-old Konstantin Krugovikhin (1815–?), while a student at the Academy, offered a typical scene in *Landscape and Hunter in Pavlovsk Park* (1837) of a clump of birches, a dog, and a lone officer facing away from the viewer.[143] In the same year, Ignaty Shchedrovsky, his fellow student, produced *The Hunters,* a photo-like representation. In the foreground, drawn from a low perspective, the diagonal postures of the two sportsmen are replicated — according to an old formula — by two listing trees. A horseman stands on the horizon. A village at the left is indistinct and the idyllic atmosphere is enhanced by the contrast of the rosy dawn sky and the rich green vegetation. The same artist's *Landscape with Hunters* (1847) has a mounted nobleman, his servant on foot carrying the gun, asking a peasant for directions — a common scene in literature and in real life. The unrivaled guide through this world is Ivan Turgenev's *Notes of a Hunter,* whose imagery may have been partly shaped by pictures like those described above. But his keen up-close observation tells us much more than do landscape artists about rural society. Turgenev matches the visuals of gun-bearing serfs but adds their habit of running behind the master's conveyance or horse. Unlike the graphic art of the era, he describes the ragged garments of the peasants and their lapses in servility that regularly occurred in remote places, taverns, and post houses.[144]

There are no paintings of nobles on foot or horseback surveying the field work of their peasants, consulting with a steward, or engaging in many other noble pursuits in the great outdoors. But artists sometimes found on the Russian highways and byways much material for genre art. Picturing modes of travel could combine some social commentary with landscape, dramatic action, and current vehicular technology. B. Swebach, a Swiss who worked in Russia in the 1820s, idealized a winter sledge in *Troika* (1819; GRMFZh, 168). N. E. Sverchkov's *Travelers* (1855) juxtaposes the swift course of a tarantas with an officer or official on board and a mounted escort out in front hurtling along on business as the relatively immobile peasants watch it go by (GRMFZh, 5833). A strong sense of what things were like in the post houses described so often in literature is offered in V. V. Samoilov's 1854 *Posting Station* (GRMFZh, 3735). In a rural hamlet, the church and the rough wooden station house flank the muddy road where a wheel is being changed in a setting of utter desolation. Just as bleak is Gruzinsky's *On the Road* (1859; GRMFZh, 9150), with a *telega* or village cart carrying a lone soldier sitting on straw and a driver up front. The unsprung cart looks like an upside-down coffin.

While artists painstakingly sought new objects to put on canvas, the distribution of graphic art widened with the growth of new reproductive techniques. The establishment of the first lithographic workshop in Petersburg in 1816 quickened mass output of cheap reproductions. The Society for the Encouragement of Artists, declaring that "national honor" demanded sharing pictures of Russian popular life, commissioned such scenes, lithographed them, and then sent them off not only to the provincial art schools but to artists in Mogilëv, Orël, Tula, Pskov, Simbirsk, Yaroslavl, Vyatka, Kharkov, Irkutsk, and other places. Through this and other channels, works by Venetsianov, Orlovsky, and others reached a broad public. Ignaty Shchedrovsky (1815–70), the son of a poor official, went to St. Petersburg in 1833, attended the Academy, and became a Free Artist. In the 1830s, at the behest of the society, he executed thirty-six *Scenes of Russian National Life*. In the 1840s he produced more such scenes in *Here Are Our People!* (*Vot nashi!*), whose very title indicated a determination to introduce the Russian people to themselves. The album went into three editions and popularized the "everyday life genre" (*bytovoi zhanr*) that would flourish in the last half of the century. All this was supplemented with book illustrations that matched the content of the physiologies and provincial sketches and reached into the places they were describing and depicting.[145]

Petersburg: Cityscape, City Folk

A kind of visual database for Imperial Russia's most important city exists in a book of 231 superb reproductions entitled *Pushkin's Petersburg,* conveniently divided into the periods 1800–1820 and the 1820s to 1830s. Other published and archival visual sources help fill the gap up to the 1850s.[146] Although little changed in actual Petersburg society, a great deal did in visual human geography. As time progressed, staffage figures of lower-class urbanites — small, distant, often turned away from the viewer, and clad in nondescript garb — get bigger, closer, and more legible as individual human beings. New sections of the city, back streets, and courtyards come into view, filled with socially diverse people. Elite spaces remain that way most of the time: Palace, Admiralty, and Mikhailovsky Squares; the Swan Canal, the English Embankment, and the gated and restricted Summer Garden. Exceptions for the first two are made for parades and folk fairs. Sadovaya Street from the Nevsky down to and including Haymarket Square are favorite sites for artists who want to capture the steaming and bubbling life of the lower classes. Men, women, and children move through the streets and sidewalks, courtyards and squares — jostling, bargaining, and clearly making raucous noise. The largest mixed assemblies appear at festival time near the Admiralty and in suburban Ekaterinhof. Congregations of every class intermix especially often along the Nevsky at the canal intersections, on bridges, and at the Kazan Cathedral, the City Duma, Gostiny Dvor, and the Anichkov Palace. Parades, far from diminishing, have grown in frequency and in numbers — as have spectators from among commoners.

The discovery of the countryside and provinces and their mysterious inhabitants had its analogue in a kind of excavation of the "unknown city." For a long time, academic art by convention or design had tended to treat the urban masses as passive spectators, ignoring or marginalizing their occupations, their spontaneity, and the everyday material goods surrounding them. But side by side with the monumental rendering of the capital, other representations — including those by academy-trained artists — began to unveil a city less Venetian, more Russian, though sometimes marked by official rhetoric even when the subject is the throb of commerce as in I. A. Ivanov's *Gostiny Dvor* (1815), where ordinary citizens are flanked by a marching platoon and a guard post.[147]

V. R. Zotov, a theater man with a keen eye, ear, and nose, called the bridges of St. Petersburg "our Roman forum," where the lower classes hung about at the four corners to trade, gossip, meet up, or idle away the hours.[148] Bridges indeed loomed large in the physiology of St. Petersburg, and they attracted more than just the plebs. F. Ya. Alexeev's view of Kazan Cathedral from across the Nevsky Prospect in the 1810s foregrounds the upper and lower worlds of the great city: gentlemen and townsmen look down from the bridge at the washerwomen up to their knees in the waters of the Catherine Canal. Sadovnikov, in an 1830 watercolor of the Anichkov Bridge over the Fontanka Canal, wrought an engaging and complex composition of the crowd in conversation groups that included a red-nosed merchant, a peasant couple, vendors, assorted gentry and military, a bridge guard, and sundry conveyances. Many views captured watch boats sailing beneath the bridge. Lesser-known works jumbled balcony viewers, marching troops, noble families in carriages with footmen, and the grittier world of people washing and working along the canals.[149]

The new urban art, though always bearing traces of the old, distinguished itself for the most part by differentiating social types more sharply than before and thus endowing them with clear markers of identity. Massed scenes depicted commoners at play; both the panoramic paintings and the focused genre works showed people in the act of commerce and even physical labor. Urban entertainments naturally attracted many kinds of representation. Foreign eyes exoticized them, Russian popular prints showed "the people" to themselves, and Russian professional artists found new subjects and objects to celebrate. The acceleration of urban literary exploration began in the 1840s with a burst of feuilletons and "physiological sketches"; and literary works about the low, the lower, and the lowest depths were sometimes called daguerreotypes because of their photographic or documentary realism. These verbal and illustrated "local-color sketches of urban life and social types"[150] were quickly imitated by writers of fiction. The physiologies and the 1846 *St. Petersburg Collection*, with works by Nekrasov, Dostoevsky, and others, were criticized as the "natural school" by Bulgarin, who coined the term; and they were conversely praised by Belinsky and other Westernizers.[151] Although one of the main works of this epoch, the 1845 *Physiology of St. Petersburg*, had poor graphics, better artists began following the trend.

Alexander Orlovsky (Orlowski, 1777–1832), a Polish-born artist in Russian service since 1802, earned the name "quick pencil" for his impressions of Petersburg street life. He met the everyday of common people head-on in scores of anecdotal scenes decades before Fedotov, and with greater range. His corpus included an 1808 oil painting of a staggering drunk. His 1820 pictures titled *Coachmen's Bazaar* and *Cabbies' Market* put expressive features on the drivers' faces and pictured a dozen animated conversations and transactions whose tone can almost be "read" from the skillfully captured gesturing of autonomous individuals. His *St. Petersburg Winter Market* (1820s) pulsates with livestock, horses, dogs, tradesmen, women, goods, and sleds bunched near a wooden cabin on the stone-framed square — a veritable re-creation of a village in the midst of the granite capital (fig. 63). Orlovsky seemed to delight in crafting the details and rough textures of the buildings and the athletic movements of his subjects.[152] The kinds of realia not often shown and less remembered from prose treatments are abundant and memorable in graphics: a heated guard booth; a snack stand with vodka tumblers at the ready; booths for milk, tobacco, and fuel — items so utterly familiar to residents of the capital that it was perhaps natural for only the visual artist to have seen their value as signifiers. Memoirs and stories about theater rarely mention what theatergoers saw dozens or scores of times: the coachmen's fire pavilions near the theaters where the drivers drank tea, chatted, and kept warm as their masters enjoyed opera or ballet inside.[153]

The gap between the social visibility of certain types and their near absence in literature is greatest in the case of the street vendors and physical laborers. Speaking generally of Europe, Peter Burke observed that "images offer particularly valuable evidence of practices such as street trading which were rarely recorded because of their relatively unofficial nature."[154] *Nosilshchiki* — street vendors with portable trays of fruit or dry goods — were omnipresent in Petersburg and other cities, and from the 1820s onward inhabit lithographs, paintings, and later on photographs and postcards. They sometimes pose alone as "types" and sometimes stand amid the monumental architecture of the capital.[155] Foodstuff dominated the trade of peddlers, mostly peasants from nearby villages, uncountable though licensed. Venetsianov in the 1810s drew some vivid scenes of interclass bargaining in *Near the St. Petersburg Bourse* and *Horse Market in St. Petersburg,* the latter at least hinting at a class-leveling effect in the marketplace. *The Magic Lantern,* an 1817 journal attributed to him, bulges with pictures of street vendors that were later copied onto porcelain statuettes.[156] Gruzinsky's *Street Scene* (1861) adds another touch of realism to his picture of a woman selling eggs and herrings from her sleigh: two drunks blissfully asleep in a classic pose beneath a lamppost (GRMFZh, 1445).

Haymarket Square, the city's busiest venue for street trade, served as a lively setting for the "slum" novels of Krestovsky and Dostoevsky.[157] Neither has the exuberance of an 1820 lithograph of the busy Sadovaya Street, at a point near the Haymarket, where officers, vendors, women, and men engage in an endless bustle of buying and selling, haranguing, begging, and solicitation among a rich mosaic of social types.[158] Adrian Volkov's *Haymarket,* done at the time in which the above-mentioned novels are set, even more vividly captures the excitement of men changing the wheel of a diligence, semicriminal elements lurking around, and fun-lovers on a rampage near the picturesque Haymarket Church (GRMFZh, 2636). Volkov (1827–74) achieved notoriety and a minor silver medal at the Academy for a related work, *Glutton Row in St. Petersburg* (1858), which delves even deeper into the tawdry yet animated life of the capital, with haggling traders and drunks staggering and prone in a dismal courtyard.[159]

When it came to depicting work in the city, artisanry and hard physical labor fell far behind commercial activity in representation. The caretaker or building and yard man (*dvornik*), found in almost every residential building, appears rarely, and even more rarely at work. V. I. Dahl's *Janitor* (1844), garbed in peak cap, vest, shirt, and apron, presides over the doors and gates of his empire — entryways, staircases, and the courtyard littered with broken-down coaches — and sweeps with a long broom.[160] The courtyard represented what one scholar has called "the great democratizing pause in the otherwise overly official Imperial capital"; and its *dvornik* (as a police informant) the link between courtyard and officialdom.[161] Scenes of wharves, river and canal banks, and bridges almost always contain some kind of work, including that of washerwomen, ferrymen, and occasionally shipbuilders. In Benjamin Patersen's *Police Bridge* of the 1810s, three stonemasons on the Moika near Nevsky Prospect are at work in a clear division of tasks — one wheeling, one crushing, and one shaping — as a well-dressed gentry couple look the other way. In an 1820s lithograph, about a hundred men are building supports for the new St. Isaac's Bridge across the Neva at Senate Square.[162] Aside from these, very little gang work made it to canvas or print by Russian artists.

Large-scale collective labor appeared even more rarely in urban art. Over a hundred "factories" — enterprises defined as employing sixteen or more workers — operated in St. Petersburg at the end of this era. I have found no scenes of work inside these, which included the state arsenal and the shipbuilding and repair shops. Thousands of workers performed arduous labor in teams every day across the city under the public's gaze. In 1839 alone, some six thousand laborers toiled continuously in the construction of the enormous St. Isaac's Cathedral, and an unknown number were at work rebuilding the Winter Palace, recently consumed by fire, at top speed in time for a royal wedding.[163] Theaters, circuses, and other buildings that burned down had to rebuilt. But the intensive, bone-killing labor on these construction sites was ignored in favor of the superstructures and materials. One of Sadovnikov's late 1830s or early 1840s watercolors of the building of St. Isaac's Cathedral (1818–58) shows the scaffolding and the caravan of stone-hauling horses — but no work-ers. The only depiction of laborers was done by the architect of that church, the Frenchman Auguste Montferrand. His 1830s watercolor, *At the Con-struction of St. Isaac's Cathedral,* prominently features about forty workmen straining with levers and pulleys at the base of the massive half-finished struc-ture as well-dressed gentry look on. The grunt and pain of urban labor had yet to find either realistic or even poetic treatment among Russian artists.[164]

It has long been noted that beggars almost disappeared from Russian art after the eighteenth century. Ivan Eremenev (or Ermenëv, 1746 or 1749?–1790), the son of a stable boy, finished the Academy of Arts in 1767. Between working on baroque historical and biblical studies, he did eight watercolors known as *The Poor* (mid-1760s–1775). *Dinner,* a peasant family around a common bowl, has been discussed above. *Poor Woman with Little Girl* and *Blind Singers* are drenched in misery. *Beggars* (early 1770s) depicts an old (though ageless) man and woman halting along with the help of canes — he with a hobo bag, she stooped over and dressed in patched clothes.[165] Their open-mouthed agony recalls not only Hogarth but even Goya. As a whole, these pictures depicted the suffering of lower-class people at a descriptive level found not only among none of Eremenev's contemporaries but in the work of no other artist until the 1850s. Orlovsky's *Poor Peasants at a Carriage* (1816) does not come close; less still do the occasional staffage beggars planted among the crowds in other urban pictures.

Where have all the poor gone in the reign of Nicholas I? Indigent people appeared in prints and journal illustrations, but hardly at all in painting. Expressive culture dealing with poverty is an interpretive minefield. It raises the problem of definition. The characters in Dostoevsky's epistolary novella whose title is usually translated as *Poor Folk* were unfortunate or "afflicted people" rather than completely impoverished ones. Their cramped and vulnerable lives were lived inside four walls. If we identify the poorest of the poor with home-lessness and beggary, another factor surfaces. Overreacting Petersburg police believed and reported that many beggars were fakes, members of criminal gangs who made a living — meager as it might have been — with tin cups and canes on the streets or at church doors. Indeed, the state considered this fluid mass who came in and out of the city at will a public menace. It was not easy to distinguish "pious pilgrims and deserving poor" from "itinerant thieves."[166] It may be that, since the periodic police round-up campaigns were known to the public, painters shied away from such a problematic subject for art — even when capturing in genre the lesser-known corners of urban life. Certainly arbiters of taste frowned upon mixing high art with harsh realities.[167]

One may stroll along the Nevsky with Gogol or hear a character in Ivan

Goncharov's *Oblomov* a few decades later say: "Not to go to Ekaterinhof on the first of May? . . . Everyone will be there!" without ever feeling the brimming activity that made St. Petersburg and its entertainment suburbs so vital. A lithograph after an 1835 sketch of Thimm, set on St. Petersburg's St. Isaac's Square, the massive and nearly completed cathedral in the background, does just this. The subject is a folk fair to mark the pre-Lenten festivities. All the usual amusements are on hand for socially mixed citizens on fairground rides or lining up for tickets to the booth show. Thimm's large picture combines several genres: a perspective study that uses the Admiralty spire and symmetrical buildings as the frame; a military parade whose mounted guards are shooing pedestrians away from a cortege of gentry; and the huge double ice-hill in the center, flanked by Leman's Circus and a booth theater.[168] The richness of information in this picture and its compositional strategy convey the experience of a moment in the heart of the city that no other medium except film could capture.

Not even graphic artists could recreate the city's noise, odors, temperature, and atmosphere. V. R. Zotov tells us for example that Gorokhovaya Street smelled of freshly baked bread, while from other sites emanated the aroma of leather boots, eggs, kvass, or mushrooms.[169] Missing also from urban pictorial representation is the sound track, what a contemporary collection of pictures called "the cries of Petersburg:"[170] the cacophonous symphony of barking dog, vendor's pitch, drill sergeant's sharp command, hooves of carriage horses, cabmen's cries, the jangle of spurs, the creaking and clanking of gear, and the report of the daily cannon shot across the river. Earlier cityscapists who celebrated the momentous and magnificent city of stone and water were content to maintain a dignified silence. But as the midcentury drew near, artists at least attempted to suggest the tactile, kinetic, and olfactory emanations of the city, and to "score" their graphic dramas with implied sounds, the reverse of what opera and, later, film composers sought to do.

The quest for the whole metropolis was of course never completed. As in the provinces, certain sectors of human experience failed to make it to the canvas, sketch paper, or print shop. There were things, as Bulgarin put it in 1845, "from which the well-bred person averts his eyes." Such things included the public display of serfs for sale in the city's courtyards in the 1790s.[171] The omissions cannot simply be attributed to the dark repression of the tsars and their censors. Training in the conventions, opportunity, and personal taste came into play. The lag in representing industrial scenes reflected comparative economic history, and in this Russia resembled many parts of Europe. Important is not so much what artists failed to depict as the new things they did depict. Gradually in the reign of Alexander I and more rapidly under his successor, "the most numerous classes" of the great metropolis had found their way into art, and, if often "typed" or caricatured, had at least emerged from the invisible realm of exclusion.

Photo Finish

Siegfried Kracauer, the early twentieth-century film psychoanalyst, likened Louis-Jacques Daguerre (1789–1851), the inventor of the daguerreotype in 1839, to the historian Leopold von Ranke, in that both of them selected, framed, and organized material for presentation — one visually, the other in print.[172] It has been variously argued that the English squire William Fox Talbot and the Russian infantry officer Alexei Grekov invented what became the photograph simultaneously with Daguerre. Certainly researchers at the Russian Academy of Sciences were already at work on light pictures. Quite remarkable was the rapid spread of the new technology via the printed word to the rest of Europe. In the United States, technological wizardry and instant marketing created an industry in Philadelphia and New York within a year of Daguerre's invention in France, and in 1840 the world's first photo studio opened in New York.[173]

Russia's photographic pioneer, Alexei Grekov (1799–1850s?), a Yaroslav gentry officer, engineer, and government official, came to St. Petersburg in 1836 to work for *Moscow News,* the government organ. He reproduced images on a metal plate and displayed his findings in 1840. He opened a studio or "Artistic Cabinet" in Moscow in 1840, and in 1841 published an anonymous pamphlet entitled *The Painter Without Brush or Paint,* showing how to make all kinds of likenesses in minutes and how to pose subjects. As Russia's first professional portrait photographer, Grekov made images "the size of a small snuffbox" and sat his subjects in a special posing chair with a cushion for the head. Unfortunately, none of his works has survived. Studios quickly appeared in other Russian towns and people lined up to have their pictures taken. Bulgarin's journal *Northern Bee* reported on Daguerre's invention; articles, books, and brochures on the subject followed. In 1858 came the first journal of photography.[174]

Sergei Levitsky (1819–98) was the first important Russian photographer to have left his work to posterity. While studying law at Moscow University, he developed an interest in chemistry, physics, and amateur photography, and obtained a camera from Grekov. Visiting Rome in 1845, he shot a group portrait of the Russian art colony. After spending four years in Paris, Levitsky returned to St. Petersburg and in 1849 opened a professional portrait studio. His work was so proficient that he garnered several international awards. In the 1850s, Levitsky's subjects included Pauline Viardot, Lev Tolstoy, Turgenev, and Glinka. The young Tolstoy poses in a Crimean War military uniform, his torso and gaze facing left. The photo of Turgenev, also in 1856, faces the other way and is much less flattering. Vladimir Stasov, despite his strong reservations about the medium, persuaded Mikhail Glinka to sit for Levitsky right before his last trip to Europe where he died. The composer stands before us in a Napoleonic posture, hand tucked in coat. Levitsky also attended an 1856 gathering of writers from all over Russia and took a group portrait of Turgenev, Tolstoy, Ostrovsky, Grigorovich, and Druzhinin. Embracing a wide political gamut, he photographed Herzen and Bakunin as well as ceremonial events of Tsar Alexander II.[175]

The popularity of portraiture grew with the opening of new studios, the shortening of exposure time, and greater accuracy in the likeness. Early works followed the traditions of the miniature oil portrait in posing and composition and soon superseded it. Like painters, photographers sought solutions to problems of pose, grouping, color, light, props, background, angles, space, and tonal nuance. Levitsky's studio, a glass pavilion with top and side lighting, drapes and wallpaper, had a table full of knick-knacks. Clients often brought their own chairs and other accessories to create a home-like backdrop. The three-quarter-face pose, slightly off center, with diagonals for dynamic effect, became standard. The hands, which seemed to glow excessively in early photos, were hidden. Some masters used color for the background, others tinted the entire print, and many held to painterly conventions for a long time. Tinting was often overdone. In black-and-white studies, clothing presented problems. Dark suits made a glaring contrast with a white background and the best cameramen sought to develop a smooth tonal transition between them. The drabness and uniformity of costumes that men in particular began wearing from the 1840s onward inhibited poetic effect. The doublets, ruffs, and powdered wigs of the deeper past were long gone, and the more recent flamboyance of revolutionary, Restoration, and romantic trappings gave way to variations on the plain black London frock coat with cravat. The male sartorial world had turned monochrome. Even painters were hard put to enliven the post-1850 men's portrait.[176]

Partly for those reasons, the quality of early photo portraits seemed to offer little threat to painters. Unlike the brush, the camera could not overcome stiffness and gracelessness of some subjects even when it tried to replicate the conventions of the canvas. The gap between purpose and outcome may have stripped such sitters of status for the viewer. A shot of P. D. Durnovo in the 1850s shows an exceptionally rigid stance, with feet together, cane and railing tightly gripped, a grim facial expression, and dull apparel. Dautendei's 1848 photo of the historian Timofei Granovsky and Levitsky's of the poet Fëdor Tyutchev are hardly more appealing. A tinted 1859 portrait of a stiff and awkward N. F. Shcherbina is not saved by his wide-awake hat and cape.[177] Female subjects did not fare much better under the camera's eye. 1850s portraits come across as perfectly uninteresting human triangles due to the shape of gowns then in fashion. K. A. Bergner's group study of the mother of Savva Mamontov with two daughters (1850s) comes out as three triangles within a triangle. Color rarely helped. In the same decade, an unknown photographer produced a jarring and grotesquely realistic tinted photo of a very solemn young woman standing against a brightly colored theatrical backdrop of ruins and vines, a pathetic attempt to conflate the sensibilities of two different eras at the moment of their divergence.[178]

Sometimes the old arty poses worked well, as in the case of the photograph of M. S. Volkonsky, son of the Decembrist, at the end of 1850s; and in that of the opera singer Enrico Tamberlink, who had the advantage of stage costume and theatrical gesturing. The portrait of the Slavophile Konstantin Aksakov in 1844 succeeds also largely because of the outlandish *murmolka* and *armyak* that he liked to wear, garments of mixed ethnic origin. Levitsky's widely reproduced study of the Westernizer Alexander Herzen, done in London in 1861, overcomes the dullness of costume and beard and captures the remnants of a romantic youth by posing the subject in a strong diagonal lean, with head on hand and legs crossed.[179] A portrait of the ten-year-old Vladimir Ershov of 1855 or 1856 evokes, in the dignity and self-confidence of his pose, the budding of a future Guards officer and aide to the tsar. In the 1850s, the photographer Bergner overcame the usual awkwardness of family groupings by posing two small children with toys on a kind of banister rail beside their young mother. The purchasing public — gentry and merchants — apparently unaffected by degrees of artistic success, flocked to the studios, the merchants moving up a social notch as some had done when they sat for oil portraits. Though photographic portraits were cheaper than those in oil, the lower classes remained largely out of the portrait studios. The sole exception I have found, by an anonymous photographer, features two working-class brothers, fireplace installers, solemnly facing the camera (fig. 64). This tinted daguerreotype, made in Moscow around 1852, is probably the first ever posed photograph of individual workers.[180]

Few of the rare early photographs of Russian genre scenes have survived. One gritty shot by a foreigner, Roger Fenton, in 1852 includes a Moscow tavern. Revealing how remote from real appearances were even the most naturalistic genre pictures of this era, the dark and misty image of a squat and nondescript tavern, a cart, a stone step, and a lunette above the door is depressing in its very ordinariness. The Russian Academy–trained V. A. Karrick (William Carrick, b. 1827 or 1830) photographed scenes of everyday life and of popular street types in Petersburg, Novgorod, the Volga, and the central provinces. A surviving 1862 Carrick photo shows peasants at the Kamenka Fair near Simbirsk wearing cylinder hats and carrying water buckets. The drab and soiled garments of Carrick's street figures in the early 1860s give a harsher and more direct look at reality than the most unflattering renditions of the critical and accusatory artists of the same period.[181] Landscape and genre held few charms for commercial photographers because it yielded little profit and required hauling expensive and heavy equipment.

However, Russian and foreign photographers did journey to the interior on government business or to satisfy their curiosity. Although there was as yet no thoroughgoing enterprise compared to the photographing of British India, for example,[182] separate expeditions were launched to capture Russia with light and lens. As early as 1843 Levitsky took camera and plates on a government assignment to examine mineral water sites in the Caucasus. He and the scientist Yu. F. Fritsche, who was using photography for research, shot topographical sites and towns, but none of their plates has survived. In the 1850s when the collodion process introduced the use of paper for better images, photography made further headway among amateurs, journalists, scientists, and ethnographers. This led the Imperial Geographical Society to use the medium in an ethnographic study of Voronezh Province. The Swede Karl Mazer, who maintained a large studio in Moscow, sailed down the Volga with his apparatus to Nizhny Novgorod and Astrakhan, taking pictures along the way. The Frenchman Alfred d'Avignon journeyed with his camera in the early 1840s to Tver, Novgorod, Vladimir, Nizhny Novgorod, Kazan, Ekaterinburg, Tobolsk, Krasnoyarsk, Irkutsk, and even to remote Kiakhta near the Chinese border. In addition to recording the Siberian lands with his camera, d'Avignon took pictures of the exiled Decembrists Volkonsky, A. V. Poggio, and N. A. Panov. Reported to the police and arrested, d'Avignon then dropped out of sight and most of his pictures of the Decembrists were destroyed. Volkonsky's, one that survived, now hangs in the Historical Museum in Moscow. One Decembrist exile, N. A. Bestuzhev, living in the Trans-Baikal region of Siberia, took up photography as an amateur hobby in the 1850s.[183]

Photography was well in place when the Crimean War broke out in 1853 making that conflict the first ever covered by photoreportage. Cameramen from the major belligerents arrived on the peninsula along with journalists, including the young Tolstoy, to record the fortunes and misfortunes of war. The more realistic English and French works caught harrowing views of the gutted buildings and torn-up streets of Sevastopol after the city was captured.

Images taken after the battles at Balaklava and the Black River show a tormented landscape of burned and twisted trees, already foreshadowing the grimness of World War I. The Russian pictures are less harsh, and they feature many a figure study in the parade portrait tradition of officers in heroic and pompous poses.[184]

While clients were ordering portrait photographs in the burgeoning salons all over Europe, the art world looked on, sometimes in dismay. "This is the end of art," said J. M. W. Turner on seeing his first daguerreotype. "I am glad I have had my day."[185.] The poet Charles Baudelaire had this to say twenty years after the invention of the new process: "I am convinced that the badly applied advances of photography, like all purely material progress for that matter, have greatly contributed to the impoverishment of French artistic genius."[186] American commentators wondered whether the new device was an art, a "factual document," a record, or an idealization. The painter Thomas Cole dismissed it completely, while another American claimed that photography had "swept away many of the illiberal distinctions of rank and wealth." Samuel Morse and hundreds of others deserted painting for it.[187]

In Russia, scientific discussions of the uses of photography were soon joined by a debate about the arts. A theater critic in 1849 used the term "daguerreotype of nature" in a flattering way to describe Shchepkin's acting. The journal *Photography* argued — in tones taken sixty years later by Lenin about cinema — that photography was the most influential of all the arts because it could reach so many people. Other voices dissented. The conservative journalist Osip Senkovsky, after seeing an Academy of Arts exhibit in 1840 of three plates dedicated to Nicholas I, declared that Daguerre was a charlatan. The St. Petersburg *Art Gazette* wrote that, though photography was useful to science, it had no relevance to art, especially to portraiture. "Talent," wrote a critic, "is better at painting pictures than sunlight." In some of the literary criticism aimed at "naturalism," the word "daguerreotype" was used as insult. Vladimir Stasov called the new medium "a cold, if also believable, summary of facts." Stasov qualified his comment. He worried that photography posed a threat to the far superior and far more genuine art of engraving and suggested that, had it appeared earlier it might have overshadowed engraving altogether. But photography, he wrote, did not embody ideas; it simply copied coldly as opposed to engraving which had warmth and life. "The world of art lies distant and unattainable to [photography] and it should not lay claim to it." Yet in 1858 he raised photography to a major element in the art world and predicted great results.[188]

Practicing artists responded in various ways. Some felt alarm at the menacing eye of the camera and were intimidated by the apparent verisimilitude of its products. Others were so enchanted by it that, like artists elsewhere, they gave up conventional art and embraced the black box. Many of these were graduates of the Academy, where painterly realism was rare. Andrei Karelin (b. 1837), the illegitimate son of a state peasant mother, attended an icon-painting school in Tambov and then the Academy from 1857. He became a photographer, as did Taras Shevchenko's friend from the Academy, Ivan Hudovsky. Lavr Plakhov, a first-class graduate of the Academy, saw a daguerreotype in Paris, stopped painting, and took his camera to the towns of Ukraine. Carrick studied architecture at the Academy before turning to photography. Kramskoi's classmates from Voronezh, M. B. Tulinov and M. I. Ponomarëv, did likewise. Andrei Denier (1820–92) audited Academy courses, opened a photo studio in the Passage on Nevsky Prospect, and brought his art training with him to the new venture. More than that, Denier converted some of his professors to at least a tolerance of the camera. In 1860–61, photographs were exhibited side by side with paintings. Denier made photo portraits of several professors, including that arch-academician Fëdor Bruni whom he persuaded to serve as judge at photographic exhibits. Along the way, Denier did portraits of the Itinerant painters Ilya Repin, Ivan Kramskoi, and Ivan Shishkin, and of the literary figures Nikolai Nekrasov, Turgenev, and Tyutchev. Shevchenko's famous photo in furs, done on his return from exile in the late 1850s, is the work of Denier.[189]

More subtle and in the long run more important than these cases of career change was photography's impact on those who remained artists. Though few were unaffected, Sergei Zaryanko and Kramskoi best illustrate the diversity of that impact. Zaryanko, the erstwhile disciple of Venetsianov who taught Vasily Perov among others at the Moscow School of Painting, took the more literal side of the master's teaching and, helped by the camera, took painterly "realism" to absurd lengths. As a painter and teacher who envisioned the artist's job as nothing less than exact reproduction, he saw the photographic image with dual vision: on the one hand, he claimed that it distorted reality; on the other, he proclaimed photography to be an auxiliary science and a useful aid to drawing. Perov said rightly that his master's work sometimes looked just like a photo. Zaryanko's three 1850s portraits hanging side by side in the Russian Museum can hardly be differentiated from tinted photographs. *The Rostovtsev Family* in particular displays photographic details in each of its parts, but is composed like a painting and is thus not only unrealistic but a failure as a work of art.[190] It was in fact the on-canvas equivalent of the grotesque tinted photograph of the young woman noted above. Zaryanko, though his influence on other artists was strong, had himself been led into an aesthetic dead end by the camera.

The future great Itinerant painter, Ivan Kramskoi (1837–87), took an opposite course, starting with photography and ending in art. As a youth in Ostrogozhsk in Voronezh Province, he apprenticed to traveling photographers, wandering from town to town on contract. One of them, Yakov Danilevsky, a converted Jew, had been a watchmaker and photographer in Kharkov. Arriving in Ostrogozhsk in the summer of 1853 as dragoon regiments were gathering for the Crimean War, Danilevsky opened a portrait studio and Kramskoi retouched the photos of officers and soldiers. When Kramskoi went on the road with Danilevsky, his mother objected to his working for a Jew, even a converted one. Kramskoi, who traveled with Danilevsky for a few years, thought little better of his boss whom he described as lacking artistic taste and, in clichéd anti-Semitic terms, as having "the character of a Jew [*zhid*]." After moving to St. Petersburg Kramskoi gained a reputation as the "god of retouching," working for Denier. Kramskoi continued retouching during his studies at the Academy of Arts in the 1860s. He even planned a photography studio in the 1860s. Instead, he used his encounter with photography as a springboard to a style and a movement that changed Russian art (chapter 9).[191]

By the 1840s at least, the Russian educated public was athirst for knowledge, stories, and pictures of their vast country. The leading journal of the 1840s, the Petersburg *Contemporary*, in its reviews of Academy exhibits, echoed Moscow Governor Senyavin and the Slavophile Khomyakov in urging painters to uncover the diverse riches of Russia.[192] Exploring the interior was not simply a matter of finding and representing new worlds. The slow shift in visualizing also brought about self-discovery. On the social level, it signaled new structures of value and self-worth. Landscapes and cityscapes became increasingly populated with real Russian people of various social backgrounds. The privileged classes remained in view, but were more and more often captured in intimate portraits and family scenes. Even the realia of interiors could produce revelation. When Venetsianov instructed his pupils to gaze carefully at the most trivial objects of an interior, it meant that ordinary things were as worthy of reproduction as the opulent props of ceremonial portraits and interiors. This probably reinforced the notion that ordinary *people* were equally worthy of representation. And since representation had been linked in the academic discourse to dignity and freedom, then the leap to the idea of general liberation may have taken root among artists as well. The natural process — no sudden revolt — of change in cognition brought into public view identities that had previously been obscured; and it led to a search for novel social types. Artists increasingly turned away from classical concerns to the here and now: from the outside to the inside, from the past to the present, from the high to the low. In one sense, the constant expansion of the artists' spatial focus — both in form and in social content — was joined to a constriction of space in generic subject matter. Of the principal modes of the artistic relationship to life, aside from self-expression — to exalt, to show, to critique — Russian art had reached the second function by the 1850s. Given the social, political, and intellectual climate of that decade, it took no great leap to reach the third mode.

PART V

Finale and Overture

When Did the Real Day Dawn?

The day passes and so does the night
— *Taras Shevchenko, 1860*

When, then, will the real day dawn?
— *Nikolai Dobrolyubov, 1860*

A relatively unnoticed but illuminating event of 1858 brings us full circle back to the hardship story of a serf musician and puts it in a new frame. The serf owner P. K. Vonlyarlyarsky of Smolensk Province, it will be recalled (chapter 2), had refused stubbornly to free his cellist and violinist. The enserfed cellist, Vikenty Meshkov, appeared as soloist in a Moscow society concert in which a count, a prince, and several other nobles performed. The attentive elite audience received him cordially. The talent exhibited by the remarkable artist impressed a reporter for the *Russian Herald,* all the more so since, he said, the serf had received only two dozen lessons and was thus largely self-taught. In a comment on social relations, the journalist wrote: "In view of the warm reception given to a serf artist by people of privilege, the mind automatically raises a question: what draws together people from utterly different rungs of the social ladder, people with nothing in common?" In reply, he posited artistic activity as a social lubricant. "An even higher feeling has brought about this movement: what we have here is the human being who has reached out a hand to another human being." To illustrate the barriers to that human commonality, the journalist noted that, while the proceeds of the event would not go to Meshkov for the purchase of his freedom, rumor had it that a wealthy unnamed music lover had offered to redeem the cellist for the sum of three thousand rubles. Vonlyarlyarsky, however—as in the past—-declined the offer and promised to free him on his own. According to Herzen's account published in *The Bell,* Vonlyarlyarsky made it clear that there had been no offer and that he would decline one if made, since he needed the two musicians to tutor his daughters. Whether Meshkov had to wait until 1861, the year of emancipation, is unknown.[1]

Narratives of Awakening

If the years 1838–48 constituted a "marvelous decade," then the slightly longer stretch from 1848 to 1861 might be named an "explosive decade." After Nicholas died in 1855, during the Crimean War, the consciousness of imminent change thickened in society and grew lyrical in its articulation. During the war, Ivan Turgenev in a letter voiced the hope that the fall of Sevastopol would prove to be the Battle of Jena for Russia and thus usher in renewal and reform, as had happened in Prussia after its devastating defeat by Napoleon. The Crimean War was a shocking revelation of Russia's apparent backwardness, not only in military prowess but in all aspects of national organization. Scores of articles poured forth a stream of hope that a new era was about to dawn; and they invoked well-established similes about a new day, light after darkness, a bright morning for society and for the nation. The euphoria of expectation was palpable. A new journal devoted to sustaining the mood called itself *Daybreak*. Some took up another metaphor: when Ostrovsky's *The Storm* appeared in 1859, the heavy climatic atmosphere in the final act followed by the crack of thunder and teeming rain was seen as emblematic of cleansing away the filth of the past. In 1857, Dobrolyubov (fig. 66) compared his country to Ilya Muromets of Russian epic who had slumbered for thirty years—a sly jab at the reign of Nicholas I—and then woke up brimming with strength to accomplish great deeds. The radical exile Herzen, who had founded his paper *The Bell* as an alarm clock, exclaimed that the country was "suddenly awakened." Russians' developing interest in their own country sharpened; they wished to know not only where it was going, but what it actually was. When emancipation came in 1861, Mikhail Shchepkin exclaimed "I don't want to die. The times are good. Everything is moving forward. One must live." Sofya Soboleva had a character in an 1863 story recall the moment when the dawn brought not only light but a general awakening of people, of life, of new forces:

> Even in the drawing-rooms of our provincial town, the words "the modern world," "emancipation," "progress" had become common currency. "Thank God," I thought. It felt as though a huge forest had woken from its enchanted sleep. Millions of voices had begun to mutter, to chatter, to make noises that might only be half-articulate as yet, but which were already distinct. And every now and then some fully formed note would sound amidst that disorganized racket, with the promise of a delightful harmony in time.[2]

The new tsar, Alexander II, set the reform process going with statements of intent to bring about emancipation of the serfs; and with the enunciation of *glasnost,* the lifting of the more absurd aspects of Tsar Nicholas's censorship and a modest allowance of public discussion in the press. Scholars have argued for a century and a half over what made the tsar move to free the serfs. No single cause can be reasonably isolated. Russia's economic lag, its recent defeat by smaller European powers fighting on its own soil, and the escalating and worrisome incidence of peasant disorder combined to persuade the monarch that the time for delay was past. Historians must take seriously his oft-quoted warning to the gentry that "if we do not emancipate the peasants from above, they might do it themselves from below." Even ninety years after the bloody Pugachëv uprising, the very thought of another one could still bring shivers of alarm. The number of peasant disturbances had grown exponentially in the last years of Nicholas I. One hundred thirty-nine murders of landowners and stewards and seventy failed attempts occurred in the years 1836–51; in 1852–55 alone the combined number was fifty-nine.[3]

The easing of censorship brought an explosion of new journals and increased circulation of older ones, though theater censorship remained stringent. One hundred fifty new newspapers appeared in 1856–60. The unofficial pages of the government provincial gazettes came alive with material that went beyond the usual doses of information on shows and entertainments, thus helping to weaken the line between the state and the public sphere. The new dispensation allowed the sometimes strident and always trenchant views of radical journalists to spread far and wide. Nikolai Chernyshevsky preached a shadowy version of peasant land redistribution bordering on socialism. Herzen's talk of a populist "Russian socialism" came in illegally across the frontiers. Nikolai Dobrolyubov and Dmitry Pisarev glossed the plays of Ostrovsky and the novels of Goncharov and Turgenev with social and rebellious readings. In his famous 1860 review of Turgenev's *On the Eve,* Dobrolyubov catalogued a long line of useless and superfluous literary characters whose real counterparts, he claimed, populated the Russian social landscape. He titled his review "When, then, will the real day dawn?"[4] Within a half-dozen years after the Crimean War, Dr. Nikolai Pirogov had opened the "woman question" to public gaze and M. L. Mikhailov and Chernyshevsky had enlarged its implications.[5]

The deluge of words did not dry up on the page. Salons had been buzzing for a decade about the fictions of Grigorovich and Turgenev on the peasant question. Serfdom became the holy issue of issues. The notion of liberating a mass of humanity naturally opened a whole discourse on "freedom" and justice — for Negro slaves in America; for Italians from the Habsburg yoke; and for Russian priests, women, young people, and all the downtrodden and destitute, the insulted and humiliated. Russian towns and cities were swept with a breath of bracing air and deafened with the clamor of optimistic rhetoric. A new generation of students turned words into deeds in a series of university disturbances that lasted well into the 1860s and helped feed the even more dedicated bands of outright revolutionaries who endeavored to upset the state and introduce a form of socialism across the land.[6]

Amidst the maelstrom of liberation talk, subtler movements accompanied the forces of emancipation and the attendant reforms: limited social convergence, the swelling of a merchant interest in national culture, and professional assertion — all intimately tied to creative activity. The introduction of self-government in provincial and district bodies — the zemstvos — threw together divergent social classes in deliberative institutions and spawned widespread openings for professional agronomists, physicians, and other specialists. The new law courts, judicial procedures, juries, and justices of the peace brought people of all classes into public and official venues, surrounded by a burgeoning legal profession.[7] Grassroots movements of social activism that sprung up in the capitals and provincial towns multiplied spaces where people of diverse backgrounds purposely mingled. In the 1860s, student groups, radical circles, and even residential communes were open to men and women, Russians and non-Russians (including Jews), nobles and those at or near the bottom of the social scale. The intelligentsia ran Sunday Schools for workers in the years 1859–62. A Literary Fund with branches in Saratov, Ekaterinoslav, Grodno, Odessa, Taganrog, Tambov, Tver, and Vilna had a mixed ethnic and social makeup.[8] Most such organizations were battered and eventually closed down as seditious; but their spontaneous formation revealed a movement toward social interaction, leaping over traditional boundaries.

By the time of emancipation, the juridical class or *soslovie* system had been slowly eroding. Already in the eighteenth century, alongside clergy, merchants, townspeople, and peasants — themselves subdivided — the vaguely defined *raznochintsy* had emerged and the gentry had ramified into as many as six categories. Even this elaboration of terms could not accommodate the variety of social and occupational divisions springing up all around. The state, in the words of Gregory Freeze, "was gradually impelled to make new, larger loopholes and to deviate significantly from the basic principle of post-Petrine social policy."[9] Although juridical lines continued to divide society, symbolic forces pointed the other way. Up until the 1850s, for example, gentry men maintained the shaven face which distinguished them from merchants, peasants, and most other members of the lower orders. In 1849, during an official dynastic celebration, the tsar had issued an order banning gentry beards. As Richard Wortman interprets this act, "the beard symbolized a coming together of elite and people in a national culture whose features were not defined by the autocratic power."[10] The ban did not last, and in subsequent decades it became more difficult to represent clear markers between social classes in art, photography, and on the stage. Both the slight but real diminution of social barriers and the clarification and spread of professional identities flowed into the continuing development of a Russian national feeling.

The merchant estate, complex and varied, does not permit universal generalizations about its role in culture. For example, among the fifty or so wealthy serf industrialists who had made their fortunes on *obrok* and had been emancipated by 1861,[11] only a fraction ventured to support the arts. The patrons who appear in the coming pages lived mostly in Moscow, the center of Russia's domestic wholesale trade, in greater numbers than in the capital.[12] Most Moscow merchants possessed no self-conscious or unified cultural doctrine, no armory of ideas, nor even the language to construct an ideology. Yet during the Crimean War, an active segment was converted to an alliance with Slavophilism on account of its conservative monarchism and hostility to Western liberalism. Personal bonds, journals, patriotic banquets, and shared views on national economic self-sufficiency drove the alliance. The Slavophile Ivan Aksakov saw the merchants "as a link between the peasantry and the upper classes." The Official Nationalist Mikhail Pogodin — like Polevoi before him — shared some of the Slavophile views and praised the "remarkable, benevolent Moscow merchants" for their financial contributions to the war effort. Apollon Grigorev, prophet of the emerging "ideology of the soil" or Native Soil conservatism (*pochvennichestvo*), hailed the merchantry as inclusive, bearded, moneyed, and ready to patronize both art and commerce; broader than the gentry elite; more energetic than the peasants, and thus a capacious carrier of values and the embodiment of the Russian national spirit. In this vague blend of nationalisms, their sometimes foggy intellectual formulations were downplayed, and merchant capitalists were happy to pick and choose from all of them — in politics and in art — without being bothered by nuances.[13]

Ironically, at the moment of the first wave of a continuing intellectual assault upon merchants that made previous satirical jibes seem like innocent fun, a number of merchants emerged as vital agents in "nationalizing" the arts of Russia. The denizens of the "kingdom of darkness" often bore the standard of conservative progress, Russian patriotism, and artistic patronage. One scholar has argued that merchant cultural consumption, being largely theatrical and visual, lay outside both the literary mainstream and the "verbal, secularized culture of Russia's intelligentsia." She rightly stresses some parallels between merchant and peasant ways of life, however much they may have differed in income and occupation: the love of visual culture — icon and *lubok* — and eager participation in folk fairs. Merchants were singularly active in patronizing and supporting theater and the graphic arts, more so than either literature or music. Yet the best-known patrons of art music were the widow of an industrialist, Nadezhda von Meck, who subsidized Tchaikovsky; and the timber merchant Mitrofan Belyaev, who later sponsored some members of the Mighty Five.[14] There were other exceptions: merchants who, emulating what they saw as their intellectual betters, scheduled literary evenings as well as performances at the Moscow Merchant Club; those who in 1844 offered to buy a house for the playwright and fabulist Ivan Krylov; and the great millionaire art buyer, Kozma (Kuzma) Soldatenkov, who had a close personal friendship with Nikolai Rubinstein. Members of the Moscow Hunting Society, founded in 1863, included Rubinstein, Stanislavsky (when he was still Alexeev) and the merchant-patrons Savva Mamontov, Tretyakov, Soldatenkov, and others.[15]

The rise of professionalism generated its own possibilities and problems for creative artists. Even in the realm of revolutionary violence, the disastrous amateur plotting of the Decembrists was about to be replaced by circles that would blossom into a professional underground of propagandists and later of terrorists.[16] Definitions of professionalism usually speak of formal training, standards, mutual communication in print or meetings, some self-governance, the satisfaction of pride in performance, and an avid desire for respect from state and society — in other words for status. Russian professionals also sought relative freedom from the entanglements of state control, in return for which they preached a self-defined debt to society — thus their strong links to the values of the intelligentsia. Bureaucratic arrogance towards free professions lessened somewhat after emancipation, though it never eroded completely. Physicians, engineers, and lawyers walked the long road to professional independence as they built group identities outside the constricting coils of chanceries and regiments.[17]

For creative artists, serfdom, foreign specialists, and the proliferation of artistic amateurs had long stood as obstacles to status. Even before the serfs were freed in 1861, the campaigns against amateurism and foreign domination intensified. As of 1861, Peter the Great's approach to imbibing foreign culture remained in place to a large degree, not only in the content of the imports, but in the mode of receiving it: bringing foreigners to Russia, sending Russians abroad. Skills in ship design and ordnance were high on Peter's shopping list; Catherine II and her successors added cultural products and talent to that list. At the moment of emancipation, Germans were still very visible in the instrumental music world, French and Italian figures in opera and ballet. Ironically, the call for the upgrading of professional training for Russians generated a contradiction, because in some realms of artistic expression, notably instrumental music and graphic art—neither requiring native proficiency in the Russian language—professionalism came to be identified in some quarters as antinational.

Nationhood in Counterpoint

When Anton Rubinstein returned to Russia from Europe in 1858, the classical music scene did not look promising. Glinka had held his "last salon" at his sister's home in the summer of 1854 and bid what were to be his farewells to Lvov, Serov, Dargomyzhsky, Ulybyshev, and Balakirev. Glinka died in Berlin in 1857. As with Beethoven in Germany in the late nineteenth century, all parties claimed Glinka as their idol. A biographer of Tchaikovsky has written of *Ruslan and Lyudmila* that "no other work has ever had such a seminal importance in the annals of Russian music." Yet at the moment of Glinka's death, no one seemed ready to take up his work on a grand scale or to act as the central figure of Russian musical life. Dargomyzhsky and Serov had not yet proven themselves, and were temperamental and standoffish to boot. The Mighty Five had yet to emerge, and the seventeen-year-old student Peter Ilich Tchaikovsky still sat on the benches in law school. None displayed much organizational energy. Mikhail Vielgorsky had died in 1856; and General Lvov was beset by jealousy and had delegated much of his Capella work to his assistants. Rubinstein, a prophet returning from the wilderness, was an outsider still snubbed for his Vienna article demeaning Russian music (chapter 3).[18]

The birth of the Russian Musical Society and the St. Petersburg Conservatory, both dedicated to Russian music and to professionalized higher education, proved the catalyst that generated a burst of creative energy as well as a querulous flood of invective. Claims to the idea of establishing a higher music school have been made by and for many. Friedrich Scholtz, who worked in the Capella and in the Imperial Theaters, as early as 1819 had hatched plans for a "conservatory" in the form of free classes in his home. But he died in the cholera epidemic of 1830. Vladimir Stasov, no admirer of Grand Duchess Elena Pavlovna, noted that she broached the idea of a Russian conservatory to Clara and Robert Schumann in 1844. In 1849, the ex-serf composer Daniil Kashin set up a school in Moscow for all social classes at free or low-cost tuition, but died a year later. The violinist Afanasev claimed that he wrote a proposal for a conservatory in the 1850s that Mikhail Vielgorsky and Lvov brushed off; and that it was given by the Tula landowner and cellist V. A. Kologrivov to his friend Anton Rubinstein. Another Rubinstein friend, N. D. Kashkin, reported that the Russian Musical Society scheme arose from the Rubinstein brothers at a family holiday gathering. Elena Pavlovna and Anton Rubinstein often discussed a conservatory at the Mikhailovsky Palace and in Nice. In 1858, the talk turned to action. Rubinstein, upon his return, though spurned privately by other composers, possessed a major European reputation. Feeling unfulfilled as Elena Pavlovna's court pianist, he launched a musical salon at his Petersburg flat on the Fontanka where he and others aired their dreams about the future of Russian musical life (fig. 67).[19]

The founders of the Russian Musical Society, going beyond the efforts of existing Petersburg organizations, aspired, in the words of its charter, "to effect the spread of musical education in Russia, facilitate the development of all branches of musical art, and encourage talented Russian composers, performers, and music teachers." The society, a protoconservatory in disguise, sought to perform the functions of the Academy of Arts and the Theater School, but with a national outreach to acquaint the public with Russian and foreign musical art in schools and branches all over the country. Largely the brainchild of Rubinstein and Kologrivov, the society was launched in the home of Matvei Vielgorsky in 1859. To avoid delays, it adopted the 1847 charter of the Vielgorskys' now defunct Symphonic Society. On the board sat Rubinstein, Kologrivov, Kashkin, Dmitry Stasov (Vladimir's brother), and the Grand Duchess, who secured donations from the imperial family and aristocrats. Lvov declined to join the prize committee and forbade his singers from appearing with the Russian Musical Society. The society, under august sponsorship, held its first rehearsals (though only for two hours a week) at the Mikhailovsky Palace. The inaugural season of 1859–60 obtained first-rate musicians from St. Petersburg's musical forces.[20] At the first concert in November the audience heard Glinka's *Ruslan and Lyudmila* overture, Rubinstein's G Minor Piano Concerto, the finale of Handel's *Jephta,* an excerpt from Mendelssohn's unfinished *Lorelei,* and Beethoven's Fifth Symphony. A capacity audience of about nine hundred filled the Gentry Club. To the ten concerts per year were added chamber performances. Flushed with success after the first season, the Russian Musical Society organizers dedicated the box office receipts to the campaign for a conservatory of music.[21]

On the eve of emancipation, foreigners, state employees, serfs, and dilettantes had made up the Russian musical community rather than a professional body of free artists. It was still natural to identify amateurs as Russians and professionals as foreigners (mostly ethnic Germans). In the 1860s, popular fiction continued to poke fun at domestic music lessons. A character in the Sofya Soboleva story cited above snidely dismissed the ubiquitous piano lessons for young girls which "flooded Russia with bad lady musicians and with incompetent music mistresses." In January 1861, Rubinstein, in the very midst of his conservatory campaign, addressed musical amateurism at large in a blistering article in *The Age,* tersely titled "Concerning Music in Russia." Amateurs, he wrote, were poorly trained by foreign tutors who, to mollify the parents, exposed pupils to easy tunes rather than rigorous exercises. Amateurs could take up music as a hobby or avocation since they scorned fame and faced no critical response or shortage of money. Between the lines, one can easily discern Rubinstein's desire to turn the tables on patronizing attitudes towards artistic public performance, an attitude that had prevented noblemen like Mikhail Buturlin from singing and General Lvov from playing the violin in a public venue. That attitude derived from pride of birth rather than achievement. As for state schools, Rubinstein believed that both the theater and Court Capella, the only musical training centers in Russia, produced mere "civil servants' rather than "free artists."[22] With all his faults, his volcanic temper, and his colossal ego, Rubinstein had the wit and courage to challenge the very core of the Russian social code.

Projecting his own experience, Rubinstein believed that making good music required full-time dedication, hard work, some suffering and sacrifice, and a desire for personal success, fame, and even money — as well as a willingness to face critics. Russia needed a market place of competition, an updraft of talent from every class and element, and a rigorous training system that would eventually replace foreigners with competent Russian musicians. Rubinstein did not hesitate to unveil the dirty word "ambition" — pride of profession and an upward trajectory. A telling incident of 1850, described with angry astonishment in his autobiography, had revealed to him in a flash the harsh truth about his place in the ascriptive society he lived in. After making his confession at the Kazan Cathedral, he identified himself in the confessional register as "artist." The deacon challenged Rubinstein's title since he was attached to no school, theater, or government body. In the end, the pianist known all over Europe simply had to write "son of a merchant." The deacon's persistent query, "What then are you?" and society's obsession with rank showed Rubinstein that, since he was no noble, official, military man, teacher, or theater employee, and had received no diploma at the hands of his private teachers, he was in a sense a "nobody." This, he claimed, fueled his determination to create in Russia the title Free Artist for the independent professional musician, equivalent to that of Free Artist of the Academy of Arts with its concomitant status.[23]

Rubinstein's crusade transcended his undeniable personal ambition[24] as he fought to upgrade the status and proficiency of musicians, convinced as he was that Russia could not advance much further in musical glory without dedicated professional institutions. The hundred-year rise and fall of serf orchestras had produced precious few serious musicians and only one great composer who had been exposed to them — Glinka. Teachers, composers, performers of music enjoyed no civil rights as such unless employed by the school system or the Imperial Theaters.[25] Real talent was often squandered for lack of subsidized high-level musical training for the gifted poor. Apollon Gussakovsky (1841–75), in part a victim of this lack, was a promising composer, a portion of whose symphony was well received at the Petersburg University concerts in 1861. But, afflicted with tuberculosis and impoverished by the need to support a large family, he died at the age of thirty-four without having fulfilled his early promise, and was much lamented by Balakirev, Stasov, Musorgsky, and others.[26] By creating a conservatory and the social networks around it, Rubinstein hoped to achieve professionalism for musicians: specialized higher knowledge, group consciousness, and at least a partial acceptance in society of the more outstanding musical figures.

Resistance to building another imperial school for the arts surfaced in various forms, some of them bizarre. When Odoevsky tried to raise money for a conservatory in 1859 from Grand Duchess Maria Nikolaevna, she replied: "Oh, I cannot understand music. It grates on my nerves. And where would the money come from?" Rubinstein's 1860 petition to the Ministry of Education was turned down. His public appeal in the press backfired because of its antidilettante tone. Elena Pavlovna then lobbied in the highest circles and the Ministry of the Court gave its assent. In October 1861, eight months after the emancipation of the serfs, the conservatory was chartered, though variants on the term "school" were sometimes used to describe it. A year later it opened with classes held at first in the Mikhailovsky Palace and in private homes. In 1869, a regular base was found and in 1896 the conservatory took up abode in the place where it stands today — Theater Square, the site of the old St. Petersburg Bolshoi Stone Theater and opposite the Mariinsky Theater.[27]

Born in the postserfdom era, the St. Petersburg Conservatory became the first higher school with open admissions for pupils of both genders and all classes and nationalities, including Jews, who could leave the Pale to study music. Literate children fourteen and above with musical talent could apply, and scholarships were available for the poor. All enjoyed exemption from taxes and army service; graduates, like those of the Academy, earned the coveted title Free Artist.[28] Despite Rubinstein's determination to "Russianize" the musical profession, German music was privileged and a shortage of qualified Russians led to hiring foreign instructors for the time being.[29] The conservatory's mission of training teachers, players, and singers of both sexes to make a respected professional livelihood was also meant to help fill the "silent provinces" with good music. One of its first pupils, the twenty-one-year-old Tchaikovsky, moved to Moscow in 1865, where Nikolai Rubinstein would open the that city's conservatory in 1866. The Moscow Conservatory was by no means a mere extension of Anton's St. Petersburg achievement. Nikolai Rubinstein, a more gregarious type than his brother, had propagandized for it to his friends, who included playwright Alexander Ostrovsky, the "Ostrovsky stars" Prov Sadovsky and Lyubov Nikulina-Kositskaya, and the editors of the *Muscovite*. Alexei Verstovsky, to his credit, supported the conservatory as well, though he died on the eve of its opening.[30]

Rubinstein's triumph in creating the St. Petersburg Conservatory exceeded his personal fame as a virtuoso. He needed to routinize his charisma through an institution. The musical star of prereform Russia had been but a satellite still orbiting around the real stars — emperor, grand duchesses, aristocrats. With the conservatory in place, Rubinstein's star quality could no longer be overshadowed in quite the same way. Tendentious as it might sound, the Soviet musicologist Boris Asafiev's notion that Rubinstein's struggle represented one between "lordly culture" and "*raznochintsy* culture" is essentially true.[31] After the Revolution of 1917, all institutions bearing the designation "Imperial" were renamed. The St. Petersburg and Moscow conservatories would, by ordinary rules of courtesy and historical accuracy, have been named after the Rubinstein brothers. Instead they were and remain named after, respectively, Rimsky-Korsakov and Tchaikovsky. There is of course little to debate about the musical eminence of these two pairs; the Rubinsteins did not achieve long-lasting renown as composers outside Russia. Considerations of ethnic origin probably played no role in the Soviet naming. But ethnic origins did become an issue in the 1860s when a Russian musical identity was being constructed. The conservatory, seen as a godsend to some musical figures, looked to others like a threat.

Vladimir Stasov (1824–1906), the most vocal opponent of Rubinstein's vision and one of the most influential voices in late nineteenth-century Russian culture, vigorously promoted both the Mighty Five circle of composers and the Itinerant school of painters. Son of a prominent Petersburg architect, well traveled, and steeped in European culture, Stasov played four-hand piano arrangements at home and possessed an impressive technical musical knowledge. As a student in the 1830s and 1840s, he found a vibrant musical environment at the School of Jurisprudence, founded in 1835 and set in an imposing edifice on the Fontanka opposite the Summer Garden, where Tchaikovsky dropped out and where — a generation later — Lenin persevered for a law degree. The director, a music lover, engaged Henselt, Knecht, and Schuberth, among others, to teach music there. Tsar Nicholas visited the "aviary" in the dorm where students squeaked out their sounds on various instruments. An official complained that the "lazy and proud schoolboys who were incapable of composing a report, . . . danced and sang magnificently" and gave school concerts. Stasov conducted "duels" at the piano with Alexander Serov. Stasov claimed that the training at the school was better than that later provided at the conservatory, allegedly because the teaching was "freer."[32] Thus was planted the seed of Stasov's antiprofessionalism.

Stasov hosted scholars, artists, and musicians (including Rubinstein) at his home, frequented concerts, and lectured on music history. A cultural organizer, Stasov wrote that "systematization, arranging in categories, had always been my passion in everything." And as a freelance cultural critic, he reveled in polemics. "A person can only write well if he is in flames."[33] Stasov remained inflammatory to the end of his long life. Like Rubinstein, he detested the influence of Italian opera in Russia and wanted to improve musical life, but their means conflicted. A polemic crystallized around Rubinstein's January 1861 article, "Concerning Music in Russia," which provoked a storm. Stasov responded within a month. Though he later poured venom on aristocratic dilettantes, Stasov now defended them because, though lazy and bereft of talent, they and their bad music caused no harm to Russian musical culture and occupied only limited social space, as opposed to bad music from so-called professionals. He opposed Rubinstein over the linked issues of ambition and academic preparation. Ambition, born of greed and the profit motive, stained the escutcheon of exalted creativity; and giving musicians the status of Free Artists would simply provide "bait" for those who aspired to title and privilege rather than to a life in art. A conservatory, said Stasov, would embody these evils and strangle spontaneous creativity with academic rules. Stasov claimed that Europe was now coming to recognize that "academies and conservatories serve only as breeding grounds for talentless people and aid the establishment in art of harmful ideas and tastes." In a retrospective article of 1883 that achieved the status of scripture for a century, Stasov reiterated his arguments against academic degrees and titles and criticized Rubinstein's conservatory as the undesirable equivalent of the Academy of Arts.[34] No one seemed to notice at the time that three or four generations of amateur music-making were consigned to the trash bin by both Stasov and Rubinstein.

The pedagogical tussle hardened into a war over national authenticity that was sharpened by personal animosities. Some of the fault lay with Rubinstein, who with his arrogant personality did not take kindly to contradiction. In later years, Konstantin Stanislavsky noted Rubinstein's "lava-like temperament."[35] While in company, Rubinstein could hold his tongue; when he picked up the pen, he too often dipped it in acid. But his adversaries surpassed him in venom and saw him as another Stolz who tried to outshine all the lazy Russian Oblomovs. Rubinstein's draconian work habits and demands for punctuality, scheduling, and discipline seemed a standing insult to the allegedly more relaxed "Russian" manner. Stasov socialized with Rubinstein at musical events, but down deep he disdained him. "Mr. Rubinstein," he wrote in 1861, "is a foreigner, with nothing in common either with our national character or our art," an obvious reference to his family name, foreign training, and perhaps his Jewish origins.[36] Though Stasov employed what was by this time the less polite *zhid* as well as the neutral *evrei* (Jew) in his various references to Rubinstein, his anti-Semitism was selective rather than sweeping. For example, in speaking of the young composer Serov's "Jewish talent," Stasov patronizingly praised the "good" side of his Jewishness in contrast to Rubinstein's.[37] Rubinstein's alleged "foreignness" — his European training and musical contacts — outweighed his specific Jewishness for Stasov whose hostility would have been the same had Rubinstein been an ethnic German. Rubinstein's association with the German-born Elena Pavlovna also counted against him, although both men disliked her. Stasov, alluding to the despised Offenbach, called the grand duchess "la belle Hélène," and her "German party" — "archreactionary" foes of Russian national culture.[38]

Stasov's colleagues displayed even greater rudeness: Musorgsky called Rubinstein Tupinstein ("Dullstone"), the conservatory a German Musical Ministry, and Elena Pavlovna Auntie Alyona (or Alëna, a sometimes affectionate, but in this case dismissive, diminutive of Elena). He also blasted Rubinstein's concept of the "artist" as a bombastic and imported token of "fame and money." Balakirev dubbed Rubinstein a "musical Baltic German general."[39] Stasov was wont to contrast Rubinstein's origins with the provincial and purely Russian ones of Glinka, Dargomyzhsky, Balakirev, Rimsky-Korsakov, and even Musorgsky, who had come to St. Petersburg at age ten. In fact, Balakirev descended from Tatars. As for the remaining members of the Five: the Petersburg-born Alexander Borodin's biological father had a Tatar lineage;[40] and César Cui's family background was part French and part Lithuanian, and he had studied with the Polish composer Stanislaw Moniuszko.

Stasov himself was born in St. Petersburg; when he heard that his family might have had a Prussian ancestry, he exclaimed: "Germans indeed! How unpleasant."[41] Stasov's schoolmate Alexander Serov was partly Jewish. A grandfather, Karl Gablitz (Hablitz, Gablits, 1752–1821) of Königsberg, had converted to Orthodoxy and served with distinction under Catherine II as senator, state councillor, vice governor, scientist, and explorer. On learning of their Jewish ancestry, Serov and his sister ironically exclaimed "We are Jews!" As a mature composer, Serov became an outspoken anti-Semite. He called the Russian Musical Society the Jew *Musikverein* and the conservatory the Piano Synagogue. In an 1862 article on Rubinstein, Serov described the Russian musical scene as "virgin soil" exploited by foreign seekers of the "Promised Land" who resembled the Jewish tavern keeper, Yankel, in Gogol's *Taras Bulba*. Serov never joined Stasov's camp, but maintained an unrelenting animosity to the Rubinsteins.[42]

It was against this culturally turbulent background that the assembly of Russian musical genius came into being that came to be known in translation as the Mighty Five or Mighty Little Handful (*Moguchaya kuchka*): Balakirev, César Cui (Tsesar Kyui, 1835–1918), Musorgsky, Borodin, and Rimsky-Korsakov, three of whom were to achieve lasting fame outside Russia. Stasov originally coined the term in a review of a concert organized by Balakirev in 1867 for a Pan-Slav meeting to designate the composers on the program: Balakirev, Glinka, Dargomyzhsky, and Rimsky-Korsakov. While Stasov served as prophet and defender of the faith, it was Mily Balakirev (1836–1910) who inspired and organized the composers' circle, which came into being between 1856 when he met Cui and 1862 when he met Borodin. It was at first called simply *pyatero* or the Five. Later both designations took hold. In any case, the achievements of the Mighty Five are central to Russian musical history from the 1860s onward up to today and have been analyzed in hundreds of scholarly studies. Though long exposed by disinterested investigators, various myths persist about the Five: they held to a unified ideology; as idealists, they lacked economic or career motives; they and only they produced authentic, national, and folkish Russian music; and their foes were foreign-inspired intriguers.[43]

After coming to St. Petersburg from Nizhny Novgorod where he had cut his musical teeth, Balakirev made a name for himself in public concerts as a pianist and composer (fig. 68). His first major work, the 1855–56 Piano Concerto in F-sharp Minor, resonates with the styles of Schumann, Chopin, and Mendelssohn (whom Balakirev later contemptuously called "Mendel"), with barely discernable Russian overtones. Balakirev, a neurotic bundle of contradictions and an extreme Russian chauvinist, disliked Jews, Germans, Poles, and Catholics. He promoted the use of "eastern" motifs that he discovered during a visit to the Caucasus, out of which came his *Islamey: Fantasy on Oriental Themes*. Though he despised Europe, Balakirev wrote one of his best works, *King Lear,* with a European style and subject matter. An avid reader of Belinsky and Chernyshevsky, he distrusted the aristocratic elite and its amateurism, touted self-teaching and spontaneous inspiration, and proclaimed the *narod* the fount of art. Yet his politically reactionary views made him fear the masses. Though a dyed-in-the-wool nationalist, Balakirev hated Russia's vaunted center, Moscow, yet aspired to write a Kremlin Symphony.[44]

Balakirev, sharing Stasov's views on Rubinstein and the conservatory, longed to create a specifically Russian school of musical culture. Both he and Gavriil Lomakin have been credited with the idea of a private "counter-conservatory," the Free Music School. The word "free" (*besplatnaya*) in the title meant "free of charge" and had nothing to do with Rubinstein's notion of Free (*svobodnyi*) Artist. The school was inspired by the Sunday schools for the common people that flourished in St. Petersburg in the early 1860s. With permission of the city administration, the Free School opened in 1862. It issued no diplomas initially and had no official state sponsorship, though it did attract the patronage of Grand Duke Nikolai Alexandrovich and later of the tsar himself. The free tuition and the evening and Sunday schedule allowed for a broad admissions policy which attracted not only the middle classes, but shop clerks, seamstresses, chambermaids, and even factory workers. Lomakin taught vocal and Balakirev instrumental music. The curriculum allowed European music, but taught at a lower level than at the conservatory. Balakirev had had no systematic training and he preached to his disciples that they did not need it either.[45] There are indications that Musorgsky nourished an aristocratic contempt for hard work and serious application, although Rimsky-Korsakov's claim that "he gave himself over to [music] only in his leisure hours"[46] must be treated skeptically. Some of the others in the Five also proudly flaunted their indifference to formal training. The conflicting visions of the Rubinstein and Stasov camps about Russian musical life and its role in society came into sharp relief in the contrast between the conservatory and the Free Music School.

The musical schism of the 1860s, despite its sometimes absurd rhetorical posturing, probably enriched rather than hindered musical advancement in Russia. Each side doubled its efforts to outdo the other. Prior to 1861, most would-be composers who aspired to further heights had to pass through the hands of foreigners in Russia or abroad. With the growth of aspiring amateur composers and nonserf musicians came a demand for Russian home-grown education. Both the conservatories and the Free School in their different ways help fill this need.

The Volga Generation

Ironically, the reign of the new tsar, Alexander II, constricted rather than expanded public theatrical performance space by stiffening a regulatory process begun under his father. From the 1840s several directives had issued forth from the Ministry of the Court, designed to protect the ticket sales of the Imperial Theaters by limiting, forbidding, or controlling virtually all public entertainments in the capitals without prior permission of the Directorate. The campaign culminated in an 1854 law that placed all entertainment in the two capitals — balls, masquerades, concerts, and some charity affairs — under the Directorate, which now had the power to grant permits, control the repertoire, and garner one-fourth of the profits. Violators were reprimanded. The Crimean War had generated many benefit concerts in gentry, merchant, and artisan clubs outside the purview of Directorate; and the use of imperial artists in these caused dismay, since they repeated numbers already performed on the stages of the Imperial Theaters. Henceforth only charity concerts fell outside this law which was confirmed by Tsar Alexander Il in 1862.[47]

In 1856–58 a Committee to Review the Deficit of the Imperial Theaters, chaired by Count V. F. Adlerberg and including director Gedeonov and writer Vladimir Sollogub, addressed the theater monopoly question and the financial problems that regularly plagued the theater system which, despite subsidies, was deep in debt. The spending pattern continued to show a preference for Petersburg over Moscow and for foreign productions over Russian ones. At the top stood ballet, followed by the three foreign companies, Russian opera, and, at the bottom, Russian drama. The level of monetary support ranged from 193,448 rubles per year for the ballet to 44,232 for Russian drama. Italian paychecks averaged 3,000 rubles per year; Russian, 1,140. More alarming, the entire outlay exceeded that of comparable European theaters. This unpleasant fact was lucidly revealed to the committee by Sollogub whom it had sent to study the theater system of Berlin, Vienna, and Paris for the 1857 season. He argued that the state's historical role in Russian theater as a product of theater's court origins was now obsolete. The cause of the deficit and decline of Russian theater was its lack of artistic freedom and choice. In prophetic terms, he insisted that the spread of Russian railways and the freeing of the lower classes would require new kinds of theatrical life. Otherwise, he warned, "only brilliant ballets and foreign spectacles" and not national art could flourish. Alluding to the swollen budgets for spectacles, Sollogub showed that, in number of performances, Russian drama in Petersburg had in 1857 outstripped all other genres. He proposed ending the monopoly by allowing private theaters to coexist beside the Imperial Theaters.[48]

Count Adlerberg, a conservative, publicly endorsed Sollogub's suggestions, but sent a secret memo to the tsar taking the opposite view. Adlerberg conceded the recreational function of theater, but strongly asserted its ideological role as a molder of public opinion and a moral force deflecting people from harmful pursuits such as card playing and idle talk that could lead to antistate activity. The Revolutions of 1848 and the Petrashevsky affair were barely a decade in the past. Adlerberg was also disturbed by the recent flood of plays critical of serfdom. To him, extending theater meant promoting a radical mood, since private theaters would become pulpits for antigovernment propaganda. He urged that the state monopoly be retained — especially since the French and German companies in Petersburg could not exist without a subsidy. Neither he nor others mentioned the competitive drain on audiences that a private sector would produce. Reading between the lines, a Soviet scholar not unreasonably interpreted the reverence for foreign productions among conservatives as suitably apolitical and attuned to aristocratic taste. Director Gedeonov echoed Adlerberg and raised the familiar lament about the anarchy of provincial theaters. Tsar Alexander II heeded their advice.[49] The monopoly had been put in place piecemeal by various administrative orders and practices. Now, in 1858, it was codified and remained in force until 1882, in the reign of Tsar Alexander III.

It is highly doubtful that eliminating the Imperial Theaters monopoly would have spelt financial disaster. After 1882 and the end of the monopoly, the new Mariinsky Theater in St. Petersburg and the Moscow Bolshoi saw their greatest age, with operas of Borodin, Musorgsky, Rimsky-Korsakov, and Tchaikovsky, and the last-named's triumphs in the Marius Petipa ballets. The Alexandrinsky Theater, graced by the popular Maria Savina, continued to draw crowds; and in Moscow, Russian drama flourished at the Maly. But, during the reign of Tsar Alexander II, while theaters proliferated in the provinces, those in the capitals were frozen.

Actors got a well-deserved jump in official status from Tsar Nicholas I, but not much change in their image. When Vasily Karatygin died in 1853, Tsar Nicholas, genuinely moved by the loss of his favorite, attended the church service and a few days later inquired of the actor's brother about the death. Mikhail Shchepkin, by virtue of his dignity and engaging personality, had not only won hearts among all classes on and off stage, but also a certain social recognition. At a farewell banquet for him on the eve of his journey to Europe in 1853, Official Nationalists, Slavophiles, and Westernizing liberals converged to congratulate him. Mikhail Pogodin organized the affair and the toast was given by fellow Moscow University historian, Timofei Granovsky: "Honor and glory to this Russian artist who has worked in the field of art for practically half a century without growing weak in spirit, without his zeal flagging." In 1855, Shchepkin was feted again at the Moscow School of Painting and Sculpture for his fifty years on the stage, the first such testimonial to an actor. To an audience of actors, artists, and literary figures, the sculptor Ramazanov praised him for inspiring all artists. Shchepkin was also the first actor and the first ex-serf admitted to the exclusive English Club. But Shchepkin was an exception. Russia was still far from the moment when actors were universally adulated and received by all ranks of society, who would harken with reverence to their utterances about "my public" and the theater as a temple of art.[50]

Gedeonov's sour complaint about the uncontrolled growth of provincial theaters was on the mark. In 1842, the Ministry of Internal Affairs had reiterated the order to privately owned commercial theaters to submit their repertoires through the governors to the Third Section for approval; and Gedeonov grumbled at the number of those theaters functioning under capricious local authorities. It had become clear that previous efforts to control provincial performances had been ineffective. Theaters could be found in every province except Olonets in the far north and Tobolsk, Amur, Trans-Baikal, the Maritime Provinces, and Yakutia in the east. A few years after the emancipation, Konstantin Pobedonostsev described how a theater was established in a provincial town on the Dnieper River by occupying a disused military building, raising about five thousand rubles in the town, and using 350 convicts for the construction! In his view, the enterprise was essential for raising civic consciousness and teaching moral lessons. Petrovskaya cites the average seating capacity of provincial theater as four or five hundred, though conceding low attendance in some. She also claims that, in the larger empire—in places like Tiflis, Vladikavkaz, and Kishinёv—theater served as an arm of Russian influence from the 1860s, a subject awaiting further scholarly investigation. In subsequent decades, the provincial theater network grew apace, aided by the spread of railways. When the monopoly ended in the capitals, Popular Theaters arose there, designed by intelligentsia, state, industrialists, and church to bring "proper" culture to the urban masses and deflect them from the tavern. From 1888 to 1905, these fell under a special censorship which denied them the production of certain works allowed in other theaters. This measure had a curious effect on nationwide theatergoing. Works such as *Faust, Maria Stuart, Hamlet, The Barber of Seville,* and Molière's *Don Juan* continued to show on provincial stages open to all classes, but could not until 1906 be presented to Moscow's and Petersburg's lower classes who frequented the Popular Theaters.[51]

The provinces also played another role in the continuing transformation of Russian theatrical life. Most of the recent plays that disturbed Count Adlerberg showed the darker shades of life in outlying regions. Their authors were part of a great mid-century flurry of interior exploration. The state made little use of those having everyday contact with the Volga lands, the far north, the Urals, and the frontier zones: merchants and *obrok* serf cattle dealers and traders.[52] Under Nicholas I, the Ministries of War, the Navy, Internal Affairs, and State Domains sponsored statistical, ethnographic, hydrographic, and geographical studies and sent out research teams of scientists, journalists, novelists, portrait painters, and even a few pioneer photographers — people with a keen eye for detail — to examine the economic and social conditions of city and country life. The Imperial Geographical Society (founded in 1845) launched a systematic study of all the tsar's lands and peoples by means of questionnaires sent out to priests, teachers, officials, landowners, seminarians, merchants, and even peasants — about local language, material culture, and folkways. Under the new tsar, the Naval Ministry, headed by the dynamic Admiral Grand Duke Konstantin, combined topographical and riverine research with ethnographic study. In launching the so-called Literary Expeditions of 1855–62, he harnessed the talents of writers for missions to the interior to examine local life. Their reports were published in the *Naval Review* (*Morskoi sbornik*). Among those commissioned was, ironically, M. L. Mikhailov — novelist, publicist, and one of the first prominent radicals to be jailed and exiled by the new regime. In November 1855 he set out from Petersburg and sojourned in Ufa, the Urals, and Orenburg, his native turf. What he saw simply deepened the sense of a brutal, unjust, and rotten system that he had already discovered as a writer.[53]

The team assigned to inspect the length of the Volga River had a direct resonance in Russian culture: the dramatists Alexei Potekhin, Alexei Pisemsky, and Alexander Ostrovsky. To Ostrovsky was assigned the sector of the river from near its source down to Nizhny Novgorod, about eight hundred miles. Potekhin sailed from the Oka to the Volga and thence downriver to Saratov. Pisemsky took on the lower reaches and the lands around Astrakhan.[54] They observed close up and absorbed details on church services, home life, evening gatherings, feasts, and other occasions. Much has been made, and rightly so, of the Volga journeys as formative experiences for these writers, though some of their plays were written and staged before the Literary Expedition. The government chose them as writers who were already conversant with Russia's back county. Potekhin and Pisemsky had attended the same gymnasium in Kostroma Province, and Ostrovsky summered there from the 1840s onward. The three mingled at Moscow University and in journalism circles. After their return to Moscow, these three men—a kind of 1850s "Volga generation"—used recent observations of provincial life to expand their gallery of dramatic figures and introduce situations previously unknown on the Russian stage.

Alexei Potekhin (1829–1908), son of a poor noble who worked as an estate steward, grew up in the peasant villages of Kostroma where he developed an eye for detail. Beginning in 1851, he wrote ethnographic sketches of the various social types he encountered, and incorporated some of his findings into his early plays. The Literary Expedition of 1856 widened his angle of vision. In Moscow, Potekhin moved in Slavophile and Native Soil circles and was close to Ostrovsky and the *Muscovite*. Potekhin's plays—which he called "muzhik [peasant] drama"—expressed a kind of Slavophile respect for the peasants, minus the romanticism. Potekhin depicted them as generally honest, morally superior to the gentry, richly emotional, but also prone to violence. The raw drinking sequences he put on stage offended some audiences. Potekhin's corpus of the 1850s, though burdened with plots that hardly rose above melodrama, offered the first cycle of serious plays about village life in a realistic setting, using authentic staging of folk songs and dances, and recognizable peasant orality.[55]

When Potekhin's first play, *Man's Judgment, Not God's,* appeared in the *Muscovite* in 1853, the censors read it as a sharp indictment of serfdom and tried to keep it off the boards. But Grand Duke Konstantin found it impressive and, with Pogodin, arranged its staging in Moscow and St. Petersburg in 1854. Lyubov Nikulina-Kositskaya, the ex–house serf and former provincial actress who well knew the dark side of village life as well as intergenerational conflict (see chapter 6), played the daughter who runs away from a fanatically religious father. Village intolerance and superstition suffuse the play, and the father puritanically controls his daughter's love life. In the resolution, the father, on finding his missing child, becomes more humane and tolerant, and patronizingly announces to her: "You are forgiven by me and by God." The daughter repents and renounces marriage to enter a convent where she will serve the Lord and her father. The jilted groom obligingly discovers that he has always loved martial heroes and battle songs and joins the army. "I am off to serve Tsar-Batyushka [Little Father] and Orthodox Matyushka-Rossiya [Mother Russia]."[56]

In *The Sheepskin Coat and the Soul of a Human* (1854), an unpleasant female landowner persecutes her well-educated governess who is trying to raise money to redeem her brother from serfdom. Attempts to force the governess into an unwanted marriage fail, and the brother eventually gains his freedom. This was probably the first Russian drama to treat the struggle for individual serf emancipation. The censors removed a line in the printed version about the peasants' superiority to the upper classes and kept it from the stage until 1865.[57] *Another's Wealth Avails Me Naught* (1855) appeared on stage at the very end of Nicholas I's reign. Set at a rural posting station, the play centers around a complex and plausible peasant youth who combines a violent temper with an inner decency. During a father-son battle over money, the boy is prevented by his conscience from murdering the old man. Potekhin wrote later of the performance that the actor Martynov, playing the young man, became a peasant "in face, expression, dress, movement, voice timbre, speech — all of it was peasant [*muzhitskoe*]." Potekhin's world, never before seen on stage, anticipated the grimmer dramas of Pisemsky and much later Lev Tolstoy. Some in the audience thought it offended good taste: a character speaks of "Furrin' wine, Jamaker rum they calls it and they drinks it wit' tea. . . . Smells like bedbug [juice]. What stuff!" Yet *Another's Wealth* was well received at the Alexandrinsky. Critics have not been kind to Potekhin: even at the time, Apollon Grigorev distinguished between the art of Ostrovsky and the lesser genres of specialists like Potekhin whose works he dismissed as "genre-ism in the worst sense of the word." Soviet critics would later fault Potekhin, no muckraker, for his failure to inject a political message into his realism.[58]

With Alexei Pisemsky's harrowing drama *A Bitter Fate* (1859), we arrive at another major turning point in the relationship between public expression and social reality. His blend of sexual and social strains in the landlord-serf world reached print and then the stage. The version passed by the censor opened up an unprecedented vista of rustic violence that far surpassed Potekhin's. A bare plot summary gives little inkling of the force contained in this play. While a serf is away in St. Petersburg, his wife has an affair with the young gentry master back on the estate and gives birth to the master's child. When the husband finds out, the drama intensifies in confrontations among the three sides of the triangle, during which several relatively peaceful solutions are aired. But in a shocking dénouement, the husband hurls the infant to the floor and kills it. Pisemsky's treatment of a far from rare situation is no simple indictment of an evil landowner availing himself of a vulnerable serf woman. They are both complicated individuals in love with each other. The husband is driven by an overweening pride, displayed even among his peers, that moves him to the terrible deed. In fact, he, rather than the lord, is the agent of cruelty. The landowner, a provincial Hamlet, feels genuine chagrin and sorrow for the wronged husband. In the end, the peasant man runs away, returns to give himself up, and repents.

Remarkably, *Bitter Fate* passed through the print censorship in 1859. One plot variant that the author considered for a time had the peasant husband actually organizing a group of violent bandits to wreak vengeance upon the estate by killing the steward, one of the less attractive figures in the final version. In the draft that Pisemsky first submitted to the censors, clearly his real choice, he set up an all too plausible solution whereby the peasant husband slays the landowner. The censors delayed, alluding to the uncertain mood of the countryside on the eve of emancipation and the recent spate of gentry and steward murders. Two incidents involving sex and violence had occurred in Pisemsky's own Chukhlomsky District of Kostroma, both on the estate of the landowner Ermolaev. In 1847, a house serf, returning from off-farm work, developed doubts about the paternity of the child born in his absence and killed it. In 1857 — two years before *Bitter Fate* appeared in print — another house serf on the same estate, incensed at the landowner's beating and sexual abuse of his wife and other village women, stabbed him.[59] The resemblance between the details of these cases and Pisemsky's drama leave no doubt that he conflated them for his plot.

In *Bitter Fate,* the shift in victim from the serf owner to his child, though technically deflecting violence from gentry to illegitimate commoner, came closer to the harsh realities of the rural world than anything even imaginable in previous Russian drama. The old costume plays about boyar poisonings and executions and the tinsel terrors of the imported melodramas must have seemed pallid escapism compared to the exposition of village tension and latent ferocity suggested in Pisemsky's work. He had moved the power of the serf owner into the background, and had foregrounded what Lev Tolstoy would later call "the power of darkness" — the elemental peasant force that could erupt in violence. If Count Adlerberg had feared the plays on serfdom prior to 1858, what might he have thought about Pisemsky's truly disturbing piece had it reached theater audiences before 1863? Although *Bitter Fate* received an Uvarov prize — the highest award for drama — in 1860, it could not be staged until two years after the emancipation, and then only after some resistance from the censors.[60]

The "cumulative catalogue of the oppression of peasants" had been growing since the 1840s in the published fiction of Grigorovich, Turgenev, and a few others who had slipped through the censors. Drama was a different story. Pisemsky's scenes of lethal manorial conflict — bereft as they were of a deus ex machina or kindly noble *raisonneur* — could not have been tolerated on stage as long as serfdom existed. Potekhin and Pisemsky, both displaying vague

Slavophile and Native Soil leanings, joined those who were seeking to put real peasants on the page and the canvas. They made their characters speak in something like authentic Russian diction and invested them with dignity and sometimes potential violence. Their treatments of village life constituted the most important breakthrough in the history of peasant representation in the arts, including painting, to that moment. However stylized for the theater were their peasant characters, they strode the stage in a way utterly different from the fraudulent ones that had done so in the past and that had been created by myths, metaphysical visions, imported frumpery, and wartime patriotism.[61]

Alexander Ostrovsky (1823–86) made a more enduring theatrical break-through (fig. 69). Of gentry origin on his Swedish mother's side, this quintes-sentially middle-class son of a lawyer of clerical background was born on the Malaya Ordynka in the heart of merchant Moscow. Ostrovsky withdrew from the law faculty of Moscow University in 1843 and, following his father, began working as a minor official in the courts. There he became conversant with business dealings and the merchant way of life, knowledge that he put to use in his dramas. Interested in books and theater since childhood, Ostrovsky fre-quented almost daily Pechkin's coffee house, which was across the street from his offices. He animated a group known as the Young Editors of the *Muscovite* who met to dine, hear new literary works, and sing Russian folk songs. At various times, Gogol, Mikhail Pogodin, Stepan Shevyrëv, Alexei Khomyakov, and Shchepkin attended. The *Muscovite* was associated with the Native Soil ideology. In the early 1850s, the Young Editors' circle mingled with adherents of Official Nationalism and Slavophilism, an affiliation where personal friend-ships often blurred the lines dividing those currents. Around Russian pancakes at Pogodin's, old feuds could be overshadowed by elective affinities in a quest for an authentic Russian national culture. It was to this audience that Os-trovsky read some of his earliest works.[62]

Ostrovsky received his commission to capture in words the everyday life of the peoples of the Upper Volga for the *Naval Review*. Already an established playwright, He embarked on an 1856–57 journey of ethnographic explora-tion that took him through waterways and forest roads to dozens of Volga provincial towns. Although he submitted his report in dry technical language replete with sketches of various rivercraft, Ostrovsky gained much insight about provincial Russia from his watery excursion. In the deep interior, he observed local customs, scenes, folk sayings, and speech patterns which he kept in a card file and later incorporated into his plays. A sojourn in Torzhok provided the setting for *The Storm*. A half dozen "Volga" plays were based on this material.[63]

Ostrovsky's early prose sketches of Moscow life resemble the documentary-like feuilletons and physiologies of the time as well as the art of the inner city. His first phase as a dramatist, the merchant cycle, lasted until 1860, the year of *The Storm,* after which he branched out to portray other walks of life. The first full-length effort of the merchant period, *It's a Family Affair, We'll Settle it Ourselves* (1850) drew a dismal picture of the domestic life of an Old Believer Moscow merchant, a family despot, drunk, and crooked businessman. He scoffs at the law and despises the poor as well as uppity merchants who live in manor houses. His daughter, like the painter Fedotov's *Choosy Bride,* spurns her own class; takes piano, French, and dancing lessons; and aspires to marry an officer. She ends up with her father's clerk and together they swindle the larcenous father who lands in jail. The almost unrelieved harshness of the action and the personages got the play banned from production (as written) until 1860 and won the author police surveillance. Despite the ban, the printed version of *Family Affair* circulated so rapidly that Taras Shevchenko in December 1850 played in an amateur performance of it in the barracks of an expeditionary force on a peninsula of the Aral Sea! Moscow merchants who read or heard about Ostrovsky's play were incensed, all the more so since it captured certain authentic aspects of their life.[64]

Don't Get into Another's Sleigh (1853), the first Ostrovsky play to reach the stage, contrasted an honorable merchant with his daughter's heartless aristocratic suitor. As the title poetically indicates, this work mocked social-climbing merchants and their children. As the first realistic portrait of ordinary merchant life on the Russian stage, it enjoyed a triumph in Moscow where it won back the favor that Ostrovsky had lost among the business community due to *Family Affair.* The Petersburg theater authorities were at first reluctant to show it but did so in 1853. Tsar Nicholas loved it: "Ce n'est pas une pièce," he said, "c'est une leçon."[65] *Sleigh* was followed rapidly in 1854 by *Poverty Is Not a Vice,* which treats again the familiar struggle between merchant father and daughter. The villain is a rich Europeanized merchant suitor. The hero, Lyubim Tortsov, one of the great characters in Russian drama, is the drunken but good-hearted brother of the obstreperous merchant father. His intervention enables true love to triumph for the daughter and a poor clerk. Tortsov, who uses colloquial Russian language, speech patterns, and gestures, has remained a plum role for actors ever since; and the sets and props of this play set a new standard for realistic stage settings.

Ostrovsky's masterpiece, *The Storm* (1859), ranks with the works of Fonvizin, Griboedov, Gogol, and Chekhov. It has been translated many times and much later was made into an opera, *Katya Kabanova,* by Leoš Janáček. In a Volga town, much like the ones Ostrovsky had recently surveyed in the Literary Expedition, the overbearing Volga merchant Dikoi (savage) endorses in-equality and despises the lower classes, women, and the young. He is con-trasted with an impoverished seminoble nephew, with his European education and mannerisms. The central character, Katya Kabanova, is tyrannized by her mother-in-law, a merchant's widow. Locked in a loveless marriage, Katya dreams of release. "Why don't people fly like birds?" she asks, echoing a familiar metaphor in fiction about women seeking emancipation from repres-sive and claustrophobic surroundings. Katya finds this liberation in an adul-terous love affair with Dikoi's nephew and then kills herself by leaping into the raging Volga River in the midst of a thunderstorm. The play, praised for a century and a half for its dramatic power, catapulted Ostrovsky into perma-nent fame and success (he was the co-recipient of the Uvarov Prize in 1860), and further enhanced the reputation of the ex-serf Nikulina-Kositskaya who played the role of Katya Kabanova at the Maly Theater. This work and its predecessors also led to a schism within the theater establishment and set off a scorching debate about Ostrovsky among the Russian intelligentsia.[66]

Writing twenty-five years after the event, the chronicler of Russian theater A. I. Wolf said about the premiere of Ostrovsky's *Sleigh* at the Alexandrinsky Theater, February 19, 1853: "From that day, rhetoric, insincerity, and Gal-lomania gradually began to disappear from Russian drama. Characters spoke on stage as they did in real life. A whole new world opened up for audiences. . . . Actors suddenly appeared who knew how to impersonate simply and naturally an ordinary Russian person."[67] In the same season, the brilliant French tragedienne Rachel, "the last great paragon of neoclassical declama-tion," appeared in Russia and her cadences brought a moment of nostalgia. But the short-lived discussion of her style showed once again that it had long ago become archaic.[68] When Vasily Karatygin passed away in 1852 he had already been overshadowed by his younger colleague and pupil, Alexander Martynov (1816–60). In honing his skills, Karatygin had been a bookish scholar; Martynov, like an ethnographer, haunted marketplaces to learn the speech patterns and gestures of Petersburg street life. His versatility and expe-rience on the road enabled him to succeed as the coachman in Potekhin's *Another's Wealth Avails Me Naught*, and most famously in the early plays of Ostrovsky.[69] Wolf's punctuation mark of 1853 is exaggerated: Gallomania on stage had long been in decline and "rhetorical insincerity" — often spoken in Russian accents — did not disappear from the drama stage.

Nevertheless, while several styles of dramatic acting coexisted on the eve of emancipation, a major shift in theatrical culture had occurred, particularly in Moscow. Looking back from the vantage point of World War I, theater histo-rian N. N. Ignatov argued that Ostrovsky's public was "not satisfied with all-human [i.e. eternal or universal] truths, but needed a special truth related to a given type in a particular environment." And when "the public began demanding realistic drama, [actors] appeared, fully equipped to play types and characters from life that corresponded to reality." In short, said Ignatov, "dramatists and performers both responded to the same change in the psyche of the spectator."[70] Ignatov does not explain how and why that public made a shift or how performers detected it. Such mechanisms remain a mystery for almost all times and places. One can only suggest that, in the first instance, part of the literate playgoing public had become used to reading, hearing conversations, and seeing pictures about themselves and other social communities and now were ready to watch themselves on stage as well. Twenty years of debate in the thick journals and salon talk had clearly overflowed from the gentry intelligentsia to a wider public; and a decade of further ferment in the Crimean War and the rumors of emancipation and reform had escalated desires. Actors, directors, and dramatists had good ears and could feel the shift. Zeitgeist cannot explain it all. Individual wills and styles of the creators and performers coincided with streams of public curiosity.

The schism over Ostrovsky at the Moscow Maly Theater erupted long before *The Storm* broke over Russia in 1860. The two camps divided over content and acting styles. The Muscovite camp which embraced Ostrovsky's realistic treatment of merchant life in Moscow and the provinces included Nikulina, Sadovsky, and Kolosova, all of whom had registered success in Ostrovsky's plays. The Western camp, which respected older traditions ranging from Molière to Gogol, set Shumsky and Lensky, among others, against Ostrovsky. Ironically, the most distinguished voice among them had for years been considered by the public the quintessential Russian national and "natural" actor: Mikhail Shchepkin. This venerable ex-serf and veteran of the provincial circuit disliked *The Storm* and sniffed at what he and his colleagues called the vodka, greased boots, and "stinking fur coats" of merchants on stage. This was more than a reaction of one generation to another, of an established star to new challengers. Shchepkin did not seek pure "naturalism" on stage because he believed that theater required distance. He tried for a modification of the older declamatory style and closer communication with the public; and his roles reflected a deep sympathy for the underdog or the "little man." But, just as he feared the radicalism of his friend Herzen, Shchepkin stopped short of sleazy revelations, sweeping social criticism, and muckraking on stage. Shchepkin's sense of theatrical decorum was scandalized by what he saw as vulgarity in the new dramatic culture. The divergence over tastes blossomed into nasty feuds.[71]

The quarrel exacerbated the personal rivalry between Shchepkin and the rising star of the Ostrovsky productions, Prov Sadovsky (Ermilov, 1818–72). As a fourteen-year-old from a middle-class family in Ryazan Province, Sadovsky had taken to the road with his actor uncle and had roamed for years on the circuit through Tula, Kaluga, Ryazan, Elets, Lebedyan, Voronezh, and Tambov. Shchepkin discovered him in Kazan and brought him to the Moscow Maly in 1839. During the Crimean War, Sadovsky, a fiery Slavophile, forged another link between Slavophilism, theater, and the Moscow merchants. At Pechkin's coffee house, he regaled merchants with patriotic recitations "until the tears came." Sadovsky found a friendly reception in the circle of Ostrovsky, Pogodin, and the Young Editors. As Lyubim Tortsov in *Poverty Is Not a Vice,* a role made for him, Sadovsky achieved a spectacular success. When Shchepkin attempted the same role, merchant audiences made it clear that they preferred Sadovsky's Tortsov. The two actors drifted apart. Characteristically, the provinces echoed Moscow's choice. A Voronezh journalist as early as 1854 wrote that Ostrovsky's corpus required a new kind of acting, one of "naturalism and simplicity." And an observer at the Barsov actors' hiring hall recalled that, after Ostrovsky's *Poverty,* the scouts there began to seek out Tortsovs rather than Hamlets. The torch had passed from the old and beloved standard bearer Shchepkin.[72]

The coming generation viewed all this as a triumph of "realism" on stage and thus of "truth." Realistic acting is a matter of contemporary perception. Theater, by definition, is always illusionary, though it may range from extreme stylization (Kabuki, Noh, or Meyerhold's "Biomechanics") to attempts at representation in a natural manner through dramaturgical plausibility, familiar-sounding diction, and authentic costumes and sets. Yet even the most realistic theatrical speech is terser (or more long-winded), more vivid, eloquent, epigrammatic than the everyday speech of the age in which it is performed. And it is ephemeral. Shchepkin may have poked fun at the baroque postures and gesticulations of his colleagues, but the actors of his own time and the "realistic" ones for decades afterwards did not turn their backs to the audience until Stanislavsky adapted the Fourth Wall to Russian theater at the end of the century, a style in which the cast only looked at or spoke to each other and not the audience. One sees the same kind of transition from declamatory to realistic acting that unfolded in the 1850s in the silent cinema of Russia from 1908 to 1917.[73] The fundamental change in theater, as Anatoly Altschuller put it, was the victory of the dramatist over the actor: "Whereas in 1820 it could be said that many characters were created as much by the actors as by the playwright, by about 1850, when Ostrovsky's plays began to appear, the persona of the author had become central in the creation of theatre."[74]

Critics have correctly stressed Ostrovsky's realism, attention to everyday life, authentic sets, and social commentary; but they sometimes obsess on his merchant cycle at the expense of Ostrovsky's universality and rich diversity of dramatic motifs and characters. Following on the fourteen merchant plays ending with *The Storm,* came thirty-three plays of great variety in theme, social content, and style.[75] None the less, that cultural clash of the late 1850s and early 1860s is essential to understanding Ostrovsky's relation to social history. The issue was often blurred, adherents often changed sides, and all camps were divided within themselves. The question that generated heat was whether Ostrovsky was for or against the merchantry. This turned into a "national" problem because the long-despised commercial class began to re-place the peasantry as the emblem of Russianness. Since despotism and cor-ruption cohabited with decency and simplicity in Ostrovsky's reading of the Russian merchants' collective soul, the scope for interpretation was wide. He managed to win the approval of some merchants, Westernizers, Slavophiles, and Native Soil conservatives — and the enmity of others among those fluid groups. And of course, they divided over favorites among the plays. Critics who demanded a social or national interpretation of the arts made their own particular selection. From an esthetic point of view, their opinions are irrele-vant. Ostrovsky has lasted as the most-performed playwright in Russian his-tory because of his art and not his messages.

Westernized liberals who, like Shchepkin, held to older European tradi-tions, were unimpressed. The more radical among them, happy with what they saw as Ostrovsky's exposure of an evil universe in their midst, harped on the merchant characters' negative qualities. The locus classicus of this ex-posure was a series of seminal essays by Nikolai Dobrolyubov. In "The King-dom of Darkness" (1859) he meticulously catalogued all the merchants' vices portrayed in the Ostrovsky plays up to that date: cheating, philistinism, petty tyranny at the office, soul-destroying oppression in the dark recesses of the home, and ill-treatment of the weak — especially poor people and women.[76] Based on this interpretation, he handed down a sweeping indictment of the merchant world implied in the title of his review. In Ostrovsky's *The Storm,* Dobrolyubov perceived a bright "Ray of Light in the Kingdom of Darkness" (1860): Katya Kabanova's allegedly rebellious gesture of suicide.[77] Dobrolyu-bov did not invent the abuses: they are all found in the plays and existed in real life as well. But he fashioned them into a potent and one-sided panorama of stereotypes that would haunt the reputation of an entire class of people right down to and beyond the Revolution of 1917. Ostrovsky's negative images of merchants in the early plays dissolved in the more complicated scenarios of later ones. But Dobrolyubov's image was stamped into the outlook of the Russian intelligentsia and much of the creative community. Their hostility to capitalism, business, and petty bourgeois philistinism endured.

Ostrovsky's professional trajectory was not much affected by tendentious readings of his works. His support widened from the Slavophile and Native Soil schools to the merchants themselves, and to the entire theatergoing nation. The Russian playwright least known in the West became the best known in his native land. Slavophiles, with some exceptions, admired Ostrovsky because they saw bright elements of Russian life mixed in with the dark. *Sleigh, Poverty,* and the 1855 *You Can't Live as You Like* seemed like affirmations of Russianness and a rejection of decadent Western ways.[78] The Slavophiles were moving out from their airy salon debates and the fat journals into a large public sphere and adding the merchants to the *narod* as vessels of Russianness. Prophets of the Native Soil were even keener in their adoption of Ostrovsky who, as an original member of the *Muscovite*'s editorial board, was one of them. To Apollon Grigorev, merchants formed a natural bridge between the *narod* and western European culture. Ostrovsky, their poet, could reach a higher realism than that of accusatory criticism. For Grigorev in 1860, Ostrovsky was "a poet who can play all the tunes of popular life in every key."[79] Ostrovsky, scenic realism, and the merchantry combined into a socio-cultural vehicle of Russianism.

How did merchants respond to their would-be poet? Their "Ostrovsky-ism," hardly universal, did not spring up at once. Early in Nicholas I's reign, one of them wrote to the theater administration that "it is more pleasant to see kings, dukes, and other heroes on stage than simple gentry folk whom we see every day." We may assume that this fussy man of commerce would have enjoyed seeing his own kind even less. Even when present at all on the stage, merchants had not come off very well, whether in Matinsky's *St. Petersburg Gostiny Dvor* (1779), Plavilshchikov's *Shop Clerk* (1804), or Gogol's *Marriage* (1842). The big merchants protested Ostrovsky's *Family Affair,* but the weaker middle- and lower-ranked merchants who did not identify with its villainous characters embraced Ostrovsky.[80] As his characters and situations developed, the merchants adopted him as their own and remained the heart of his public for generations. The fact that so many actors and even some writers came of merchant stock may have been a factor. Yet surely some of Ostrovsky's plays bolstered those traditionalists who opposed emulation of the gentry. Upward climbers had been constantly ridiculed on stage,[81] but such ridicule could be found in Ostrovsky as well.

The rest of the nation joined the flood of spectators who flocked to see Ostrovsky's works. He was "a defining event in the life of the Russian theater," wrote Ignatov. "Kings, dukes, and marquesses had to doff their fine raiment and turn over their throne to the Russian bearded merchant in a long tunic and stovepipe boots." The Maly Theater in Moscow, once the House of Shchepkin, became the House of Ostrovsky in the playwright's own lifetime. Since

1853, all forty-seven of his plays have been at different times staged here. Far more than a local Muscovite hero, Ostrovsky in fact became *the* Russian national playwright, and his works were put on again and again in St. Petersburg and across the empire on the imperial and amateur stages and in the private, provincial, and Popular Theaters that sprouted up after the emancipation of the serfs in 1861 and the lifting of the theater monopoly in 1882. Part of the attraction was Ostrovsky's avoidance of tricks and declamation aimed at applause; his use of Russian gestures, customs, songs, and proverbs; and his insistence on actors' plain dress and hairdos rather than stylized society coiffures and fancy costumes. He replaced the standard pair of divans, some chairs, a table, and a chandelier with a more realistic stage set. For this reason, some critics likened him to an explorer who had discovered a new country — his own. The visible triumph of Ostrovsky and of Russianness on stage led him and others vainly to keep certain imported works off Russian stages. Like the adherents of other dramatic styles that harden into "schools," they failed to realize that audiences could enjoy adaptations of French farces without eroding their admiration for the products of real Russian culture.[82]

The victory of Ostrovsky did not account for the subsequent history of theater as a whole. Musical genres and lavish spectacles continued to attract audiences as did domestic and imported farces. And, as in other countries, the innovators of serious drama held idealism and realism pretty much in equal reverence, the one for moral uplift, the other to show the need for it.[83] What is important about the shift in repertoire is the expansion on stage of Russian themes and characters. In the 1850s only about 10 percent of the plays passed by censors dealt with Russian life; by 1860 they predominated. The national deluge would have made the heart of Plavilshchikov sing. His old tirade against "Dido languishing for love of Aeneas and Iarbas" was echoed by a Kharkov critic who in 1858 announced that even mediocre plays taken from contemporary Russian life were more in demand than those about "the antics of dukes, marquesses, and prelates, or about the Italian stiletto, English spleen, and French caustic wit."[84] The *Contemporary* observed in November 1857 that "Russian theater is gradually coming alive," alluding to Ostrovsky on Moscow life and the staging of Shchedrin on provincial life.[85] "Coming alive" in essence meant "becoming Russian." In the 1850s, Potekhin, Pisemsky, and Ostrovsky introduced Russian types, manners, and idioms that had previously seldom been seen on stage. The theater had joined literature and art in the continuing quest for naturalist representation and in the search for a mirror to match the photographic "realities" of the daguerreotypes. Audience willingness to see art represent Russian life brought, one by one, the social organisms of Russia before the public gaze.

Mutiny on the Embankment

In his famous 1883 article, "Twenty-Five Years of Russian Art," Vladimir Stasov wrote of the 1850s: "Along with the opening of the new reign and the accession of Alexander II to the throne, an enormous change in Russian art occurred, a break with the past and a coursing off in new directions. To the extent that artists no longer resembled previous ones, so neither did their works. A new period emerged, a new world was born."[86] For Stasov, the "real day" had dawned, and the Academy of Arts remained enwrapped in twilight. Here and in other writings, he launched a broadside against false art, classicism, and eclecticism which he identified with the Academy and which had nothing to do with Russia.[87] Stasov, indulging in lyrical exaggeration, ignored or forgot the long decades of preparation, the overlap, the continuing interplay of influences, the stops and goes. He argued that both music and art had taken a major leap forward at the same time. By the 1860s, the image of a stuffy prereform Academy was already embedded in fiction. In the Soboleva story quoted above, a young artist "poured vitriol on painters who lavished their labors on aping rich satins and velvets"—a clear reference to old-fashioned parade portraiture—and praised "the unshowy paintings of the Russian genre painters." To complete what was already a cliché, the idealistic painter extolled true art and lamented his poverty as he lay dying of consumption in the presence of his love.[88]

These, among many such examples, point to a neat and satisfying turning point, but that point had a dull edge. Schematic periodization can restrict the imagination as well as help organize the mind. A long-standing view of nineteenth-century art as a two-period epoch—before and after 1863 (the revolt of the Academy of Arts)—was challenged and corrected long ago by dozens of Soviet studies of a "middle period," roughly 1840–70.[89] But even this stretch of time needs to be sliced. A transitional decade between the death of Fedotov and the secession anticipated the harsh side of the critical realism that sometimes engaged the Itinerants. But in this decade and long after, artists worked in many different styles: academic classicism, romanticism, realism, Biedermeier, and an Italian "salon" art of sentimental genre pictures. Like the rage for Italian opera, this was part of Russia's cultural shopping around Europe. Portraits, landscapes, and genre works hung together on walls public and private. Popular graphics and photography were shaping some styles and the latter was stealing patrons away from the easel painters. Eclecticism ruled: the eve of the new day had a mottled, multicolored sky and not the dark obscurantist pall of myth-makers. Apollon Maikov in 1857 recognized and lamented the fact that the real day had not dawned.[90]

The "heroization" of a native revolt owed much to the maligning of its alleged foe: the Academy of Arts. There is much truth in the picture of the Academy as a drag on cultural change. Academies normally protect tradition as long as they can and there is no questioning the decadence of that tradition in Russia by the 1850s. The great names in and out of academia were dying off: Kiprensky in 1836, Venetsianov in 1847, Bryullov and Fedotov in 1852, Tropinin in 1857, and Ivanov in 1858. Mediocre traditionalists held sway. For example, A. T. Markov (1802–78), after spending a decade abroad, gained the rank of professor in 1842 for his painting *The Coliseum,* a pallid, cliché-ridden, traditional treatment. T. A. Neff (originally Timoleon Karl von Neff) a Dresden-trained painter, descended to what Savinov called "cheap salonism" to please the taste of court circles.[91] When the boarding school of the Academy closed in 1840, only day students were admitted, thus widening the social gulf in education among Academy students. Ivan Kramskoi recalled his envy of educated people. He and other artists such as Repin and Perov belonged to estates that were subject to tax, recruitment, and even corporal punishment, with little chance for mobility or travel.[92] Academy degrees could shatter the juridical bonds but not erase social inferiority. As late as the 1850s, an obser-vant English visitor noted that artists, as opposed to writers, possessed little repute or status.[93]

With all that, the winds of change that rose after the Crimean War blew through the musty halls of the Academy. Tsar Alexander II, though he reg-ularly visited Academy exhibits and ordered pictures, was much less intrusive than his father. In 1859 Fëdor Tolstoy was kicked upstairs as assistant presi-dent and Prince Gagarin, an amateur Byzantinist, replaced him as vice presi-dent. The new Conference secretary F. F. Lvov (1820–95), who was also secretary of the Society for the Encouragement of Artists, reopened the board-ing school and introduced more student choice of genre and theme. Prior to 1859, genre had been discouraged but not prohibited. Now it was openly permitted, though only for the silver medal. The Academy even bent the rules on this in the 1860s and was inundated by social thematics in dozens of genre works by now mostly forgotten painters — variously known as exposers, ac-cusers, and muckrakers — whose critical approach went beyond the social satire of Fedotov. When they endeavored to exhibit social evils, the Academy's response was far from uniformly negative.[94] Alexei Korzukhin won a medal for *A Drunken Father;* V. V. Pukirev gained a professorship for *Unequal Mar-riage* (1862) depicting a May-December wedding.[95] Far bolder was the work of V. I. Yakobi (1834–1902), a provincial noble and graduate of Kazan Uni-versity who served in the Crimean War. At the Academy he won a medal for his bleak study of poverty and desperation in *Beggars' Festival* (1859) and a major gold medal for the politically charged *Prisoners' Rest Stop* (1861). One of the very first public depictions of exile, it is a harrowing scene of crowds of suffering convicts and families, with a dying man — obviously a member of the intelligentsia, perhaps a radical — stretched out on a wagon. When M. L. Mikhailov was arrested in 1861, his friend Yakobi managed to do a portrait of him in shackles (the original has not survived), lithograph copies of which were broadcast far and wide.[96]

The most celebrated of the accusatory painters, Vasily Perov (1833 or 1834–1882), the illegitimate son of a poor noble in Tobolsk, was given the name Perov (*pero* means pen) for his fine handwriting. He studied at the Arzamas school intermittently, and in 1852 or 1853 entered the Moscow School of Art where he imbibed the ultrarealist Sergei Zaryanko's doctrine of direct observation of real objects. Since the Moscow school could not award medals until 1865, Perov's came from the St. Petersburg Academy. His works created turbulence even as they won medals. *The Arrival of the Police Inspector* (1857) depicted a cabin, with an official about to interrogate a young peasant who is tightly held by a village elder. It contained strong pictorial suggestions of official corruption and abuse of a probably innocent man. The drunken official has apparently received as a bribe a basket of eggs on the floor behind him. As in Saltykov-Shchedrin's *Provincial Sketches* (1856–57), to which the painting is often compared, bureaucratic iciness is set against the humanity of the underdog. Beyond the anecdotal treatment of a single event, one could easily read an indictment of serfdom and the "system." *Arrival* is commonly held to have launched the era of critical realism in Russian painting and, in the words of Elizabeth Valkenier, represented "a quantum jump from Fedotov's satirical treatment of various classes and their foibles to an exposé of institutions that oppressed the people." And yet this work by a pioneer of the "accusatory genre" (*oblichitelnyi zhanr*) in Russian art was awarded in 1858 a major silver medal by the Academy, and the canvas was purchased by the merchant Gerasim Khludov.[97]

Perov produced three notorious scenes of religious life in 1860–62. Anti-clericalism, though brewing for some time among segments of the Westernizing intelligentsia, had not been reflected in high art. Perov's mentor Zaryanko in fact painted in the 1850s a perfectly reverent scene of faculty and uniformed students at worship the law school chapel (GRMFZh, 3660). Perov took a different and shocking line. His *Village Easter Procession* (1861) mocked a rural observance of the most joyful of Orthodox Church holidays, with its procession of icons, blessed eggs, kisses, and exclamations of "Christ has risen!" (fig. 70). Two of the parishioners lie drunk, another holds the icon upside down, and the inebriated priest can hardly stand. Both the preliminary sketch and the oil version were rejected by the Academy of Arts, the latter in the competition for a gold medal. Pavel Tretyakov bought the painting and showed it at the Society for the Encouragement of Artists until the Holy Synod had it removed. Tretyakov was warned of trouble in store for buying it, Perov was placed under surveillance, and the government forbade any reproduction of the painting until 1905.[98] Perov's *Village Sermon* (1861) was hardly less offensive: out of nine figures in the church only the child is paying attention; a nobleman dozes, his wife is flirting with a younger man, a peasant is scratching his ear, and a group in the background is distracted by a reading of the Emancipation Decree of 1861. Contrary to the statute on genre scenes, the controversial painting won a major gold medal, was exhibited at the Academy, and was sold to the merchant patron Kozma Soldatenkov. An 1862 work completed the assault: *Tea Drinking in Mytishchi* shows a corpulent and arrogant priest refusing alms to a begging veteran. Thus Perov, a man from a provincial background, challenged the academic canon and offended religious sensibility in public by offering three aspects of religious life in the countryside: robotic ritual in the midst of alcoholic stupor, everyday hypocrisy and routine observance, and ecclesiastical unconcern for the poor. This turn in art coincided with a current for reform of the clergy in the late 1850s.[99]

Perov's anticlerical paintings were the first of their kind in the history of Russian easel art; *Arrival* was the first attack on serfdom on canvas, and the last until emancipation. Later artists would take up such inflammatory subjects as the sale of a serf woman and the Pugachëv revolt. To the modern viewer, Perov's early works may seem only suggestive compared to these. But so great was public anxiety over the coming emancipation that Perov's pictures were bitterly attacked. Yet he was one of the first painters patronized by merchants who were otherwise conservative elements in Russian society. The Petersburg Academy, far from ostracizing Perov, appointed him a professor there in 1870, the very year he became one of the founders of the Itinerant school.[100] When viewed together, his work and that of the lesser-known "accusers" offer the most striking panorama to that time of the underbelly of Russian society.

The accusatory painters came, in one way or another, through the Academy of Arts rather than as rebels against it. Although they were sometimes associated with political radicals, there was little connection between them. N. N. Shumova stressed the friendships of the painters Zhuravlëv, Vereshchagin, Peskov, and Shishkin with revolutionaries, and that of Yakobi with radical writer M. L. Mikhailov, though the latter had many associations with people, including Anton Rubinstein, who were not themselves radical.[101] Nikolai Chernyshevsky's 1855 master's thesis proclaimed the function of art to mirror nature, the material world, and real human experience. Alexander Herzen, in emigration, turned an 1858 obituary of Alexander Ivanov into a manifesto demanding that painters condemn social evil. His friend Nikolai Ogarëv urged painters to expose and denounce the abuses of Russian society and the state. Ivan Dmitriev (1840–67) not only took up the doctrine, but also jeered at early realism for pallidly criticizing drunkenness and limited social problems instead of attacking its deeper ills. The intellectual and programmatic relationship of the painters with the ideology of emerging radicals who viewed art through a socially conscious prism was in fact problematic. Elizabeth Valkenier stresses the differences between the artistic generation of the 1860s and that of the 1870s, the Itinerants, especially those of the 1880s onward. Painters of the 1860s were closer to liberals and social nihilists than to political radicals and deep philosophical critics of the regime and the social order.[102]

The "mutiny of the fourteen" against the Academy of Arts in 1863 in some ways resembled the mutiny of Stasov and the Five against the Conservatory, though the former revolted against a hundred-year-old institution rather than one that was just being born. The snide critics notwithstanding, the Academy had by no means become a general object of disapprobation. The ex-serf, revolutionary artist, and state convict Taras Shevchenko, upon his release in 1857, resided at the Academy in modest quarters and became an Academician of engraving. An Academy exhibit of his pictures in 1860 included a self-portrait as a fierce patriotic Ukrainian hetman with a Zaporozhian moustache. This bold work caused an uproar in the reactionary press, especially when it was purchased by Grand Duchess Elena Pavlovna, the liberal salon dynast who had recently freed the serfs on her Karlovka estate. The artist, who owed his freedom and his training to the Academy, died in 1861, right after the February 19 rescript freeing the serfs, and lay in state in the chapel of the Academy. The funeral journey became a major event as it passed through St. Petersburg and Moscow to Kiev, the final resting place.[103]

Art mutinies and schisms were nothing new in Europe. In 1823, the Society of British Artists, seeking "publicity and profit" in a clientele of middle-class patrons, challenged the British Royal Academy. Critics divided over whether this was a healthy development or a cheap pandering to vulgar taste and thus a menace to high art and noble taste. In 1856 occurred the secession of the Macchaioli ("daubers") from the Academy in Florence, led by Telemaco Signorini and Raffaello Sernesi, among others, some of whom went on to fight in the Risorgimento war of 1859. Dedicated to spontaneity and the application of blocks of paint directly to canvas without the prior sketch, the Daubers rejected the polished and finished academic mode and opposed, in the words of one account, the "potentially stultifying procedures taught in the Acad-

emy." The more famous art revolt, the 1863 *Salon des refusés*, resulted from
the French Academy's rejection of the work of a group of young painters who
then, with the blessing of Napoleon III, set up a counter-salon.[104]

In Russia, the struggle was actually brought on by the reform process in the
Academy. In 1862, a resolution to equalize all genres was hotly discussed,
revised, and finally rejected — the rejection being the occasion if not the trigger
of the 1863 revolt. In the following year, two themes were announced for the
annual competition: in history, "The Feast of the Gods at Valhalla"; in genre,
"The Liberation of the Serfs." When a group of students requested a change in
the history theme, they were denied. Fourteen of them challenged Gagarin and
Lvov in the Conference Hall and withdrew from the Academy. Only two of
these — Zhuravlëv and Peskov — had any radical associations and most of the
others never became members of the Itinerant school which is often wrongly
conflated with the "revolt of the fourteen." They received their diplomas but
no medal, stipend, or trip abroad. The secession from the gold medal competition meant the loss of court patronage and state service emoluments. Thus,
the mutineers identified professionalism with personal expression and self-
determination rather than defining it in terms of state sponsorship.[105]

The story of the Itinerants is the best-known chapter in nineteenth-century
Russian art history. Though it falls outside the confines of this book, certain of
its features throw light on the preceding period. The main link between the
"mutiny of the fourteen" and the Itinerants, Ivan Kramskoi, while still working as a photographic retoucher for Denier, entered the Academy in 1856 and
a year later won a silver medal for his *Death of the Wounded Lensky,* inspired
by Pushkin's *Eugene Onegin.*[106] A friend called the evenings at Kramskoi's
where students sketched and discussed art the "new Russian academy."[107]
After the revolt of 1863 Kramskoi taught for the Society for the Encouragement of Artists. He formed a cooperative association (*artel*) with his fellow
secessionists who lived together in a shared apartment — a communal idea
popular among nihilists, radicals, and art-minded people of the 1860s, including Musorgsky. In 1865, Kramskoi's group mounted its first traveling exhibit
to the Nizhny Novgorod Fair where they showed genre works dealing with
peasants, soldiers, servants, and the urban poor. Only four of the original *artel*
group became members of the Itinerants or *Peredvizhniki*, founded in 1870
and officially titled the Association of Traveling Art Exhibits. As with the Five,
myths have been woven tightly around the group's history.[108]

The Itinerants did not consistently maintain a radical stance in art. After
some friction with the Academy of Arts, peaceful coexistence returned in the
1870s. Ilya Repin and other Itinerants accepted posts there in the 1890s.
Others moved in Academic circles and worked in traditional genres of paint-

ing. The jubilee celebrations of the arch-Academic Karl Bryullov in 1899 brought together Academy professors including Repin, to praise the once famous artist. While mavericks such as Alexander Benois denounced Bryullov's heritage, Ilya Repin gave a pro-Bryullov speech, only a fragment of which survives.[109] In the content of their paintings, the Itinerants produced some accusatory canvases, but also took up politically neutral genres: landscape, history, and some portraits of by no means progressive figures. In general they diluted the social in favor of the national.[110] Landscape, which the critic Ivan Dmitriev had called a reactionary diversion in 1863 and which Stasov saw as irrelevant, featured prominently in their offerings. More than half of the forty-seven pictures shown in 1871 by the Itinerants were landscapes. Peasants almost but not quite disappeared from landscape after the 1860s. No simple dichotomy existed between a Russian and an international school, for the "national" camp divided from the 1870s onward into positive and critical.[111]

In a masterful study of European realism embracing literature, social discourse, and art, Linda Nochlin offered a working definition of what realism meant to mid-century European artists: "truthful, objective and impartial representation of the real world, based on meticulous observation of contemporary life." She also uses or attributes to others terms and phrases such as "mundane," "mirroring everyday reality," a mode of "stripping [the artists'] minds, and their brushes, of second-hand knowledge and ready-made formulae," "matter-of-fact representations," and "scrupulous notation." Nineteenth-century realism — unlike numerous earlier practices of "visual veracity" — implied not only verisimilitude but also contemporaneity and a wider range of subject matter.[112] This vivid lexicon indicates the variety of meanings of "realism" for Russians who created, viewed, and wrote about art at mid-century. The word could be applied to "lifelike" representations of biblical, historical, and mythological figures; to contemporary subject matter; or, for some, only to depictions of the sordid — poverty, drunkenness, exploitation, impiety, corruption, and a dozen other indictable practices. To a radical critic such as Ivan Dmitriev, for example, a "realistic" landscape was not real but reactionary since it was a waste of time and deflected attention from social maladies. For others, realism meant portraying what was truly Russian. The Itinerants shuttled back and forth between "good" Russian reality such as Savrasov's *The Rooks Have Returned* and the "bad" as in Perov's *Last Tavern on the Road*. What most realists had in common was the use of a Russian national vocabulary in their work in the way of props, setting, costume, and gestures.

The great British art patrons of the mid-nineteenth century — manufacturers, bankers, lawyers, shipbuilders, textile manufacturers, railroad men, wholesalers — had a strong preference for "realism": social drama, domestic scenes, moral uplift, and diversions such as sport. Illusion, technical crafts-manship, and polish seemed to appeal to men whose fortunes often swung on technological achievements. A finished product symbolized both workman-ship and a good work ethic. Furthermore, the new rich were more than ready to purchase new art and had little affection for the neoclassical masters. At mid-century at least, well-off Englishmen were less patronizing (in the psycho-social sense) toward artists than the old gentry clientele, and displayed a cer-tain respect for artists as professionals, though later — with more confidence and more money — they tended to become domineering. Businessmen also (with several exceptions) owned moderate-sized homes whose walls could accommodate genre and portraits — but not large historical canvases.[113] Rus-sian merchants, many of whom had acquired superb collections of ancient Russian icons, also largely avoided academic and neoclassical works in favor of what was to them Russian "modernism" — that is, the contemporary works of the realists. Arno Mayer has argued that Russia and England were excep-tions to his thesis that the European bourgeoisie patronized only traditional art.[114] Merchants began rather early the leap from purchase of portraits to an essentially different act of buying art. Motives varied. Kozma Soldatenkov — the "Moscow Medici" — an Old Believer who married a French Catholic, collected a wide selection of Russian art, ranging from Bryullov to Perov. Vera Mamontova began collecting in the 1850s. Gerasim Khludov founded a mu-seum holding the works of Bryullov, Fedotov, and Aivazovsky — a wholly unideological assortment. Others included the Morozovs, Ivan Shchukin, and the Botkins, most of them close acquaintances and even relatives by blood or marriage.[115]

The major figure of Russian art patronage of the late nineteenth century, Pavel Tretyakov (1832–98), embodied many of the aspects of collecting asso-ciated with his class and milieu. Born in the Zamoskvorechie district of Mos-cow, the heartland of Russia's merchantry, Tretyakov became an avid reader and, for a time, theatergoer: on his first visit to St. Petersburg in 1852 at age twenty, he attended fourteen theater performances. At age eighteen, he had become head of a huge textile firm upon the death of his father. He began purchasing Dutch masters in 1854 and a few years later shifted to Russian art. On seeing the collection (which he later bought) of F. I. Pryanishnikov, an officer of the Society for the Encouragement of Artists, Tretyakov vowed to create his own Russian collection as a cultural "nation-building" enterprise. He met Vasily Perov in 1860 and bought a number of his controversial works as well as Yakobi's *Prisoners' Rest Stop*. Tretyakov's admiration for Russian art stemmed from his patriotism, itself conditioned on the one hand by a conservative antiforeignism and a suspicion of bureaucracy and aristocracy (he declined an offer of ennoblement from Tsar Alexander III); and on the other by a public-spirited aspiration to make Russia's cultural treasures available to all. Overarching this was Tretyakov's search for personal and family recognition outside the ranks of the state. His tastes were fairly catholic—indeed sometimes more so than those of the Itinerants whom he vigorously patronized—in terms of genre and style. "Poetry and truth" were what he demanded of genre, landscape, or history. He financed portraits of people as different as Shchepkin, Ostrovsky, the nationalist Mikhail Katkov, and the Pan-Slav ideologists Rostislav Fadeev and Nikolai Danilevsky. Keeping a promise he made in 1860, Tretyakov opened in 1881 the gallery in Moscow (fig. 71) that bears his name and that eventually achieved world renown.[116]

What did the new brand of patronage mean to the artists, Itinerants and others? The word "freedom" had in the course of the nineteenth century come to mean several different things to creative figures and their supporters: juridical release for serfs and other obligated classes so that they could pursue a life in the arts; the professional designation of Free Artist; and the less specific notion of independence from powerful patrons and from the art market in general so that painters could follow their own creative impulses. The last category was of course the one that entoiled most artists in western Europe. The popular image that has come down to us on that score is precisely one of impoverished geniuses fighting for the right to work as artists. In reality, artists were caught in the dilemma of wanting to paint according to their personal lights and at the same time make a living—not always compatible desires. Relieved of the earlier disabilities after 1861, Russian artists joined the ranks of artists everywhere in facing (and loudly complaining about) that dilemma.

Arrivals, Departures

At a stretch, one might read Ivan Goncharov's 1859 novel *Oblomov* as a metaphor for Russia's struggle to awaken on the eve of emancipation. Just as his house serf Zakhar constantly tried to rouse his master from bed and was rudely rebuffed, so the peasant question nagged at dormant Russia. Oblomov had good instincts: arousal from his bed always ended the sweet reverie of his manorial utopia. After 1861, that utopia and its real-life serenity and seigniorial power were gone with the wind. As a Russian gentrywoman learned with shock and anger after news of emancipation, her serf woman could no longer—like those in Venetsianov's *Morning of a Country Lady*—be commanded to bring products or perform duties.[117] Landowners had feared a new *Pugachëvshchina* in the wake of emancipation, though it did not come to pass; like their European counterparts in earlier times, they also feared—or claimed to fear — the decline of manners and culture if serfs were manumitted; and they predicted an onrush of vulgarity and materialism.[118] Ironically, some nobles revealed a materialism of their own by demanding compensation for the training given to their house serfs.[119] But though serfdom ended, the elaborate structure of deference that had helped sustain it continued in existence. Freedom meant, theoretically, mobility and choice of vocation, though numerous obstacles to that choice remained — poverty, illiteracy, and the restraining power of the village commune. Tragically, in the 1930s communism would impose old and new obstacles — ascription and the Stalinist passport system — upon the peasant grandchildren of the liberated serfs of the 1860s.[120] And by then, the content and the styles of the art they chose to work in would be determined by government. Braving the obstacles, free Russian peasants of the late nineteenth century would make their careers in all the arts, though how and how many remains a subject inviting further investigation. For the peasants and for the other members of the lower reaches of society, the opportunities opened, as they did for the elite who more and more began taking up professions in the arts in violation of a fading gentry code. As for gentry amateurism, the great butt of professional artists, it continued to flourish right up to the Revolution as it did among other classes.

The subsequent history of the national expansion of musical, theatrical, and fine art production has been well chronicled. The capital conservatories, staffed in the late nineteenth century by Russian men and women, ethnic minorities (especially Jews), and foreigners signified a "modern" sense of national culture, taught and created by diverse people and rooted in both Russian and European traditions. Its various provincial counterparts developed along local lines as well as reflecting standards set in the center. Local Russian musical societies and orchestras followed suit.[121] Even before the theater monopoly ended, several houses, with disguised names to avoid the law, came and went in the capitals. When the lid came off in 1882, commercial houses proliferated. These and the new Popular Theaters grew rapidly in the provinces as well, where the network of theaters was already firmly established.[122] Well-heeled patrons like Savva Mamontov organized their own theaters; in his case a private opera (1885). The number of art galleries in St. Petersburg alone grew to sixty-two by 1871. The Moscow art market by 1900, though having no dense network of auctions, dealers, and appraisers, was a blaze of intellectual give and take. The Maecenases — merchants, manufacturers, and railroad magnates, Russian and non-Russian (including Jewish) — had dethroned the aristocracy as collectors and as shapers of taste, which now leaned toward modern Russian and European art. In the provinces, by 1915 twenty-eight museums, galleries, or collections possessed holdings originally in the Academy of Arts.[123] The Academy and the Itinerants outdid each other in provincial showings. From 1870 to the end of the regime their number grew enormously. In 1884–94, the Itinerants showed twenty-two hundred pieces, and the Academy over four thousand. The Academy tended to show more works, but the Itinerants probably had more viewers, though this is hard to estimate. The figures jumped in the 1890s as a result of greater press coverage and more interaction between artists and society, the spread of the art market, and provincial art schools in the late nineteenth century.[124]

All of this brought a steady expansion of public cultural space and with it a closer contact among classes. Mingling of diverse groups as such does not necessarily entail harmony, as is clear from social practices and experience in prisons, armies, and schools. So what was the social significance of public space? To a certain extent, an elite Republic of Taste was being crowded — though not replaced — by new publics with new tastes and more sites for seeing and for buying art and performance. This provided a classic exemplar of Habermas's "public sphere" where culture and wide discussion of its qualities act as an inclusive force in society.[125] The extension of the arts from the private into the public sphere broadened popular participation. This hardly meant a steady rise in enlightenment or morality among social classes, but it did bring a widening of their experience and their outlooks. The sheer act of gaining entry to previously forbidden or otherwise inaccessible places and seeing new things added an increment, however slight, of dignity and honor to those previously denied them.

In the broad reaches of the land outside the capitals, the process was accelerated by that great engine of modernity, the railroad, whose cultural impact awaits serious study and whose network was both anticipated and utilized by traveling artists (fig. 72). Not everyone welcomed the train. In Ostrovsky's *The Storm,* the old peasant woman Fëklyushka likened the railroad train to an "iron devil." As early as 1853, Metropolitan Filaret identified it with the Antichrist, as did many another antimodernist in years to come.[126] Yet, even before Filaret thundered, the railroad passenger car was already being used as a setting for comedy. The 1852 vaudeville "Railroad" revolved around a love affair on the way from Moscow to St. Petersburg, with episodes in Tver and Vyshny Volochok. The setting caught on in the coming years in fiction and drama.[127] The railroad station, that dominant site of arrivals and departures, may be taken as an emblem for the things that were being left behind and the new destinations for the world of the Russian arts. But the railroad also had a much more direct and powerful meaning. For, although it did not bind together the far-flung communities of the nation as it did in Britain or France, it did — as in those nations — extend the reach of culture in a dramatic way over the next fifty years.

The "revolt" in the worlds of art did not mean revolution against the arts —

though that idea floated prominently in the writings of journalists such as Pisarev and in fictional characters such as Bazarov. Calls for throwing Pushkin and Raphael out the window were common in this discourse. At another level, at a meeting of young people in the early 1860s, nihilist men and women were saying that music and theater were for the affluent and that musicians were of less use to the people than shoemakers. A woman, angered at a member's admiration for Liszt, Chopin, and Glinka, said "they are founding conservatories and giving out scholarships while the people stagnate in ignorance." In the same decade, the painter Repin visited the "anti-salon" of Valentina Serova, mother of the well-known painter, wife of the composer, and herself a composer. Repin noted that the nihilists in attendance talked all the way through a piano recital and put their rudeness on display. At least one young radical hoped that the theater would become a scene of political ferment. On March 5, 1861, the eve of the public announcement of emancipation which had been decreed weeks earlier, Pëtr Kropotkin and his fellow officers rushed to the Italian opera's last performance of the season, believing that "some manifestation was sure to take place there" — in their meaning, a protest. But the only manifestation took the form of hurrahs and a singing of "God Save the Tsar."[128] Political revolution in theater — a pallid one at that — would have to wait until 1905.

What of the well-known schisms and rebellions within the arts? These insurrections — when not invented — have been greatly exaggerated. The nearly parallel myths about the Itinerants and the Mighty Five persisted in Soviet and Western scholarship and among cultural consumers for such a long time that it is still difficult to dislodge them, even though Elizabeth Valkenier, Robert Ridenour, and Richard Taruskin have provided definitive demolition. The myths set up a distinct and long-lasting polarity between Itinerants and Academy and between the Five and the Conservatory — in each case pitting heroic patriots against reactionary cosmopolitans. In fact, both of the insurgent movements were originally anchored to social-professional issues as much as to those of national expression; and while they rejected or claimed to reject academic systems, they also sought artistic and social status and recognition within academic institutions. The Itinerants and the Mighty Five over time went through several reversals, or, depending on one's view, experienced similar maturation. The artists engaged in all genres of painting: history (notably Russian history), landscape, genre, political and social commentary, and portraits of people of various political coloring. The musicians also branched out into styles and genres, such as chamber music, that were alien to the early notions of the Five. In painting, the national came to dominate over the socially critical. For composers, social criticism was almost never an issue; but, one might argue that, unlike the Itinerants, they became less rather than more national. Itinerants and Mighty Five patrons included merchants and the state: Repin painted a renowned collective portrait of the State Council; Rimsky-Korsakov filled the Imperial Theaters with his operas. These mutations were accompanied by a conservative stance: Repin and others objected to the early work of Valentin Serov; survivors of the Five did the same for some emerging composers.

Rimsky-Korsakov as early as 1871 became a professor at the Petersburg Conservatory, while simultaneously heading the Free Music School. He later befriended Tchaikovsky, a favorite target of some in the Mighty Five, and came to view his friend Stasov's canonical account of a fundamental schism as fiction. "A special 'Russian music'," he said in the 1880s, "does not exist." By the end of that decade, the Five had essentially dissolved with the death of Musorgsky and Borodin and the formation of the Belyaev Circle—which Cui and Balakirev repudiated. This circle, patronized by the wealthy merchant Mitrofan Belyaev, soon become the dominant musical school, with close links to the Conservatory. The Itinerant painters similarly diversified, diluted much of the social commentary of their earlier works, and accepted patronage from patriotic merchants and the Russifying Tsar Alexander III. In the 1890s, four of them took up posts at the Academy of Arts. Well before this, in Taruskin's words alluding to both the Itinerants and the Five, "the mavericks of the 1860s were becoming the establishment of the 1880s." For good measure, it can be noted that the once censored playwright Alexander Ostrovsky ended up as an official of the Imperial Theaters.[129]

This is not to argue that no "real days" or fundamental changes dawned; it was just that the weather, fickle as usual, always brought surprises and unexpected tomorrows. Looking afresh at the century or so before the emancipation, one might be tempted to see it as an almost ahistorical period, a tranquil time before the great blows and change points so familiar to us from that segment of prerevolutionary history that has won the most scholarly attention—the years 1855–1917, with their Great Reforms, a continuous revolutionary movement, industrialization, urban technologies, the 1905 upheavals, and those of World War I and the Russian Revolution. The grand sweep of events from the fires in St. Petersburg in the early 1860s to the Petrograd eruptions of 1917, the rhythmic waxing and waning of economic life and its ugly social consequences, the brilliant cultural effusions of the Silver Age—these have pressed the historical muse to the service of drama, a drama whose final curtain bore the hammer and sickle upon its crest and whose main inspiration has often been teleological and apocalyptic. No comparable historiosophical terminals lay in wait at the end of the period covered in these pages. Neither the blood-drenched kurgans of Crimea nor the great awakening of civic consciousness in the late 1850s could match in scope or misery the fatal year 1917. The lack of a vivifying and motivating telos bestows upon this period a certain supposed emptiness, an appearance of flotation as of a sleeping community cut loose from world-historical processes, more suited to investigation by anthropologists than to the analyses of historians. But this is a misleading picture. Stasis is a relative concept; in fact, all is forever flowing, at however glacial a tempo. After all, the import of the preceding chapters lies not in the dénouement of its story but in its unrolling, the lives lived, the arts created and experienced.

Russia was still in many ways a big importer of culture in the early nineteenth century. One might even say without undue exaggeration that Russia was the object (but not victim) of an uncoordinated three-power occupation: the Germans in music, the French in theater, and the Italians in art. In the second half of the century, the importing continued, but the export factor took on world significance — especially in literature, music, and ballet. Russian creative figures came to be more than welcome in European and American cultural venues. Throughout the nineteenth and early twentieth centuries, painters went to Rome, composers and performers roved the European capitals, French-speaking Russian enthusiasts thronged the Comédie française and the Opéra. As I hope to have demonstrated, the earlier period contained its own complexities. The great changes of the postemancipation period did not occur suddenly but were preceded by long preparation in all fields. Nor were they simply a wave of revolts from below by creative minds; the ever-present state, wrapped in its own ambivalence about the arts, took away with one hand — but often gave with the other — the medals, the patronage, the education, and the permissions that eroded its own ascriptive cultural system.

When, then, did the real day dawn? No answer is possible because Dobrolyubov, in posing the question, like all visionaries dreamed of a permanent bright new day in human relationships — a noble hope indeed — rather than the painful odyssey of incremental reform, alternating with the disillusion and reversion that are the lot of our humanity. What awaited Russia were many dawns and many dusks, numerous arrivals and departures throughout the next half-century which was to be the most glorious and spectacular period of its cultural history and which awaits its social historian. One may say that the days passed as did the nights — and the real day kept dawning.

Abbreviations

Notation of files and file groups varies from archive to archive, with "inv." sometimes used for "op.", "n." for "ed. kh.," etc. In the notes, f. = fond.

Volume and issue numbers and pagination in old Russian journals are inconsistent and irregular. I have supplied information when it exists.

BE	*Balet: entsiklopediya* (Moscow, 1981)
BESII	*Bolshoi entsiklopedicheskii slovar izobrazitelnogo iskusstva*, 4 v. (St. Petersburg, 2000)
CASS	*Canadian-American Slavic Studies*
CSP	*Canadian Slavonic Papers*
DS	*Dvoryanskoe sobranie*
EE	*Evreiskaya entsiklopediya*, 13 v. (St. Petersburg, n.d. [pre-1917])
EIT	*Ezhegodnik Imperatorskikh Teatrov* (St. Petersburg, 1890–1915)
ELG	*Entsiklopediya literaturnykh geroev* (Moscow, 1997)
EO	A. S. Pushkin. *Eugene Onegin*, ed. Vladimir Nabokov, 4 v. (Princeton, 1964)
ERJ	*Encyclopedia of Russian Jewry* (Jerusalem, 1998–)
ERZ	*Entsiklopediya russkoi zhivopisi* (Moscow, 1999)

ESBE	*Entsiklopedicheskii slovar: Brokgauz-Efron*, 86 v. (St. Petersburg, 1890–1907)
ESG	*Entsiklopedicheskii slovar: Granat*, 60 v. (reprint, Moscow, 1993)
GASO	Gosudarstvennyi Arkhiv Smolenskoi Oblast, Smolensk
GR	*Goroda Rossii: entsiklopediya* (Moscow, 1994)
GRMFZh	Gosudarstvennyi Russkii Muzei, Fond Zhivopisi XVIII–Pervoi Poloviny XIX veka, St. Petersburg
GTsMMKF	Gosudarstvennyi Tsentralnyi Muzei Muzykalnoi Kultury imeni M. I. Glinki, Fonoteka, Moscow
GTsMMKRO	Gosudarstvennyi Tsentralnyi Muzei Muzykalnoi Kultury imeni M. I. Glinki, Rukopisnyi Otdel, Moscow
GTsTMRO	Gosudarstvennyi Tsentralnyi Teatralnyi Muzei imeni A. A. Bakhrushina, Rukopisnyi otdel, Moscow
IIRR	*Iz istorii realizma v russkoi zhivopisi*, ed. K. V. Mikhailova et al. (Moscow, 1982)
IRD	*Istoriya russkoi dramaturgii: XVII–pervaya polovina XIX veka* (Leningrad, 1982)
IRDT	*Istoriya russkogo dramaticheskogo teatra*, 7 v. (Moscow, 1977–87)
IRI	*Istoriya russkogo iskusstva*, 3d ed., 3 v. (Moscow, 1991)
IRLPD	Institut Russkoi Literatury (Pushkinskii Dom), St. Petersburg
IRM1	*Istoriya russkoi myzyki*, 3 v. (Moscow, 1960)
IRM2	*Istoriya russkoi myzyki*, 10 v. (Moscow, 1986–)
ISAKh	*Imperatorskaya S.P.B. Akademiya Khudozhestv: kratkii istoricheskii ocherk* (St. Petersburg, 1914)
IV	*Istoricheskii vestnik*
JGO	*Jahrbücher für Geschichte Osteuropas*
JMH	*Journal of Modern History*
KA	*Krasnyi arkhiv*
KS	*Kievskaya starina*
ME	*Muzykalnaya entsiklopediya*, 6 v. (Moscow, 1973–82)
MERSH	*Modern Encyclopedia of Russian and Soviet History* (Gulf Breeze, 1976–)
MERSL	*Modern Encyclopedia of Russian and Soviet Literatures* (Gulf Breeze, 1977–)
MTV	*Muzykalnyi i teatralnyi vestnik*
MPES	*Muzykalnyi Peterburg: Entsiklopedicheskii slovar, XVIII vek*, 3 v. (St. Petersburg, 1996–99)

MQ	*Musical Quarterly*
n.d.	no date of publication
NG	*New Grove Dictionary of Music and Musicians*, 20 v. (London, 1995)
n.p.	no place of publication
OSP	*Oxford Slavonic Papers*
OZ	*Otechestvennye zapiski*
PSS	*Polnoe sobranie sochinenii i pisem: sochineniya*
RA	*Russkii arkhiv*
RB	*Russkii balet: entsiklopediya* (Moscow, 1997)
RBS	*Russkii biograficheskii slovar*, 19 v. (St. Petersburg, 1896–1913)
REE	*Rossiiskaya evreiskaya entsiklopediya* (Moscow, 1994–)
RGALI	Rossiiskii Gosudarstvennyi Arkhiv Literatury i Iskusstv, Moscow
RGBRO	Rossiiskaya Gosudarstvennaya Biblioteka imeni V. I. Lenina, Rukopisnyi Otdel, Moscow
RIIE	*Russkoe iskusstvo: illyustrirovannaya entsiklopediya* (Moscow, 2001)
RKh	*Russkie khudozhniki: entsiklopedicheskii slovar* (St. Petersburg, 1998)
RM	*Russkaya mysl*
RNBFF	Rossiiskaya Natsionalnaya Biblioteka, Filial, Fonoteka, St. Petersburg
RNBOE	Rossiiskaya Natsionalnaya Biblioteka, Otdel Estampov, St. Petersburg
RNBRO	Rossiiskaya Natsionalnaya Biblioteka, Rukopisnyi Otdel, St. Petersburg
RP	*Repertuar russkago teatra i panteon vsekh evropeiskikh teatrov* (continuation of RRT; title varies)
RPis	*Russkie pisateli, 1800–1917: biograficheskii slovar* (Moscow, 1989–)
RR	*Russian Review*
RRT	*Repertuar russkago teatra*
RS	*Russkaya starina*
RV	*Russkii vestnik*
SEEJ	*Slavonic and East European Journal*
SEER	*Slavonic and East European Review*
SG	*Starye gody*
SGE	*Soobshcheniya Gosudarstvennogo Ermitazha* (title varies)

SIRIO	*Sbornik Imperatorskago Russkago Istoricheskago Obshchestva*
SM	*Sovetskaya muzyka*
s.p.	separate pagination
SPBGTB	Sankt-Peterburgskaya Gosudarstvennaya Teatralnaya Biblioteka
SPBKF	Sankt-Peterburgskaya Gosudarstvennaya Konservatoriya imeni N. A. Rimskogo-Korsakova, Fonoteka
SR	*Slavic Review*
TE	*Teatralnaya entsiklopediya*, 5 v. (Moscow, 1961–67)
TMV	*Teatralnyi i muzykalnyi vestnik* (continuation of MTV).
VE	*Vestnik Evropy*

Notes

Introduction

1. See the works of historians Roosevelt, Lincoln, Norris, and Ely cited in the chapters. Their excellent contributions have yet to be incorporated into social or general history. Ropert, *La misère et la gloire,* focuses on ideas, literature, and architecture.

2. For a masterful example of not ignoring those works, see Brooks, *When Russia Learned to Read.*

3. Becker, *Art Worlds,* passim.

4. Williams, *Long Revolution,* 45.

5. *Ocherki russkoi kultury XIX veka,* 5. For discussions of the public sphere and the arts in eighteenth-century Europe, see Blanning, *Culture of Power,* 2; and Crow, *Painters and Public Life in Eighteenth-Century Paris.*

6. Weintraub and Kumar, *Public and Private in Thought and Practice,* 17; and Weintraub, "The Theory and Politics of the Public/Private Distinction," ibid., 101–42. Weintraub's term for what I mean by public space is "sociability," which requires no politics, no mutual obligations, or even solidarity — except the momentary one of a shared experience. It often requires social distance alongside physical proximity. On this see Lovell, *Summerfolk,* 41 n. 40.

7. Rogger, *National Consciousness in Eighteenth-Century Russia.*

8. Wortman, *Scenarios of Power,* 1; Riasanovsky, *Nicholas I and Official Nationality;* idem, *Image of Peter the Great;* Gasiorowska, *Image of Peter the Great in Russian Fiction;* Whittaker, *Origins of Modern Russian Education.*

9. Lotman, *Besedy o russkoi kulture;* idem, *Roman A. S. Pushkina "Evgenii Onegin";*

idem, *Semiotics of Russian Cultural History;* idem, *Velikosvetskie obedy;* see also Todd, *Fiction and Society in the Age of Pushkin;* idem, *Literature and Society in Imperial Russia.*

Chapter 1. Town and Country

1. The Sollogub quip, "Petersburg is a dot on the map of Russia; the fashionable world is a dot on the map of Petersburg," is from an 1840 society tale cited by Pursglove, "V. A. Sollogub and *High Society*" in Cornwell, *Society Tale,* 71.

2. Volkov, *St. Petersburg,* 44; Lincoln, *Sunlight at Midnight.*

3. Yatsevich, *Pushkinskii Peterburg,* 80–83; "Russkii Muzei: Avtobiografiya," St. Petersburg TV, Channel 2, January 22, 1998; *Russkii Muzei Imperatora Aleksandra III; Petrov, Russkii Muzei; Russian Museum;* Ivanova, "Mikhailovskii Dvorets," 256–58; Stites, "Circles on a Square."

4. See Ward, *Moscow and Leningrad,* vol. 2, for addresses. The older chatty and charming works of popular writers such as Pylyaev, Yatsevich, and Stolpyansky — full of errors as they are — entwine the topographical with the anecdotal and biographical, and give the reader a sense of historical place. Yatsevich, *Pushkinskii Peterburg;* Stolpyanskii, *Muzyka* and *Staryi Peterburg i Obshchestvo Pooshchreniya Khudozhestv;* Pylyaev, *Staroe zhite* and *Zabytoe proshloe okrestnostei Peterburga.*

5. Rozanov, *Muzykalnyi Pavlovsk;* Massie, *Pavlovsk.* On these and other important sites of entertainment, see Lovell, *Summerfolk.* The Russian word *vokzal,* from the eighteenth-century London entertainment complex, Vauxhall, came to mean simply railway station.

6. Goncharov, "Pisma stolichnogo druga k provintsialnomu zhenikhu" in Oksman, *Feletony sorokovykh godov,* 39–84; Lotman, "Russkii dendizm" in *Besedy o russkoi kultury,* 90–102, 123–35. For a minute description of the round in *bonne société,* see Arnold, *Vospominaniya,* 1:16–21.

7. Karamzin, "Letters of a Russian Traveler" in Segel, *Literature of Eighteenth-Century Russia,* 1:421; Tyutcheva cited in Shevyrëv, "Kulturnaya sreda stolichnogo goroda" in *Ocherki russkoi kultury XIX veka,* 122 n. 58; Khvoshchinskaya in Clyman, *Russia Through Women's Eyes,* 81. Club and restaurant life allowed a much looser mode of social behavior. See *Stoletie S.-Peterburgskago Angliiskago sobraniya.*

8. Bourdieu, *Distinction.*

9. Karlinsky, *Gogol,* 109.

10. Skalkovskii, *Vospominaniya,* 1–9; Lincoln, *Vanguard of Reform,* 16–17, 20; Wirtschafter, *Structures of Society;* idem, *Social Identity in Imperial Russia.*

11. Krestovskii, *Peterburgskyya trushchoby.* This book reproduces authentic slum jargon and captures big-city underlife with its scenes of misery in jails and hospitals. For this, Krestovsky was accused by some of "photographing reality." Ashcroft, "*Peterburgskie trushchoby,*" 163–75; Elets, *Biografiya Krestovskogo,* 163–75.

12. Shevyrëv, "Kulturnaya sreda stolichnogo goroda," 73, 78.

13. Custine, *Letters from Russia,* 49; graphics in RNBOE; Shevyrëv, "Kulturnaya sreda stolichnogo goroda," 75.

14. Jahn, "St. Peterburger Heumarkt," 162–77.

15. Cited in Shevyrëv, "Kulturnaya sreda stolichnogo goroda," 119 n. 38. Though done a few years after this period, P. Vereshchagin's canvas of a Moscow market scene captures its vitality: Ovsyannikov, *Kartiny russkogo byta*, 294.

16. Herzen, *My Past*, 10.

17. Gershenzon, *Griboedovskaya Moskva*, 73–79.

18. Edwards, *Russians at Home*, 346–48; *Moskovskoe Kupecheskoe Sobranie*, 11–13; Blagovo, *Razskazy babushki*, the memories of Elizaveta Yankova (1768–1861).

19. The literature on merchants is huge. See Buryshkin, *Moskva kupecheskaya*; Rieber, *Merchants and Entrepreneurs in Imperial Russia*; Owen, *Capitalism and Politics in Russia*; Ruckman, *Moscow Business Elite*, 8–9. West, *Merchant Moscow*; Kelly, "Teacups and Coffins" in Marsh, *Women in Russia and Ukraine*, 55–77.

20. Sollogub, *Tarantas*, 84. *Moskovskoe Kupecheskoe Sobranie*, 14–25. For other clubs: Butorov, *Sobirateli i metsenaty Moskovskogo Angliiskogo Kluba*; Smith, *Working the Rough Stone*; Bremner, *Excursions in the Interior of Russia*, 1:216; Lotman, *Velikosvetskie obedy*, 34–35. Merchants at English gentry affairs were put in roped-off areas at concerts and clubs well into the nineteenth century: Bramsted, *Aristocracy and the Middle Classes in Germany*, 150–99. Sumptuary laws, though not enforced, dictated that carriages of burghers be one-horse: Gurowski, *Russia as It Is*, 145–61.

21. Wirtschafter, *Social Identity*, 81–82 *Moscow Business Elite*, 1–48, for social identity, relations, and imagery.

22. Edwards, *Russians at Home*, 155–57; Owen, *Capitalism and Politics in Russia*, 23.

23. Ruane, "Caftan to Business Suit," 53–60. For attitudes to dress in the Zamoskvorechie District of Moscow, see Alexander Ostrovsky's ironic sketch in his *Polnoe sobranie sochinenii*, 1:34–35.

24. Herzen, *My Past*, 82, 94; Dmitriev, "Studencheskiya vospominaniya," 225–33; Friedman, "In the Company of Men," 129–30. Universities' jails in fact represented a degree of independence from the state's law-enforcement agencies.

25. For an engaging account of the French emigration, see Haumant, *Culture française en Russie*, especially chaps. 14–16 and p. 337; Piggott, *John Field*, chaps. 3–7; Buturlin, "Zapiski," RA, 5–8 (1897) 597 n.

26. Roosevelt, *Russian Country Estate*; Blum, *Lord and Peasant in Russia*, 349.

27. GASO, f. 1, op. 7, d. 9; Lincoln, *Vanguard of Reform*, 130–32.

28. Rak, "Aleksandr Aleksandrovich Shakhovskoi" in Levitt, *Early Modern Russian Writers*, 348–55 (qu. 351).

29. Roosevelt, *Russian Country Estate*; Cavender, "Nests of Gentry."

30. Roosevelt, *Russian Country Estate*, 144; Kots, *Krepostnaya intelligentsiya*, 17; Shchepkina, *Vospominaniya*, 45–46; Zhdanov, *Putevyya zapiski po Rossii*, 130–31.

31. Some middle and poor nobles, masters of a hundred souls or less, engaged grotesquely in social mimicry by nailing up four Doric columns topped by a classical pediment to their humble wooden cabins as a sign of their membership in the "well-born caste": Marasinova, "Kultura russkoi usadby," 273.

32. *Ocherki russkoi kultury*, 5–11; V. A. Koshelëv, "O 'literaturnoi' provintsii i 'literaturnoi provintsialnosti'," in Belousov, *Russkaya provintsiya*, 37–55 (qu. 49).

33. Kurmachëva, *Krepostnaya intelligentsiya*, 121, citing serf prices in selected provinces; Petersburg house serfs sold for three hundred to seven hundred rubles in the 1790s:

Stolpyanskii, "Torgovlya lyudmi v starom Peterburge," 214; Kots, *Krepostnaya intelligentsiya,* 30; Jones, *Emancipation of the Russian Nobility;* Confino, *Domaines et seigneurs en Russie;* Raeff, *Origins of the Russian Intelligentsia.*

34. Roosevelt, *Russian Country Estate;* Marasinova, "Kultura russkoi usadby," 265–377; Dmitrieva, *Zhizn usadebnogo mifa.*

35. Bobkov, "Iz zapisok byvshago krepostnogo cheloveka."

36. Keppen, *Devyataya reviziya,* 199–200, 207–8; Kolchin, *Unfree Labor,* 161.

37. Field, *End of Serfdom,* 44.

38. Troinitskii, *Serf Population in Russia,* 13, 73–79.

39. The provincial figures are estimates for 1859 in D. M., "Neskolko slov o dvorovykh lyudyakh," 46–54 (s.p.): Kursk, 43,017; Orël, Ryazan, Tambov, Tver, Tula, 20–40,000; Vilna, Vladimir, Voronezh, Kaluga, Moscow, Novgorod (an error: Nizhny Novgorod is undoubtedly meant), Penza, Poltava, Pskov, Saratov, Simbirsk, Kharkov, Yaroslav, 10–20,000; Vitebsk, Grodno, Ekaterinoslav, Kazan, Mogilëv, Novgorod, Orenburg, Perm, Samara, St. Petersburg, Kherson, Tauride, 5–10,000. A study of Tver Province counts 43,000 house serfs as against a gentry population of about 10,000 for 1847: Cavender, "Nests of Gentry," 20. For distribution of provincial orchestras and theaters, see chaps. 2, 3, and 6 of the present book. Merchants also had house serfs which they acquired illegally by registering them in another owner's name: Nikitenko, *Up from Serfdom,* 126.

40. For parade culture on estates, see Stites, *Revolutionary Dreams,* 20–21; Shipov, "Istoriya moei zhizni"; Sverbeev, *Zapiski,* 2:7–44; Vodovozova, *Na zare zhizni,* 1:159; Merder, "Otzhivye tipy," 537–52.

41. Marrese, *Woman's Kingdom,* 125; Bushnell, "Did Serf Owners Control Serf Marriage?"

42. Maza, *Servants and Masters in Eighteenth-Century France.*

43. Bobkov, "Iz zapisok byvshago krepostnogo cheloveka"; Arakcheev: Kots, *Krepostnaya intelligentsiya,* 88–89; Kondakov, *Spisok,* 385; Wrangel, *Vospominaniya;* Letkova, "Krepostnaya intelligentsiya," 184–85, 190–92. A fascinating and learned study of corporal punishment for law-breakers does not touch on the private or domestic beatings that were beyond the reach of the law and claimed many more victims: Schrader, *Languages of the Lash.*

44. On conscription, see Sverbeev, *Zapiski,* 2:27–44. Wirtschafter, *From Serf to Russian Soldier,* 3–25, provides a clear picture of the variety and complexity of recruitment practices. Manorial serfs were generally subject to a rota that put men eligible by age and family size up to the front of the line.

45. Herzen, *My Past,* 13, 15; Roosevelt, *Russian Country Estate,* 183–89; Kots, *Krepostnaya intelligentsiya,* 20; Lotman, *Semiotics of Russian Cultural History,* 57–58; Panaeva, *Vospominaniya,* 100–101 and n. 2. A housemaid in Griboedov's *Woe from Wit* speaks of the gentry and "the worst of all, the master's temper and the master's love" (Act I): Griboedov, PSS, 2:6.

46. Kolchin, *Unfree Labor,* 143 (guardianships); Shchepetov, *Iz zhizni krepostnykh krestyan,* 47 (Pestel); Nikitenko, *Up from Serfdom,* 59; D. M., "Neskolko slov o dvorovykh lyudyakh," 52. Literature on serf abuse: *Krepostnichestvo i volya,* a collection of atrocity stories; and Melgunov, *Krepostnoe pravo.*

47. Aksakov, *Years of Childhood,* 225–27.

48. Wachtel, *Battle for Childhood,* 105–25.

49. Curtiss, *Russian Army Under Nicholas I;* Wirtschafter, *From Serf to Russian Soldier;* Zelnik, *Labor and Society in Imperial Russia;* Haywood, *Russia Enters the Railway Age.* As a corrective to the myth of female owners as more abusive than males, see Marrese, *Woman's Kingdom,* 231–32.

50. Kurmachëva, *Krepostnaya intelligentsiya* (schooling); Nikitenko, *Diary of a Russian Censor,* xiii; Purlevskii, "Vospominaniya krepostnago, 1800–1868"; Douglass quoted by Peter Kolchin in the introduction to Nikitenko, *Up from Serfdom,* xvii; Bohac, "Everyday Forms of Resistance"; Kurmachëva records a few scattered cases of resistance and one of flight by educated or artistic serfs (*Krepostnaya intelligentsiya,* 298–99).

51. Zablotskii-Desyatovskii, *Kiselëv,* 2:255 on Tsar Nicholas; Passenens, *Russie et l'esclavage,* 2:86 and passim; Letkova, "Krepostnaya intelligentsiya." Disobedience and debauchery were common verdicts on lower-class suicide in the era of serfdom. See Morrisey, "In the Name of Freedom."

52. Kots, *Krepostnaya intelligentsiya;* Kurmachëva, *Krepostnaya intelligentsiya,* though weighted toward serfs engaged in literary, educational, and scientific-technical realms, also contains useful information on serf artists and an exhaustive historiography.

53. Savelov, "Dvoryanskoe soslovie."

54. Roosevelt, *Russian Country Estate;* Marasinova, "Kultura russkoi usadby."

55. The pioneering work is Semevskii, *Krestyanskii vopros v Rossii,* 1:316–17, 396–97, and passim. See Blum, *Lord and Peasant in Russia;* Kolchin, *Unfree Labor;* Moon, *Russian Peasants and Tsarist Legislation,* 80–112, for a detailed analysis of the 1847 decree; Rimsky-Korsakov, *My Musical Life,* 17; Moon, *Russian Peasantry, 1600–1930,* 148 (Sheremetev); Emmons, *Russian Landed Gentry,* 80 (Unkovsky).

56. Ruud, *Fighting Words,* 92–93; Melgunov, *Krepostnoe pravo,* contains excerpts from Herzen, Turgenev, Belinsky, Shevchenko, Shchepkin, Nekrasov, Shchedrin. Grigorovich, and others. For an older view of "abolitionist" literature, see Dodge, "Abolitionist Sentiment in Russia, 1762–1855." After emancipation, according to Alexander Pypin, some four thousand works on peasants issued forth from the presses in the decades 1858–78, a corpus that awaits analysis: Donskov, *Changing Image of the Peasant,* 7 n. 2.

57. Belinsky, *Selected Philosophical Works,* 386–87, 474–75. Belinsky, who spent his youth in Penza Province amid abusive serf owners, put his observations into an unpublished, unstaged, and very talky play, "Dmitry Kalinin" (1831): *Polnoe sobranie sochinenii,* 1:417–503; Nechaeva, "'Dmitrii Kalinin' i krepostnaya deistvitelnost." See also Vetrinskii, *Vissarion Grigorevich Belinskii,* 28–29.

58. Nikitenko, *Up from Serfdom,* 201.

59. Cavender, "Nests of Gentry," 164 and passim.

60. Field, *End of Serfdom,* 44; Dodge, "Abolitionist Sentiment," 318–44 and passim.

61. Prostakov got his freedom in 1828 at age 80, won the title Free Artist in 1838 for his project of the Church of Christ the Savior in Moscow, and apparently died in 1854 at age 106: Kots, *Krepostnaya intelligentsiya,* 88; Kondakov, *Spisok,* 376; Bobkov, "Iz zapisok byvshago krepostnogo cheloveka," 749; Turgenev, "Pëtr Petrovich Karataev" in *Zapiski okhotnika,* PSS, 4:250–51.

62. Kropotkin, *Memoirs of a Revolutionist,* 44 (see his impassioned thoughts on serfdom's evils, 38–48); Shipov, "Istoriya moei zhizni," 147–48; Jesse, *Notes of a Half-Pay,* 2:281–82.

63. Nikitenko, *Up from Serfdom,* 128–29 (qu. 128), 153–54, 171, 194–95 (qu. 194),

and passim. V. M. Nikitenko, the father, was a choral singer for N. P. Sheremetev. He learned languages, law, and music and suffered constantly in servitude. At seventeen his voice changed and he was sent as a clerk to a distant estate. His haphazard education "only fired his imagination." He became a teacher, got embroiled constantly in litigation, and served in menial, though responsible jobs. A female landowner he worked for reached a point where his efficiency, which advantaged her, was outweighed by the power he had accrued and thus his presumed (and presumptuous) independence which she would not brook: Nikitenko, *Up from Serfdom*, 8–11 (qu. 11). 97, and passim.

64. Buturlin, "Zapiski," RA, 5–8 (1897) 192–93; Zhdanov, *Putevyya*, 26–28.

65. The entries I examined are Astrakhan, Elets (then in Orël Province), Kaluga, Kazan, Kharkov, the Korennaya settlement, Kursk, Nizhny Novgorod, Omsk, Penza, Poltava, Saratov, Smolensk, Tambov, Tula, Tver, Vladimir-on-the-Klyazma, Voronezh, Yaroslavl—all entered alphabetically in Gagarin, *Vseobshchii geograficheskii slovar*.

66. See Karlinsky, *Gogol*, 165–66.

67. Numbers: Lincoln, *Vanguard of Reform*, 113; spas: Roosevelt, *Russian Country Estate*, 202.

68. Alexander, *Bubonic Plague in Early Modern Russia;* McGrew, *Russia and the Cholera*, 45–46, 50–51, 78–79, and passim.

69. For a case study, see Litvinova, "Sozdanie dvoryanskikh soslovnykh organov v voronezhskoi gubernii, 1785–1801 gg.," 57–77; Yablochkov, *Istoriya dvoryanskago sosloviya v Rossii*, 541–47; Emmons, *Russian Landed Gentry;* Aksakov, *Years of Childhood*. For a sense of small town life in the late eighteenth century, see Stites, "The Veselukha Tower." I find "Gentry Club" the least unsatisfactory term for this organization, its venue, and its social-cultural function. Variants include House of the Nobility and *Assemblée de la noblesse*.

70. Buturlin's unit in Orël in the 1820s: "Zapiski," RA, 5–8 (1897) 192; Zhdanov, *Putevyya*, 65–68; Nikitenko, *Diary*, xiii; Kramskoi: see chap. 8; orgies: "Orlovskii starozhil," *Bylyya chudaki v orlovskoi gubernii*, 33; Karlinsky, *Gogol*, 133; billeting in Ryazan province, 1820s: Rostislavov, *Provincial Russia*, 182–84.

71. But apparently not everywhere: "social life for the gentry in Tver' did not revolve around the balls in the provincial and district capitals, though festivities in those towns attracted gentry revelers": Cavender, "Nests of Gentry," 344.

72. A. F. Veltman's novel, *Serdtse i dumka*, offers a vivid description of a district town ball. For provincial capital balls—including those at election time—see F. v. E. [F. A. von Ettinger], *Bashnya Veselukha;* Shalikov, *Drugoe puteshestvie v Malorossiyu*, 154–57; Orlovskii starozhil, *Bylyya chudaki*, 50; Roosevelt, *Russian Country Estate*, 200–202. Election rules in Romanovich-Slavatinskii, *Dvoryanstvo v Rossii*, 436–38. For charitable activities: Lindenmeyr, *Poverty Is Not a Vice*, 116, see also 109–10.

73. Mironov, *Russkii gorod v 1740–1860-e gody*, 80–193; idem, *Social History of Imperial Russia;* Koshman, "Gorod i obshchestvenno-kulturnaya zhizn," 53–54; Kaiser, *Reinterpreting Russian History*, 272 (market days); Artynov, *Vospominaniya krestyanina*, 60–61.

74. Christian, "*Living Water*," chaps. 2–4, 10–11.

75. Monasteries and pilgrimages: Hilton, *Russian Folk Art*, 44; Artynov, *Vospominaniya krestyanina*, 20–27 (Tikhvin); Chulos, "Religious and Secular Aspects of Pilgrimage

in Modern Russia," 21–58 (Voronezh). See chap 6 of the present work for the Korennaya Monastery. Fistfights: among many accounts, see Rostislavov, *Provincial Russia*, pp. 182–84.

76. Numbers and rules: Kaiser, *Reinterpreting Russian History*, p. 272; Rozman, *Urban Networks in Russia*, 119–20; Orlovsky, *Limits of Reform*, 26.

77. Fëdorov, "Krestyanin-otkhodnik," one of many treatments of this issue.

78. Zablotskii-Desyatovskii, *Kiselëv;* Druzhinin, *Gosudarstvennye krestyane;* Rozen (Rosen), *Zapiski dekabrista,* 293; Mazour, *First Russian Revolution;* idem, *Women in Exile;* and Zetlin, *Decembrists,* 300.

79. Tsar Nicholas qu. in Koshman, "Gorod," 40; *Istoriya zheleznodorozhnogo transporta Rossii,* 1:43–47; Fitzpatrick, *Great Russian Fair,* 171–72; Melnikov, *Stoletie nizhegorodskoi yarmarki,* 39–40.

80. Stroganov, "Provintsializm/Provintsialnost" in Belousov, *Russkaya provintsiya,* 30–37. See also Klubkova, "Russkii provintsialnyi gorod i stereotipy provintsialnosti," ibid., 20–30.

81. Varneke, *Istoriya,* 451 (Kulikov); Veltman, *Serdtse i dumka,* 49–59.

82. Lounsbery, "No This Is Not the Provinces'."

83. Vereshchagin, "Zhenskiya mody aleksandrovskago vremeni."

84. Lotman, "Lyudi 1812 goda," *Besedy o russkoi kultury,* 326–30.

85. Gershenzon, *Griboedovskaya Moskva,* 14–18; Smirnov, *Nizhegorodskaya starina,* 391.

86. Evtuhov, "*Gubernskie Vedomosti* and Local Culture."

87. Kozlyakov, "Kulturnaya sreda provintsialnogo goroda," 125–202; Raab, "City of Perm."

88. For some recent insights on local studies then and now, see Evtuhov, *Kazan, Moscow, St. Petersburg*; Raleigh, *Provincial Landscapes: Local Dimensions of Soviet Power*; Baschmakoff, *Modernization in the Russian Provinces*. Baschmakoff takes up marginal and didactic discourses, spatial self-representation, and travel literature in her work. See also her "Lokalnyi tekst, golos pamyati i poetika prostranstva" (ms.).

Chapter 2. The Domestic Muse

1. The original: Passenens, *Russie et l'esclavage,* 2:91–92; Yatsevich distorts Passenens in *Pushkinskii Peterburg,* 110n. Giovanni Battista Viotti (1755–1824) was a prolific composer, famed teacher, and court musician to Marie Antoinette. The concerto in the story is not identified, but an example of one is *Kontsert N. 22 dlya skripki s orkestrom lya minor,* and a violin and harp sonata on *Vera Dulova, arfa* (Melodiya, 33 S-10–13745–6): GTsMMKF. Viotti featured as the admired hero of the fictional Polykarp, serf waiter, butler, and ex-violinist, in Turgenev's *Zapiski okhotnika:* PSS, 4:201.

2. Puzyrevskii, *Imperatorskoe Russkoe Muzykalnoe Obshchestvo,* 3.

3. Corbin, *Village Bells,* 289 and passim; Lokhanskii, "Russkie kolokolnye zapevy"; Williams, *Bells of Russia.* For rhapsodic reports of a visitor on the "rich sweetness" of the bell sound, see Bremner, *Excursions in the Interior of Russia,* 1:121–22.

4. For a sampling of Glinka: *Glinka Romances, Patrioticheskaya pesnya,* and *M. Glinka: romansy.* The literature on popular song writers is immense. Nikolai Andreevich

Titov was popularly known as "the grandfather of the Russian romance." Boris Gasparov and Catherine Evtuhov (a descendant), personal communication.

5. Hodge, *Double Garland and* "Mutatis Mutandis." See also Brown, "Native Song," 57–84.

6. Stolpyanskii, *Muzyka,* 132, 135–37, 212; Vorontsov, "Muzyka," 472–80; Vyazemsky: EO, 2:385.

7. Stolpyanskii, *Muzyka,* 148–95; Muzalevskii, *Russkoe fortepyannoe iskusstvo,* 82; Fedosyuk, *Chto neponyatno u klassikov,* 238.

8. Clementi: Parakilas, *Piano Roles,* 77–93; Piggott, *John Field,* chap. 3.

9. Muzalevskii, *Russkoe fortepyannoe iskusstvo,* 243. In the United States during this period, pianos where being hauled by mule teams and canal boats across the mountains from the eastern seaboard to Pittsburgh and beyond: Tawa, *High-Minded and Low-Down,* 71.

10. Ivanov, "List v Rossii" in GTsMMKRO, f. 364, inv. 223, n. 8871.

11. Wortman, *Scenarios of Power,* 1.

12. Lvov, "Zapiski"; Bers, "Lvov"; Korf, "Materialy," 47; *Aleksei Fëdorovich Lvov;* Shtakelberg, "Russkii narodnyi gimn"; Shilder, *Imperator Nikolai Pervyi,* 1:26 and 474 n. 21, lays to rest the notion that Nicholas had and retained a childhood dislike of music. Volkov, *St. Petersburg,* 25, has Nicholas playing the flute. Lvov also organized summer chorales at Peterhof at which the emperor sang.

13. After Maria Fëdorovna died in 1828, Tsar Nicholas's brother Mikhail replaced classical music with the sounds of drums and martial music and the spectacle of drill. Charles Timberlake, "Pavlovsk Palace and Park," MERSH, 27:101–3; Rozanov, *Muzykalnyi Pavlovsk,* 1–22; Swartz, "Women Patrons and Performers"; Arnold, *Vospominaniya,* 2:138–39; Muzalevskii, *Russkoe fortepyannoe iskusstvo,* 131–32.

14. *Severnaya pchela,* quoted in Stolpyanskii, *Muzyka,* 146. The editor, the conservative Faddei Bulgarin, elsewhere commented sourly that "even" daughters of lower civil servants and artisans were taking up piano: cited in Khoprova, *Ocherki,* 4; see Leppert, *Music and Image,* for class blurring through music and resentment of it in eighteenth-century England. Greene, "Mid-Nineteenth-Century Domestic Ideology," 78–97.

15. Wirtschafter, *Social Identity,* 18–19.

16. Family relations: Tovrov, *Russian Noble Family;* Hammarberg, "Flirting with Words" (qu. 298); Stolpyanskii, *Muzyka,* 141–46; Glagoleva, "Dream and Reality of Russian Provincial Young Ladies," 64. Glagoleva also cites a real-life gentry woman who bemoaned the time wasted by young girls at the keyboard (p. 54). For domesticity and music elsewhere: Loesser, *Men, Women, and Pianos;* Leppert, *Music and Image;* Smith, *Ladies of Leisure;* Welter, "Cult of True Womanhood."

17. Muzalevskii, *Russkoe fortepyannoe iskusstvo,* 241; Buturlin, "Zapiski," RA, 5–8 (1897) 188; Glinka: Zetlin [Tsetlin], *The Five,* 27. For European male taboos about music and dance, see Leppert, *Music and Image,* chap. 2.

18. Muzalevskii, *Russkoe fortepyannoe iskusstvo,* 103, 138.

19. Shalikov, *Puteshestvie v Malorossiyu,* 185; *Damskii zhurnal* (1823–33). For more on Shalikov, see Hammarberg, "Flirting with Words"; Campbell, *Odoevsky,* 63–64; Hodge, *Double Garland,* 191–92, passim; *Russkaya elegiya,* 223; Schönle, *Authenticity and Fiction.*

20. Shchepkina, *Vospominaniya*, 20.

21. *Zhdanovich at the Piano* (1849). A Soviet art historian, attempting to link the "realism" of Fedotov with Dostoevsky, rather oddly compared Zhdanovich to Varvara in *Poor Folk*: Rakova, "Russkii kamernyi portret." It might be more apt to compare her to the girl in Ingres, *The Stamatey Family* (1818) where the piano is part of the daughter's identity in the family circle. See also Vanslov, *Istoriya russkogo iskusstva*, 1:284.

22. Stolpyanskii, *Muzyka*, 153–63; Grigorev, *My Literary and Moral Wanderings*, 55. See the painter Vasily Tropinin's *Guitarist* [GRMFZh, 5230]. The harp, almost always associated with women, declined at the turn of the nineteenth century: Stolpyanskii, *Muzyka*, 150–53.

23. Findeizen, *Ocherk*, 3–4; Muzalevskii, *Russkoe fortepyannoe iskusstvo*, 104–5, 243–44; Stolpyanskii, *Muzyka*, 193–94; Piggott, *John Field*, chaps. 3–7; Norris, *Russian Piano Concerto*, 14–15.

24. Muzalevskii, *Russkoe fortepyannoe iskusstvo*, 234–44; Natanson, *Iz muzykalnogo proshlogo*, 1–38; Karlinsky, *Gogol*, 12; Belyakov, *Opernaya i kontsertnaya deyatelnost*, 180; Artynov, *Vospominaniya krestyanina*, 56.

25. Citron, *Gender*, 104–8; Bourdieu, *Distinction*; Chuikina, "Professionalnaya reintegratsiya dvoryanstva."

26. ME, 1:223.

27. Arnold, *Vospominaniya*, 2:198–202. For one of many examples of intelligentsia views on intellectual enthusiasm, see Annenkov, *Extraordinary Decade*, 137.

28. Goffman, *Presentation of Self*.

29. See the standard works on salon and social behavior: Aronson, *Literaturnye kruzhki*; Brodskii, *Literaturnye salony*. The psychology of upper-class behavior in society is explored in Lotman, *Semiotics of Russian Cultural History*, *Besedy o russkoi kultury*, and *Velikosvetskie obedy*; see also Shepard, "Society Tale." A splendid if exaggerated visual treatment of the aristocratic soirée can be seen in the opening of Sergei Bondarchuk's 1967 film of Tolstoy's *War and Peace*.

30. Stasov, *Selected Essays*, 155.

31. Leppert, *Music and Image*, 11. Bers, "Lvov," 158, and references in note 12 above. The son of a serf who played violin as a stiffener in many quartets of the time claimed that Lvov poorly understood the Beethoven Golitsyn quartets: Afanasev, "Vospominaniya," 35.

32. Biographical notes and service records of the brothers in RGALI, f. 191, op. 2, ed. kh. 224 and f. 1925, op. 2, ed. kh. 30; diplomas and honors in IRLPD, f. 50: Vielgorskie. See Shcherbakova, *Vielgorskie*; Skonechnaya, *Moskovskii Parnas*, 138–46; Sokolov, *Ryadom s Pushkinym*, 131; Bugrov, *Svet kurskikh ramp*, 2:10; "Knyaz kompozitor," 4. Mikhail's son Iosif died in spite of Gogol's loving care in Rome at the age of twenty-three in 1838: Karlinsky, *Gogol*.

33. Shcherbakova, *Vielgorskie*, qu. 18; Aronson, *Literaturnye kruzhki*, 193–98, 285–87; Brown, *Glinka*, 80–81; Afanasev, "Vospominaniya," IV, 41 (Aug. 1890) 272; Yatsevich, *Pushkinskii Peterburg* (1931) 83, 90–96 (qu. 92). Vielgorsky also hosted a musical salon in Moscow in 1823–26.

34. Sollogub, *Peterburgskie Stranitsy*, 139, 142–43, 211–12 (qu. 212). On Sollogub, see Pursglove, "V. A. Sollogub" in Cornwell, *Society Tale*. Muraveva, *Kak vospityvali russkogo dvoryanina*, 131–32, on Vielgorsky's good manners.

35. Campbell, *Odoevsky;* Panaeva, *Vospominaniya,* 113; Cornwell, *Odoevsky,* esp. pp. 121–59, for the musical life; and idem, "Vladimir Odoevskii" in Cornwell, *Society Tale,* 9–19.

36. Aronson, *Literaturnye kruzhki,* 171–82, 280–83; Ledkovsky, "Avdotiya Panaeva."

37. Bramsted, *Aristocracy and the Middle-Classes in Germany,* 151ff.; Aronson, *Literaturnye kruzhki,* 70–71(Botkin). At the dawn of the twentieth century, when King Edward VIII took British tea mogul Sir Thomas Lipton on a cruise, someone caustically remarked that the king "had gone yachting with his grocer": Cannadine, *Pleasures of the Past,* 157. Norms of eighteenth- and early nineteenth-century English etiquette held that music study for men could be not only ungentlemanly, but also unmanly and even un-English — the last due to the rash of foreign teachers: Leppert, *Music and Image,* chap. 2. Leppert also observes that aristocrats could be portrayed as musicians, but as ones without exertion: 136 and passim.

38. Kuznetsov, *Glinka,* 38–50 (qu. 43). Further details in Hodge, *Double Garland,* 217–20 and passim; Aronson, *Literaturnye kruzhki,* 224–34, 292–96; Yatsevich, *Pushkinskii Peterburg* (1931) 148–53; Nikitenko, *Diary,* 77. Yury Arnold who once received a grievous insult there offers the most hostile account in *Vospominaniya,* 2:29, 243–44. Panaev in Brodskii, *Literaturnye salony,* 237–45 and Sollogub in *Peterburgskie Stranitsy,* 312 are also scorching. One source puts Kukolnik's flat, nicknamed the Stock Exchange, on No. 8 Glukhoe Street: Shevchenko, *Povest,* 68. See Ward, *Moscow and Leningrad,* 2:6–57, 148 and Orlova, *Glinka's Life,* for other locations.

39. Glinka's wife: Yatsevich, *Pushkinskii Peterburg* (1931) 149; for an honest discussion of Glinka's sexual life, see Brown, *Glinka.* Glinka's setting of Kukolnik's verses is on *M. Glinka: Proshchanie s Peterburgom.*

40. Arnold, *Vospominaniya,* 2:243.

41. A dispassionate but largely negative view of the troika's evenings is given by Kukolnik's friend, the Penza Province noble V. A. Insarskii: *Zapiski,* 71–72, which also attributes Kukolnik's artistic decline to his wild life.

42. Ward, *Moscow and Leningrad,* 2:150–51; Belza, *Shimanovskaya.* Elena Szymanowska (Maria's sister): "Dnevnik." Musical examples of Szymanowska in Szymanowska, "Nocturne." For other salons: Bers, "Lvov," 158; Levashëva, "Muzyka v kruzhke A. A. Delviga."

43. Fairweather, *Pilgrim Princess;* Gorodetzky, "Princess Zinaide Volkonsky"; Tomei, *Russian Women Writers,* 1:151–60.

44. Brodskii, *Literaturnye salony,* 172–74; Buturlin, "Zapiski," RA, 1–4 (1897) 237 and 5–8 (1897) 177–78, 549–51, for these and other domestic productions of Italian opera in Moscow; Fairweather, *Pilgrim Princess,* 194–215; Nechkina, *Dvizhenie Dekabristov,* 2:433. For the context of women's salons, see Bernstein, "Women on the Verge of a New Language." Genishta's (Jeništa's) setting of Pushkin's "The Day Star Is Now Extinguished" (Pogaslo dnevnoe svetilo) is recorded on radio by Georgii Vinogradov with Georgii Orentrikher at piano: GTsMMKF.

45. Muzalevskii, *Russkoe fortepyannoe iskusstvo,* 133–34; Revyakin, *Moskva,* 356; Afanasev, "Vospominaniya," IV, 41 (July 1890) 34; Bezekirskii, *Iz zapisnoi knizhki,* 9–10. For Europe, see Young, *Concert Tradition,* 60–61, and Weber, *Music and the Middle Class,* 31.

46. Afanasev, "Vospominaniya," IV, 41(July 1890) 26–29. For Perm Province in this era, see Raab, "City of Perm." Gatsiskii, "Ulybyshev." Haydn's *Creation* is prominently featured in Ulybyshev's utopian vision of the future: see chapter 3 of the present work.

47. Shcherbakova, *Vielgorskie*, 34 (qu.); Wirtschafter, *Social Identity*, 21 (qu.).

48. See the argument for the salon as amateur infrastructure in Vienna: Kahn, *Cosmopolitan Culture*, 157.

49. RBS, 9:532–33; Vigel, *Zapiski*, 231–32; Kots, *Krepostnaya intelligentsiya*, 111; Malnick, "Russian Serf Theatres," 393–94; Livanova, *Glinka*, 1:29.

50. Dolgorukii, *Puteshestvie*, 86; IRDT, 3:158–59.

51. Lending musicians: Ivanov, "Vospominaniya," IV (Oct. 1891) 64–69, 73–76; Shchepkin story: Kots, *Krepostnaya intelligentsiya*, 125–26. Whatever the truth of this anecdote, it raises the issue of a perceived or imagined sexual menace from below. The subject of a love affair between a male serf and his master's wife made it into a play written after the emancipation, A. I. Sumbatov-Yuzhin's *Sergei Satilov* (1883): McReynolds, *Russia at Play*, 62. Some gentry women were known to use underlings sexually: Odessa grand ladies would sometimes bring back *cavalieri servanti* from their visits to Italy: Seletskii, "Zapiski," KS, 8 (Mar. 1884) 450–51.

52. Purlevskii, "Vospominaniya krepostnago"; advertisement reproduced in Kaiser, *Reinterpreting Russian History*, 295. Teachers: Kots, *Krepostnaya intelligentsiya*, 51, 106–8; Findeizen, *Ocherk*, 3–4; Albrekht, *Proshloe i nastoyashchee orkestra*, 37; Turgenev: PSS, 4:39 and 7:123–295; Kots, *Krepostnaya intelligentsiya*, 106–8; Karolina Pavlova, "At the Tea-Table," in Kelly, *Anthology*, 30–70.

53. Kropotkin, *Memoirs of a Revolutionist*, 22; Kots, *Krepostnaya intelligentsiya*, 92–97; Letkova, "Krepostnaya intelligentsiya," 172; Rybkin, *Generalissimus Suvorov*, 64; Raikes, *City of the Czar*, 1:203; the priest: [A. I. Rozanov], "Zapiski selskago svyashchennika," RS (Jan. 1880) 67; Afanasev, "Vospominaniya," IV, 41(July 1890) 38–40.

54. Glagoleva, "Dream and Reality of Russian Provincial Young Ladies," 51–52.

55. Sukhodolov, "Graf N. P. Sheremetev," 100. See Gronow, *Sociology of Taste*, 137.

56. Bezekirskii, *Iz zapisnoi knizhki*, 2; letter of Mikhail Vielgorsky to Aleksei Verstovskii: GTsTMRO, f. 53, n. 81. n.d. The magnate I. D. Shepelev, apparently an exception, treated his Russian professional conductor as a near equal: Afanasev, "Vospominaniya," IV, 41 (July 1890) 43. Panchulidze's orchestra: Gavril Gerakov, *Putevyya zapiski*, 36. In the 1830s, Panchulidze's ensemble passed to his son who took it to Penza where it lasted to the 1850s: Ya. K. Evdokimov, "Muzykalnoe proshloe Saratova (do 1917 goda)" in Shteinpress, *Iz muzykalnogo proshlogo*, 147.

57. Panaev's story, "Akteon," quoted by Ugo Persi, "Traektoriya russkoi muzykalnoi kultury (konets XVIII–pervaya polovina XIX v." in Belousov, *Russkaya provintsiya*, 66; Buturlin, "Zapiski," RA, 5–8 (1897) 42; Baryatinsky: Fëdorov, *Marino*, 70–74 and passim; "Knyaz kompozitor," 4; Galagan: Seletskii, "Zapiski," KS, 8 (Aug. 1884) 622–23.

58. The Tarnovsky estate formed the setting of Shevchenko's story "Muzykant": Shevchenko, *Povest*, 163, 201. Glinka had come to the region hunting voices for the Court Capella: Orlova, *Glinka's Life*, 192–205; *Pamyati Glinki*, 531–32; Roosevelt, *Russian Country Estate*, passim; Kots, *Krepostnaya intelligentsiya*, 30.

59. Burgess, "Russian Public Theatre Audiences," 168; Roosevelt, *Russian Country Estate*, 202–3; Shenig, "Vospominaniya," 303–6; Brown, *Glinka*, 21; Vinnitskii, "Razskazy"; Shcherbakova, *Vielgorskie*, 30–39.

60. Glagoleva, *Russkaya provintsialnaya starina,* 120 (with coverage of private orchestras also); Ruban, *Zabitye imena,* 27; Krylov cited in Kelly, *Refining Russia,* 70–71; Kots, *Krepostnaya intelligentsiya,* 103; Brown, *Glinka,* 143; Roosevelt, *Russian Country Estate,* 103; Buturlin, "Zapiski," RA, 5–8 (1897) 574–75.

61. Lomakin, "Avtobiograficheskiya zapiski," RS (Mar. 1886) 645–66; Kots, *Krepostnaya intelligentsiya,* 104–6; Nikitenko, *Diary,* introduction; idem, *Up from Serfdom,* 6–7.

62. Kuznetsov, *Iz istorii,* 67–70; Roosevelt, *Russian Country Estate,* 240, 284; Herzen's amusing account: *My Past,* 539–49. Golitsyn's father had commissioned quartets from Beethoven.

63. Muzalevskii, *Russkoe fortepyannoe iskusstvo,* 116; Kots, *Krepostnaya intelligentsiya,* 100–103; Afanasev, "Vospominaniya," IV, 41 (July 1890) 23–24 (on Dolgoruky); Boiledieu, *Le Calife de Bagdad.* Spohr even heard a horn band doing a Glück overture: *Musical Journeys,* 34. Mme. De Stael counted twenty horns in the Naryshkin band, whose players went by the names of the notes they played (do, re, fa, etc.): Henri Troyat, *Pushkin,* tr. N. Amphoux (New York, 1970) 7.

64. Passenens, *Russie et l'esclavage,* 2:3; Kelly, *Refining Russia,* 114 (Derzhavin); Brown, *Glinka,* 26 and n. 1.

65. Vrangel, "Arakcheev i iskusstvo"; Bugrov, *Svet kurskikh ramp,* 1:17.

66. Kots, *Krepostnaya intelligentsiya,* 110; Glagoleva, "Dream and Reality of Russian Provincial Young Ladies," 59; Letkova, "Krepostnaya intelligentsiya," 163–64; Romanovich-Slavatinskii, *Dvoryanstvo v Rossii,* 334–36.

67. Pylyaev, "Den Generalissimusa Suvorova" in *Staroe zhite,* 297–310; Roosevelt, *Russian Country Estate,* 146–47; Letkova, "Krepostnaya intelligentsiya," 171; Kots, *Krepostnaya intelligentsiya,* 96, 98, 110; Passenens, *Russie et l'esclavage,* 2:90; Bakarev, "Usadba nachala XIX v.," 257; "Knyaz kompozitor," 4 (Baryatinsky).

68. Kots, *Krepostnaya intelligentsiya,* 110.

69. I have found no verifiable details on Kashin's manumission. Simon Karlinsky claims he was freed because of a concert version of an opera by Sergei Glinka for Alexander I's coronation: *Russian Drama,* 191. See Hodge, *Double Garland,* passim, and chapter 3 of the present work; Fëdorovskaya, *Davydov,* passim. Fragments on his life in Muzalevskii, *Russkoe fortepyannoe iskusstvo,* 243–44; Stolpyanskii, *Muzyka,* 140–41; Norris, *Russian Piano Concerto* (1994), who calls him probably "the first true Russian nationalist" composer. A sample of his musical folk adaptation is "Variations on a Russian Theme" (GTsMMKF).

70. Shcherbakova, *Vielgorskie,* 40; Gozenpud, *Dom Engelgardta,* 157. Prince Alexander Kurakin, the brother of Alexei, was a member of the Petersburg Philharmonic Society: *Kratkii obzor,* see list of sponsors. Vielgorsky organized concerts to raise Semënov's redemption money: Sokolov, *Ryadom s Pushkinym,* 132.

71. Chemerovtsov: Kurmachëva, *Krepostnaya intelligentsiya,* 160, 341–42 (the deposition). Herzen's news item in *Kolokol* (Feb. 1, 1859) 280. Comment in Budaev, "Materialy"; Kots, *Krepostnaya intelligentsiya,* 41. The Vonlyarlyarskys (originally Von Lar-Lar) hailed from the Black Forest in Germany but had been Russianized for centuries. A descendant claimed that his ancestors had been benevolent landowners: Vonlyarlyarskii, *Moi vospominaniya.* The Kamensky story is from Melgunov, *Krepostnoe pravo,* 233–34,

unreferenced but attributed to "Count Delagard" who may have been one of the Franco-Swedish de la Gardie family (see an alternate version of the murder in chapter 6 of the present book). Elena Kots throughout her 1926 book relates sad cases of talent drowned in alcohol, serfs cheated out of promised freedom, and skilled musicians diverted to other labor.

72. Vodovozova, *Na zare zhizni,* 1:156–97. Vaska's wife, an educated housemaid, suffered similar reversals.

73. Mariya Nikoleva (one of Finogen's gentry pupils), "Cherty starinnago byta," 148–49; Kots, *Krepostnaya intelligentsiya,* 122–23, and 124–26 for a few more victim tales; Roosevelt, *Russian Country Estate,* 267.

74. Nikitenko, *Diary,* intro., 211–12 n. 2; idem, *Up from Serfdom,* 6–8 (qu. 6); ME, 2:182–83; Persi, "Traektoriya russkoi muzykalnoi kultury" in Belousov, *Russkaya provintsiya,* 68–69; Seaman, *History of Russian Music,* 72–73, 115–16; Vsevolodskii-Gerngross, *Teatr v Rossi,* 26; Shchepetov, *Iz zhizni krepostnykh krestyan,* 39.

75. On this painful issue, see Christian, *"Living Water".* Herzen, *My Past,* 213.

76. Tourgeneff, *Russie et les russes,* 1:147–53 (qu. 147); Confino, *Domaines et seigneurs,* 74, 86, 140. Vodovozova, *Na zare zhizni,* 1:162–63. On the problem of uneven education among serfs, Nikolai Nekrasov built his sad poem "On the Road" around a marriage between a humble coachman and an educated serving girl: Nekrasov, *Sobranie sochinenii,* 1:889–90. There was no parallel in the American antebellum slave culture to the serf orchestra or theater, although field hands and house slaves would sing or dance on occasion in the master's home: Tawa, *High-Minded and Low-Down,* 47, 191, and passim; Peter Kolchin, *Unfree Labor.*

77. Shchepkina, *Vospominaniya,* 21–26; Kropotkin, *Memoirs of a Revolutionist,* 44–45; Dolgorukii, *Puteshestvie,* 196–97.

78. Pavlov, *Imeniny.* The army-as-freedom theme is anticipated in Alexander Radishchev's famous antiserfdom travel notes: see "Gorodnya" in *Journey,* 201–12.

79. *Kompozitor Glinka.*

80. For the huge Soviet literature on Glinka, see Brown, *Glinka.* Church bells and composition: Lokhanskii, "Russkie kolokolnye zapevy." Glinka's sister reported that, after his European travels, he could never bear to behold the misery of serfdom on his own estate: Shestakova, "M. I. Glinka," 598.

81. Kann-Novikova, "Glinka na Smolenshchine," 213–34; Dobrokhotov, "Krestyane sela Novospasskogo o Glinke," 361–67. The sculptor Stepanov tells of a malicious rumor that Glinka's musical collaborator was his valet Yakov: [P. A. Stepanov], "Vospominaniya," 38–58.

82. Kann-Novikova, "Glinka na Smolenshchine"; Abraham, *On Russian Music,* 256. A fair-minded and informed discussion of "folk" influence can be found throughout Brown, *Glinka.* Alluding in print to the unquestionable influence of Mozart on Glinka could ruin a Soviet musicologist's career in Stalin's time: see Volkov, *St. Petersburg,* 65.

83. Alfimov, *Smoliane,* 353–60; Kann-Novikova, "Glinka na Smolenshchine"; Brown, *Glinka,* 31; Persi, "Traektoriya russkoi muzykalnoi kultury" in Belousov, *Russkaya provintsiya,* 68; Rimskii-Korsakov, "Iz vospominanii," 2:140–42.

84. Campbell, *Russians on Russian Music,* xiv. Ironically, Glinka's home province of Smolensk remained what some would call a backwater in terms of classical music. It had

no institutionalized concert life until well after Glinka's death and the emancipation of the serfs (the first Symphonic Society was founded there in 1909 by a cellist, Yuliya Saburova, and the future Soviet science fiction writer, Alexander Belyaev). Like most creative people, Glinka returned to the capital where he had gotten his schooling. It was the only place — outside Moscow — where his music could have a wide audience and influence over the musical culture of the time.

Chapter 3. In Search of a Concert Hall

1. Johnson, *Listening in Paris*, 216, 218 (qu.) and passim; idem, "Musical Experience," 191–226.

2. Quoted in Campbell, *Russians on Russian Music*, 39.

3. See Fradkina, *Zal Dvoryanskogo Sobraniya*, 40, 53–66, 80, and passim (qu. 54); Serov in MTV, 11 (Mar. 11, 1856) 201–2.

4. Adorno, *Sociology of Music*, 1–20; Fradkina, *Zal Dvoryanskogo Sobraniya*, 55–56. Cf. the similar pot-pourri musical performances in early nineteenth-century Lvov and Cracow cited in Pekacz, *Music in the Culture of Polish Galicia*. Quite a different and untypical impression of Philharmonia programming appeared on a live 1997 Russian television broadcast from the Great Hall in a recreation of an 1847 concert there: Haydn's Symphony No. 88, an aria from Mozart's *Clemenza di Tito*, Beethoven's Fantasy for Piano, Orchestra, and Chorus, a solo piano piece by Adolphe Henselt, and Mendelssohn's *Midsummer Night's Dream* overture: St. Peterburg TV, Nov. 25., 1997, with commentary and contemporary graphics.

5. At a Petersburg concert in March 1859, the young Nikolai Rimsky-Korsakov noted that the conductor declined the audience demand to repeat the scherzo from Mendelssohn's *Midsummer Night's Dream*: Rimskii-Korsakov, "Iz vospominanii," 2:145.

6. Arnold, *Vospominaniya*, 3:48–51. Lazarev-Lazareff caused similar scenes in Dresden and Berlin and later spent time in the Balkans where, he claimed, the insurgent Slavs offered him a tsar's crown: Arnold, 3:51–55.

7. For historical pictures, see *Leningradskaya . . . Filarmoniya*.

8. Láng, *Music in Western Civilization*, 721–23, 961–62, 970–72; Nettel, *Orchestra in England*, 73–111; Donakowski, *Muse for the Masses;* Weber, *Music and the Middle Class;* Young, *Concert Tradition*.

9. Findeizen *Ocherk*, 1–3; Stolpyanskii, *Muzyka*, 5–21, 103; Ward, *Moscow and Leningrad*, 2:143. Smith, *Working the Rough Stone*, 79, says that two of the musical clubs had hundreds of members.

10. Background: Soubies, *Histoire de la musique en Russie*, 37–60. Spohr, *Musical Journeys*, 34; Arnold, *Vospominaniya*, 1:22. For Karamzin's 1801 translation of the Haydn libretto, based on Milton and Genesis, see Baehr, *Paradise Myth*, 268 n. 77. See also Petrovskaya, *Muzykalnoe obrazovanie*, 296–97.

11. IRLPD, f. 50, n. 173: St. Petersburg Philharmonic Society letter to Mikhail Vielgorskii, May 1, 1852; Spohr, *Musical Journeys*, 34; Gozenpud, *Dom Engelgardta*, 21–28, on the impact of the *Creation* on Russian musicians; Johnson, *Listening in Paris*, for speculation about the Paris reception; *Kratkii obzor; Filarmonicheskoe Obshchestvo*, 1–5, a very admiring post-Soviet summary; and three useful surveys by violinist and presi-

dent of the Philharmonia, 1881–86, Evgenii Albrekht: *Obshchii obzor* (1884), *Obshchii obzor* (1902), and *Proshloe i nastoyashchee orkestra*.

Alexander Ulybyshev, in his utopian sketch "Dream" (1819), featured Haydn's *Creation* as the appropriate music to celebrate civic rectitude and social justice: the text in *Vzglyad skvozd stoletiya*, 91–99; tr. in Raeff, *Decembrist Movement*, 60–66. Commentary in Stites, *Revolutionary Dreams*, 25 and 260 n. 61.

12. The current name is the Glinka Small Hall, a branch of the St. Petersburg Philharmonia. Concert hall historical placards and program notes for a concert, December 1997; *Malyi zal; Sankt-Peterburg—Petrograd—Leningrad;* Ward, *Moscow and Leningrad,* 2:20; Kuznetsov, *Iz istorii,* 107n.

13. Albrekht, *Obshchii obzor* (1884); *Filarmonicheskoe Obshchestvo,* 6–67; Stolpyanskii, *Muzyka,* 22–24; Fradkina, *Zal Dvoryanskogo Sobraniya,* 7–16; Gozenpud, *Dom Engelgardta,* 232, passim; *Malyi zal; Sankt-Peterburg—Petrograd—Leningrad.* For the European difficulties in finding permanent concert space, see Kahn, *Cosmopolitan Culture,* 149.

14. Campbell, *Odoevsky,* 274; *Desyat let simfonicheskoi muzyki,* 3; Albrekht, *Obshchii obzor* (1884) 3–21; *Kratkii obzor; Findeizen, Ocherk;* ME, 1:450. The total list of 203 concerts from 1802 to 1902 shows that the Philharmonia did not increase its offerings after emancipation.

15. Stolpyanskii, *Muzyka,* 26; Gozenpud, *Dom Engelgardta,* 64; Arnold, *Vospominaniya,* passim.

16. IRLPD, f. 50, n. 166, membership certificate to the Society for Matvei Vielgorskii, Jan. 29, 1827; and n. 173, a letter to Mikhail Vielgorskii, May 1, 1852; Albrekht, *Obshchii obzor* (1884) 3–21; Gozenpud, *Dom Engelgardta,* 12: Arnold, *Vospominaniya,* 2:171. An absence report on the theater orchestra of 1859 contained one clearly Slavic name out of eleven: GTsTMRO, f. 222, n. 91a. Court musicians, at least in the time of Paul, were paid professionals, mostly Italian and French: RGALI, f. 872, op. 1, ed. kh. 54, N. P. Yusupov to Paul in 1798 on fees for the musicians playing at Pavlovsk, Gatchina, and Peterhof.

17. Riasanovsky, *Image of Peter the Great,* 65.

18. Tawa, *High-Minded and Low-Down,* 125; Blaukopf, *Musical Life in a Changing Society,* qu. 203; Kahn, *Cosmopolitan Culture,* passim.

19. The most reliable study is Dunlop, *Russian Court Chapel Choir;* Ershov, *Stareishii russkii khor;* Kazachkov, "Dva stilya," 82–83. The Capella's 1790s concerts offered the works of Sarti, the court conductor; and Haydn, Mozart, Handel, Gossec, and Pergolesi: Fëdorovskaya, *Kompozitor Stepan Davydov;* Campbell, *Odoevsky,* 359 (qu.).

20. Barbier, *World of the Castrati;* Ruban, *Zabitye imena,* 27; ME, 3:239–40; Listova, *Varlamov,* 8–14; Lincoln, *Between Heaven and Hell,* 96.

21. *Russkie kompozitory,* 36–42; Dunlop, *Russian Court Chapel Choir,* 5–15, 109–18, passim; Ward, *Moscow and Leningrad,* 2:147, 255.

22. Dunlop, *Russian Court Chapel Choir,* 15–26, 114–18; *Aleksei Fëdorovich Lvov,* 25 (Berlioz qu.); Bers, "Lvov"; Kazachkov, "Dva stilya," 82–83. In 1839, the Marquis de Custine was powerfully impressed by the Capella's control of dynamics, its deep emotion, and its "nuances of expression": Custine, *Letters from Russia,* 67.

23. V. Bogdanov-Berëzovskii's introduction to Glinka, *Zapiski,* 1–20 (qu. 11). Sol-

logub, *Peterburgskie stranitsy,* 292–93, saw Glinka's appointment as a humiliation. Dunlop, *Russian Court Chapel Choir,* 93. See also Ugo Persi, "Traektoriya russkoi muzykalnoi kultury" in Belousov, *Russkaya provintsiya,* 69–70.

24. *Kratkii istoricheskii ocherk ... Patrioticheskago Obshchestva; Pyatidesyatiletie ... Patrioticheskago Zhenskago Obshchestva;* Lindenmeyr, *Poverty Is Not a Vice,* 111. Program of 1837 with names of performers in GTsTMRO, f. 53, n. 461; Shalikov in *Damskii zhurnal,* 5 (May, 1823) 210. Sontag, retired from the stage after her marriage to a titled Italian diplomat, could no longer sing to ticketed audiences.

25. Panaeva, *Vospominaniya,* 68; Ridenour, *Nationalism,* 11; Stolpyanskii, *Muzyka,* 37.

26. Nikoltsev, "Iz istorii," 110–35; Olkhovskii, *Peterburgskie istorii,* 160–69. On student life, Whittaker, *Origins of Modern Russian Education,* 174–76. Schuberth: Campbell, *Great Cellists;* Rubinstein, *Autobiography,* 58. By some accounts, Schuberth was the first Russian conductor to face the orchestra, but the singer I. A. Melnikov recalls seeing Schuberth facing the audience and flapping his arms up and down like a bird: Melnikov, "Zapiski," RS, 137 (Jan. 1909) 63–64. Rubinstein is said to have stood sideways.

27. Ilin, "Borodin," 340 and passim; Paskhalov, *Rubinshtein;* Barenboim, *Rubinshtein,* 1:139.

28. Egorov, "Reaktsionnaya politika tsarizma." Flynn, *University Reform,* 204, says that many of the gentry majority were poor until the mid-1830s, after which rich and aristocratic students appeared.

29. Data on the Symphonic Society conflict: *Moskovskaya Konservatoriya,* 12; Shcherbakova, *Vielgorskie,* 69–82; ME, 5:21. In the above-cited letter to Mikhail Vielgorsky of May 1, 1852, the Philharmonic Society thanked him for many years of "la haute protection": IRLPD, f. 50, n. 173. Matvei: Ginzburg, *Russkoe violonchelnoe iskusstvo,* 278–330; IRLPD, f. 50, n. 125 (Cécile Cherubini to Matvei Vielgorskii, May 18, 1842) and No. 134 (Pauline Viardot to Matvei Vielgorskii, 1845–52); Campbell, *Great Cellists.*

30. Lunin cited in Eidelman, *Conspiracy,* 14; Shteinpress, "Matvei Yurevich Vielgorskii"; Shcherbakova, *Vielgorskie,* 69–82; Ginzburg, *Russkoe violonchelnoe iskusstvo,* 278–330. The *Theme and Variations* performed on radio in 1965 by Svyatoslav Knushevitsky and Naum Valter: GTsMMKF.

31. Bers, "Lvov," 146–47, 166; record jacket notes for Lvov, *Violin Concerto,* SPBKF; Gozenpud, *Dom Engelgardta,* 172.

32. The Lvov concerto, *Concert dans le mode d'une scène dramatique* (1840), is played by Sergei Stadler with Vladislav Chernushenko and the Leningrad Philharmonia on *A. Lvov; A. Arenskii* (SPBKF). The "rediscovery" recalls the 1950s revival of the Hungarian Carl Goldmark's violin concerto which, though written in a different era, it resembles in places. The Lvov work was long known to Soviet musicians; the date of the recording (1987) suggests that it was an offshoot of glasnost. See Rosen, *Romantic Generation,* 590–94, for religious kitsch.

33. Shtakelberg, "Russkii narodnyi gimn"; *Aleksei Fëdorovich Lvov,* 3–14; Bers, "Lvov," 146–47; Krutov, *Bozhe, tsarya khrani;* Wortman, *Scenarios of Power,* 1:389–90.

34. *Aleksei Fëdorovich Lvov,* 3–14 (qu. 11).

35. Albrekht, *Obshchii obzor* (1884) xi (qu.); Ridenour, *Nationalism*, 10; *Moskov-skaya Konservatoriya*, 13; Dunlop, *Russian Court Chapel Choir*, 91; Bers, "Lvov," 156–57; *Filarmonicheskoe Obshchestvo*, 6–7.

36. Journal survey in Hodge, *Double Garland*, 16–17. Kozlovsky dance pieces performed by V. Kornachev and the Vladimir Chamber Ensemble: GTsMMKF, also released on Melodiya S-90 20665 001 (1990). Two of his aria-like songs, "A Cruel Fate" and "Little Bee," display a wide range of moods (performed by Evgeniya Martynovskaya). Kozlovsky set Derzhavin's "Let the Thunder of Victory be Heard," a semiofficial anthem until Lvov's "God Save the Tsar": Boris Gasparov, personal communication.

37. Zhilin's "Waltz" performed by S. Ponyatovskii, viola, and T. Sergeeva, piano; his "Kak na dubochke dva golubtsy" on piano by Dmitrii Blagoi: GTsMMKF. See also Muzalevskii, *Russkoe fortepyannoe iskusstvo*, 91–97; Nikolaev, *Dzhon Fild*, 13–22, 140–43.

38. Cornwell, *Odoevsky*, 138, 144 (qu.), 158; Bernandt, "Odoevskii"; Campbell, *Russians on Russian Music*, 47–53. See Odoevskii, *Muzykalno-literaturnoe nasledie*, 88–102, for a sampling of his reviews and comments. On musical hierarchy: Weber, *Music and the Middle Class*, for Europe; Levine, *Highbrow/Lowbrow*, for the United States. For British sensitivity to imported music, see Young, *Concert Tradition*, 172–74.

39. Lichtenfeld, "Triviale und anspruchsvolle Musik"; Ridenour, *Nationalism*, 5–24; Pylyaev, *Zabytoe proshloe*, 497; Rozanov, *Muzykalnyi Pavlovsk*, 47–57; Campbell, *Russians on Russian Music*, 42–43; TE, 3:857; Cornwell, *Odoevsky*, 141, 334 n. 94; Ward, *Moscow and Leningrad*, 2:154, 253; Gerald Seaman, "Moscow and St Petersburg," 255 (the press).

40. Natanson, *Iz muzykalnogo proshlogo*, 38–120; Andreev, *Moskovskii Universitet*, 69, 75, 108–9. For another school concert site, see Medvedev, "Dnevnik," 119–20.

41. Verstovskii, "Avtobiografiya"; Hodge, *Double Garland*, 208; GTsTMRO, f. 53, n. 463; Shtakelberg, "Russkii narodnyi gimn." Verstovsky also conducted at a short-lived Moscow Musical Assembly in 1834: *Moskovskaya Konservatoriya*, 19. Monster concerts: Mikhnevich, *Ocherk*, 340.

42. GTsTMRO, f. 53, n. 73, 77, 81, 188–94, 244; GTsTMRO, f. 222, unnumbered; IRLPD, f. 50, n. 130.

43. Bezekirskii, *Iz zapisnoi knizhki*, 1–15. Other details in GTsTMRO, f. 24. I have seen only one of Bezekirsky's scores, a coronation march in B major for orchestra marked by a predictable gambit: one measure of trombone and tuba, the melodic line repeated in a measure of horns, followed by one of trumpets, and then strings and winds into a tutti: score in GTsMMKRO, f. 170, inv. 3, n. 4821.

44. Buturlin, "Zapiski," RA, 9–10 (1897) 257. One of many instances of stretching the concept of public performance by aristocrats was a Moscow charity concert of 1840 or 1841 at the Gentry Club with amateur performers and the Bolshoi Theater orchestra doing opera excerpts: ibid., 259–60.

45. Ginzburg, *Anri Vetan*, 57–60; Katski's reports to Verstovsky in 1850–54 in GTsTMRO, f. 53, n. 188–94; Wieniawski's for Feb. 2, 1858, GTsTMRO, f. 53, n. 66; Reiss, *Wieniawski*, 40–41 (for Liszt, see below, notes 67–71); Afanasev, "Vospomina-niya," IV, 41 (Aug. 1890) 255–76.

46. Bezekirskii, *Iz zapisnoi knizhki,* 15–18; Glagoleva, *Russkaya provintsialnaya starina,* 123–24; Bugrov, *Svet kurskikh ramp,* 2:20–25; Natanson, *Iz muzykalnogo proshlogo,* 35–37 (Uglich); *Panteon,* (1852) 7 (Kostroma); Vorontsov, "Muzyka," 460–80.

47. Ya. K. Evdokimov, "Muzykalnoe proshloe Saratova" in Shteinpress, *Iz muzykalnogo proshlogo,* 148–53.

48. *Damskii zhurnal,* 5 (Jan. 1833) 75–77; Lincoln, *Conquest of a Continent,* 147–48 (Irkutsk); GTsMMKRO, f. 40, d. 264 (Tobolsk); Shteinpress, "Muzyka v Orenburge 125 let nazad" in Shteinpress, *Iz muzykalnogo proshlogo,* 125–42; Skonechnaya, *Moskovskii Parnas,* 58–59.

49. Hamm, *Kiev,* 145; Insarskii, *Zapiski,* 73–74 (Taganrog); Wieniawski to Verstovskii, Feb. 2, 1858, GTsTMRO, f. 53, n. 66; Reiss, *Wieniawski,* 41.

50. Belyakov, *Opernaya i kontsertnaya deyatelnost,* 179–86; Smirnov, *Nizhegorodskaya starina,* 434–37; Gatsiskii, *Nizhegorodskii teatr,* 46–53; Boborykin, *Vospominaniya,* 1:101–2; Rimsky-Korsakov, *My Musical Life,* 29; Fitzpatrick, *Great Russian Fair,* 178.

51. Program: GTsMMKRO, f. 40, d. 264. For Alyabev's instrumental work see Dobrokhotov, *Alyabev: kamerno-instrumentalnoe tvorchestvo;* Seletskii, "Zapiski," KS, 8 (Mar. 1884) 449–50, 453. Bezekirskii, *Iz zapisnoi knizhki,* 17; Katsanov, "Iz istorii muzykalnoi kultury Odessy (1794–1855)" in Shteinpress, *Iz muzykalnogo proshlogo,* 393–459 (430–31 on Gold). See Milstein, *From Russia to the West.*

52. Coldicott, "Performance Practice in Beethoven's Day," 87–91; Lichtenfeld, "Triviale und anspruchsvolle Musik"; Weber, *Music and the Middle Class,* 16–22 (qu. 22), 51, passim.

53. Sennett, *Fall of Public Man,* 200; for the popularity of virtuosos in Vienna, see Kahn, *Cosmopolitan Culture,* 150; Weber, *Music and the Middle Class.*

54. Shcherbakova, *Vielgorskie;* Skonechnaya, *Moskovskii Parnas,* 138–46; Lindenmeyr, *Poverty Is Not a Vice,* 116–18.

55. An errant French utopian socialist, Dominique Tajan-Rogé, who played cello at the Petersburg opera in 1836–48, moonlighted in the salons where he "was paid poorly in rubles and generously in rudeness": Locke, *Music, Musicians, and the Saint-Simonians,* 220.

56. Piggott, *John Field,* chaps. 3–7 (see esp. pp. 28, 41, 97); Nikolaev, *Dzhon Fild,* 1–70; Muzalevskii, *Russkoe fortepyannoe iskusstvo,* 86, 104–13; Natanson, *Iz muzykalnogo proshlogo,* 68–69; Kuznetsov, *Glinka,* 3–8; Norris, *Russian Piano Concerto,* 10–16.

57. Nikolaev, *Dzhon Fild,* 69.

58. Musical analysis in Piggott, *John Field,* chaps. 12–20; Hudson, *Stolen Time,* 199–211; Kallberg, *Chopin at the Boundaries.* Meyerhold: Golub, *Recurrence of Fate,* 138. Ten nocturnes by Field: Svetlana Potanina, piano, 1979: GTsMMKF. The music of Chopin, an active anti-Russian émigré, was not banned in Russia; sheet music circulated and critiques of performances of his music appeared under Nicholas I: Swartz, "Chopin as Modernist."

59. Belza, *Shimanovskaya,* 3–124.

60. Taylor, *Schumann,* 230–31; Stasov, *Selected Essays,* 142–46.

61. Haugen, *Ole Bull,* 58 (qu.), 74, 148; Linge, *Ole Bull,* 102–3; Schwarz, *Great*

Masters, 226 (qu.), 231–32; Herresthal, *Norwegische Musik,* 17–18; Stolpyanskii, *Muzyka,* 63–64.

62. Ginzburg, *Anri Vetan,* 19–42; Vieuxtemps-Verstovskii, letters of Feb. 17 and 24, 1848: GTsTMRO, f. 53, n. 92, 93; Bergmans, *Henry Vieuxtemps,* qu. 19; Kufferath, *Henri Vieuxtemps;* Radoux, *Vieuxtemps.*

63. Schwarz, *Great Masters,* 226; Reiss, *Wieniawski;* Duleba, *Wieniawski,* 38–43, 59–69, 150–53, and passim, with clippings and priceless illustrations. His *Souvenir: is on Vospominanie o Moskve,* SPBKF.

64. Bezekirskii, *Iz zapisnoi knizhki,* 7–8. The episode is not mentioned in the Russian or Polish biographies I have seen. Another virtuoso worthy of note, the Belgian cellist Adrien-François Servais (1807–66), called by Berlioz "the Paganini of the 'cello," made six concert tours in Russia from 1839 until his death, playing in small villages as well as large urban centers. He was lauded by, among others Odoevsky and Nicholas I: liner notes by Kenneth Slowik to the CD: *Servais: Souvenirs & Caprices.*

65. Gozenpud, *Dom Engelgardta,* 224–29; Stolpyanskii, *Muzyka,* 68–69; Holoman, *Berlioz,* 383–89; Cornwell, *Odoevsky,* 151–53; Stasov, *Selected Essays,* 146 n. 2.

66. Berlioz, *Autobiography,* 2:257–89 (270 for the Moscow events); undated letter from Berlioz to Verstovsky: GTsTMRO, f. 53, n. 32; Fradkina, *Zal Dvoryanskogo Sobraniya,* 15.

67. Walker, *Liszt,* 1:286 n. 3, 374–77; Taylor, *Liszt,* 81–82; Nikitenko, *Diary,* 86; Stasov, *Selected Essays,* 121 (qu.), 122.

68. Senelick, *National Theater,* 353; Ivanov, "List v Rossii," unidentified clip in GTsMMKRO, f. 364, inv. 223, n. 8871.

69. Weilguny, *Liszt,* pl. 103; Walker, *Liszt,* 378.

70. Anecdotes: Taylor, *Liszt,* p. 83; Walker, *Liszt,* 378. Two years later, in 1849, those troops put down the Hungarian revolution. Liszt also spoke out for Polish independence, though not in the tsar's presence.

71. Metzner, *Crescendo of the Virtuoso,* 292 (for Liszt, see pp. 136–59).

72. The theme of the musical demon was well established in European fiction. In Dostoevsky's bizarre tale, the mad violinist admires Kukolnik and detests "foreign prodigies," who he claims are all "Jews running after Russian money": Dostoevsky, "Netotchka Nezvanova" in *The Friend of the Family,* 206–358. See Herzen, *My Past,* 99. In M. L. Mikhailov's "The Violinist" (1853), the son of a serf, an obsessed musician, tries to steal the superior violin of a visiting nobleman and destroys it instead: "Skripach" in *Sochineniya* (1915) 2:131–50.

73. On the discordant images of Russia in this age, see Malia, *Russia Under Western Eyes;* and Goldfrank, *Origins of the Crimean War.*

74. "Liszt, Schumann and Berlioz in Russia" in Stasov, *Selected Essays,* 117–42 (qu. 121).

75. Leppert, "Cultural Control" (Schumann qu. 265); Blanning, *Culture of Power,* 10. I have not been able to include the impact of visiting opera singers and ballerinas, for which see: Buckler, *Literary Lorgnette;* and Taruskin, "Italyanshchina" in *Defining Russia Musically,* 186–235.

76. Johnson, *Listening in Paris,* 263.

77. For a survey of child prodigy performers in Russia, see Stolpyanskii, *Muzyka,* 94–98, and throughout Shteinpress, *Iz muzykalnogo proshlogo.*

78. The "Melody," overplayed for decades, was demoted to semiclassical status by the canon-makers, along with Rachmaninov's Prelude in C sharp minor and Sibelius' "Valse triste." "Zhelanie" ("If This is but a Dream") often shared billing with "Donkey Serenade," and "Ah, Sweet Mystery of Life" in American radio concerts. Recordings of Rubinstein, some not easily available elsewhere, are stored in SPBKF and include "Barcarole" (1853), "Pevets" (1849–50), "Noch" (1852), "Zhelanie" (1850), and "Romans-Melodiya." A revealing contrast between the skills of Glinka and Rubinstein at adapting folk themes are the former's *Kamarinskaya* and the latter's *Russkaya* (SPBKF), an orchestral excursion into folk dance rhythms and melody.

79. RNBRO, f. 654, A. G. Rubinshtein, opis 1, ed. kh. 1, a copy of the baptismal certificate at the Nikolskaya Church in Berdichev, June 28, 1831; Rubinstein, *Autobiography*, 1–5; Bowen, *"Free Artist,"* 3. For the milieu: Stanislawsky, *Tsar Nicholas I and the Jews*; Klier, *Russia Gathers Her Jews*. The best biography, dating from the time of Khrushchev, is Barenboim's *Rubinshtein*, a magisterial work based on international archives and a huge source base, though understandably reticent on the Jewish issue, overly negative on Grand Duchess Elena Pavlovna, and somewhat unfair to the musical contribution of aristocratic patrons and amateurs. I have chiefly relied on it for the facts (family background, 1:3–17). Findeizen, *Rubinshtein*, the first serious biography, is occasionally patronizing on Rubinstein's Jewish origins but contains important details. Paskhalov, *Rubinshtein*, is a lighter treatment. The previously cited *Autobiography* is only moderately self-revealing; Barenboim appends the original in vol. 1 of his work, pp. 397–421.

80. Barenboim, *Rubinshtein*, 1:17–27.

81. RNBRO, f. 654, A. G. Rubinshtein, opis 1, ed. kh. 4: notes on first Moscow recital, 11 July, 1839; Findeizen, *Rubinshtein*, 9; Natanson, *Iz muzykalnogo proshlogo*, 100; Barenboim, *Rubinshtein*, 1:28–83; Rubinstein, *Autobiography*, 40–55.

82. Lincoln, *Vanguard of Reform*, 148–62; idem, "Circle of Grand Duchess Yelena Pavlovna"; Barenboim, *Rubinshtein*, 1:84–291. Karl Bryullov's brilliant portrait, *Elena Pavlovna and Daughter* (1830), hangs in the Russian Museum.

83. Matvei Vielgorsky wrote to Rubinstein calling him a "first-class talent," fully deserving the appointment to the court: RNBRO, f. 142, ed. kh. 125; Shcherbakova, *Vielgorskie*, 83; Barenboim, *Rubinshtein*, 1:84–160; Rubinstein, *Autobiography*, 61–2; *Muzyka v XIX veke*, 26–28.

84. Barenboim, *Rubinshtein*, 1:87, 161–219 (Glinka qu., 183–84). The unexpurgated letter to V. P. Engelhardt, Nov. 27, 1855 in Glinka, *Polnoe sobranie pisem*, 465–66 (qu. 466). Sometime at midcentury, the word *evrei* replaced *zhid* as the neutral term and the latter became a slur (Boris Gasparov, personal communication), though it is not clear when that happened and how different kinds of people used the words. Soviet scholars avoided staining the reputation of sacrosanct Russian cultural figures, many of whom were anti-Semitic in a rather routine way. The numerous Soviet Jewish musicologists were probably happy to avoid the vexing Jewish issue in Russian and Soviet life and culture altogether. See also Rubinstein, *Autobiography*, 77; Norris, *Russian Piano Concerto*, 21–53 (p. 36); and Olkhovsky, *Stasov*, 86. In any case, the memory of the Rubinstein brothers suffered no opprobrium even in the worst years of Soviet anti-Semitism, c. 1948–1953.

85. Rubinstein, *Autobiography*, 81–83; Barenboim, *Rubinshtein*, 1:161–219; Findeizen, *Rubinshtein*, 43–47.

Chapter 4. Inside the Capital Stages

1. Senelick, "Theatre," 264. See the documents illuminating these developments in Senelick, *National Theater*.

2. Senelick, "Theatre," 265; Wortman, *Scenarios of Power*, 1:181–92; Baehr, *Paradise Myth*; Custine, *Letters from Russia*, 73.

3. Borovsky, "Organization of the Russian Theatre" in Leach, *History of Russian Theatre*, 41–56; Drizen, *Materialy*; idem, *Stoletie Imperatorskikh Sanktpeterburgskikh Teatrov*. Varneke, *Istoriya*, 1–117, still remains useful. An inferior translation, *History*, contains material not in the other work. I have consulted both. See also *F. G. Volkov*; Yartsev, *Osnovanie i osnovatel russkago teatra*; and Vsevolodskii-Gerngross, *Istoriya teatralnago obrazovaniya*, 1.

4. Bocharnikova, *Bolshoi teatr*, 4–6; Kuznetsova, *Bolshoi teatr*, 10–29; Starikova, *Teatralnaya zhizn starinnoi Moskvy*; Zagoskin, "Kontsert besov"; Blagovo, *Razskazy babushki*, 205; Seaman, "Moscow and St. Petersburg." A mockup of the Petrovsky and its rotunda is displayed at the Bakhrushin Theater Museum in Moscow. Lo Gatto, *Storia del teatro russo*, 1:135, apparently believed Maddox's story that he was once an Oxford professor of mathematics. For a fine summary of the complex eighteenth-century theatrical scene, see Wirtschafter, *Play of Ideas*, 2–28.

5. TE, 3:762, 646 — both entries by the prolific popularizer of circus and theater history Yu. Dmitriev; Varneke, *Istoriya*, 106, 127, 316; Senelick, *National Theater*, 318.

6. The most reliable guide to the houses of St. Petersburg is Petrovskaya, *Teatralnyi Peterburg*, 71, 81–85, 100–121. See also "Zdanie teatralnoe," TE, 2:767–79, with excellent floor plans; and the beautifully illustrated Taranovskaya, *Arkhitektura teatrov Leningrada*, 57–112.

7. Petrovskaya, *Teatralnyi Peterburg*, 125–26, 151–55. Observations of the backstage based on my tour of the Alexandrinsky Theater in April 2002.

8. Raikes, *City of the Czar*, 1:104; Haumant, *Culture française en Russie*, 347–51.

9. Kuznetsova, *Bolshoi teatr*, 35; Varneke, *Istoriya*, 316–17; Blagovo, *Razskazy babushki*, 206; TE, 1:642; Burgess, "Russian Public Theatre Audiences," 169.

10. Bocharnikova, *Bolshoi teatr*, 6; Kuznetsova, *Bolshoi teatr*, 45–54; Chayanova, *Torzhestvo muz*; Shteinpress, *Alyabev*, 127–32; Zarubin, *Bolshoi Teatr*, 36–37. GTsMMKF: a recording of Alyabev's portion of the "Prolog" (1825) by the All-Union Radio Chorus and Orchestra. I have not heard Verstovsky's musical contribution.

11. *Istoricheskaya spravka o Bolshom Teatre*; Edwards, *Russians at Home*, 164, 178–86 (qu. 181).

12. *Gosudarstvennyi Akademicheskii Malyi Teatr*, a brief official introduction; *Istoricheskaya spravka o Bolshom Teatre*. Observations of the backstage based on my tour of the Maly Theater in December 1997.

13. TE, 1:447; Vsevolodskii-Gerngross, *Teatr v Rossii*, 40; Taneev, "Iz proshlogo imperatorskikh teatrov," 851.

14. Mikhnevich, *Ocherk,* 308–10; Vsevolodskii-Gerngross, *Teatr v Rossii,* 31–38; Roosevelt, *Russian Country Estate,* 263.

15. Buturlin, "Zapiski," RA, 1–4 (1897) 437 and note (qu); Vsevolodskii-Gerngross, *Teatr v Rossii,* 36–38; R. M. Zotov, "Zapiski," IV (July 1896), 26–50.

16. Panaeva, *Vospominaniya,* 18, 63, passim; Bezekirskii, *Iz zapisnoi knizhki,* 13–15; Afanasev, "Vospominaniya," IV, 41 (Aug. 1890) 271–72. The singer Darya Leonova echoed Afanasev's opinion: "Vospominaniya artistki," IV (Jan. 1891) 132.

17. Ungurianu, "Zagoskin," 344–55. Dates differ on Verstovsky's appointments: see Listova, *Varlamov,* 25; Verstovskii, "Avtobiografiya," a useful but self-promoting account; "A. N. Verstovskii"; Dobrokhotov, *Verstovskii,* 13–24; Levashëva, "A. N. Verstovskii"; RGBRO, f. 411, n. 95 (promotion certificate). V. Drezen's painting in GTsMMKRO, f. 364, op. 218, n. 8871.

18. Dobrokhotov, *Verstovskii,* 13–24; Afanasev, "Vospominaniya," IV, 41 (July 1890) 37; Shteinpress, *Stranitsy,* passim; Ivanov, "Vospominaniya," IV (Dec. 1891) 326.

19. Senelick, *National Theater,* 352; RGBRO, f. 411, n. 333, 415, 421; GTsMMKRO, f. 364, inv. 218, n. 41 and 42. Part of this record was published in "Perepiska A. N. Verstovskago s A. M. Gedeonovym" in EIT, 2 (1913) 33–55.

20. Opochnin, *Teatralnaya starina,* 149–86; Pogozhev, *Stoletie organizatsii,* 1/1:133–4, 313–16; Roosevelt, *Russian Country Estate,* 263–65; Kuznetsov, *Iz istorii,* 67–68; Dynnik, *Krepostnoi teatr,* 68–75.

21. Wesling, *Napoleon,* 1.

22. Vsevolodskii-Gerngross, *Istoriya teatralnago obrazovaniya,* 443–52, found data on social origins for only nine of about 150 to 160 pupils at the Imperial Theater School from 1783 to 1800: children of performers, townspeople, a clerk, a servant, and a "Tula musician." On foundlings in Russia, see Ransel, *Mothers of Misery,* 31–62. Empress Maria Fëdorovna cut back on the cultural training of foundlings after 1797; consequently, their recruitment probably fell off. See Rosslyn, "Female Employees in the Russian Imperial Theatres," for an informative account of the social background of eighteenth-century actresses. See also Martorella, *Sociology of Opera,* 16.

23. Opochnin, *Teatralnaya starina,* 149–86: Drizen, *Materialy,* 222–26; Muzalevskii, *Russkoe fortepyannoe iskusstvo,* 234–35; Kots, *Krepostnaya intelligentsiya,* 99; Albrekht, *Proshloe i nastoyashchee orkestra,* 37–62; Listova, *Varlamov,* 19–51 (qu. 19); Afanasev, "Vospominaniya," IV, 41 (July 1890) 36–37 and (Aug. 1890) 272.

24. Senelick, *National Theater,* 359; Grossman, *Pushkin,* 24; Ozarovskii, "Khram Talii i Melpomeny," 516–17; Levitt, "Illegal Staging of Sumarokov's *Sinav i Truvor.*" The best discussion of authorial identities is in Wirtschafter, *Play of Ideas,* 36–47.

25. EO, 2:85; Swift, *Loftier Flight;* Grossman, *Pushkin,* 98–131; Panaeva, *Vospominaniya,* 35; Zotov, cited by Adamson, "Russian Imperial Ballet," 184; R. M. Zotov, "Zapiski," IV (Nov. 1896) 402, 422. For Didelot's creative side, see Slonimskii, *Didlo.*

26. Ch. Didelot, "Observations, demandes, et réglements relatifs à la danse," Mar. 22, 28, 31, 1828, in IRLPD, f. 50, Vielgorskie, ed. kh. 19.

27. Volkov, *St. Petersburg,* 64; Arnold, *Vospominaniya,* 2:128–30. Another son of Cavos conducted a St. Petersburg orchestra: Soubies, *Histoire de la musique en Russie,* 64–65.

28. Malnick, "Shakhovskoi," qu. 37, 51; Rak, "Shakhovskoi"; Karlinsky, *Russian Drama,* 228–49.

29. Vsevolodskii-Gerngross, *Teatr v Rossii*, 40.

30. A. V. Karatygin, "Russkii teatr v tsarstvovanie Aleksandra I," 258; Panaeva, *Vospominaniya*, 23–24, 62, 76; Bezekirskii, *Iz zapisnoi knizhki*, 24; Afanasev, "Vospominaniya," IV, 41 (July 1890) 40; Varneke, *Istoriya*, 421–22.

31. Opochnin, *Teatralnaya starina*, 34–73; Nikitenko, *Diary*, 28 and passim; Panaeva, *Vospominaniya*, 23–24, 36, 76; Vsevolodskii-Gerngross, *Teatr v Rossii*, 106–7; Burdin, "Vospominaniya artista," 145; Grossman, *Pushkin*, 10, 49; R. M. Zotov, "Zapiski," IV (Nov. 1896) 412–16; Kubasov, "Teatralnyya intrigi," 293–96.

32. Buckler, *Literary Lorgnette*, 71; Panaeva, *Vospominaniya*, 52–55, 76; Varneke, *Istoriya*, 305; Grossman, *Pushkin*, 50–52.

33. Panaeva, *Vospominaniya*, 26, 37, 57–58. Panaeva's novel, co-authored with her lover Nekrasov, *Dead Lake* (1851), describes backstage jealousies and rivalries: see Ruth Sobel's piece on Panaeva in Tomei, *Russian Women Writers*, 1:299–304. Albrekht, *Proshloe i nastoyashchee orkestra*, 43–44; Afanasev, "Vospominaniya," IV, 41 (July 1890) 37 and (Aug. 1890) 272; Yurkevich, "Iz vospominanii," 171–72; R. M. Zotov, "Zapiski," IV (Aug. 1896) 320–21.

34. The opera house in seventeenth-century France was popularly known as the "academy of love": Blanning, *Culture of Power*, 81. Opochnin, *Teatralnaya starina*, 94–112; Malnick, "Shakhovskoi," 33; R. M. Zotov, "Zapiski," IV (July 1896) 47–48 and (Aug. 1896) 313. See also Senelick, "Erotic Bondage," 25; and Rosslyn, "Petersburg Actresses."

35. Grossman, *Pushkin*, 10 (qu.), 54; Dobrolyubov, "Razvrat Nikolaya Pavlovicha," 64–68. Rafail Zotov tells that the tsar regularly went backstage between the acts to talk to actresses, but is mute on any other relations: "Zapiski," IV (Aug. 1896) 319.

36. Panaeva, *Vospominaniya*, 38–44, 47. Rafail Zotov claimed that the Miloradovich-Telesheva affair was platonic: "Zapiski," IV (July 1896) 39. See Rak, "Shakhovskoi," for a slightly different view. In 1828, Orest Kiprensky painted her portrait and adorned it with symbols of national simplicity, religion, and purity: Gray, *Russian Genre Painting*, 79 and n. 34, fig. 11. For continuing amorous ballet liaisons in the twentieth century, see Frame, *St. Petersburg Imperial Theaters*, 105.

A celebrated duel originated in a theatrical liaison. Avdotiya Istomina (1799–1848), dance soloist at the St. Petersburg Bolshoi Stone, had by 1817 become an object of jealousy. After a spat with her lover Vasily Sheremetev, she went off to visit Griboedov, a fervent admirer, and his friend A. P. Zavadovsky. Out of this incident, a four-way duel ensued in which Zavadovsky killed the jealous Sheremetev, the "injured" party and challenger. The second part, between A. I. Yakubovich and Griboedov, took place in Tiflis months later. Yakubovich's bullet struck Griboedov in the hand — done purposely, some said, in order to ruin his piano playing: Grossman, *Pushkin*, 54–60; Reyfman, *Ritualized Violence Russian Style*, 77–78; Kelly, *Diplomacy and Murder in Teheran*. Ironically, Istomina became a patron herself when as an older woman, she tried to promote her young lover: Panaeva, *Vospominaniya*, 40–42.

37. R. M. Zotov, "Zapiski," IV (Oct. 1896) 38; Vsevolodskii-Gerngross, *Teatr v Rossii*, 138, misquotes Zotov's two hundred figure as twenty. In fact some of the weaker Russian ballet graduates ended up in the provinces. Karsavina, *Theatre Street*.

38. A. E. Asenkova, "Kartiny proshedshago: zapiski russkoi artistki." See also Varneke, *Istoriya*, 140–42; R. M. Zotov, "Zapiski," IV (Oct. 1896) 39. For a vividly contras-

tive picture of life in a military school, see Krylov, "Kadety sorokovykh godov," 943–47. The Moscow Theater school admitted serfs as external pupils — a practice unknown in St. Petersburg — into the 1840s: Medvedev, *Vospominaniya,* 38.

39. Panaeva, *Vospominaniya,* 47–48, 56–57, 66–67; Natarova, "Recollections" in Wiley, *Century of Russian Ballet,* 135–69; V. R. Zotov, "Peterburg v sorokovykh godakh," IV (Jan. 1890) 48–49; Insarskii, "Vospominaniya," 303–14; R. M. Zotov, "Zapiski," IV (Dec. 1896) 766.

40. See note 39 above, and Swift, *Loftier Flight,* 108; Natarova, "Recollections" in Wiley, *Century of Russian Ballet.* Panaeva, *Vospominaniya,* 40–44n, 73–44, 121–23; Grossman, *Pushkin,* 53. Stanislavsky, *My Life in Art,* 97–99.

41. Buturlin, "Zapiski," RA, 5–8 (1897) 597–98.

42. Vitale, *Pushkin's Button,* 30 (qu.), 132; Karlinsky, "Russia's Gay History and Literature," 88 (Pushkin qu.); "Gomoseksualizm v russkoi kulture," 104–7; and *Gogol,* 56–58. A few sketchy facts can be found in Healey, "Moscow"; and Tuller, *Cracks in the Iron Closet,* 88.

43. Viola, "Popular Resistance in the Stalinist 1930s."

44. Senelick, *Serf Actor,* 223–24; Herzen, *My Past,* xvi.

45. Vsevolodskii-Gerngross, *Teatr v Rossii,* 107–9; Taneev, "Iz proshlogo imperatorskikh teatrov," 878; Solovëv: Senelick, *National Theater,* 359–61. The actor F. A. Burdin left a favorable and even unctuous view of stage life of the era, stressing the gifts, salaries, medical care, and pensions: "Vospominaniya," 145–47.

46. Swift, *Loftier Flight,* 82; R. M. Zotov, "Zapiski," IV (Aug. 1896) 306–7; Natarova, "Recollections" in Wiley, *Century of Russian Ballet,* 158; Ignatov, *Teatr i zriteli,* 1:74; Sobel on Panaeva in Tomei, *Russian Women Writers,* 1:299–304. An atypical defense of actors as ordinary moral human beings appeared in the light-hearted fashion journal *Babochka,* 44 (June 1829) 175–76. Actors of the German theaters experienced similar isolation: Gubkina, *Nemetskii muzykalnyi teatr,* 93–97. In Old Regime France, actors were held excommunicate during their careers on stage: Blanning, *Culture of Power,* 80.

47. Vigel, *Zapiski,* passim; Senelick, *National Theater,* 318 n. 2 (with different terms); Burdin, "Vospominaniya," 148; TE, 2:868. For the fluid social context of these ranks, see Wirtschafter, *Structures of Society,* 32, 34, 76–77, 135, 137, 173 n. 37.

48. Nikitenko, *Diary,* 193; Senelick, *National Theater,* 380–81 and n. 1 (qu.). Viardot: Meshcherskii, "Iz moei stariny," 496; Buckler, *Literary Lorgnette,* 79–80, 82.

49. The negative view of A. V. Karatygin, "Russkii teatr v tsarstvovanie Aleksandra I," 258–59 is countered by V. R. Zotov, "Peterburg v sorokovykh godakh," IV (Mar. 1890) 563–64. Further glosses in Vsevolodskii-Gerngross, *Teatr v Rossii,* 50–51; Grossman, *Pushkin,* 9; Varneke, *Istoriya,* 138–40.

50. Varneke, *Istoriya,* 134; Medvedeva, *Ekaterina Semënova;* Panaeva, *Vospominaniya,* 25. Bolina: Vigel, *Zapiski,* 258–59. Dozens of French, Italian, and Iberian performers married titled men in this era.

51. The most interesting treatment of Russian opera audiences is Buckler, *Literary Lorgnette.* The theater encounter between Natasha Rostova and Anatol Kuragin occurs in Book VIII, chap. 9 of *War and Peace.*

52. Lighting caused numerous fires until gas arrived in 1863: Kuznetsova, *Bolshoi*

teatr, 76; Grossman, *Pushkin,* 14–16; Ozarovskii, "Khram Talii i Melpomeny," 516–17 (qu.). Seating terminology varies widely in and out of Russia: see Fedosyuk, *Chto neponyatno u klassikov,* 238–39; Buckler, *Literary Lorgnette,* 26–27.

53. Grossman, *Pushkin,* 26–29 (quotes 29); Panaeva, *Vospominaniya,* 151. Almost all evidence of the size and makeup of audiences is impressionistic. Even in the best-documented theaters in the world for this period, those of London, exact computation is impossible: Donohue, *Theatre in the Age of Kean.*

54. Edwards, *Russians at Home,* 181, commenting on the reopened Moscow Bolshoi in 1856. In the late eighteenth century, Moscow theater subscribers were expected to illuminate, furnish, and even wallpaper their own loges to which they were given keys: Pylyaev, *Staroe zhite,* 254. Buckler, *Literary Lorgnette,* passim.

55. Buckler, *Literary Lorgnette,* 28; Grossman, *Pushkin,* 17 (qu.); Varneke, *History,* 68 (qu. Empress Elizabeth). Tolchënov: David Ransel, private communication (and see chapter 6 of the present work); in the eighteenth century, commoners were allowed into court performances when the royal family was not in residence: Wirtschafter, *Play of Ideas,* 14. Ignatov, *Teatr i zriteli,* 72–73.

56. R. M. Zotov, "Zapiski," IV (Oct. 1896) 31; Lough, *Paris Theatre Audiences,* 188, 195, 226 (qu.); Grossman, *Pushkin,* 20 (qu.). For earlier appeals to the parterre in Russian theaters, see Wirtschafter, *Play of Ideas,* 45.

57. Lower attendance in September–October prevailed because merchants were still busy at the fairs and the "shuttling" landowners were waiting for snow to provide transportation to the capitals: Ignatov, *Teatr i zriteli,* 72–73; Petrovskaya, *Teatralnyi Peterburg,* 119, 121. In 1839, the Moscow Bolshoi had five tiers with sixteen boxes. Sumarokov, *Progulka po 12-ti guberniyam,* 90–91.

58. Ably analyzed in Buckler, *Literary Lorgnette,* 32–33. Bulgarin refers to no particular theater.

59. Dobrokhotov, *Verstovskii,* 24; Petrovskaya, *Teatralnyi Peterburg,* 126–27 (Nekrasov qu. 126). See Von Geldern, *Entertaining Tsarist Russia,* 47. Gogol's vignette on ticket fever at the Alexandrinsky box office has been quoted endlessly.

60. Blagovo, *Razskazy babushki,* 203.

61. *Finland and Russia,* 509, quoting Custine; Skonechnaya, *Moskovskii Parnas,* 49; Herzen, *My Past,* 41 and n. 4. Pushkin episodes: Kelly, *Refining Russia,* 74; Grossman, *Pushkin,* 63. Griswold, *Renaissance Revivals,* 111.

62. Ignatov, *Teatr i zriteli,* 60; *Elixir:* Edwards, *Russians at Home,* 185–86 (for the coronation, see Wortman, *Scenarios of Power,* 2:44); Lough, *Paris Theatre Audiences,* 192ff., 200; Burgess, "Russian Public Theatre Audiences," 164.

63. Grossman, *Pushkin,* 54; A. V. Karatygin, "Russkii teatr v tsarstvovanie Aleksandra I," 258; Vitale, *Pushkin's Button,* 28.

64. Accounts of the episode (but not the punishment) vary. See A. V. Karatygin, "Russkii teatr v tsarstvovanie Aleksandra I," 272 (his son V. A. Karatygin was a participant); Kubasov, "Teatralnyya intrigi," 296–304; Shatskov, "Katenin," 107–18.

65. Panaeva, *Vospominaniya,* 38–39. The brothers were sons of Jehuda Leib ben Noah (or Lev Nikolaevich Nevakhovich, 1776–c. 1831), a converted and assimilated spokesman for Jewish enlightenment and emancipation who, while still a Jew, advocated tolerance and had patriotic plays staged in St. Petersburg: Fishman, *Russia's First Modern*

Jews, 127–28; Klier, *Russia Gathers Her Jews,* 51–52, 125–26; EE, 11:622–24; Haberer, *Jews and Revolution,* 5. Mikhail Nevakhovich's (1817–50) *Jumble (Eralash)* was the first caricature collection in Russia (St. Petersburg, 1846–47). Through his daughter, he was the grandfather of Ilya, Ivan, and Lev Mechnikov: REE, 2:322. Alexander, with Rafail Zotov, worked in the Repertoire Department of the Imperial Theater in the 1830s and 1840s: V. R. Zotov, "Peterburg v sorokovykh godakh," IV (Apr. 1890) 103–4. The Jewish origin of the Nevakhovich brothers was not an issue in these disputes.

66. Ignatov, *Teatr i zriteli,* 71–72; Burgess, "Russian Public Theatre Audiences," 179–80, 166. For a lively view of American theater audiences, see Levine, *Highbrow/Lowbrow.*

67. Pustynnik, "Teatralnaya publika." The author, later speaking of the Bolshoi Stone, used the term *gulyane* ("folk fair") to describe the audience's exit. Buckler, *Literary Lorgnette,* 33–35, offers an imaginative and convincing literary reading of this piece.

68. Burgess, "Russian Public Theatre Audiences," 171, 175; Fedosyuk, *Chto neponyatno u klassikov,* 240; Wirtschafter, *Play of Ideas,* 24–25; EO, 1:106; 2:4; Edwards, *Russians at Home,* 164–85; Mally, *Revolutionary Acts,* 18; Zaitsev, *Taras Shevchenko,* 45.

69. Grossman, *Pushkin,* 33–34; Pustynnik, "Teatralnaya publika," 750; Johnson, *Listening in Paris,* 29.

70. Lough, *Paris Theatre Audiences,* 209, passim; Ignatov, *Teatr i zriteli,* 70–73; Grossman, *Pushkin,* 16; *Otello:* Rosen, *Romantic Generation,* 602; *Don Giovanni:* Gertsen, *Sochineniya,* 1:337. Levine cites similar instances in *Highbrow/Lowbrow,* 30.

71. P. V. Medvedev, "Dnevnik," 67 and passim; Kostenetskii, "Vospominaniya iz moei studencheskoi zhizni," RA, 1 (1887) 105; Bobkov, "Iz zapisok byvshago krepostnogo cheloveka," IV (May 1907) 468.

72. Altschuller, "Actors and Acting," 114; Buckler, *Literary Lorgnette,* 28, citing Danilov in *O teatre.*

73. Wirtschafter, *Play of Ideas,* ix–x and passim. See my discussion of sociability in the introduction to this book. Dramatist Gnedich naively believed that "some good plays and actors could imperceptibly change the way of thinking and behavior of our servants, artisans, and workers and could get them out of the pubs and into the theater": Grossman, *Pushkin,* 28.

74. Pushkin, *Eugene Onegin,* Book XXII, 11–12, in EO, 1:106; Raikes, *City of the Czar,* 1:105; Pustynnik, "Teatralnaya publika," 750. For visual treatments of the coachmen's pavilions in the early nineteenth century, see *Pushkinskii Peterburg.* pls. 77–78. Close-up views can be seen in an 1820s lithograph by K. P. Beggrov (ibid., pl. 83); and in one by Vasily Sadovnikov from 1836 reproduced in Shevchenko, *Povest,* 224–25. See also *Nouvelle collection: quarante-deux vues de Saint-Pétersbourg et de ses environs* (St. Petersburg, 1826) in RNBOE, Sobranie I. I. Rybakova, Ei-227.

75. Edgerton, "Ambivalence as the Key to Kniazhnin's Tragedy"; Wachtel, *Obsession with History,* 19–45. For a brief overview of censorship in this period, see Drizen, *Materialy,* 93–149.

76. Borovsky, "Emergence of the Russian Theatre" in Leach, *History of Russian Theatre,* 79; *Olinka:* Pylyaev, *Staroe zhite* 256–57; Drizen, *Materialy,* 123–24; Kozlyakov, "Kulturnaya sreda provintsialnogo goroda," 134–35 (qu. 135), puts the *Dido* episode in

a larger context. See also "Tsenzura v tsarstvovanie Imperatora Nikolaya I," RS (July 1901) 151–67; and Wirtschafter, *Play of Ideas,* 25–28.

77. Drizen, *Materialy,* 124; Swift, *Popular Theater,* 128; Senelick, *Russian Comedy,* ix–x; idem, *National Theater,* 355; "Tsenzura v tsarstvovanie Imperatora Nikolaya I," RS (Sept. 1901) 643–68.

78. V. R. Zotov, "Peterburg v sorokovykh godakh," IV (Jan. 1890) 45.

79. Smirnova, "Iz zapisok," 79 n. 2. This is an amusing anecdote, but I found no such anachronistic passage in the play: Aksakov, *Osvobozhdenie Moskvy.*

80. Kozlyakov, "Kulturnaya sreda provintsialnogo goroda," 134–35; Senelick, *Russian Dramatic Theory,* xxv (qu. from censor), 29–59; and *Serf Actor,* 179–80. See also Nikitenko, *Diary,* 85; and Choldin, *Fence Around the Empire.*

81. IRDT, 2:27 (qu.), and see pp. 27–31 for more on journalism. Translated excerpts from Pnin in Raeff, *Russian Intellectual History,* 126–58. *Vestnik Evropy, Severnyi vestnik, Dramaticheskii vestnik,* and *Zhurnal dramy* were among periodicals that covered theater in the first decades of the century. See Rodina, "L'évolution du théâtre russe," 212–29; TE, 2:707 and 5:135–38.

82. Grossman, *Pushkin,* 18; Stolpyanskii, *Muzyka,* 33–36; Senelick, *Russian Dramatic Theory,* xviii.

83. Ruud, *Fighting Words,* 65; Schleifman, "Russian Daily Newspaper"; V. R. Zotov, "Peterburg v sorokovykh godakh," IV (Mar. 1890) 566–68 (qu. 568); (Apr. 1890) 92–115; Nikitenko, *Diary,* 94 (Viardot incident); Drizen, *Materialy,* 136–37; Evreinov, *Krepostnye aktëry,* 19 n. 1 (Gedeonov).

84. Zhikharëv, *Zapiski;* Cassiday, "Reflections of the St. Petersburg Theater"; Vigel, *Zapiski;* Christoff, *Introduction,* vol. 3: *Aksakov,* 10.

85. Stolpyanskii, *Muzyka,* 33–36. As late as the 1930s, British censors forbade suicide in plays, since it suggested a lapse of British justice: Roger Lewis, *Laurence Olivier,* 181. Preliminary censorship was not abolished there until the late twentieth century.

86. Frame, *St. Petersburg Imperial Theaters.*

87. Gnedich cited in Zhikharëv, *Zapiski,* 2:196–97; Aksakov in Brodskii, *Literaturnye salony,* 122–27; Christoff, *Aksakov,* 12; Listova, *Varlamov,* 31.

88. Galakhov, "Literaturnaya kofeinya v Moskve," RS, 17 (Apr. 1886) 181–98; Senelick, *Serf Actor,* 70–71; Feoktistov, "Glava iz vospominanii"; Dmitriev, "Studencheskiya vospominaniya," 3–5 (s.p.).

89. Wirtschafter, *Play of Ideas,* 20; Dmitrieva, *Zhizn usadebnogo mifa,* 236–85.

90. Malnick, "Russian Serf Theatres," 393–96; Dynnik, *Krepostnoi teatr,* 57–60; Senelick, "Erotic Bondage," 25; Glagoleva, *Russkaya provintsialnaya starina,* 127–28.

91. Blagovo, *Razskazy babushki,* 204; Buturlin, "Zapiski," RA, 5–8 (1897) 199; Grot in Clyman, *Russia Through Women's Eyes,* 8; Arnold, *Vospominaniya,* 1:25–26; Shchepkina, *Vospominaniya,* 23, 116–17; Kropotkin, *Memoirs of a Revolutionist,* 15–16; "Lëgkii sposob ustroistva domashnyago teatra," RP, 7 (1842) 58–60, 77 (s.p.). For many more examples of home performances, see Roosevelt, *Russian Country Estate.*

92. Cited in Mally, *Revolutionary Acts,* 215.

93. Velyashev, *Opisanie prazdnika.* For the context, see Wortman, *Scenarios of Power,* 1:15–34; and Baehr, *Paradise Myth,* passim.

94. Borovsky, "Organization of the Russian Theatre" in Leach, *History of Russian*

Theatre, 47; Pylyaev, *Staroe zhite,* 265; Kelly, *Refining Russia,* 27 (Smolny); Ramazanov, "Vospominaniya o Karle Pavloviche Bryullove," 26; Vsevolodskii-Gerngross, *Teatr v Rossii,* 147; Giesemann, *Kotzebue in Russland,* 9; Karlinsky, *Gogol,* 12–13.

95. Skalkovskii, *Vospominaniya molodosti,* 112–14; Natanson, *Iz muzykalnogo proshlogo,* 86, 88. Senelick, *Serf Actor,* 108. For student off-campus theater in Kharkov in 1840, see Seletskii, "Zapiski," KS, 8 (Jan. 1884) 295.

96. Catriona Kelly, "Popular, Provincial, and Amateur Theatres, 1820–1900" in Leach, *History of Russian Theatre,* 137; Buturlin, "Zapiski," RA, 5–8 (1897) 217 and passim.

97. Translated in Von Geldern, *Entertaining Tsarist Russia,* 95.

98. Lotman, *Semiotics of Russian Cultural History,* 67–94; Thompson, "Patrician Society, Plebeian Culture," 382–405 (qu. 389); Maza, *Servants and Masters in Eighteenth-Century France,* 238–41, 294–95.

99. Elias, *Civilizing Process,* 16 and passim; Wortman, *Scenarios of Power,* 1; *Parizhskie teatry;* Sennett, *Fall of Public Man,* 174–76; Wortman, "Theatricality, Myth, and Authority," 48–52.

100. Ozarovskii, "Khram Talii i Melpomeny," 516–17, describes an 1829 handbook, *Bouquet, a Pocketbook for Theater Lovers,* which contained information about the theater houses, habits, and costumes, the last largely French. See also Hughes, "From Caftans to Corsets," 17–32.

101. Goscilo, "Keeping A-Breast of the Waist-Land."

Chapter 5. An Unfolding Drama

1. Senelick, *Russian Dramatic Theory,* xvii, 24 (qu.); Griswold, *Renaissance Revivals,* 6–9.

2. Altschuller, "Actors and Acting," 104; Varneke, *Istoriya,* 100–110. To take three male stars of the eighteenth century: Shusherin was the son of a poor official, Pomerantsev aspired to be a clerk, and Plavilshchikov came from a merchant family. When Pylyaev, *Staroe zhite,* 254, called these three "actor aristocrats," he was referring to their status in the theater, not their social origin. See also Zhikharëv, *Zapiski,* 1:272–73 (commentary).

3. Varneke, *Istoriya,* 91–97, 315; Buckler, "Divas in the Drawing Room," 79.

4. Grossman, *Pushkin,* 42–47; Shatskov, "Katenin," 107–18; Sirotinin, "Semënova," 481. Pushkin claimed that Alexandra Karatygina admitted not understanding a word of her lines if written in verse: Senelick, *Russian Dramatic Theory,* 6.

5. The prominent prerevolutionary (and later Soviet) theater scholar, Vsevolod Vsevolodsky-Gerngross, in his earliest analysis of actors' performance in this era, gave more or less equal weight to social and educational factors: *Teatr v Rossii,* 105–9. In the Soviet years, however, he tilted towards a more sociological explanation of actors' performance.

6. A factor even in modern times. Actor Laurence Olivier, the Anglican, and director Ingmar Bergman, the Lutheran, both imbibed the oratorical styles of their preacher fathers: Lewis, *Laurence Olivier;* Bergman, *The Magic Lantern.*

7. Senelick, *National Theater,* 372–74. Vsevolodskii-Gerngross, *Iskusstvo deklamatsii,* traces its musical and poetic genealogy.

8. Skonechnaya, *Moskovskii Parnas*, 96; *Mimica* (*Mimika*) excerpted in Senelick, *National Theater*, 216–18; Shchepkina, *Vospominaniya*, 228: Senelick, *Serf Actor*, 28; a performance of *Talanty i poklonniki* at the Maly Theater, Moscow, October, 1997.

9. Zhikharëv, *Zapiski*, 2:206; Grossman, *Pushkin*, 86 (qu.).

10. A common plot idea from Dostoevsky's "Netochka Nezvanova" to Clifford Odets' *Country Girl*.

11. Varneke, *Istoriya*, 428–43 (cf. pp. 437–36 of this book with his *History*, 262); Altschuller, "Actors and Acting," 107; TE, 3:979–83; Buturlin, "Zapiski," RA, 5–8 (1897) 542 (qu.); Afanasev, "Vospominaniya," IV, 41 (July 1890) 37–38.

12 Rodina, "L'évolution du théâtre russe," 223–24; TE, 3:645–49; Senelick, *Serf Actor*, 59–60.

13. Dmitriev, "Studencheskiya vospominaniya," 233–39; Galakhov, "Literaturnaya kofeinya v Moskve," RS, 17 (Apr. 1886) 188–97.

14. Varneke, *Istoriya*, 422–28, 440–42, 499 (qu.); Volkov, *St. Petersburg*, 27–28; Monas, *Third Section*, 96; Buturlin, "Zapiski," RA, 5–8 (1897) 542 n. 1.

15. "Zhurnal P. A. Karatygina" in GTsTMRO, f. 108, n. 14; Honour, *Neo-classicism*, 34. The story inspired many eighteenth-century century visual and literary works. A translation by Catherine II and others of Marmontel's novel on the subject reached its fifth edition by the early nineteenth century: Zorin, *Kormya dvuglavogo orla*, 183. The work was still a hit in popular theaters at the turn of the twentieth century: Swift, *Popular Theater*, 161. Donizetti's opera *Belisario* (1836) gained renown in Europe as well, but I have seen no record of its Russian performance. In 1836, in faraway Mexico City, General Santa Ana is said to have dreaded going to this interminable opera, but was encouraged by an aide who told him there would be horses on stage! Harrigan, *The Gates of the Alamo*, 177.

16. Varneke, *Istoriya*, 442 (Grigorev qu.); see Aksakov's verdict in Senelick, *National Theater*, 333–34; Rodina, "L'évolution du théâtre russe" 224; Altschuller, "Actors and Acting," 110–11; TE, 2:1137–39; Arnold, *Vospominaniya*, 2:177–78 (banquet); Buturlin, "Zapiski," RA, 5–8 (1897) 542.

17. Senelick, *Serf Actor*, 26–29; Malnick, "Actors Shchepkin and Sosnitsky," 295–96; Varneke, *Istoriya*, 498.

18. *Mikhail Semënovich Shchepkin*, 1:198 and 2:386 (quotes). For a scrupulous charting of Shchepkin's complexity and growth through the years, see Senelick, *Serf Actor*, 129–47.

19. Skonechnaya, *Moskovskii Parnas*, 102; Senelick, *Serf Actor*, 130. Review of *Sailor* by V. A. Dyachenko (1843) in Senelick, *National Theater*, 338–39, and Belinsky's appreciation, ibid., 337–38.

20. Reminiscences about Shchepkin and others at the Pechkin coffee house by Afanasy Fet in Brodskii, *Literaturnye salony*, 362–65; Dmitriev, "Studencheskiya vospominaniya," 233–39; *Moskovskii Universitet*, 98, 109, passim. See also Altschuller, "Actors and Acting," 121; Shchepkina, *Vospominaniya*, 193–247; Senelick, *Serf Actor*, 70, 108 (Moscow life) and 197–202, 221–22 (Herzen); *Mikhail Semënovich Shchepkin*, 1:198 (qu.); Malia, *Herzen*, 392.

21. Schuler, *Women in Russian Theater*, 61–68.

22. Stanislavsky, *My Life in Art*, 10 (qu.), 80–88.

23. A prime example is Aseev, "Zhivye traditsii." See Senelick, *Serf Actor,* passim, for a corrective.

24. Cited in Marasinova, "Kultura russkoi usadby," 308–9. On Grech, see Roosevelt, *Russian Country Estate,* 330–31.

25. Zorin, *Kormya dvuglavogo orla,* 31–64; Vrangel, "Romantizm v zhivopisi aleksandrovskoi epokhi," 380; Grossman, *Pushkin,* 11. For the classical background, see Wes, *Classics in Russia;* Harold Segel, "Classicism"; Kahn, "Readings of Imperial Rome."

26. G. S. Kirk in Homer, *The Iliad,* tr. R. Fitzgerald (Oxford, 1984), xv (qu.); Bruford, *Culture and Society in Classical Weimar,* 360–69.

27. Green, "Italian Scandal as Russian Tragedy," 394 (qu).

28. "V. A. Ozerov" in Gerbel, *Russkie poety,* 121–27; Mark Altshuller, "Ozerov"; Karlinsky, in *Russian Drama,* 207–13, argues homosexuality as a reason for Ozerov's mental breakdown and other miseries.

29. Sergei Uvarov describes the rehearsal atmosphere at Olenin's in Brodskii, *Literaturnye salony,* 39–42. Wes, *Classics in Russia,* 132–33; Whittaker, *Origins of Modern Russian Education,* 15; Stuart, *Aristocrat-Librarian.* A painting of the Olenin estate interior shows that his company also engaged in such nonaesthetic pastimes as cards and sewing: Roosevelt, "Country House as a Setting and Symbol," 50.

30. *Edip v afinakh, tragediya v 5 d.* in Ozerov, *Tragedii,* 1–59; Altshuller, "Ozerov"; A. D. P. Briggs, "Writers and Repertoires, 1800–1850" in Leach, *History of Russian Theatre,* 86; Nikitenko, *Up from Serfdom,* 136; Shevchenko, *Povest,* 90; Buturlin, "Zapiski," RA, 1–4 (1897) 400–401.

31. Honour, *Neo-classicism,* 65; Tolstoy, *The Tolstoys,* 169.

32. Cassiday, "Northern Poetry for a Northern People," 240–66 (qu. 251).

33. *Fingal, tragediya v 3 d.* in Ozerov, *Tragedii,* 60–101. Karlinsky's assessment in *Russian Drama,* 199–200. Incidental music and monologue from *Fingal:* GTsMMKF, orchestral original, Mag-1612.

34. Briggs, "Writers and Repertoires" in Leach, *History of Russian Theatre,* 89.

35. *Dmitrii Donskoi, tragediya v 5 d.* in Ozerov, *Tragedii,* 102–73 (qu. 106). See also Karlinsky, *Russian Drama,* 200–201; Altshuller, "Ozerov"; Rodina, "L'évolution du théâtre russe," 217–19; A. V. Karatygin, "Russkii teatr v tsarstvovanie Aleksandra I," 262; Sirotinin, "Semënova," 475. Rapturous reports on Donskoi's reception in Zhikharëv, *Zapiski,* 2:88–96 and Vigel, *Zapiski,* 255. In the 1820s, V. V. Selivanov and his brother read, reread, memorized, and declaimed whole scenes from Ozerov's *Donskoi,* and even got to perform in it: *Predaniya i vospominaniya,* 171.

36. Ignatov, *Teatr i zriteli,* 59.

37. Karatygin, "Yakovlev"; Grossman, *Pushkin,* 86–88.

38. Grossman, *Pushkin,* 74; Zetlin, *Decembrists,* 118. The best biography: Medvedeva, *Ekaterina Semënova,* which lists all her roles with illustrations of costumes and gestures. See also Sirotinin, "Semënova," 475–77.

39. Varying accounts in Medvedeva, *Semënova;* Haumant, *Culture française en Russie,* 207–9. See also Ward, *Moscow and Leningrad,* 2:23–24.

40. Pushkin in Senelick, *Russian Dramatic Theory,* 5; Grossman, *Pushkin,* 85; Sirotinin, "Semënova," 480–503; Buturlin, "Zapiski," RA, 5–8 (1897) 543–44.

41. Rodina, "L'évolution du théâtre russe," 213 (qu.); N. V. Koroleva, in "Dekabristy i teatr," insists that the Decembrists admired only the historical models and not the style of classical drama. See Lotman, *Semiotics of Russian Cultural History,* 95–149; Volk, *Istoricheskie vzglyady Dekabristov,* 193; Anatole Mazour, *First Russian Revolution,* 131.

42. Lough, *Paris Theatre Audiences,* 242, passim.

43. Vodovozova, *Na zare zhizni,* 1:474.

44. Karlinsky, *Gogol,* 147–48. The tragedies of Alexander Pushkin and Mikhail Lermontov had little impact on the theatrical life of their own time. Lermontov's romantic and tragic masterpiece *Masquerade* (1835–36), which treated aristocratic decadence and the jealousy-induced murder of an innocent wife, was censored for its "indecent criticism of costume balls at the Engelhardts' house" (Varneke, *History,* 237) and it remained unstaged in its original form until 1862. Pushkin's *Boris Godunov* (1825) and the "little tragedies" — universally recognized works of genius — had little success.

45. Kostenetskii, "Vospominaniya," RA, 3 (1887) 346.

46. Vsevolodskii-Gerngross, *Teatr v Rossii,* passim; Pylyaev, *Staroe zhite,* 281–96. For the nationalist background, see Martin, *Romantics, Reformers, Reactionaries.*

47. Kryukovskii, *Pozharskoi;* Zhikharëv, *Zapiski,* 2:315–18. See Dunning, *Russia's First Civil War,* for the historical background. For intelligent commentary: Zorin, *Kormya dvuglavogo orla,* 157–186 and his " 'Beskrovnaya pobeda' Knyazya Pozharskogo." *Pozharskoi* was chosen to open the Alexandrinsky Theater in 1832.

48. Hodge, "Susanin, Two Glinkas, and Ryleev"; Ginzburg, *Russkii muzykalnyi teatr,* 234–38; Rak, "Shakhovskoi"; R. M. Zotov, "Zapiski," IV (Oct. 1896) 48. The last minute Cossack rescue device would endure and resurface many times in popular war melodrama: see Stites, *Russian Popular Culture,* 36, for a film example from World War I.

49. Vsevolodskii-Gerngross, *Teatr v Rossii,* 156; Krasovskaya, *Istoriya russkogo baleta,* 35. The two parts are often cited as a single unified work with one title: *Universal Militia, or Love of Country* (*Vseobshchee opolchenie, ili Lyubov k otechestvu*); Varneke, *Istoriya,* 345. The term "universal" refers to the liability for service of all.

50. Fuller, *Strategy and Power in Russia,* 191 (qu.); Martin, *Romantics, Reformers, Reactionaries,* 6off., 98, and passim.

51. Pylyaev, *Staroe zhite,* 283–85; Lotman, "Lyudi 1812 goda" in *Besedy o russkoi kultury,* 330; Vrangel, "Romantizm v zhivopisi," 384.

52. Martin, "Response of the Population of Moscow."

53. Wortman, *Scenarios of Power,* 1:256 (qu.); IRLPD, f. 371, N. V. Kukolnik, opis 1: "Kratkaya biograficheskaya spravka N. V. Kukolnika"; Kukolnik, "Iz vospominanii"; Gerbel, *Russkie poety.*

54. Kukolnik, *Ruka vsevyshnyago otechestvo spasla,* in *Sochineniya dramaticheskiya,* 1:141–238; IRLPD, f. 371, n. 141, censor's copy with a few parts crossed out; Rydel, "Kukol'nik." The anti-Polish feelings among a broad spectrum of educated Russians were exacerbated by Europe's negative reaction to the suppression of the Polish uprising of 1830.

55. Danilov, *Ocherki,* 248–49 (qu.); Senelick, *National Theater,* 359 n. 3; Wortman, *Scenarios of Power,* 1:388–95. On the wave of dynastic loyalty in 1866, see Gleason, *Young Russia,* 329–34. A recent scholar argues somewhat unconvincingly that the

work's popularity has been overstated: an impressive sixteen performances in 1834, but only seventeen in the years 1835–48: Kiseleva, "Zhizn za tsarya," 176.

56. Kukolnik, *Knyaz Mikhail Vasilevich Skopin-Shuiskii* in *Sochineniya*, 1:239–48 (qu. 245). For the tangled roles of Skopin-Shuisky and Lyapunov in the Time of Troubles, see Dunning, *Russia's First Civil War*.

57. Kukolnik, *Knyaz Daniil Vasilevich Kholmskii* in *Sochineniya*, 2:375–511. Its music is on the cassette: Glinka, *Aragonskaya khota, Vals Fantasiya, Simfoniya na dve Russkie temy*. Musical analysis in Brown, *Glinka*, 164–73.

58. On Sannazaro (*Yakobi San Nazar*, in Russian), see Clark, *Landscape into Art*, 56–57. I have not read the play. Turgenev, PSS, 4:206. Materials on the later life in IRLPD, f. 371: N. V. Kukolnik: Opis 1: "Kratkaya biograficheskaya spravka N. V. Kukolnika." See also Sazhin, "Iz biografii pisatelya N. V. Kukolnika," and Kirichinskii, *Zabytyi poet-nationalist*, a panegyric.

59. Hodge, "Susanin"; idem, *Double Garland*, 150–52 and passim; Glinka, *Zapiski*, 1–20; Yurkevich, "Iz vospominanii," 163 (qu.).

60. Arnold, *Vospominaniya*, 2:128–30. A reviewer for the *Northern Bee* reported a comment Glinka made while writing *Susanin*: "Cavos? Russian music? Only imitation, no more": Yurkevich, "Iz vospominanii," 163. Zetlin, *The Five*, 33; Glinka, *Zapiski* (1953) 1–20.

61. Campbell, *Russians on Russian Music*, 3, 7; Haskell, *Attentive Listener*, 103, on various reactions to the opera; Christoff, *Introduction*, vol. 1: *Xomjakov*, 77.

62. Arnold, *Vospominaniya*, 2:128–30, claims that the opera was originally titled *A Death for the Tsar*.

63. Wortman, *Scenarios of Power*, 1:390–95; Kiseleva, "Zhizn za tsarya," 173–85.

64. Nikitenko, *Diary*, 47–48; Ruud, *Fighting Words*, 70; White, "Polevoi"; Mikhailova, "Vopros o teatralnoi monopolii," 84.

65. Polevoi, *Dedushka russkogo flota, Dramaticheskiya sochineniya*, 97–162; *Parasha Sibirachka*, ibid., 47–96, both with commentary. Background on Brandt in Hughes, *Russia in the Age of Peter the Great*, 81. Herzen, *My Past*, 116–17; TE, 3:456, for a Soviet assessment.

66. Figures from Volf, *Khronika peterburgskikh teatrov*, 2:iv–v of the appendix; Polevoi, *Ugolino* (St. Petersburg, 1838).

67. Wirtschafter, *Play of Ideas*, 156 (qu.); see also pp. 147–71 for the "Moral Monarchy." plays. Her "Drama and Society in Imperial Russia, 1740s to 1790s" (ms.) contains some additional detail. Polevoi's speech and merchant orientation: Owen, *Capitalism and Politics in Russia*, 19, 235 n. 86.

68. Herzen, *My Past*, 291 and n. 10.

69. Swift, *Popular Theater*, 281.

70. Ungurianu, "Zagoskin"; RPis 2:304–6. During the Crimean War the house serf Bobkov witnessed an unnamed 1855 drama repeating the familiar theme of landlords praising recruits and recruits shouting their willingness to die for Russia: Bobkov, "Iz zapisok byvshago krepostnogo cheloveka," IV (June 1907) 741.

71. Cumberland, *The Jew*; *Karantin* in Khmelnitskii, *Sochineniya*, 2:275–327 (qu. 278). It featured music by Verstovsky.

72. Levitina, *Russkii teatr i Evrei*, 1:34, 67, 119–20, 127–28, 137–39, 142, 231 n. 17.

In the incidental music for *Kholmsky*, Glinka composed a "Jewish" melody for Rachel in a singing contest with a Russian woman: Brown, *Glinka*, 167. This curious scene highlights the widely held prejudice of many Russians that Jews could not really release themselves in gaiety (in the eyes of Russian males, this alleged reserve was the result of temperance): Kukolnik, *Kholmskii, Sochineniya dramaticheskiya*, 2:415–17.

73. Dynnik, *Krepostnoi teatr*, 151–52; Lough, *Paris Theatre Audiences*, 237–38 (Beaumarchais); Varneke, *Istoriya*, 191 (Plavilshchikov).

74. Mandel, *Kotzebue*; Karlinsky, *Russian Drama*, 191–92; Stites, "Misanthrope."

75. Kotzebue, *Menschenhass und Reue* in *August von Kotzebue: Schauspiele*, 43–126 (qu. 72). The earliest Russian translation I found is *Nenavist k lyudyam i raskayanie*, 4th ed. (Orël, 1826). German, but not Russian, audiences were scandalized by the forgiveness of Meinau's wife: Coleman, "Kotzebue and Russia," 342.

76. Giesemann, *Kotzebue in Russland*, 104, 119, 175; Aksakov, *Sobranie sochinenii*, 1:325; Vsevolodskii-Gerngross, *Istoriia russkogo teatra*, 2:29, 58–59, 64–65; Karatygin, *Zapiski*, 91–92; Varneke, *Istoriya*, 431–32.

77. Küchelbecker quoted in *Istoriia russkoi dramaturgii*, 258; R. M. Zotov in Vsevolodskii-Gerngross, *Istoriya russkogo teatra*, 2:30. A contemporary claimed that young Moscow merchants read all of Kotzebue's plays in translation more than once: Selivanov, *Predaniya i vospominaniya*, 248–49. The provincial peasant-merchant Alexander Artynov is rhapsodic in his memory of a Moscow performance in the late 1820s of Kotzebue's *Child of Love*: *Vospominaniya krestyanina*, 86.

78. Dyukanzh [Ducange], *Tereza, ili zhenevskaya sirota, melodrama*, tr. of *Thérèse, ou l'orphéline de Genève*. See Stites, "Misanthrope" for additional references.

79. Caigniez, *Pie voleuse*. The title page also indicates a ballet as well as music by Piccinni. Commentary in Rahill, *World of Melodrama*, 56–63; and Ginisty, *Mélodrame*, 121–38, 219.

80. The Russian translation by Valberkh is *Soroka-Vorovka, ili palezosskaya sluzhanka* (St. Peterburg, 1816). See also IRDT, 2:280, 288; Gozenpud, *Opernyi slovar*, 389–90; Kimbell, *Italian Opera*, 358, 563; Osbourne, *Rossini*, 198–201; Weinstock, *Rossini*, 498, 77.

81. TE, 3:787–90.

82. Laqueur, "Bodies, Details, and the Humanitarian Narrative."

83. R. M. Zotov, "Zapiski," IV (Oct. 1896) 32–33 and (Nov. 1896) 419, 422.

84. Senelick, *Russian Comedy*, ix.

85. Maza, *Servants and Masters in Eighteenth-Century France*, 229–43 and passim.

86. Varneke, *History*, 64–65.

87. Newlin, "Rural Ruses," 307, and idem, *Voice in the Garden*, 13, 20, 24, passim.

88. Berkov, *Istoriya russkoi komedii*, 318; Karlinsky, *Russian Drama*, 99–101; Varneke, *Istoriya*, 186–87, 198–99. See also Rogger, *National Consciousness*, 141. The term *bobyl* also implies a loner.

89. Simmons, *English Literature and Culture in Russia*, 158 (qu.) and passim; Baehr, *Paradise Myth*, 151–52; Karlinsky, *Russian Drama*, 188–92; Fanger, "Peasant and Russian Literature," 239; Van Regemorter, "Deux images idéales de la paysannerie russe." Donskov, *Changing Image of the Peasant*, gives a useful review of the literature on the subject and a learned discussion of rustic language in drama.

90. Quoted in Donskov, *Changing Image of the Peasant*, 38. The italics, quite appropriate, are Donskov's.

91. *Anyuta*: Wirtschafter, *Play of Ideas*, 87. Libretto by Mikhail Popov and music by Evstignei Fomin (1761–1800) or by Vasily Pashkevich (Paszkiewicz; 1742–1800). See also Shatz, "Noble Landowner in Russian Comic Operas," 26–27.

92. Nikolev, *Rozana i Lyubim* (1778, music by Ivan [Iosif] Kertselli) in *Rossiiskii featr*, unnumbered volume, 1–109 (qu. 32); Abraham, *On Russian Music*, 256. Wirtschafter, in *Play of Ideas*, counts thirty-four performances of *Rozana* in Moscow in 1778–1800 and four in Petersburg in 1780–82: p. 229 n. 18.

93. Knyazhnin, *Sochineniya*, 2:109–38, tr. in Segel, *Literature of Eighteenth-Century Russia*, 2:374–93. The music is by V. A. Pashkevich. Shatz, "Noble Landowner in Russian Comic Operas," 31–32.

94. Karlinsky, *Russian Drama*, 144. For this play and others on recruitment, soldiers, and soldiers' wives, see Wirtschafter, *Play of Ideas*, 89–95, 229 n. 26.

95. Borovsky, "Emergence of the Russian Theatre" in Leach, *History of Russian Theatre*, 74; Woodhouse, "Tales from Another Country." For the limits of permitted satire in visual culture, see Dianne Farrell, "Laughter Transformed: the Shift from Medieval to Enlightenment Humor in Russian Popular Prints" in Bartlett, *Russia and the World of the Eighteenth Century*, 157–70.

96. Excerpts in Von Geldern, *Entertaining Tsarist Russia*, 57–65. See Wirtschafter, "Drama and Society"; Dostoevsky, *House of the Dead*, 184–204.

97. Karlinsky, *Russian Drama*, 122–23.

98. Ibid., 95 (qu. on Sumarokov), 172–76 (on *Chicanery*); Wirtschafter, *Play of Ideas*, 133–35, 238–39 n. 50; idem, "Drama and Society" (performance history).

99. Wirtschafter, *Play of Ideas*, 118–20. See her discussion of this play and of G. N. Gorodchaninov's *Mitrofanushka in Retirement* (1800) in "Military Service and Social Hierarchy." On the psychological urge that sent some nobles into voluntary service, see Newlin, *Voice in the Garden*, 66.

100. This play, *Modnaya lavka*, and *Lessons to Daughters* in Krylov, *Sochineniya*, 2 v. (Moscow, 1956) 1:333–438. See Senelick's witty translation of the first, *The Milliner's Shop*, in his *Russian Satiric Comedy*, 25–65; Stennik, "Krylov." For eighteenth-century Gallophobia, see Rogger, *National Consciousness*.

101. Quoted in Borovsky, "Russian Theatre in Russian Culture" in Leach, *History of Russian Theatre*, 11.

102. Shakhovskoi, "Polubarskie zatei," undated ms., SPBGTB; Sakhnovskii, *Krepostnoi usadebnyi teatr*, 52–60. See also Rak, "Shakhovskoi"; Karlinsky, *Russian Drama*, 232; Roosevelt, *Russian Country Estate*, 151–52. The earliest known spoof of amateur theater was the anonymous 1790 comedy, *A Queer Gathering*: Varneke, *History*, 110, 141. Baumgarten, *Spätklassische russische Komödie*, offers a detailed analysis of sources, formal structures, and intertextuality. For Mikhail Zagoskin's *Noble Theater* (1827), a send-up of gentry amateur theatricals, see chap. 6 of the present work.

103. Confino, *Société et mentalités collectives*, 99–133 (qu. 122). See also Blum, *Lord and Peasant in Russia*, 409–12.

104. Shakhovskoi, *Pustodomy*, in the collection of comic stage works by various authors *Stikhotvornaya komediya*, 2:231–363. At least one eighteenth-century play, Vol-

kov's *Upbringing*, saw the promotion of "improved methods of cultivation" as a legitimate aspect of noble service: Wirtschafter, "Military Service and Social Hierarchy," 227.

105. Shakhovskoi, *New Sterne* (excerpts), tr. in Von Geldern, *Entertaining Tsarist Russia*, 31–41.

106. For example Sheridan's *School for Scandal* (1777); Karlinsky, *Russian Drama*, 232–34.

107. Shakhovskoi, *Urok koketam, ili lipetskie vody* in *Stikhotvornaya komediya*, 2:7–146 (qu. 48). For the literary background, see Rak, "Shakhovskoi"; Whittaker, *Origins of Modern Russian Education*, 29–33; Karlinsky, *Russian Drama*, 235–39; Grossman, *Pushkin*, 132–40 (qu. 132).

108. Sumarokov, *Progulka po 12-ti guberniyam*, 138–41.

109. Julie Cassiday expertly analyzes the connection between the spa as social site and Shakhovskoi's treatment of it: "*The Lipetsk Spa*: Placing the 'Caustic Shakhovskoi' in Context" (ms.). See also the introduction to Cornwell, *Society Tale*; and Joe Andrew, "Another Time, Another Place: Gender and the Chronotope in the Society Tale" ibid., 127–51.

110. See Moser, *Antinihilism*.

111. Potekhin, *Sochineniya*, 12:322.

112. "Emansipirovannaya zhenshchina," RP, 2 (1845) 219–40. On George Sand in Russia, see Stites, *Women's Liberation Movement*, 19–25. Shakhovskoi offered an ironic panorama of social-cultural images for the ideal wife in *The Married Fiancée* (1818): bluestocking, dummy, housekeeper, party girl, and gushy sentimentalist: Karlinsky, *Russian Drama*, 240–44.

113. Matinsky: Kots, *Krepostnaya intelligentsiya*, 112–13. The opera: Ginzburg, *Russkii muzykalnyi teatr*, 83–99 (summary and excerpts); and Mooser, *L'opéra comique français en Russie*, 175. The music was written by Pashkevich.

114. Wirtschafter, *Play of Ideas*, 107.

115. Ibid., 97–100. Chernavskoi's plot remarkably resembles that of the 1916 Evgenii Bauer film, *Life for a Life*.

116. Varneke, *Istoriya*, 200. Plavilshchikov wrote at least one other play on this theme: Wirtschafter, *Play of Ideas*, 42 and 97–100, for a discussion of the genre.

117. Tsinkovich-Nikolaeva, "Kupecheskaya tema v repertuare," 110–26 (qu. 117).

118. TE, 2:158. Karlinsky, *Gogol*, 171–72, 184 (qu.). I have regrettably read no works by Grigorev.

119. Karlinsky, *Russian Drama*, 274 (qu.); Varneke, *Istoriya*, 364–92; Kosny, "Vodevil D. T. Lenskogo"; Rodina, "L'évolution du théâtre russe."

120. Batyushkov quoted in Kozlyakov, ""Kulturnaya sreda provintsialnogo goroda," 134. Zagoskin, *G——n Bogatonov, ili provintsial v stolitse* (the saucy Anyuta's lines: 87–88, 102, 113); *M. N. Zagoskin: biograficheskii ocherk*, 26–30 (qu. 29); *Syn otechestva*, 39 (1817) 88–102. See also Ungurianu, "Zagoskin"; and Karlinsky, *Russian Drama*, 262, who delightfully translates Bogatonov as Moneybags. Molière, *Le bourgeois gentilhomme* (1670; Paris, 1998).

121. "Dom na Peterburgskoi Storone," in RP, 2 (1843) 92–119 (qu. 118). See comment in Lovell, *Summerfolk*, 52 n. 83, and 55–56 for satires on dacha life.

122. Arnold, *Vospominaniya*, 2:174; A. F. Koni, *Vospominaniya o pisatelyakh*, 11–12.

F. A. Koni, *Peterburgskie kvartiry* in *Teatr F. A. Koni.*, 2:1–110. Belinsky, who famously hated most light entertainment, admired this play. Renting and apartment living became a regular feature of graphics in popular periodicals, such as the *Illustrated Family Pages* in the 1850s (*Illyustrirovannyi semeinyi listok*, 1859–61, passim).

123. See Galakhov, "Literaturnaya kofeinya v Moskve" (Apr. 1886) 185 and Ivanov, "Vospominaniya," IV (Oct. 1891) 89, for Lensky's offstage sociability.

124. Borzikov (from *borzoi,* a Russian breed of hound) was a code name for Koni since the censors did not allow Lensky to use the name "Loshadka" (*kon* and *loshad* are Russian words for horse): Beskin, "Lev Gurych Sinichkin." An excellent translation of *Sinichkin* is available in Senelick, *Russian Comedy,* 1–58. See also Karlinsky, *Russian Drama,* 276–77.

125. As described by friend and admirer Mikhail Buturlin in "Zapiski," RA, 5–8 (1897) 543.

126. Kosny, "Towards a Poetics of Classical Russian Vaudeville," 190–99. See also his "Vodevil D. T. Lenskogo," 367.

127. Swift, *Popular Theater,* 140; Beskin, "Lev Gurych Sinichkin"; and *Lev Gurych Sinichkin,* WMNB Video.

128. Wirtschafter, *Play of Ideas,* esp. ix–x, 13, 173 (qu.), 174–76, 207 n. 41; idem, "Drama and Society."

Chapter 6. Playing the Provinces

1. Petrovskaya, *Teatr i zritel provintsialnoi Rossii,* 5. See also McReynolds, *Russia at Play,* a study that reinforces Petrovskaya's opinion and which she also quotes.

2. Sennett, *Fall of Public Man,* 207; Heather Nathans, "Forging a Powerful Engine"; Sterne, *A Sentimental Journey* (1768; London, 1995), 23. For provincial theater, in addition to the notes below, one may start with the chapters entitled "Provintsialnyi teatr" in vols. 1–4 of IRDT; Danilov, *Russkii dramaticheskii teatr,* 1:147–58 and 2:156–70; Petrovskaya, *Teatr i zritel provintsialnoi Rossii,* 5–102 (covering 1850 to 1870). For an old but detailed province-by-province bibliography, see A. M. Bryanskii, "K istoriografii russkogo provintsialnogo teatra," in Danilov, *O teatre,* 153–76.

3. Video: The Pyatnitsky Folk Ensemble, on *Russian Folk Song and Dance.*

4. Dynnik, *Krepostnoi teatr,* 35. Serious research on serf theater, manorial and otherwise, began in the early Soviet period: Sakhnovskii, *Krepostnoi usadebnyi teatr;* Kots, *Krepostnaya intelligentsiya;* and the Dynnik book. Many of the anecdotes about abuse of serf performers can be traced to Evreinov, *Krepostnye aktëry,* and further back to Pylyaev, *Staroe zhite,* and to Ekaterina Letkova, "Krepostnaya intelligentsiya," which draws heavily from De Passenens (1822), Vigel, and other travelers. M. D. Kurmachëva, *Krepostnaya intelligentsiya,* includes theatrical serfs.

5. The print in Kuznetsov, *Iz istorii,* 69; Burgess, "Fairs and Entertainers in 18th-Century Russia," 99. To world audiences, the best-known depiction of serfs performing for the masters is in Tchaikovsky's opera *Eugene Onegin* (1879). On the Tolstoy episode, see Figes, *Natasha's Dance.*

6. Yu. V. Sobolev, manuscripts in RGALI, f. 860, op. 1, ed. kh. 348; Dynnik, *Krepostnoi teatr,* 35–37; Roosevelt, *Russian Country Estate,* 129–53 (esp. 139) and passim.

The most recent work expands Dynnik's narrow definition to include cases of amateurs, professionals, and serfs performing together in looser manorial settings: Dmitrieva, *Zhizn usadebnogo mifa*, 236–85. Her table, pp. 466–519, adds some items to Dynnik but is also incomplete.

7. Grossman, *Pushkin*, 62; Pylyaev, *Staroe zhite*, 279; Dynnik, *Krepostnoi teatr*, 66.

8. Pylyaev, *Staroe zhite*, 255, 276; Mikhnevich, *Ocherk*, 303–4; Blagovo, *Razskazy babushki*, 203. See also Roosevelt, *Russian Country Estate*, 39–45; Sakhnovskii, *Krepostnoi usadebnyi teatr*, 52; Dynnik, *Krepostnoi teatr*, passim; Malnick, "Russian Serf Theatres," 399.

9. IRDT, 2:205–6; N. P. Sheremetev, 1792 correspondence with I. A. Dmitrevsky and S. A. Sandunov on their training of his serf actors: RA (May 1896) 202–6; Senelick, *Serf Actor*, 9–10; Roosevelt, *Russian Country Estate*, 64–65, 135–37; Sakhnovskii, *Krepostnoi usadebnyi teatr*, 45; Malnick, "Russian Serf Theatres," 396–98; Kots, *Krepostnaya intelligentsiya*, 154–56; Pylyaev, *Staroe zhite*, 252. On Shcherbatov, fierce defender of serfdom and noble rights but a foe of luxury, see Walicki, *History of Russian Thought*, 26–31.

10. Herzen, *My Past*, 67; Varneke, *History*, 103; Kots, *Krepostnaya intelligentsiya*, 20; Milyukov, *Dobroe staroe vremya*, 93–95 (qu. 95).

11. *Karta krepostnogo teatra*, wall map, in GTsTMRO; V. A. Koshelëv, "O 'literaturnoi' provintsii i 'literaturnoi provintsialnosti'," in Belousov, *Russkaya provintsiya*, 49–50.

12. Ryabkov, *Smolenskii krai*, 66ff.; Ivanov, "Pervye spektakli," 3; Sakhnovskii, *Krepostnoi usadebnyi teatr*, 41; Senelick, "Erotic Bondage," 27 (qu.).

13. IRDT, 2:16; Orlovskii starozhil, *Bylyya chudaki*, 108–9; Kuznetsov, *Iz istorii*, 52; Senelick, "Russian Serf Theatre"; Kots, *Krepostnaya intelligentsiya*, 158–59, a reproduction of the *affiche*; Sakhnovskii, *Krepostnoi usadebnyi teatr*, 44.

14. Pylyaev, *Staroe zhite*, 278; Anchipolovskii, *Staryi teatr: Voronezh*, 92 (Turgeneva); Sakhnovskii, *Krepostnoi usadebnyi teatr*, 51.

15. Leskov, "Make-Up Artist." Leskov's narrator is unsure which of the Kamensky counts the events concerned. See also McLean, *Leskov*, 438–41; Buturlin, "Zapiski," RA, 5–8 (1897) 201; Kots, *Krepostnaya intelligentsiya*, 41; Orlovskii starozhil, *Bylyya chudaki*, 11–12.

16. Tula: Glagoleva, *Russkaya provintsialnaya starina*, 126–28; Kots, *Krepostnaya intelligentsiya*, 153; Roosevelt, *Russian Country Estate*, 237–38; Ryazan and Ryumin: Rostislavov, *Provincial Russia*, 213.

17. Rybkin, *Generalissimus Suvorov*, 64; Dynnik, *Krepostnoi teatr*, 95–96; Borovsky, "Emergence of the Russian Theatre" in Leach, *History of Russian Theatre*, 63; Malnick, "Russian Serf Theatres," 405–6.

18. RBS, 2:566–69; IRDT, 2:417, mistakenly limits the theater's lifetime to the years 1806–29; Kollar, "Ocherk istorii muzykalnogo teatra v Nizhnem Novgorode"; Zhdanov, *Putevyya*, 51–52; Feoktistov, "Glava iz vospominanii," 101–4; Afanasev, "Vospominaniya," IV, 41 (July 1890) 38–40 and (Aug. 1890) 258–59; Smirnov, *Nizhegorodskaya starina*, 435; Murav, "Theater of Sukhovo-Kobylin," 16–17; Kots, *Krepostnaya intelligentsiya*, 145–46; Roosevelt, *Russian Country Estate*, 138–39.

19. Saratov: Gerakov, *Putevyya zapiski*, 35–36; Ya. K. Evdokimov, "Muzykalnoe

proshloe Saratova" in Shteinpress, *Iz muzykalnogo proshlogo*, 147–49. Simbirsk: Pylyaev, *Staroe zhite*, 262–63; Sakhnovskii, *Krepostnoi usadebnyi teatr*, 44. Penza: Vigel, *Zapiski*, 91, 147–49; Vsevolodskii-Gerngross, *Teatr v Rossii*, 141–42; Kots, *Krepostnaya intelligentsiya*, 131; Dynnik, *Krepostnoi teatr*, 46.

20. Fëdorov, *Marino*, 68–69; Sakhnovskii, *Krepostnoi usadebnyi teatr*, 27–31; Dynnik, *Krepostnoi teatr*, 63, 118; Nikitenko, *Up from Serfdom*, 161–62.

21. Shalikov, *Puteshestvie v Malorossiyu*, 74–85, 215–52. Though he does not touch on this incident, Andreas Schönle's analysis of Shalikov's journeys helps explain why such self-absorbed sentimental travelers rarely perceived the realities of serfdom: *Authenticity and Fiction*, 88–98.

22. Roosevelt, *Russian Country Estate*, 263; Dynnik, *Krepostnoi teatr*, 47: Krasovskaya, *Russkii baletnyi teatr*, 77–78. I have not inquired into Polish manorial theaters in Ukraine and Belorussia.

23. Gatsiskii, *Nizhegorodskii teatr*, 9–19; Smirnov, *Nizhegorodskaya starina*, 403–6; Melnikov, *Stoletie nizhegorodskoi yarmarki*, 23–24; Kollar, "Ocherk istorii muzykalnogo teatra v Nizhnem Novgorode," 295.

24. Kots, *Krepostnaya intelligentsiya*, 139 (qu.); and Belyakov, *Opernaya i kontsertnaya deyatelnost*, 1–16.

25. Gerakov, *Putevyya zapiski*, 21; Melnikov, *Stoletie nizhegorodskoi yarmarki*, 49; Gatsiskii, *Nizhegorodskii teatr*, 9–19; Selivanov, *Predaniya i vospominaniya*, 165–67; Pylyaev, *Staroe zhite*, 258–62.

26. Vigel, *Zapiski*, 172–74; Aksakov, *Sobranie sochinenii*, 1:318–27; Pylyaev, *Staroe zhitie*, 264 (Tatars).

27. Vyazemskii cited in Kots, *Krepostnaya intelligentsiya*, 129–30; Vigel, *Zapiski*, 148. See also Pylyaev, *Staroe zhite*, 276–77; Vsevolodskii-Gerngross, *Teatr v Rossii*, 141–42; Varneke, *Istoriya*, 126; Dynnik, *Krepostnoi teatr*, 195; IRDT, 2:420.

28. Chernov, *Literaturnye mesta orlovskoi oblasti*, 33–34.

29. First-hand accounts: Ertaulov, "Vospominaniya"; Buturlin, "Teatr grafa Kamenskago v Orle," 1707–12; Zhirkevich, "Zapiski," 565–73, 579–80. Other details in Orlovskii starozhil, *Bylyya chudaki*, 14–15; Kots, *Krepostnaya intelligentsiya*, 142–45; Pylyaev, *Staroe zhite*, 266–72; and Letkova, "Krepostnaya intelligentsiya," 165.

30. Orlovskii starozhil, *Bylyya chudaki*, 19–20, is the only source for this.

31. *Mikhail Semënovich Shchepkin*, 2:153; Gertsen, "Soroka-Vorovka: povest," *Sochineniya*, 1:327–50, 502–7. For more detail, see Stites, "Misanthrope." Chernov, "Krepostnye aktrisy orlovskogo teatra"; Putintsev, "Krepostnaya aktrisa Kuzmina," 190–95; Grits, "K istorii 'Soroki-vorovki'," 655–60; IRDT, 2:288, 423–26, 523.

32. Gerakov, *Prodolzhenie putevykh zapisok*, 122–23; Ertaulov, "Vospominaniya"; Dolgorukii, *Puteshestvie*, 6; and the sources in notes 30 and 31 above. One of the earliest provincial newspapers, *Drug Rossian* (1816–18), reviewed the performances at the Orël theater.

33. Ivanov, "Vospominaniya," 64–89; Roosevelt, *Russian Country Estate*, 141–42; Moser, *Pisemsky*, 3, 5; Medvedev, *Vospominaniya*, 97–107.

34. Kots, *Krepostnaya intelligentsiya*, 127; Sobolev, RGALI, f. 860, op. 1, ed. kh. 348.

35. Dynnik, *Krepostnoi teatr*, 106, 232–34; Leichtentritt, *Music, History, and Ideas*, 182 (Cherubini); Mooser, *L'opéra-comique français*, 123–36; Lepskaya, *Repertuar Sheremetevykh krepostnykh teatrov*, 8–51, and the catalogue of performances.

36. Vigel, *Zapiski*, 82–83. *Semi:* Kuznetsov, *Iz istorii*, 67–70 (illust., p. 69). Krasov-skaya, *Istoriya russkogo baleta*, 7; Mikhnevich, *Ocherk*, 307; Buturlin, "Zapiski," RA, 1–4 (1897) 400–401, 420–21.

37. Letkova, "Krepostnaya intelligentsiya," 164, and Dynnik, *Krepostnoi teatr*, 226–27, both citing *Zhurnal dramaticheskii*.

38. Zagoskin, *Blagorodnyi teatr*, 31 (qu.).

39. Vodovozova, *Na zare zhizni*, 1:83–86, 157.

40. Letkova, "Krepostnaya intelligentsiya," 163; Pylyaev, *Staroe zhite*, 279.

41. For the impact of gentry private power on the condition of the serf population, see Pipes, *Property and Freedom*, 190–200. See the thoughtful comments on motivations by Wortman: "Theatricality, Myth, and Authority," 48–52.

42. *V okrestnostyakh Moskvy*, 327–32; Varneke, *Istoriya*, 483–84; Kelly, *Refining Russia*, 92 and n. 22. Largesse and ruinous spending were of course the habits only of those possessing great wealth, as Michael Confino has emphasized: *Société et mentalités collectives*, 375.

43. Malnick, "Russian Serf Theatres," 399 (Wilmot); Dynnik, *Krepostnoi teatr*, 77–78; Kots, *Krepostnaya intelligentsiya*, 153; Pylyaev, *Staroe zhite*, 275–76.

44. Komarovskii, "Iz zapisok," 1278–79; Haxthausen, *Russian Empire*, 1:227 (in fact the actors he saw were ex-serfs—see below); Senelick, "Erotic Bondage," 28; Kots, *Krepostnaya intelligentsiya*, 134; Medvedev, *Vospominaniya*, 167; Goffman, *Presentation of Self*, 22–24; Letkova, "Krepostnaya intelligentsiya," passim. For the extent of mixed serf-amateur production, see Dmitrieva, *Zhizn usadebnogo mifa*, 259–60 and the table, 466–519.

45. Roosevelt, *Russian Country Estate*, 105–6; idem, "Emerald Thrones and Living Statues"; Kots, *Krepostnaya intelligentsiya*, 20 (serf ball); Herzen, *My Past*, 13; Hodge, *Double Garland*, 185 (hunchbacks).

46. [A. I. Rozanov], "Zapiski selskago svyashchennika," RS (Jan. 1880) 67–68; Dynnik, *Krepostnoi teatr*, 28; Orlovskii starozhil, *Bylyya chudaki*, 108–9.

47. Roosevelt, *Russian Country Estate*, 263; Senelick, "Erotic Bondage," 24–34 (qu. 29); Nikulina-Kositskaia, "Notes," 140–41.

48. Kugushev, *Kornet Otletaev*, 216 and 206 quotes. Pylyaev cites Kugushev's relative, V. S. Taneev, as the model for this tale: *Staroe zhite*, 278. For a nuanced note on Kugushev: RPis, 3:196–97. Later novels, both set at the time of the Crimean War, took up the theme. Sergei Atava's *Menacing Shadows* (1888), an exposé of gentry evil seducers, drew on his own prereform life: Atava [S. N. Terpigorev], *Potrevozhennyya teni*, also an expanded version in *Sobranie sochinenii*, 3:5–721. G. A. Machtet's *And One in the Field Is a Warrior* (a reference to a once famous Friedrich Spielhagen novel) combines all the horrors of theatrical erotic bondage, as seen though the eyes of a lackey: *I odin v pole voin* in *Polnoe sobranie sochinenii*, 5:5–185 (see pp. 112–13). The misuse of female serf performers was taken up in Soviet ballets: ballet master Fëdor Lopukhov and composer K. A. Korchmarev, *The Serf Ballerina* (1927); and L. M. Lavrovsky, *Katerina* (1935), with the music of Anton Rubinstein and Adolphe Adam: Krasovskaya, *Istoriya russkogo baleta*, 25; Lopukhov, *Shestdesyat let v balete*.

49. Roosevelt, *Russian Country Estate*, 107–9, with portrait by N. I. Argunov; Malnick, "Russian Serf Theatres," 408; IRDT, 2:212–13; Sukhodolov, "Graf N. P. Sheremetev"; Douglas Smith, personal communication.

50. Sibiryakov: Negorov, "Krepostnoi teatr," *Teatr i iskusstvo*, 7 (Feb. 15, 1911) 153; Guseva: Medvedev (her nephew), *Vospominaniya*, 137.

51. IRDT, 2:217.

52. Qu. in Pylyaev, *Staroe zhite*, 260. Dolgorukii rendered a slightly more qualified judgment on the serfs of the Kamensky theater a few years later: Dolgorukii, *Puteshestvie*, 7–10, 197–98.

53. Kots, *Krepostnaya intelligentsiya*, 136, 138 (qu.); Gatsiskii, *Nizhegorodskii teatr* 9–19; Senelick, "Erotic Bondage," 30–31. Illustration of a punishment instrument in Smirnov, *Nizhegorodskaya starina*, 403.

54. See IRDT, vols. 2, 3, and 4, for numerous examples of successful actors; Vyazemsky's views cited in Dmitrieva, *Zhizn usadebnogo mifa*, 275; Evreinov, *Krepostnye aktëry*, 4, 24, 39, and passim; Malnick, "Russian Serf Theatres," 393 (qu.), 407–8.

55. Hoch, *Serfdom and Social Control*; Field, *Rebels in the Name of the Tsar*; Frierson, *Peasant Icons*.

56. Letkova, "Krepostnaya intelligentsiya," 171–72; Bystrov: Bugrov, *Svet kurskikh ramp*, 1:30; Turgenev, PSS, 4:86; Medvedev, *Vospominaniya*, 54. *Raisonneur*: in a play, the voice of moral judgment.

57. A prime example is Shchepetov, *Iz zhizni krepostnykh krestyan*, 41–43. See also the contrasting but mutually complementary views of Priscilla Roosevelt and Laurence Senelick in RR, 50/1 (Jan. 1991) 1–34.

58. Catherine cited by Roosevelt in *Russian Country Estate*, 138.

59. Borovsky, "Organization of the Russian Theatre" in Leach, *History of Russian Theatre*, 45; idem, "Emergence of the Russian Theatre," ibid., 64; Wirtschafter, *Play of Ideas*, 18–19; Sakhnovskii, *Krepostnoi usadebnyi teatr*, 9; Smith, *Working the Rough Stone*, 77–78; Varneke, *Istoriya*, 117–32; IRDT, 2:191–204, covering the years 1800–1812.

60. Glagoleva, *Russkaya provintsialnaya starina*, 118–19, 123, 133, 145; idem, "Dream and Reality of Russian Provincial Young Ladies," 36–41; Bernstein, "Women on the Verge of a New Language," 210–11.

61. Lavrov, *Stsena*, 121.

62. Medvedev, *Vospominaniya*, 136, 138; Edwards, *Russians at Home*, 163.

63. Ivanov, "Vospominaniya," IV (Oct. 1891) 73–76; Medvedev, *Vospominaniya*, 90–96; IRDT, 4:220–21; Zhdanov, *Putevyya*, 193–95; *Yaroslavskiya gubernskiya vedomosti*, (Mar. 3, 1856) 73. See also (Feb. 4, 1856) 39–41, (Mar. 3, 1856) 74, and (Mar. 10, 1856) 83. Information on topography and population in provincial towns as of 1843 is drawn from Gagarin, *Vseobshchii geograficheskii slovar*, and Shaw, *Landscape and Settlement in Romanov Russia*, 257.

64. Zhdanov, *Putevyya*, 48; Bobkov, "Iz zapisok byvshago krepostnogo cheloveka," IV (June 1907) 738.

65. Koshman, "Gorod i obshchestvenno-kulturnaya zhizn," 35; Selivanov, "Teatr v Tambove," 22–27 (s.p.); Zhdanov, *Putevyya*, 77; Lavrov, *Stsena*, 86–97, 103.

66. Vigel, *Zapiski*, 88; *Ocherki istorii voronezhskogo kraya*, 444–52 (qu. 446) and 460–80; Anchipolovskii, *Staryi teatr: Voronezh*, 1–120; IRDT, 4:38–40.

67. Glagoleva, *Russkaya provintsialnaya starina*, 23, 123–25; Gerakov, *Prodolzhenie putevykh zapisok*, 153; Kvitka, "Dvoryanskie vybory"; Ignatov, *Teatr i zriteli*, 306–7; Lavrov, *Stsena*, 135–38.

68. Lavrov, *Stsena*, 142–43; Medvedev, *Vospominaniya*, 48–62; Boborykin, *Vospominaniya*, 1:104 (Miloslavsky); Glagoleva, *Russkaya provintsialnaya starina*, 124–27 (qu. 126).

69. Buturlin, "Zapiski," RA, 8 (1898) 536; Smirnova, "Iz zapisok," 77; Senelick, *Serf Actor*, 171; Petrovskaya, *Teatr i zritel provintsialnoi Rossii*, 36.

70. Murzakevich, *Istoriya goroda Smolenska*, 113–20; Ryabkov, *Smolenskii krai*, 66ff.; A. Ivanov, "Pervye spektakli"; GASO, f. I, op. 1, d. 186.

71. *Putevoditel ot Moskvy do S.-Peterburga i obratno*, 108–21; Haywood, *Russia Enters the Railway Age, 1842–1855*.

72. Haywood, *Beginnings of Railway Development*, 75; Gohstand, "Geography of Trade," 333–39; Fitzpatrick, *Great Russian Fair*, 174; Melnikov, *Stoletie nizhegorodskoi yarmarki*, 1–95.

73. Gatsiskii, *Nizhegorodskii teatr*, 21–24; Belyakov, *Opernaya i kontsertnaya deyatelnost*, 19–23; Kollar, "Ocherk istorii muzykalnogo teatra v Nizhnem Novgorode," 298–99; Bremner, *Excursions in the Interior of Russia*, 2:213–16. The son of one of Shakhovskoi's actresses, Alexei Mikhailov (1818–60), was freed no later than 1838 and went on to the Academy of Arts to study with Bryullov: Gosudarstvennyi Russkii Muzei, *Zhivopis XVIII–pervoi poloviny XIX vekov*, 46.

74. Zhdanov, *Putevyya*, 202–3; Haxthausen, *Russian Empire*, 1:228; Belyakov, *Opernaya i kontsertnaya deyatelnost*, 19–28; Medvedev, *Vospominaniya*, 181 (Queen Mary); Gatsiskii, *Nizhegorodskii teatr*, 33–37, 44–45.

75. For similar events in the United States at this period, see Preston, *Opera on the Road*, 99–148. Boborykin, *Vospominaniya*, 1:58.

76. IRDT, 3:161–66 and 4:223–25; Kruti, *Russkii teatr v Kazani*, 90–149; Boborykin, *Vospominaniya*, 1:103–7.

77. E. V. Maiburov, "Muzykalnaya zhizn Ekaterinburga" in Shteinpress, *Iz muzykalnogo proshlogo*, 22–77; IRDT, 4:240–42; Medvedev, *Vospominaniya*, 194.

78. Medvedev, *Vospominaniya*, 194, 216–48; Lavrov, *Stsena*, 106–7; IRDT, 4:222–23.

79. Moser, *Pisemsky*, 68; Zaitsev, *Shevchenko*, 213; Medvedev, *Vospominaniya*, 252–53.

80. Vsevolozhskii, *Puteshestvie*, 1:10; Zhdanov, *Putevyya*, 97.

81. Bugrov, *Svet kurskikh ramp*, 1:14–19; *Kurskii oblastnoi dramaticheskii teatr*; Vnukova, "Kurskii dramaticheskii teatr"; *Kursk: kraevedcheskii slovar-spravochnik*, 140–42; IRDT, 2:225–26; Senelick, *Serf Actor*, 11, 18, 103; Lavrov, *Stsena*, 155–61.

82. Klinchin, *Rybakov*, 11–24; Lavrov, *Stsena*, 155–61; Zhdanov, *Putevyya*, 101–4.

83. Flynn, *University Reform*, 153–54. Disorders among students — drink, theft, fighting — were common at the time. Seletskii, "Zapiski," KS, 8 (Jan. 1884) 259–60; IRDT, 4:227 (Rosen qu.); Haxthausen, *Russian Empire*, 1:396.

84. Senelick, *Serf Actor*, 38–39, 46–47; Lavrov, *Stsena*, 133; Kots, *Krepostnaya intelligentsiya*, 131; Zhdanov, *Putevyya*, 142–46.

85. Zaitsev, *Shevchenko*, 101; Hamm, *Kiev*, 147 and passim; Zhdanov, *Putevyya*, 150, 161–62; Buturlin, "Zapiski," RA, 5–8 (1897) 592; Gerakov, *Prodolzhenie putevykh zapisok*, 85; *Panteon* (1852) 3; "Bogdanov Artistic Family" in Wiley, *Century of Russian Ballet*, 197; IRDT, 4:226 (Engelhardt).

86. De-Ribas (the grandson of a Neapolitan consul in Odessa), *Staraya Odessa*, 88–93

and passim; Herlihy, *Odessa*, 137, 141–42; idem, "Commerce and Architecture in Odessa." Opera: Gozenpud, *Russkii opernyi teatr;* Taruskin, *Defining Russia Musically,* 188–90; Buckler, *Literary Lorgnette,* 4–5; Zipperstein, *Jews of Odessa,* 65–66. Memoirs: Jesse, *Notes of a Half-Pay,* 1:199; Seletskii, "Zapiski," KS, 8 (Mar. 1884) 451–52; Buturlin, "Zapiski," RA, 5–8 (1897) 28; Vsevolozhskii, *Puteshestvie,* 1:100; Gerakov, *Prodolzhenie putevykh zapisok,* 64–78.

87. IRDT, 4:229–36; Senelick, *Serf Actor,* 173–74.

88. *Panteon* (1852) 11 (Kishinëv); IRDT, 4:228–29; Senelick, *Serf Actor,* 174–76; Lavrov, *Stsena,* 114–20.

89. Pskov is mentioned as a stopping point for troupes, but I have no details. The observant Zhdanov, *Putevyya,* 22, cites the absence of gentry in the town of Novgorod; Ivanov, "Vospominaniya," IV (Oct. 1891) 76–78 (Vologda); Parkinson quoted in Hartley, *Social History,* 194; Giesemann, *Kotzebue in Russland,* 73–74.

90. Borovsky, "Organization of the Russian Theatre" in Leach, *History of Russian Theatre,* 54, and "Emergence of the Russian Theatre," ibid., 65 (qu.); IRDT, 4:242–45.

91. Filonov, "V novo-cherkasskom teatre," 69–82; Klinchin, *Rybakov,* 51; Medvedev, *Vospominaniya,* 63–71, 148–76.

92. Mikhailova, "Vopros o teatralnoi monopolii," 76–86; Danilov, *Russkii dramaticheskii teatr,* 2:156; Petrovskaya, *Teatr i zritel provintsialnoi Rossii,* 29. My list: Archangel, Astrakhan, Dünaburg, Dvinsk, Ekaterinburg, Irbit, Kazan, Kerch, Kharkov, Kherson, Kiev, Kishinëv, Kostroma, Kursk, Mogilëv, Morshansk, Nikolaevsk, Nizhny Novgorod, Novocherkassk, Odessa, Orël, Orenburg, Penza, Perm, Poltava, Pskov, Rostov-on-Don, Rybinsk, Saratov, Sevastopol, Shemyaka, Simbirsk, Simferopol, Smolensk, Staraya Rusa, Stavropol, Taganrog, Tambov, Tula, Tver, Ufa, Vilna, Vladimir, Vologda, Voronezh, Voznesensk, Vyatka, Vyshny Volochok, Yaroslavl, Zhitomir.

93. Lavrov, *Stsena,* 168–70; Medvedev, *Vospominaniya,* 128–47, 177–88; Gorbunov, *Sochineniya,* 3:24, 224, passim. I have found no connection between Barsov's Inn and the serf actors of that name, nor data on when the hiring hall began functioning. A Kursk scholar believes that the connection is probable but not provable: Yurii Bugrov, conversation, Kursk, July, 2003.

94. Lavrov, *Stsena,* 103, 143–44. M. L. Mikhailov's novel *Pereplëtnye ptichki, Sochineniya* (1915), 2:83, vividly describes a colorful three-wagon caravan full of costumes and effects. Medvedev, *Vospominaniya,* 192–93, 268; Zhdanov, *Putevyya,* passim; Fitzpatrick, *Great Russian Fair,* 172.

95. Gohstand, "Geography of Trade," 329 (qu.); Rozman, *Urban Networks,* 120; Barenboim, *Rubinshtein,* 1:43; Burgess, "Fairs and Entertainers in 18th-Century Russia," 95–113; Nekrylova, *Russkie narodnye gorodskie prazdniki.*

96. Dolgoruky cited in Vsevolodskii-Gerngross, *Teatr v Rossii,* 147, 151. The prince noted some years later that in Ukraine the streets were also a Babel of languages: Dolgorukii, *Puteshestvie,* 87–88. Shalikov, *Drugoe puteshestvie v Malorossiyu,* 89–95; Herzen, *My Past,* 171–73 (Tyufyaev); Christoff, *Introduction,* vol. 3: *Aksakov,* 64–65. An exciting evocation of days at a country fair is offered in Egor Klassen's novel, *Provintsialnaya zhizn,* 3 v. (Moscow, 1843) 1:53–131. See also Selivanov, "Teatr v Tambove."

97. Herlihy, "South Ukraine as an Economic Region," 316; Gohstand, "Geography of Trade," 339–46 (map, p. 340); Dynnik, *Krepostnoi teatr,* 47; Zaitsev, *Shevchenko,* 113.

98. Lysykh, "Istoriya kurskoi korenskoi yarmarki," 7–8; Ieromonakh Leonid, "Korennaya yarmarka", 34–35; Gohstand, "Geography of Trade," 344; Rozman, *Urban Networks,* passim; Zhdanov, *Putevyya,* 97–99; Lavrov, *Stsena,* 161–63; Senelick, *Serf Actor,* 25. The fair still functions.

99. Gorshkov, "Serfs on the Move: Peasant Seasonal Migration."

100. Szwankowski, *Teatr Wojciecha Boguslawskiego,* 212, 239; see also Ratajczak, "Teatr prowincjionalny i prowincja teatralna"; Saunders, *Ukrainian Impact on Russian Culture;* IRDT, 2:399–402.

101. Vsevolodskii-Gerngross, *Teatr v Rossii,* 151; IRDT, 2:402–10, 461; TE, 5:925–26; Senelick, *Serf Actor,* 35–39.

102. IRDT, 3:166–77; TE, 3:868–69.

103. Letkova, "Krepostnaya intelligentsiya," 157–59; Senelick, *Serf Actor,* 1–20, 136 (qu.); Shchepkin, "Zapiski"; Osykov, *Ya rodilsya v sele Krasnom.*

104. Senelick, *Serf Actor,* 20–54; Shchepkin, "Zapiski," 93–128; Malnick, "Actors Shchepkin and Sosnitsky," 293.

105. Senelick, *Serf Actor,* 69–248 passim; Laskina, *Mochalov,* 152; Rybakov in Lavrov, *Stsena,* 132; Rossiev, "M. S. Shchepkin, gastrolër," 60–67.

106. Klinchin, *Rybakov,* passim; Lavrov, *Stsena,* 124–30; IRDT, 3:193–99.

107. Ivanov, "Vospominaniya"; Haywood, *Beginnings of Railway Development,* 1–17(Rybinsk and the river systems).

108. Ivanov, "Vospominaniya," IV (Oct. 1891) 67, 71–72; (Nov. 1891) 323–32, and passim.

109. Medvedev, *Vospominaniya,* 27–28, 75–87, 97–107, 120, and passim; TE, 3:758.

110. Petrovskaya, *Teatr i zritel provintsialnoi Rossii,* 98; Mikhailov, *Pereplëtnye ptichki, Sochineniya* (1915), 2:1–296. Boborykin, *Za polveka,* 327. See also Fateev, *Mikhail Mikhailov,* 128–30. Medvedev, *Vospominaniya,* 138–43, 183–86; Ivanov, "Vospominaniya," IV (Nov. 1891) 338–45 and (Dec. 1891) 583–88; IRDT, 4:252–53; Kruti, *Russkii teatr v Kazani,* 102.

111. Lavrov, *Stsena,* 7–40, 48–78 (qu. 50 and 67). As a member of the *meshchanstvo* (a townsman) he was required constantly to account for his movements to the police.

112. Ibid., 86–97, 103–5, 114–24.

113. Ibid., 94, 105, 120–21, 144, 161–63.

114. Ibid., 164–66 (list of his provincial roles), 196–206 (qu. 197), 217–18. Not all provincials passed their Moscow auditions. An earlier actor, anticipating Ernst Neizvestny's famous confrontation with Khrushchev, responded thus to criticism of his "realistic" delivery: "Your Excellency, a general's rank does not suffice to make judgments on art." He was dismissed: Efros, *Shchepkin,* 27.

115. TE, 1:1052; IRDT, 3:201–3.

116. Nikulina-Kositskaia, "Notes," 109–57.

117. Bulgarin, *Ivan Vyzhigin,* 3:131; Nikulina-Kositskaya, "Notes," 150. This version corrects the biographical dates in the original: "Zapiski." For the Volga references, see RS (Feb. 1878) 296–97. See also Varneke, *Istoriya,* 579–81.

118. "Bogdanov Artistic Family" in Wiley, *Century of Russian Ballet,* 188–213; Insarskii, *Zapiski,* 132–33; *Illyustrirovannyi semeinyi listok,* 63–64 (Feb. 14, 1860) 103–6; RB, 65–66.

119. Arnold, *Vospominaniya*, 2:101–3; Selivanov, "Teatr v Tambove," 27; R. M. Zotov, "Zapiski," IV (Oct., 1896) 36.

120. *Panteon* (Mar. 1852) 2 (s.p.); Anchipolovskii, *Staryi teatr: Voronezh*, 95 (Sokolov). Entrepreneur N. I. Ivanov describes how personal connections worked in getting into the Moscow theater: "Vospominaniya," IV (Oct. 1891) 85–87. The pathway from provincial circuits to stardom in the capitals was common throughout Europe. From the provinces Isidoro Maiquez (d. 1820) went to Madrid; Karoly Megyeri (1799–1842) and Marton Lendvay (1807–58) to Pest; Johann Brockmann (1745–1812) to Vienna; Ludwig Devrient (1784–1832) to the Royal Theater in Berlin; and Edmund Kean from Wales and Exeter to London. For the last, see Donohue, *Theatre in the Age of Kean*.

121. Medvedev, *Vospominaniya*, 132.

122. Lavrov, *Stsena*, 133; Medvedev, *Vospominaniya*, 234, 261–62; Vnukova, "Kurskii dramaticheskii teatr" 59 (tavern drinking). Artists were not above cheating. One provincial performer signed on to play twenty-four instruments which turned out to be twenty-four drums: "Bogdanov Artistic Family" in Wiley, *Century of Russian Ballet*, 194–95. Managers and actors used cheap devices to fill the seats, such as *affiches* showing fires, bridges destroyed, daggers, poison, and other horrors that appeared nowhere in the production: Filonov, "V novo-cherkasskom teatre," 80. One actor chose for his benefit a work centered around 1812; he borrowed cannons from the garrison and placed them in front of the theater to suggest a lavish spectacle, thus angering the full house when no ordnance appeared on stage: Lavrov, *Stsena*, 160–61.

123. Bulgarin, *Ivan Vyzhigin*, 3:115–42 (qu. 124). The novel was translated as *Ivan Vejeeghen* and excerpted in Von Geldern, *Entertaining Tsarist Russia*, 65–74.

124. Veltman, "*Provintsialnye aktëry*," *Biblioteka dlya chteniya*, 10 (1835) 108–43. The vaudeville, *Neistovyi Roland v bezumnom dome*, was a translation of *Roland furieux*, a send-up of Ariosto. Soviet scholars, unwilling to admit such a humble provenance for the idea behind Gogol's masterpiece, instead attributed it to a twenty-word fragment by Pushkin. But the similarities between Veltman's tale and *Inspector General* are too obvious to be ignored.

125. Mikhailov, *Pereplëtnye ptichki*, *Sochineniya* (1915), 2:1–296. The Soviet edition, *Sochineniya* (1958) 2:124–392, contains useful commentary, pp. 550–57. Except for tales of exploitation, most Soviet accounts of provincial theater tend to ignore the life of actors outside their stage roles. The narratives of theater life are male-dominated and thus incomplete and even distorted. Gender in the postemancipation period is skillfully explored in Schuler, *Women in Russian Theater*, and her present research holds promise for a deeper understanding of life on stage in the pre-emancipation period.

126. Petrovskaya, *Teatr i zritel provintsialnoi Rossii*, 38–39; Drizen, *Materialy*, 132–33; Mikhailova, "Vopros o teatralnoi monopolii"; Golub, *Recurrence of Fate*, 134 (*Woe from Wit*); Danilov, *Russkii dramaticheskii teatr*, 2:158; IRDT, 3:152–53. Enterprising scholars seem to find more illegal performances of *Woe from Wit* each year.

127. To take but two comparative examples, see Pies, *Theater in Schleswig*; Pekacz, *Music in the Culture of Polish Galicia*.

128. For the complete list, see Artynov, *Vospominaniya krestyanina*, 140.

129. Ivanov, "Vospominaniya," IV (Oct. 1891) 74; Moser, *Pisemsky*, 55; Boborykin, *Vospominaniya*, 1:56–59; IRDT, 3:150–51; Seletskii, "Zapiski," KS, 8 (Jan. 1884) 259–60.

130. At a performance in Kaluga of *Dmitry Donskoi* in the 1830s, the gallery clapped with furor to recall the lead who appeared in sandals and bowed to the four corners of the theater with his hand over his heart: Smirnova, "Iz zapisok," 79.

131. IRDT, 3:151; Levine, *Highbrow/Lowbrow,* 15 and passim.

132. Ozarovskii, "Khram Talii i Melpomeny," 522–23.

133. Smirnov, *Nizhegorodskaya starina,* 436; Gatsiskii, "Aleksandr Dmitrievich Uly-byshev," 55–56, 66.

134. Medvedev, *Vospominaniya,* 257–59; Senelick, *Serf Actor,* 76; M. I. Semevskii [Mikhail Se——vskii], "Progulka v Nizhnii Novgorod," RV (Aug. 1860) 295–96 (Ry-binsk); Ivanov, "Vospominaniya," IV (Oct. 1891) 70 and (Nov. 1891) 333, 340.

135. Senelick, *Serf Actor,* xiii (qu.), 53. See also IRDT, 3:153–58.

136. Filonov, "V novo-cherkasskom teatre"; IRDT, 3:169–73, for one of numerous examples cited throughout these volumes; Kruti, *Russkii teatr v Kazani,* 97 (Aksakov). For a sample of Belinsky on theater, see an excerpt in Senelick, *Russian Dramatic Theory,* 60–70.

137. Kapkanishchikov: "Kniga pamyati Alekseya Petrovicha Kapkanishchikova," *Iz istorii voronezhskogo kraya,* 181–206 (see 188–89, 201–2). Boborykin, *Vospomina-niya,* 1:56–59; the Kursk peasant: Bugrov, *Svet kurskikh ramp,* 1:25–26. For Popular Theaters — enterprises created by the intelligentsia, state, church, and private organiza-tions to promote culture for the lower classes — see Swift, *Popular Theater,* especially pp. 266–84; and Thurston, *Popular Theater,* who discusses peasant reactions to theatrical performances and readings in the 1860s to 1880s (pp. 10, 68–73, 101–15). For parallels in reading tastes, see Brooks, *When Russia Learned to Read.*

138. Tolchënov: Ransel, "Eighteenth-Century Russian Merchant Family"; idem, "En-lightenment and Tradition."

139. Orlovskii starozhil, *Bylyya chudaki,* 14–15 (Kamensky); Ivanov, "Vospomina-niya," IV (Oct. 1891) 71 (Shiryaev); Merzlyakov, "Poseshchenie teatra," on divinity students. It seems unlikely that the Jewish theatergoers were only those under the influ-ence of the growing Haskalah (Enlightenment) movement flowing in from Austria and the Germanies. For the breadth of audience reception in the Popular Theaters of later times, see Swift, *Popular Theater,* 205–31. Though seldom noted, acting (and dancing for females) outside the calendric ritual cycle was considered sinful in the norms of peasant culture: Dmitrieva, *Zhizn usadebnogo mifa,* 276.

140. Senelick, *Serf Actor,* 11.

141. "Bogdanov Artistic Family" in Wiley, *Century of Russian Ballet,* 192–93.

142. Wortman, *Scenarios of Power,* 1:306–8 and passim. Under Nicholas I, governors in some towns appointed local directorates composed of minor officials to oversee theater schedules and repertoires, while leaving artistic management to theater staff. The social power system of the Imperial Directorate was only roughly replicated. Directors had their female "favorites," and actors who insulted one could be dismissed. More often they got detailed to guard duty, as in Voronezh where, in Medvedev's words, "nearly everyone in town would come to see Hamlet on duty in the watchtower." Memoirs testified to the decency of most officials toward theater people: IRDT, 3:25; Medvedev, *Vospominaniya,* 195 (qu.) and passim; Lavrov, *Stsena,* 139.

Chapter 7. Academic Vistas

1. The eighteenth-century European art flow into Russia is told in splendid illustrative detail in Cracraft, *Petrine Revolution in Russian Imagery.*

2. Repin, *Dalëkoe blizkoe,* 121. The description comes from my visits in 1989 and 1997–98 and from three illustrated books: Litovchenko, *Nauchno-issledovatelskii muzei;* Lisovskii, *Akademiya khudozhestv;* and *Imperatorskaya Akademiya Khudozhestv* (1997). Plakhov, *Coachmen's Room at the Academy of Arts:* GRMFZh, 5204. See the painting of the antique gallery by G. K. Mikhailov from the 1830s in Alekseeva, *Khudozhniki,* 215.

3. Prehistory in Cracraft, *Petrine Revolution in Russian Imagery,* 234–42. See also note 2 above, and McConnell, "Catherine the Great and the Fine Arts"; Munro, "Academy of Fine Arts." Mikhail Piotrovsky, Director of the State Hermitage Museum, lecture on October 8, 1999 at the National Museum of Women in the Arts in Washington, D. C.

4. Quote: *Finland and Russia,* 484; ISAKh, 13–14. Unlike the Paris Academy, the Petersburg Academy housed all the arts in one building: Hamilton, *Art and Architecture,* 228. See also Boime, *Academy and French Painting.* For foundlings, see chap. 4 and Ransel, *Mothers of Misery,* 31–62.

5. Painting reproduced in Shevchenko, *Povest,* 290. Administrative details and biographies: Kondakov, *Yubileinyi spravochnik.* See also Limonov, *Rossiya pervoi poloviny XIX v. glazami inostrantsev,* 713 n. 19.

6. ISAKh, 21–32; Moleva, *Russkaya khudozhestvennaya shkola,* 19–44; Choiseul-Gouffier, *Historical Memoirs,* viii; Stroganov: Sarabianov, *Russian Art,* 12; Kots, *Krepostnaya intelligentsiya,* 83–86; Hunter-Stiebel, *Stroganoff,* 145–56; Petrov, *Sbornik materialov,* 1:44.

7. Solntsev, "Moya zhizn," RS (Feb. 1876) 311–23, a favorable account; A. Zotov, "Puti razvitiya russkogo iskusstva," 73, a more critical one. A good balanced study in English is Stuart *Aristocrat-Librarian,* see pp. 111–12. For Labzin's mystical contacts, see Etkind, "Umirayushchii sfinks"; and Labzina, *Days of a Russian Noblewoman.*

8. Korf, "Materialy," 45; ISAKh, 32–46.

9. Valkenier, *Russian Realist Art,* 4–7. In 1840, the closing of the boarding school reduced the educational level of Academy students.

10. ISAKh, 29 (both qu.); Kondakov, *Yubileinyi spravochnik,* 1:288; Yunge (his daughter), "Iz moikh vospominanii"; idem, *Vospominaniya,* the book version; and Tolstoy, *Tolstoys,* 146–72 and passim (silhouette, 175).

11. Nikitenko, *Diary,* 45; Yunge, "Iz moikh vospominanii," VE, 40/1–2 (Jan.–Feb. 1905) 804 (qu.).

12. Savinov, *Akademiya Khudozhestv,* 1–25; ISAKh, 24.

13. Perkins, "Mobility in the Art Profession," 225–33 (230 n. 29); Solntsev, "Moya zhizn," RS (Jan. 1876) 116–28.

14. Bowlt, "Russian Painting," 117–18; Moleva, *Russkaya khudozhestvennaya shkola,* 9; A. Zotov, "Puti razvitiya russkogo iskusstva," 77. For a detailed administrative history of the Academy to 1863, see Petrov, *Sbornik,* vols. 1–3.

15. Flynn, *University Reform,* 75–80. See also Friedman, "In the Company of Men, 25, 29–30, 61ff. Obligated classes: those who were taxable and liable for military service.

16. Ruban, *Zabitye imena,* 28 (qu.), 29. Subsequent rulings in Petrov, *Sbornik,* 1:93–94, 114–15.

17. A. Zotov, "Puti razvitiya russkogo iskusstva," 73; Kots, *Krepostnaya intelligentsiya,* 52. Similar arrangements involved, apparently, no tension: cf. the Smolensk landowner who sent a young house serf to the Moscow English Club to learn culinary art in order for him to return to employment in his kitchen: Mariya Nikoleva, "Cherty starinnago byta," RA, 10 (1893) 169. See also Gray, *Russian Genre Painting,* ix.

18. The decree: Kurmachëva, *Krepostnaya intelligentsiya,* 111; Vrangel, "Arakcheev i iskusstvo," 439–71 (qu. 458). See also Jenkins, *Arakcheev.*

19. Moleva, *Russkaya khudozhestvennaya shkola,* 347 n. 32, reproduces only a somewhat misleading portion of this correspondence with Arakcheev. The full version is in "Aleksei Nikolaevich Olenin," esp. 284–88, letter of Olenin to Arakcheev, Dec. 16, 1817 (qu. 286–87). Additional comment in Stuart, *Aristocrat-Librarian,* 103–4. A decade later, reacting to the suicide of a serf art student, General Benckendorff, chief of the political police, echoed Olenin's view that "only free men should be allowed to study the fine arts." Morrisey, "In the Name of Freedom," 289 (see chapter 8 of the present work).

20. Stuart *Aristocrat-Librarian,* 148.

21. V. I. Semevskii, *Krestyanskii vopros v Rossii,* 1:399.

22. Starr, "Russian Art and Society," 104.

23. Martin, *Romantics, Reformers, Reactionaries,* 98.

24. A. Zotov, "Puti razvitiya russkogo iskusstva," 73; Petrov, *Sbornik,* 3:3.

25. Selected data on social origins from 1764 in Petrov, *Sbornik,* 1:159–71. Other eighteenth- and all nineteenth-century figures: Perkins, "Mobility in the Art Profession," 225–33 (her figures for 1833–39 refer only to state-supported students). In contrast to the eighteenth century, very few graduates of serf origin became prominent. Other sources show the children of merchants of various guilds as Academy students. See also Savinov, *Akademiya Khudozhestv,* 1–25.

26. Perkins, "Mobility in the Art Profession"; Maegd-Soep, *Emancipation of Women,* 97; Tomei, *Russian Women Writers,* 1:350; Kondakov, *Spisok,* 192; Petrov, *Sbornik,* 1:426.

27. Moleva, *Russkaya khudozhestvennaya shkola,* 20–21; Shevchenko, *Povest,* 38 n. 21; Stuart, *Aristocrat-Librarian,* 99–100; Valkenier, *Russian Realist Art,* 1–3; Yakovkina, *Istoriya russkoi kultury,* 212–13.

28. Solntsev, "Moya zhizn," RS (Jan. 1876) 116–28 and (Feb. 1876) 315–16, 318; Moleva, *Pedagogicheskaya sistema Akademii Khudozhestv,* 135; Moleva, *Russkaya khudozhestvennaya shkola,* 39. The Blagoveshchensky (later Nikolaevsky) Bridge between Vasilevsky Island at the Academy and the English Embankment did not open until 1853: lithograph in Lotman, *Velikosvetskie obedy,* 110.

29. Valkenier, *Russian Realist Art,* 14.

30. Seryakov, "Moya trudovaya zhizn." Kots, *Krepostnaya intelligentsiya,* 52, 78–83, like most others who wrote about Seryakov, omits Bulgarin's role. Throughout, the capitalized term "Academician" refers to an honorific title granted by the Academy which came with government rank and the chance of a low-ranking teaching post. I use "academician" in the usual sense of one teaching at or professing the norms of the Academy.

31. Solntsev, "Moya zhizn"; Belozerskaya, "Fëdor Grigorevich Solntsev."

32. Zaitsev, *Shevchenko*, 41–57, 115, passim; Shevchenko, *Povest*, 39 (qu.), 116–18. This autobiographical novella of 1855 (*The Artist* in English) offers a colorful picture of life inside the Academy.

33. F. F. Lvov, "Obshchestvo Pooshchreniya Khudozhnikov," 633–54 (qu. 635).

34. Moleva, *Russkaya khudozhestvennaya shkola*, passim; Savinov, *Akademiya Khudozhestv*, 1–25; Ramazanov, "Vospominaniya o Karle Pavloviche Bryullove," 19; Solntsev, "Moya zhizn," RS (Jan. 1876) 119–28; Boime, *Academy and French Painting*, 19–21; ISAKh, 24–25.

35. Alekseeva, *Venetsianov*, 28–29. The drawings got Venetsianov's application for an Academy position rejected: Gray, *Russian Genre Painting*, 89.

36. Petrov, *Sbornik*, 1:119; Kondakov, *Yubileinyi spravochnik*, 1:159; Valkenier, *Russian Realist Art*, 1–6; Stuart *Aristocrat-Librarian*, 99; Norman, "Pavel Tret'iakov (1832–1898)," 70.

37. Savinov, *Akademiya Khudozhestv*, 35.

38. Edwards, *Russians at Home*, 346–47.

39. Mme. de Staël's *Corinne, a Story of Italy;* Sarabianov, *Russian Art*, 44.

40. Bowlt, "Russian Painting," 122–23; Taylor, "Russian Painters and the Pursuit of Light"; Kondakov, *Spisok*, 5, 126.

41. Morozov, *Russkaya khudozhestvennaya fotografiya*, 12 (ill.); Shevchenko, *Povest*, 335; Tomei, *Russian Women Writers*, 1:288 (Kologrivova); unsigned and unidentified newspaper clipping in RGALI, f. 191, ed. kh. 2057 (scandals).

42. ISAKh, 42 (qu.); Bowlt, "Russian Painting," 123.

43. Mai, "Poussin, Félibien, und Lebrun: zur Formierung der französischen Historienmalerei an der Académie Royale de Peinture et de Sculpture in Paris" in Mai, *Historienmalerei in Europa*, 9–25; Pevsner, *Academies of Art*, 89–101: Barrell, "Public Prospect and the Private View," 35; Burke, *English Art*, 90–119, 236–39; Leppert, *Art and the Committed Eye*, 41.

44. Shevchenko, *Povest*, 166.

45. For interesting commentary, see Savinov, "Akademicheskaya zhivopis."

46. Reproduction in Moleva, *Russkaya khudozhestvennaya shkola*, pl. 44. The Notbek hangs in the Circular Gallery of the Academy (see also Litovchenko, *Nauchno-issledovatelskii muzei*, 13). For an interesting speculation on viewers of homoerotic art, see Collins, *Leonardo*, 180–81 and passim.

47. Ramazanov, "Vospominaniya o Karle Pavloviche Bryullove"; Hare, *Art and Artists of Russia*, 179; Gagarin, "Vospominaniya," 899.

48. Edward Bulwer-Lytton's once world-famous novel, *The Last Days of Pompeii*, appeared a year after Bryullov completed his canvas and was translated into Russian in 1836. Gagarin, "Vospominaniya," 899; Pacini, *L'ultimo giorno di Pompeii*, score and libretto. Commentary in Sarabianov, *Russian Art*, 58–60; Bowlt, "Russian Painting," 125.

49. RGALI, f. 191, ed. kh. 2057 (P. A. Efremov, materials on Karl Bryullov); Hudson, *Rise of the Demidov Family*, 113–14; MERSH, 9:52–54; Volkov, *St. Petersburg*, 62.

50. Olkhovskii, *Peterburgskie istorii*, 17 (Nekrasov); Swift, *Popular Theater*, 37–38 (circus).

51. Unsigned, "Gigant russkago iskusstva," RGALI, f. 191, ed. kh. 2057; Ramazanov, "Vospominaniya o Karle Pavloviche Bryullove," 1–4; Savinov, *Bryullov*, 102.

52. On patroness-ward relationship among the Russian gentry, see Kelly, *Refining Russia,* 43–44. For the Bryullov-Samoilova liaison, see Regina, "Karl Briullov's Portrait."

53. The poet Yuliya Zhadovskaya, *Polnoe sobranie sochinenii,* 1:138; Nikitenko, *Diary,* 78.

54. Insarskii, *Zapiski,* 74–75; Shevchenko, in *The Artist,* often gives an impression of Bryullov's moderation; Sarabianov, *Russian Art,* 62.

55. RGALI, f. 191, ed. kh. 2057 (revival). According to some accounts, Bryullov once gave up waiting for Tsar Nicholas I to appear for a portrait sitting when the monarch was twenty minutes late. The artist explained his breach of court etiquette by saying that he knew of the tsar's punctuality and therefore thought that he was not coming at all: Sarabianov, *Russian Art,* 57.

56. Baehr, *Paradise Myth,* and Wortman, *Scenarios of Power,* 1; Savinov, *Akademiya Khudozhestv,* 23; Paulson, *Beautiful, Novel, and Strange,* 305.

57. RKh, 220–22 (Egorov).

58. OZ (Mar. 1858) cited in Lotman, *Velikosvetskie obedy,* 284; Boborykin, *Vospominaniya,* 1:176; Gray, *Russian Genre Painting,* 107–9. The agony of Ivanov's composition is summarized in Sarabianov, *Russian Art,* 70–72. Commentary: Bowlt, "Russian Painting," 127–28.

59. Werner Busch, "Über Helden diskutiert Man nicht: zum Wandel des Historienbildes im englischen 18. Jahrhundert" in Mai, *Historienmalerei,* 57–76.

60. Kondakov, *Spisok,* 116; Hamilton, *Art and Architecture,* 228; Lebedev, *Russkaya istoricheskaya zhivopis,* unpaginated; Cracraft, *Petrine Revolution in Russian Imagery,* 246–47.

61. Tr. in Segel, *Literature of Eighteenth-Century Russia,* 1:459–69 (qu. 459). For other contemporary articles along these lines, see Vrangel, "Romantizm v zhivopisi aleksandrovskoi epokhi," SG (July–Sept. 1908) 383.

62. A. Zotov, "Puti razvitiya russkogo iskusstva," 70.

63. ISAKh, 28, Savinov, *Akademiya Khudozhestv,* 28.

64. Vrangel, "Romantizm v zhivopisi," 383–87; Aptekar, *Russkaya istoricheskaya zhivopis;* Zorin, *Kormya dvuglavogo orla,* 160–61.

65. Ivanchin-Pisarev, *Otechestvennaya galleriya,* 1:153 and 2:1–77; Kohlman, *On Senate Square, December 14, 1825.* Reproduced many times: see Shevchenko, *Povest,* 228. A. Zotov, "Puti razvitiya russkogo iskusstva," 70.

66. Burke, *Eyewitnessing,* 51, 53, 143–44. The battle paintings (a so-named branch of the art profession) dealing with more recent events were much better but not much more interesting.

67. Pevsner, *Academies of Art,* 234; IIRR, 11.

68. Burke, *Eyewitnessing,* 26; Leppert, *Art and the Committed Eye,* 9, 165, and idem, *Music and Image,* chap. 8. For self-control as a badge of nobility, see Elias, *Civilizing Process.*

69. Galagin: Ruban, *Zabitye imena,* 38–39; the Kochubei picture may have been commissioned by his survivors since he died in 1834 and the piece is roughly dated to the mid-1830s: Alekseeva, *Khudozhniki,* 213; Glebov: Marasinova, "Kultura russkoi usadby," 296, 309.

70. See *Portretnaya miniatyura,* 1. Among many treatments, Andreeva, *Pervye khudozhniki Peterburga,* and Hare, *Art and Artists of Russia,* 114–15. I have also drawn from

Grand Duke N. M. Romanov's *Russkie portrety XVIII i XIX vekov*, which contains about one thousand portrait reproductions. For its importance, see Cockfield, *White Crow*, 77.

71. Cannadine, *Aspects of Aristocracy*, 27–34.

72. Bonnell, *Iconography of Power*, 154. Ironically, many of the portraits of the Stalin era possessed exactly this quality.

73. Hare, *Art and Artists of Russia*, 119 and pl. 71; Yatsevich, *Pushkinskii Peterburg*, 27–28. Comment and reproductions in Baehr, *Paradise Myth*, 80–82, 121; Roosevelt, *Russian Country Estate*, 126–27; *Portret v russkoi zhivopisi XVIII–XIX vekov*. Hamilton, *Art and Architecture of Russia*, 229.

74. Bowlt, "Russian Painting," 114; Roosevelt, *Russian Country Estate*, 127–28; *Portret v russkoi zhivopisi*, unnumbered reproduction. Kurakin the censor: Gray, *Russian Genre Painting*, 81 n. 44. See also Richard Brompton's 1781 portrait showing a cross-legged Kurakin with a walking stick, leaning on a rocky surface in a very vague landscape. Here the subject is so obviously happy that he has gone beyond the conventional restraint: Cross, *By the Banks of the Neva*, 308–13 (ill. 313).

75. Reproduction: plate ix of IRI, 1. See Leppert, *Music and Image*, 161–62. Borovikovsky's enchanting miniatures in *Portretnaya miniatyura*, 1:120–32.

76. The painter became a devotee of Ekaterina Tatarinova, Lutheran-born and Smolny-educated widow of a military hero. She hosted a "ship" or chapter of the Petersburg Khlysty and Skoptsy religious sectarians, the latter known for their practice of self-castration. Along with Nikita Fëdorov, a peasant prophet and musician from the Cadet Corps, she conducted "raptures" in the Mikhailovsky Castle, where adepts attired in white garments sang and uttered prophecy: Sarabianov, *Russian Art*, 27; Yatsevich, *Pushkinskii Peterburg*, 118–20. For the mystical currents, see Etkind, "Umirayushchii sfinks" and Engelstein, *Castration and the Heavenly Kingdom*, 41.

77. Sarabyanov, *Kiprenskii*; Hare, *Art and Artists of Russia*, 173–74; Kots, *Krepostnaya intelligentsiya*, 68–69. There are many versions of the murder story. Reproductions: *Portret v russkoi zhivopisi*, unnumbered; *Portretnaya miniatyura*, 2:16.

78. The question which of three Davydov brothers is here represented is still debated. IRI, 1, pl. xi; Kirsanova, *Kostyum v russkoi khudozhestvennoi kulture*, 158–60; idem, *Rozovaya ksendreika*, and Fedosyuk, *Chto neponyatno u klassikov*.

79. Sarabyanov, *Russian Art*, 30, 32.

80. Rosenthal, *Prospects for the Nation*, 1–12 and passim.

81. Barrell, "Public Prospect and the Private View"; Ann Pullan, "For Publicity and Profit" in Rosenthal, *Prospects for the Nation*, 261–84. Other British scholars have interpreted the panoramic outlook as rational or leveling and opposed to the "organic" and picturesque views which represented the natural development of English politics: Ann Bermingham, "System, Order, and Abstraction: the Politics of English Landscape Drawing around 1795" in Mitchell, *Landscape and Power*, 83.

82. Honour, *Neo-classicism*, 161.

83. See for example his *Pastoral Landscape* (c. 1650) and comment in Janson, *History of Art*, 592–93; Clark, *Landscape into Art*, 54–73.

84. Newlin, "Rural Ruses," 307; idem, *Voice in the Garden*, 20, 24, 41, 104–5 (watercolors), and passim.

85. IIRR, pl. 46 and text.

86. Roosevelt, *Russian Country Estate,* 83, 127–28.

87. Some of the dates and attributions are contested. Illustrations in Roosevelt, *Russian Country Estate,* 76, 170, 293; Shevchenko. *Povest,* 162; IIRR, pls. 78–80, 90, 94, 136. See also Roosevelt, "Country House as a Setting and Symbol," 43–44; and Shchepetov, *Iz zhizni krepostnykh krestyan,* 49.

88. See for example Roosevelt, *Russian Country Estate;* and Cavender, "Nests of Gentry."

89. Roosevelt, *Russian Country Estate,* 111 (Poltoratsky); IIRR, pls. 110 and 129 (*View of a Town with Fortress Wall* is undated and anonymous). For more on suburban representation, see Lovell, *Summerfolk.*

90. On the urban genre in early modern Europe, see Burke, *Eyewitnessing,* 84. For an introduction to the literature on the Petersburg myth and "text," see Hellberg, *Imperial Imprints;* Kaganov, *Images of Space;* and Sidney Monas, "St. Petersburg and Moscow as Cultural Symbols" in Stavrou, *Art and Culture,* 26–39.

91. Volkov, *St. Petersburg,* 16.

92. *Pushkinskii Peterburg.*

93. Sadovnikov, *Vidy Peterburga,* a set of twenty-four unnumbered reproductions. See also *Panorama Nevskogo Prospekta,* lithographs based on Sadovnikov's watercolors, 1830–35. The most spectacular book of reproductions, Gusev, *Sankt-Peterburg,* privileges the official city and gives some attention to the humbler quarters. See also Lure, *Blistatelnyi Peterburg.*

94. RKh, 673; Gray, *Russian Genre Painting,* 84–85. The Chernetsov canvas contains a remarkable gallery of notables, including many of the people in this book.

95. Lotman, *Velikosvetskie obedy,* 32. *Parade on Palace Square:* GRMFZh, 3726. Additional parade scenes: "Paradnyi Peterburg" in Gusev, *Sankt-Peterburg,* 59–71.

96. Since no residences except the royal family's Marble Palace faced Mars Field, it was hard to find interior spaces from which to view the spectacle. The opera singer Darya Leonova wangled a place in the Pavlovsk Guards barracks to see a parade there: Leonova, "Vospominaniya artistki Imperatorskikh Teatrov," IV (Jan. 1891) 133. See also *Nouvelle collection* in RNBOE, Sobranie I. I. Rybakova, Ei-227. For more on the routines, costumes, and functions of parade culture, see Keller, *Prazdnichnaya kultura Peterburga.* The magnificence of the uniforms of that era is illustrated in Bespalova, *Kostyum v Rossii,* 173–206.

97. Herzen, *My Past,* 290; Kondakov, *Spisok,* 222; see a portrait of Shebuev at work in 1831 by I. I. Vistelius in *Portretnaya miniatyura,* 2:94.

98. Savinov, *Akademiya Khudozhestv,* 28–35; Lisovskii, *Akademiya khudozhestv,* 3–10; and Litovchenko, *Nauchno-issledovatelskii muzei.*

99. Yunge, "Iz moikh vospominanii," VE, 40/1–2 (Jan.–Feb. 1905) 805–6; Timofeev, *Khudozhnik.*

100. Pevsner, *Academies of Art,* 221–23, 239 (qu.). For commentary on the European shift, see also Friedlaender, *David to Delacroix,* 129.

101. Sarabianov, *Russian Art,* 11.

102. Macleod, *Art and the Victorian Middle Class,* 11.

103. West, "Romantic Landscape in Early Nineteenth-Century Russian Art." A British

critic, commenting on a Russian art exhibit in London in 1862, observed "a collection of all the various influences under the weight of which Russian art has developed to its present, very inferior level." Cited in Valkenier, *Russian Realist Art*, 57.

104. Savinov, "Akademicheskaya zhivopis"; idem, *Akademiya Khudozhestv*, 19; Vrangel, "A. V. Stupin i ego ucheniki," 435.

105. L. M. Tarasov, "Pavel Antonovich Ritstsoni" in Leonov, *Russkoe iskusstvo* (1958), 263–74.

106. Gray, *Russian Genre Painting*, 20–31, 36–44; Hunter-Stiebel, *Stroganoff*; Gorodetzky, "Princess Zinaide Volkonsky," 101. Shevchenko and friends were once politely turned away at the Yusupov Palace: *Povest*, 232. In its proposal of 1824, the Society for the Encouragement of Artists stated that "the glory of Russia or its reputation demands the establishment of a Russian museum or gallery devoted to the Russian school of art. . . . A Russian museum would strengthen in the public mind its love for art and would engender respect for our own natural talents": Komelova, "Peterburgskoe Obshchestvo Pooshchreniya Khudozhestv"; Moleva, *Russkaya khudozhestvennaya shkola*, 249.

107. Starr, "Russian Art and Society," 96, 100; Bowlt, "Russian Painting," 122; Vrangel, "Iskusstvo i gosudar Nikolai Pavlovich," 53–163 (qu. 57); Gray, *Russian Genre Painting*, 31 (Sapieha). Nicholas also purged the works of Ivanov *père* from the Academy: Hare, *Art and Artists of Russia*, 183.

108. Shevchenko, *Povest*, 230 (with a reproduction of the ticket); Ge cited in Shumova, *Russkaya zhivopis*, 26. Ilya Repin, on entering the Academy in 1863, was told by Fëdor Lvov that the frock coat rule was long gone: Repin, *Dalëkoe blizkoe*, 124. See also Kuznetsov, *Ermitazh*; Shapiro, *Ermitazh i ego shedevry* and *Ermitazh: putevoditel*. Gray, *Russian Genre Painting*, 19, dates the end of the ticket system to 1866.

109. Wes, *Classics in Russia*, 134; Stuart *Aristocrat-Librarian*, passim; Batyushkov, "Progulka v Akademiyu Khudozhestv," 160 (qu.). See also Serman, *Konstantin Batyushkov*, 106–8.

110. Solntsev, "Moya zhizn," RS (Feb. 1876) 313; Starr, "Russian Art and Society," 95–96; Nikitenko, *Diary*, 20; Raikes, *City of the Czar*, 1:66; Ramazanov, "Vospominaniya," 56. The ragged but steady evolution from a limited audience into an art public in France is meticulously traced in Crow, *Painters and Public Life*.

111. Alpers, "Museum as a Way of Seeing," 26; Carol Duncan, "Art Museums and the Ritual of Citizenship" in Karp, *Exhibiting Cultures*, 88–103; Becker, *Art Worlds*, 119; Cracraft, *Petrine Revolution in Russian Imagery*, 252–7.

112. Perkins. "Noble Patronage"; Ward, *Moscow and Leningrad*, 2:115 (art shops). The provincial icon market, however, flourished: Veliky Ustyug in the far north, famous for its icons, had five market squares, a Gostiny Dvor, hundreds of kiosks, and an annual three-day fair in June where a large quantity of art changed hands: Hilton, *Russian Folk Art*, 43–44.

113. Shumova, *Russkaya zhivopis*, n.p. (Pzhetslavsky). Fiction about artists, modeled after the German *Künstlernovellen* and other forms, became popular in Russia in the 1830s and 1840s. N. A. Polevoi's "The Painter" (1833) deals with an idealistic, romantic painter of a minor official family and his conflicts with aristocratic society: White, "Polevoi."

114. Gray, *Russian Genre Painting*, 45–68; Bowlt, "Russian Painting," 117.

Chapter 8. Exploring the Interior

1. Ely, *This Meager Nature,* 19 and passim.

2. Gray, *Russian Genre Painting,* 58. This book is especially incisive on European models and influences, particularly of the Dutch masters and the contemporary Düsseldorf school, on Russian art.

3. Hilton, *Russian Folk Art,* 25, 203–4.

4. Stupin, "Sobstvennoruchnyya zapiski"; Kornilov, *Arzamasskaya shkola zhivopisi;* idem, "Aleksandr Vasilevich Stupin"; Moleva, *Russkaya khudozhestvennaya shkola,* 171–94; Kots, *Krepostnaya intelligentsiya,* 20, 56–58, 73–77.

5. Moleva, *Russkaya khudozhestvennaya shkola,* 189; numbers: Kurmachëva, *Krepostnaya intelligentsiya Rossii,* 112.

6. Zaitsev, "Vospominaniya starogo uchitelya," 667–68 (qu.).; Roosevelt, *Russian Country Estate,* 187. The punishment meted out in a church school in Arzamas in 1848 provides a stark contrast to the humanism of Stupin's establishment: see Freeze, *Parish Clergy in Nineteenth-Century Russia,* 138; and the school scenes in Rostislavov, *Provincial Russia.* Myasnikov: Stupin, "Sobstvennoruchnyya zapiski," 409; Zaitsev, "Vospominaniya starogo uchitelya," 669; Kornilov, *Arzamasskaya shkola zhivopisi,* 9–10. Morrisey, "In the Name of Freedom," has produced fascinating speculation about motives and understandings of this episode. The motive of another suicide is not recorded: Hilton, *Russian Folk Art,* 205–6.

7. Morrisey, "In the Name of Freedom," 281; ISAKh, 40; Zaitsev, "Vospominaniya starogo uchitelya," 668–69; Kondakov, *Spisok,* 190; Kots, *Krepostnaya intelligentsiya,* 56; Vrangel, "A. V. Stupin i ego ucheniki." Maria Zhukova (1804–55), daughter of a minor civil servant family in Arzamas, studied drawing at the school, earned money as an artist, and did copying at the Hermitage: Tomei, *Russian Women Writers,* 1:183–98. Sollogub, *Tarantas,* 134.

8. Gray, *Russian Genre Painting,* 69. For the life: Leonteva, *Venetsianov.* The storage attic of the Russian Museum contains his portraits which are rarely seen in the public collections. Soviet curators naturally privileged the artist's genre and peasant studies. For some of the originals: GRMFZh, 5170, 5178, 3633, 3638, 5149, 5173. Reproductions of these and others in Alekseeva, *Khudozhniki shkoly Venetsianova,* tr. as *Venetsianov and His School,* passim. Some of the reproductions in Alekseeva are woodcuts or other versions of Venetsianov's pictures by his disciples.

9. Moleva, *Russkaya khudozhestvennaya shkola,* 195–219 (qu. 197, 198, 199).

10. *Aleksei Gavrilovich Venetsianov* (1957), 3. For additional details, see Mashkovtsev, "Venetsianov"; Savinov, *Venetsianov.*

11. Gray, *Russian Genre Painting,* 80.

12. Moleva, *Russkaya khudozhestvennaya shkola,* 204–11 (qu. 206); Alekseeva, *Khudozhniki,* 5–180.

13. Hare, *Art and Artists of Russia,* 175–79; Alekseeva, *Khudozhniki,* 351–2; Hilton, *Russian Folk Art,* 208–12; Zhitnev in *Portretnaya miniatyura,* 2:230, and in Alekseeva, *Khudozhniki,* 185.

14. Makarov: Moleva, *Russkaya khudozhestvennaya shkola,* 304, 307–10 (qu. 309); Nadezhdin: ibid., 310–14 (qu. 312), 382–83 n. 13; Kurmachëva, *Krepostnaya intel-*

ligentsiya, 112. The sample of social origins is very selective, since few data are given for the others in a list of about one hundred. The most obscure provincial art school, in Voronezh, was founded in the 1810s by F. F. Churikov, an Academy graduate: Moleva, *Russkaya khudozhestvennaya shkola,* 315–17.

15. The name indicates Polish origin, possibly Bójalski. See Kondakov, *Spisok,* 27; Moleva, *Russkaya khudozhestvennaya shkola,* 317–19, 384 n. 22.

16. Sumarokov, *Progulka po 12-ti guberniyam,* 80.

17. Moleva, *Russkaya khudozhestvennaya shkola,* 326–30 (qu. 326–27); Dmitrieva, *Moskovskoe Uchilishche,* 8–29.

18. Moleva, *Russkaya khudozhestvennaya shkola,* 335; Dmitrieva, *Moskovskoe Uchilishche,* 12–15.

19. Dmitrieva, *Moskovskoe Uchilishche,* 60, 82 (qu.); Gray, *Russian Genre Painting,* 157. The Stroganov school, resembling a military barracks, trained artisans for the porcelain and faïence factory: Kots, *Krepostnaya intelligentsiya,* 58; Sumarokov, *Progulka po 12-ti guberniyam,* 80.

20. ISAKh, 42 (qu.); Dmitrieva, *Moskovskoe Uchilishche,* 26–27, 48. I have not seen the texts of any promissory documents made by serf owners.

21. Dmitrieva, *Moskovskoe Uchilishche,* 75–76.

22. Ibid., 28–29; Pogodin letter, excerpted in Kohn, *Mind of Modern Russia,* 60–68.

23. Dmitrieva, *Moskovskoe Uchilishche,* 27–28, 73; Valkenier, "Intelligentsia and Art," 156. For Shevyrëv's exaltation of Russian nature, see Ely, *This Meager Nature,* 118–21.

24. Dmitrieva, *Moskovskoe Uchilishche,* 18, 34–39, 57–58; RNBRO, f. 861, I. I. Shishkin, n. 2, ms. biography of Mokritsky. For Zaryanko's theoretical positions, see Muratov, *Zaryanko,* 93–109.

25. Dmitrieva, *Moskovskoe Uchilishche,* 51–53.

26. RNBRO, f. 861, I. I. Shishkin: n. 1, "Biografiya" from *Knizhki Nedeli* (Nov. 1899) 7–35 and (Dec. 1899) 42–68; n. 165, ticket, 1855, from Ministry of the Court School of Painting and Sculpture of the Moscow Art Society to Shishkin for a trip to Vyatka to show his works; Dmitrieva, *Moskovskoe Uchilishche,* 53; RKh, 702–7.

27. Moleva, *Russkaya khudozhestvennaya shkola,* 326–41; Dmitrieva, *Moskovskoe Uchilishche,* 3–4 and passim.

28. Dmitrieva, *Moskovskoe Uchilishche,* 78–81; P. V. Medvedev, "Dnevnik," 8 and passim. Purchase by private patrons by no means meant that the pictures were widely seen. One patron, General Samsonov, doted on the pupils and bought up their works, but stored them in a large empty mansion in the suburbs of the city: Dmitrieva, *Moskovskoe Uchilishche,* 47.

29. Starr, "Russian Art and Society," 101–3 and passim; idem, *Decentralization and Self-Government in Russia;* Moleva, *Russkaya khudozhestvennaya shkola,* 319 and passim.

30. As claimed by Koshman, "Gorod i obshchestvenno-kulturnaya zhizn," 32.

31. Hilton, *Russian Folk Art,* 198; Buturlin, "Zapiski," RA, 1–4 (1897) 400–401; Kots, *Krepostnaya intelligentsiya,* 77–78.

32. Ruban, *Zabitye imena,* 27–28; Roosevelt, *Russian Country Estate,* 125.

33. West, "Romantic Landscape in Early Nineteenth-Century Russian Art," 38 n. 16.

34. Sivkov, "Krepostnye khudozhniki."

35. Argunovs: RKh, 41–42, and Roosevelt, *Russian Country Estate,* 62–63; Kurmachëva, *Krepostnaya intelligentsiya,* 120. Shibanov: RIIE, 565–66, and Hilton, *Russian Folk Art,* 200. Sazonov: Kurmachëva, *Krepostnaya intelligentsiya,* 130; Haxthausen, *Russian Empire,* 1:235.

36. Kots, *Krepostnaya intelligentsiya,* 47–50; Ruban, *Zabitye imena,* 35; Marasinova, "Kultura russkoi usadby," 290–91; Hilton, *Russian Folk Art,* 204.

37. [A. I. Rozanov], "Zapiski selskago svyashchennika," RS, 27 (Mar. 1880) 465–66; Semevskii, *Krestyanskii vopros v Rossii,* 1:396–97; Letkova, "Krepostnaya intelligentsiya," 177. The agonizingly romantic hero of A. V. Timofeev's novel, *Khudozhnik,* progresses from serf lackey to freeman, struggling along the way from physical punishment, lost love, poverty, class tension, and dilemmas about genres. On suicide: Morrisey, "In the Name of Freedom."

38. The earliest source for this case is a footnote in Ramazanov, "Vasilii Andreevich Tropinin," 54 n. 1. N. N. Vrangel wrongly conflated the two Polyakovs by inserting material about A. V. Polyakov (see below) into Ramazanov's footnote which he quotes: *Venok mertvym,* 64–65. The two lives had radically different outcomes, and Ramazanov would certainly have known enough about A. V. Polyakov's case to have identified him properly. Ramazanov also tells of a serf who hanged himself in the master's garden.

39. Prilezhaeva-Barskaya, *Krepostnoi khudozhnik;* Ramazanov, "Vasilii Andreevich Tropinin."

40. Petinova, *Tropinin.*

41. Ibid. In this otherwise sound study, the author argued unconvincingly that Tropinin's Moscow female subjects resembled characters in the plays of Ostrovsky. The notion seems to be an effort to link Tropinin with Moscow cultural nationalism. There are such links, but the Ostrovsky one is not. In any case, Tropinin's reputation as a Russian national artist rests as much on his genre depictions of the everyday and of humble Russian social types such as *A Poor Old Man* (1824). See also Kots, *Krepostnaya intelligentsiya,* 63–68; Kondakov, *Spisok,* 199; RKh, 613–16; G. V. Zhidkov, "Vasilii Andreevich Tropinin," in Leonov, *Russkoe iskusstvo* (1954), 221–38; and Volgina, *Vasilii Tropinin.*

42. For the life and work: Obukhov, *Soroka;* and A. N. Savinov, "Grigorii Vasilevich Soroka, 1823–64." Pictures: Obukhov, *Soroka,* 46 fig. 19; Alekseeva, *Khudozhniki,* 329; *Portret v russkoi zhivopisi.*

43. Obukhov, *Soroka,* 51, reasonably suggests that this work displays an internal spiritual and emotional life in turmoil.

44. Hilton, *Russian Folk Art,* 207–9; *Krestyanskoe dvizhenie v Rossii v 1796–1825 gg.,* 659.

45. Savinov, "Grigorii Vasilevich Soroka," 644; *Aleksei Gavrilovich Venetsianov* (1980), 41, 304 n.1.

46. With Alexander Sanin in the title role: Yury Tsivian, personal communication.

47. Kondakov, *Spisok,* 174; RKh, 547–49; Sadovnikov, *Vidy Peterburga,* introduction.

48. Ruban, *Zabitye imena,* 29–30.

49. Timofeev, *Khudozhnik;* Kots, *Krepostnaya intelligentsiya,* 31, 51, 53–54.

50. Moleva, *Russkaya khudozhestvennaya shkola,* 334; Dmitrieva, *Moskovskoe Uchilishche,* 25.

51. Stolpyanskii, *Staryi Peterburg i Obshchestvo Pooshchreniya Khudozhestv,* 3–9 (qu. 5), a valuable account, though containing errors. Sobko, *Kratkii istoricheskii ocherk Imperatorskago Obshchestva Pooshchreniya Khudozhestv,* 3–11; Komelova, "Peterburgskoe Obshchestvo Pooshchreniya Khudozhestv," 34–36; Golubeva, "Iz istorii Obshchestva Pooshchreniya Khudozhnikov," 67–72. The change of the last word of the society's names from "Arts" to "Artists" accounts for the variation in these titles.

52. Komelova, "Peterburgskoe Obshchestvo Pooshchreniya Khudozhestv," 34.

53. Moleva, *Russkaya khudozhestvennaya shkola,* 221.

54. Perkins. "Noble Patronage," 439; Sobko, *Kratkii istoricheskii ocherk Imperatorskago Obshchestva Pooshchreniya Khudozhestv,* 7–10; Norman, "Pavel Tret'iakov (1832–1898)," 126–27; Stolpyanskii, *Staryi Peterburg i Obshchestvo Pooshchreniya Khudozhestv,* 56–75.

55. *Nekrologiya . . . Tomilova;* Shumova, *Russkaya zhivopis.* The twenty-nine numbered pages of text are followed by several hundred unnumbered pages, in no chronological or alphabetical order, of reproductions and commentary. My references to this part of the book thus contain no page numbers.

56. Stolpyanskii, *Staryi Peterburg i Obshchestvo Pooshchreniya Khudozhestv,* 56–57; Golubeva, "Iz istorii Obshchestva Pooshchreniya Khudozhnikov," 71–72 n. 18; Zaitsev, *Shevchenko,* 41; Moleva, *Russkaya khudozhestvennaya shkola,* 376 n. 6; Kots, *Krepostnaya intelligentsiya,* 71–72; Hilton, *Russian Folk Art,* 205.

57. Ruban, *Zabitye imena,* 28 (ellipsis in the original).

58. See note 38 above; Kondakov, *Spisok,* 156; Kots, *Krepostnaya intelligentsiya,* 71; Moleva, *Russkaya khudozhestvennaya shkola,* 223–24, 376 n. 7; Golubeva, "Iz istorii Obshchestva Pooshchreniya Khudozhnikov"; Sokolov, *Ryadom s Pushkinym,* 297–99. Svinin: Danilov, "Dedushka russkikh istoricheskikh zhurnalov."

59. Zaitsev, *Shevchenko.* Shevchenko's autobiographical novella *The Artist* provides sometimes imagined details: Shevchenko, *Povest,* 35–38, 45, 49, 51. 71. All quotations are my translations of the Russian text.

60. Seletskii, "Zapiski," in KS, 8 (Aug. 1884) 621–22.

61. Zaitsev, *Shevchenko,* 28–38 (qu. 35, 37). Zaitsev (ibid., 225–26) cites F. P. Tolstoy's daughter, who wrote that their home "had been the real headquarters for all the efforts that had been made to free Shevchenko"; Shevchenko, *Povest,* 82–138 (qu. 82). The novella spins out the story in slow stages, with many pauses and setbacks, as in a melodrama. See also Sokolov, *Ryadom s Pushkinym,* 132.

62. Shevchenko, *Povest,* 77–268; Zaitsev, *Shevchenko,* 165–219.

63. Boime, *Academy and French Painting,* 136; Christiana Payne, " 'Calculated to Gratify the Patriot': Rustic Figure Studies in Early-Nineteenth-Century Britain" in Rosenthal, *Prospects for the Nation,* 61–78 (qu. 64). See also Sam Smiles, "Dressed to Till: Representational Strategies in the Depiction of Rural Labour, c. 1790–1839," ibid., 79–95.

64. Solkin, "The Battle of the Ciceros"; Bermingham, "Reading Constable," 100.

65. Ely, *This Meager Nature.* This superb study meticulously traces the changing views

of landscape in fiction, travel literature, and art. Many of the landscapes he discusses and that I do not treat are either unpeopled or date from after emancipation. See also his "Critics in the Native Soil," 254, 260.

66. Custine, *Letters from Russia,* 26.

67. Kondakov, *Spisok,* 213 (Khudyakov). The works cited in the following pages are found in printed reproductions, and on the walls of the Tretyakov Gallery in Moscow, the Russian Museum in St. Petersburg, and a few other museums. Works in the Russian Museum's unhung storage collection are referenced by painting number in parentheses as [GRMFZh]. My selection is, I believe, representative of the hundreds of canvases and other graphic works I studied there.

68. *V okrestnostyakh Moskvy,* pls. 163–64.

69. The opening paragraph of "Kasyan s Krasivoi Mechi," *Zapiski okhotnika,* PSS, 4:114–33.

70. IIRR, introduction and plates. Except for Venetsianov, the painters named in this paragraph are not treated in Ely, *This Meager Nature.*

71. Shumova, *Russkaya zhivopis,* 21–22. See Ely, *This Meager Nature,* for Savrasov and other early landscapists.

72. IIRR, pl. 68.

73. Chernetsov, *Puteshestvie po Volge;* G. V. Smirnov, "Grigorii Grigorevich Chernetsov (1802–1865); Nikanor Grigorevich Chernetsov (1805–1879)" in Leonov, *Russkoe iskusstvo* (1954) 545–70; Moleva, *Russkaya khudozhestvennaya shkola,* 223 and pl. 152; Ely, *This Meager Nature,* 76–78; idem, "Origins of Russian Scenery."

74. Ely, *This Meager Nature,* 165.

75. Burke, *Eyewitnessing,* 137; Nochlin, *Realism,* 34, 47, 57; Brettell, *Painters and Peasants,* 14–18 and passim.

76. Barrell, *Dark Side of the Landscape,* 5, 21–22, 89–129, and passim; Alun Howkins, "Land, Locality, People, Landscape: the Nineteenth-Century Countryside" in Rosenthal, *Prospects for the Nation,* 97–114. A historian, Howkins intertextualizes the visual material with literary works.

77. Gray, *Russian Genre Painting,* 72. I have not seen these works.

78. For a sense of that reality, see Hoch, *Serfdom and Social Control.*

79. Barrell, *Dark Side of the Landscape,* 12, 16 (qu.); Clarke, *Absolute Bourgeois,* 93; Brettell, *Painters and Peasants,* 34–35.

80. Hilton, *Russian Folk Art,* 212–14; Zapotocky, "Venetsianov and the Slavophiles"; Hare, *Art and Artists of Russia,* 176; see also Alekseeva, *Khudozhniki,* passim; Hilton, *Russian Impressionism* (qu., n.p.).

81. Cited in Ely, "Critics in the Native Soil," 259.

82. Newlin, "Rural Ruses," 306. See also idem, *Voice in the Garden,* passim.

83. Alekseeva, *Khudozhniki,* 45.

84. Ibid., 55, 61, 71.

85. Baxandall, *Painting and Experience in Fifteenth-Century Italy,* 77–81.

86. Netting, "Images and Ideas in Russian Peasant Art."

87. Alekseeva, *Khudozhniki,* 41, 59, 64, 96, and female nudes, 310–11; Gray, *Russian Genre Painting,* 80; Zaitsev, *Shevchenko,* 229.

88. Alekseeva, *Khudozhniki*, 49 and 50–51; Leonteva, *Venetsianov*, 23–24, 31.

89. Venetsianov's *Girl with a Sickle* (1820) corrects the error but takes the subject no closer to the task suggested by that implement: Alekseeva, *Khudozhniki*, 81, 95, 98.

90. Alekseeva, *Khudozhniki*, 63. See also Roosevelt, "Country House as a Setting and Symbol," 48–49.

91. Roosevelt, *Russian Country Estate*, 170–71.

92. IIRR, pls. 100, 102; Alekseeva, *Khudozhniki*, 291. 292–93, 295–96, 326.

93. Roosevelt, *Russian Country Estate*, 219 fig. 156.

94. Repr. in Alekseeva, *Khudozhniki*, 285–87; Obukhov, *Soroka*, 22–23 fig. 5.

95. Sosnina, *Russkii traditsionnyi kostyum*, 23–24.

96. IIRR, pl. 68; Alekseeva, *Khudozhniki*, 156–60; Kondakov, *Spisok*, 55.

97. Myrone, *Representing Britain*, 42; Alekseeva, *Khudozhniki*, 101, 137–39; Brettell, *Painters and Peasants*, 13–17.

98. Plakhov: Alekseeva, *Khudozhniki*, 195, 206 (and see also 198. 199, 204, 205). Plakhov may have been inspired by various European models: Gray, *Russian Genre Painting*, 128 fig. 36. Cf. the English work by Joseph Wright, *Iron Forge* (1772), which is far more animated and dramatic, with the smith's family proudly looking on: Myrone, *Representing Britain*, 54.

99. Sadovnikov, *Vidy Peterburga*, introduction.

100. Harris, *Great Urals*, 11–13.

101. Hudson, *Rise of the Demidov Family*, 113 and passim; Vedenetsky: Kondakov, *Spisok*, 34; pictures, IIRR, pls. 62, 74. Demidov also used other members of the Khudoyarov serf family to paint operations of the factory: Hilton, *Russian Folk Art*, 204–5.

102. IIRR, pl. 73. Such scenes were rare in painting, nor did artists try to portray the steam engines or the railways and tramlines that roared and hissed in a few factories and mines in the Urals and elsewhere: Haywood, *Beginnings of Railway Development*, 51–61. For social makeup and status of industrial serfs, see Zelnik, *Labor and Society in Imperial Russia*; and Crisp, *Studies in the Russian Economy*, 64. Apparently no fiction presented the factory devouring the soul of robotic workers until Kuprin's "Moloch" and Alexander Serafimovich's "At the Factory" — both 1899.

103. Gray, *Russian Genre Painting*, 153 fig. 52, 73 fig. 6, 74 fig. 7. For other domestic scenes, see Venetsianov's *Nastya and Masha* (1820s) in Alekseeva, *Venetsianov*, 16; and Rostislav Felitsyn, *On the Cabin Porch* (1855), a somewhat folksy study of two little village girls in a salon-style treatment of everyday life (GRMFZh, 3828). Bowl-dipping was standard practice among clergy as well as peasantry and no indicator of poverty: Rostislavov, *Provincial Russia*, 84.

104. Alekseeva, *Khudozhniki*, 249.

105. See also his *View of Yuriev Monastery on the Volga* (1851) in RKh, 672; and Tropinin, *Wedding in the Village of Kukavka, in Podolia*.

106. *Traktir* (via Polish from the Latin *tracto* = "I treat" or "take care of"); variants on this were called *kharchevnya, kabak, piteinyi dom, pogrebka*, or, in Ukraine, *shinky* and *korchny*: Fedosyuk, *Chto neponyatno u klassikov*, 227–30; Christian, *"Living Water"*.

107. Reproduced also in IIRR, pl. 138. The taboo on tavern scenes in eighteenth-century century British painting was part of a rule (often broken) that represented the

peasant way of life as hard-working and deserving of "honest" relaxation. Hogarthian rampage was allowed only in prints.

108. Turgenev, *Zapiski okhotnika*, PSS, 4:225–44.

109. L. M. Tarasov, "Pavel Antonovich Ritstsoni" in Leonov, *Russkoe iskusstvo* (1958) 263–74, with illustrations (qu. 267, 271); Shumova, *Russkaya zhivopis*, n.p. After looking at Chernetsov's works, Nicholas left the exhibition saying that the Academy "needs stricter examinations and awards": ISAKh, 44. It is not clear that all these tavern scenes were set in rural areas.

110. IIRR, pls. 140, 145; Shevchenko, *Povest*, 194–95 (Sternberg); Shumova, *Russkaya zhivopis*, n.p. (Popov).

111. Besides Hoch and Rostislavov, see, for a later period: Worobec, *Peasant Russia: Family and Community in the Post-Emancipation Period* (Princeton, 1991); idem, *Possessed: Women, Witches, and Demons in Imperial Russia* (Dekalb, 2001); and Frank, *Crime, Cultural Conflict, and Justice in Rural Russia.*

112. Starr, "Russian Art and Society," 105; Hilton, *Russian Folk Art*, 218.

113. Wirtschafter, *From Serf to Russian Soldier*, 22–23, 34, and passim.

114. Fedosyuk, *Chto neponyatno u klassikov*, 197; Kondakov, *Spisok*, 22.

115. Alekseeva, *Khudozhniki*, 154–55.

116. Alekseev's Poltava in a woodcut version in Alekseeva, *Khudozhniki*, 241; Krendovsky's in ibid., 237–40.

117. Hilton, *Russian Folk Art*, 25, 203–4; Cracraft, *Petrine Revolution in Russian Imagery*, 248; Ransel, "Neither Nobles nor Peasants."

118. *Yaroslavskie portrety XVIII–XIX vekov*, 5–15 and figs. 119, 51, 101. See Kozlyakov, "Kulturnaya sreda provintsialnogo goroda," 159.

119. *Yaroslavskie portrety XVIII–XIX vekov*, passim; Romanov, *Russkie portrety XVIII i XIX vekov*. On merchant dress and status, see Owen, *Capitalism and Politics in Russia*, 10, 23; and Ruane, "Caftan to Business Suit."

120. Kozlyakov, "Kulturnaya sreda provintsialnogo goroda," 125.

121. Alekseeva, *Khudozhniki*, 218.

122. *Portret v russkoi zhivopisi*, unnumbered reproduction.

123. Discussion and illustration in Kelly, *Refining Russia*, 96–97.

124. Valkenier, "Intelligentsia and Art," 158; Gray, *Russian Genre Painting*, 137 (qu.); Sarabyanov, *Fedotov*; Kirsanova, *Rozovaya ksendreika*, 111–12.

125. Shumova, *Russkaya zhivopis*, 8, 11; A. O., "Neskolko slov o Fedotove" in *Svetopis*, 12 (Dec. 1858) 229–31.

126. Volodina, *Russian Interior*, 24; Demidenko, *Interer v Rossii*, 137; Gray, *Russian Genre Painting*, 125–30 (qu. 26); Sarabianov, *Russian Art*, 53–55.

127. Dynnik, *Krepostnoi teatr*, 175–76.

128. See for example the 1850 interior by an unknown artist on the estate of the Filosofovs: Roosevelt, *Russian Country Estate*, 174.

129. Ya. P. Balmen in the 1830s thus recorded estate life in Chernigov Province: Marasinova, "Kultura russkoi usadby," 331–33.

130. I wish to thank Kira Vladimirovna Mikhailova of the Russian Museum for an inch-by-inch analysis of this large canvas.

131. Roosevelt, *Russian Country Estate,* 180.

132. Rand, *Intimate Encounters;* Myrone, *Representing Britain.*

133. Bowlt, "Russian Painting," 128–29.

134. A survey of high society table habits contains many menus, but very few pictures of dining: Lotman, *Velikosvetskie obedy.*

135. For this and other interiors, see Demidenko, *Interer v Rossii;* Volodina, *Russian Interior;* Gray, *Russian Genre Painting,* 94 fig. 22, 126 fig. 34; Alekseeva, *Khudozhniki,* 269.

136. Shevchenko, *Povest,* 104–5, 163; Roosevelt, "Country House as a Setting and Symbol," 50.

137. For example, in Turgenev's *Notes of a Hunter* and Gogol's *Dead Souls.*

138. Karlinsky, *Gogol,* 154; Sarabianov, *Russian Art,* 88–89; A. Zotov, "Puti razvitiya russkogo iskusstva," 79; Valkenier, "Intelligentsia and Art," 158 (Maikov); Hamilton, *Art and Architecture of Russia,* 242.

139. Gray, *Russian Genre Painting,* 136 fig. 39.

140. Alekseeva, *Khudozhniki,* 333. Chernyshev, the son of a soldier, had been an NCO trainee. With the help of V. A. Perovsky, the military governor of Orenburg, he was discharged from service due to ill health in 1841. The Society for the Encouragement of Artists helped him enter the Academy: Shumova, *Russkaya zhivopis,* n.p.

141. Cf. Philip Reinagle's *Members of the Carrow Abbey Hunt* (1780) and hundreds of hunting prints in eighteenth-century England where that sport was already institutionalized and clubby: Myrone, *Representing Britain,* 48. Russian hunt clubs emerged only after emancipation: McReynolds, *Russia at Play,* 82–87.

142. Roosevelt, *Russian Country Estate,* 177. See also *Duck Hunt,* by an unknown artist, showing three hunters firing as a peasant loads their guns, a crude popular blend of landscape and genre: IIRR, pl. 92.

143. IIRR, pl. 118; Kondakov, *Spisok,* 102.

144. IIRR, pls. 84, 85. Turgenev, *Zapiski okhotnika,* passim. On the hunt, see the interesting remarks in Brouwer, *Character in the Short Prose of Turgenev,* 79–90; idem, "Turgenev's *Sportsman's Sketches* as an Artistic Whole," 71–72, 77; and Ely, *This Meager Nature,* 129–32.

145. Komelova, "Peterburgskoe Obshchestvo Pooshchreniya Khudozhestv," 34–36; Golubeva, "Iz istorii Obshchestva Pooshchreniya Khudozhnikov," 67–72; Kondakov, *Spisok,* 230 (Shchedrovsky); Kozlyakov, "Kulturnaya sreda provintsialnogo goroda," 159. D. Begichev's *Provincial Scenes* (1840) was illustrated by K. K. Klodt; for those who illustrated Gogol's *Dead Souls,* see Agin, *Sto chetyre risunki.*

146. *Pushkinskii Peterburg.* There are two versions of this book, both published in Leningrad in 1974, but with different paginations. For more art depicting the capital in this era, see Sadovnikov, *Vidy Peterburga; Neva Symphony; Vues de Pawlowsk par Thurner* (n.p., c. 1820), etching or *eau-forte* works; RNBOE, unnumbered and untitled chromolithograph views of St. Petersburg, 1820s: RNBOE, Sobranie I. I. Rybakova, En-237k. Some of the pictures here cited can now be found in the recent Gusev, *Sankt-Peterburg;* Buckler, *Mapping St. Petersburg,* appeared too late for me to incorporate its rich observations.

147. *Pushkinskii Peterburg,* pl. 33.

148. V. R. Zotov, "Peterburg v sorokovykh godakh," IV (Feb. 1890) 324–27.

149. *Pushkinskii Peterburg*, pl. 42 (see also pls. 5–6, 9–10, 13, 14, 29, 32, 34; *Gorod glazami khudozhnikov*, 62–63, 73–74; and "Reki i kanaly" in Lure, *Blistatelnyi Peterburg*, 269–93.

150. Frank, *Dostoevsky*, 119: Fanger, *Dostoevsky and Romantic Realism*, 134–36 and passim.

151. Volkov, *St. Petersburg*, 37–38.

152. RKh, 444–46; Belza, *Shimanovskaya*, 91; *Pushkinskii Peterburg*, pls. 64 and 65 (see also pls. 66 and 67); Lotman, *Velikosvetskie obedy*, 197. Orlovsky's 1809 *Views of Popular St. Petersburg Shopkeepers* and *Russian Cries*, both published in London, are cited in Gray, *Russian Genre Painting*, 154. Another collection came out in 1825–26: *Notebooks on the Theme of Russian Popular Life (Tetrady na temu russkogo narodnogo byta)*. Grigorii Kaganov has noted the "hidden villages and provincial towns inside St. Petersburg": lecture, Renvall Institute, Helsinki University, November 13, 2001.

153. See chapter 4 and note 74 there.

154. Burke, *Eyewitnessing*, 185 and passim. See also Gohstand, "Geography of Trade," 355–57.

155. See two examples by Sadovnikov in Lotman, *Velikosvetskie obedy*, 80 and 81; and the lithograph of an urban street force, wares on head, made in the 1830s in *Cris de Pétersbourg*: RNBOE: Kollektsiya I. I. Rybakova, papka 10.

156. Gray, *Russian Genre Painting*, 78; Alekseeva, *Venetsianov*, pls. 11, 12; Hare, *Art and Artists of Russia*, 176. Other trading scenes: Gusev, *Sankt-Peterburg*, 276–83 (especially the unflattering lithographs of merchants at Gostiny Dvor and elsewhere by R. K. Zhukovskii, part of his series *Russian National Life*, pp. 278–79).

157. See chapter 1.

158. *Pushkinskii Peterburg*, pl. 60.

159. L. M. Tarasov, "A. M. Volkov" in Leonov, *Russkoe iskusstvo* (1958), 631–46 (figs. 635, 637). See also A. F. Chernyshev, *Petersburg Marketplace* (1851) in Alekseeva, *Khudozhniki*, 331; and a lithograph of street sellers at the great Vauxhall in Ekaterinhof near the capital in *Nouvelle collection: quarante-deux vues de Saint-Pétersbourg et de ses environs* (St. Petersburg, 1826): RNBOE, Sobranie I. I. Rybakova, Ei-227. For the Haymarket milieu, see Jahn, "St. Peterburger Heumarkt."

160. *Fiziologiya Peterburga*, with engravings by Thimm, Agin, *Sto chetyre risunki*, pp. 38–50. Dostoevsky's *Poor Folk* (1846) contains one of the many vignettes of the courtyard in the fiction of the era.

161. Ruble, "St. Peterburg's Courtyards and Washington's Alleys," 3.

162. *Pushkinskii Peterburg*, pls. 5–6, 9–10, 13, 14, 29, 32, 34. Patersen (variant spellings, 1750–1815), a Swedish Russophile, spent many years in Petersburg from 1787. See also the lithograph *Ferry Slip* (1841) by the Academy's Ferdinand Perrot of the boat dock at the Academy of Arts with ferrymen at work and passengers embarking: Lotman, *Velikosvetskie obedy*, 39.

163. Custine, *Letters from Russia*, 38–39.

164. Sadovnikov, *Vidy Peterburga*, No. 5; Shevchenko, *Khudozhnik*, 372 (Montferrand). For depictions of work processes in European art, which were well developed by the eighteenth century, see Craske, *Art in Europe*, 126–27.

165. RKh, 223–24; Kondakov, *Spisok*, 67; Gray, *Russian Genre Painting*, 152–53 fig. 51.

166. Jahn, *Fromme Pilger, artige Arme, und streunende Gauner.*

167. On such objections in literature, see Herman, *Poverty of the Imagination*, 216 n. 11 and passim.

168. For this and other examples ranging from 1832 to 1857, see Nekrylova, *Russkie narodnye gorodskie prazdniki*, 90, 142–43, 162–63, 166–67.

169. V. R. Zotov, "Peterburg v sorokovykh godakh," IV (Feb. 1890) 324–27.

170. *Cris de Pétersbourg:* RNBOE: Kollektsiya I. I. Rybakova, papka 10 (possibly modeled after *Cries of London* which I have not seen). For many more contemporary graphic representations of the city, see RNBOE: Sobranie Rybakova, papka 7, "Martynov, A. E.: aquarelles" (reprinted and with commentary in Martynov, *Saint-Pétersbourg*; and *Vidy S.-Peterburga i okrestnostei.*

171. Bulgarin cited in Ely, *This Meager Nature*, 38–39. Courtyard sales: Stolpyanskii, "Torgovlya lyudmi v starom Peterburge," 42. See also Leblanc, "Teniers, Flemish Art, and the Natural School Debate."

172. Burke, *Eyewitnessing*, 23.

173. Stapp, *Robert Cornelius;* Jenkins, *Images and Enterprise.*

174. Morozov, *Russkaya khudozhestvennaya fotografiya*, 7–10; Barchatova [Barkhatova], "Die ersten Photographien in Russland," 24–29; Lotman, *Velikosvetskie obedy*, 109. The most sumptuous of recent collections is Barkhatova, *Russkaya fotografiya.*

175. Morozov, *Russkaya khudozhestvennaya fotografiya*, 10–13, 34–38; RNBOE, Sobranie Levitskogo: early Russian photographs; Saburova, "Frühe Meister," 31–40.

176. Morozov, *Russkaya khudozhestvennaya fotografiya*, 14–18, 39–40; Saburova, "Frühe Meister"; Lotman, *Velikosvetskie obedy*, 52–54. Compare the renowned Isabey 1814 oil portrait of Sergei Volkonsky, the Decembrist (in Mazour, *Women in Exile*, 58) with an 1856 photograph of him (in Lotman, *Velikosvetskie obedy*, 50). See also Alfred d'Avignon's photograph of Volkonsky, taken in Irkutsk in 1845: Barkhatova, *Russkaya fotografiya*, 37.

177. Lotman, *Velikosvetskie obedy*, 56–57. See cover of Roosevelt, *Apostle of Russian Liberalism;* Tyutchev in RNBOE, Sobranie Levitskogo; Shcherbina in Barkhatova, *Russkaya fotografiya*, 36.

178. Females: Barkhatova, *Russkaya fotografiya*, 38 top right; Barchatova [Barkhatova], *Portrait of Tsarist Russia*, 39, 41. The tinted photo recalls Walter Benjamin's remark about "the retouched negative . . . the bad painter's revenge against photography": "Little History of Photography," 515.

179. Christoff, Introduction, vol. 3: *Aksakov*, 10, 102, 132; Barchatova, *Portrait of Tsarist Russia*, 48. The Herzen photo is found in many books about nineteenth-century revolutionary Russia, e.g. Yarmolinsky, *Road to Revolution*, facing p. 34.

180. Lyons, *Russia in Original Photographs*, 4; Barkhatova, *Russkaya fotografiya*, 25 top (workers), 38 top left; idem, *Portrait of Tsarist Russia*, 42 (workers), 52.

181. Obolensky, *Russian Empire: a Portrait in Photographs*, 45, 164 (Fenton; Carrick: Kamenka Fair); Morozov, *Russkaya khudozhestvennaya fotografiya*, 53; Lyons, *Russia in Original Photographs*, 38–39 (Carrick).

182. Exhibit, "British Photography in India," Sackler Gallery, Washington, D.C., Spring, 2000. See also Ryan, *Picturing Empire;* Cannadine, *Ornamentalism.*

183. Morozov, *Russkaya khudozhestvennaya fotografiya*, 18–20; Saburova, "Frühe Meister."

184. *Krymskaya voina, 1853–1856;* Barkhatova, *Russkaya fotografiya,* 39.

185. Cited in Crofton, *Dictionary of Art Quotations,* 141.

186. Cited in Janson, *History of Art,* 907.

187. Williams, *Confounding Images: Photography and Portraiture,* 8, 17, 38, 41.

188. OZ, 11 (1849) 138 (s.p.)—Shchepkin; F. Ponomarëv, "Istorii fotografii," *Svetopis,* 1 (Jan. 1858); Yurkevich, "Iz vospominanii peterburgskago starozhila," 160–61 (Senkovsky). Yurkevich erroneously puts the show in 1837. Quotations: Saburova, "Frühe Meister," 34 (Stasov); Morozov, *Russkaya khudozhestvennaya fotografiya,* 23 (*Art Gazette*) and 27 (Stasov).

189. *Andrei Osipovich Karelin;* Zaitsev, *Shevchenko,* 244; Morozov, *Russkaya khudozhestvennaya fotografiya,* 14, 30–31, 33, 53; Krivtsova, "Iz istorii khudozhestvennoi zhizni."

190. Gray, *Russian Genre Painting,* 158; Morozov, *Russkaya khudozhestvennaya fotografiya,* 29. See also Zaryanko's "parado-realist" portrait of General K. A. Shilder (1845) in Alekseeva, *Khudozhniki,* 255 (reproductions do not do justice to the distortion displayed in this work); and G. Yu. Smirnov, "Sergei Konstantinovich Zaryanko" in Leonov, *Russkoe iskusstvo* (1958), 369–86. Reproduced here are lesser-known works such as the portrait of the singer Osip Petrov in 1849 (p. 375) and a study of the Law School lobby in 1840–41 (p. 371).

191. Kramskoi, *Ivan Nikolaevich Kramskoi,* 3–40 (autobiographical notes and a memoir by M. B. Tulinov), qu. 21 (see above, chapter 3, note 84, for the word *zhid;* L. M. Afanasev, "Izobrazitelnoe iskusstvo" in *Ocherki istorii voronezhskogo kraya,* 452–60; Morozov, *Russkaya khudozhestvennaya fotografiya,* 32–33. The famous nightscapist Arkhip Kuindzhi also started out as a photo retoucher. Ivan Shishkin used the medium as a guide in painting: Ely, *This Meager Nature,* 187.

192. Valkenier, "The Intelligentsia and Art," 157.

Chapter 9. When Did the Real Day Dawn?

1. RV (Feb. 1858) 236–39. The report is also cited, with a few errors, in Lotman, *Velikosvetskie obedy,* 269. Herzen in *Kolokol* (Feb. 1, 1859) 280. The subsequent lot of the Meshkov brothers remains a mystery. Vikenty was not self-taught. He had played abroad and both brothers had studied at a private music school in Kursk and had performed at the Gentry Club in that town in 1850: Bugrov, *Svet kurskikh ramp,* 2:18–19.

2. Turgenev: Confino, *Société et mentalités collectives,* 294 n. 1; Dobrolyubov, *Sobranie sochinenii,* 2:120; Herzen: Petrovskaya, *Teatr i zritel provintsialnoi Rossii,* 10; Efros, *Shchepkin,* 56; Soboleva, "Pros and Cons: the Thoughts and Dreams of Madame Count Counsellor Lisitsyna" in Kelly, *Anthology of Russian Women's Writing,* 89.

3. Field, *End of Serfdom;* Emmons, *Russian Gentry.* Figures in Confino, *Société et mentalités collectives,* 295 n. 5.

4. Balmuth, *Censorship in Russia,* 42, 78, 126; Burmistrova, *Provintsialnaya gazeta;* Dobrolyubov in *Selected Philosophical Essays,* 389–441.

5. Engel, *Mothers and Daughters;* Tishkin, *Zhenskii vopros v Rossii v 50–60gg XIX v.;*

Stites, *Women's Liberation Movement*; Maegde-Soep, *Emancipation of Women*; Rosenholm, *Gender Awakening*.

6. Egorov, "Reaktsionnaya politika tsarizma v voprosakh universitetskogo obrazovaniya." See Gleason, *Young Russia*; Brower, *Training the Nihilists*; Venturi, *Roots of Revolution*; Belliustin, *Description of the Clergy in Rural Russia*.

7. Emmons, *Zemstvo in Russia*; Frieden, *Russian Physicians*; Wortman, *Development of a Russian Legal Consciousness*.

8. Zelnik, "Sunday School Movement in Russia, 1859–1862"; Kimball, "Conspiracy and Circumstance in Saratov, 1859–1864."

9. Freeze, *Parish Clergy in Nineteenth-Century Russia*, 146. See also Wirtschafter, *Social Identity*, 23–24 and passim.

10. Wortman, *Scenarios of Power*, 1:402.

11. Mikhail Shatsillo, "Labor Relations in Merchant Moscow" in West, *Merchant Moscow*, 88.

12. Starr, "Russian Art and Society," 98.

13. Owen, *Capitalism and Politics in Russia*, 29–52; Dowler, *Dostoevsky, Grigor'ev, and Native Soil Conservatism*, passim. Nicholas Riasanovsky and others long ago traced the common ground of the "nationalist" wing of Official Nationalism and the Slavophiles: see his *Nicholas I and Official Nationality in Russia* and "Pogodin and Sevyrëv in Russian Intellectual History."

14. Clowes, "Merchants on Stage and in Life," 147; Taruskin, *Stravinsky*, 1:46.

15. Bradley, "Merchant Moscow After Hours," 134; Nikitenko, *Diary*, 102.

16. An observation made long ago by Michael Karpovich in the introduction to Zetlin, *Decembrists*, 7.

17. Balzer, *Russia's Missing Middle Class*; Clowes, *Between Tsar and People*.

18. Shestakova, "Poslednye gody zhizni i konchina M. I. Glinki"; Dennis, *Beethoven in German Politics*; Brown, *Tchaikovsky*, 1:18; see also *P. I. Chaikovskii*, a photographic record; Findeizen, *Rubinshtein*, 47–57.

19. Shteinpress, *Alyabev*, 150 (Scholtz); Stasov, *Selected Essays*, 144; Norris, *Russian Piano Concerto*, 18–19, 191 n. 29 (Kashin); Afanasev, "Vospominaniya," IV, 41 (Aug. 1890) 274; Barenboim, *Rubinshtein*, 1:246–59; E. Barutcheva, "Anton Rubinshtein i Peterburgskaya Konservatoriya: tri vstrechi" in *Anton Grigorevich Rubinshtein: sbornik statei*, 27–36.

20. Puzyrevskii, *Imperatorskoe Russkoe Muzykalnoe Obshchestvo*, 4–5, 7 (qu.); idem, *Ocherk pyatidesyatiletiya deyatelnosti S.-Peterburgskoi Konservatorii*, 8–32; Findeizen, *Ocherk*, 11–17; Dunlop, *Russian Court Chapel Choir*, 93. Lvov was apparently miffed at not being appointed to the board of the Russian Musical Society.

21. Rubinstein, *Autobiography*, 85–102; Ridenour, *Nationalism*, 35–37; Findeizen, *Ocherk*, 17–29.

22. Soboleva: Kelly, *Anthology of Russian Women's Writing*, 89, 91 (qu.); Rubinstein article translated as "The State of Music in Russia" in Campbell, *Russians on Russian Music*, 64–73; G. Nekrasova, "Rubinshtein i 'Moguchaya kuchka'" in *Anton Grigorevich Rubinshtein*, 36–46.

23. Rubinshtein, *Avtobiograficheskiya vospominaniya*, 46–47; idem, *Autobiography*, 91–92.

24. Stressed by Taruskin: *Stravinsky,* 1:46.

25. Findeizen, *Ocherk,* 9. See also Wirtschafter, *Social Identity,* 87 and passim for the status of other professions.

26. Gozenpud, "Pogibshii talant (A. S. Gussakovskii)."

27. Campbell, *Odoevsky,* 145 (Maria Nikolaevna); Rubinstein, *Autobiography,* 103–11; "Russkii Muzei: Avtobiografiya," St. Petersburg TV, Channel 2, Jan. 22, 1998. According to Rubinstein, the organizers avoided the word "conservatory" out of a fear of "kvass patriotism" among antiforeign opponents: *Avtobiograficheskiya vospominaniya,* 51.

28. Ridenour, *Nationalism,* 37–40. For Jews living in St. Petersburg, see Nathans, *Beyond the Pale.*

29. Olkhovsky, *Stasov,* 94.

30. A. L. Revyakin, *Moskva v zhizni i tvorchestve A. N. Ostrovskogo,* 358, 362. European conservatories, though names varied, had begun to proliferate in the eighteenth century — usually growing out of singing academies. Italy had the oldest ones. Leipzig opened a *Singakademie* in 1771. France followed embryonically in 1783 and fully in 1795 with the Paris Conservatoire, the first modern national, secular conservatory. These were followed by Prague, Vienna, and Graz in the 1810s; Milan in 1824; Britain in 1830; an upgraded Leipzig school in 1843; Munich in 1846; Berlin and Dresden in the 1850s; Frankfurt in 1861; St. Petersburg in 1862 and Moscow in 1866: NG, 6:18–21.

31. Asafiev cited in Barenboim, *Rubinshtein,* 1:132. At the unveiling of the statue of Anton Rubinstein at the St. Petersburg Conservatory in 1902, speakers called him "a great Russian artist and a major public figure" and "a musical *Tale of Bygone Years,* a fanatic of musical life": GTsMMKRO, f. 59, inv. 117, n. 7848; inv. 116, n. 7848.

32. Stasov, "Uchilishche pravovedeniya"; Zetlin, *The Five,* 1–19; Wortman, *Development of a Russian Legal Consciousness,* 201 (qu.), 204–22. Stasov, like Rubinstein, had a close brush with the law in 1849 by attending the Petrashevsky Circle: *Delo Petrashevtsev,* 2:149, 224, and 3:412: Zetlin, *The Five,* 49–52. There exists as yet no satisfactory critical biography of Stasov. Soviet studies were too tolerant of his nationalist diatribes; Olkhovsky's volume is useful but somewhat schematic. The best guide to Stasov's mythologizing role in Russian music and art is to be found throughout Taruskin, *Stravinsky,* vol. 1; and Ridenour, *Nationalism.*

33. Stasov qu.: *Selected Essays,* 7, and Olkhovsky, *Stasov,* 10.

34. Articles in Campbell, *Russians on Russian Music,* 73–80 (qu. 78); and Stasov, *Selected Essays,* 81–84 and passim.

35. Stanislavsky, *My Life in Art,* 110.

36. In Campbell, *Russians on Russian Music,* 74.

37. Stasov, "Uchilishche pravovedeniya," 581 and 599–600 (his use of both *zhid* and *evrei*). For these slippery terms, see chapter 3, note 84.

38. Olkhovsky, *Stasov,* 88, 171 n. 9. For the intelligentsia's hatred of Jacques Offenbach, whose operettas were beginning to sweep Russia in the 1860s, see Billington, *Mikhailovsky and Russian Populism,* 76–78.

39. Barenboim, *Rubinshtein,* 1:236; Nekrasova, "Rubinshtein i 'Moguchaya kuchka'," 38, 41.

40. Not Georgian, as is commonly held: Popova, *Borodin,* 9–10.

41. Olkhovsky, *Stasov,* 13.

42. Serov: ERJ, 1:367–68; REE, 1:253; Stasov, "Uchilishche pravovedeniya," 599–600; Ridenour, *Nationalism,* 65–108; Campbell, *Russians on Russian Music,* 80–85; Taruskin, *Musorgsky,* 97, 99 n. 6, 379.

43. For one of numerous Soviet treatments, see Gordeeva, *Moguchaya kuchka.* For expert demythologization, see Ridenour, *Nationalism,* 81–92; Taruskin, *Stravinsky,* vol. 1; and idem, *Defining Russian Musically.*

44. Garden, *Balakirev,* 22–51; Norris, *Russian Piano Concerto,* 56–60; Piano Concerto in F-sharp minor on M. *Balakirev, N. Medtner, Igor Zhukov;* Zetlin, *The Five,* 56–59.

45. Ridenour, *Nationalism,* 127–29; Olkhovsky, *Stasov,* 91–93; Zetlin, *The Five,* 128–31; Garden, *Balakirev,* 22–51.

46. Rimsky-Korsakov, *My Musical Life,* 17–29, 60 (qu.).

47. Taneev, "Iz proshlogo imperatorskikh teatrov," 872–86; S. S. Danilov, "Materialy po istorii russkogo zakonodatelstva o teatre" in Danilov, *O teatre,* 177–200 (see pp. 179–80).

48. Mikhailova, "Vopros o teatralnoi monopolii," 79.

49. Ibid.; Swift, *Popular Theater,* 48–49. The state theater monopoly in England ended in 1843, but in fact had long been unofficially encroached on by various performance sites: Donohue, *Theatre in the Age of Kean.* By 1850 there were twenty-one theaters in London and about seventy-five in the provinces: Williams, *Long Revolution,* 261–63. The monopoly in France ended in 1864 and in the Germanies in the late 1860s.

50. Volf, *Khronika peterburgskikh teatrov,* 1:162; Roosevelt, *Apostle of Russian Liberalism,* 158; Senelick, *Serf Actor,* 217, 224.

51. Mikhailova, "Vopros o teatralnoi monopolii"; Petrovskaya, *Teatr i zritel provintsialnoi Rossii,* 18, 26, 28–29; Pobedonostsev, *Sochineniya,* 80–82; Swift, *Popular Theater,* 118 and passim.

52. Shipov, "Istoriya moei zhizni," RS (May 1881) 133–48 (a neglected example of an informed serf trader); Knight, "Science, Empire, and Nationality"; *Istoricheskii ocherk deyatelnosti Korpusa Voennykh Topografov, 1822–1872* (St. Petersburg, 1872).

53. Maksimov, "Literaturnaya ekspeditsiya"; Clay, *Ethos and Empire;* Konstantin: Lincoln, *Vanguard of Reform,* 141–48; Fateev, *Mikhail Mikhailov,* 162–68. For the Volga journey of the Chernetsov brothers, see above, chapter 8.

54. Clay, *Ethos and Empire,* passim; Morozov, "A. A. Potekhin" in *Minuvshii vek,* 392–415 (405–6); Moser, *Pisemsky,* 67–73; Hoover, *Ostrovsky,* 23–24.

55. Potekhin, "Iz teatralnykh vospominanii" in *Sochineniya,* 12:319–38. Ethnographic stories ibid., vol. 12. General works: Morozov, "A. A. Potekhin" in *Minuvshii vek;* Glinskii, "Aleksei Antipovich Potekhin"; S. V. Kastorskii, "Pisatel-dramaturg A. A. Potekhin"; and Donskov, *Changing Image of the Peasant,* 43–66.

56. Potekhin, *Sud lyudskoi — ne bozhii,* 77 (qu.); idem, "Iz teatralnykh vospominanii," *Sochineniya,* 12:322.

57. Kastorskii, "Pisatel-dramaturg A. A. Potekhin," 185 n. 19.

58. Potekhin, "Iz teatralnykh vospominanii," *Sochineniya,* 12:326, 332; review by V. Stoyunin in MTV (Jan. 1, 1856) 29; Morozov, "A. A. Potekhin" in *Minuvshii vek;*

Kastorskii, "Pisatel-dramaturg A. A. Potekhin," 195, cites performance figures on the immense popularity of this play in the years 1855–81. See also *Tinsel* (written during the Literary Expedition and published in 1858), so scathing an indictment of provincial corruption that it was not staged till the 1870s: Potekhin, *Mishura*. Grigorev, *Teatralnaya kritika*, 202–4 (qu. 202) and passim.

59. Pisemskii, "Gorkaya sudbina"; Milovidov, "Dve chukhlomskikh dramy."

60. Moser, *Pisemsky*, 94–104. The ending that Pisemsky adopted was suggested to him by the actor Martynov. Lower-class reaction to this play is hard to come by. P. V. Medvedev makes no mention of *Bitter Fate*, but he saw Pisemsky's *Hypochondriac* in 1857 in a full house when the author was called on stage three times: "Dnevnik." *Bitter Fate* did better in the provinces that in the capitals.

61. Woodhouse, "Tales from Another Country," 181 (qu.); see also Jenkins, "Pisemsky's *Bitter Fate*"; Cynthia Marsh, "Realism in the Russian Theatre, 1850–1882" in Leach, *History of Russian Theatre*, 149.

62. Hoover, *Ostrovsky*, 15–32; Ward, *Moscow and Leningrad*, 2:200, 263; Dowler, *Dostoevsky, Grigor'ev, and Native Soil Conservatism*, 27–28 and passim; N. V. Berg, "Salon E. Rostopchinoi," in Brodskii, *Literaturnye salony*, 410–23.

63. Ostrovskii, "Puteshestvie po Volge ot istokov do Nizhnego-Novgoroda" in *Polnoe sobranie sochinenii*, 10:322–47, 630–33; GTsTMRO, f. 200, n. 2679 (letter of commission) and nn. 3245–94 (sketches, unnumbered); Hoover, *Ostrovsky*, 23–24.

64. Ostrovsky, *Plays*, 213–305; Hoover, *Ostrovsky*, 33–37; Kate Sealy Rahman, "Aleksandr Ostrovsky—Dramatist and Director" in Leach, *History of Russian Theatre*, 168; Zaitsev, *Shevchenko*, 203. *Family Affair* was produced in Irkutsk in 1858 while under the ban: S. S. Danilov, *Russkii dramaticheskii teatr*, 2:158. The morose quality of the original *Family Affair* proved no obstacle to staging it as a musical comedy at the Koleso theater in Moscow in our own time: *Teatralnyi Zhurnal*, 2 (1999) 30–32.

65. Burdin, "Vospominaniya," 146; Hoover, *Ostrovsky*, 42.

66. *The Storm* in Reeve, *Anthology of Russian Plays*, 1:315–74 (qu. 329); Stites, *Women's Liberation Movement in Russia*, 47.

67. Volf, *Khronika peterburgskikh teatrov*, 1:156–57.

68. Senelick, *Russian Dramatic Theory*, xx.

69. Varneke, *History*, 367–79; Altschuller, "Actors and Acting," 111–12. For a still useful review of the Ostrovsky team, see Varneke, *Istoriya*, 571–94.

70. Ignatov, *Teatr i zriteli*, 336, 337, 338.

71. Senelick, *Serf Actor*, 185–92; Malnick, "Actors Shchepkin and Sosnitsky," 307–8.

72. Varneke, *Istoriya*, 571–78; Owen, *Capitalism and Politics in Russia*, 35 (Pechkin's). See a recollection of Sadovsky written forty years after his performances as Tortsov in Senelick, *National Theater*, 365–66; Voronezh: Petrovskaya, *Teatr i zritel provintsialnoi Rossii*, 73; Gorbunov, *Sochineniya*, 3:24.

73. *Early Russian Cinema*.

74. Altschuller, "Actors and Acting," 104–5, 114.

75. Kate Sealy Rahman, "Aleksandr Ostrovsky—Dramatist and Director" in Leach, *History of Russian Theatre*, 166–81.

76. For example in *Poor Bride* (1852): Hoover, *Ostrovsky*, 37–40.

77. Dobrolyubov, *Selected Philosophical Essays*, 218–373 and 549–635.

78. Hoover, *Ostrovsky,* 40–42. See also Christoff, *Introduction,* vol. 3: *Aksakov,* 344; Senelick, "Theatre," 267.

79. Dowler, *Dostoevsky, Grigor'ev, and Native Soil Conservatism,* 12, 33, 121, 127; Senelick, *National Theater,* 368; see also Feoktistov, "Glava iz vospominianii."

80. Ignatov, *Teatr i zritel,* 332 (qu.), 334.

81. As noted by Edwards in *Russians at Home,* 155–57. For a welcome corrective to the Ostrovsky-Dobrolyubov depiction of merchant women, see Muriel Joffe and Adele Lindenmeyr, "Daughters, Wives, and Partners: Women of the Moscow Merchant Elite" in West, *Merchant Moscow,* 95–108.

82. Ignatov, *Teatr i zriteli,* 332 (qu.); Hoover, *Ostrovsky,* 132–38; Swift, *Popular Theater,* 217, 220, 223–24.

83. For an example from an earlier period see Jules Guex, *Théâtre et la société française.*

84. Petrovskaya, *Teatr i zritel provintsialnoi Rossii,* 40–41 (qu. 41).

85. Cited in Lotman, *Velikosvetskie obedy,* 154.

86. Stasov, *Izbrannye sochineniya,* 2:51. See Valkenier, *Russian Realist Art,* 56–62, for a judicious treatment of Stasov.

87. Cited in A. Zotov, "Puti razvitiya russkogo iskusstva," 71.

88. Kelly, *Anthology of Russian Women's Writing,* 71–113 (qu. 80).

89. Shumova, *Russkaya zhivopis.*

90. Gray, *Russian Genre Painting,* 7.

91. Savinov, "Akademicheskaya zhivopis," 121–28.

92. Valkenier, "Peredvizhniki," 249–50. The theme of social inferiority runs through her *Russian Realist Art,* where she argues convincingly that it played a much greater role than politics in the emergence of the realist generation.

93. Edwards, *Russians at Home,* 154.

94. ISAKh, 45; Valkenier, *Russian Realist Art,* 18; Gray, *Russian Genre Painting,* 162–63.

95. Gray, *Russian Genre Painting,* 163. As an unprecedented public comment on this common practice, Pukirev's canvas set off a big discussion: Maegd-Soep, *Emancipation of Women,* 96–97.

96. Shumova, *Russkaya zhivopis,* 11, and unnumbered plates; Fateev, *Mikhail Mikhailov;* IIRR, introduction, 1–15, and plates. Many of the "forgotten" works are stored in the attic archive of the Russian Museum.

97. Gray, *Russian Genre Painting,* 155–59; Dmitrieva, *Moskovskoe uchilishche,* 90; Valkenier, "Intelligentsia and Art," 161. A fine collection of his reproductions can be found in Shumova, *Vasily Perov.*

98. Hilton, "Art of Ilia Repin." 1:22; Norman, "Pavel Tret'iakov (1832–1898)," 74.

99. Norman, "Pavel Tret'iakov (1832–1898)," 72. See Gray, *Russian Genre Painting,* 160–62 and figs. 56–58 for further analysis. Clerical ferment: Belliustin, *Description of the Clergy in Rural Russia.*

100. Gray, *Russian Genre Painting,* 175.

101. Shumova, *Russkaya zhivopis,* 11.

102. The whole issue is handled with great insight in her *Russian Realist Art,* 18–23, and in "Peredvizhniki," 247–65.

103. Zaitsev, *Shevchenko*, 252–68. See Grabowicz, *Poet as Mythmaker*, 8–11 and passim, for Shevchenko's deep ambivalences about life, authority, and creativity. On Elena Pavlovna: Lincoln, "Circle of Grand Duchess Yelena Pavlovna"; idem, *Vanguard of Reform*, 148–62; idem, "Karlovka Reform."

104. Ann Pullan, "For Publicity and Profit" in Rosenthal, *Prospects for the Nation*, 264; Florence: *International Herald Tribune* (July 15–16, 2000) 7; Boime, *Academy and French Painting*, 15, 63, 100, 180; Becker, *Art Worlds*, 95.

105. The artists also suffered police interrogation and surveillance. Valkenier, *Russian Realist Art*, 33–34; Norman, "Pavel Tret'iakov (1832–1898)," 121, 124. The seceders: Ivan Kramskoi, V. V. Venig, A. K. Grigorev, N. D. Dmitrev-Orenburgsky, F. S. Zhuravlëv, A. I. Korzukhin, K. V. Lemokh, N. S. Shustov, N. P. Petrov, A. D. Kitovchenko, K. E. Makovsky, A. I. Morozov, M. I. Peskov, and V. P. Kretyan — a sculptor.

106. Norman, "Pavel Tret'iakov (1832–1898)," 121.

107. Krivtsova, "Iz istorii khudozhestvennoi zhizni," 94.

108. Valkenier, *Russian Realist Art*, 37–134, offers the best demythologization. See also Ezerskaya, *Peredvizhniki*.

109. Sternin, *Khudozhestvennaya zhizn Rossii*, 29–30.

110. Valkenier, "Peredvizhniki," 255, 259; idem, "Intelligentsia and Art," 153–71.

111. Ely, *This Meager Nature*, 255, 257, 265.

112. Nochlin, *Realism*, 13 and passim.

113. Macleod, *Art and the Victorian Middle Class*, passim, based on a sample of 146 males.

114. Mayer, *Persistence of the Old Regime*.

115. Norman, "Pavel Tretiakov and Merchant Art Patronage," 93–95; "Kozma Terentevich Soldatenkov (1818–1901)" in *Sobirateli i metsenaty*, 272–86.

116. Norman, "Pavel Tret'iakov (1832–1898)." This dissertation is indispensable for an understanding of the art world in the late nineteenth century.

117. Field, "The Year of Jubilee" in Eklov, *Russia's Great Reforms, 1855–1881*, 40–41.

118. Blum, *End of the Old Order*, 329.

119. Field, *End of Serfdom*, 208.

120. Fitzpatrick, "Ascribing Class," and her numerous other works on the Stalin period.

121. The Russian Musical Society opened branches in Moscow, Kiev, and Kazan in the 1860s; in Kharkov, Pskov, Nizhny Novgorod, Saratov, Omsk, Tobolsk, and Tomsk in the 1870s; and in Tambov, Tiflis, and Odessa in the 1880s. By the early twentieth century, about forty towns had affiliates: Findeizen, *Ocherk*, 17–29. For the spread of provincial orchestras, see ME, 4:795.

122. Petrovskaya, *Teatr i zritel provintsialnoi Rossii*, passim.

123. Ely, *This Meager Nature*, 171; Bowlt, "Moscow Art Market" in Stavrou, *Art and Culture*, 108–28; *Imperatorskaya Akademiya Khudozhestv: Muzei*, i–xxvi; Norman, "Pavel Tretiakov and Merchant Art Patronage," 93, 98, 105.

124. Sternin, *Khudozhestvennaya zhizn Rossii*, 19–28.

125. David Solkin has applied this interpretation to art publics in *Painting for Money*, 2–3, 247–76, and passim.

126. Golub, *Recurrence of Fate,* 29; Filaret: F. D. Bobkov, "Iz zapisok byvshago krepostnogo cheloveka," IV (May 1907) 472.

127. V. V. Lvov, "Zheleznaya doroga"; Leikin, *Aktëry-lyubiteli.*

128. Vodovozova, *Na zare zhizni,* 2:73–75 (qu. 74); Repin cited in Kelly, *Refining Russia,* 105; Kropotkin, *Memoirs of a Revolutionist,* 105–6.

129. Taruskin, *Stravinsky,* 1:23–75 (qu. 64). The once militant member of the Mighty Five, César Cui, became director of the Russian Musical Society a few years after Rubinstein, its founder, stepped down; Valkenier, *Russian Realist Art,* passim.

Bibliography

Archival Materials

MOSCOW

RGBRO: Rossiiskaya Gosudarstvennaya Biblioteka imeni V. I. Lenina, Rukopisnyi Otdel
Fond 411, A. N. Verstovskii.

RGALI: Rossiiskii Gosudarstvennyi Arkhiv Literatury i Iskusstv
Fond 191, op. 1, ed. kh. 2057: P. A. Efremov, materials on Karl Bryullov; op. 2, ed. kh. 224: on the Vielgorskii brothers.
Fond 794, op. 1, ed. kh. 113: Karl Lyudvig Didlo (Charles-Louis Didelot).
Fond 860, op. 1, ed. kh. 348: Yu. V. Sobolev, typescripts.
Fond 872: V. Ya. Stepanova: archival notes on Imperial Theater management, 1752–1820.
Fond 952: Mikhail Glinka, musical score.
Fond 1915, op. 1, n. 1, 737: Police reports on Aleksandr Alyabev.
Fond 1925, op. 2, ed. kh. 30: Service records of Mikhail and Matvei Vielgorskii.
Fond 2729, op. 1, ed. kh. 3: V. D. Tikhomirov, autograph papers on Didelot, Perrot, St. Léon, Petipa.

GTsTMRO: Gosudarstvennyi Tsentralnyi Teatralnyi Muzei imeni A. A. Bakhrushina, Rukopisnyi otdel
(All followed by opis 1; items unnumbered.)
Fond 24, V. V. Bezekirskii.

Fond 53, A. N. Verstovskii.

Fond 108, P. A. Karatygin.

Fond 143, D. T. Lenskii.

Fond 178, P. S. Mochalov.

Fond 200, A. N. Ostrovskii.

Fond 222, Ludwig (Louis) Maurer.

Karta Krepostnogo Teatra. Large-format, colored wall map, unnumbered and undated (but 1920s), catalogued under title.

GTsMMKRO: Gosudarstvennyi Tsentralnyi Muzei Muzykalnoi Kultury imeni M. I. Glinki, Rukopisnyi Otdel.

Fond 40, A. A. Alyabev, d. 264–66: ms. programs.

Fond 59, Anton Rubinshtein.

Fond 170, V. V. Bezekirskii, op. 3, ed. kh. 4621: Coronation March.

Fond 255, Dzhon Fild (John Field).

Fond 364, Aleksei Verstovskii: inv. 218, n. 8871: correspondence, Verstovskii-Gedeonov; and 214–17, 219, 222–35, 285–88.

GTsMMKF: Gosudarstvennyi Tsentralnyi Muzei Muzykalnoi Kultury imeni M. I. Glinki, Fonoteka.

(Magnetic tapes recorded live, some unidentified by date or performance, with catalogue numbers where present; lyricist in parentheses when known, followed by performer(s), if any.)

Alyabev, Aleksandr. *Prolog* (1825). All-Union Radio Chorus and Orchestra.

——. "Solovei" (A. I. Delvig). Antonina Nezhdanova and piano. DI-13392.

——. *Volshebnyi Baraban: vodevil* (1827). N. Rabinovich, Leningrad Radio Symphony Orchestra.

Davydov, Stepan. "Kaby zavtra" and song from *Lesta, Dneprovskaya rusalka*. Soprano and piano.

Field, John. Ten Nocturnes. Svetlana Potanina, recorded on All-Union Radio, 1979.

Fomin, E. Overture to *The Miller, Wizard, Deceiver, and Matchmaker*. V. Kornachev, the Vladimir Chamber Ensemble. Also on Melodiya S-90 20665 001 (1990).

——. Two arias from *Amerikanets*. Opera. Svetlana Erofeeva and chamber orchestra.

Genishta, Iosif [Osip Jeništa]. "Elegiya: pogaslo dnevnoe svetilo" (Pushkin). Georgii Vinogradov, tenor, and Georgii Orentirikher, piano.

Kashin, Daniil. "Devitsy-krasavitsy" (Pushkin). G. Sakharova, soprano, with balalaikas. "Twelve Variations for Harp," Olga Erdeli, harp.

——. "Variations on a Russian Theme." Galina Barkova, harp.

——. Variations on "Vo sadu li, v ogorode." Dmitrii Blagoi, piano.

——. "Ya ne znala ni o chëm v svete" (A. F. Merzlyakov). Lyudmila Zykina, voice, R. Bromberg, piano.

——. "Zashchitnikam Petrov Grada." Male voices of the All-Union Radio Song Ensemble.

Kozlovskii, Osip [Jozef Kozlowski]. Incidental music to *Fingal* (Ozerov). Soprano and harp.

———. Two polonaises. V. Kornachev, the Vladimir Chamber Ensemble. Also on Melodiya S-90 20665 001 (1990).

———. Two songs, "Prezhestokaya sudbina" and "Pchëlka."

Varlamov, Aleksandr. "Beleet parus odinokii" (Lermontov). I. S. Kozlovskii. DI-6095.

———. "Krasnyi sarafan" (N. G. Tsyganov). I. Arkhipova. DI-5842.

———. "Vdol po ulitse metelitsa metët" (folk lyrics). Nikolai Gedda, tenor.

Verstovskii, Aleksei. *Askoldova Mogila.* Opera. The Taras Shevchenko Academic Theater Orchestra and Opera Company of Kiev, 1959.

———. "Chërnaya shal" (Pushkin). I. S. Kozlovskii, Gennadii Rozhdestvenskii, Bolshoi Symphony Orchestra, 1959. DI-18145.

———. *Kto brat, kto sestra? opera-vodevil* (libretto, Aleksandr Griboedov and P. A. Vyazemskii). Dramatic Theater of the All-Union Radio Committee.

———. "Staryi muzh" (Pushkin, from "The Gypsies"). L. Myasnikova and piano. DI-16559–16560.

Vielgorskii, Matvei. *Tema i Variatsii.* Svyatoslav Knushevitskii, cello, and Naum Valter, piano (radio, 1965).

Zhilin, Aleksei. "Kak na dubochke dva golubtsy." Dmitrii Blagoi, piano.

———. "Waltz." S. Ponyatovskii, viola, and T. Sergeeva, piano.

ST. PETERSBURG

RNBRO: Rossiiskaya Natsionalnaya Biblioteka, Rukopisnyi Otdel

Fond 142, Vielgorskie: ed. kh. 125: Matvei: On the appointment of Anton Rubinshtein as pianist to Her Imperial Majesty, 1852.

Fond 539, V. F. Odoevskii, op. 2, n. 43, 44: notes.

Fond 654, Anton Rubinshtein, op. 1, ed. kh. 1: copy of his baptismal certificate at the Nikolskaya Church in Berdichev, 28 June, 1831; ed. kh. 4: notes on first Moscow recital, July 11, 1839; unnumbered: eight programs in his hand (mostly in German).

Fond 739, V. V. Stasov.

Fond 861, I. I. Shishkin, n. 1, "Biografiya" from *Knizhki Nedeli* (Nov. 1899) 7–35 and (Dec. 1899) 42–68; n. 2, ms. biog. of Apollon Mokhritskii; n. 165, ticket, 1855, from Ministry of the Court School of Painting and Sculpture of the Moscow Art Society to Shishkin for a trip to Vyatka.

RNBOE: Rossiiskaya Natsionalnaya Biblioteka, Otdel Estampov

Sobranie (sometimes Kollektsiya) Rybakova. Papka 7, Martynov, A. E.: aquarelles; untitled, chromolithograph views of St. Petersburg, 1820s, En-237k.

———. Papka 10: *Cris de Pétersbourg* [1830s]; *Nouvelle collection: quarante-deux vues de Saint-Pétersbourg et de ses environs,* 1826, black and white lithographs, Ei-227.

Sobranie Sergeya Levitskogo: early Russian photographs.

Vues de Pawlowsk par Thurner (1820s), etchings, unnumbered.

RNBFF: Rossiiskaya Natsionalnaya Biblioteka, Filial, Fonoteka

Rubinshtein [Rubinstein], Anton. *Demon.* Opera. A. Melik-Pashaev and the Bolshoi Theater (1950).

SPBKF: Sankt-Peterburgskaya Gosudarstvennaya Konservatoriya imeni N. A. Rimskogo-Korsakova, Fonoteka.

(Magnetic tapes and vinyl records, some unidentified by date or performance, with catalogue numbers where present; lyricist in parentheses when known, followed by performer, if any.)

Alyabev, Aleksandr. *Uvertyura.* DI-8917.

Bortnyanskii, D. S. *Kheruvimskaya pesnya.* DI-11661.

———. *Sokol.* Opera.

Fomin, E. *Suita iz opery "Orfei."* DI-14899.

Glinka, Mikhail. *Kamarinskaya; Ruslan i Lyudmila.* Opera. IIA2.

Haydn, Joseph. *Sotvorenie Mira.* DI-7502.

Kozlovskii, Osip [Jozef Kozlowski]. Incidental music to *Fingal* (Ozerov). Orchestral original. Mag-1612. IIA1.

Lvov, Aleksei. "Bozhe tsarya khrani." IIA3.

———. Violin Concerto (1840). Sergei Stadler, violin, with Vladislav Chernushenko and the Leningrad Philharmonia Orchestra. On *A. Lvov; A. Arenskii,* Melodiya, stereo, S-10-25083–005. Folder Lyadov, 26978.

Rubinshtein [Rubinstein], Anton. "Barcarole" (1853), DI-8598. Piano; "Pevets" (1849–50), DI-16527; "Noch" (1852), DI-16527; "Zhelanie" (1850), DI-13006; "Romans-Melodiya," DI-6305.

———. *Dramaticheskaya simfoniya* (No. 4). B. Khaikin and the Bolshoi Theater Orchestra. Folder Rubinshtein, No. 5771.

———. *Russkaya.* DI-5828.

Vielgorskii, Matvei. *Tema i variatsii.* Cello. DI-5525.

Viotti, Giovanni Battista. Sonata for Harp and Violin in B Major. On *Vera Dulova, arfa.* Melodiya, stereo, 33: C-10–13745–6.

Wieniawski, Henryk. *Vospominanie o Moskve.* Andrei Korsakov, violin, and Iolanta Miroshnikova, piano. On *G. Venyavskii,* Melodiya, stereo, S-10–19161–2. Folder Venyavskii, 10438. IIB1.

SPBGTB: Sankt-Peterburgskaya Gosudarstvennaya Teatralnaya Biblioteka

Manuscript copy of A. A. Shakhovskoi, "Polubarskie zatei" (undated).

IRLPD: Institut Russkoi Literatury (Pushkinskii Dom)

Fond 371: N. V. Kukolnik, op. 1. "Kratkaya biograficheskaya spravka N. V. Kukolnika"; n. 141, censor's copy of *Ruka vsevyshnyago otechestva spasil* (1834); n. 125, War Ministry to Kukolnik, Nov. 13, 1846; n. 127, Kukolnik to War Ministry, Sept. 12, 1848; n. 41, "Rech v Taganroge," Apr. 1861; n. 21, "Zhizn russkikh gorodov: 1, Voronezh," 1849.

Fond 50: Vielgorskie, ed. kh. 19. Ch. Didelot, "Observations, demandes, et réglements relatifs à la danse," Mar. 22, 28, 31, 1828; n. 125, Cécile Cherubini to Matvei Vielgorskii, May 18, 1842; n. 130, Bernhard Romberg to Matvei Vielgorskii, June 12, 1840; n. 134, Pauline Viardot to Matvei Vielgorskii, 32 letters, 1845–52; n. 166, membership certificate to the St. Petersburg Philharmonic Society for Matvei Vielgorskii, Jan. 29, 1827; n. 173, St. Petersburg Philharmonic Society letter to Mikhail Vielgorskii, May 1, 1852.

GRMFZh: Gosudarstvennyi Russkii Muzei, Fond Zhivopisi XVIII — Pervoi Poloviny XIX veka

Undisplayed paintings.

SMOLENSK

GASO: Gosudarstvennyi Arkhiv Smolenskoi Oblast

Fond I, Kantselyariya smolenskogo gubernatora: op. 1, d. 13, 15, 20, 23, 34, 102, 111, 349; op. 4, d. 129; op. 7, d. 9, 186.
Fond 1260: Inv. opis n. I (1812–96).

Published Works

PRIMARY PUBLISHED SOURCES

Afanasev, N. Ya. "Vospominaniya," IV, 41 (July 1890) 23–48; (Aug. 1890) 255–76.

Agin, A. and E. E. Bernardskii. *Sto chetyre risunki k poeme N. V. Gogolya "Mertvyya dushi."* 2d ed. St. Petersburg, 1892.

Aksakov, Konstantin. *Osvobozhdenie Moskvy v 1612 godu.* Moscow, 1848.

Aksakov, Sergei. *The Family Chronicle.* Tr. M. C. Beverley. New York, 1961.

———. *Sobranie sochinenii.* 4 v. Moscow, 1895–1900, mixed editions.

———. *Years of Childhood.* Tr. Alec Brown. New York, 1960.

Aleksandrov, A. [Durova]. "Dva slova iz zhiteiskago slovarya," OZ, 7/1 (1839) 38–52.

Aleksei Gavrilovich Venetsianov. Moscow, 1957. Reproductions.

Aleksei Gavrilovich Venetsianov: stati, pisma, sovremenniki o khudozhnike. Leningrad, 1980.

"Aleksei Nikolaevich Olenin," RS (Oct. 1875) 280–96.

Alyabev, A. *Shest romansov.* Moscow, 1834.

Andrei Osipovich Karelin: tvorcheskoe nasledie. Nizhnii Novgorod, 1990. Early photographs.

Annenkov, P. V. *The Extraordinary Decade: Literary Memoirs.* Ed. A. P. Mendel. Tr. I. R. Titunik. Ann Arbor, 1968.

Arkhiv Direktsii Imperatorskikh Teatrov, 1746–1801 gg. 4 v. St. Petersburg, 1892.

Arnold, Yurii. *Vospominaniya.* 3 v. Moscow, 1892–93.

Aronson, M. and S. Reiser, eds. *Literaturnye kruzhki i salony.* Leningrad, 1929.

Artynov, Aleksandr. *Vospominaniya krestyanina sela Ugodich, Yaroslavskoi gubernii Rostovskago uezda.* Moscow, 1882.

Atava, Sergei [S. N. Terpigorev]. *Potrevozhennyya teni.* St. Petersburg, 1888.

———. *Sobranie sochinenii.* 6 v. St. Petersburg, n.d.

Babochka. Journal of the 1820s.

Bakarev, V. A. "Usadba nachala XIX v.: iz zapisok arkhitektora," KA, 5 (1936) 254–62.

Batyushkov, K. N. "Progulka v Akademiyu Khudozhestv" in *Sochineniya Batyushkova.* 2 v. St. Petersburg, 1850, 1:131–68.

Belinskii, V. G. *Polnoe sobranie sochinenii.* 13 v. Moscow, 1953–59.

Belinsky [Belinskii], V. G. *Selected Philosophical Works.* Moscow, 1948.

Belliustin, I. S. *Description of the Clergy in Rural Russia: the Memoir of a Nineteenth-Century Parish Priest.* Ed. Gregory Freeze. Ithaca, 1985.

Benckendorf [Benkendorf], A. Kh. "Zapiski Grafa A. Kh. Benkendorfa (1832–1837gg.)" in Shilder, *Imperator Nikolai Pervyi*, 2:647–764.

Bergman, Ingmar. *The Magic Lantern*. New York, 1988.

Berkov, P. N. *Istoriya russkoi komedii XVIII v.* Leningrad, 1977.

Berlioz, Hector. *Autobiography*. Tr. R. Holmes. 2 v. London, 1884.

Bezekirskii, V. V. *Iz zapisnoi knizhki artista, 1850–1910*. St. Petersburg, 1910.

Blagovo, Dmitrii. *Razskazy babushki: iz vospominanii pyati pokolenii*. St. Petersburg, 1885.

Bobkov, F. D. "Iz zapisok byvshago krepostnogo cheloveka," IV (May) 446–74; (June) 734–64; (July) 142–64; all 1907.

Boborykin, P. D. *Vospominaniya*. 2 v. Leningrad, 1965.

——. *Za polveka (moi vospominaniya)*. Ed. B. P. Kozmin (Moscow, 1929).

Bremner, Robert. *Excursions in the Interior of Russia*. 2d ed. 2 v. London, 1840.

Brodskii, N. L., ed. *Literaturnye salony i kruzhki: pervaya polovina XIX veka*. Leningrad, 1930.

Bulgarin, Faddei. *Ivan Vejeeghen*. 2 v. Philadelphia, 1832.

——. *Ivan Vyzhigin*. 4 v. St. Petersburg, 1829.

Burdin, F. A. "Vospominaniya artista ob imperatore Nikolae Pavloviche," IV, 23 (Jan. 1886) 144–53.

Buturlin, M. D. "Teatr grafa Kamenskago v Orle v 1827 i 1828 godakh," RA, 7/10 (1869) 1707–12.

——. "Zapiski," RA, 1–4 (1897) 213–47, 396–444, 579–652; 5–8 (1897) 5–74, 177–256, 541–601; 9–10 (1897) 33–106, 237–82; 8 (1898) 529–90.

Caigniez, L.-C. and J. M. T. Baudouin d'Aubigny, *La pie voleuse, ou la servante de Palaiseau: mélodrame historique*. Paris, 1815. Tr. as [Kene], *Soroka Vorovka, ili palezosskaya sluzhanka*. St. Petersburg, 1816.

Campbell, Stuart, ed. *Russians on Russian Music 1830–1880: An Anthology* Cambridge, 1994.

Chaikovskii, Modest. *Zhizn Petra Ilicha Chaikovskogo*. 3 v. Moscow, 1900–1902.

Chernetsov, Grigory and Nikanor. *Puteshestvie po Volge*. Moscow, 1970.

Choiseul-Gouffier, Comtesse de. *Historical Memoirs of Alexander I and the Court of Russia*. Chicago, 1901.

Clyman, Toby and Judith Vowles, eds. *Russia Through Women's Eyes: Autobiographies from Tsarist Russia*. New Haven, 1996.

Cumberland, Richard. *The Jew* (1794) in L. I. Newman, ed., *Richard Cumberland: Critic and Friend of the Jews*. New York, 1919, pp. 61–124.

Custine, Astolphe, Marquis de. *Journey for Our Time: The Russian Journals*. Ed. and tr. P. P. Kohler. Chicago, 1951.

——. *Letters from Russia*. Ed. and tr. Robin Buss. London, 1991.

Dal, Vladimir. *Tolkovyi slovar zhivogo velikorusskogo yazyka*. 4 v. St. Petersburg, 1903–9.

Damskii zhurnal. Moscow, 1827–33.

Delo Petrashevtsev. 3 vols. Moscow, 1937–51.

D. M. "Neskolko slov o dvorovykh lyudyakh," OZ, 119/7 (July 1858) 46–54.

Dmitriev, Nikolai. "Studencheskiya vospominaniya o Moskovskom Universitete,"

Nedalëkoe proshloe. St. Petersburg, 1865 (167–247). Also signed N. D. in OZ, 122 (July 1858) 81–95; (Sept. 1858) 1–42; (Jan. 1859) 1–14; all s.p.

Dobrolyubov, N. G. "Razvrat Nikolaya Pavlovicha i ego priblizhnykh lyubimtsev," *Golos minuvshego,* 1 (Jan. 1922) 64–68.

——. *Selected Philosophical Essays.* Moscow, 1948.

——. *Sobranie sochinenii.* 9 v. Moscow, 1961–64.

Dolgorukii, I. M. *Puteshestvie v Kiev v 1817 godu.* Moscow, 1870.

Dostoevskii, Fëdor. *The House of the Dead.* Tr. C. Garnett. New York, 1959.

——. "Nyetochka Nezvanov" in *The Friend of the Family.* Tr. of *Netochka Nezvanova* by Constance Garnett. New York, 1949.

Dyukanzh, Viktor [Victor Ducange]. *Tereza, ili zhenevskaya sirota.* Moscow, 1833.

Edwards, Sutherland. *The Russians at Home: Unpolitical Sketches.* 2d ed. London, 1861.

E., F. v. [F. A. von Ettinger]. *Bashnya Veselukha, ili Smolensk i zhiteli ego shestdesyat let nazad* (1845). Smolensk, 1992.

Ertaulov, Gurii. "Vospominaniya o nekogda znamenitom teatre Grafa S. M. Kamenskago v g. Orle," *Delo* (June 1873) 184–219.

Feoktistov, E. M. "Glava iz vospominianii," ed. B. Modzalevskii in *Atenei,* bk. 3. Leningrad, 1926, pp. 84–114.

F. G. Volkov i russkii teatr ego vremeni: sbornik materialov. Moscow, 1953.

Filonov, A. G. "V novo-cherkasskom teatre" in Filonov, *Ocherki Dona.* St. Petersburg, 1859, pp. 69–82.

Finland and Russia. London, 1849 (Vol. 2 of *Handbook for Northern Europe*).

Fiziologiya Peterburga. Ed. V. I. Kushelov. Moscow, 1991.

Gagarin, G. G. "Vospominaniya knyazya G. G. Gagarina o Karle Pavloviche Bryullove," *Novoe vremya* (Dec. 14, 1899). Tr. from a French ms. of 1849.

Gagarin, S. P. *Vseobshchii geograficheskii slovar.* 3 v. Moscow, 1843.

Galakhov, A. D. "Literaturnaya kofeinya v Moskve v 1830–1840 gg.," RS, 17 (Apr. 1886) 181–98; (June 1886) 691–706.

Gatsiskii, A. S. "Aleksandr Dmitrievich Ulybyshev," RA, 1 (1886) 55–68.

——. *Nizhegorodskii teatr (1798–1867).* Nizhny Novgorod, 1867.

Gerakov, Gavril. *Prodolzhenie putevykh zapisok po mnogim guberniyam, 1820-go i nachala 1821-go.* Petrograd [*sic*], 1828.

——. *Putevyya zapiski po mnogim rossiiskim guberniyam, 1820.* Petrograd [*sic*], 1828.

Gertsen [Herzen], Aleksandr. *Sochineniya.* 9 v. Moscow, 1955.

Ginzburg, S. L., ed. *Russkii muzykalnyi teatr, 1700–1835 gg.: khrestomatiya.* Leningrad, 1941.

Glinka, Mikhail. *Polnoe sobranie pisem.* Ed. N. Findeizen. St. Petersburg, 1907.

——. *Zapiski.* Ed. V. Bogdanov-Berezovskii. Leningrad, 1953. Tr. as *Memoirs* by R. Mudge. Westport, 1980.

Goncharov, Ivan. *Oblomov.* Tr. D. Magarshack. London, 1954.

——. "Pisma stolichnogo druga k provintsialnomu zhenikhu" in Yu. G. Oksman, ed., *Feletony sorokovykh godov.* Moscow, 1930, pp. 39–88.

Gorbunov, I. F. *Sochineniya,* 3 v. St. Petersburg, 1904–7.

Gorod glazami khudozhnikov: Peterburg — Petrograd — Leningrad v proizvedeniyakh zhivopisi i grafiki. Leningrad, 1978.

Gosudarstvennaya Tretyakovskaya Galereya: istoriya i kollektsii. Moscow, 1986.

Gosudarstvennyi Russkii Muzei. *Zhivopis XVIII–nachalo XX veka.* Leningrad, 1980.

Gosudarstvennyi Russkii Muzei. *Zhivopis XVIII–pervoi poloviny XIX vekov: novye postupleniya, 1977–1987.* Leningrad, 1990.

Griboedov, A. S. *Polnoe sobranie sochinenii,* 3 v. St. Petersburg, 1911–17.

Grigorev, Apollon. *My Literary and Moral Wanderings.* Tr. R. Matlaw. New York, 1962.

——. *Teatralnaya kritika.* Ed. A. Ya. Altshuller et al. Leningrad, 1985.

Grigorovich, D. V. "Derevnya," *Povesti i razskazy,* 7 v. St. Petersburg, 1872, 1:3–71.

——. *Polnoe sobranie sochinenii.* 12 v. Moscow, 1896.

Gurowski, Adam de. *Russia As It Is.* 2d ed. New York, 1854.

Haxthausen, August von. *The Russian Empire, Its People, Institutions, and Resources* (1856). Tr. R. Farie. 2 v. London, 1968.

——. *Studies on the Interior of Russia.* Ed. S. Frederick Starr. Tr. Eleanore Schmidt. Chicago, 1972.

Herzen [Gertsen], Alexander. *My Past and Thoughts.* Ed. D. Macdonald. Berkeley, 1982.

Illyustrirovannyi semeinyi listok, 1859–61.

Insarskii, V. A. "Vospominaniya V. A. Insarskago: trevogi v teatralnom upravlenii," RS (Oct. 1874) 303–14.

——. *Zapiski Vasiliya Antonovicha Insarskago.* St. Petersburg, 1914.

Ivanchin-Pisarev, Nikolai. *Otechestvennaya galleriya.* 2 v. Moscow, 1832.

Ivanov, N. I. "Vospominaniya teatralnogo antreprenër," IV (Oct.) 64–89; (Nov.) 321–45; (Dec.) 581–605; all 1891.

Jesse, William. *Notes of a Half-Pay in Search of Health: Russia, Circassia, and the Crimea in 1839–40.* 2 v. London, 1841.

Kaiser, Daniel and Gary Marker, eds. *Reinterpreting Russian History: Readings, 860–1860s.* New York, 1994.

Kapkanishchikov, A. P. "Kniga pamyati Alekseya Petrovicha Kapkanishchikova" in *Iz istorii voronezhskogo kraya,* 181–206.

Karatygin, A. V. "Russkii teatr v tsarstvovanie Aleksandra I, 1801–1825: iz zhurnala," RS (Oct. 1880) 257–75.

Karatygin, P. A. "Dom na Peterburskoi Storone," RP, 2 (1843) 92–119.

——. *Zapiski.* Leningrad, 1929.

Karsavina, Tamara. *Theatre Street.* London, 1930.

"Kartiny proshedshago: zapiski russkoi artistki," *Muzykalnyi i teatralnyi vestnik* (Sept. 15) 492–94; (Sept. 22) 492–95; (Oct. 6) 529–52; (Oct. 27) 578–80; (Nov. 24) 642–44; (Dec. 15) 699–700; (Dec. 22, 1857) 709–15; (Dec. 29) 720–25; all 1857.

Katalog arkhivnikh fondov gosarkhiva Smolenskoi oblasti i ego filiala v g. Vyazme (Dosovetskii period). Smolensk, 1989.

Keller, E. E. *Prazdnichnaya kultura Peterburga: ocherk istorii.* St. Petersburg, 2001.

Kelly, Catriona, ed. *An Anthology of Russian Women's Writing, 1777–1992.* Oxford, 1994.

Keppen, Pëtr. *Devyataya reviziya: izsledovanie o chisle zhitelei v Rossii v 1851 godu.* St. Petersburg, 1857.

Khmelnitskii, Nikolai. *Sochineniya.* 3 v. St. Petersburg, 1849.

Khrapovitskii, A. I. "Dnevnik," RS (Feb. 1879) 341–56.

Knyazhnin, Ya. B. *Sochineniya*. 2 v. St. Petersburg, 1847–48.

Kohn, Hans, ed. *The Mind of Modern Russia: Historical and Political Thought of Russia's Great Age*. New York, 1955.

Kolokol. 1857–67.

Komarovskii, E. F. "Iz zapisok," RA (Oct. 1867) 1276–1330.

Koni, A. F. *Vospominaniya o pisatelyakh*. Leningrad, 1965.

Koni, F. A. *Teatr F. A. Koni*. 4 v. St. Petersburg, 1870–71.

Kostenetskii, Yakov. "Vospominaniya iz moei studencheskoi zhizni," RA, 1 (1887) 98–117; 2 (1887) 229–42; 3 (1887) 321–49; 5 (1887) 73–81; 6 (1887) 217–42.

Kotzebue, August von. *Die deutschen Kleinstädter* (1803). Ed. H. Schumacher. Berlin, 1964.

———. *Menschenhass und Reue: Schauspiel in fünf Aufzügen* in Jürg Nathes, ed., *August von Kotzebue: Schauspiele*. Frankfurt/Main, 1972), pp. 43–126. Tr. as [Kotsebu], *Nenavist k lyudyam i raskayanie*. 4th ed. Orël, 1826.

———. *Das merkwürdigste Jahr meines Lebens* (1803). Munich, 1965. Tr. as [Kotsebu], *Dostopamyatnyi god moei zhizni*. 2 v. N.p., 1879.

Kozlov, I. I. *Polnoe sobranie stikhotvorenii*. Leningrad, 1963.

Kramskoi, Ivan. *Ivan Nikolaevich Kramskoi: ego zhizn, perepiska, i khudozhestvenno-kriticheskiya stati*. St. Petersburg, 1888.

Kratkii istoricheskii ocherk deistvii S.-Peterburgskago Zhenskago Patrioticheskago Obshchestva. St. Petersburg, 1848.

Krepostnichestvo i volya. Moscow, 1911.

Krestovskii, V. V. *Peterburgskyya trushchoby*. 4 v. St. Petersburg, 1864.

Kropotkin, P. A. *Memoirs of a Revolutionist*. Ed. J. A. Rogers. New York, 1962.

Krylov, I. A. *Sochineniya*. 2 v. Moscow, 1956.

Krylov, N. A. "Kadety sorokovykh godov," IV (Sept. 1901) 943–47.

Krymskaya voina, 1853–1856 — geroicheskaya oborona Sevastopolya: pervye foto-reportazhi. Moscow, 1977. Photos.

Kryukovskii, Matvei. *Pozharskoi, tragediya v trëkh deistviyakh*. 2d ed. St. Petersburg, 1810.

Kugushev, Grigory. *Kornet Otletaev: povest*. Moscow, 1853.

Kukolnik, N. V. "Iz vospominanii," IV, 45/7 (July, 1891) 79–99.

———. *Sochineniya dramaticheskiya*. 3 v. St. Petersburg, 1851–52.

Kvitka, G. F. "Dvoryanskie vybory" in *Dramaticheskiya sochineniya*. 2 v. St. Petersburg, 1862, 2:1–218.

Labzina, Anna. *Days of a Russian Noblewoman: The Memories of Anna Labzina, 1758–1821*. Ed. G. Marker and R. May. DeKalb, 2001.

Lavrov, I. I. *Stsena i zhizn v provintsii i v stolitse*. Moscow, 1889.

Leonova, Darya. "Vospominaniya artistki Imperatorskikh Teatrov," IV (Jan.) 120–44; (Feb.) 326–51; (Mar.) 632–59; (Apr. 75–83); all 1891.

Leskov, N. S. "The Make-Up Artist" in *The Enchanted Pilgrim and Other Stories*. Tr. D. Magarshack. Westport, 1977, pp. 283–303.

Limonov, Yu. A., ed. *Rossiya pervoi poloviny XIX v. glazami inostrantsev*. Leningrad, 1991.

Liszt, Franz. *Selected Letters*. Ed. and tr. A. Williams. Oxford, 1998.

Lomakin, G. Ya. "Avtobiograficheskiya zapiski," RS (Mar.) 645–66; (June) 675–89; (Aug.) 465–85; all 1886.

Lopukhov, Fëdor. *Shestdesyat let v balete.* Moscow, 1966.

Lvov, A. F. "Zapiski Alekseya Fëdorovicha Lvova," RA, 4 (1884) 225–60 and 5 (1884) 65–114.

Lvov, F. F. "Obshchestvo Pooshchreniya Khudozhnikov v 1850–1862 gg.," RS (July 1881) 633–54.

Lvov, V. V. "Zheleznaya doroga: shutka-vodevil v 1 deistvii," *Raut* (1852) 339–61.

Lyons, Marvin. *Russia in Original Photographs, 1860–1920.* London, 1977.

"Lyubopytnyi prikaz Knyazya A. B. Kurakina," RA, 11 (1893) 387–93.

Machtet, G. A. *Polnoe sobranie sochinenii.* 10 v. St. Petersburg, 1911–13.

Maksimov, Sergei. "Literaturnaya ekspeditsiya," RM (Feb. 1890) 17–50.

Martynov, Andrei. *Saint-Pétersbourg.* Text by Dominique Fernandez. Paris, 1994.

Medvedev, P. M. *Vospominaniya.* Leningrad, 1929.

Medvedev, P. V. "Dnevnik Pavla Vasilevicha Medvedeva, 1854–1864 gg." Transcribed from archival documents by Jeffrey Burds.

Melgunov, S. P., ed. *Krepostnoe pravo i krestyanskaya zhizn.* Moscow, 1911.

Melnikov, I. A. "Zapiski," RS, 137 (Jan. 1909) 55–66; (Feb. 1909) 349–64.

Mërder, N. I. "Lyudi bylago vremeni: iz razskazov Very Ivanovny Annenkovoi i drugikh starozhilov," RA, 1 (1906) 105–21.

——. "Otzhivye tipy," IV (Mar. 1890) 537–52.

Merzlyakov, M. "Poseshchenie teatra," *Biblioteka dlya chteniya,* 31 (June, 1864) 1–40; s.p.

Meshcherskii, A. V. "Iz moei stariny," RA (1901) 95–118 and 470–504.

Mikhailov, M. L. *Sochineniya.* 3 v. Petrograd, 1915.

——. *Sochineniya.* 3 v. Moscow, 1958.

Milstein, Nathan. *From Russia to the West: The Musical Memoirs and Reminiscences.* Ed. S. Volkov. New York, 1990.

Milyukov, A. P. *Dobroe staroe vremya.* St. Petersburg, 1872.

Morozov, P. *Minuvshii vek.* St. Petersburg, 1902.

Moskovskii Universitet v vospominaniyakh sovremennikov (1755–1917). Moscow, 1989.

Murzakevich, Nikifor. *Istoriya goroda Smolenska.* Ed. I. I. Orlovskii. Smolensk, 1903.

Mussorgsky [Musorgskii], Modest. *The Mussorgsky Reader: A Life of Modest Petrovich Mussorgsky in Letters and Documents.* Ed. and tr. J. Leyda. New York, 1947.

Myrone, Martin. *Representing Britain, 1500–2000: 100 Works from the Tate Collections.* London, 2000.

Nekrasov, N. A. *Sobranie sochinenii.* 4 v. Moscow, 1979.

Nekrologiya pokoinago chlena vysochaishe utverzhdënnago Obshchestva Pooshchreniya Khudozhnikov kollezhskago sovetnika i kavalera Alekseya Romanovicha Tomilova. St. Petersburg, 1849.

Neva Symphony: Leningrad in Works of Graphic Art and Painting. Leningrad, 1975.

Nikitenko, A. V. *Diary of a Russian Censor.* Tr. H. Jacobson. Amherst, 1975.

——. *Up from Serfdom: My Childhood and Youth in Russia, 1804–1824.* Tr. H. Jacobson. New Haven, 2001.

Nikitin, Pavel. *Istoriia goroda Smolenska.* Smolensk, 1848.

Nikoleva, Mariya. "Cherty starinnago dvoryanskago byta," RA, 9 (1893) 107–20; 10 (1893) 129–96.

Nikulina-Kositskaya, Lyubov. "Notes" in Clyman, *Russia Through Women's Eyes,* 108–57.

———. "Zapiski," RS (Jan.) 65–80; (Feb.) 281–304; (Mar.) 611–24; all 1878.

Odoevskii, V. F. *Muzykalno-literaturnoe nasledie.* Moscow, 1956.

Ogarëv, N. P. *Izbrannye proizvedeniya.* 2 v. Moscow, 1956.

Onnore, I. I. "Odinadtsat let v teatre," RS (Jan. 1910) 95–108.

Ostrovskii, A. N. *Plays.* Tr. G. R. Noyes. New York, 1917.

———. *Polnoe sobranie sochineniya.* 10 v. Moscow, 1973–78.

Osykov, B. *Ya rodilsya v sele Krasnom.* Belgorod, n.d.

Ozerov, V. A. *Tragedii.* St. Petersburg, 1907.

Pacini, Giovanni. *L'ultimo giorno di Pompeii: melodramma tragico.* Naples, 1825.

Palma [P. Alminskii]. *Aleksei Slobodin: semeinaya istoriya.* St. Petersburg, 1873.

Panaeva, Avdotiya. *Vospominaniya, 1829–1870.* Ed. K. Chukovskii. 2d ed. Leningrad, 1928.

Panorama Nevskogo Prospekta. St. Petersburg, 2003. Lithographs based on Sadovnikov.

Panteon. Journal.

Parizhskie teatry, ili sobranie zamechatelneishikh teatralnykh kostyumov. Moscow, 1829.

Passenens, M. P. D. de. *La Russie et l'esclavage.* 2 v. Paris, 1822.

Pavlov, N. F. *Imeniny* (1835). St. Petersburg, 1922.

"Perepiska A. N. Verstovskago s A. M. Gedeonovym" in EIT (1913), 2:33–55.

Petrov, P. N., ed. *Sbornik materialov dlya istorii Imperatorskoi S.-Peterburgskoi Akademii Khudozhestv za sto let eya sushchestvovaniya.* 4 v. St. Petersburg, 1864–87.

P. I. Chaikovskii. Moscow, 1978. A photographic record.

Pisemskii, A. F. "Gorkaya sudbina" in Pisemskii, *Polnoe sobranie sochinenii.* 24 v. St. Petersburg, 1895–96, 23:55–109.

Pobedonostsev, K. P. *Sochineniya.* St. Petersburg, 1996.

Pocock, Isaac. *The Magpie, or the Maid? a Melo Drame.* London, 1816.

Polevoi, Nikolai. *Dramaticheskiya sochineniya N. A. Polevogo iz russkoi istorii.* St. Petersburg, 1899.

Portret v russkoi zhivopisi XVIII–XIX vekov. Moscow, 1988. Reproductions.

Portretnaya miniatyura: iz sobraniya Gosudarstvennogo Russkogo Muzeya, XVIII–nachalo XX veka. Ed. K. V. Mikhailova and G. V. Smirnov. 2 v. Leningrad, 1974.

Potekhin, A. A. *Mishura.* Moscow, 1858.

———. *Sochineniya.* 12 v. St. Petersburg, 1904.

———. *Sud lyudskoi—ne bozhii: drama iz narodnago byta.* Moscow, 1855.

P. R., "Zapiski starogo aktëra," RS (Jan.) 113–37; (Feb.) 387–413; (March) 560–75; all 1905.

[Purlevskii, Savva]. "Vospominaniya krepostnago, 1800–1869," RV (July 1877) 320–47 and (Sept. 1877) 34–67.

Pushkin, A. S. *Eugene Onegin: A Novel in Verse.* Tr. V. Nabokov. 4 v. Princeton, 1964.

———. *Sobranie sochinenii.* 10 v. Moscow, 1974–75.

Pushkinskii Peterburg. Leningrad, 1974. Graphics.

Pustynnik, P. "Teatralnaya publika," *Literaturnaya gazeta,* 46 (Nov. 13, 1847) 727–31.

Putevoditel ot Moskvy do S.-Peterburga i obratno. 2d ed. Moscow, 1847.

Radishchev, Aleksandr. *A Journey from St. Petersburg to Moscow.* Ed. R. Thaler. Tr. L. Wiener. Cambridge, Mass., 1958.

Raeff, Marc, ed. *Russian Intellectual History: An Anthology.* New York, 1966.

Raikes, Thomas. *The City of the Czar; or, a Visit to St. Petersburg in the Winter of 1829–30.* 2 v. Philadelphia, 1838.

Ramazanov, Nikolai. "Vospominaniya o Karle Pavloviche Bryullove," *Moskvityanin,* 16 (Aug. 1852) 1–28.

Reeve, F. D., ed. *An Anthology of Russian Plays.* 2 v. New York, 1961.

Repin, Ilya. *Dalëkoe blizkoe.* Leningrad, 1982.

Rimskii-Korsakov, V. N. "Iz vospominanii i materialov semeinogo arkhiva" in *Rimskii-Korsakov: issledovaniya, materialy, pisma.* 2 v. Moscow, 1954, 1:113–76.

Rimsky-Korsakov [Rimskii-Korsakov], Nikolai. *My Musical Life.* Tr. J. Joffe. New York, 1936.

Romanov, N. M. *Russkie portrety XVIII i XIX vekov.* 5 v. St. Petersburg, 1905–9; reprint Moscow, 1999–2000. Reproductions.

Rossiya-Russia. Journal.

Rossiiskii featr. 43 v. St. Petersburg, 1786–1794.

Rostislavov, Dmitrii. *Provincial Russia in the Age of Enlightenment: The Memoir of a Priest's Son.* Ed. A. Martin. DeKalb, 2002.

[Rozanov, A. I.]. "Zapiski selskago svyashchennika" (title varies), RS (Mar. 1879) 554–62; (Nov. 1879) 433–60; (Jan. 1880) 39–78; (Mar. 1880) 456–94.

Rozanov, I. and N. Sidorov, eds. *Komicheskaya opera XVIII veka.* Moscow, 1913.

Rozen [Rosen], A. E. *Zapiski dekabrista.* Irkutsk, 1984.

Rubinshtein [Rubinstein], Anton. *Avtobiograficheskiya vospominaniya A. G. Rubinshteina, 1829–1889 gg.* 2d ed. St. Petersburg, 1889.

Rubinstein [Rubinshtein], Anton. *Autobiography of Anton Rubinstein, 1829–1889.* Tr. A. Delano. Boston, 1890.

———. *Conversation on Music.* Tr. J. P. Morgan. New York, 1892.

Russkaya elegiya kontsa XVIII–nachala XIX v: antologiya. Moscow, 1983.

Russkii teatr. N.p., n.d. 1840s. A collection of two dozen plays and vaudevilles.

Sadovnikov, V. *Vidy Peterburga: akvareli V. Sadovnikova.* Leningrad, 1970.

Saltykov-Shchedrin, M. E. *The Golovevs.* Tr. I. P. Foote. Oxford, 1986.

———. *Gubernskie ocherki, 1856–1857* in *Sobranie sochinenii.* 20 v. Moscow, 1965–77, vol. 2.

Segel, Harold, ed. *The Literature of Eighteenth-Century Russia.* 2 v. New York, 1967.

Seletskii, P. D. "Zapiski," KS, 8 (Jan.) 247–96; (Mar.) 443–64; (Apr.) 609–43; (May) 77–87; (June) 239–66; (July) 484–504; (Aug.) 609–26; (Sept.) 82–103; all 1884.

Selivanov, I. "Teatr v Tambove," RP, 16 (1842) 22–27; s.p.

Selivanov, V. V. *Predaniya i vospominaniya.* St. Petersburg, 1881.

Semevskii, M. I. [Mikhail Se——vskii]. "Progulka v Nizhnii Novgorod," RV (July) 16–23, (Aug.) 281–303, and (Sept.) 128–43; all 1860.

Senelick, Laurence, ed. *National Theater in Northern and Eastern Europe, 1746–1900.* New York, 1991.

——, ed. *Russian Comedy of the Nikolaian Era*. Amsterdam, 1997.

——, ed. *Russian Dramatic Theory from Pushkin to the Symbolists*. Austin, 1981.

——, ed. *Russian Satiric Comedy: Six Plays*. New York, 1983.

Seryakov, L. A. "Moya trudovaya zhizn," RS (Sept.) 161–184; (Oct.) 339–66; (Nov.) 506–16; all 1875.

Shakhovskoi, A. A. *Komedii, stikhotvoreniya*. Leningrad, 1961.

——. *Lomonosov, ili rekrut stikhotvorets*. St. Petersburg, 1816.

——. *Sochineniya*. St. Petersburg, 1898.

Shalikov, P. I. *Drugoe puteshestvie v Malorossiyu*. Moscow, 1804.

——. *Puteshestvie v Malorossiyu*. Moscow, 1803.

Shchepkin, M. S. "Zapiski" in *Mikhail Semënovich Shchepkin: zhizn i tvorchestvo*. 2 v. Moscow, 1984, 1:50–128.

Shchepkina, Aleksandra. *Vospominaniya*. Moscow, 1915.

Shenig [Schönig?], N. I. "Vospominaniya," RA, 3 (1880) 267–325.

Shestakova, L. I. "M. I. Glinka," RS (Dec. 1884) 593–604.

——. "Poslednye gody zhizni i konchina M. I. Glinki," RS (Dec. 1870) 610–32.

Shevchenko, Taras. *Povest Tarasa Shevchenko "Khudozhnik": illyustratsii, dokumenty*. In Russian and English. Kiev, 1989.

Shipov, N. N. "Istoriya moei zhizni: razskaz byvshago krepostnago krestyanina," RS (May) 133–48; (June) 221–40; (July) 437–78; (Aug.) 665–78; all 1881.

Skalkovskii, K. A. *Vospominaniya molodosti, 1843–1869*. St. Petersburg, 1906.

Smirnova, A. O. "Iz zapisok," RA, 9–12 (1895) 77–90.

Smolenskiya gubernskiya vedomosti. 1853.

Sollogub, V. A. *Peterburgskie stranitsy vospominanii*. St. Petersburg, 1993.

——. *The Tarantas* (1845). Tr. W. E. Brown. Ann Arbor, 1989.

Solntsev, F. G. "Moya zhizn i khudozhestvenno-arkheologicheskie trudy," RS (Jan.) 109–28; (Feb.) 311–23; (Mar.) 617–44; (May) 147–60; (June) 263–302; all 1876.

Spohr, Ludwig. *The Musical Journeys of Louis Spohr*. Tr. H. Pleasants. Norman, 1961.

Staël, Mme. de. *Corinne, a Story of Italy*. Philadelphia, 1880.

Stanislavsky [Stanislavskii], Konstantin. *Building a Character*. Tr. E. Hapgood. New York, 1987.

——. *My Life in Art*. Tr. J. J. Robbins. London, 1924.

Stasov, V. V. *Izbrannye sochineniya*. 2 v. Moscow, 1937.

——. *Selected Essays on Music*. Tr. F. Jonas. New York, 1968.

——. "Uchilishche pravovedeniya sorok let tomu nazad, 1836–42," RS (Dec. 1880) 1015–42; (Feb. 1881) 393–422; (Mar. 1881) 573–602; (June 1881) 247–79.

[Stepanov, P. A.] P. S. "Vospominaniya o M. I. Glinke," RS (July 1871) 38–58.

Stephens, J. L. *Incidents of Travel in Greece, Turkey, Russia, and Poland* (1838). 7th ed. 2 v. New York, 1849.

Stikhotvornaya komediya, komicheskaya opera, vodevil kontsa XVIII–nachala XIX vek. 2 v. Leningrad, 1990.

Stupin, A. V. "Sobstvennoruchnyya zapiski o zhizni" in *Shchukinskii sbornik*. 5 vols. Moscow, 1902–6, 3:369–482.

Sumarokov, Pavel. *Progulka po 12-ti guberniyam s istoricheskimi i statisticheskimi zamechaniyami v 1838*. St. Petersburg, 1839.

Sushkov, N. V. "Kartiny russkago byta v starinu," *Raut* (1852) 463–71.

Sverbeev, D. N. *Zapiski*. 2 v. Moscow, 1899.

Svetopis: khudozhestvennyi zhurnal. St. Petersburg, 1858–59.

Syn otechestva.

Szymanowska, Elena. "Dnevnik Eleny Shimanovskoi," ed. I. Karasinskaya in Igor Belza, ed., *Russko-Polskie muzykalnye svyazy*. Moscow, 1963, pp. 82–118.

Szymanowska, Maria. "Nocturne" in James Briscoe, ed., *Historical Anthology of Music by Women*. Bloomington, 1987, pp. 103–8.

Tchaikovsky [Chaikovskii], P. I. *Tchaikovsky: A Self-Portrait*. Ed. A. Orlova. Tr. R. M. Davison. Oxford, 1990.

Timofeev, A. V. *Khudozhnik*. 3 v. St. Petersburg, 1834.

Tolstoy, L. N. *Voina I Mir*. Moscow, 2003.

Tomei, Christine, ed. *Russian Women Writers*. 2 v. New York, 1999.

Troinitskii, A. *The Serf Population in Russia According to the 10th National Census* (1861). Tr. E. Herman. Newtonville, 1982.

Tsebrikov, M. *Materialy dlya geografii i statistiki Rossii, sobranye ofitserami generalnago shtaba. Smolenskaya guberniya*. St. Petersburg, 1862.

Tourgeneff [Turgenev], N. *La Russie et les russes*. 3 v. Paris, 1847.

Turgenev, Ivan. *Polnoe sobranie sochinenii i pisem: sochineniya*. 15 v. Moscow, 1960–68.

———. *Sketches from a Hunter's Album*. Tr. R. Freeborn. London, 1990.

Valk, S. N., ed. *Krestyanskoe dvizhenie v Rossii v 1796–1825gg.: sbornik dokumentov*. Moscow, 1961.

Vazem, E. O. *Zapiski baleriny Sankt-Peterburgskogo Bolshogo Teatra, 1867–1884*. Ed. N. A. Shuvalov. Leningrad, 1937.

Veltman, A. F. *Serdtse i dumka* (1838). Moscow, 1986.

Velyashev, A. P. *Opisanie prazdnika dannogo v Moskve 19 maiya . . .* Moscow, 1814.

Verstovskii, A. N. *Askoldova mogila: romanticheskaya opera* (1835). Ed. B. Dobrokhotov. Moscow, 1963. Piano and voices.

———. "Avtobiografiya." Ed. B. Modzalevskii, in *Biryuch petrogradskikh gosudarstvennykh akademicheskikh teatrov*. Vol. 2, Petrograd, 1920, pp. 227–41.

———. *Gromoboi: opera*. Piano arrangement by A. Dubuque. M, n.d.

Vidy S.-Peterburga i okrestnostei: litografirovannoe izdanie Obshchestva Pooshchreniya Khudozhestv (1821–1826). Leningrad, 1960. Commentary by G. Komelova.

Vigel, F. F. *Zapiski*. Moscow, 2000.

Vinnitskii, F. N. "Razskazy iz bylogo vremeni," *Chteniya v Imperatorskom Obshchestve Istorii i Drevnostei Rossiiskikh pri Moskovskom Universitete* (Jan.–Mar. 1874) 63–110.

Vodovozova, E. N. *Na zare zhizni*. 2 v. Moscow, 1964.

Volodina, T. *Russian Interior*. Moscow, 2000. Reproductions.

Von Geldern, James and Louise McReynolds, eds. *Entertaining Tsarist Russia: Tales, Songs, Plays, Movies, Jokes, Ads, and Images from Russian Urban Life, 1779–1917*. Bloomington, 1998.

Vonlyarlyarskii, V. *Moi vospominaniya, 1852–1939*. Berlin, 1939.

Vrangel [Wrangel], Nikolai. *Vospominaniya (ot krepostnogo prava do bolshevikov)*. Berlin, 1924.

Vsevolozhskii, N. S. *Puteshestvie chrez yuzhnuyu Rossiyu, Krym, i Odessii . . . na 1836 i 1837 godakh.* 2 v. Moscow, 1839.

Vzglyad skvozd stoletiya. Moscow, 1977.

Wallace, Donald Mackenzie. *Russia.* New York, 1905.

Wiley, Roland, ed. *A Century of Russian Ballet: Documents and Accounts, 1810–1910.* Oxford, 1990.

———. *Tchaikovsky's Ballets: Swan Lake, Sleeping Beauty, Nutcracker.* Oxford, 1985.

Wilmot, Martha and Catherine Wilmot. *The Russian Journals.* Ed. Marchioness of Londonderry and H. M. Hyde. London, 1935.

Yakhontov, A. N. "Peterburgskaya italyanskaya opera v 1840-kh godakh," RS (Dec. 1886) 735–48.

Yaroslavskie portrety XVIII–XIX vekov: Yaroslavl, Pereslavl-Zalesskii, Rostov Yaroslavskii, Rybinsk, Uglich. Moscow, 1984. With commentary.

Yaroslavskiya gubernskiya vedomosti.

Yunge, Ekaterina. "Iz moikh vospominanii 1843–1860," VE, 40/1–2 (Jan.–Feb.) 767–806; 40/3–4 (Mar.–Apr.) 138–89 and 763–94; 40/5–6 (May–June) 256–91; all 1905.

———. *Vospominaniya, 1843–60.* Reprint of the above, St. Petersburg, n.d.

Yurkevich, P. I. "Iz vospominanii Peterburgskago starozhila," IV, 10 (Oct. 1882) 156–74.

Zagoskin, Mikhail. *Askoldova mogila.* 3 v. Moscow, 1833.

———. *Blagorodnyi teatr, komediya v chetyrëkh deistviyakh.* Moscow, 1828.

———. *G—n Bogatonov, ili provintsial v stolitse* in *Polnoe sobranie sochinenii.* Vol. 5 Petrograd, n.d., pp. 72–126.

———. "Kontsert besov" in *Nezhdannye gosti.* Moscow, 1994, pp. 90–102.

Zaitsev, I. K. "Vospominaniya starogo uchitelya," RS (June, 1887) 662–712.

Zhadovskaya, Yuliya. *Polnoe sobranie sochinenii.* 3 v. St. Petersburg, 1885–94.

Zhdanov, Mikhail. *Putevyya zapiski po Rossii v 20-i gubernyakh.* St. Petersburg, 1843.

Zhikharëv, S. P. *Zapiski sovremennika.* 2 v. Leningrad, 1989.

Zhirkevich, I. S. "Zapiski," RS (Aug. 1875) 554–80.

Zhurnal peshekhodtsev ot Moskvy do Rostova, i obratno v Moskve. Moscow, 1830.

Zotov, R. M. "Zapiski," IV (June) 762–97; (July) 26–50; (Aug.) 301–21; (Sept.) 593–616; (Oct.) 27–53; (Nov.) 400–427; (Dec.) 765–96; all 1896.

Zotov, V. R. "Peterburg v sorokovykh godakh," IV (Jan.) 29–53; (Feb.) 324–43; (Mar.) 553–72; (Apr.) 92–115; (May) 290–319; (June) 535–59; all 1890.

SECONDARY WORKS

Abraham, Gerald. *On Russian Music* (1939). New York, 1980.

———. "V. V. Stasov: Man and Critic" in Stasov, *Selected Essays on Music.*

Adamson, Andy. "The Russian Imperial Ballet" in Leach, *History of Russian Theatre,* 182–98.

Adorno, Theodor. *Introduction to the Sociology of Music.* Tr. E. B. Ashton. New York, 1976.

Albrekht [Albrecht], E. K. *Obshchii obzor deyatelnosti vysochaishe utverzhdënnago S.-Peterburgskago Filarmonicheskago Obshchestva.* St. Petersburg, 1884.

———. *Obshchii obzor stoletnoi yubilei S.-Peterburgskago Filarmonicheskago Obshchestva.* St. Petersburg, 1902.

————. *Proshloe i nastoyashchee orkestra (ocherk sotsialnogo polozheniya muzykantov)*. St. Petersburg, 1886.

————. *S.-Peterburgskaya Konservatoriya*. St. Petersburg, 1891.

Alekseeva, Tatyana. *Khudozhniki shkoly Venetsianova*. Moscow, 1982.

————. *Venetsianov and His School*. Tr. C. Justice and Yu. Kleiner. Leningrad, 1984.

Aleksei Fëdorovich Lvov: ego gimn i deyatelnost. St. Petersburg. 1908.

Alexander, John. *Bubonic Plague in Early Modern Russia*. Baltimore, 1980.

Alfimov, Evgenii and A. Mishin, eds. *Smoliane*. Moscow, 1980.

Alpers, Svetlana. "The Museum as a Way of Seeing" in Karp, *Exhibiting Cultures*, pp. 25–32.

Altschuller, Anatoly. "Actors and Acting, 1820–1850" in Leach, *History of Russian Theatre*, 104–23.

Altshuller, Mark, "Vladislav Aleksandrovich Ozerov" in Levitt, *Early Modern Russian Writers*, 265–72.

Anchipolovskii, Zinovii. *Staryi teatr: Voronezh, 1787–1917*. Voronezh, 1996.

Anderson, Roger and Paul Debreczeny, eds. *Russian Narrative and Visual Art: Varieties of Seeing*. Gainesville, 1994.

Andreev, A. Yu. *Moskovskii Universitet v obshchestvennoi i kulturnoi zhizni Rossii nachala XIX veka*. Moscow, 2000.

Andreeva, Vera. *Pervye khudozhniki Peterburga*. Leningrad, 1989.

Anton Grigorevich Rubinshtein: sbornik statei. St. Petersburg, 1997.

"A. N. Verstovskii," *Niva*, 30/9 (1899) 177–78.

"A. N. Verstovskii," *Radio-programmy* (Aug. 11, 1936).

Aptekar, M. *Russkaya istoricheskaya zhivopis*. Moscow, 1939.

Arapov, Pimen. *Letopis russkago teatra*. St. Petersburg, 1861.

Art du ballet en Russie, 1738–1940. Paris, 1991.

Asafev, B. "Kompozitor iz pleyady slavyano-rossiiskikh bardov Aleksei Nikolaevich Verstovskii," SM, 8–9 (1946) 73–80.

Aseev, B. "Zhivye traditsii," *Teatralnaya zhizn*, 16 (Aug. 1963) 22–25.

Ashcroft, Irina. "*Peterburgskie trushchoby*: A Russian Version of *Mystères de Paris*," *Revue de littérature comparée*, 53/2 (Apr.–June 1979) 163–75.

Austin, Paul. *The Exotic Prisoner in Russian Romanticism*. New York, 1997.

Baehr, Stephen. *The Paradise Myth in Eighteenth-Century Russia: Utopian Patterns in Early Secular Russian Literature and Culture*. Stanford, 1991.

Bakhrushin, Yu. A. *Istoriya russkogo baleta*. 3d ed. Moscow, 1977.

Balmuth, Daniel. *Censorship in Russia, 1865–1905*. Washington, 1979.

Balzac dans l'Empire russe. Paris, 1993.

Balzer, Harley, ed. *Russia's Missing Middle Class: The Professions in Russian History*. Armonk, 1996.

Barbier, Patrick. *The World of the Castrati*. Tr. M. Crosland. London, 1996.

Barchatova [Barkhatova], Elena. "Die ersten Photographien in Russland" in *Russische Photographie*, 24–29.

Barenboim, L. *Anton Grigorevich Rubinshtein: zhizn, artisticheskii put, tvorchestvo, muzykalno-obshchestvennaya deyatelnost*. 2 v. Leningrad, 1957–62.

Barkhatova, Elena, et al., eds. *A Portrait of Tsarist Russia: Unknown Photographs from the Soviet Archives*. New York, 1989.

——, et al. *Russkaya fotografiya seredina XIX–nachalo XX veka.* Moscow, 1996.

Barratt, Glynn. *The Rebel on the Bridge: A Life of the Decembrist Baron Andrey Rozen (1803–84).* London, 1975.

Barrell, John. *The Dark Side of the Landscape: The Rural Poor in English Painting, 1730–1840.* Cambridge, 1980.

——. "The Public Prospect and the Private View: The Politics of Taste in Eighteenth-Century Britain" in Pugh, *Reading Landscape,* 19–40.

Barsukov, N. *Zhizn i trudy M. I. Pogodina.* 22 v. St. Petersburg, 1888–1910.

Barrett, Thomas. "The Remaking of the Lion of Dagestan: Shamil in Captivity," RR, 53/3 (1994) 353–66.

Bartlett, Roger, Anthony Cross, and Karen Rasmussen, eds. *Russia and the World of the Eighteenth Century.* Columbus, 1988.

Barzun, Jacques. *Berlioz and his Century.* New York, 1956.

Baschmakoff, Natalia. "Lokalnyi tekst, golos pamyati i poetika prostranstva" (ms.).

Baschmakoff, Natalia and Paul Fryer, eds. *Modernization in the Russian Provinces.* Helsinki, 2000.

Baumgarten, Caroline. *Die spätklassische russische Komödie zwischen 1805 und 1822: Studien zu Sachovskoj, Zagoskin, Chmel'nickij, und Griboedov.* Munich, 1998.

Baye, Joseph. *Smolensk: les origines: l'épopée de Smolensk en 1812 après des documents inédits.* Paris, 1912.

Baxandall, Michael. *Painting and Experience in Fifteenth-Century Italy: A Primer in the Social History of Pictorial Style.* Oxford, 1972.

Beaumont, Cyril. *The Complete Book of Ballets.* New York, 1938.

Becker, Howard. *Art Worlds.* Berkeley, 1982.

Belchikov, N. F. *Taras Shevchenko (zhizn i tvorchestvo).* Leningrad, 1956.

Belousov, A. F. and T. V. Tsivyan, eds. *Russkaya provintsiya: mif—tekst—realnost.* Moscow, 2000.

Belozerskaya, N. A. "Fëdor Grigorevich Solntsev," RS, 18 (June 1887) 713–37.

Belyakov, B. N., V. G. Blinova, and N. D. Bordyug, *Opernaya i kontsertnaya deyatelnost v Nizhnem-Novgorode—gorode Gorkom (1798–1980).* Gorky, 1980.

Belza, Igor. *Mariya Shimanovskaya.* Moscow, 1956.

Benjamin, Walter. "Little History of Photography" in *Selected Works,* ed. M. W. Jennings. 3 v. Cambridge, Mass, 1999, 2:507–30.

Bergmans, Paul. *Henry Vieuxtemps.* Turnhoud, 1920.

Bermingham, Ann. "Reading Constable" in Pugh, *Reading Landscape,* 97–120.

Bernandt, G. "V. F. Odoevskii—muzykalnyi pisatel," SM, 8 (1939) 49–54.

Bernstein, Lina. "Women on the Verge of a New Language: Russian Salon Hostesses in the First Half of the Nineteenth Century" in Goscilo, *Russia,* 209–24.

Bers [Behrs], A. A. "Aleksei Fëdorovich Lvov kak muzykant i kompositor," RS, 31/102 (Apr. 1900) 145–68.

Beskin, Emil. "Lev Gurych Sinichkin," *Novyi zritel,* 50 (1924) 3–5.

Bespalova, E. P., ed. *Kostyum v Rossii XV–nachalo XX veka.* Moscow, 2000.

Billington, James. *Mikhailovsky and Russian Populism.* Oxford, 1958.

Biograficheskiya svedeniya o chlenakh Akademii i voobshche khudozhnikakh, umershikh v 1875–1878 gg. St. Petersburg, 1879.

Biograficheskiya svedeniya o chlenakh Akademii i voobshche khudozhnikakh, umershikh v 1873–1875 gg. St. Petersburg, 1876.

Blanning, T. C. W. *The Culture of Power and the Power of Culture: Old Regime Europe, 1660–1789.* New York, 2002.

Blaukopf, Kurt. *Musical Life in a Changing Society: Aspects of Musical Sociology.* Portland, 1992.

Bloom, Peter, ed. *Music in Paris in the 1830s.* Stuyvesant, 1987.

Blum, Jerome. *The End of the Old Order in Rural Europe.* Princeton, 1978.

———. *Lord and Peasant in Russia from the Ninth to the Nineteenth Century.* Princeton, 1961.

Bocharnikova, Ella. *Bolshoi teatr: kratkii istoricheskii ocherk.* Moscow, 1987.

Bohac, Rodney. "Everyday Forms of Resistance: Serf Opposition to Gentry Extractions, 1800–1860" in Esther Kingston-Mann et al., eds., *Peasant Economy, Culture, and Politics of European Russia, 1800–1921.* Princeton, 1991, pp. 236–60.

Boime, Albert. *The Academy and French Painting in the Nineteenth Century.* New Haven, 1986.

Bonnell, Victoria. *Iconography of Power: Soviet Political Posters under Lenin and Stalin.* Berkeley, 1997.

Botkina, A. P. *Pavel Mikhailovich Tretyakov.* Moscow, 1986.

Boulton, Marjorie. *The Anatomy of Drama.* London, 1960.

Bourdieu, Pierre. *Distinction: A Social Critique of the Judgment of Taste.* Tr. R. Nice. Cambridge, Mass., 1984.

Bowen, Catherine Drinker. *"Free Artist": The Story of Anton and Nicholas Rubinstein.* New York, 1939.

Bowlt, John. "Nineteenth-Century Russian Caricature" in Stavrou, *Art and Culture,* 221–36.

———. "Russian Painting in the Nineteenth Century" in Stavrou, *Art and Culture,* 113–39.

Bozhe, tsarya khrani. St. Petersburg, [1990].

Bozhe, tsarya khrani: russkii narodnyi gimn (1910). Novgorod, 1991.

Bradley, Joseph. "Merchant Moscow After Hours: Voluntary Associations and Leisure" in West, *Merchant Moscow,* 133–43.

Bramsted, Ernest, *Aristocracy and the Middle Classes in Germany: Social Types in German Literature, 1830–1900* (1937). Chicago, 1964.

Bratton, Jackie, Jim Cook, and Christine Gledhill, eds. *Melodrama: Stage, Picture, Screen.* London, 1994.

Brettell, Richard and Caroline Brettell. *Painters and Peasants in the Nineteenth Century.* Geneva, 1983.

Brooks, Jeffrey. *When Russia Learned to Read: Literacy and Popular Literature, 1861–1917.* Princeton, 1985.

Brooks, Peter. *The Melodramatic Imagination: Balzac, Henry James, Melodrama, and the Mode of Excess.* New Haven, 1976.

Brouwer, Sander. *Character in the Short Prose of Ivan Sergeevič Turgenev.* Amsterdam, 1996.

———. "Turgenev's *Sportsman's Sketches* as an Artistic Whole" in De Haard, *Semiotic Analysis,* 67–84.

Brower, Daniel. *Training the Nihilists: Education and Radicalism in Tsarist Russia.* Ithaca, 1975.

Brown, David. *Mikhail Glinka: A Biographical and Critical Study.* London, 1974.

——. *Tchaikovsky.* 4 v. London, 1978–91.

Brown, Edward J. *Stankevich and His Moscow Circle, 1830–1840.* Stanford, 1966.

Brown, Malcolm. "Native Song and National Consciousness in Nineteenth-Century Russian Music" in Stavrou, *Art and Culture,* 57–84.

Brown, William E. *A History of Russian Literature of the Romantic Period.* 4 v. Ann Arbor, 1986.

Bruford, W. H. *Culture and Society in Classical Weimar, 1775–1806.* Cambridge, 1962.

Buckler, Julie. "Divas in the Drawing Room: Opera as Literature in Prerevolutionary Russia." Harvard University Dissertation, 1996.

——. *The Literary Lorgnette: Attending Opera in Imperial Russia.* Stanford, 2000.

——. *Mapping St. Petersburg: Imperial Text and Cityshape.* Princeton, 2005.

——. "Melodramatizing Russia: Nineteenth-Century Views from the West" in McReynolds, *Imitations of Life,* 2002, 55–78.

Budaev, D. I. and M. N. Levitin, eds. *Istorii zhivye golosa (episody iz proshlogo Smolenska).* Smolensk, 1992.

——. "Materialy iz smolenskoi gubernii na stranitsakh gertsenskogo 'Kolokola'" in Koshelëv, *Smolenskii krai,* 34–42.

Bugrov, Yu. A. *Svet kurskikh ramp,* 3 v. Kursk, 1995–2002.

Burbank, Jane and David Ransel, eds. *Imperial Russia: New Histories for the Empire.* Bloomington, 1998.

Burgess, Malcolm. "Fairs and Entertainers in 18th-Century Russia," *Slavonic Review,* 38 (1959) 95–113.

——. "Russian Public Theatre Audiences of the 18th and Early 19th Centuries," SEER, 37/88 (Dec. 1958) 160–83.

Buryshkin, Pavel. *Moskva kupecheskaya.* New York, 1954.

Burke, Joseph. *English Art, 1714–1800.* Oxford, 1976.

Burke, Peter. *Eyewitnessing: The Uses of Images as Historical Evidence.* Ithaca, 2001.

Burmistrova, L. P. *Provintsialnaya gazeta v epokhu prosvetitelei (gubernskie vedomosti Povolzhya i Urala, 1840–1850 gg.).* Kazan, 1985.

Bushnell, John. "Did Serf Owners Control Serf Marriage? Orlov Serfs and Their Neighbors, 1773–1861," SR, 52/3 (Fall 1993) 419–45.

Butorov, Aleksei. *Sobirateli i metsenaty Moskovskogo Angliiskogo Kluba.* Moscow, 2002.

Campbell, Joseph. *The Hero with a Thousand Faces.* London, 1988.

Campbell, Margaret. *The Great Cellists.* London, 1988.

Campbell, Stuart. *V. F. Odoevsky and the Formation of Russian Musical Taste in the Nineteenth Century.* New York, 1989.

Cannadine, David. *Aspects of Aristocracy.* New Haven, 1994.

——. *Ornamentalism: How the British Saw Their Empire.* London, 2001.

——. *Pleasures of the Past.* London, 1997.

Carpenter, Ellon. "Women Music Scholars in the Soviet Union" in J. L. Zaimont, ed. *The Musical Woman,* vol. 3. Westport, 1991, pp. 456–516.

Cassiday, Julie. "Northern Poetry for a Northern People: Text and Context in Ozerov's *Fingal,*" SEER, 78/2 (Apr. 2000) 240–66.

——. "Reflections of the St. Petersburg Theater and Russian Theatricality in S. P. Zhikharev's *Zapiski sovremennika.*" Ms.

Cavender, Mary. "Nests of Gentry: Family, Estate, and Local Loyalties in Provincial Tver', 1820–1860." University of Michigan Dissertation, 1997.

Chayanova, Olga. *Torzhestvo muz.* Moscow, 1925.

Chernov, N. "Krepostnye aktrisy orlovskogo teatra," *Teatralnaya zhizn,* 4 (1961) 28–29.

——. *Literaturnye mesta orlovskoi oblasti.* Orël, 1959.

Choldin, Marianna Tax. *A Fence Around the Empire: Russian Censorship of Western Ideas Under the Tsars.* Durham, 1985.

Christian, David. *"Living Water": Vodka and Russian Society on the Eve of Emancipation.* Oxford, 1990.

Christiansen, Rupert. *Prima Donna: A History.* 2d ed. London, 1995.

Christoff, Peter. *Introduction to Nineteenth-Century Russian Slavophilism: A Study in Ideas.* Vol. 1: *A. S. Xomjakov.* The Hague, 1961. Vol. 2: *I. V. Kireevskij.* The Hague, 1972. Vol. 3: *K. S. Aksakov.* Princeton, 1983. Vol. 4: *Iu. F. Samarin.* Boulder, 1991.

Chto chitat o smolenskoi oblasti. Smolensk, 1979.

Chudinova, I. A. "Peterburg—zvuchashchii gorod" in *Geografiya iskusstva: sbornik statei.* Moscow, 1996, pp. 137–53.

Chuikina, Sofiya. "Professionalnaya reintegratsiya dvoryanstva." Paper, Renvall Institute, Helsinki, 1998.

——. "Sotsialnaya sreda pomestnogo dvoryanstva." European University of St. Petersburg M.A. Thesis, 1997.

Chulos, Chris, "Orthodox Identity at Russian Holy Places" in Chulos and Timo Pirainen, eds., *National Identity in Contemporary Russia.* Aldershot, 1999, pp. 1–24.

——. "Religious and Secular Aspects of Pilgrimage in Modern Russia" *Byzantium and the North,* 9 (1999) 21–58.

Citron, Marcia. *Gender and the Musical Canon.* Cambridge, 1993.

Clark, Kenneth. *Landscape into Art.* London, 1949.

Clark, Peter. *British Clubs and Society: The Origins of an Associational World.* Oxford, 2000.

Clarke, T. J. *The Absolute Bourgeois: Artists and Politics in France, 1848–1851.* Greenwich, 1973.

Clay, Catherine. *Ethos and Empire: The Ethnographic Expedition of the Imperial Russian Naval Ministry, 1855–1862.* Ann Arbor, 1989.

Clowes, Edith, Samuel Kassow, and James West, eds. *Between Tsar and People: Educated Society and the Quest for Public Identity in Later Imperial Russia.* Princeton, 1991.

Clowes, Edith. "Merchants on Stage and in Life: Theatricality and Public Consciousness" in West, *Merchant Moscow,* 147–59.

Cockfield, Jamie. *White Crow: The Life and Times of the Grand Duke Nicholas Mikhailovich Romanov, 1859–1919.* Westport, 2002.

Coldicott, Anne-Louise. "Performance Practice in Beethoven's Day" in Barry Cooper, ed., *The Beethoven Compendium.* London, 1991, pp. 280–89.

Coleman, Arthur. "Kotzebue and Russia," *Germanic Review,* 5/4 (Oct. 1930) 323–41.

Collins, Bradley. *Leonardo, Psychoanalysis, and Art History.* Evanston, 1997.

Confino, Michael. *Domaines et seigneurs en Russie vers la fin du XVIIIe siècle.* Paris, 1963.

———. *Société et mentalités collectives en Russie sous l'ancien régime.* Paris, 1991.

Corbin, Alain. *Village Bells: Sound and Meaning in the French Countryside.* Tr. M. Thom. New York, 1998.

Cornwell, Neil. *The Life, Times, and Milieu of V. F. Odoevsky, 1804–1869.* London, 1986.

———, ed. *The Society Tale in Russian Literature.* Amsterdam, 1998.

Cracraft, James. *The Petrine Revolution in Russian Imagery.* Chicago, 1997.

Craske, Michael. *Art in Europe.* Oxford, 1997.

Crisp, Olga. *Studies in the Russian Economy Before 1914.* London, 1976.

Crofton, Ian, ed. *A Dictionary of Art Quotations.* London, 1988.

Cross, Anthony. *By the Banks of the Neva: Chapters in the Lives and Careers of the British in Eighteenth-Century Russia.* Cambridge, 1997.

Crosten, William. *French Grand Opera: An Art and a Business.* New York, 1948.

Crow, Thomas. *Painters and Public Life in Eighteenth-Century Paris.* New Haven, 1985.

Curtiss, J. S. *The Russian Army Under Nicholas I.* Durham, 1965.

Dahlhaus, Carl, ed. *Studien zur Trivialmusik des 19. Jahrhunderts.* Regensburg, 1967.

Danilov, N. I. "Teatr" in *Ocherki istorii voronezhskogo kraya,* pp. 444–52.

Danilov, S. S. *Ocherki po istorii russkogo dramaticheskogo teatra.* Moscow, 1948.

———, and S. S. Mokulskii, eds. *O teatre: sbornik statei.* Leningrad, 1940.

———. *Russkii dramaticheskii teatr XIX veka.* 2 v. Leningrad, 1957–74.

Danilov, V. V. "Dedushka russkikh istoricheskikh zhurnalov," IV (July 1915) 109–29.

De Haard, Eric et al., eds. *Semiotic Analysis of Literary Texts: to Honour Jan van der Eng on the Occasion of his 65th Birthday.* Amsterdam, 1990.

Demidenko, Yuliya. *Interer v Rossii: traditsii, moda, stil.* St. Petersburg, 2000.

Dennis, David. *Beethoven in German Politics, 1870–1989.* New Haven, 1996.

De-Ribas, A. *Staraya Odessa: istoricheskie ocherki i vospominaniya.* Odessa, 1913.

Deshkova, Irina. *Illyustrirovannaya entsiklopediya baleta v rasskazakh i istoricheskikh anekdotakh.* Moscow, 1995.

Desyat let simfonicheskoi muzyki, 1917–1927. Leningrad, 1928.

Dmitrieva, E. E. and O. N. Kuptsova, *Zhizn usadebnogo mifa: utrachennyi i obretennyi rai.* Moscow, 2003.

Dmitrieva, N. *Moskovskoe Uchilishche Zhivopisi, Vayaniya, i Zodchestva.* Moscow, 1951.

Dobrokhotov, Boris. *A. A. Alyabev.* Moscow, 1947.

———. *A. A. Alyabev: kamerno-instrumentalnoe tvorchestvo.* Moscow, 1948.

———. *A. A. Alyabev: tvorcheskii put.* Moscow, 1966.

———. *A. N. Verstovskii.* Moscow, 1949.

———. "Krestyane sela Novospasskogo o Glinke" in *M. I. Glinka: sbornik statei,* pp. 361–67.

Dobysh, G. *Zvëzdy russkoi stseny.* Moscow, 1992.

Dodge, William R. "Abolitionist Sentiment in Russia, 1762–1855." University of Wisconsin Dissertation, 1950.

Donakowski, Conrad. *A Muse for the Masses: Ritual and Music in an Age of Democratic Revolution*. Chicago, 1972.

Donohue, Joseph. *Theatre in the Age of Kean*. Oxford, 1975.

Donskov, Andrew. *The Changing Image of the Peasant in Nineteenth Century Drama*. Helsinki, 1972.

Dowler, Wayne, *Dostoevsky, Grigor'ev, and Native Soil Conservatism*. Toronto, 1982.

Drizen, N. V. *Materialy k istorii russkago teatra*. Moscow, 1905.

———. *Stoletie Imperatorskikh Sanktpeterburgskikh Teatrov*. St. Petersburg, n.d.

Druskin, M. S. and Yu. V. Keldysh, eds. *Ocherki po istorii russkoi muzyki, 1700–1825*. Leningrad, 1956.

Druzhinin, N. M. *Gosudarstvennye krestyane i reforma P. D. Kiselëva*. 2 v. Moscow, 1946–58.

Duleba, Wladyslaw. *Wieniawski*. Cracow, 1974.

Dunlop, Carolyn. *The Russian Court Chapel Choir, 1796–1917*. Amsterdam, 2000.

Dunning, Chester. *Russia's First Civil War: The Time of Troubles and the Founding of the Romanov Dynasty*. University Park, 2001.

Dynnik, Tatyana. *Krepostnoi teatr*. Leningrad, 1933.

Edgerton, William. "Ambivalence as the Key to Kniazhnin's Tragedy, *Vadim Novgorodskii*" in Bartlett, *Russia and the World*, 306–15.

Efros, N. *M. S. Shchepkin* (1920). Moscow, 2001.

Egorov, Yu. N. "Reaktsionnaya politika tsarizma v voprosakh universitetskogo obrazovaniya v 30–50-kh gg. XIX v.," *Istoricheskie nauki*, 3 (1960) 60–75.

Eidelman, Natan. *Conspiracy Against the Tsar: A Portrait of the Decembrists*. Tr. C. Carlile. Moscow, 1985.

Eklov, B., J. Bushnell, and L. Zakharova, eds. *Russia's Great Reforms, 1855–1881*. Bloomington, 1994.

Elets, Yu. *Biografiya Krestovskogo*. St. Petersburg, 1898.

Elias, Norbert. *The Civilizing Process: The History of Manners* (1939). Tr. E. Jephcott. New York, 1978.

Elizarova, N. A. *Teatry Sheremetevykh*. Moscow, 1944.

Ely, Christopher. "Critics in the Native Soil: Landscape and Conflicting Ideals of Nationality in Imperial Russia," *Ecumene*, 7/3 (2000) 253–70.

———. "The Origins of Russian Scenery: Volga River Tourism and Russian Landscape Aesthetics," SR, 62/4 (Winter 2003) 666–82.

———. *This Meager Nature: Landscape and National Identity in Imperial Russia*. DeKalb, 2001.

Emmons, Terence. *The Russian Landed Gentry and the Peasant Emancipation of 1861*. Cambridge, 1968.

Emmons, Terence and Wayne Vucinich, eds. *The Zemstvo in Russia*. New York, 1982.

Engel, Barbara. *Mothers and Daughters: Women of the Intelligentsia in Nineteenth-Century Russia*. Cambridge, 1983.

Engelstein, Laura. *Castration and the Heavenly Kingdom: A Russian Folk Tale*. Ithaca, 1999.

Ershov, A. *Stareishii russkii khor*. Leningrad, 1978.

Etkind, Aleksandr. "Umirayushchii sfinks: krug Golitsyna-Labzina i Peterburgskii period russkoi misticheskoi traditsii," *Studia slavica finlandensia*, 13, (1996) 17–46.

Evreinov, Nikolai. *Krepostnye aktëry: istoricheskii ocherk.* St. Petersburg, 1911.

Evtuhov, Catherine. "The *Gubernskie Vedomosti* and Local Culture, 1838–1860." Ms., 1999.

Evtuhov, C., B. Gasparov, A. Ospovat, and M. Von Hagen, eds. *Kazan, Moscow, St. Petersburg: Multiple Faces of the Russian Empire.* Moscow, 1997.

Ezerskaya, N. A. *Peredvizhniki i natsionalnye khudozhestvennye shkoly narodov Rossii.* Moscow, 1987.

Fairweather, Maria. *The Pilgrim Princess: A Life of Princess Zinaida Volkonsky.* London, 1999.

Fanger, Donald. *Dostoevsky and Romantic Realism: A Study of Dostoevsky in Relation to Balzac, Dickens, and Gogol.* Cambridge, Mass., 1967.

——. "The Peasant and Russian Literature" in Wayne Vucinich, ed., *The Peasant in Nineteenth-Century Russia.* Stanford, 1968, pp. 231–62.

Fateev, P. S. *Mikhail Mikhailov — revolyutsioner, pisatel, publitsist.* Moscow, 1969.

Fëdorov, S. I. *Marino Knyazei Baryatinskikh.* Kursk, 1994.

Fëdorov, V. A. "Krestyanin-otkhodnik v Moskve (konets XVIII–pervaya polovina XIX v.)" in *Russkii gorod.* Moscow, 1976, pp. 165–80.

Fëdorovskaya. L. A. *Kompozitor Stepan Davydov.* Leningrad, 1977.

Fedosyuk, Yu. A. *Chto neponyatno u klassikov, ili Entsiklopediya russkogo byta XIX veka.* Moscow, 1998.

Fellinger, Imogen. "Die Begriffe *Salon* und *Salonmusik* in der Musikanschauung des 19. Jahrhunderts" in Dahlhaus, *Studien,* 131–41.

Field, Daniel, *The End of Serfdom: Nobility and Bureaucracy in Russia, 1855–1861.* Cambridge, Mass., 1976.

——. *Rebels in the Name of the Tsar.* Boston, 1989.

Fifty Russian Artists. Moscow, 1985.

Figes, Orlando, *Natasha's Dance: A Cultural History of Russia.* New York, 2002.

Filarmonicheskoe Obshchestvo Sankt-Peterburga, 1802–1915, 1992–1997. St. Petersburg, 1997.

Findeizen [Findeisen], N. F. *Anton Grigorevich Rubinshtein.* Moscow, 1907.

——. "The Earliest Russian Operas," MQ, 19/3 (July, 1933) 331–40.

——. *Mikhail Ivanovich Glinka.* Moscow, 1896.

——. *Ocherk deyatelnosti S.-Peterburgskago otdeleniya Imperatorskago Russkago Muzykalnago Obshchestva (1859–1909).* St. Petersburg, 1909.

Fishman, David. *Russia's First Modern Jews: The Jews of Shklov.* New York, 1995.

Fitzpatrick, Anne. *The Great Russian Fair: Nizhnii Novgorod, 1840–90.* London, 1990.

Fitzpatrick, Sheila. "Ascribing Class: The Construction of Social Identity in Soviet Russia," JMH, 65/4 (1993) 745–70.

Fleishman, Avrom. "Three Ways of Thinking About Fiction and Society" in *Russianness: Studies on a Nation's Identity.* Ann Arbor, 1990, pp. 183–95.

Flynn, James. *The University Reform of Tsar Alexander I, 1802–1835.* Washington, 1988.

Fradkina, Eleonora. *Zal Dvoryanskogo Sobraniya: zametki o kontsertnoi zhizni Sankt-Peterburga.* St. Petersburg, 1994.

Frame, Murray. *The St. Petersburg Imperial Theaters: Stage and State in Revolutionary Russia, 1900–1920.* Jefferson, 2000.

Frank, Joseph. *Dostoevsky: The Seeds of Revolt*. Princeton, 1976.

Frank, Stephen. *Crime, Cultural Conflict, and Justice in Rural Russia, 1856–1914*. Berkeley, 1999.

Freeze, Gregory. *The Parish Clergy in Nineteenth-Century Russia: Crisis, Reform, Counter-Reform*. Princeton, 1983.

Frid, E. L., ed. *Russkaya muzykalnaya literatura*. Pt. 2. 3d ed. Leningrad, 1970.

Frieden, Nancy. *Russian Physicians in an Era of Reform and Revolution, 1856–1905*. Princeton, 1981.

Friedman, Rebecca. "In the Company of Men: Student Life and Russian Masculinity, 1825–1855." University of Michigan Dissertation, 2000.

Friedlaender, Walter. *David to Delacroix*. Cambridge, Mass., 1952.

Frierson, Cathy. *Peasant Icons: Representations of Rural People in Late Nineteenth-Century Russia*. New York, 1993.

Fuller, William. *Strategy and Power in Russia, 1600–1914*. New York, 1992.

Garden, Edward. *Balakirev*. New York, 1967.

Gasiorowska, Xenia. *The Image of Peter the Great in Russian Fiction*. Madison, 1979.

Genêt-Delacroix, Marie Claude. *Art et état sous la IIIe République*. Paris, 1992.

Gerbel, Nikolai, ed. *Russkie poety v biograficheskakh i obraztsakh*. St. Petersburg, 1873.

Gerould, Daniel, ed. *Melodrama*. New York, 1980.

Gershenzon, Mikhail. *Griboedovskaya Moskva*. 2d ed. Moscow, 1916.

Giesemann, Gerhard. *Kotzebue in Russland: Materialien zu einer Wirkungsgeschichte*. Frankfurt, 1968.

Ginisty, Paul. *La mélodrame*. Paris, n.d.

Ginzburg, L. S. *Anri Vetan* [Henry Vieuxtemps]. Moscow, 1983.

———. *Russkoe violonchelnoe iskusstvo do 60-kh godov XIX veka*. Moscow, 1957.

Glagoleva, Olga. "Dream and Reality of Russian Provincial Young Ladies, 1700–1850," *Carl Beck Papers in Russian and East European Studies*, 1405 (Jan. 2000).

———. *Russkaya provintsialnaya starina: ocherki kultury i byta tulskoi gubernii XVII–pervoi poloviny XIX vv*. Tula, 1993.

Gleason, Abbott. *Young Russia: The Genesis of Russian Radicalism in the 1860s*. Chicago, 1983.

Glinskii, B. "Aleksei Antipovich Potekhin," IV, 11–12 (1908) 987–1004.

Goffman, Erving. *The Presentation of Self in Everyday Life*. New York, 1959.

Gohstand, Robert. "The Geography of Trade in Nineteenth-Century Russia," *Studies in Russian Historical Geography*, 2 (1983) 329–74.

Goldfrank, David. *The Origins of the Crimean War*. London, 1994.

Golub, Spencer. *The Recurrence of Fate: Studies in Theater History and Culture*. Iowa City, 1994.

Golubeva, E. "Iz istorii Obshchestva Pooshchreniya Khudozhnikov," *Iskusstvo*, 10 (1961) 67–72.

Gordeeva, Evgeniya. *Moguchaya kuchka*. Moscow, 1966.

Gorodetzky, Nadejda. "Princess Zinaide Volkonsky," OSP, 5 (1954) 93–106.

Gorshkov, Boris. "Serfs on the Move: Peasant Seasonal Migration in Pre-Reform Russia, 1800–61," *Kritika*, 1/4 (Fall 2000) 627–56.

Goscilo, Helena. "Keeping A-Breast of the Waist-land: Women's Fashion in Early Nineteenth-Century Russia" in Goscilo, *Russia*, 31–63.

——, and Beth Holmgren, eds. *Russia, Women, Culture.* Bloomington, 1996.

Gosudarstvennyi Akademicheskii Malyi Teatr segodnya. Moscow, 1997.

Gozenpud, Abram. *Dom Engelgardta: iz istorii kontsertnoi zhizni Peterburga pervoi poloviny XIX veka.* St. Petersburg, 1992.

——. *Opernyi slovar.* Moscow, 1965.

——. "Pogibshii talant (A. S. Gussakovskii)," SM, 4 (Apr. 1951) 76–83.

——. *Russkii opernyi teatr XIX veka (1857–1872).* Leningrad, 1971.

——. *Russkii opernyi teatr XIX veka (1836–1850).* Leningrad, 1969.

Grabowicz, George. *The Poet as Mythmaker: A Study of Symbolic Meaning in Taras Ševčenko.* Cambridge, Mass., 1982.

Gray, Rosalind. *Russian Genre Painting in the Nineteenth Century.* Oxford, 2000.

Green, Michael. "Italian Scandal as Russian Tragedy: Kheraskov's *Venetsianskaia Monakhinia*" in Bartlett, *Russia and the World,* 388–99.

Greene, Diana. "Mid-Nineteenth-Century Domestic Ideology in Russia" in Marsh, *Women and Russian Culture,* 78–97.

Griswold, Wendy. *Renaissance Revivals: City Comedy and Revenge Tragedy in the London Theatre, 1576–1980.* Chicago, 1986.

Grits, T. S. "K istorii 'Soroki-vorovki'," *Literaturnoe nasledstvo,* 63 (1965) 655–60.

Gronow, Jukka. *The Sociology of Taste.* London, 1997.

Grossman, Leonid. *Pushkin v teatralnykh kreslakh: kartiny russkoi stseny, 1817–1820.* Leningrad, 1926.

Gubkina, N. V. *Nemetskii muzykalnyi teatr v Peterburge v pervoi treti XIX veka.* St. Petersburg, 2003.

Guex, Jules. *Le théâtre et la société française de 1815 à 1848.* Paris, 1900.

Gusev, V. and E. Petrova. *Sankt-Peterburg: portret goroda i gorozhan.* St. Petersburg, 2003.

Haberer, Erich. *Jews and Revolution in Nineteenth-Century Russia.* Cambridge, 1995.

Hall, James. *Illustrated Dictionary of Symbols in Eastern and Western Art.* London, 1994.

Hamburg, Gary. *Boris Chicherin and Early Russian Liberalism, 1828–1866.* Stanford, 1992.

Hamburger, Klára. *Liszt.* Budapest, 1987.

Hamilton, George Heard. *The Art and Architecture of Russia.* Baltimore, 1954.

Hamm, Michael. *Kiev: A Portrait, 1800–1917.* Princeton, 1993.

Hammarberg, Gitta. "Flirting with Words: Domestic Albums" in Goscilo, *Russia,* 297–320.

Hare, Richard. *The Art and Artists of Russia.* London, 1965.

Harris, James R. *The Great Urals: Regionalism and the Evolution of the Soviet System.* Ithaca, 1999.

Hartley, Janet. *Alexander I.* London, 1994.

——. *A Social History of the Russian Empire, 1650–1825.* London, 1999.

Haskell, Henry, ed. *The Attentive Listener: Three Centuries of Music Criticism.* Princeton, 1996.

Harrigan, Stephen. *The Gates of the Alamo.* New York, 2000.

Harvard Dictionary of Music. 2d ed. Ed. Willi Apel. Cambridge, 1969.

Haugen, Einar and Camilla Cai. *Ole Bull: romantisk musiker og kosmopolitisk nordmann*. Oslo, 1992.

Haumant, Émile, *La culture française en Russie, 1700–1900*. Paris, 1910.

Hays, Michael and Anastasia Nikolopoulou, eds. *Melodrama: The Cultural Emergence of a Genre*. New York, 1996.

Haywood, Richard. *The Beginnings of Railway Development in Russia in the Reign of Nicholas I, 1835–1842*. Durham, 1969.

——. *Russia Enters the Railway Age, 1842–1855*. Boulder, 1998.

Healey, Don. "Moscow" in David Briggs, ed., *Queer Sites: Gay Urban Histories since 1600*. London, 1999, pp. 38–60.

Heiser, Edmund, *Literary Portraits in the Works of Dostoevskij*. Munich, 1989.

Hellberg, Elena. *Imperial Imprints*. Helsinki, 2004.

Herlihy, Patricia. "Commerce and Architecture in Odessa in Late Imperial Russia" in William Brumfield et al., eds., *Commerce in Russian Urban Culture, 1861–1914*. Washington, 2001, pp. 180–94.

——. *Odessa: A History, 1794–1914*. Cambridge, Mass., 1986.

——. "The South Ukraine as an Economic Region in the Nineteenth Century" in I. S. Koropeckyj, ed., *Ukrainian Economic History: Interpretive Essays*. Cambridge, Mass., 1991, pp. 308–38.

Herman, David. *Poverty of the Imagination: Nineteenth-Century Russian Literature about the Poor*. Evanston, 2001.

Herresthal, Harald. *Norwegische Musik*. Oslo, 1987.

Hickey, Michael. "Smolensk in Revolution." Northern Illinois University Dissertation, 1993.

Hilton, Alison. "The Art of Ilia Repin: Tradition and Innovation in Russian Realism." 2 v. Columbia University Dissertation, 1979.

——. *Russian Folk Art*. Bloomington, 1995.

——. "Russian Folk Art and 'High' Art in the Early Nineteenth Century" in Stavrou, *Art and Culture*, 237–54.

——. *Russian Impressionism*. Forthcoming.

Hirsch, Julia. *Family Photographs: Content, Meaning, and Effect*. New York, 1981.

Hoch, Steven, *Serfdom and Social Control*. Chicago, 1986.

Hodge, Thomas. *A Double Garland: Poetry and Art-Song in Early Nineteenth-Century Russia*. Evanston, 2000.

——. "Mutatis Mutandis: Poetry and the Musical Romance in Early Nineteenth Century Russia." Stanford University Dissertation, 1992.

——. "Susanin, Two Glinkas, and Ryleev: History-Making in *A Life for the Tsar*" in Wachtel, *Intersections and Transpositions*, 3–19.

Holde, Arthur. *Jews in Music*. London, 1960.

Holden, Anthony. *Tchaikovsky*. London, 1995.

Holoman, D. Kern. *Berlioz*. Cambridge, Mass., 1989.

Honour, Hugh. *Neo-classicism*. Harmondsworth, 1968.

Hoover, Marjorie. *Alexander Ostrovsky*. Boston, 1981.

Hudson, Hugh. *The Rise of the Demidov Family and the Russian Iron Industry in the Eighteenth Century*. Newtonville, 1986.

Hudson, Richard. *Stolen Time: The History of Tempo Rubato.* Oxford, 1994.

Hughes, Lindsey. "From Caftans to Corsets: The Sartorial Transformation of Women During the Reign of Peter the Great" in Peter Barta, ed., *Gender and Sexuality in Russian Civilization.* London, 2001, pp. 17–32.

———. "N. A. Lvov and the Russian Country House" in Bartlett, *Russia and the World,* 289–300.

———. *Russia in the Age of Peter the Great.* New Haven, 1998.

Hunt, Lynn. *The Family Romance of the French Revolution.* Berkeley, 1992.

Hunter-Stiebel, Penelope. *Stroganoff: The Palace and Collections of a Russian Noble Family.* New York, 2000.

Huttunen, Tomi, Pekka Pesonen, and Sanna Turoma. "Modernism and Postmodernism: Means of Understanding 20th Century Russian Culture" in Markku Kangaspuro, ed., *Russia: More Different than Most.* Helsinki, 1999, pp. 29–44.

Ieromonakh Leonid. "Korennaya Yarmarka" (1876) in *Korennoi pustina chetyre veka,* 1 (1997) 34–35.

Ignatov, I. N. *Teatr i zriteli,* vol. 1: *Pervaya polovina XIX st.* Moscow, 1916.

Ilin, M. "Borodin" in *Izbrannye proizvedeniya.* 3 v. Moscow, 1962, 3:315–63.

Imperatorskaya Akademiya Khudozhestv: Muzei. Petrograd, 1915.

Imperatorskaya Akademiya Khudozhestv: vtoraya polovina XVIII, pervaya polovina XIX veka. Moscow, 1997.

Isakov, S. K. et al. *Akademiya Khudozhestv: istoricheskii ocherk.* Moscow, 1940.

Istoricheskaya spravka o Bolshom Teatre v svyazi s Imperatorskimi Moskovskimi teatrami. Moscow, 1900.

Istoricheskii ocherk Smolenska. St. Petersburg, 1894.

Istoriya dorevolyutsionnnoi Rossii v dnevnikakh i vospominaniyakh. 2 v. Moscow, 1977–78.

Istoriya russkogo dramaticheskogo teatra. 7 v. Moscow, 1977–87.

Istoriya russkoi dramaturgii: XVIII–pervaya polovina XIX veka. Leningrad, 1982.

Istoriya zhelkznodorozhnogo transporta Rossii, vol. 1: *1836–1917.* St. Petersburg, 1994.

Ivanov, A. "Pervye spektakli," *Rabochii put* (Smolensk), Aug. 22, 1972, p. 3.

Ivanova, E. A. "Mikhailovskii Dvorets" in *Iz istorii muzei: sbornik statei i publitkatsii.* St. Petersburg, 1995, pp. 256–58.

Iz istorii kultury kurskogo kraya. Kursk, 1995.

Iz istorii smolenskogo kraya. Smolensk, 1958.

Iz istorii voronezhskogo kraya—k dvukhstoletiyu voronezhskogo kraevedeniya: sbornik statei, no. 8. Voronezh, 2000.

Jahn, Hubertus. *Fromme Pilger, artige Arme, und streunende Gauner: Bettelei, Armut, und soziale Imagination in Russland.* Erlangen University *Habilitationsschrift,* 1998.

———. "Der St. Peterburger Heumarkt im 19. Jahrhundert: Metamorphosen eines Stadtviertels," JGO, n.s. 44 (1996) 162–77.

Janson, H. W. *History of Art.* 5th ed. Rev. A. Janson. New York, 1995.

Jenkins, Maya. "Pisemsky's *Bitter Fate:* The First Outstanding Drama of Russian Peasant Life," CSP, 3 (1958) 76–88.

Jenkins, Michael. *Arakcheev: Grand Vizier of the Russian Empire.* New York, 1969.

Jenkins, Reese. *Images and Enterprise: Technology and the American Photographic Industry, 1839–1925.* Baltimore, 1975.

Johnson, James H. *Listening in Paris: A Cultural History.* Berkeley, 1995.

——. "Musical Experience and the Formation of a French Musical Public," JMH, 64 (June 1992) 191–226.

Jones, Robert. *The Emancipation of the Russian Nobility.* Princeton, 1973.

Kaganov, Grigory. *Images of Space: St. Petersburg in the Visual and Verbal Arts.* Tr. S. Monas. Stanford, 1997.

Kahn, Andrew. "Readings of Imperial Rome from Lomonosov to Pushkin," SR, 52/4 (Winter 1993) 745–68.

Kahn, Bonnie. *Cosmopolitan Culture: The Gilt-Edged Dream of a Tolerant City.* New York, 1987.

Kallberg, Jeffrey. *Chopin at the Boundaries: Sex, History, and Musical Genre.* Cambridge, Mass., 1996.

Kann, P. Ya. *Progulki po Peterburgu.* St. Petersburg, 1994.

Kann-Novikova, E. "Glinka na Smolenshchine," *Literaturnyi Smolensk,* 13 (1954) 213–34.

Karatygin, P. A. "Aleksei Semënovich Yakovlev, 1773–1817," RS (Oct., 1880) 276–85.

Karlinsky, Simon. "Gomoseksualizm v russkoi kulture i literature: kratkii obzor," *Literaturnoe obozrenie,* 11 (1991) 104–7.

——. *Russian Drama from Its Beginnings to the Age of Pushkin.* Berkeley, 1985.

——. "Russia's Gay History and Literature from the Eleventh to the Twentieth Centuries" in Winston Leyland, ed., *Gay Roots: Twenty Years of Gay Sunshine.* San Francisco, 1991, pp. 81–104.

——. "Russia's Gay Literature and Culture: The Impact of the October Revolution" in Martin Duberman et al., eds. *Hidden from History: Reclaiming the Gay and Lesbian Past.* New York, 1989, pp. 347–64, 552–59.

——. *The Sexual Labyrinth of Nikolai Gogol.* Cambridge, Mass. 1976.

Karp, Ivan and Steven Lavine, eds. *Exhibiting Cultures: The Poetics and Politics of Museum Display.* Washington, 1991.

Kastorskii, S. V. "Pisatel-dramaturg A. A. Potekhin" in *Iz istorii russkikh literaturnykh otnoshenii XVIII–XX vekov.* Moscow, 1959, pp. 177–98.

Kazachkov, S. "Dva stilya — dve traditsii," SM, 2 (Feb. 1971) 80–88.

Keldanay-Mohr, Irmgard. *Unterhaltungsmusik als soziokulturelles Phänomen des 19. Jahrhunderts.* Regensburg, 1977.

Kelly, Catriona. *Refining Russia: Advice Literature, Polite Culture, & Gender from Catherine to Yeltsin.* Oxford, 2000.

——. "Teacups and Coffins: The Culture of Russian Merchant Women, 1850–1917" in Marsh, *Women in Russia and Ukraine,* 55–77.

Kelly, Laurence. *Diplomacy and Murder in Teheran: Alexander Griboyedov and Imperial Russia's Mission to the Shah of Persia.* London, 2002.

Kendall, Alan. *Tchaikovsky: A Biography.* London, 1988.

Khoprova, T. et al. *Ocherki po istorii russkoi muzyki XIX veka.* Leningrad, 1960.

Kimball, Alan. "Conspiracy and Circumstance in Saratov, 1859–1864" in Rex Wade and Scott Seregny, eds., *Politics and Society in Provincial Russia: Saratov, 1590–1917.* Columbus, 1989, pp. 28–48.

Kimbell, David. *Italian Opera.* Cambridge, 1991.

Kimerling, Elise. *See* Wirtschafter, Elise Kimerling

Kirichinskii, E. N. *Zabytyi poet-nationalist*. Kharkov, 1910. On Kukolnik.

Kirsanova, R. M. *Kostyum v russkoi khudozhestvennoi kulture, 18–pervoi poloviny 20 vv*. Moscow, 1995.

———. *Rozovaya ksendreika i dradelamovoi platok: kostyum — veshch i obraz v russkoi literature XIX v*. Moscow, 1989.

———. *Stsenicheskii kostyum i teatralnaya publika v Rossii XIX veka*. Kaliningrad, 1997.

Kiseléva, Lyubov. "Zhizn za tsarya: slovo — muzyka — ideologiya v russkom teatre 1830-kh godov," *Rossiya-Russia*, 3 (1999) 173–85.

Kleberg, Lars. "Litteraturen och vardagslivet: En Presentation av Jurij Lotmans arbeten inom *semiotika povedenija*," *Svantevit*, 2 (1980) 119–34.

Klier, John. *Russia Gathers Her Jews*. DeKalb, 1986.

Klinchin, A. P. *Mikhail Semënovich Shchepkin*. Moscow, 1964.

———. *Nikolai Khrisanfovich Rybakov*. Moscow, 1972.

Knight, Nathaniel. "Science, Empire, and Nationality: Ethnography in the Russian Geographical Society, 1845–1853" in Burbank, *Imperial Russia*, 108–41.

"Knyaz kompozitor," *Kurskaya pravda*, Feb. 28, 2003, p. 4.

Kogan, L. A. *Krepostnye volnodumtsy*. Moscow, 1966.

Kogut, Adolf [Adolph Kohut]. *Znamenitye Evrei*. Tr. A. A. Frek. 2 v. Odessa, 1902.

Kolchin, Peter. *Unfree Labor: American Slavery and Russian Serfdom*. Cambridge, Mass., 1987.

Kollar, V. A. "Ocherk istorii muzykalnogo teatra v Nizhnem Novgorode" in Shteinpress, *Iz muzykalnogo proshlogo*, 298–303.

Komelova, G. "Peterburgskoe Obshchestvo Pooshchreniya Khudozhestv i ego deyatelnost v 20–40-kh gg. XIX v.," *Soobshcheniya Gosudarstvennogo Ermitazha* (1958) 34–36.

———. *Russkaya gravyura i litografiya XVIII–nachala XX vv*. Leningrad, 1960.

Kondakov, S. N., ed. *Spisok russkikh khudozhnikov*. St. Petersburg, 1914 (v. 2 of the following).

———. ed. *Yubileinyi spravochnik Imperatorskoi Akademii Khudozhestv, 1764–1914*. 2 v. St. Petersburg, 1914.

Korf, M. "Materialy i cherty k biografii Imperator Nikolya I i k istorii ego tsarstvovaniya" in SIRIO, 98 (1896) 1–100.

Kornilov, P. E. "Aleksandr Vasilevich Stupin" in Leonov, *Russkoe iskusstvo* (1954) 155–68.

———. *Arzamasskaya shkola zhivopisi*. Leningrad, 1947.

Koroleva, N. V. "Dekabristy i teatr" in *Dekabristy i russkaya kultura*. Leningrad, 1975, pp. 231–66.

Koshelëv, Ya. R., ed. *Smolenskii krai v istorii russkoi kultury*. Smolensk, 1973.

Koshman, L. V. "Gorod i obshchestvenno-kulturnaya zhizn" in *Ocherki russkoi kultury XIX veka*, 12–72.

Kosny, Witold. "Towards a Poetics of Classical Russian Vaudeville" in Andrew Donskov et al., eds., *Slavic Drama: the Question of Innovation*. Ottawa, 1991, pp. 190–99.

———. "Vodevil D. T. Lenskogo 'Lev Gurych Sinichkin'" in De Haard, *Semiotic Analysis*, 365–76.

Kotelnikova, I. "A. M. Prevo—kommissioner Obshchestva Pooshchreniya Khudozhestv: izdatel pervoi poloviny XIX v.," *Soobshcheniya Gosudarstvennogo Ordena Lenina Ermitazha*, 18 (1967) 9–11.

Kots, E. S. *Krepostnaya intelligentsiya*. Leningrad, 1926.

Kozlyakov, V. N. and A. A. Sevastyanova. "Kulturnaya sreda provintsialnogo goroda" in *Ocherki russkoi kultury XIX veka*, 125–202.

Krasovskaya, Vera. *Istoriya russkogo baleta*. Leningrad, 1978.

———. *Russkii baletnyi teatr ot vozniknoveniya do serediny XIX veka*. Leningrad, 1958.

Kratkii obzor deyatelnosti S.-Peterburgskago Filarmonicheskago Obshchestva. St. Petersburg, 1902.

Krivtsova, M. A. "Iz istorii khudozhestvennoi zhizni vtoroi poloviny XIX–nachala XX vv.: M. I. Ponomarëv" in *Iz istorii voronezhskogo kraya*, 93–102.

Kruti, I. A. *Russkii teatr v Kazani*. Moscow, 1958.

Krutov, V. V. *Bozhe, tsarya khrani: istoriya pervogo rossiiskogo gimna*. Moscow, 1998.

Kubasov, Ivan. "Teatralnyya intrigi v 1822 godu," RS (Nov. 1901) 293–304.

Kufferath, Maurice. *Henri Vieuxtemps: sa vie et son oeuvre*. Brussels, 1882.

Kurmachëva, M. D. *Krepostnaya intelligentsiya Rossii vtoraya polovina XVIII–nachalo XIX veka*. Moscow, 1983.

Kurskii oblastnoi dramaticheskii teatr im. A. S. Pushkina. Kursk, 1979.

Kursk: kraevedcheskii slovar-spravochnik. Kursk, 1977.

Kuznetsov, Evgenii. *Iz istorii proshlogo russkoi estrady*. Moscow, 1958.

Kuznetsov, K. A. *Glinka i ego sovremenniki*. Moscow, 1926.

Kuznetsov, Yu. *Ermitazh*. Leningrad, 1965.

Kuznetsova, A. I. and V. Ya. Libson. *Bolshoi Teatr: istoriya sooruzheniya i rekonstruktsiya zdaniya*. 2d ed. Moscow, 1995.

Láng, Paul Henry. *Music in Western Civilization*. New York, 1941.

Laqueur, Thomas. "Bodies, Details, and the Humanitarian Narrative" in Lynn Hunt, ed., *The New Cultural History*. Berkeley, 1989, pp. 176–204.

Laskina, M. N. *P. S. Mochalov: letopis zhizni i tvorchestva*. Moscow, 2000.

Layton, Susan. *Russian Literature and Empire*. Cambridge, 1994.

Leach, Robert and Victor Borovsky, eds. *A History of Russian Theatre*. Cambridge, 1999.

Lebedev, A. K. *Russkaya istoricheskaya zhivopis do Oktyabrya 1917 goda*. Moscow, 1962.

Leblanc, Ronald. "Teniers, Flemish Art, and the Natural School Debate," SR, 50/3 (Fall 1991) 576–89.

Lebrecht, Norman. *When the Music Stops: Managers, Maestros, and the Corporate Murder of Classical Music*. London, 1996.

Ledkovsky, Marina. "Avdotiya Panaeva: Her Salon and Her Life," *Russian Literature Triquarterly*, 9 (Spring 1974) 423–32.

Leichtentritt, Hugo. *Music, History, and Ideas*. Cambridge, Mass., 1938.

Leikin, N. A. *Aktëry-lyubiteli*. 2d ed. St. Petersburg, 1892.

Leningradskaya Gosudarstvennaya Ordena Trudovogo Krasnogo Znameni Filarmoniya imeni D. D. Shostakovicha. Leningrad, 1991.

Leonov, A. I., ed. *Russkoe iskusstvo: ocherki o zhizni i tvorchestve khudozhnikov. Pervaya polovina devyatnadtsatogo veka*. Moscow, 1954.

———. ed. *Russkoe iskusstvo: ocherki o zhizni i tvorchestve khudozhnikov. Seredina devyatnadtsatogo veka.* Moscow, 1958.

Leonteva, G. K. *Aleksei Gavrilovich Venetsianov.* Leningrad, 1980.

———. *Karl Briullov: Artist of Russian Romanticism.* St. Petersburg, 1996.

Leppert, Richard. *Art and the Committed Eye: The Cultural Functions of Imagery.* Boulder, 1996.

———. "Cultural Control, Idolatry, and the Piano Virtuoso: Franz Liszt" in Parakilas, *Piano Roles,* 252–81.

———. *Music and Image: Domesticity, Ideology, and Socio-Cultural Formation in Eighteenth-Century England.* Cambridge, 1988.

Lepskaya, Liya. *Repertuar Sheremetevykh krepostnykh teatrov.* Moscow, n.d.

Letkova, Ekaterina. "Krepostnaya intelligentsiya," OZ (Nov. 1883) 157–98.

Levashëva, O. E. "A. N. Verstovskii," SM, 6 (1949) 65–73.

———. "Muzyka v kruzhke A. A. Delviga," *Voprosy muzykovedeniya: ezhegodnik,* 2 (1955) 323–60.

Levine, Lawrence. *Highbrow/Lowbrow.* Cambridge, Mass., 1988.

Levitina, Viktoriya. *Russkii teatr i Evrei.* 2 v. Jerusalem, 1988.

Levitt, Marcus, ed. *Early Modern Russian Writers: Late Seventeenth and Eighteenth Centuries.* Detroit, 1995.

———. "The Illegal Staging of Sumarokov's *Sinav i Truvor* in 1770 and the Problem of Authorial Status in Eighteenth-Century Russia," SEEJ, 43/2 (1999) 299–323.

Lewis, Roger. *The Real Life of Laurence Olivier.* London, 1996.

Lichtenfeld, Monika. "Triviale und anspruchsvolle Musik in den Konzerten um 1850" in Dahlhaus, *Studien,* 143–50.

Lincoln, W. Bruce. *Between Heaven and Hell: The Story of a Thousand Years of Artistic Life in Russia.* New York, 1998.

———. "The Circle of Grand Duchess Yelena Pavlovna, 1847–1861," SEER, 48/112 (July 1970) 373–87.

———. *Conquest of a Continent: Siberia and the Russians.* New York, 1994.

———. *In the Vanguard of Reform: Russian Enlightened Bureaucrats, 1825–1861.* De-Kalb, 1982.

———. "The Karlovka Reform," SR, 28/3 (Sept. 1969) 463–70.

———. *Nicholas I: Emperor and Autocrat of All the Russias.* Bloomington, 1978.

———. *Sunlight at Midnight: St. Petersburg and the Rise of Modern Russia.* New York, 2000.

Lindenmeyr, Adele. *Poverty Is Not a Vice.* Princeton, 1996.

Linge, Ola. *Ole Bull: livshistoria—mannen—kunstnaren.* Oslo, 1953.

Lisovskii, V. G. *Akademiya khudozhestv.* St. Petersburg, 1997.

Listova, N. *Aleksandr Varlamov: ego zhizn i pesennoe tvorchestvo.* Moscow, 1968.

Litovchenko, E. N. *Nauchno-issledovatelskii Muzei Rossisskoi Akademii Khudozhestv.* St. Petersburg, 1996.

Litvinova, T. N. "Sozdanie dvoryanskikh soslovnykh organov v voronezhskoi gubernii, 1785–1801 gg." in *Iz istorii voronezhskogo kraya,* 57–77.

Livanova, Tamara and Vladimir Protopopov. *Glinka: tvorcheskii put.* 2 v. Moscow, 1955.

Livanova, Tamara. *Muzyka doglinskogo perioda*. Moscow, 1946. Popular essay.

Locke, Ralph. *Music, Musicians, and the Saint-Simonians*. Chicago, 1986.

Loesser, Arthur. *Men, Women, and Pianos*. New York, 1951.

Lo Gatto, Ettore. *Storia del teatro russo*. 2 v. Florence, 1963.

Lohr, Eric and Marshall Poe, eds. *The Military and Society in Russia, 1450–1917*. Leiden, 2002.

Lokhanskii, V. V. "Russkie kolokolnye zapevy" in B. V. Raushenbakh, ed., *Kolokola: istoriya i sovremennost*. Moscow, 1985, pp. 18–27.

Lokshin, D. *Vydayushchiesya russkie khory i ikh direzhëry*. Moscow, 1953.

——. *Zamechatelnye russkie khory i ikh direzhëry*. Moscow, 1963.

Lotman, Yurii. *Besedy o russkoi kulture: byt i traditsii russkogo dvoryanstva (XVIII–nachalo XIX veka)*. St. Petersburg, 1994.

——. *Roman A. S. Pushkina "Evgenii Onegin"*. Leningrad, 1980.

——. *Semiotics of Russian Cultural History*. Ed. A. D. and A. S. Nakhimovsky. Ithaca, 1985.

—— and E. A. Pogasyan. *Velikosvetskie obedy*. St. Petersburg, 1996.

Lough, John. *Paris Theatre Audiences in the Seventeenth and Eighteenth Centuries*. Oxford, 1957.

Lounsbery, Anne. " 'No This Is Not the Provinces': Provinciality and Russian National Identity in Gogol's *Dead Souls*." Ms.

Lovell, Sephen. *Summerfolk: A History of the Dacha, 1710–2000*. Ithaca, 2003.

Lukomskii, G. and V. Lukomskii. *Kostroma*. Kostroma, 1913.

Lure, F. M. *Blistatelnyi Peterburg*. St. Petersburg, 2002.

Lysykh, V. N. "Istoriya kurskoi korenskoi yarmarki," *Kurskaya byl* (June 2003) 7–8.

Macleod, Dianne. *Art and the Victorian Middle Class: Money and the Making of Cultural Identity*. Cambridge, 1996.

Maegd-Soep, Carolina. *The Emancipation of Women in Russian Literature and Society*. Ghent, 1978.

Mai, Ekkehard and Anke Repp-Eckert, eds. *Historienmalerei in Europa: Paradigmen in Form, Funktion, und Ideologie*. Mainz, 1990.

Malia, Martin. *Alexander Herzen and the Birth of Russian Socialism*. New York, 1965.

——. *Russia Under Western Eyes*. Berkeley, 1999.

Mally, Lynn. *Revolutionary Acts: Amateur Theater and the Soviet State, 1917–1938*. Ithaca, 2000.

Malnick, Bertha. "A. A. Shakhovskoi," SEER, 32/78 (Dec. 1953) 29–51.

——. "The Actors Shchepkin and Sosnitsky," SEER, 38/91 (June 1960) 289–313.

——. "Russian Serf Theatres," SEER, 30/75 (June 1952) 393–411.

Malyi zal imeni M. I. Glinki. St. Petersburg, 1997.

Mandel, Oscar. *August von Kotzebue, the Comedy, the Man*. University Park, 1990.

Marasinova, E. N. and T. P. Kazhdan. "Kultura russkoi usadby," *Ocherki russkoi kultury XIX veka*, 265–377.

Marrese, Michelle. *A Woman's Kingdom: Noblewomen and the Control of Property in Russia, 1700–1861*. Ithaca, 2002.

Marsh, Rosalind, ed. *Women and Russian Culture: Projections and Self-Perceptions*. New York, 1998.

——, ed. *Women in Russia and Ukraine.* Cambridge, 1996.

Martin, Alexander. "The Response of the Population of Moscow to the Napoleonic Occupation of 1812" in Lohr, *Military and Society,* 469–89.

——. *Romantics, Reformers, Reactionaries: Russian Conservative Thought and Politics in the Reign of Alexander I.* DeKalb, 1997.

Martinsen, Deborah, ed. *Literary Journals in Imperial Russia.* Cambridge, 1997.

Martorella, Rosanne. *The Sociology of Opera.* New York, 1982.

Mashkovtsev, N. G. "Aleksei Gavrilovich Venetsianov" in Leonov, *Russkoe iskusstvo* (1954) 571–96.

Massie, Suzanne. *Land of the Firebird: The Beauty of Old Russia.* New York, 1980.

——. *Pavlovsk: The Life of a Russian Palace.* London, 1990.

Mayer, Arno. *The Persistence of the Old Regime.* New York, 1981.

Mayor, A. Hyatt. *Prints and People: A Social History of Printed Pictures.* New York, 1971.

Maza, Sarah. *Servants and Masters in Eighteenth-Century France.* Princeton, 1983.

Mazour, Anatole. *The First Russian Revolution, 1825* (1937). Stanford, 1964.

——. *Women in Exile: Wives of the Decembrists.* Tallahassee, 1975.

McConnell, Allen. "Catherine the Great and the Fine Arts" in Ezra Mendelsohn and Marshall Shatz, eds., *Imperial Russia, 1700–1917, State, Society, Opposition: Essays in Honor of Marc Raeff.* DeKalb, 1988, pp. 37–57.

McGrew, Roderick. *Russia and the Cholera, 1823–32.* Madison, 1965.

McLean, Hugh. *Nikolai Leskov: The Man and His Art.* Cambridge, Mass., 1977.

McReynolds, Louise and Joan Neuberger, eds. *Imitations of Life: Two Centuries of Melodrama in Russia.* Durham, 2002.

McReynolds, Louise. *Russia at Play: Leisure-Time Activities at the End of the Tsarist Era.* Ithaca, 2002.

Medvedeva, Irina. *Ekaterina Semënova: zhizn i tvorchestvo tragicheskoi aktrisa.* Moscow, 1964.

Meeks, Carroll. *The Railroad Station: An Architectural History.* New Haven, 1956.

Mellers, Wilfrid. *The Masks of Orpheus: Seven Stages in the Story of European Music.* Manchester, 1987.

Melnikov, A. P. *Stoletie nizhegorodskoi yarmarki, 1817–1917.* [Nizhny Novgorod, 1917].

Metzner, Paul. *Crescendo of the Virtuoso: Spectacle, Skill, and Self-Promotion in Paris During the Age of Revolution.* Berkeley, 1998.

M. I. Glinka: sbornik statei. Moscow, 1958.

Mikhailova, R. F. "Vopros o teatralnoi monopolii v 1856–1858 gg.," *Istoricheskie nauki,* 3 (1960) 76–86.

Mikhail Semënovich Shchepkin: zhizn i tvorchestvo. 2 v. Moscow, 1984.

Mikhnevich, Vladimir. *Ocherk istorii muzyki v Rossii v kulturno-obshchestvennom otnoshenii.* St. Petersburg, 1879.

Milovidov, Ivan. "Dve chukhlomskikh dramy," RS (Nov. 1889) 335–60.

Milyukov, P. N. *Outlines of Russian Culture,* Ed. M. Karpovich. 3 v. Philadelphia, 1942.

Mimoza [pseudonym]. "Opera nashikh babushek," *Moskovskaya gazeta,* Sept. 20, 1910, p. 4.

Mironov, Boris. *Russkii gorod v 1740–1860-e gody.* Leningrad, 1990.

——. *A Social History of Imperial Russia, 1700–1917.* 2 v. Boulder, 2000.

Mitchell, W. J. T., ed. *Landscape and Power.* Chicago, 1994.

M. N. Zagoskin: biograficheskii ocherk. St. Petersburg, 1889.

Moleva, N. and E. Belyutin. *Pedagogicheskaya sistema Akademii Khudozhestv XVIII veka.* Moscow, 1956.

——. *Russkaya khudozhestvennaya shkola pervoi poloviny XIX veka.* Moscow, 1963.

Monas, Sidney. *The Third Section: Police and Society in Russia under Nicholas I.* Cambridge, Mass., 1961.

Moon, David. *The Russian Peasantry, 1600–1930: The World the Peasants Made.* London, 1999.

——. *Russian Peasants and Tsarist Legislation on the Eve of Reform: Interaction Between Peasants and Officialdom, 1825–1855.* London, 1992.

Mooser, R. Aloys. *L'opéra comique français en Russie au XVIII siècle.* Geneva, 1954.

Morov, A. G. *Tri veki russkoi stseny.* Moscow, 1978.

Morozov, Sergei. *Russkaya khudozhestvennaya fotografiya: ocherki iz istorii fotografii, 1839–1917.* Moscow, 1955.

Morrisey, Susan. "In the Name of Freedom: Suicide, Serfdom, and Autocracy in Russia," *SEER*, 82/2 (Apr. 2004) 268–91.

Moser, Charles. *Antinihilism in the Russian Novel of the 1860s.* The Hague, 1964.

——. *Pisemsky: A Provincial Realist.* Cambridge, Mass., 1969.

Moskovskaya Konservatoriya, 1866–1966. Moscow, 1966.

Moskovskoe Kupecheskoe Sobranie: istoricheskii ocherk. Moscow, 1914.

Munro, George. "Academy of Fine Arts," MERSH, 1:17–19.

Muratov, A. M. *Sergei Konstantinovich Zaryanko.* St. Petersburg, 2003.

Murav, Harriet. *Russian Legal Fictions.* Ann Arbor, 1998.

——. "The Theater of Sukhovo-Kobylin." Ms.

Muravëva, O. S. *Kak vospityvali russkogo dvoryanina.* Moscow, 1995.

Muzalevskii, V. I. *Russkoe fortepyannoe iskusstvo: XVIII–pervaya polovina XIX veka.* Leningrad, 1961.

Muzyka v XIX veke. St. Petersburg, 1901.

Natanson. V. *Iz muzykalnogo proshlogo Moskovskogo Universiteta.* Moscow, 1955.

Nathans, Benjamin. *Beyond the Pale: The Jewish Encounter with Late Imperial Russia.* Berkeley, 2002.

——. "Habermas' 'Public Sphere' in the Era of the French Revolution," *French Historical Studies*, 16/3 (Spring 1990) 620–644.

Nathans, Heather. "Forging a Powerful Engine: Building Theaters and Elites in Post-Revolutionary Boston and Philadelphia" in *Explorations in Early American Culture* (*Pennsylvania History*, 56 [1999]) 111–43.

Nechaeva, V. S. "'Dmitrii Kalinin' i krepostnaya deistvitelnost" in her *V. G. Belinskii: nachalo zhiznennogo puti i literaturnoi deyatelnosti, 1811–1830.* Moscow, 1949, pp. 307–26.

Nechkina, M. V. *Dvizhenie Dekabristov.* 2 v. Moscow, 1955.

Negorov, N. "Krepostnoi teatr," *Teatr i iskusstvo*, 6 (Feb. 6) 131–34; 7 (Feb. 15) 151–54; 8 (Feb. 20) 171–74; 9 (Feb. 27) 191–94; 10 (Mar. 6) 211–14; all 1911.

Nekrylova, Anna. *Russkie narodnye gorodskie prazdniki, uveseleniya, i zrelishcha: konets XVIII–nachalo XX veka*. 2d ed. Leningrad, 1988.

Nettel, Richard. *The Orchestra in England: A Social History*. London, 1972.

Netting, Anthony. "Images and Ideas in Russian Peasant Art," SR, 35/1 (Mar. 1976) 48–68.

Neuberger, Joan and Valerie Kivelson, eds. *Visual Documents of Russian History and Culture*. Forthcoming.

Newlin, Thomas. "Rural Ruses: Illusion and Anxiety on the Russian Estate, 1775–1815," SR, 57/2 (Summer 1998) 295–319.

———. *The Voice in the Garden: Andrei Bolotov and the Anxieties of Russian Pastoral, 1738–1833*. Evanston, 2001.

Nikolaev, A. A. *Dzhon Fild*. Moscow, 1979.

Nikoltsev, G. D. and L. A. Shilov, "Iz istorii muzykalnoi zhizni Peterburgskogo Universiteta" in *Ocherki po istorii Leningradskogo Universiteta*, 4 (Leningrad, 1982) 110–135.

Nochlin, Linda. *Realism*. Harmondsworth, 1971.

Norman, John. "Alexander II as a Patron of Russian Art" in Norman, ed., *New Perspectives on Russian and Soviet Artistic Culture*. London, 1994, pp. 25–40.

———. "Pavel Tretiakov and Merchant Art Patronage, 1850–1900" in Clowes, *Between Tsar and People*, 93–107.

———. "Pavel Tret'iakov (1832–1898): Merchant Patronage and the Russian Realists." Indiana University Dissertation, 1989.

Norris, Jeremy. *The Russian Piano Concerto*. Bloomington, 1994.

Norris, Stephen. "Images of 1812: The Patriotic War in Russian Culture." Ms., 2000.

———. "Russian Images of War: The Lubok and Wartime Culture, 1812–1917." University of Virginia Dissertation, 2002.

Obolenskaya, S. V. "Obraz nemtsa v russkoi narodnoi kultury XVIII–XIX vv.," *Odissei: chelovek v istorii* (1991) 160–85.

Obolensky [Obolenskaya], Chloe. *The Russian Empire: A Portrait in Photographs*. New York, 1979.

Obukhov, V. *Grigorii Soroka*. Leningrad, 1982.

Ocherki istorii voronezhskogo kraya. Voronezh, 1961.

Ocherki russkoi kultury XIX veka: obshchestvenno-kulturnaya sreda. Moscow, 1998.

Oksman, Yu. G. *Feletony sorokovykh godov*. Moscow, 1930.

Olkhovskii, Evgenii. *Peterburgskie istorii: gorod i intelligentsiya v minuvshem stoletii (1810-e–1910-e gody)*. St. Petersburg, 1998.

Olkhovsky, Yuri. *Vladimir Stasov and Russian National Culture*. Ann Arbor, 1983.

Opochnin, E. N. *Russkii teatr: ego nachalo i razvitie*. 5 v. St. Petersburg, 1887.

———. *Teatralnaya starina*. Moscow, 1902.

Orlova, Alexandra. *M. I. Glinka: letopis zhizni i tvorchestva*. Moscow, 1952. Tr. as *Glinka's Life in Music: A Chronicle* by R. Hoops. Ann Arbor, 1998,

Orlovskii starozhil [pseudonym]. *Bylyya chudaki v orlovskoi gubernii*. 2d ed. Orël, 1919.

Orlovsky, Daniel. *The Limits of Reform: The Ministry of Internal Affairs in Imperial Russia, 1802–1881*. Cambridge, Mass., 1981.

Osbourne, Richard. *Rossini*. London, 1986.

Osetinskii, O. "Khudozhestvennyi rukovoditel Malogo Teatra, narodnyi artist SSSR Yurii Solomin," *Vek*, 41/356 (1999) 9. Interview.

Ovsyannikov, Yu. M. *Kartiny russkogo byta*. Moscow, 2000.

Owen, Thomas. *Capitalism and Politics in Russia: A Social History of the Moscow Merchants, 1855–1905*. Cambridge, 1981.

Ozarovskii, Yu. "Khram Talii i Melpomeny (teatr aleksandrovskoi epokhi," SG (July–Sept. 1908) 513–28.

Pallot, Judith and Dennis Shaw. *Landscape and Settlement in Romanov Russia, 1613–1917*. Oxford, 1990.

Pamyati Glinki, 1857–1957: issledovaniya i materialy. Moscow, 1958.

Panofsky, Erwin. *The Iconography of Coreggio's Camera di San Paolo*. London, 1961.

——. *Studies in Iconology: Humanist Themes in the Art of the Renaissance* (1939). New York, 1962.

Parakilas, James, ed. *Piano Roles: Three Hundred Years of Life with the Piano*. New Haven, 2000.

Paskhalov, V. I. *Anton Grigorevich Rubinshtein*. Moscow, 1989.

Pastukhova, Z. I. *Po smolenshchine*. Moscow, 1985.

Paulson, Ronald. *The Beautiful, Novel, and Strange*. Baltimore, 1996.

Pekacz, Jolanta. *Music in the Culture of Polish Galicia, 1772–1914*. Rochester, 2002.

Perkins, Etta. "Mobility in the Art Profession in Tsarist Russia," JGO, n.s. 39/2 (1991) 225–33.

——. "Noble Patronage, 1740s–1850," CASS, 23/4 (Winter 1989) 429–42.

Perrot, Michelle, ed. *From the Fires of Revolution to the Great War*. Vol. 5 (1990) of *A History of Private Life*. Ed. Philippe Ariès et al. 5 v. Cambridge, Mass., 1987–91.

"Pervaya gubernskaya vystavka v Rossii" in *Materialy po izucheniyu smolenskoi oblasti*. Moscow, 1967.

Petinova, Elena. *Vasilii Andreevich Tropinin*. Leningrad, 1987.

Petrov, G. F. *Russkii Muzei*. Leningrad, 1972.

Petrovskaya, Ira. *Istochnikovedenie istorii russkoi muzykalnoi kultury XVIII–nachalo XX veka*. Moscow, 1983.

——. *Muzykalnoe obrazovanie i muzykalnye obshchestvennye organizatsii v Peterburge, 1801–1917: entsiklopediya*. St. Petersburg, 1999.

——, and V. Somina, *Teatralnyi Peterburg: nachalo XVIII veka–oktyabr 1917 goda*. St. Petersburg, 1994.

——. *Teatr i zritel provintsialnoi Rossii vtoraya polovina XIX veka*. Leningrad, 1979.

Pevsner, Nikolaus. *Academies of Art, Past and Present* (1940). Cambridge, 1973.

Pies, Eike. *Das Theater in Schleswig, 1618–1839*. Kiel, 1970.

Piggott, Patrick. *The Life and Music of John Field, 1782–1837: The Creator of the Nocturne*. London, 1973.

Pipes, Richard. *Property and Freedom*. New York, 1999.

——. *Russia Under the Old Regime*. New York, 1974.

Pogozhev, V. P. *Stoletie organizatsii Imperatorskikh Moskovskikh Teatrov*. 2 v. St. Petersburg, 1906–8.

Popova, Tatyana. *Borodin*. 2d ed. (Moscow, 1960).

Preston, Katherine. *Opera on the Road: Traveling Opera Troupes in the United States, 1825–1860*. Urbana, 1993.

Prilezhaeva-Barskaya, B. *Krepostnoi khudozhnik: o zhizni khudozhnika V. A. Tropinina.* Leningrad, 1956. A children's book.

Propp, Vladimir. *The Morphology of Folktales.* 3d ed. Austin, 1971.

Pugh, Simon, ed. *Reading Landscape: Country — City — Capital.* Manchester, 1990.

Putintsev, V. "Krepostnaya aktrisa Kuzmina," *Voprosy literatury,* 9 (Sept. 1963) 190–95.

Puzyrevskii, A. I. *Imperatorskoe Russkoe Muzykalnoe Obshchestvo v pervyya 50 let ego deyatelnosti (1859–1909).* St. Petersburg, 1909.

——. *Ocherk pyatidesyatiletiya deyatelnosti S.-Peterburgskoi Konservatorii.* St. Petersburg, 1912.

Pyatidesyatiletie S.-Peterburgskago Zhenskago Patrioticheskago Obshchestva. St. Petersburg, 1862.

Pylyaev, M. I. *Staroe zhite* (1892). St. Petersburg, 2000.

——. *Zabytoe proshloe okrestnostei Peterburga.* St. Petersburg, 1996.

Raab, Nigel. "The City of Perm: Emancipation before the Emancipation." Ms., 1999.

Radoux, J. Théodore. *Vieuxtemps.* Paris, [1895].

Raeff, Marc. *The Origins of the Russian Intelligentsia.* New York, 1966.

——. *The Decembrist Movement.* Englewood Cliffs, 1966.

Rahill, Frank. *The World of Melodrama.* University Park, 1967.

Rak, V. D. "Aleksandr Aleksandrovich Shakhovskoi" in Levitt, *Early Modern Russian Writers,* 348–55.

Rakova, M. "Russkii kamernyi portret vtoroi chetverti XIX veka" in *Ocherki po istorii russkogo portreta pervoi poloviny XIX veka.* Moscow, 1966.

Raleigh, Donald, ed. *Provincial Landscapes: Local Dimensions of Soviet Power.* Pittsburgh, 2001.

Ramazanov, Nikolai. "Vasilii Andreevich Tropinin," RV, 11 (1861) 50–83.

Rand, Richard et al. *Intimate Encounters: Love and Domesticity in Eighteenth-Century France.* Princeton, 1997.

Ransel, David. "An Eighteenth-Century Russian Merchant Family in Prosperity and Decline" in Burbank, *Imperial Russia,* 256–80.

——. "Enlightenment and Tradition: The Aestheticized Life of an Eighteenth-Century Provincial Merchant" in Laura Engelstein and Stephanie Sandler, eds., *Self and Story in Russian History.* Ithaca, 2000, pp. 305–29.

——. *Mothers of Misery: Child Abandonment in Russia.* Princeton, 1988.

——. "Neither Nobles nor Peasants: Primitivist Portraiture and the Emergence of the Merchant Estate" in Neuberger, *Visual Documents.*

Ratajczak, Dobrochna. "Teatr prowincjonalny i prowincja teatralna w XIX stuleciu" in *Polski teatr: prowincjialny rekonesans.* Lodz, 1987, pp. 11–33.

Regina, Kristen. "Karl Briullov's Portrait of Countess Samoilova." University of Maryland M.A. Thesis, 2002.

Reiss, Jozef. *Wieniawski.* Cracow, 1985.

Revutskii, D. "T. G. Shevchenko i ukrainskaya narodnaya pesnya," SM, 3 (1939) 81–93.

Revyakin, A. I. *Moskva v zhizni i tvorchestve A. N. Ostrovskogo.* Moscow, 1962.

Reyfman, Irina. *Ritualized Violence Russian Style: The Duel in Russian Culture and Literature.* Stanford, 1999.

Riasanovsky, Nicholas. *The Image of Peter the Great in Russian History and Thought.* New York, 1985.

———. *Nicholas I and Official Nationality in Russia, 1825–1855.* Berkeley, 1959.

———. "Pogodin and Ševyrëv in Russian Intellectual History," *Harvard Slavic Studies,* 4 (1957) 148–67.

———. *Russia and the West in the Teaching of the Slavophiles.* Cambridge, Mass., 1952.

Rice, Tamara. *Russian Art.* Middlesex, 1949.

Ridenour, Robert. *Nationalism, Modernism, and Personal Rivalry in Nineteenth-Century Russian Music.* Ann Arbor, 1981.

Rieber, Alfred. *Merchants and Entrepreneurs in Imperial Russia.* Chapel Hill, 1982.

Rodina, T. M. "L'évolution du théâtre russe de 1800 à 1850," *Cahiers d'histoire mondiale,* Special number (1958) 212–29.

Rogger, Hans. *National Consciousness in Eighteenth-Century Russia.* Cambridge, Mass., 1960.

Romanovich-Slavatinskii, A. V. *Dvoryanstvo v Rossii ot nachala XVIII veka do otmeny krepostnago prava.* St. Petersburg, 1870. 2d ed. Kiev, 1912.

Roosevelt, Priscilla. *Apostle of Russian Liberalism: Timofei Granovsky.* Newtonville, 1986.

———. "The Country House as a Setting and Symbol in Nineteenth-Century Literature and Art" in Anderson, *Russian Narrative and Visual Art,* 41–62.

———. "Emerald Thrones and Living Statues: Theater and Theatricality on the Russian Estate," RR, 50/1 (Jan. 1991) 1–23.

———. *Life on the Russian Country Estate: A Social and Cultural History.* New Haven, 1995.

———. "Tatiana's Garden: Noble Sensibilities and Estate Park Design in the Romantic Era," SR, 49/3 (Fall 1990) 335–49.

Ropert, André. *La misère et la gloire: histoire culturelle du monde russe de l'an mil à nos jours.* Paris, 1992.

Rosen, Charles. *The Romantic Generation.* Cambridge, Mass., 1995.

Rosenholm, Arja. *Gendering Awakening: Femininity and the Russian Woman Question of the 1860s.* Helsinki, 1999.

Rosenthal, Michael, Christiana Payne, and Scott Wilcox, eds. *Prospects for the Nation: Recent Essays in British Landscape, 1750–1880.* New Haven, 1997.

Rosselli, John. *Music and Musicians in Nineteenth-Century Italy.* London, 1991.

Rossiev, Pavel. "M. S. Shchepkin, gastrolër," EIT, 3 (1912) 60–67.

Rosslyn, Wendy. "Female Employees in the Russian Imperial Theatres (1785–1825)" in Rosslyn, ed. *Women and Gender in 18th-Century Russia.* Aldershot, 2003, pp. 257–77.

———. "Petersburg Actresses On and Off Stage (1775–1825)" in Anthony Cross, ed. *St Petersburg, 1703–1825.* London, 2003, pp. 119–47.

Rozanov, A. S. *M. I. Glinka.* 2d ed. Moscow, 1987.

———. *Muzykalnyi Pavlovsk.* Leningrad, 1978.

Rozman, Gilbert. *Urban Networks in Russia, 1750–1800.* Princeton, 1976.

Ruane, Christine. "Caftan to Business Suit: The Semiotics of Russian Dress" in West, *Merchant Moscow,* 53–60.

———. "The Discourse of Clothes Shopping in Pre-Revolutionary Russia." Ms.

Ruban, V. V. *Zabitye imena: rasskazy ob ukrainskikh khudozhnikakh XIX–nachala XX veka.* Kiev, 1990.

Ruble, Blair. "St. Peterburg's Courtyards and Washington's Alleys: Officialdom's Neglected Neighbors." Kennan Institute Occasional Papers, No. 285.

Ruckman, Jo Ann. *The Moscow Business Elite: A Social and Cultural Portrait of Two Generations, 1840–1905.* DeKalb, 1984.

Russian Museum: Survey of the Collection. St. Petersburg, 1992.

Russische Photographie, 1840–1940. Berlin, 1993.

Russkie kompozitory. Chelyabinsk, 2001.

Russkii Muzei Imperatora Aleksandra III. St. Petersburg, n.d.

Ruud, Charles. *Fighting Words: Imperial Censorship and the Russian Press.* Toronto, 1982.

Rybkin, N. *Generalissimus Suvorov: zhizn ego v svoikh votchinakh.* Moscow, 1874.

Ryabkov, G. T. *Smolenskii krai v period feodalizma (vtoroi poloviny XVIII–pervoi poloviny XIX vv.).* Smolensk, 1984.

Ryan, James R. *Picturing Empire: Photography and the Visualization of the British Empire.* London, 1997.

Rydel, Christine. "Nestor Vasil'evich Kukol'nik" in Rydel, *Russian Literature* (1999), 67–78.

——. ed. *Russian Literature in the Age of Pushkin and Gogol: Poetry and Drama.* Detroit, 1999.

——. ed. *Russian Literature in the Age of Pushkin and Gogol: Prose.* Detroit, 1998.

Saburova, Tatyana. "Frühe Meister der russischen Photographie" in *Russische Photographie,* 31–40.

Sadie, Stanley, ed. *History of Opera.* London, 1989.

Sakhnovskii, V. G. *Krepostnoi usadebnyi teatr.* Leningrad, 1924.

Samson, Jim. *The Music of Chopin.* London, 1985.

Sankt-Peterburg—Petrograd—Leningrad. St. Petersburg, 1992.

Sarabianov [Sarabyanov], Dmitri. *Russian Art from Neoclassicism to the Avant-Garde: Painting, Sculpture, Architecture.* London, 1990.

Sarabyanov, Dmitrii. *Orest Adamovich Kiprenskii.* Leningrad, 1982.

——. *Pavel Andreevich Fedotov.* Leningrad, 1985.

——. *Russkaya zhivopis XIX veka.* Moscow, 1959.

Saunders, David. *The Ukrainian Impact on Russian Culture.* Edmonton, 1985.

Savelov, A. M. "Dvoryanskoe soslovie v ego bytom i obshchestvennom znachenii," DS, 5 (1996) 59–69.

Savinov, A. N. "Akademicheskaya zhivopis" in I. E. Grabar, ed., *Istoriya russkogo iskusstva.* 13 v. Moscow, 1953–64, 8/2:110–28.

——. *Akademiya Khudozhestv.* Moscow, 1948.

——. *Aleksei Gavrilovich Venetsianov: zhizn i tvorchestvo.* Moscow, 1955.

——. "Grigorii Vasilevich Soroka, 1823–64" in Leonov, *Russkoe iskusstvo* (1954) 643–52.

——. "Istoricheskaya zhivopis," *Istoriya russkogo iskusstva,* 7:162–92.

——. *Karl Pavlovich Bryullov.* Moscow, 1966.

Sazhin, V. N. "Iz biografii pisatelya N. V. Kukolnika" in *Issledovanie pamyatnikov pismennoi kultury v sobraniyakh i arkhivakh.* Leningrad, 1985, pp. 105–12.

Schleifman, Nurit. "A Russian Daily Newspaper and Its New Readership: *Severnaia Pchela,*" *Cahiers du monde russe et soviétique,* 28/2 (Apr.–June 1987) 127–44.

Schönle, Andreas. *Authenticity and Fiction in the Russian Literary Journey, 1790–1840.* Cambridge, Mass., 2000.

——. "The Scare of the Self: Sentimentalism, Privacy, and Private Life in Russian Culture, 1780–1820," SR, 57/4 (Winter 1998) 723–46.

Schrader, Abby. *Languages of the Lash: Corporal Punishment and Identity in Imperial Russia.* DeKalb, 2002.

Schuler, Catherine. *Women in Russian Theater: The Actress in the Silver Age.* London, 1996.

Schwarz, Boris. "Beethoveniana in Soviet Russia," MQ, 47/1 (Jan. 1961) 4–21.

——. *Great Masters of the Violin.* New York, 1983.

Seaman, Gerald. *History of Russian Music.* Oxford, 1967.

——. "Moscow and St Petersburg" in Alexander Ringer, ed., *The Early Romantic Era.* London, 1990, pp. 236–58.

Seddon, J. H. *The Petrashevtsy.* Manchester, 1985.

Segel, Harold. "Classicism and Classical Antiquity in Eighteenth- and Early Nineteenth-Century Russian Literature" in John Garrard, ed., *The Eighteenth Century in Russia.* Oxford, 1973, pp. 48–71.

Semënov, V. P., ed. *Rossiya: polnoe geograficheskoe opisanie nashego otechestva,* vol. 9: *Verkhnee Podneprove i Belorussiya,* St. Petersburg, 1905.

Semevskii, V. I. *Krepostnoe pravo i krestyanskaya reforma v proizvedeniyakh M. E. Saltykova.* Rostov-on-Don, [1900].

——. *Krestyanskii vopros v Rossii v XVIII i pervoi polovine XIX veka.* 2 v. St. Petersburg, 1888.

Senelick, Laurence. "The Erotic Bondage of Serf Theatre," RR, 50/1 (Jan. 1991) 24–34.

——. "Russian Serf Theater and the Early Years of Mikhail Shchepkin," *Theater Quarterly,* 10/38 (1980) 8–16.

——. *Serf Actor: The Life and Art of Mikhail Shchepkin.* Westport, 1984.

——. "Theatre" in Nicholas Rzhevsky, ed., *The Cambridge Companion to Modern Russian Culture.* Cambridge, 1998, pp. 264–98.

Sennett, Richard. *The Fall of Public Man.* New York, 1977.

Serman, Ilya. *Konstantin Batyushkov.* New York, 1974.

Shapiro, Yu. *Ermitazh i ego shedevry.* Leningrad, 1973.

——. *Ermitazh: putevoditel.* Leningrad, 1983.

Shatskov, Vladimir. "Pavel Aleksandrovich Katenin" in Rydel, *Russian Literature* (1999), 107–18.

Shatz, Marshall. "The Noble Landowner in Russian Comic Operas of the Time of Catherine the Great: The Patriarchal Image," CASS, 3/1 (Spring 1969) 22–38.

Shaw, Dennis and Judith Pallot. *Landscape and Settlement in Romanov Russia, 1613–1917.* Oxford, 1990.

Shchepetov, K. N. *Iz zhizni krepostnykh krestyan Rossii XVII–XIX vekov.* Moscow, 1963.

——. *Krepostnoe pravo v votchinakh Sheremetevykh (1708–1885).* Moscow, 1947.

Shcherbakova, T. *Mikhail i Matvei Vielgorskie: ispolniteli, prosvetiteli, metsenaty.* Moscow, 1990.

Shepard, Elizabeth. "The Society Tale and the Innovative Argument in Russian Prose Fiction of the 1820s," *Russian Literature,* 10 (1981) 111–62.

Shestakova, Nataliya. *Progulki po teatralnoi Moskve.* Moscow, 1989.

Shevyrëv, A. P. "Kulturnaya sreda stolichnogo goroda: Peterburg i Moskva" in *Ocherki russkoi kultury XIX veka,* 73–124.

Shilder, N. K. *Imperator Aleksandr Pervyi: ego zhizn i tsarstvovanie.* 2 v. St. Petersburg, 1903.

———. *Imperator Nikolai Pervyi.* 2 v. St. Petersburg, 1903.

Shtakelberg [Stackelberg], K. K. "Russkii narodnyi gimn," IV, 137(July 1914) 115–131.

Shteinpress, Boris. *A. A. Alyabev v izgnanii.* Moscow, 1959.

———, ed. *Iz muzykalnogo proshlogo: sbornik ocherkov.* Moscow, 1960.

———. "Matvei Yurevich Vielgorskii," SM, 8–9 (1946) 73–80.

———. *Stranitsy iz zhizni A. A. Alyabeva.* Moscow, 1956.

Shubin, V. F., ed. *Aleksandrinskii — Pushkinskii — Aleksandrinskii.* St. Petersburg, 1995.

Shumova, M. N. *Russkaya zhivopis pervoi poloviny XIX veka.* Moscow, 1978.

———. *Russkaya zhivopis serediny XIX veka.* Moscow, 1984.

———. *Vasily Perov.* Leningrad, 1989.

Shurygina, Lyudmila. *Pervye shagi.* Smolensk, 1963.

Simmons, Ernest. *English Literature and Culture in Russia (1553–1840).* Cambridge, Mass., 1935.

Sirotinin, A. N. "Ekaterina Semënovna Semënova," IV (Sept. 1886) 474–508.

Sivkov, K. V. "Krepostnye khudozhniki v sele Arkhangelskom: stranitsa iz istorii krepostnoi intelligentsii nachala XIX v.," IV, 6 (1940) 195–214.

Skonechnaya, Ada. *Moskovskii Parnas.* Moscow, 1983.

Slavyanskaya mifologiya: entsiklopedicheskii slovar. Moscow, 1995.

Slonim, Marc. *Russian Theater from the Empire to the Soviets.* Cleveland, 1961.

Slonimskii, Yu. *Didlo.* Leningrad, 1958.

Smirnov, D. *Nizhegorodskaya starina.* Nizhny Novgorod, 1995 (reprint).

Smirnov, I. A. *Smolensk — gorod russkoi slavy.* Moscow, 1982.

Smith, Bonnie. *Ladies of Leisure.* Princeton, 1981.

Smith, Douglas. *Working the Rough Stone: Freemasonry and Society in Eighteenth-Century Russia.* DeKalb, 1999.

Smolenskaya oblast: kraevedcheskii slovar. Moscow, 1978.

Smolenskaya starina. Smolensk, 1911–12, 1916.

Sobirateli i metsenaty Moskovskogo Angliiskogo Kluba. (Moscow, 2002).

Sobko, N. *Kratkii istoricheskii ocherk Imperatorskago Obshchestva Pooshchreniya Khudozhestv.* St. Petersburg, 1890.

Sokolov, Vadim. *Ryadom s Pushkinym.* Moscow, 1998.

Solkin, David. "The Battle of the Ciceros: Richard Wilson and the Politics of Landscape in the Age of John Wilkes" in Pugh, *Reading Landscape,* 41–65.

———. *Painting for Money: The Visual Arts and the Public Sphere in Eighteenth-Century England.* New Haven, 1993.

Sosnina, N. and I. Shangina. *Russkii traditsionnyi kostyum.* St. Petersburg, 1998.

Soubies, Albert. *Histoire de la musique en Russie.* Paris 1898.

Squire, P. S. *The Third Department: The Establishment and Practices of the Political Police in the Russia of Nicholas I.* Cambridge, 1968.

Stanislawsky, Michael. *Tsar Nicholas I and the Jews.* Philadelphia, 1983.

Stanyukovich, Vladimir. *Domashnyi krepostnoi teatr Sheremetevykh XVIII vek.* Leningrad, 1927.

Stapp, William. *Robert Cornelius: Portraits from the Dawn of Photography* Washington, 1983.

Starikova, L. M. *Moskva starodavnyaya.* Kaliningrad, 2000.

———. *Teatralnaya zhizn starinnoi Moskvy.* Moscow, 1988.

Starr, S. Frederick. *Decentralization and Self-Government in Russia, 1830–1870.* Princeton, 1972.

———. "Russian Art and Society, 1800–1850" in Stavrou, *Art and Culture,* 87–112.

State Russian Museum: Guidebook. St. Petersburg, 1997.

Stavrou, Theofanis, ed. *Art and Culture in Nineteenth-Century Russia.* Bloomington, 1983.

Stennik, Yu. V. "Ivan Andreevich Krylov" in Levitt, *Early Modern Russian Writers,* 197–207.

Sternin, G. Yu. *Khudozhestvennaya zhizn Rossii na rubezhe XIX–XX vekov.* Moscow, 1970.

Stites, Richard. "Circles on a Square: The Heart of St. Petersburg Culture in the Early 19th Century" in Neuberger, *Visual Documents.*

———. "The Creative Provinces in Early Nineteenth Century Russia" in Baschmakoff, *Modernization in the Russian Provinces,* 306–23.

———. "The Domestic Muse: Music at Home in the Twilight of Serfdom" in Wachtel, *Intersections and Transpositions,* 187–205.

———. "The Misanthrope, the Orphan, and the Magpie: Imported Melodrama in the Twilight of Serfdom" in McReynolds, *Imitations of Life,* 25–54.

———. *Revolutionary Dreams.* New York, 1989.

———. *Russian Popular Culture.* Cambridge, 1992.

———. "The Veselukha Tower: Social and Cultural Space in Old Smolensk" in Arja Rosenholm and Natalia Baschmakoff, eds., *Aspektija: Festschrift for Professor Marja Leinonen.* Tampere, 1995, pp. 295–305.

———. *The Women's Liberation Movement in Russia.* Princeton, 1978.

Stoletie S.-Peterburgskago Angliiskago Sobraniya. St. Petersburg, 1870.

Stolpyanskii, P. N. *Muzyka i muzitsirovanie v starom Peterburge* (1926). Leningrad, 1989.

———. *Staryi Peterburg i Obshchestvo Pooshchreniya Khudozhestv.* Leningrad, 1928.

———. "Torgovlya lyudmi v starom Peterburge," *Nasha starina,* 1 (Jan. 1916) 30–43; 3 (Mar. 1916) 204–20. I have not seen the Feb. issue.

Stuart, Mary. *Aristocrat-Librarian in Service to the Tsar: Aleksei Nikolaevich Olenin and the Imperial Public Library.* Boulder, 1986.

Sukhodolov, V. N. "Graf N. P. Sheremetev i Praskovya Zhemchugova," *Otechestvo: kraevedcheskii almanakh.* Moscow, 1994, pp. 99–108.

Surits, E., ed. *Russkii balet i ego zvëzdy.* Moscow, 1998.

Swann, Alfred. "The Nature of the Russian Folk-Song," MQ, 29/4 (1943) 498–516.

Swartz, Anne. "Chopin as Modernist in Nineteenth-Century Russia" in John Rink and Jim Samson, eds., *Chopin Studies,* vol. 2. Cambridge, 1994, pp. 35–49.

———. "Women Patrons and Performers in St. Petersburg, 1820–1840." Ms.

Swift, E. Anthony. *Popular Theater and Society in Tsarist Russia.* Berkeley, 2002.

Swift, Mary Grace. *A Loftier Flight: The Life and Accomplishments of Charles-Louis Didelot, Balletmaster.* Middletown, 1974.

Szwankowski, Eugeniusz. *Teatr Wojciecha Bogulslawskiego w latach 1799–1814.* Wroclaw, 1954.

Taneev, S. V. "Iz proshlogo imperatorskikh teatrov, 1825–1856," RV, 184/8 (Aug. 1886) 851–86.

Taranovskaya, M. Z. *Arkhitektura teatrov Leningrada.* Leningrad, 1988.

Taras Shevchenko, 1814–1861: A Documentary Biography of Ukraine's Poet Laureate and National Hero. Washington, 1960.

Tarasulo, Itzhak. "Peasant Revolts against Landlords in Russia in 1812." Ms.

Tarle, Evgenii. *Napoleon's Invasion of Russia.* New York, 1942.

Taruskin, Richard. *Defining Russia Musically: Historical and Hermeneutical Essays.* Princeton, 1997.

———. *Musorgsky: Eight Essays and an Epilogue.* Princeton, 1993.

———. "Realism as Preached and Practiced: The Russian Opera Dialogue," MQ, 56/3 (July 1970) 431–54.

———. *Stravinsky and the Russian Traditions: A Biography of the Works through Mavra.* 2 v. New York, 1996.

Tawa, Nicholas. *High-Minded and Low-Down: Music in the Lives of Americans, 1800–1861.* Boston, 2000.

Taylor, Joshua. "Russian Painters and the Pursuit of Light" in Stavrou, *Art and Culture,* 140–52.

Taylor, Ronald. *Franz Liszt.* London, 1986.

———. *Robert Schumann.* London, 1982.

Teatr Opery i Baleta imeni S. M. Kirova. Leningrad, 1976.

Teatr: spravochnye i bibliograficheskie izdaniya. Moscow, 1983.

Thompson, E. P. "Patrician Society, Plebeian Culture," *Journal of Social History,* 7/4 (Summer 1974) 382–405.

Thorpe, Richard. "Academic Theater in Revolutionary Russia." Princeton University Dissertation, 1990.

Thurston, Gary. *The Popular Theater Movement in Russia, 1862–1919.* Evanston, 1998.

Timofeev, Grigorii. *A. A. Alyabev: ocherk zhizni i tvorchestva.* Moscow, 1912.

Tishkin, G. A. *Zhenskii vopros v Rossii v 50–60gg XIX v.* Leningrad, 1984.

Todd, William Mills. *Fiction and Society in the Age of Pushkin.* Cambridge, Mass., 1986.

Tolstoy, Nikolai. *The Tolstoys: Twenty-Four Generations of Russian History.* London, 1983.

Tovrov, Jessica. *The Russian Noble Family: Structure and Change.* New York, 1987.

Trainin, V. Ya. *Aleksandr Aleksandrovich Alyabev, 1787–1851.* Leningrad, 1968.

Trofimov, I. T. *Pisateli Smolenshchiny.* Smolensk, 1959.

"Tsenzura v tsarstvovanie Imperatora Nikolaya I," RS (July) 151–67; (Aug.) 397–404; (Sept.) 643–48; all 1901.

Tsinkovich-Nikolaeva, V. "Kupecheskaya tema v repertuare Aleksandrinskogo Teatra, 1832–1842 godov" in *Traditsii stsenicheskogo realizma: Akademicheskii Teatr Dramy im. A. S. Pushkina.* Leningrad, 1980, pp. 110–26.

Tuller, David. *Cracks in the Iron Closet: Travels in Gay and Lesbian Russia.* Boston, 1996.

Ungurianu, Dan. "Mikhail Nikolaevich Zagoskin" in Rydel, *Russian Literature* (1998), 344–55.

Valkenier, Elizabeth. *Ilya Repin and the World of Russian Art.* New York, 1990.

———. "The Intelligentsia and Art" in Stavrou, *Art and Culture,* 153–71.

———. "The Peredvizhniki and the Spirit of the 1860s," RR, 3 (1975) 247–65.

———. *Russian Realist Art, the State, and Society: The Peredvizhniki and Their Tradition.* Ann Arbor, 1977.

Van Regemorter, J. L. "Deux images idéales de la paysannerie russe à la fin du XVIIIe siècle," *Cahiers du monde russe et soviétique,* 11/1 (Jan.–Mar. 1968) 5–19.

Vanslov, V. V. et al. *Istoriya russkogo iskusstva.* 3 v. Moscow, 1991.

Varneke, Boris. *History of the Russian Theater* (1939). Tr. B. Brasol. New York, 1951.

———. *Istoriya russkago teatra.* 2d expanded ed. [St. Petersburg, 1914].

Venturi, Franco. *Roots of Revolution: A History of the Populist and Socialist Movements in Nineteenth Century Russia.* New York, 1966.

Vereshchagin, V. "Zhenskiya mody aleksandrovskago vremeni," SG (July–Sept. 1908) 472–93.

Vetrinskii, Ch. *Vissarion Grigorevich Belinskii.* St. Petersburg, n.d.

Viola, Lynne. "Popular Resistance in the Stalinist 1930s: Soliloquy of a Devil's Advocate," *Kritika,* 1/1 (Winter 2000) 45–70.

Vitale, Serena. *Pushkin's Button.* New York, 1995.

Vnukova, T. A. "Kurskii dramaticheskii teatr im. A. S. Pushkina: stareishii v Rossii" in *Iz istorii kultury kurskogo kraya,* 56–73.

V okrestnostyakh Moskvy: iz istorii russkoi usadebnoi kultury XVIII–XIX vekov. Moscow, 1979.

Volf, A. I. *Khronika peterburgskikh teatrov s kontsa 1826 do nachala 1855 goda.* 2 v. St. Petersburg, 1877.

Volgina, Yu. I. *Vasilii Tropinin.* Moscow, 2000.

Volk, S. S. *Istoricheskie vzglyady Dekabristov.* Moscow, 1958.

Volkov, Solomon. *St. Petersburg: A Cultural History.* New York, 1995.

Vorontsov, Yu. V. "Muzyka" in *Ocherki istorii voronezhskogo kraya,* 460–80.

Vrangel [Wrangel], N. N., S. Makovskii, and A. Trubnikov. "Arakcheev i iskusstvo," SG (July–Sept. 1908) 439–71.

Vrangel [Wrangel], N. N. "A. V. Stupin i ego ucheniki," RA, 1 (1906) 432–48.

———, "Iskusstvo i gosudar Nikolai Pavlovich," SG (July–Sept. 1913) 53–163.

———. "Romantizm v zhivopisi aleksandrovskoi epokhi," SG (July–Sept. 1908) 377–438.

———. *Venok mertvym: khudozhestvenno-istoricheskiya stati.* St. Petersburg, 1913.

Vsevolodskii-Gerngross, Vsevolod. *Iskusstvo deklamatsii.* Leningrad, 1925.

———. *Istoriya russkogo teatra.* 2 v. Leningrad, 1929.

———. *Istoriya teatralnago obrazovaniya v Rossii.* St. Petersburg, 1913.

———. *Teatr v Rossii v epokhu Otechestvennoi Voiny.* St. Petersburg, 1912.

Wachtel, Andrew. *The Battle for Childhood: Creation of a Russian Myth.* Stanford, 1990.

——, ed. *Intersections and Transpositions: Russian Music, Literature, and Society.* Evanston, 1998.

——. *An Obsession with History: Russian Writers Confront the Past.* Stanford, 1994.

Wade, Rex and Scott Seregny, eds. *Politics and Society in Provincial Russia: Saratov, 1590–1917.* Columbus, 1989.

Walicki, Andrzej. *A History of Russian Thought from the Enlightenment to Marxism.* Tr. H. Andrews-Rusiecka. Stanford, 1979.

Walker, Alan. *Franz Liszt,* vol. 1: *The Virtuoso Years, 1811–1847.* 2d ed. Ithaca, 1987.

Ward, Charles. *Moscow and Leningrad: A Topographical Guide to Russian Cultural History.* 2 v. Munich, 1989–92.

Warner, Elizabeth. *The Russian Folk Theater.* The Hague, 1977.

Weber, William. *Music and the Middle Class: The Social Structure of Concert Life in London, Paris, and Vienna.* London, 1975.

Weilguny, Hedwig and Willy Handrich. *Franz Liszt.* Leipzig, 1980.

Weinstock, Herbert. *Rossini: A Biography.* New York, 1968.

Weintraub, Jeff. "The Theory and Politics of the Public/Private Distinction" in Weintraub and Krushan Kumar, eds. *Public and Private in Thought and Practice: Perspectives on a Grand Dichotomy.* Chicago, 1997, pp. 101–42.

Welter, Barbara. "The Cult of True Womanhood, 1800–1860," *American Quarterly,* 18 (Summer 1966) 151–74.

Wes, Marinus. *Classics in Russia, 1780–1855.* Leiden, 1992.

Wesling, Molly. *Napoleon in Russian Cultural Mythology.* New York, 2001.

West, James et al., eds. *Merchant Moscow: Images of Russia's Vanished Bourgeoisie.* Princeton, 1998.

West, James. "The Romantic Landscape in Early Nineteenth-Century Russian Art and Literature" in Anderson, *Russian Narrative and Visual Art,* 11–40.

White, Mary Jo. "Nikolai Alekseevich Polevoi" in Rydel, *Russian Literature* (1998) 272–80.

Whittaker, Cynthia. *The Origins of Modern Russian Education.* DeKalb, 1984.

Williams, Edward. *The Bells of Russia: History and Technology.* Princeton, 1985.

Williams, Raymond. *The Long Revolution.* London, 1961.

Williams, Susan S. *Confounding Images: Photography and Portraiture in Antebellum American Fiction.* Philadelphia, 1997.

Wirtschafter, Elise Kimerling. "Drama and Society in Imperial Russia, 1740s to 1790s." Ms.

——. *From Serf to Russian Soldier.* Princeton, 1990.

——. "Military Service and Social Hierarchy: The View from Eighteenth-Century Russian Theater" in Lohr, *Military and Society,* 221–40.

——. *The Play of Ideas in Russian Enlightenment Theater.* DeKalb, 2003.

——. *Social Identity in Imperial Russia.* DeKalb, 1997.

——. *Soldiers' Children, 1719–1856: A Study of Social Engineering in Imperial Russia.* Berlin, 1982.

——. *Structures of Society: Imperial Russia's "People of Various Ranks".* DeKalb, 1994.

Woodhouse, Jenny. "Tales from Another Country: Fictional Treatments of the Russian Peasantry, 1847–1861," *Rural History,* 2/2 (1991) 171–86.

Worbs, Hans Christoph. "Salonmusik" in Dahlhaus, *Studien,* 121–30.

Worobec, Christine. *Peasant Russia: Family and Community in the Post-Emancipation Period.* Princeton, 1991.

———. *Possessed: Women, Witches, and Demons in Imperial Russia.* DeKalb, 2001.

Wortman, Richard. *The Development of a Russian Legal Consciousness.* Chicago, 1976.

———. *Scenarios of Power: Myth and Ceremony in Russian Monarchy.* 2 v. Princeton, 1994–2000.

———. "Theatricality, Myth, and Authority," RR, 50 (Jan. 1991) 48–52.

Yablochkov, Mikhail. *Istoriya dvoryanskago sosloviya v Rossii.* St. Petersburg, 1876.

Yakovkina, N. I. *Istoriya russkoi kultury XIX vek.* St. Petersburg, 2000.

———. *Ocherki russkoi kultury pervoi poloviny XIX veka.* Leningrad, 1989.

Yarmolinsky, Avrahm. *Road to Revolution.* New York, 1959.

Yartsev, A. A. *Osnovanie i osnovatel russkago teatra (F. G. Volkov).* Moscow, 1900.

Yatsevich, A. *Pushkinskii Peterburg.* Leningrad, 1931; expanded ed. St. Petersburg, 1993.

Young, Percy. *The Concert Tradition.* London, 1965.

"Yubilei narodnoi opery," *Niva,* 41/37 (1910) 619–20. On Verstovsky.

Zablotskii-Desyatovskii, A. P. *Graf P. D. Kiselëv i ego vremya.* 4 v. St. Petersburg, 1882.

Zaitsev, Pavlo. *Taras Shevchenko: A Life.* Ed. G. Luckyj. Toronto, 1988.

Zapotocky, Christine. "Venetsianov and the Slavophiles." Ms.

Zarubin, V. I. *Bolshoi Teatr: pervye postanovki oper na russkoi stsene, 1825–1993.* Moscow, 1994.

Zetlin [Tsetlin], Mikhail. *The Decembrists.* Tr. G. Panin. New York, 1958.

———. *The Five* (1959). Westport, 1975.

Zelnik, Reginald. *Labor and Society in Imperial Russia, 1855–1870.* Stanford, 1971.

———. "The Sunday School Movement in Russia, 1859–1862," JMH, 27 (June 1965) 151–70.

Zheleznodorozhnyi transport: entsiklopediya. Moscow, 1995.

Zipperstein, Steven. *The Jews of Odessa: A Cultural History, 1794–1881.* Stanford, 1985.

Zorin, Andrei. " 'Beskrovnaya pobeda' Knyazya Pozharskogo," *Novoe literaturnoe obozrenie* 38/4 (1999) 111–28.

———. *Kormya dvuglavogo orla: literatura i gosudarstvennaya ideologiya v Rossii v poslednei treti XVIII–pervoi treti XIX veka.* Moscow, 2001.

Zotov, A. "Puti razvitiya russkogo iskusstva pervoi poloviny XIX veka," *Iskusstvo,* 15/2 (Mar.–Apr. 1952) 70–79.

RECORDINGS (SEE ALSO "ARCHIVES" ABOVE)

Balakirev, Mily. Piano Concerto in F-sharp Minor on *M. Balakirev, N. Medtner, Igor Zhukov.* LP Melodiya S 10 04993 4.

Boiledieu, François-Adrien. *Le Calife de Bagdad.* Musidisc CD MUS 201852.

Bortnyansky, Teplov, Kozlovsky: Songs and Chamber Music. CD OPS 30–179 HM 90.

Field, John. *Piano Music, Nocturnes and Sonatas.* CD Naxos, 8.550761.

Glinka, Mikhail. *Aragonskaya khota, Vals Fantasiya, Simfoniya na dve Russkie temy.* CD Record, 90. Also contains incidental music to N. Kukolnik, *Prince Kholmskii;*

Vospominaniya o letnoi nochi v Madride; Pervonachalnaya polka; Andante cantabile i rondo. Evgenii Svetlanov and the State Philharmonic Orchestra.

——. *Glinka Romances*. LP Melodia S 10–12089–90. Evgenii Nesterenko, bass; Evgenii Shenderovich, piano.

——. *M. Glinka: Proshchanie s Peterburgom*. LP Melodiya, R10.

——. *M. Glinka: Romansy*. Cassette Extraphone, 97012. Galina Pisarenko, voice; Vera Shubina, piano.

——. *Patrioticheskaya pesnya*. LP RSFSR Aprelevskii Zavod Gramplastinok.

Lvov, Alexei. Two versions of "God Save the Tsar" on *The Rise and Fall of the Russian Empire*. CD. David Schimmelpenninck, comp.; Nicolas Picolas, producer.

Moskva: muzykalnye uveseleniya. A. Verstovskii. Marina Filippova, mezzo-soprano. IML CD 080.

Rubinstein [Rubinshtein], Anton. *Piano Music*. 2 CDs Marco Polo 8.223176, 8.223177. Banowetz.

Servais: Souvenirs & Caprices. Deutsche Harmonium Mundi, 77108–2-RG. CD ddd 1990/1988. Liner notes by Kenneth Slowik.

Viotti, Giovanni Battista. *Kontsert N. 22 dlya skripki s orkestrom lya minor*. LP Melodiya, stereo 33 C 10–09931–2. Oleg Krysa, violin; Mark Ermler with the USSR Academic Symphony Orchestra.

Von Geldern, James and Louise McReynolds, eds. *Entertaining Tsarist Russia*. CD, Bloomington, 1998.

FILM, VIDEO

Kompozitor Glinka. Moscow, 1952. Dir. Grigorii Alexandrov; music arranged by V. Shebalin and conducted by Evgenii Mravinskii; V. Smirnov as Glinka, Yurii Lyubimov as Dargomyzhskii, Svyatoslav Rikhter as Franz Liszt, Lyubov Orlova as Glinka's sister. Folk dances by the Igor Moiseev ensemble.

Baryshnya-krestyanka. Moscow, 1995. Video. Dir. Aleksei Sakharov.

Early Russian Cinema. 10 video cassettes, 26 films. New York, 1992.

Lev Gurych Sinichkin. 1956. WMNB Video.

Oblomov. Moscow, 1980. Dir. Nikita Mikhalkov.

Russian Folk Song and Dance. Video Kultur, V 1107.

Voina i mir. Moscow, 1967. Dir. Sergei Bondarchuk.

WEBSITES

Theater

www.alincom.com/bolshoi/history/history.htm
www.IMRC/russianart/theater.htm

Art

www.USC.edu/dept/LA
www.rusmuseum.ru/e-hist.html
www.ROLLINS.edu/Foreign_Lang/Russian/travex.html

Index

emancipation, 384; on gesture in acting, 176; Jewish roles of, 198–99; on
Karatygin, 178; life on the road, 258;
Maly Theater and, 148; Moscow acting style and, 179–81; at Moscow merchant clubs, 295; at Pechkin's Coffeehouse, 167; provincial theater and,
232, 246, 247; realism and, 275; Repnin's theater and, 253; reputation of,
399–400; rivalry with Sadovsky, 408–
9; serf theater of Wolkenstein and,
229; on serf-run theaters, 252; in Shakhovskoi plays, 211; southern circuit
of, 254–55; struggles to gain freedom,
39; tales of serf misery, 73; as Western-
izer, 410
Shchepkina, Alexandra, 27, 61, 83
Shcherbatov, Mikhail, 225, 290
Shcherbina, N. F., 374
Shchukin, Ivan, 420
Shebuev, Vasily, 284, 302, 303, 313
*Sheepskin Coat and the Soul of a
Human, The* (Potekhin), 402–3
Shepelev, D. D., 228–29
Shepelev, I. D., 228
Shepherd and Peasant Girl (Khudyakov),
344
Sheremetev, Count N. P., 36, 74, 81, 225;
as corrupt despot, 82; manorial theater
of, 240; serf choir of, 98
Sheremetev, D. N., 76, 338, 339
Sheremetev, P. B., 168, 225, 333
Sheremetev family, 76, 106, 146, 224
Sheremetev Theater, 131
Sheridan, Richard Brinsley, 212, 228, 246
Shevchenko, Taras, 37, 39, 150, 377,
383; Academy of Arts and, 293–94,
417; on Astrakhan, 251; classical
drama and, 184; "Dream, The," 349–
50; freedom from serfdom, 336, 340–
42; on Greco-Roman history, 298; at
Hermitage, 317; provincial theater
and, 259; theater and, 159, 406
Shevyrëv, Stepan, 123, 137, 219, 328–
29, 405

Shibanov, Mikhail, 333, 354
Shipov, N. N., 31, 38
Shirai, D. I., 230
Shiryaev, Andrei, 234, 278
Shiryaev, V. G., 322, 341
Shishkin, Ivan, 310, 329–30, 348, 416
Shishkov, A. S., 167, 212
Shmelkov, P. M., 329
*Shooting of Russian Patriots by the
French in Moscow, The* (attrib.
Shebuev), 302
Shop Clerk (Plavilshchikov), 214
Shostakovich, Dmitry, 91
Shteinpress, Boris, 101, 134
Shumova, N. N., 416
Shusherin, Yakov, 183
Shuvalov, Ivan, 284, 288, 289
Shuvalov family, 224, 318
Siberia, 57, 63, 110, 255–56, 321, 375
Siberian exile, 31, 34, 46, 286; Dos-
toevsky in, 209; for homosexuals, 148;
for musicians, 69; for playwrights,
162, 200
Sibiryakov, Ivan, 241
Sievers, Jacob, 255
Signorini, Telemaco, 417
Silver Age, 140, 304, 425
Sinelnikov, Viktor, 33
Skalkovsky, K. A., 170
Skavronsky, Count Pavel, 71
Skopin-Shuisky, Mikhail, 194
Skotti, 329
Slavophilism, 26, 136, 165, 195, 244,
400; duel between capital cities and,
177; merchant alliance with, 387;
Moscow School of Art and, 328; Official Nationalism merged with, 9; peasantry viewed by, 348; photography
and, 378; provincial life and, 276; Rus-
sian art and, 301; theater and, 167,
405, 409, 410, 411; Time of Troubles
and, 198; utopia of, 323; wartime
patriotism and, 192; Young Editors
and, 405
Slavyansky, Fëdor, 324, 344, 362